NEWCOMER'S HANDBOOK

FOR MOVING TO AND LIVING IN

Seattle

Including Bellevue, Redmond, Everett, and Tacoma

4th Edition

FIRST BOOKS

503-968-6777
www.firstbooks.com

Newcomer's Handbook for Moving to and Living in Seattle
4th Edition

Newcomer's Handbook® and First Books® are registered trademarks of First Books.

Authors: Monique Vescia (4th edition), Maria Christensen (3rd edition), Monica Fischer (2nd edition), and Amy Bellamy (1st edition)
Editor: Linda Franklin
Series Editor: Linda Franklin
Cover and interior design: Erin Johnson Design
Interior layout and composition: Emily Dueker
Maps provided by Jim Miller/fennana design
Photographs by Monique Vescia

ISBN-13: 978-1-937090-28-9
ISBN-10: 1-937090-28-0

Printed in the USA on recycled paper.

Published by First Books®, 503-968-6777, www.firstbooks.com.

What readers are saying about Newcomer's Handbooks:

I recently got a copy of your Newcomer's Handbook for Chicago, and wanted to let you know how invaluable it was for my move. I must have consulted it a dozen times a day preparing for my move. It helped me find my way around town, find a place to live, and so many other things. Thanks.

– Mike L.
Chicago, Illinois

Excellent reading (Newcomer's Handbook for San Francisco and the Bay Area) ... balanced and trustworthy. One of the very best guides if you are considering moving/relocation. Way above the usual tourist crap.

– Gunnar E.
Stockholm, Sweden

I was very impressed with the latest edition of the Newcomer's Handbook for Los Angeles. It is well organized, concise and up-to-date. I would recommend this book to anyone considering a move to Los Angeles.

– Jannette L.
Attorney Recruiting Administrator for a large Los Angeles law firm

An exceptional book for relocators. However, even non-relocators will find it very enjoyable. It features great coverage of the city of Portland, including the very desirable West Hills and Bridlemile sections, as well as its incorporated suburbs, yet it also covers unincorporated areas...as well as the often-overlooked towns of Wilsonville and Happy Valley, and Vancouver, Washington and its suburbs. Many great ideas for education, dining, house-hunting, shopping, health/fitness, and recreation are included in this book. DON'T PASS THIS BOOK UP UNDER ANY CIRCUMSTANCES!!!!!!!!!!

– "The Footpath Cowboy"
(on amazon.com)

In looking to move to the Boston area, a potential employer in that area gave me a copy of the Newcomer's Handbook for Boston. It's a great book that's very comprehensive, outlining good and bad points about each neighborhood in the Boston area. Very helpful in helping me decide where to move.

– no name given (online submit form)

We were considering moving to Portland, Oregon and recently took a scouting mission there to see whether that was an idea worth pursuing. This book proved invaluable and I would highly recommend it to anyone considering the same thing. Its neighborhood descriptions were spot on and helped us focus our search.

– L. Gillespie
New York, New York (on amazon.com)

TABLE OF CONTENTS

WELCOME TO SEATTLE, ONE OF THE MOST LIVABLE URBAN AREAS in the world! No doubt you've heard about the rain, but there's a lot more to the "Emerald City" than that. Part of the Pacific Northwest, Seattle is one of the most beautiful and lush regions in the United States. On a clear day, from atop every one of Seattle's many hills, you can view snow-capped mountains—including majestic Mount Rainier to the southeast—crystal-clear lakes, or the magnificent Puget Sound.

Don't be daunted by the rumors you've heard about Seattle and rain. While it's certainly true that the city has its share of rainy days, much of Seattle's rain is really a fine mist or drizzle. Often a day that starts off cloudy becomes bright and sunny by afternoon. Winters are wet but mild, averaging about five inches of rain per month from November to January, with temperatures seldom falling below the low- to mid-30s. Summers are comfortably warm, typically in the mid-70s. Spring and fall are cool but often sunny, and you'll enjoy some of the most spectacular views during these seasons, with snowy mountains set against a backdrop of radiantly clear, sunlit blue sky. Surprisingly, some residents prefer the cooler days, and as summer ends will tell you that they're relieved to be done with the weeks of "hot" temperatures. Most appreciate the rain, understanding that it is an indispensable factor in creating some of the wonderful characteristics of this area, such as the abundant green expanses, colorful rhododendrons, and plentiful lakes and waterways.

Situated between two bodies of water and two mountain ranges, Seattle has stunning vistas that can be enjoyed throughout the city. To the west is Puget Sound, an inland saltwater sea that connects to the Pacific Ocean. The Sound is what makes Washington immediately recognizable on every map of the United States, creating the Olympic Peninsula. Running along the middle of the peninsula are the Olympic Mountains (the "Olympics"), which are surrounded by forests and small logging towns. From Seattle, one can see the Olympics clearly, and recognize The Brothers, a twin-peaked mountain in the center of the range.

East of the city lies Lake Washington, 22 miles long and part of a system of lakes in the Seattle area that were formed by glaciers. Other lakes within the city include Lake Union, just north of downtown and connected by man-made channels to Lake Washington and Puget Sound, as well as Green Lake, Haller Lake, and Bitter Lake, all located in the north end of the city. All of these lakes are fed by mountain streams created by melting snow in the Cascades, a volcanic mountain range that runs the length of the state and separates Western and Eastern Washington. Mount Rainier is part of the Cascade Range, as are many smaller mountains that can be seen from vantage points throughout the city.

All of these natural wonders contribute to the abundant recreational opportunities that make Seattle a favorite of outdoor enthusiasts. From early spring to late summer, residents hike and camp in both the Cascades and the Olympics. There is water-skiing in nearby lakes, kayaking on the Sound, and fishing along the many rivers and streams. More intrepid adventurers travel to the eastern side of the Cascades for rock-climbing and bouldering, or head into the mountains for challenging mountain-climbing on Mount Rainier, Mount Baker, Mount Adams, or The Brothers. In the winter several popular ski resorts in the Cascades offer downhill skiing, snowboarding, and cross-country skiing. Those resorts on Snoqualmie Pass are just an hour drive from Seattle on I-90; others are slightly farther away on Mount Baker, Stevens Pass, and Mount Rainier.

Beneath the natural beauty, however, are problems. Puget Sound may sparkle on a clear day, but pollution is damaging the health of the waterway and its inhabitants. A large fish kill occurred during the summer of 2010 in Hood Canal, an offshoot of Puget Sound, caused in part by sewage runoff that helped to drastically drop oxygen levels. Red tide is common, which prompts shellfish harvesting bans. Puget Sound orcas (killer whales) were classified as an endangered species in 2005. Cleanup programs exist, but it remains to be seen if they will be enough to reverse the damage. If you take advantage of the many water-based recreational activities, remember to minimize your "footprint" just as you would do on land. Don't toss litter in the water or dump human waste overboard. Think about kayaking instead of power boating, and support organizations that are working to minimize pollution, such as the Puget Sound-keeper Alliance.

In addition to the mild weather and the natural beauty of the area, Seattle and its swiftly growing surrounding communities also share a dynamic economy. Bill Gates, one of the world's richest individuals, lives ten minutes east of Seattle in Medina. Fifteen miles north and east of Seattle lies the town of Red-mond, home to Gates' company, Microsoft. National giants with large offices in nearby Bellevue include Eddie Bauer, T-Mobile, and Expedia. In the five years between 2003 and 2008, Seattle's economy showed impressive growth, especially in the areas of technology and health care.

The effects of the financial crisis and recession of 2008–2009 were certainly felt in the Seattle area, though many believe the city escaped the worst of the crash as a result of its diverse economy and the health of local corporate giants like Microsoft, Starbucks, and Amazon. Nonetheless, between 2008 and 2011 many residents watched their homes steadily lose value and their IRAs shrink. A majority of the city's cherished arts organizations lost funding, social services programs had to be cut or scaled back, and libraries and community centers had to close. Despite these setbacks, the Puget Sound Region remains one of the swiftest growing areas of the country, and per-capita income in Seattle is 25% above the U.S. average.

Since the beginning of the new millennium, the local economy and beautiful surroundings have brought thousands of newcomers to Seattle. From 2000 to 2010, King, Snohomish, Kitsap, and Pierce counties, which make up the Seattle metropolitan area, added over 400,000 new residents. According to the 2010 Census, Seattle's population is currently at 612,000, a nearly 9% increase since the previous count, and growth in nearby cities such as Renton, Issaquah, and Auburn has been far more dramatic. By 2014 the population of the metropolitan area is expected to top 5 million people.

To accommodate the influx, and to decrease urban sprawl and its negative environmental impacts, city townhouses and condominiums have slowly replaced single-family houses with large yards in neighborhoods such as Ballard and Fremont. The demand for condos in downtown Seattle areas like Belltown and South Lake Union is high, with properties snapped up before construction is finished. Seattle is one of the country's most educated cities, according to a study by the Brookings Institution. A high percentage of college graduates are attracted to a hip, urban lifestyle in Seattle and are helping to drive the demand for downtown living. While some Seattle homes are still affordable for middle-income and first-time homebuyers, housing prices have continued their relentless upward march. With the increased demand for housing, some formerly overlooked Seattle neighborhoods, like South Park, Beacon Hill, and the Central District, are now being revitalized, with old homes remodeled and new houses built in these areas. Other newcomers, especially those with families, are opting for homes outside the city limits.

Seattle entered the national spotlight in the 1990s, making espresso (Starbucks), "grunge" music (Nirvana, Pearl Jam), microbrews (Red Hook), and software (Microsoft) a daily part of U.S. culture. In recent years, the city's residents have added fine dining and Major League Soccer to their list of favorite leisure pursuits. Growth, prosperity, and the innovative culinary talents of chefs such as Ethan Stowall, Matt Dillon, and Tom Douglas and have given rise to a thriving restaurant scene. The Seattle Sounders soccer team, first established in 2007, played its inaugural match in 2009, and went on to win the U.S. Open

Cup an unprecedented three years in a row between 2009 and 2011. On game days, passersby are treated to intermittent and thunderous roars from the fans crowding CenturyLink Field in SoDo, where the team plays its sold-out home matches. In addition, Seattle has a nationally recognized performing arts community, including the Seattle Symphony, the Seattle Opera, and the Pacific Northwest Ballet, as well as several theatrical companies including the Seattle Repertory Theatre, and A Contemporary Theater (ACT).

As newcomers soon learn, conversations here, which used to revolve primarily around microbrews, coffee, computers, and the weather, now lament the traffic. The Texas Transportation Institute's annual study of 75 urban areas listed Seattle as having the 10th worst commute time in 2009. The institute also estimated that travelers in the region experience 44 hours of delay each year. Your daily commute is an extremely important factor to consider when choosing a place to live here, especially if your route includes either of the two bridges. Highway 520 and Interstate 90 run along bridges that span Lake Washington, connecting Seattle with the Eastside communities, which include Bellevue, Kirkland, Issaquah, Renton, Redmond, and Woodinville. Both bridges create traffic bottlenecks during rush hour, and these transit headaches will be exacerbated when the 520 bridge replacement project gets under way in 2012. On the bright side, the views of Lake Washington and Mount Rainier from the bridge decks are amazing!

As Seattle continues to grow, another point of concern for new and old residents alike is personal safety. Happily, in the past several years, Seattle's crime rates have declined in most neighborhoods, due in part to strong community involvement. Auto thefts and car prowls—car break-ins and burglary—continue to plague residents of certain areas despite efforts by local police agencies. No matter which neighborhood you choose, take precautions to avoid becoming a target: lock your car and remove valuables, and park in well-lighted areas. As in any major city, be sure to take reasonable precautions when in unfamiliar surroundings. Keep money and other possessions out of sight, and avoid exploring new neighborhoods after dark. Consider getting a steering wheel locking device or a security system. (For more tips on keeping safe in Seattle, see the **Safety** section in **Getting Settled**.)

LOCAL LINGO

While you won't hear a distinctive accent when people talk here, the Northwest is loaded with Native American place names, which can be difficult to pronounce correctly. In addition, many places have nicknames or shortened names. As with most slang, there are no general rules, but if you remember that the main freeway is "I-5" and not "the I-5" and that when people say "the mountain is out," it's a general statement about how nice the weather is (since

Mt. Rainier is in view), you'll be talking like a native in no time. The following list is not comprehensive, but it will give you a head start.

Alki: pronounced "AL koye"; a popular beach and recreation area where the founders of the city first landed. The word means "eventually," or "by and by" in Chinook jargon.

The Ave: short for University Way NE, the main business street in the University District. Queen Anne locals also refer to Queen Anne Avenue as the Ave.

The Eastside: encompasses all the cities east of Lake Washington, including Bellevue, Issaquah, Kirkland, and Redmond.

Geoduck: this large clam with a long neck is pronounced "gooey-duck." Watch for it on menus around the city.

Issaquah: city on the Eastside pronounced "ISS-a-kwah"

The Locks: boats pass through the Ballard Locks to and from Puget Sound and Lake Union, officially known as the Hiram M. Chittenden Locks, which generally no one remembers.

The Market: the Pike Place Market. Note that it is not correct to say "Pike's" or "Pike Street" when using the full name.

Mossback: slang term for someone who has lived in the Northwest for many years, long enough to have grown moss on their back.

Nordy's: affectionate shortening of Nordstrom, the department store that originated in Seattle. Note that while "Nordy's" works as a nickname, it is not correct to say "Nordstrom's."

The Pass: there are several passes over the Cascade Mountains, but in Seattle and the surrounding areas, if you say "the Pass," everyone will assume you're talking about Snoqualmie Pass, an hour east of the city.

Pill Hill: the nickname for First Hill, home to hospitals and medical clinics.

Puyallup: pronounced "pyew-AL-up" (as in gallop), this city south of Seattle is home to the popular, annual Puyallup Fair.

SAM: the Seattle Art Museum, say it like the name "Sam."

Sammamish: pronounced "suh-MAM-ish," a lake and town on the Eastside.

Sequim: pronounced "Skwim," a town on the Olympic Peninsula, known for the lavender grown there and as the driest city in western Washington.

Snoqualmie: pronounced "snow-KWAL-me."

The Sound: Puget Sound is never "Puget's Sound" and saying "the Puget Sound" will rarely work in conversation. Just go with "the Sound" and people will know what you're talking about.

Sunbreaks: feature of local weather reporting, used to describe those brief moments when the sun manages to elbow its way through the clouds. "Expect showers in the afternoon, followed by possible sunbreaks later in the day."

The 12th Man: term coined by the Seattle Seahawks organization to collectively describe the team's most loyal fans. The number 12 has been retired from Seahawks team uniforms.

Utilikilt: Inspired mutation of the kilt and the cargo pant, sold in the Utilikilt store in Pioneer Square. Sported by a select group of local men secure enough in their masculinity to wear this garment with pride. Great for showing off your leg tattoos.

UW: Shortened, and pronounced "U-Dub," as a nickname for the University of Washington.

WSU: pronounced "Wa-zoo" as a nickname for Washington State University in eastern Washington, especially good to know during the Apple Cup, the annual football battle between the rivals UW and WSU.

WHAT TO BRING

- **A detailed map**; although most of Seattle proper is on a straightforward grid, many of the major streets don't follow the rules. You can purchase a handy laminated Rand McNally fold-out map or the comprehensive Thomas Brothers Road Atlas of the Pacific Northwest. If you have a smart phone or PDA, there are apps, such as King County iMAP (www.kingcounty.gov/operations/GIS/Maps/iMAP.aspx), that put all kinds of geographic information at your fingertips.

- **A car**; public transportation (buses, light rail, ferries) is available, but it can be time consuming to explore the city without a car. Buses stop at nearly every block, and transferring buses can cause long delays. If a car is not possible, expect to spend some time getting used to the bus routes and schedules; and don't try to travel around at night by bus without checking the schedule beforehand—many buses stop running or change routes early in the evening.

- **An umbrella or rain hat**; most likely it will be raining when you arrive. Also bring a lightweight but warm jacket. Temperatures and weather conditions can vary sharply during the day, going from sunny and warm to cold and rainy within a few minutes. However, after you've been here a while, you may find yourself adopting the local disdain for umbrellas and a relaxed attitude about getting wet (it's a fact of life).

- **A cell phone**, which is convenient for contacting potential landlords from the road. If you plan to search the classifieds for your new abode, get a jump on the competition by picking up the Sunday edition of *The Seattle Times* on Friday night. The paper is available at most grocery and convenience stores.

- **A good attitude and a smile**; while most people in Seattle are helpful and outgoing, you'll notice a layer of reticence when meeting strangers. Some have dubbed the phenomenon the "Seattle Freeze," noting that people are very polite but not particularly friendly. A little effort can thaw the freeze, so consider joining activity or social groups as a way to meet people when you get here. With a little patience and a calm demeanor you'll be able to get help from just about anybody in Seattle. So stop in, have a latte, and stay for a while or forever. Welcome to Seattle, a wonderful place to live!

HISTORY

Seattle was founded on its present site in February 1852, four months after the first party of white settlers landed the schooner *Exact* on Alki Point, in what is now known as West Seattle. This group, known as the Denny Party, included Arthur Denny and his family, his brother David, as well as the Lows, the Bells, the Borens, and the Terrys. Many of the city streets are named after these founders of Seattle. In early 1852 Denny, Low, and Boren set out in a canoe to find a more sheltered area for their settlement. They crossed Elliott Bay and, measuring the depth of the bay using a piece of rope and a horseshoe, chose a harbor for their new city (Seattle) just west of what is now Pioneer Square.

Seattle is named for Chief Sealth, a Salish Indian. Dr. David "Doc" Maynard, who arrived in 1852 and started Seattle's first store and hospital, was instrumental in naming the city. Maynard was a friend of Chief Sealth's and suggested Seattle as a more easily pronounced version of the Chief's name. Maynard thought the original name for the settlement, Duwamps, a derivative of the name for one of the Indian tribes that lived around Elliott Bay, the Duwampish or Duwamish, might not attract visitors or new settlers to the area. The other nearby tribe, the Salish or Suquamish, lived between the Bay and what is now Lake Washington. There may have been additional tribes in the Seattle area, but because Native Americans around the Puget Sound were a loose-knit group, it is not clear how many separate tribes were here originally. What is clear, however, is that all of the area tribes were jointly represented by Chief Sealth. These tribes remained in the area until 1855 when, after some minor skirmishes between the settlers and the Indians, they were relocated to the Suquamish Indian Reservation across Puget Sound. Chief Sealth's farewell speech is an oft-quoted piece of Seattle history, and an inspiring reminder of the great Native American leader.

Henry Yesler, another of Seattle's most prominent and influential citizens, arrived in the fall of 1852, soon after Doc Maynard. Yesler was a tight-fisted businessman who, in 1853, built a sawmill, cookhouse, and a meeting hall, all firsts for the new city. The sawmill initially received its supply of lumber from the heavily wooded hills east of the settlement, areas that are now a part of the city. The trees were pushed to the mill down a slick wooden slipway, built into the side of a hill in downtown Seattle. The term "skid road" or "skid row," coined for this innovative contrivance, quickly became synonymous with the run-down streets and rowdy behavior of the mill workers who lived in that area.

On June 6, 1889, near what is now 1st Avenue and Madison Street, a glue pot caught fire in a carpenter's workshop, starting the Great Seattle Fire.

Coming after an unusual late spring drought, the fire quickly burned down every building within a 60-acre area. Soon after the fire, city officials passed an ordinance requiring that new buildings be constructed of bricks or stone. The buildings destroyed in the fire were swiftly rebuilt under these new regulations. Surprisingly, the result of the fire was a strengthened city economy, as the rebuilding projects provided much needed business to local bricklayers and builders. The sawmill was not adversely affected because demand for lumber was still great in California, and most of what was produced at Yesler's mill was shipped to San Francisco. However, the fire and subsequent renovations did have one strange consequence. The city, taking advantage of the opportunity to correct some of the drainage problems that had plagued downtown, constructed streets at a level 12 feet higher than they had been before the fire. However, some merchants rebuilt businesses at their original level, leading to sharp inclines between the city-owned streets and the privately owned sidewalks. Eventually the city put in new sidewalks at the higher street level, and the first floors of these downtown buildings became basements and open spaces. For many years these spaces were used as an underground mall, housing legitimate businesses; they later became infamous as opium dens, brothels, and moonshine establishments. Today, the Seattle Underground Tour is a popular tourist attraction that takes visitors through some of the original labyrinthine tunnels under downtown.

During the late 1800s, gold was discovered in several nearby locations, including the Fraser River in British Columbia, Boise and Coeur d'Alene in Idaho, and the Sultan and Skagit rivers in Washington. Though gold was never present in Seattle itself, the city served many of these locations as a supplier of prospecting goods. In 1877, the Seattle & Walla Walla Railroad was constructed to transport coal (which had replaced lumber as the city's major export) from Renton to Seattle. Then in 1893, the Great Northern Railroad placed its western terminus in Seattle, and the Northern Pacific Railroad Co. bought land in Seattle, extending its western route from Tacoma to Seattle. These events nicely positioned the manufacturers and merchants of Seattle, who were able to reap immense profits during Canada's Klondike gold rush. The rush, which officially began in the summer of 1897 when the steamer *Portland* docked in Seattle carrying "a ton of gold," brought prospectors through Seattle, many of whom geared up here for their expeditions. Seattle also benefited from the gold rush by opening its first assay office, establishing the city as a regional financial center as well as a port and manufacturing city.

By the 20th century, Seattle was a prosperous city with both an expanding population and business community. The need for more space inspired the Denny Regrade project, which began in 1907. Originally, in addition to First Hill, Capitol Hill, and Queen Anne Hill, there was another hill located at the north end of the city center, known as Denny Hill. The hill (actually a bluff overlooking Elliott Bay) prevented easy expansion of the downtown, standing, as it did, 190 feet above the level of nearby Pioneer Square. In 1898 some of the western side of the hill had been carted away to fill in around Western Avenue and Alaskan Way. In 1907, the project of regrading the entire hill began in earnest, primarily funded by private property owners. The dirt was hauled away and dumped into Elliott Bay, creating much of the current Seattle waterfront as well as the land that connects Downtown with the Duwamish River neighborhoods. Completed in 1931, the Denny Regrade is now the site of much of downtown, including the Belltown neighborhood.

The Seattle population has increased steadily since the early 1900s and the city has spread out, enveloping many communities that were originally sub-urbs. When Seattle hosted the World's Fair in 1962, it built a 74-acre campus that featured the Space Needle and the International Fountain. Today this site, known as Seattle Center, is home to dozens of arts, science, and sports organizations, including Key Arena, the Seattle Opera, and the Pacific Science Center, as well as the Monorail to downtown, a relic of the Fair.

Since the 1980s the area has been regularly ranked as one of America's most livable cities, and the resulting influx of newcomers has added to an already growing population. Washington's natural resources have so far provided for such basic needs as water and electricity, and, until recently, the size of the city has provided for plenty of open space and housing, as well as a pleasant small town culture. Today, much of that is changing as Seattle braces for additional population growth and expansion issues such as adequate public transportation and affordable in-city housing.

SEATTLE ADDRESS LOCATOR

Before going into the neighborhood profiles, we have provided tips for get-ting around Seattle and the Eastside, and then metro-wide county information, which should prove helpful as you begin your search for a home.

While most Seattle streets stick to a grid pattern, running east-west or north-south, others seem to meander aimlessly through several neighbor-hoods. The information here will give you a good starting point for finding your way around the city, but a map or street atlas is highly recommended. The guidelines below apply only to streets within Seattle proper, or immediately north or south of the city limits. Other suburbs and communities use different methods for assigning addresses. The Thomas Guide for Metropolitan Puget Sound covers the Seattle metropolitan area, as well as cities in King, Pierce, and Snohomish counties. You can get one at a bookstore or office supply outlet, or order online at www.shopfirstbooks.com.

The **center of the Seattle grid** is at 1st and Yesler. Street names outside downtown are provided with a North, East, South, West, NE, NW, SE, SW location tag. The tag indicates location relative to the center. Downtown streets have no location tag, and run northwest-southeast (parallel to the shore of Elliott

Bay) or northeast-southwest. Outside the downtown area, most Seattle streets run north-south or east-west. Street and house numbers increase as you move away from downtown.

North-south streets are called "avenues" with the location tag at the end; for instance, 24th Avenue NW or 32nd Avenue South. Roads that run east-west are "streets" with the location tag at the beginning; for instance, NE 49th Street or SW Spokane Street. Most avenues in the city are numbered. South of the Lake Washington Ship Canal (which bisects the city north of downtown, and connects Lake Washington and Lake Union to the Puget Sound), most streets have names rather than numbers, such as Union Street or East Aloha Street. North of the ship canal, streets are numbered. Location tags are assigned as follows:

North of Denny Way, as far as the Lake Washington Ship Canal, streets are labeled:

- **West** if they are located west of 1st Avenue North, in Magnolia and parts of Queen Anne;
- **North** if they are located directly north of downtown, on Queen Anne and around Lake Union or between 1st Avenue North and Eastlake Avenue East;
- **East** if they are located east of Lake Union, in Eastlake and Montlake.

North of the Lake Washington Ship Canal, streets are labeled:

- **NW** if they are located north of the ship canal and west of 1st Avenue NW, in Ballard and Broadview;
- **North** if they are directly north of downtown between 1st Avenue NW and 1st Avenue NE, in Phinney Ridge, Green Lake, Wallingford, and Northgate;
- **NE** if they are north of the ship canal and east of 1st Avenue NE, in Lake City, the University District and Sand Point.

South of Yesler Way, all streets are labeled:

- **South** if they are located south of downtown and east of 1st Avenue South, in Rainier Valley, Mount Baker and Beacon Hill;
- **SW** if they are located southwest of downtown and west of 1st Avenue South, in West Seattle.

Between the Lake Washington Ship Canal and Yesler Way, and east of Lake Union, all east-west–running streets are labeled East, including those in Madrona, Leschi, the Central District, Capitol Hill, and Madison Park. However, north-south streets in this area have no location tags.

Several main thoroughfares don't follow all of the above rules. For example:

- **Martin Luther King Jr. Way:** "MLK" begins at Madison Street at the north end of the Central Area, and runs south through the Central Area, Madrona, Leschi, Beacon Hill, Mount Baker, and Rainier Valley.
- **Boren Avenue/Rainier Avenue South:** Boren Avenue runs northwest-southeast over First Hill. South of Jackson Street, Boren Avenue becomes Rainier Avenue South, and continues southeast through the south end of the Central Area and into the Rainier Valley.
- **Madison Street:** One of the city's most convenient streets, Madison Street runs east from downtown, through First Hill and Capitol Hill, and along the north end of the Central Area to Madison Park on Lake Washington.

Useful highways within Seattle are listed below. Be careful of these "thoroughfares" at rush hour:

- **Interstate 5:** I-5 runs north-south through the city and is the most commonly used thoroughfare in Seattle.
- **Interstate 90:** I-90 begins at Safeco Field in downtown Seattle and runs east. The I-90 bridge is the only roadway to Mercer Island, and has more lanes in either direction than the Highway 520 bridge to the north.
- **Highway 520:** a state highway connecting I-5 (at the north end of Capitol Hill) with the Eastside communities of Bellevue, Kirkland, and Redmond; the 520 bridge is always packed during rush hour.
- **Highway 99:** running parallel to, but west of, I-5 through Seattle, Highway 99 begins as Aurora Avenue in the north end, where it is a major thoroughfare lined with strip malls, inexpensive hotels, and other businesses. Crossing the Lake Washington Ship Canal into the city, Highway 99 runs through the Battery Street Tunnel and becomes the Alaskan Way Viaduct, a large stacked highway along the waterfront subject to frequent closures. (The aging Viaduct will eventually be replaced by a deep-bore tunnel.) South of the waterfront, Highway 99 becomes East Marginal Way South and eventually Pacific Highway.
- **Highway 522:** commonly known as Lake City Way NE, Highway 522 begins at NE 75th Street, runs northeast through the Lake City neighborhood to Lake Washington, and eventually turns into Bothell Way NE at the north end of the lake.
- **West Seattle Freeway:** the West Seattle Freeway connects both I-5 (at Beacon Hill) and Highway 99 with the West Seattle peninsula.

GETTING AROUND THE EASTSIDE

There are two highways that transport travelers from Seattle to the Eastside via a pair of floating bridges: Interstate 90, via the I-90 bridge, and Highway 520, via the Evergreen Floating Bridge. This bridge is scheduled for replacement between 2012 and 2014, which will impact commuters who rely on this arterial. Interstate 90 brushes up against the Mount Baker neighborhood, crosses Lake Washington to Mercer Island, and passes through Bellevue, Issaquah, and Snoqualmie before crossing the Cascade Mountains into Eastern Washington. Highway 520 begins in Montlake north of downtown Seattle, crosses Lake Washington and passes through Bellevue and Kirkland before its end in Redmond.

Interstate 405 runs north-south from Renton in the south to Lynnwood in the north, and is commonly used as a connector to either I-90 or Highway 520, as well as other less traveled roads on the Eastside. Other primary thoroughfares include the Redmond–Fall City Road (Highway 202), which connects Kirkland, Redmond, Fall City, Snoqualmie and North Bend; Highway 522 runs from Bothell to Monroe and passes through Woodinville.

It's no secret that traffic in the Seattle area is a challenge. The Eastside may be worse. Dramatic growth over the last decade has flooded the community's streets and highways with commuters. There are ways to avoid the rush hour headache, however. If your employer offers flexible hours, consider working outside the standard 8 a.m. to 5 p.m. You may want to carpool with your co-workers. The diamond (carpool) lanes offer quicker commutes and relief from stop-and-go traffic. See the **Transportation** chapter for information on Metro Transit carpool programs. King County, which encompasses the Eastside, offers a comprehensive online commuting resource called "My Commute," complete with traffic cams and flow maps, at gismaps.kingcounty.gov/MyCommute. If you must drive to the city during rush hour, there isn't much you can do but grin and bear it.

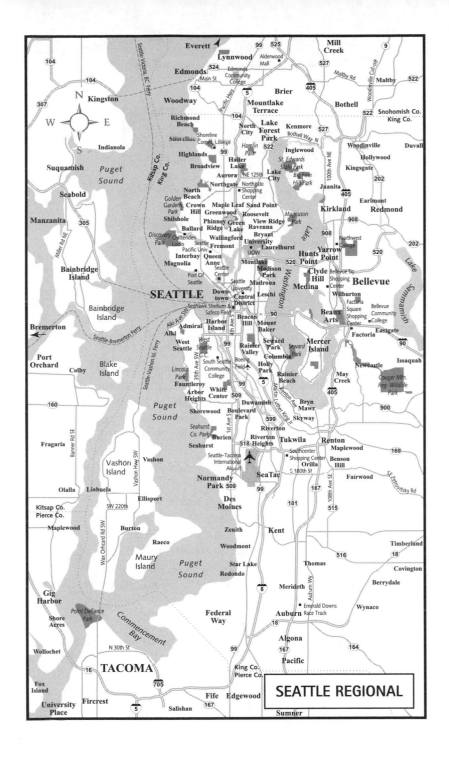

SEATTLE REGIONAL

SEATTLE AREA COUNTIES

KING COUNTY

King County is one of the largest counties in the United States, covering more than 2,200 square miles and serving nearly 2 million residents. The county stretches from Bothell and Shoreline in the north to Enumclaw in the south. Bordered by Puget Sound to the west, the county includes Vashon Island. The county's eastern border abuts the Cedar and Green River watersheds, as well as the Alpine Lakes Wilderness.

Cities served by King County include, from north to south: Bothell, Kenmore, Lake Forest Park, Shoreline, Woodinville, Duvall, Skykomish, Redmond, Kirkland, Carnation, Bellevue, Seattle, Sammamish, Mercer Island, Snoqualmie, Issaquah, North Bend, Renton, Burien, Tukwila, Sea-Tac, Des Moines, Kent, Maple Valley, Federal Way, Black Diamond, Auburn, and Enumclaw.

Outside the cities, the county provides services to regions that lie in "unincorporated King County." In addition to what is available to all county residents, like courts, public health, and property tax appraisals, the county may also provide additional local services, like land-use regulation, emergency management, and county parks.

County Executive: elected to a four-year term by county voters; King County Chinook Building, 401 5th Ave, Ste 800, Seattle, 206-296-4040, www.kingcounty.gov/exec

County Council: the Metropolitan King County Council consists of 9 members who represent geographic districts throughout the county; King County Courthouse, 516 3rd Ave, Rm 1200, Seattle, 206-296-1000, www.kingcounty.gov/council

County Maps, King County KCGIS Center: www.kingcounty.gov/operations/
GIS/Maps

Government: King County Courthouse, 516 3rd Ave, Seattle, 206-296-0100,
www.kingcounty.gov

Libraries: the King County Library System is the busiest library system in the
United States, with 22.4 million items checked out. The system includes 46
libraries and a traveling library center; 960 Newport Way NW, Issaquah, 425-
369-3200, www.kcls.org

Sheriff: King County Sheriff's Office, 516 3rd Ave, Room W-150, Seattle, 206-
296-4155, www.kingcounty.gov/safety/sheriff

Online: www.kingcounty.gov

KITSAP COUNTY

Kitsap County is located on Kitsap Peninsula, across the Puget Sound from
Seattle. One of the state's smallest counties, it is bordered by Hood Canal on
the west, Puget Sound on the east, and Mason and Pierce counties to the south.
The county seat is located in the town of Port Orchard. The city of Bremerton,
home of the Puget Sound Naval Shipyard, has been undergoing a revitalization
of its waterfront and downtown core and is becoming a more attractive option
for those who work in Seattle but find Seattle home prices too expensive. It's
a 60-minute ferry ride between Bremerton and Colman Dock on the Seattle
waterfront, but many commuters take advantage of passenger-only ferries.

Bainbridge Island is only a 35-minute ride to Seattle and continues to be
home to many commuters.

County Board of Commissioners: one commissioner is elected from
each of three districts; 614 Division St, Port Orchard, 360-337-7146,
www.kitsapgov.com/boc

County Clerk: an elected official who serves as the county's administrative
and financial officer; 614 Division St, MS-34, Port Orchard, 360-337-7164,
www.kitsapgov.com/clerk

Government: 614 Division St, Port Orchard, 360-337-5777, www.kitsapgov.com

Libraries: the Kitsap Regional Library System includes nine community branches, a bookmobile and outreach services; 1301 Sylvan Way, Bremerton,
360-405-9119, www.krl.org

Sheriff: Kitsap County Sheriff's Office, 614 Division St, MS-37, Port Orchard, 360-
337-7101, www.kitsapgov.com/sheriff

Online: www.kitsapgov.com

PIERCE COUNTY

South of King County is Pierce County, a region of 1,790 square miles with a population of about 815,000. The county's primary city is **Tacoma**. The northern border of Pierce County is located just south of Federal Way, and a bit north of Tacoma, about a 40-minute drive from Seattle midday or in the evening, and well over an hour during rush hour. For that reason, few commuters make the trek from Tacoma to Seattle each day, although more Seattleites have moved to Pierce County in recent years as they seek lower home prices.

Outside of Tacoma, Pierce County is a mix of rural communities and new housing developments. The county is also home to the largest military installation on the West Coast of the United States: Joint Base Lewis-McChord (a 2010 amalgamation of Fort Lewis Army Base and McChord Air Base), which consists of 415,000 acres that house and/or employ over 100,000 soldiers and civilians.

County Council: consists of seven members who are elected in their respective districts; 930 Tacoma Ave S, Rm 1046, Tacoma, 253-798-7777, www.co.pierce.wa.us

County Executive: elected official serves as the chief executive officer of the county; 930 Tacoma Ave S, Rm 737, Tacoma, 253-798-7477, www.co.pierce.wa.us

Government: 930 Tacoma Ave S, Tacoma, 253-798-7272, www.co.pierce.wa.us

Libraries: the Pierce County Library System includes 17 neighborhood branches and three bookmobiles; 3005 112th St E, Tacoma, 253-536-6500, www.piercecountylibrary.org

Sheriff: 930 Tacoma Ave S, Tacoma, 253-798-7530, www.co.pierce.wa.us

Online: www.co.pierce.wa.us

SNOHOMISH COUNTY

Snohomish County is located north of King County. It covers just over 2,000 square miles and borders the Puget Sound to the west, Chelan County to the east, and Skagit County to the north. At its southern boundary is **Bothell**, which straddles the border of King and Snohomish counties. Other Snohomish County cities are **Edmonds, Mountlake Terrace, Lynnwood**, and **Everett**, which has served as the county seat since 1897.

Between 2000 and 2010, Snohomish County grew by about 17%, to over 704,000 residents. By the year 2025 it is expected that the county will have grown by 49%, adding nearly 350,000 new residents.

County Council: the five members of the council are elected to four-year terms; 3000 Rockefeller, Everett, 425-388-3494, www1.co.snohomish.wa.us/departments/council

County Executive: elected to a four-year term; 3000 Rockefeller, Everett, 425-388-3460, www1.co.snohomish.wa.us/departments/executive

Government: 3000 Rockefeller, Everett, 425-388-3411, www1.co.snohomish.wa.us

Libraries: the Sno-Isle Regional Library System serves more than half a million residents in Snohomish and Island counties through 22 community libraries, outreach vans and a bookmobile; 7312 35th Ave NE, Marysville, 360-651-7000, www.sno-isle.org

Sheriff: the Snohomish County Sheriff is elected to a four-year term; 3000 Rockefeller, Everett, 425-388-3393, http://sheriff.snoco.org

Online: www1.co.snohomish.wa.us

SEATTLE NEIGHBORHOODS

As with many large and growing U.S. cities, most of Seattle's neighborhoods began as small communities located outside the city limits. As Seattle expanded over the years, the city annexed many of these small mill towns and commerce centers. While the old village names survive as neighborhood monikers, so do many of the original neighborhood names. A good example of this can be seen in Ballard, where residents may refer to their homes as being in Shilshole, North Beach, Sunset Hill, Blue Ridge, or Crown Hill, all of which are located in the larger neighborhood of Ballard.

Downtown Seattle

As you explore Seattle, you may notice certain repeating housing styles. Most Seattle neighborhoods have only gradually grown denser and more urban, so it is common to see several types of houses on a single residential city block. Victorians dating from the late 1800s, with their turreted front rooms and ornamented rooflines, are in most downtown neighborhoods, sitting alongside Craftsman-style bungalows, Tudors, Colonials, and Northwest Moderns.

The Northwest Modern or "Classic Box" style of architecture is one of the most plentiful, introduced in Seattle around the turn of the 20th century and instantly

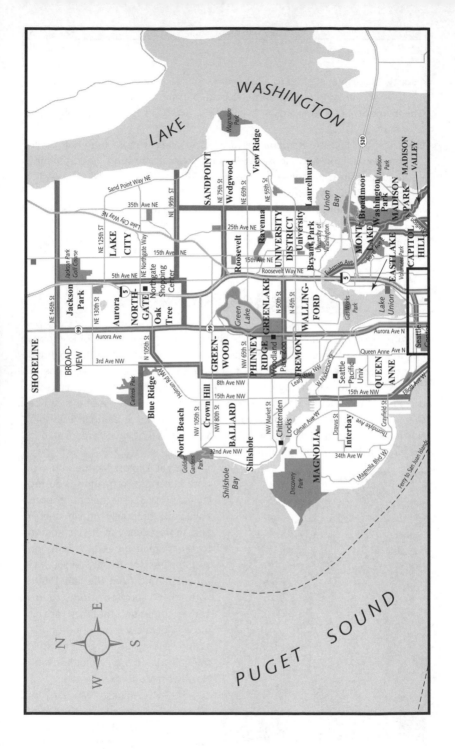

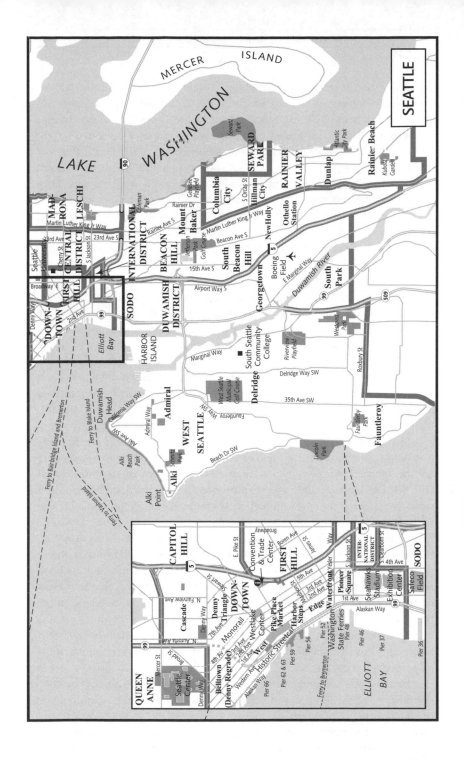

SEATTLE

MERCER ISLAND

LAKE WASHINGTON

MADRONA
LESCHI
Martin Luther King Jr Way
33rd Ave
23rd Ave S
Cherry St
S Jackson St
Seattle University
Broadway E
Denny Way
DOWN-TOWN
FIRST HILL
CENTRAL DISTRICT
2nd Ave
99
Elliott Bay
INTERNATIONAL DISTRICT
SODO
DUWAMISH DISTRICT
Airport Way S
HARBOR ISLAND
Marginal Way
BEACON HILL
15th Ave S
South Beacon Hill
Jefferson Park Golf Course
Beacon Ave S
Georgetown
Boeing Field
E Marginal Way
5
Duwamish River
99
South Park
509
Westmont 2nd
Roxbury St
Rainier Dr
Rainier Ave S
Martin Luther King Jr Way
Mount Baker
Columbia City
S Orcas St
Hillman City
NewHolly
Othello Station
RAINIER VALLEY
Dunlap
Rainier Beach
Atlantic City Park
Kubota Garden
Seward Park
SEWARD PARK
George Park Playfield
Coleman Park

Seattle University
Cherry St

South Seattle Community College
Riverview Playfield
Delridge
Delridge Way SW
35th Ave SW
West Seattle Municipal Golf Course
Fauntleroy Way SW
Faumleroy Park
Fauntleroy
Lincoln Park

Ferry to Bainbridge Island and Bremerton
Ferry to Blake Island
Ferry to Vashon Island
Duwamish Head
California Way SW
Admiral Way
Alki Beach Park
Schmitz Park
Admiral
WEST SEATTLE
Alki Ave SW
Beach Dr SW
Alki
Alki Point

CAPITOL HILL
E Pike St
Broadway
Convention & Trade Center
Boren Ave
Terry St
5th Ave
FIRST HILL
INTERNATIONAL DISTRICT
S Jackson St
S Dearborn St
5
4th Ave
SODO
Safeco Field
Exhibition Center
Eastlake Ave E
Fairview Ave E
N. Aurora Ave
99
Denny Way
Mercer St
Broad St
QUEEN ANNE
Seattle Center
Cascade
Denny Triangle
Denny Way
7th Ave
4th Ave
5th Ave
DOWN-TOWN
Belltown (Denny Regrade)
Monorail
2nd Ave
3rd Ave
Westlake
1st Ave
Pike Place Market
Harbor Steps
Historic Streetcar
Western Ave
Alaskan Way
Yesler Way
Pioneer Square
3rd Ave
2nd Ave
Washington Street
State Ferries
West Edge
Waterfront
1st Ave
Alaskan Way
Seahawks Stadium
99
Pier 36
Pier 37
Pier 46
Pier 48
Pier 52
Pier 56
Pier 59
Pier 62 & 63
Pier 66
Ferry to Bremerton
ELLIOTT BAY

19

popular with local architects and builders. Also known as the "Capitol Hill Box" because of the number of these houses in the Capitol Hill neighborhood, this style was still being built in Seattle as late as the 1940s. Classic Box houses are large two-story, four-square structures with symmetrical windows, front porches, hardwood floors, and high ceilings. The slope of the Classic Box roof starts above the entire square of the second story, so that the upstairs rooms are often the same in size and number as those below. Bungalows were introduced in Seattle in the early 1900s, appearing in the architectural pattern books that were a mainstay of local builders. In particular, the Arts-and-Crafts and Craftsman-style bungalows were popular in the city. Unlike the Classic Box, the bungalow is characterized by a sloped second-story roof, usually with one or two front gables and bracketed roof overhangs. These homes typically have three to four large bedrooms, oak or fir floors, and original built-in cabinetry.

Elaborate and symmetrical Colonials and Dutch Colonials, often referred to as "barn houses" for their distinctive shape, were built throughout Seattle in the decades between the two world wars. Tudors, recognizable for their steep roofs, arched doorways, and leaded windows, dot Seattle neighborhoods, as do simple Cape Cod cottages. Some north Seattle neighborhoods contain examples of the ranch house, also called ramblers. Built in the 1940s and 1950s and related to the Prairie School style created by Frank Lloyd Wright, these are sprawling single-story brick houses with giant picture windows. Olympic Manor, in the north end of Ballard, is built almost entirely in this style.

Seattleites are proud of where they live, a fact exemplified by the large number of community centers and organizations, neighborhood newspapers, and bustling corner coffee shops. Seattle's **Department of Neighborhoods** (206-684-0464, www.seattle.gov/neighborhoods) runs the neighborhood service centers (listed after each profile), and administers neighborhood matching funds for local projects. Community newspapers, usually free, provide valuable information about local issues, upcoming events, and activities. Every neighborhood in Seattle has at least one coffeehouse or espresso stand, which is often a good place to start your exploration of a particular area. See the neighborhood resources that follow each neighborhood profile for information about organizations, publications, post offices, nearest emergency hospitals, and public transportation routes. (Note: bus numbers are provided only for routes running through neighborhoods. Check with Metro Transit, 206-553-3000, http://metro.kingcounty.gov, for specifics on route origins and final destinations, route maps, and a trip planner.)

Unlike many other major cities, Seattle's neighborhoods do not have official borders. Those listed in this book reflect widely accepted neighborhood boundaries, many of which are guided by simple geography. For instance, many of Seattle's neighborhoods sit atop a single hill, separated by a miniature "valley" from the next neighborhood. The following neighborhood profiles are only those located within the city limits. Other communities, such as Bellevue,

Redmond, Everett, and Renton are not a part of the city, but may interest newcomers; you will find these and others profiled in the **Surrounding Communities** section.

SEATTLE—KING COUNTY

Downtown
Pioneer Square
West Edge
Pike Place Market
Harbor Steps
Belltown
Waterfront
Denny Triangle
South Lake Union

Boundaries: North: Denny Way, Mercer Street; **West:** Elliott Bay; **South:** South Royal Brougham Way, South Jackson Street; **East:** Interstate 5

Pioneer Square is perhaps the best-known and most historic of all districts in the Downtown area. Located near the site of Henry Yesler's sawmill and the original "skid road" (now Yesler Way), Pioneer Square was quickly rebuilt after the Great Seattle Fire of 1889 destroyed much of early Seattle. The Pioneer Building at 1st Avenue and James Street is one of the oldest buildings in Seattle, designed in 1889 by architect Elmer H. Fisher, at the request of Henry Yesler. Today, the brothels and gambling dens are long gone and Pioneer Square is a business and retail district. Small business offices are located in the upper floors of most of the old stone buildings. Oriental rug sellers, antique shops, sporting goods stores, sports bars, cafés, and art galleries fill the ground floor spaces.

Also home to a dynamic music scene, Pioneer Square's bars fill nightly with music-lovers and party-goers. Many of Seattle's influential bands have played in area clubs, such as the Central Saloon, Seattle's oldest bar. The New Orleans Creole Restaurant features fine blues and jazz musicians, and hipsters dance the night away at the Ibiza or Trinity Nightclub. Joint cover is offered on the weekends for those who want to visit several bars in one evening. Fat Tuesday, Seattle's Mardi Gras celebration, fills the district with revelers for a week of music and festivities (and occasional violent clashes). Pioneer Square is also a popular meeting place before Seattle sporting events.

Compared to other adjacent neighborhoods, housing opportunities in Pioneer Square are scarce. In 2008, only 1,200 apartments and condos existed in the neighborhood. Most of the apartment buildings in Pioneer Square are converted warehouses. While this is a busy, exciting part of the city, residentially

Pike Place Market

speaking, it's most appropriate for residents comfortable in a fast-paced urban environment. In the days of the Kingdome, before Safeco Field and Century-Link (formerly Qwest) Field were built, this area was an inexpensive part of the city in which to live, and as a result several homeless shelters were placed here. Today, intermingled with expensive new developments and refurbished high-tech office spaces, these residences for the down-and-out remain. In less prosperous times, Pioneer Square was home to numerous artists' residences and workspaces, but many artists were squeezed out by rising rents. In early 2000, the Washington Shoe Building, which once housed five floors of galleries and artists' studios, closed its doors. The building has been transformed into an office block with a posh, top-floor penthouse. Many of the displaced residents moved south to Georgetown, but 50 artists and their families found homes in the Tashiro Kaplan Artists Lofts located on Prefontaine Place South. The two former commercial buildings were renovated as gallery and living spaces and completed in 2004. The 619 Western Building, another haven for artists, is not expected to survive the construction of the deep-bore tunnel that will replace the Alaska Way Viaduct.

In September of 2001, the Downtown Seattle Association and then-Mayor Paul Schell christened the new **West Edge** neighborhood, an area bordered by Lenora Street to the north, Cherry Street to the south, Second Avenue to the east, and Western Avenue to the west. Essentially a marketing tool to attract more diners and shoppers, most residents continue to use more familiar down-town neighborhood names, like Pike Place and Harbor Steps, when referring to this general area.

Established in 1907, the **Pike Place Market** is Seattle's most beloved Down-town landmark. City dwellers come here first with their out-of-town guests to see the fish-throwers at the seafood stands, sample teas at Market Spice, or listen to talented street musicians. Many Seattle residents frequent Pike Place weekly for fresh fruits and vegetables, fish and shellfish, teas and coffees, and baked goods.

Local farmers who wanted to sell their produce without the involvement of middlemen organized the market. Gradually fish and meat were added to the available goods, then bakeries and cafés moved in, soon followed by folks selling jewelry, pottery, honey, flowers, kites, and coffees. Today, you can find just about anything at the Market, from the best local tomatoes and homemade jams to kitchenware and furniture. Many of these products are sold in shops in the blocks around the Market itself, or in the Corner Market Building, designed in 1912, and located at the corner of 1st Avenue and Pike Street. A few blocks south of Pike Place is the magnificent Seattle Art Museum with its notable "A Hammering Man" sculpture facing the waterfront.

A short stroll from Pike Place Market is **Harbor Steps**, one of Seattle's newer neighborhoods and a perfect example of Downtown's ongoing revitalization. Whereas many Seattle communities were named for their proximity to water (Green Lake, Eastlake), Harbor Steps was named for a wide outdoor staircase that climbs from Western Avenue, near the waterfront, to First Avenue at University Street. The Harbor Steps Apartments (www.harborsteps.com) opened in 1992 and now houses about 1,200 residents, with rents ranging from approximately $1,300 to $4,000+ per month. The complex's four high-rise towers feature private balconies and expansive glass windows, offering residents sublime views of the city, Sound, and mountains. Harbor Steps earns a Walk Score of 94 out of 100, which means you can easily accomplish all your daily errands without the use of a car. Residents range from young singles to retired couples, empty nesters, and executives moving here from around the world. The small, upscale community is also home to Harbor Steps Park, the Inn at Harbor Steps, and a selection of upscale restaurants, boutiques, and galleries.

Belltown

Located north of the Pike Place Market and centered around 2nd Avenue and Bell Street, **Belltown** is a part of the Denny Regrade, a section of Downtown created when Denny Hill was flattened in the early 1900s. The earth of the original steep bluff that stood in this area was carted off and dumped into Elliott

Waterfront

Bay, creating part of what is now the Waterfront area. Like Pioneer Square, the Belltown district is a hub for Seattle's nightlife and music scene. Twenty-somethings frequent the Venom nightclub on Western Avenue and the See Sound Lounge on Blanchard; jazz lovers can catch a show at Tula's. The Moore Theater, on 2nd Avenue, is an historic concert hall designed in 1907 by Seattle architect Edwin W. Houghton that hosts a wide range of music and cultural events.

For most of the 1970s and 1980s, Belltown was best known for its wandering homeless, drug dealers, and panhandlers, but as 2000 approached, *Sunset Magazine* declared it the "newest belle of the ball," and compared it to New York's Upper West Side. While that comparison has proved premature, the neighborhood has seen dozens of new housing developments during the last ten years, as well as the opening of the Olympic Sculpture Park. What was formerly a 9-acre industrial site now attracts residents and tourists with gorgeous views of the Sound and the Olympic Mountains, as well as major sculptures by Alexander Calder, Richard Serra, and Claes Oldenburg. Building continues at a rapid pace as Belltown has become a hip neighborhood (reflected in rising rents), attractive to young professionals, and more housing units are under construction.

High-rise condominiums facing Elliott Bay and the Olympic Mountains can be found on 1st Avenue. These amenity-rich units (high-speed Internet access, parking garages, free cable, and fitness centers) command premium rents. Condos are also pricey in trendy Belltown. *The Seattle Times* reports that at the Ellington, a 312-unit complex at First Avenue and Broad Street, condo prices range from $230,000 to nearly $800,000. The units boast gas fireplaces and views of Downtown and Elliott Bay, while the complex includes a 24/7 concierge, wireless conference room, and other upscale perks.

Only a few blocks east there are more affordable studios and one-bedrooms in buildings dating from the early 1900s. North of Pike Place, there is an assortment of apartments and low-income housing units. Like much of Downtown, home and personal security issues may make Belltown an unsuitable choice for some newcomers. People interested in living Downtown should become familiar and comfortable with the area before choosing a home here. (See the end of this profile for more on safety concerns.)

The Seattle **Waterfront**, facing Elliott Bay and the craggy snow-capped Olympic Mountains, is another lively and exciting neighborhood in Downtown. Though one of the most touristy areas of Seattle, the Waterfront has many attractions for city residents, including a free bus route (99) linking the neighborhood to the downtown retail district, Pioneer Square, and the International District. Fine restaurants featuring fresh local seafood and superior views line the piers, as do many more casual eateries and several ice cream stands.

In previous years the city's Downtown retail district has expanded, enticing shoppers back from the suburban malls. Seattle-based Nordstrom, still the dominant player in the Downtown shopping scene, occupies the spacious and remodeled former Frederick & Nelson building, and the posh Pacific Place mall currently houses upscale shops such as Michael Kors, Coach, L'Occitane, and Tiffany & Co. Nike Town and American Apparel added stores on 6th Avenue, and Anthropologie and Urban Outfitters attract shoppers to 5th Avenue. The Fairmont Olympic Hotel, on the original site of the University of Washington, offers visitors lavish accommodations close to the City Center and Rainier Square shops.

Bounded by Denny Way, Interstate 5 and 5th Avenue, the often-overlooked **Denny Triangle** neighborhood is experiencing a renaissance, similar to the 1990s redevelopment of the Belltown and Denny Regrade neighborhoods. Development plans here include a large number of new housing units; in fact, the city's comprehensive plan for the area estimates a 450% increase by 2014, to about 5,000 units. This increase in available housing is particularly noteworthy in Denny Triangle where, for years, the only recognizable landmarks were the Greyhound Bus Station and the venerable Camlin Hotel. The area already is home to multi-use high-rises with offices, condos, apartments, and hotels, including the 31-story Metropolitan Tower Apartments, bordered by Virginia Street and Seventh and Westlake avenues, and the federal courthouse. A new Whole Foods Market serves Denny Triangle residents. Also new to the area, the Cornish College of the Arts expanded and created a main campus in the vicinity of Lenora and Boren avenues. As in Belltown, rents here are rising, but the Denny Triangle Neighborhood

Denny Triangle

Association says housing will be aimed at all income levels. The mayor is proposing zoning changes that will make way for taller and narrower buildings than are now allowed in the area in exchange for developers offering some low- and middle-income housing. The city's new streetcar service bisects this neighborhood on its

South Lake Union

way between South Lake Union and Westlake Center.

Finally, northeast of Downtown, at the southern end of Lake Union, the **South Lake Union** neighborhood (formerly known as Cascade), once primarily industrial, has recently undergone a profound transformation. Paul Allen (co-founder of Microsoft), with his company, Vulcan Northwest, bought substantial acreage in the neighborhood and new mixed-use buildings have sprouted, including the huge 220 Westlake Complex and the Westlake-Terry Building. In 2010, Amazon, the world's largest online retailer, relocated its headquarters (and its 4,000 employees) to a massive 11-building complex at South Lake Union. SLU, as it is sometimes called, has become the new biotech hub in the city, with UW Medicine and ZymoGenetics setting up shop here. Other tenants of the neighborhood include REI, the retailer of outdoor gear, and the Tommy Bahama clothing company. The South Lake Union line of the Seattle Streetcar runs through SLU and connects riders to other public transit systems in the city. Lake Union Park, a new 12-acre waterfront park, celebrated its grand opening in the fall of 2010. The ultimate goal of South Lake Union's redevelopment is an urban village feel, with people living and working in the same neighborhood, and easy access to and from downtown. The Cascade P-Patch community garden at Minor Avenue North and Thomas Street, and the recently renovated Cascade Playground at the corner of Harrison Street and Pontius Avenue North help maintain the feel of a livable neighborhood.

Apartments and low-income housing units in the blocks east of Fairview Avenue include the Lakeview Apartments, erected in 2000 at the intersection of Harrison Street and Minor Avenue North. Sophisticated Federal-style brick buildings on Eastlake Avenue also offer affordable apartments and low-income housing opportunities. The new Rollin Street Flats at the corner of Westlake and Denny, the Alcyone, and the nearby Alley24 developments provide additional rental units. There are growing pains in South Lake Union, however, and many residents fear that the neighborhood will not remain affordable for long.

A cautionary note, Seattle's downtown core is a varied and lively area: a mix of modern condominiums and apartments, artists' lofts, and homeless shelters amidst busy shopping and nightlife districts. Such an urban mix is a far cry from more traditional secluded neighborhoods, and is something to consider when examining the livability of the area. Violent crimes tend to be highest in Seattle's downtown core: the Pioneer Square, International District, Central District, Denny Regrade, and Belltown neighborhoods. The section of 3rd Avenue between Pike and Pine streets downtown is a notoriously troubled area, and should be avoided. (See **Safety and Crime** in **Getting Settled** for more information.)

Website: www.seattle.gov

Area Code: 206

Zip Codes: 98121, 98101, 98104, 98109, 98134

Post Office: Main Office Station, 301 Union St, 206-748-5417

Libraries: Central Library, 1000 4th Ave, 206-386-4636, www.spl.org; Washington Talking Book and Braille Library, 2021 9th Ave, 206-615-0400, 206-615-0419 (TTY), www.wtbbl.org

Public Schools: Seattle Public Schools, 2445 3rd Ave S, 206-252-0010, www.seattleschools.org

Police: West Precinct, 810 Virginia St, 206-684-8917, www.seattle.gov/police

Emergency Hospital: Harborview Medical Center, 325 9th Ave, 206-744-3000, www.uwmedicine.washington.edu

Community Publications: Belltowner (blog), www.belltowner.com; Belltown People (blog), www.belltownpeople.com; Downtown Seattle (blog), www.downtownseattle.com/blog

Community Resources: Belltown P-Patch, 2520 Elliott Ave, 206-684-0264, www.seattle.gov/neighborhoods; Central Neighborhood Service Center, 2301 S Jackson St, Ste 208, 206-684-4767, www.seattle.gov/neighborhoods/nsc; Downtown Seattle Association, 600 Stewart St, 206-623-0340, www.downtownseattle.com; PikePlace Blog, www.pikeplacemarket.org/news_events/blog

Public Transportation: Metro Transit, 206-553-3000, http://metro.kingcounty. gov: 1– 5, 7, 10–19, 21–28, 33–37, 39, 41–43, 49, 54–57, 64, 66, 70–74, 76, 77, 79, 81–85, 98, 99, 101, 102, 106, 111, 113, 114, 116, 118–125, 131, 132, 134, 143, 150, 152, 157–159, 161, 162, 175, 177, 179, 190, 192, 196, 202, 210– 212, 214–218, 225, 229, 250, 252, 255–257, 260, 262, 265, 266, 268, 280, 301, 303, 304, 306, 308, 311, 312, 316, 355, 358, 401, 402, 404–406, 408, 410– 417, 421, 422, 424, 425, 435, 477, 600, 994; Sound Transit, 206-398-5000, www.soundtransit.org; 510, 511, 513, 522, 545, 550, 554, 577, 578, 590, 592– 595

INTERNATIONAL DISTRICT

Boundaries: **North**: South Jackson Street; **West**: 4th Avenue South; **South**: South Dearborn Street; **East**: Rainier Avenue South

Also known as Chinatown, the International District was originally home to immigrant Chinese men who, in the late 1800s, provided an inexpensive source of labor for the railroad, fish, and lumber industries. In the early 1900s, the center of the neighborhood shifted from the waterfront to its present location, just east of the new football stadium. By then, Japanese immigrants had also moved to the area, and Filipino families soon followed. Today, a blend of Asian influences flavors the International District, with residents of Chinese, Japanese, Korean, Filipino, Vietnamese, and Southeast Asian descent sharing one bustling community.

The International District, or the "I.D." as locals often call it, is located conveniently close to downtown, Pioneer Square, and the Central District, and I-5 passes right through the neighborhood. But, until recently, the appearance of Asian characters in shop windows was the only indication to visitors that they had come to a culturally diverse and distinct community. The neighborhood lacked a definitive entrance, like the ornamental gates of San Francisco's Chinatown. International District leaders created a neighborhood beautification and public art program that installed cheerful banners along 4th and 5th avenues and Jackson Street, as well as 11 large, vividly colored dragon sculptures at various street corners. The 12- to 18-foot dragons twine around light poles and attract the attention of tourists and locals alike.

Visitors frequent the area primarily for its Asian cuisine, with dozens of restaurants specializing in traditional Chinese, Japanese, and Vietnamese dishes. Herb stores, groceries, and bakeries line South King Street and surrounding side streets, and the king of all Asian markets, Uwajimaya, anchors the neighborhood at 600 5th Avenue South. The $15 million expansion and redevelopment of Uwajimaya doubled the size of the old store, and added 176 apartments and several restaurants. Rents range from just under $1,100 to nearly $2,000 per month. The huge complex serves as a bridge between the community's ancient

International District

culture and contemporary development. Before 2003, no new family housing had been added to the neighborhood in 50 years, but during the last decade 750 new subsidized and market-rate housing units have gone up. The neighborhood's newest development is the 705 Lofts complex on South Weller Street, which added 10 apartments to the area.

The heart of the International District is the site of the old Chinatown, which lies between 4th Avenue South and I-5. The main thoroughfare is Jackson Street, although many of the historic buildings and businesses are a few blocks off Jackson. Chinatown is peppered with historic hotels, many of which have been converted into low-income housing and affordable apartments for senior citizens. There are also apartments and condominiums available for middle-income families and young professionals, similar to the units at the Uwajimaya Village Apartments. On the east side of I-5, a stretch of the International District known as "**Little Saigon**" is centered around the intersection of 12th Avenue and Jackson Street. Here you'll find an inviting selection of Vietnamese groceries and take-out restaurants. The I-5 underpass on Jackson Street serves as a corridor to Little Saigon with painted and decorated freeway columns.

Crime rates here are comparable to the rest of downtown, and the area ranks fourth in the city for violent crimes.

Despite these statistics, the availability of affordable housing has drawn a growing number of people to the area. Between 2000 and 2010, the population here increased by 20%, to more than 2,500 residents. While most residents in the International District are of Asian or Pacific Island descent, others live here as well, such as a portion of King County's increasing Hispanic population. An interest in downtown living seems to be attracting younger residents to a community that in recent decades had a median age in the mid-50s.

Website: www.seattle.gov
Area Code: 206
Zip Codes: 98134, 98144, 98104, 98122
Post Office: International Station, 414 6th Ave S, 206-625-2293
Library: Central Library, 1000 4th Ave, 206-386-4636, www.spl.org
Public Schools: Seattle Public Schools, 2445 3rd Ave S, 206-252-0010, www.seattleschools.org
Police: West Precinct, 810 Virginia St, 206-684-8917, www.seattle.gov/police
Emergency Hospital: Harborview Medical Center, 325 9th Ave, 206-744-3000, www.uwmedicine.washington.edu
Community Publications: *Northwest Asian Weekly,* 412 Maynard Ave S, 206-223-5559, www.nwasianweekly.com; *Seattle Chinese Post,* 412 Maynard Ave S, 206-223-5559, www.seattlechinesepost.com
Community Resources: Central Neighborhood Service Center, 2301 S Jackson St, 206-684-4767, www.seattle.gov; Chinatown/International Dis-

trict Business Improvement Area, 507 S King St, Ste 208, 206-382-1197, www.cibia.org; Danny Woo Community Garden, Kobe Terrace Park, 221 6th Ave S

Public Transportation: Metro Transit, 206-553-3000, http://metro.kingcounty. gov: 7,14, 60, 99; International District/Chinatown Station Transit Tunnel; 41, 71–73, 74E, 76, 77, 101, 102, 106, 150, 212, 216, 217, 218, 225, 229, 255, 256, 301, 316; Sound Transit, 206-398-5000, www.soundtransit.org: 550

FIRST HILL

Boundaries: **North**: East Pike Street; **West**: I-5; **South**: Yesler Way; **East**: 12th Avenue East

First Hill, commonly referred to as "Pill Hill" because of the concentration of hospitals, clinics, and medical offices in the area, lies directly east of downtown. Seattle's elite originally settled in First Hill in the mid-1800s as the city expanded beyond the downtown boundary. Later, many affluent First Hill residents moved to more distant neighborhoods, such as Madison Park and Laurelhurst. Only a few of the early homes remain, including the Tudoresque Stimson-Green Mansion built in 1898. Other remaining structures not supplanted by medical office buildings, schools, hospitals, and hotels serve as private clubs and reception halls.

The main commercial street on First Hill is Madison Street, with an assortment of cafés, delis, hotels, and pharmacies that serve hospital and office personnel, patients, and nearby residents. George's Sausage & Delicatessen has been feeding legions of scrubs-clad workers a hearty lunch since 1983; the newly reopened Vito's is a historic bar that caters to cocktail geeks. The Sorrento Hotel on Madison Street is an exquisite brick building, constructed in 1907 and designed by well-known Seattle architect Harlan Thomas, designer of the 1929 Harborview Medical Center. Harborview, a few blocks south of Madison Street on First Hill, serves as the premier emergency care center in the Seattle area. One of the treasures of the city, the Frye Art Museum, located a block away from busy Boren Avenue, offers free admission to all.

There are few single-family houses on First Hill except for those in the area south of Harborview, which tends to be noisy due to ambulance sirens and the nearby freeway. Most First Hill residents live in apartments or condominiums facing downtown to the west or Capitol Hill to the north. The city expects to add an additional 1,400 households to the First Hill neighborhood by 2024, as employment opportunities here increase. On the west side of First Hill, an assortment of apartment buildings bordering I-5 offers views of downtown and Elliott Bay. Although freeway noise can be distracting in these residences, there

First Hill

is a nice mix of high- and low-end apartments, and many downtown professionals and doctors choose to live in the area for convenience. Elegant brick apartment buildings from the early 1900s offering secured entrances and pleasant surroundings are tucked along side streets. These buildings are only a few minutes' stroll from downtown, and the average Walk Score for the neighborhood is 94, which means all amenities are conveniently close. Also, check the north end of First Hill for a selection of brick or stucco apartment buildings that date from the late 1920s. A majority (over 78%) of First Hill residents are renters, and rents in this neighborhood average around $1,500 for a two-bedroom unit—about the same as you'll find in Ravenna and Eastlake and somewhat less than rents on Capitol Hill. Housing prices on First Hill are significantly less than those in the East Lake area.

As with nearby Capitol Hill, First Hill plays an important role in Seattle's Catholic community. Two influential Catholic schools are located here: Seattle University, a private Jesuit college on Broadway, and O'Dea Catholic High School near Madison Street.

Website: www.seattle.gov

Area Code: 206

Zip Codes: 98101, 98104, 98122

Post Office: Midtown Station, 301 Union St, 206-748-5417

Library: Central Library, 1000 4th Ave, 206-386-4636, www.spl.org

Public Schools: Seattle Public Schools, 2445 3rd Ave S, 206-252-0010, www.seattleschools.org

Police: East Precinct, 1519 12th Ave, 206-684-4300, www.seattle.gov/police

Emergency Hospital: Harborview Medical Center, 325 9th Ave, 206-744-3000, www.uwmedicine.washington.edu

Community Publication: *Capitol Hill Times*, 636 S Alaska St, 206-461-1300, www.capitolhilltimes.com

Community Resource: Yesler Community Center, 917 E Yesler Way, 206-386-1245

Public Transportation: Metro Transit, 206-553-3000, http://metro.kingcounty.gov: 2, 3, 4, 9, 12, 27, 60, 64, 84, 193, 205, 211, 303, 309, 984

CAPITOL HILL

Boundaries: North: Fuhrman Avenue East; **West**: I-5; **South**: East Pike Street; **East**: 23rd/24th Avenue East

Vibrant and diverse, Capitol Hill is one of Seattle's best-loved and most densely populated neighborhoods, where affordable (but rising) rents, offbeat retailers, and an international array of restaurants lure a rainbow of residents. It is both the center of Seattle's large gay community and a neighborhood of traditional Catholic families. At the north end, there is St. Mark's Cathedral and the Episcopal Archdiocese; at the south end is Neighbour's, a cavernous gay dance club.

Broadway is the main street of Capitol Hill. Running the length of the hill, it serves as the center of the community's commercial district, and half of the retail and restaurant businesses in the neighborhood are concentrated along this arterial. It is the place to go for lively dining or take-out; boisterous, young residents fill innumerable restaurants and bars nightly, and on summer evenings the street rings with voices late into the night. In addition to the local eateries, there are many businesses on Broadway that cater to a youthful clientele, including tattoo and body piercing shops, secondhand clothing and record stores, costume jewelers, bead shops, head shops, and gay/lesbian bookstores.

East Pike Street and East Pine Street, south of Broadway's retail core, are the center of Capitol Hill's nightlife. The area has an assortment of bars, pool halls, dance clubs, and restaurants, though this once slightly seedy district has become more refined. On East Pike Street, a collection of trendy boutiques has sprung up. The Elliott Bay Book Company, a venerable Seattle institution, was revitalized by its move from Pioneer Square to 10th Ave between Pike and Pine on Capitol Hill in 2010. A large grocery and shopping complex takes up the corner of East Pike Street and Broadway.

Fifteenth Avenue East, five blocks east of Broadway, is another Capitol Hill retail district. This area is understated and stylish but also funky and quaint, with mod boutiques, swank eateries, and cozy pubs. Fifteenth Avenue East caters to a slightly older crowd, attracting hip baby boomers and comfortably domestic gays and lesbians. The

Capitol Hill

mood here is laid-back and placid, an agreeable alternative to the constant bustle of Broadway.

To the north, Capitol Hill is filled with lovely, albeit expensive, houses, most with enchanting views. To examine the stunning vistas yourself, climb to the top of the old water tower in Volunteer Park. Homes on the eastern slope of Capitol Hill have views of the Cascades or Lake Washington; a few even offer a glimpse of Mount Rainier from a top story window. On the west side, residences look out over Lake Union, the Fremont Bridge, and the Olympic Mountains. Homes in Capitol Hill, particularly at the north end, are large and fashionable. While many are Colonials, Dutch Colonials, Victorian or Federal-style houses, the most common type of home in this area is the Northwest Modern, or "Capitol Hill Box House."

In addition to the water tower, Volunteer Park features the Seattle Asian Art Museum, a charming old water reservoir, a delightful glass conservatory, and an outdoor amphitheater for summer concerts. Homes around Volunteer Park include some of the most formal and ornate mansions in Seattle. Many are old Victorian or Federal style houses, while others are stately versions of the Northwest Modern style. Though a few homes have become unobtrusive bed and breakfasts, most are still occupied by wealthy Seattle families. Many of Capitol Hill's affluent Catholic residents live in the area and attend church at the beautiful St. Joseph's Catholic Church. Others attend St. Patrick's, at the far north end of Capitol Hill, near Roanoke Park.

South of East Aloha Street, apartments are more common and houses are smaller. Federal-style brick buildings abound in this area, subdivided into small but classic apartments, with hardwood floors and coved ceilings. Most people who live near Broadway are renters, although there are houses tucked away on the side streets that lead back toward Volunteer Park. West of Broadway, almost all of the available residences are apartments or condominiums, with many large modern apartment complexes built over I-5 and offering views of downtown and the Olympic Mountains. Rents are relatively high in this area, although many studio apartments are available. Despite its dense population, the charm of this neighborhood is that it is one of the few Seattle areas where you can walk anywhere you might need to go. In fact, having a car can be a disadvantage here, where parking is at best a challenge. By 2016, Capitol Hill will be linked to the UW via the city's expanding light rail service. The Capitol Hill Station on Broadway and transit tunnel will be completed by 2015. In addition, several bus routes connect Capitol Hill with downtown and the University District, the major hubs of the Metro bus system.

East of Broadway, residences are a haphazard mix of houses, duplexes, and apartment buildings. Homes tend to be smaller and less ornate than those on north Capitol Hill but the styles are similar—primarily Northwest Moderns, Colonials, and Victorians. Many houses here are available as single-family or multiple-tenant rentals. Apartments in this area are generally less expensive than those on the west side of the hill, depending on the building and location. East of 15th Avenue East and south of East John Street, houses and apartments are even less expensive, particularly south of the radio towers and close to the Central District. Residents here tend to be young, a mix of artists, musicians, and college students from Seattle Central Community College or Seattle University.

Website: www.seattle.gov
Area Code: 206
Zip Codes: 98102, 98112, 98122
Post Office: Broadway Station, 101 Broadway E, 206-324-5474
Library: 425 Harvard Ave E, 206-684-4715, www.spl.gov
Public Schools: Seattle Public Schools, 2445 3rd Ave S, 206-252-0010, www.seattleschools.org
Police: East Precinct, 1519 12th Ave, 206-684-4300, www.seattle.gov/police
Emergency Hospital: Swedish Medical Center, First Hill Campus, 747 Broadway, 206-386-6000, www.swedish.org
Community Publication: Capitol Hill (blog), http://blog.seattlepi.com/capitolhill; *Capitol Hill Times*, 636 S Alaska St, 206-461-1300, www.capitolhilltimes.com
Community Resources: Central Neighborhood Service Center, 2301 S Jackson St, Ste 208, 206-684-4767, www.seattle.gov/neighborhoods/nsc; Capitol Hill Community Resource Center, P.O. Box 20306, Seattle, WA 98099, 206-313-2892, http://chcrc-seattle.org; Miller Community Center, 330 19th Ave E, 206-684-4753; Capitol Hill P-Patch, 1010 E Thomas St, 206-684-0264, Thomas Street Garden P-Patch, 1010 E Thomas St; Unpaving Paradise P-Patch, E John St and Summit Ave E; www.seattle.gov/neighborhoods/ppatch
Public Transportation: Metro Transit, 206-553-3000, http://metro.kingcounty.gov: 8–12, 14, 25, 43, 49, 60, 84, 984

EASTLAKE

Boundaries: **North**: Lake Washington Ship Canal; **West**: Lake Union; **South**: East Galer Street; **East**: I-5

Just north of downtown, on the east side of Lake Union, lies the aptly named Eastlake neighborhood. Long thought of as simply an easy shortcut to downtown, Eastlake has blossomed into a charming close-knit community. Most of the retail shops and restaurants in the neighborhood are clustered along Eastlake Avenue East. Rows of houseboats share the shore of Lake Union with marine repair shops, dry docks, and National Oceanic and Atmospheric Administration

Eastlake

(NOAA) ships. To explore the appealing houseboats in Eastlake, begin at Pete's Wine Shop, located at the base of East Lynn Street, then work north or south along the shore. While the houseboats vary widely in size and luxury, all share in the daily spectacle of sailboats and seaplanes on Lake Union, and the annual Independence Day fireworks display and Christmas Ship Parade.

More traditional housing is abundant in Eastlake as well. The neighborhood has an interesting mix of apartments, condominiums, duplexes, and single-family homes. Large 1970s-style apartment buildings dot the area and offer plenty of rentals, many with views of Lake Union. More traditional brick Federal-style buildings offer both apartments and condominiums. Homes in Eastlake range from turn-of-the-century Victorians to simple Northwest Moderns. Eastlake has boomed in recent years as both a commercial and residential area, and the result has been extensive new construction throughout the area. New townhouses and apartments can be found in the few blocks between Eastlake Avenue and the lake and along Franklin Avenue East, and new condo construction continues. In 1998 the Seattle City Council voted to adopt the Eastlake Neighborhood Plan, a strategy for developing the neighborhood prepared by a committee of local residents, and business and property owners.

At the north end of Fairview Avenue, along the edge of Lake Union, are the last vestiges of the old Eastlake community. Here quaint and slightly run-down summer cottages face the lakeshore. This is the site of the Eastlake P-Patch community garden, which, like the community gardens in the International District and on Capitol Hill, is a quiet treasure for those who live here. Unfortunately, what makes this area quaint—the small number of houses—also makes it difficult to find a place to live.

Eastlake is nice. It's well located with easy access to downtown, I-5, I-90, and the 520 bridge, and it's friendly. Prospective neighbors might include university students in rental housing and apartment complexes along busy Boylston Avenue East; young professionals who rent and buy homes and condominiums along Franklin Avenue East, East Roanoke Street, and East Lynn Street; and well-to-do baby boomers who live west of Eastlake Avenue East, close to Lake Union. In addition, many older lifelong Eastlake residents still live in this community. As in much of Seattle, rents here continue to rise. They average about the same as what you'll find in Ravenna and First Hill.

Websites: www.seattle.gov, www.eastlakeseattle.org
Area Code: 206
Zip Code: 98102
Post Offices: Broadway Station, 101 Broadway E, 206-324-5474; Lake Union Mail, 117 E Louisa St
Library: Capitol Hill Branch, 425 Harvard Ave E, 206-684-4715, www.spl.org
Public Schools: Seattle Public Schools, 2445 3rd Ave S, 206-252-0010, www.seattleschools.org
Police: West Precinct, 810 Virginia St, 206-684-8917, www.seattle.gov/police
Emergency Hospital: Harborview Medical Center, 325 9th Ave, 206-744-3000, www.uwmedicine.washington.edu
Community Publications: Eastlake Avenue Blog, http://eastlakeave.com; Eastlake Neighborhood Blog, www.eastlakeblog.org
Community Resources: Montlake Community Center, 1618 E Calhoun St, 206-684-4736; Eastlake Community Council, 117 E Louisa St, www.eastlakeseattle.org, 206-322-5463; Floating Homes Association, 2329 Fairview Ave E, 206-325-1132, www.seattlefloatinghomes.org
Public Transportation: Metro Transit, 206-553-3000, http://metro.kingcounty.gov: 25, 66, 70–73, 83

QUEEN ANNE

Interbay
Lower Queen Anne
Westlake

Boundaries: North: Lake Washington Ship Canal; **West**: 15th Avenue West, Elliott Avenue West; **South**: Denny Way; **East**: Lake Union, Aurora Avenue North (Highway 99)

Situated on a hill towering 457 feet over downtown and Elliott Bay, Queen Anne is one of the oldest and loveliest residential areas in the city. In the 1890s, streetcar lines from downtown brought affluent residents up the south slope of the hill to their grand mansions. Since its origin, the Queen Anne neighborhood has flourished, remaining an idyllic residential area only minutes from downtown. Queen Anne Avenue North (locals call it "the Ave") is the main commercial street, a bustling stretch where residents gather for morning coffee and brunch in picturesque cafés, meet for lunch or dinner at local bars and restaurants, or shop in the upscale boutiques, specialty bakeries, the Thursday farmers' market and the local bookstore. Increasingly, older single-story buildings are being replaced with multi-story mixed residential and retail developments, lending a more urban quality to the neighborhood.

Surrounding the shopping district, modest Colonials and simple bungalows are home to a mix of families, older professionals, and students. In addition, formal Northwest Moderns and Tudors are home to retired folks who have lived on the hill for many years. Because of the desirability of this area, many apartment and condominium buildings have been built in recent years, replacing some older single-family dwellings. The most affordable houses and apartments are those without a view. This is a pleasant area, with well-maintained houses surrounded by lovely lawns and beautiful nearby parks. The playground at John Hay Elementary School, east of Queen Anne Avenue North, is the site of weekend basketball games; a block west of this main thoroughfare, city ballparks are host to softball games on lazy summer afternoons.

The southwest corner of Queen Anne remains an enclave for affluent and longtime residents. The homes in this area are lavish, many glimpsed only through breaks in landscaped hedges. West Highland Drive, offering unbelievable views of downtown, Elliott Bay, Mount Rainier, and the Olympic Mountains, is lined with many of the hill's original Queen Anne–style houses. In the blocks north of West Highland Drive, homes are less expensive but still well maintained. Most are modest Four Square or Queen Anne–style houses; a few are Craftsman-style bungalows. To see the merits of this neighborhood, walk or drive to Kerry Park, located on the south side of West Highland Drive. From this vantage point, the downtown cityscape and the shipping activities of Elliott Bay seem an arm's length away; in the distance, Mount Rainier towers over the city. The park is a favorite of nearby residents, who come after dark to admire the brilliant lights of downtown or to watch fireworks over the bay on Independence Day.

East of Queen Anne Avenue North, a variety of large and expensive homes share a lovely view of downtown and Mount Rainier. Many are elaborate Elizabethans and Colonials; others are large unadorned contemporary homes. Residents include a mix of wealthy entrepreneurs, foreign diplomats, and affluent professionals. In addition to breathtaking glimpses of Mount Rainier and downtown, the east side of the hill offers views of azure Lake Union and Capitol Hill. Many 1950s apartment buildings cling to this side of the hill, offering affordable rentals for young professionals. In addition, several houses and apartment buildings in the area have been remodeled and made

Queen Anne

into condominiums. Many of the people living in this corner of Queen Anne are middle-income professionals who work downtown. A word of advice: this is not the neighborhood to live in if your job is on the Eastside. Commuting from Queen Anne to the Eastside can take as much as an hour, sometimes more, during peak travel times.

The north and west sides of Queen Anne Hill are the best locations for reasonably priced rentals in the neighborhood. Many students and faculty live in Queen Anne because Seattle Pacific University (SPU) is located at the base of the hill to the north. Around the SPU campus are numerous rentals, including unpretentious apartment buildings, modest houses, tiny houseboats, and renovated storefronts. The west side of Queen Anne, including **Interbay**, a light industrial strip between Queen Anne and Magnolia, offers affordable rental apartments in modest brick and large contemporary buildings as well as rental houses and duplexes, mostly converted bungalows. Interbay is noisy and gritty, due to traffic on 15th Avenue West and the rumbling of passing trains, but some apartments here enjoy views of the Sound and the Olympic Mountains peaking over Magnolia. Amenities include a nine-hole golf course, athletic field complex, a Red Mill Burger, and a QFC grocery. Most recently, a new Whole Foods market, along with several restaurants and a liquor store, has been added, and additional developments are likely in the future. Interbay has also been identified as a possible site for a new misdemeanor jail facility, a proposal that has encountered resistance from many Queen Anne and Magnolia residents.

Apartments and condominiums are also plentiful in the **Lower Queen Anne** area, which surrounds the Seattle Center, site of the Space Needle. Built for the 1962 World's Fair, the 74-acre Seattle Center is a combination music and arts center currently undergoing a major transformation. Proposals for the space formerly occupied by the Fun Forest amusement park include a museum devoted to local glass artist Dale Chihuly and a new studio for KEXP radio station. Among the Center's many attractions are the Pacific Science Center, the Experience Music Project and Science Fiction Museum, McCaw Hall (home of the Seattle Opera), Pacific Northwest Ballet, Seattle Repertory Theatre, and Key Arena, where the Seattle Storm play. Every summer, Seattle Center is the site for Bumbershoot, a music-and-arts festival, as well as the Northwest Folklife Festival and the Bite of Seattle (see **A Seattle Year** for more details about these and other annual events) as well as a gathering place for families with children, who love to frolic in the International Fountain. In 2001, the Gates Foundation, the world's largest charitable organization, opened a new campus directly across from the Seattle Center. The $500-million, 12-acre site supports 1,200 employees and will undoubtedly spur many new developments in the area. Currently, the Lower Queen Anne area includes retail and residential districts to the north and west. Small Asian restaurants are located along Roy Street north of the Seattle Center, and cafés, bars, and restaurants cluster around Queen Anne Avenue North. Apartment buildings of all styles fill this area, from small brick buildings on Roy Street to enormous contemporary buildings along Queen Anne Avenue North. Many of the condominiums in the area were converted from former apartment buildings.

Finally, the **Westlake** area, located at the eastern base of the hill, is a commercial and increasingly residential district that runs along the west side of Lake Union. Water views and proximity to the new South Lake Union neighborhood have revitalized the area, and new housing developments along Westlake and Dexter Avenue cater to young urban professionals. Rents here tend to be higher than in other parts of Queen Anne. Westlake Avenue is lined with upscale view restaurants, private marinas, and marine shops—a combination common in Seattle's waterfront areas. A few houseboats, including the one featured in the movie *Sleepless in Seattle,* are moored here.

Though rents can vary greatly depending on which Queen Anne neighborhood you choose, figures from Dupre + Scott Apartment Advisors show that the average rent in this area for a one-bedroom apartment is now about 20% lower than the average rent in Belltown. For buyers, Queen Anne remains one of the pricier neighborhoods in Seattle, but falling home prices in the wake of the collapse of the housing market in 2008 have made this area slightly more affordable.

Website: www.seattle.gov
Area Code: 206
Zip Codes: 98109, 98119
Post Office: Queen Anne Station, 415 1st Ave N, 206-378-4000
Library: 400 W Garfield St, 206-386-4227, www.spl.org

Public Schools: Seattle Public Schools, 2445 3rd Ave S, 206-252-0010, www.seattleschools.org

Police: West Precinct, 810 Virginia St, 206-684-8917, www.seattle.gov/police

Emergency Hospital: Swedish Medical Center, Ballard, 5350 Tallman Ave NW, 206-781-6341, www.swedish.org

Community Publication: *Queen Anne News*, 636 Alaska St S, 206-461-1300, www.queenannenews.com; Queen Anne View (blog), www.queenanneview.com

Community Resources: Interbay P-Patch, 2451 15th Ave W, www.seattle.gov/neighborhoods; Queen Anne Community Center, 1901 1st Ave W, 206-386-4240, www.seattle.gov/parks; Queen Anne Help Line, 206-282-1540, www.queenannehelpline.org, Queen Anne P-Patch, 3rd Ave N and Lynn St, www.seattle.gov/neighborhoods; Queen Anne Pool, 1920 1st Ave W, 206-386-4282, www.seattle.gov/parks

Public Transportation: Metro Transit, 206-553-3000, http://metro.kingcounty.gov: 1– 4, 8, 13, 15–19, 24, 26, 28, 30, 31, 33, 45, 74, 81, 82, 994

MAGNOLIA

Boundaries: **North**: Lake Washington Ship Canal; **West**: Puget Sound; **South**: Elliott Bay; **East**: 15th Avenue West

Just west of Queen Anne is the neighborhood of Magnolia, which like Queen Anne, is both a landmark Seattle hill and a community. Rumor has it that the hill was originally named for the distinctive Madrona trees that line the bluff, which a visiting sailor mistakenly identified as magnolias. In any case, the name stuck and now designates a charming neighborhood, which, despite its proximity to downtown, is truly a residential community. It has an interesting mix of homes, mainly Northwest Moderns, Craftsman-style bungalows, and brick Tudors—many with views of the beautiful Puget Sound and craggy Olympic Mountains to the west, or of the downtown skyline and busy Elliott Bay to the southeast.

The heart of Magnolia is "the Village," a collection of restaurants, shops, bakeries, and banks that spill over McGraw Street between 32nd and 34th avenues. Families gather here for Halloween trick-or-treating and in the summer for a children's parade. Professionals frequent the neighborhood Starbucks each morning before work, or meet friends at the local pub at the end of the day. Szmania's, a critically acclaimed restaurant, is located in the Village, along with a handful of small family-friendly eateries. A marina at the south end of Magnolia is also home to several popular restaurants, which share a spectacular panorama of Elliott Bay and downtown.

Magnolia

Because of the extraordinary views and the easy commute to downtown, homes in Magnolia are fairly expensive. Along "the bluff," which traces the west edge of Magnolia from south to north, you will find especially lavish homes. More modestly sized and priced homes are located at the north end of the hill and in the middle valley where there is little or no view. Here homeowners tend to be a mix of young families, established professionals or senior citizens; many are longtime residents.

Renters in Magnolia represent all levels of income and occupations, and rental properties include luxury lofts, townhouses, and condos as well as apartments and single-family homes. Because Magnolia is not conveniently located to I-5, apartments here rent for slightly less than the Seattle average, even those with water or city views. This is particularly true for the larger, two-bedroom apartments; studio rents are comparable to other neighborhoods. You'll find many apartment buildings located at the north end of the hill, facing Ballard, as well as new developments clustered adjacent to the Village.

Nearby, on the Lake Washington Ship Canal, the Fisherman's Terminal is an energetic hub with constant activity from the fishing vessels that dock there. A memorial honors those who lost their lives in pursuit of this dangerous livelihood. Just off West Emerson Street, part of the Fisherman's Terminal was transformed into a small shopping and dining destination, featuring Chinook's restaurant and the Bay Café, a nautical-theme gallery and gift store, Wild Salmon Seafood Market, and the Highliner Tavern. Continue on this route and you'll find Discovery Park and the Hiram Chittenden Locks. The locks, which separate the Lake Washington Ship Canal from the Puget Sound, offer an easy route for foot and bicycle traffic between Magnolia and Ballard. Discovery Park, in the northwest corner of Magnolia, is Seattle's largest and most verdant park, consisting of 534 acres of meadows, forest, and beach, with clay cliffs and miles of nature trails. The nearby West Point Lighthouse was built on the northwest point of the beach in 1881 and is still a popular attraction, although the attraction is now somewhat diminished by the close proximity of the West Point Sewage Treatment Plant.

Although Magnolia is not technically a peninsula, access to the hill is limited to Dravus Street, Nickerson Street, and the Magnolia Bridge. When the bridge is closed—as it has been a few times in past years due to mudslides and an earthquake—the commute to and from Magnolia lengthens considerably. Interbay, the semi-industrial area between Magnolia and Queen Anne, effectively cuts off Magnolia from the main thoroughfare of 15th Avenue West (Elliott Avenue), so only those three streets serve as overpasses into the neighborhood. Still, Magnolia is actually quite convenient to downtown and the surrounding neighborhoods, although getting to I-5 can be difficult.

Website: www.seattle.gov
Area Code: 206
Zip Code: 98199
Post Office: Magnolia Station, 3211 W McGraw St, 206-284-5958
Library: 2801 34th Ave W, 206-386-4225, www.spl.org
Public Schools: Seattle Public Schools, 2445 3rd Ave S, 206-252-0010, www.seattleschools.org
Police: West Precinct, 810 Virginia St, 206-684-8917, www.seattle.gov/police
Emergency Hospital: Swedish Medical Center, Ballard, 5350 Tallman Ave NW, 206-781-6341, www.swedish.org
Community Publication: *Magnolia News*, 636 Alaska St S, 206-461-1300; Magnolia Voice (blog), www.magnoliavoice.com

Ballard

Community Resources: Magnolia Community Center, 2550 34th Ave NW, 206-386-4235; Magnolia Community Club, www.magnoliacommunityclub.org; Pop Mounger Pool, 2535 32nd Ave W, www.seattle.gov/parks

Public Transportation: Metro Transit, 206-553-3000, http://metro.kingcounty.gov: 19, 24, 31, 33, 994

BALLARD

Central Ballard
East Ballard
Shilshole
Loyal Heights
Whittier Heights
Crown Hill
North Beach
Olympic Manor
Sunset Hill
Blue Ridge

Boundaries: **North**: NW 110th Street; **West**: Puget Sound; **South**: Lake Washington Ship Canal; **East**: 3rd Avenue NW

Ballard is a lively and growing neighborhood located just 15 minutes north of downtown. Originally a fishing and lumbering district that sprang up on the shores of Salmon Bay, Ballard was the first community to incorporate as a city after Washington became the 42nd state, and was later annexed to Seattle in 1907. Today it comprises a collection of neighborhoods that includes Sunset Hill, Central Ballard, East Ballard, Whittier Heights, Loyal Heights, North Beach, Olympic Manor, Crown Hill, and Blue Ridge. While the majority of Ballard's new housing developments and amenities cater to young urban professionals, with plenty of spanking new condos on Market Street within walking distance of trendy shops and restaurants, the neighborhood offers a range of housing options, from pricey waterfront property with jaw-dropping views of the snow-capped Olympic Mountains to modest single-family Craftsman homes with picket fences and back alleys.

The action in **Central Ballard** centers around the main drags of Market Street and the charming diagonal stretch of Ballard Avenue NW, officially designated a historic district in 1976. This former "Shingle Capital of the World" has undergone profound changes during the first decade of the new millennium as a result of Seattle's citywide efforts to promote urban density. Longtime residents bemoan the mixed condominium and retail developments that mushroomed seemingly overnight (a local bumper sticker proclaims: "Ballard

Welcomes Our New Condo Overlords"). In 2008, Ballard lost a striking landmark, and a conspicuous example of midcentury "Googie" architecture, when the Denny's restaurant on the corner of 15th Avenue NW and Market Street was bulldozed to make way for a development that has yet to materialize, leaving an empty lot to mar the corner of a prominent intersection.

Despite these changes, one can still find vestiges of Ballard's past that lend the neighborhood its special character. At one time this community attracted immigrants from five Scandinavian countries (Denmark, Finland, Iceland, Norway, and Sweden), who gravitated to the shores of Salmon Bay during the late 19th and early 20th centuries. The annual Ballard Seafood Fest celebrates the community's roots in Scandinavian culture and the fishing industry. You can also visit the Nordic Heritage Museum and admire the carved sea serpent on roof of the Leif Erikson Lodge.

Neighborhood veterans may grouse about Ballard "blandmarks," but by and large the neighborhood's past and present pleasantly coexist. Venerable hangouts like Hattie's Hat and Conor Byrne's Pub share the street with new shops and restaurants such as La Carta de Oaxaca and Bastille.

Away from Ballard's busy shopping districts, the demographic shifts into older apartment complexes and small to medium-sized single homes on either side of the unbeautiful arterial of 15th Avenue NW, enlivened by the ubiquitous and whimsical "Henry" murals. Families in the neighborhood with children have access to both small and large neighborhood parks as well as highly rated public schools such as Whitman Middle School and Ballard High. The recently constructed Ballard Library sports a green roof and is kitty-corner from the Ballard Commons Park, where skateboarders execute ollies in the skate bowl. In a metropolis where steep hills can pose a challenge to all but the most hardcore bicyclists, portions of Ballard offer some of the flatter terrain in the city, along with easily navigable grid-like streets. An older sense of community still abides here, among the weathered Craftsman houses with the occasional chicken coop in the front yard, though crime rates do prompt residents to lock their houses and their car doors at night. If you're thinking of purchasing a home in the neighborhood, the average home price in Ballard as of 2011 was between $400,000 and $450,000.

Ballard's past is emphatically blue collar, as is evident in the more industrial sections of **East Ballard**, but the current wave of residents consists of white-collar, college-educated single professionals in their early twenties to mid-forties. Most of these residents rent their apartments and condos, and they work in a variety of services and the professional sector. The average commute from Ballard is 23 minutes—but commuting from here to the Eastside will take much longer. If you work for Microsoft, or if you're hoping to land a job there, you should consider settling in another neighborhood. Note, too, that access from Ballard to downtown and Highway 99 can be complicated when the Ballard Bridge opens to allow ships through.

On weekends, the pace in this part of the city is both lively and relaxed. The Hiram M. Chittenden Locks, an engineering marvel built in 1911 to link Puget Sound with lakes Union and Washington via the Ship Canal, is always a big hit with visitors, especially when throngs of silvery salmon muscle through the fish ladder. East of 32nd Avenue NW, the **Shilshole** section of Ballard offers modest brick Tudors and Arts-and-Crafts-style homes with a panorama of Bainbridge Island, Puget Sound, and the Olympics. **Shilshole** is best known throughout the city for the seafood restaurants that line Seaview Avenue NW, such as Ray's Boathouse and Anthony's Homeport. Seaview ends at Golden Gardens, which sounds like a retirement community but is actually a beachfront park that attracts scores of people during the warm weather for picnics, swimming, and volleyball.

Public transportation is readily available in Ballard. Several bus routes run to downtown along 15th Avenue NW and 24th Avenue NW, and there are regular routes to Wallingford and the University District that run along NW Market Street and NW 85th Street.

North of Old Ballard, on either side of 15th Ave NW between 65th and 85th streets, you'll find **Loyal Heights** and **Whittier Heights,** respectively. These residential neighborhoods of modest homes and narrow, tree-shaded streets are convenient to plenty of amenities without all the hubbub of Ballard's bustling core. One of Seattle's 12 "official" hills, **Crown Hill** begins where 15th Avenue NW meets NW 85th Street, at a busy intersection dominated by a Walgreens pharmacy and a Safeway grocery whose storefront displays Scandinavian flags. The neighborhood stretches north along 15th Avenue NW, then curves east along Holman Road. Though at first glance Crown Hill appears to be simply an accumulation of fast food outlets, auto body shops, and dry cleaning establishments, the community does have its share of hidden treasures, such as Swanson's Nursery, established in 1924, and Crown Hill Hardware, which has been here for nearly 90th years. Crown Hill's residential clusters are quiet, with well-tended yards and a mixture of brick Tudors and ramblers. Affordable homes may still be found here, particularly north of NW 85th Street.

Elegant properties with views of the Puget Sound and the Olympic Mountains are situated on the northern and western hillsides of Ballard. Many of the homes in the **North Beach** area north of NW 85th Street, such as those in the **Olympic Manor** subdivision, are sprawling 1950s ranch houses with exquisitely landscaped yards. Other more recent additions to the neighborhood include elaborate Colonials, immaculate brick Tudor cottages, and contemporary designs from the 1960s and 1970s. Homes in sections such as **Sunset Hill** have a front-row seat for breathtaking sunsets over the Olympic Mountains. In the summer months, residents watch weekend sailboat races on the Sound; during the winter holidays, colorfully lighted ships follow the shoreline as part of the annual Christmas Ship Parade.

The hillside community of **Blue Ridge** is one of the least known and most isolated neighborhoods in the city. Located on Puget Sound, north of Northwest 100th Street and south of Carkeek Park, Blue Ridge was developed during the Depression by William Boeing for some of his airplane company executives. Entirely residential, with fewer than 500 homes, the community features a club, swimming pool, tennis courts, playfields, and a private beach. Blue Ridge is a covenant community, which means there are rules and restrictions that residents are required to follow. For instance, there may be guidelines for landscaping or improvements that homeowners can make to their properties. In the past, small homes in Blue Ridge have tended to sell for about 50% higher than those in Greenwood—tack on another $200,000 for a view. Larger homes, like those originally built by William Boeing, go for seven figures.

Despite the swankier accommodations of Blue Ridge, homes in Ballard are generally more staffordable than those in nearby neighborhoods like Queen Anne and Magnolia. Renters may also find Ballard to their liking where rents are less than those in Belltown or downtown, though apartments in the neighborhood's newer developments can be pricey.

Websites: www.seattle.gov, www.inballard.com
Area Code: 206
Zip Codes: 98103, 98107, 98108, 98117, 98133, 98177
Post Office: 5706 17th Ave NW, 206-781-4656
Library: 5614 22nd Ave NW, 206-684-4089, www.spl.lib.wa.us
Public Schools: Seattle Public Schools, 2445 3rd Ave S, 206-252-0010, www.seattleschools.org
Police: North Precinct,10049 College Way N, 206-684-0850, www.seattle.gov/police
Emergency Hospital: Swedish Medical Center Ballard, 5350 Tallman Ave NW, 206-781-6341, www.swedish.org
Community Publication: *Ballard News-Tribune*, 206-461-1300; My Ballard (blog), www.myballard.com
Community Resources: Ballard Chamber of Commerce, 2208 NW Market St., 206-784-9705, www.ballardchamber.com; Ballard Community Center, 6020 28th Ave NW, 206-684-4093, www.seattle.gov/parks; Ballard Help Line and Food Bank, 206-789-7800, www.ballardfoodbank.org; Ballard Neighborhood Service Center, 5604 22nd Ave NW, 206-684-4060, www.seattle.gov/neighborhoods/nsc; Ballard P-Patch, 8527 25th Ave NW, www.seattle.gov/neighborhoods; Ballard Pool, 1471 NW 67th St, 206-684-4094, www.seattle.gov/parks; Loyal Heights Community Center, 2101 NW 77th St, 206-684-4052, www.seattle.gov/parks
Public Transportation: Metro Transit, 206-553-3000, http://metro.kingcounty.gov: 15, 17, 18, 28, 44, 46, 75, 81, 994

PHINNEY RIDGE/GREENWOOD

Boundaries: North: Holman Road NW, North 105th Street; **West**: 8th Avenue NW, 3rd Avenue NW; **South**: North 50th Street; **East**. Aurora Avenue North (Highway 99)

The Phinney Ridge and Greenwood (or "Phinneywood" as some have taken to calling it) neighborhoods are located north of Fremont, between Ballard and Green Lake. The central feature of Phinney Ridge is the Woodland Park Zoo, located southwest of Green Lake across Aurora Avenue North. If visiting, be sure to walk through the fabulous rose garden at its 50th Street entrance. Phinney Ridge, a neighborhood known for its ever-present population of young families, is a perennial favorite of lower-middle-income, white collar professionals—teachers, public servants, nonprofit organization employees, etc., creating a neighborhood reputation of liberal political views and strong community involvement. However, in more recent years, the neighborhood has become popular with more affluent professionals, and housing prices have risen accordingly.

Most Phinney Ridge residents live in Northwest Moderns or Craftsman bungalows on the west side of the hill, sharing lovely views of Ballard, the Puget Sound, and the Olympic Mountains. Apartment buildings line Phinney Avenue North along the ridge of the hill, although they taper off north of the zoo as retail shops and restaurants become more prevalent. Just north of NW 65th Street, Phinney Avenue North jogs over to become a stretch of Greenwood Avenue North and the true commercial district begins. Here the Red Mill Burger Company serves delicious burgers to people from all over Seattle; on summer evenings the line to the counter commonly stretches out the door and along the sidewalk. On Sunday mornings, another popular destination is Mae's Phinney

Phinney Ridge

Ridge Café at 65th Street, where hungry Seattle residents also fill the sidewalk during the brunch hour—you know you've found it by the large Holsteins painted on the bright green walls of the café. This area also offers a fun selection of international and vegetarian restaurants, dress shops, cozy pubs, funky coffeehouses, and card and gift shops.

The main intersection of the Greenwood neighborhood is NW 85th Street and Greenwood Avenue NW. Commercial buildings include banks, restaurants, boutiques, and well-stocked pubs, as well as the Greenwood Senior Center and the Greenwood Library.

Greenwood

Greenwood Avenue NW is also known for its antique stores, and is a comfortable and pleasant shopping district. South of NW 85th Street, the Phinney Ridge and Greenwood neighborhoods are almost identical, with roomy bungalows and Northwest Modern homes on either side of the Greenwood Avenue NW retail core. North of NW 85th Street is a collection of more modest homes. Apartment seekers will find a selection of new apartment buildings along NW 85th Street, particularly in the few blocks just west of Aurora, and apartments circa 1970 line Greenwood Avenue NW, north of NW 90th Street. Affordable cottages, modern split-level homes, and duplexes can be found tucked away from the main streets of Greenwood Avenue North and 8th Avenue NW. Average rents here tend to be lower than in nearby Seattle neighborhoods such as Queen Anne, Ravenna, and Maple Leaf. Both Greenwood and Phinney Ridge are comfortable middle-class neighborhoods and many of the residents here are young professionals and their families.

Several blocks of both Greenwood and Phinney Ridge are situated close to Aurora Avenue North, a busy state highway and commercial district with a history of drugs and prostitution; prospective residents should consider this when looking at homes in the few blocks closest to Aurora Avenue North.

Websites: www.seattle.gov, www.phinneycenter.org
Area Code: 206
Zip Codes: 98103, 98107, 98117
Post Office: Greenwood Station, 8306 Greenwood Ave N, 206-547-1406
Library: 8016 Greenwood Ave N, 206-684-4086, www.spl.org
Public Schools: Seattle Public Schools, 2445 3rd Ave S, 206-252-0010, www.seattleschools.org
Police: North Precinct, 10049 College Way N, 206-684-0850, www.seattle.gov/police

Emergency Hospital: Swedish Medical Center Ballard, 5350 Tallman Ave NW, 206-781-6341, www.swedish.org

Community Publications: Greenwood-Phinney Blog, www.phinneyridge.org; *North Seattle Herald-Outlook*, 636 S Alaska St, 206-461-1300; Phinneywood (blog), www.phinneywood.com

Community Resources: Greenwood P-Patch, 345 NW 88th St, www.seattle.gov/ neighborhoods; Greenwood Senior Center, 525 N 85th St, 206-297-0875; Phinney Neighborhood Association, 6532 Phinney Ave N, 206-783-2244, http://phinneycenter.org; Phinney Ridge P-Patch, 5926 3rd Ave NW, www.seattle.gov/neighborhoods; University Neighborhood Service Center, 4534 University Ave NW, 206-684-7542, www.seattle.gov/neighborhoods/nsc

Public Transportation: Metro Transit, 206-553-3000, http://metro.kingcounty.gov: 5, 28, 44, 48, 82, 355, 358

FREMONT

Boundaries: **North**: North 46th Street/North Market Street; **East**: Stone Way North; **West**: 8th Avenue NW; **South**: Lake Washington Ship Canal and Fremont Bridge

Ten minutes north of downtown and across from the Lake Washington Ship Canal lies the picturesque Fremont district, a small Seattle neighborhood with its central core at the intersection of Fremont Avenue North, North 35th Street, and Fremont Place North, one block north of the Fremont Bridge. From here it is less than a five-minute walk to two of Seattle's most beloved sculptures, "Waiting for the Interurban" and the "Fremont Troll," as well as Seattle's most controversial statue, Emil Venkov's "Lenin," which was originally displayed in communist Slovakia in 1988.

The self-proclaimed "Center of the Universe," Fremont charms even the most cynical of Seattle residents with its mixture of inviting shops and events. It is the home of Hale's Brewery, as well as several other microbreweries and pubs. There are art galleries galore, vintage clothing and "junk" stores, barber shops, and tattoo parlors. On the weekends, Seattle residents flock to the district for brunch and shopping, or tour the Theo Chocolate Factory. At night, Fremont's pubs overflow with a friendly and diverse crowd of locals. This area is still relatively free of tourists, despite its proximity to downtown.

During the summer, the neighborhood hosts the Fremont Sunday Market, where residents and visitors can buy goods from local artists and artisans. Also popular is the PCC Natural Market on North 34th Street, a refreshing alternative to the corporate mega-grocers. One weekend in June is devoted to the summer solstice, and includes the annual Solstice Parade and Fremont Fair. On

Fremont

summer Saturday evenings, a parking lot doubles as the site for the Fremont Outdoor Cinema. Moviegoers bring their own chairs to watch the flick, which is projected on the wall of a building bordering the lot.

The area is primarily residential, with a combination of artists, students, and young professionals calling Fremont home, though the last several years have seen rapid commercial growth here. The Quadrant Lake Union Center, located just east of the Fremont Bridge, is home to Adobe Systems, and Getty Images inhabits the Park View Building just west of the bridge. Recent housing developments have added many additional condos to the neighborhood. Despite the new construction, the neighborhood has maintained its delicate balance of bohemian culture and middle-class comfort. It is a close-knit community, formerly popular among low and middle-income families, but rising prices have pushed the neighborhood beyond the reach of many first-time homeowners.

If you'd like to rent in Fremont, your best bet is to drive, bicycle, or walk through the area looking for "For Rent" signs in windows. There is plentiful rental property here, both apartments and houses, but available units are generally snapped up before being advertised in the local newspapers. Rents in Fremont tend to be slightly higher than the city average. Fremont's shopping district contains some rental space, especially in the few blocks north of Fremont Place North, but don't limit your search to that area. To the east of Fremont Avenue, and across or under Aurora Avenue, there are additional housing opportunities. Aurora can be fairly noisy during high traffic times, so if you're sensitive to that, try to visit nearby rentals on a weekday, around 5 p.m., to experience the noise level first-hand.

A few blocks north of Fremont's shopping district is NW 39th Avenue, which is lined with large apartment buildings built during the 1950s and 1960s. Since this area is along one of the main routes between Ballard, downtown, and the University District, it can be a little noisy during high traffic times. You'll find a more traditional residential area of 1920s Craftsman-style bungalows between NW 39th and NW 46th streets, and east of Fremont Avenue North. Upper Fremont Avenue between NW 41st and NW 45th streets, sometimes called Fremont Village, is a more affordable alternative to the central retail district, listed in 2011 as one of the city's best neighborhoods by *Seattle* magazine. New restaurants and shops have opened along this stretch in recent years, though locals mourn the loss of the old Buckeroo Tavern. As with most Seattle neighborhoods near a university or college, the best time for renting is late April through early June, when students are making plans to head home for the summer. Fremont is 20 to 25 minutes by car or bus from the University of Washington, and a 5- to 15-minute walk from Seattle Pacific University, which is just across the Fremont Bridge on the north side of the Queen Anne neighborhood.

Websites: www.seattle.gov, www.fremont.com
Area Code: 206
Zip Codes: 98103, 98107
Post Office: Wallingford Station, 1329 N 47th St, 206-547-1406
Library: 731 N 35th St, 206-684-4084, www.spl.org
Public Schools: Seattle Public Schools, 2445 3rd Ave S, 206-252-0010, www.seattleschools.org
Police: North Precinct, 10049 College Way N, 206-684-0850, www.seattle.gov/police
Emergency Hospital: Swedish Medical Center Ballard, 5350 Tallman Ave NW, 206-781-6341, www.swedish.org
Community Publications: Fremont Universe (blog), www.fremontuniverse.com; *North Seattle Herald-Outlook*, 636 S Alaska St, 206-461-1300
Community Resources: Fremont Neighborhood Council, www.scn.org/fnc; Fremont Whirled-Peas (P-Patch), 3935 Woodland Park Ave N, www.seattle.gov/neighborhoods; History House, 790 N 34th St, 206-675-8875, www.historyhouse.org
Public Transportation: Metro Transit, 206-553-3000, http://metro.kingcounty.gov: 5, 26, 28, 31, 46, 82

WALLINGFORD

Boundaries: **North**: Northeast 50th Street; **West**: Aurora Avenue North (Highway 99); **South**: Lake Washington Ship Canal; **East**: I-5

A symbol of a bygone era, the old gasworks at the north end of Lake Union marks the tip of the Wallingford neighborhood. In the early 1900s, when the plant was still operational, Wallingford was a hub of industrial activity. Now

Wallingford

the neighborhood is predominantly residential, and the old plant is a beloved Seattle landmark and popular public park. Gasworks Park is a favorite for kite-flying enthusiasts because of steady winds off the lake, and for bicyclists who meet to ride the Burke-Gilman trail along Lake Union and Lake Washington. In addition, Gasworks Park is the site of one of Seattle's annual Independence Day fireworks displays. Although the fireworks can be seen from anywhere around the lake, attendees here have the added benefit of watching the fireworks to the accompaniment of music and a live television broadcast.

Despite its proximity to downtown, Wallingford exudes a quiet charm. On summer evenings, couples stroll down tree-lined streets and visit with neighbors. On Sundays, people crowd into local restaurants for brunch or catch a matinee at the Guild 45th Theater. Like nearby Fremont, Wallingford is aesthetically pleasing and community focused. Elegant Wallingford Center, an old school that was remodeled in the 1980s to become an upscale condominium and retail shopping center, is considered the crown jewel of the area. Nearby, the 45th Street Medical and Dental Clinic shares a remodeled fire station with the Wallingford branch of the Seattle Public Library. Northeast 45th Street, connecting Fremont and Ballard to the University District, offers a pleasant assortment of restaurants, travel and used bookstores, and funky boutiques.

North of Gasworks Park, on the south slope of the hill, beautifully restored homes look out over the park and the downtown skyline. Many of the Victorian and Colonial houses here were built in the early 1900s. Northwest Moderns and Craftsman bungalows were added during the 1920s. Homeowners in this area tend to be young professionals, although rental opportunities attract students from the nearby UW and Seattle Pacific University. Streets here are quiet; churches and old schools dot the area, as do corner grocery stores and coffeehouses. Spectacular views of Lake Union and downtown, as well as modestly sized homes, have attracted many middle-income families to this area. That trend is changing slowly, however, as higher real estate prices have made this neighborhood less affordable for single-income families.

North of 45th Street and close to I-5, modest and more affordable homes can be found. Most are bungalows similar to those in the south end of the neighborhood, without the panoramic views of Lake Union and downtown but occasionally with views of the tips of the Cascades to the east. The area population includes young professionals and students residing in a mix of rentals and owner-occupied houses. There are few true apartment buildings in the blocks between 45th Street and Green Lake, but they become more common as one heads toward I-5 and the University District.

Wallingford is well located for those commuting to either downtown or the Eastside. Aurora Avenue North (Highway 99) runs parallel to Stone Way, just a few blocks into the Fremont neighborhood. This is generally a good route into downtown, and even to West Seattle or the Sea-Tac Airport. Savvy Eastside commuters take a shortcut along Lake Union to bypass I-5 and catch up with Highway 520 at the Montlake entrance.

Websites: www.seattle.gov, http://wallingford.org

Area Code: 206

Zip Codes: 98103, 98105

Post Office: Wallingford Station, 1329 N 47th St, 206-547-1406

Library: 1501 N 45th St, 206-684-4088, www.spl.org

Public Schools: Seattle Public Schools, 2445 3rd Ave S, 206-252-0010, www.seattleschools.org

Police: North Precinct, 10049 College Way N, 206-684-0850, www.seattle.gov/police

Emergency Hospital: University of Washington Medical Center, 1959 NE Pacific St, 206-598-3300, http://uwmedicine.washington.edu

Community Publications: My Wallingford (blog), www.mywallingford.com; North Seattle Herald-Outlook, 636 S Alaska St, 206-461-1300, www.northseattleherald-outlook.com; Wallyhood (blog), www.wallyhood.org

Community Resources: Good Shepherd P-Patch, 4618 Bagley Ave N, www.seattle.gov/neighborhoods; Wallingford Boys and Girls Club, 1310 N 45th St, 206-547-7261; Wallingford Community Council, 2100-A N 45th St, 206-632-0645, http://wallingford.org; Wallingford Community Senior Center, 4649 Sunnyside Ave N, Ste 140, 206-461-7825, www.wallingfordseniors.org

Public Transportation: Metro Transit, 206-553-3000, http://metro.kingcounty.gov: 16, 26, 30, 31, 44, 46, 82

GREEN LAKE

Maple Leaf

Boundaries: **North**: NE 110th Street; **West**: Aurora Avenue North (Highway 99); **South**: North 50th Street; **East**: I-5

In the late 1800s trolleys connected Green Lake to downtown, creating a popular recreation spot for Seattle residents. An amusement park was opened on the west side of the lake and Woodland Park Zoo was developed at the south end. In the early 1900s, the city of Seattle annexed Green Lake and its surrounding lands, designating them a public space. Today, Green Lake is one of Seattle's most popular public parks. It is surrounded by a three-mile paved walkway that attracts bicyclists, in-line skaters, runners, and walkers. During the summer, fields at the east side of the lake fill with volleyball teams, and basketball courts offer informal but competitive pick-up games. At the south end of the lake, Woodland Park has baseball and soccer fields, lighted tennis courts, a skatepark, and a running track.

North and east of Green Lake, cozy coffee shops, fragrant bakeries, and sporting goods and bike shops provide services for visitors and residents. Most are located near the intersection of Ravenna Avenue and Green Lake Way, or a few minutes north at Green Lake Way and 80th Street. Beautiful Northwest Modern and Tudor homes line Green Lake Way, facing the lake. Even though there is heavy traffic along this main thoroughfare, the view of the lake and the popularity of the area keep up the value of these homes. Original neighborhood houses still exist, although the distance from these houses to the lakeshore increased when the lake was partially drained in the early 1900s.

The neighborhood's charm and immediate accessibility to the park make Green Lake a high demand area, which is reflected in its real estate prices. The average home price in 2009 was over $600,000, and it isn't difficult to find homes facing the lake that sell for over a million.

Homes just off the lake are the most expensive; many are elegant Colonial-style mansions with views of the lake and even of the Olympic Mountains. Recent construction has increased the number of condominiums and townhouses east of the lake, although the area remains primarily a mix of detached houses and apartments. More modest Northwest Modern and Craftsman homes line idyllic residential streets in the blocks southeast of Green Lake, bordering the Wallingford neighborhood. These homes have the advantage of proximity to Green Lake without the inconvenience of heavy traffic or summer parking problems. Northwest and west of the lake, particularly across Aurora Avenue North near the Phinney Ridge neighborhood, modest and affordable Craftsman-style bungalows and Cape Cod–style cottages line steep, quiet streets. There are few rentals available in this area, but prices for homes are often much lower than

Green Lake

those closer in to the lake. Unpretentious yet comfortable homes may be found north of 80th Street. While many of these areas seem far from the lake, most are merely a few minutes' walk away. Green Lake is one of the few Seattle neighborhoods where many residents walk to do their errands. The area around the lake is flat rather than hilly and the heavy traffic in the area makes walking a pleasant alternative to driving. The neighborhood's proximity to downtown Seattle is another selling point: commutes by car average 10 to 15 minutes, and many bus lines service the neighborhood.

While most houses around Green Lake are detached bungalows, ramblers, or duplexes, there are other options for those who would like to rent in the Green Lake area. On the southeast and east sides of the lake, particularly near Ravenna Boulevard, there are several apartment buildings and condominiums. Most are contemporary high-rise complexes; others are smaller Federal or 1950s-style apartment buildings. Many are a few blocks off the lake, surrounded by houses or other similar apartment buildings. In the smaller buildings, apartments are not often advertised in local newspapers, so prospective tenants should visit the area periodically looking for rental signs. For the best deals, try the area in the spring, when University of Washington students vacate for the summer. Dupre + Scott Apartment Advisors estimate that average monthly rent in Greenlake/Wallingford is just over $1,300.

The Green Lake neighborhood is predominantly middle-income. Southeast of the lake and across Aurora Avenue (Highway 99) to the west, couples and young families keep that part of the neighborhood hopping. These two areas have been growing rapidly as housing prices increase in the more affluent blocks north and east of Green Lake. According to the *Seattle Post-Intelligencer*, the city's Office of Management and Planning estimates that by the year 2014, the number of existing households in the Green Lake area will grow to

1,839—an increase of 400 since 1997, and a climb in density from 13.4 house-holds per gross acre to 17.2.

Just north of Green Lake is the **Maple Leaf** neighborhood, recognizable by its blue water tower decorated with enormous white maple leaves. The small retail district runs along Roosevelt Way NE and includes coffee shops, restaurants like the popular Judy Fu's Snappy Dragon, a hardware store, and many unique, independent stores. It is a neighborhood of quiet streets and modest but well-maintained homes. Most houses in the area are brick Tudors or contemporary split-levels, with small landscaped yards. Perched on a hill over I-5, many homes have views of the Olympics or Mount Rainier. Compared to other desirable neighborhoods in Seattle, housing prices in Maple Leaf are surprisingly affordable considering the neighborhood's proximity to Green Lake and I-5. Apartments in the neighborhood tend to cluster near shopping areas. Rents here for a two-bedroom unit average about $100 less per month than in Green-lake and Wallingford.

Website: www.seattle.gov
Area Code: 206
Zip Code: 98103, 98115
Post Office: Wallingford Station, 1329 N 47th St, 206-547-1406
Library: 7364 E Green Lake Dr N, 206-684-7547, www.spl.org
Public Schools: Seattle Public Schools, 2445 3rd Ave S, 206-252-0010, www.seattleschools.org
Police: North Precinct, 10049 College Way N, 206-684-0850, www.seattle.gov/police
Emergency Hospital: Northwest Hospital, 1550 N 115th St, 206-364-0500, www.nwhospital.org
Community Publications: Green Lake neighborhood blob, http://blog.seattlepi.com/ingreenlake; *North Seattle Herald-Outlook*, 636 S Alaska St, 206-461-1300, www.northseattleherald-outlook.com
Community Resources: Evans Pool, 7201 E Greenlake Dr N, 206-684-4961; Green Lake Community Center, 7201 E Green Lake Drive N, 206-684-0780, www.seattle.gov/parks; Green Lake Community Council, P.O. Box 31536, Seattle, WA 98103, www.greenlakecommunitycouncil.org; Maple Leaf Community Council, P.O. Box 75595, Seattle, WA 98175, www.mapleleafcommunity.org; Maple Leaf P-Patch, 5th Ave NE and NE 103rd St, www.seattle.gov/neighborhoods
Public Transportation: Metro Transit, 206-553-3000, http://metro.kingcounty.gov: 16, 26, 48, 64, 66, 67, 68, 72, 73, 76, 77, 79, 82, 83, 242, 243, 316, 358, 372, 373

UNIVERSITY DISTRICT

Roosevelt
Ravenna
University Park
Bryant

Boundaries: **North**: NE 75th Street; **West**: I-5; **South**: Lake Washington Ship Canal; **East**: NE 35th Street, Union Bay

In 1861, the University of Washington was founded on the present-day site of the Fairmont Olympic Hotel in downtown Seattle. Four Grecian pillars, all that remain of the original building, can now be seen on a small piece of land near the Paramount Theater (at the intersection of Pike Street and Boren Avenue). The university moved to its present location near Union Bay in 1895, intent upon shaking off its reputation as an elementary and high school—the UW graduated its first university student in 1876, but continued accepting pre-college students as late as 1897. Two influential Seattle citizens, Arthur Denny and Daniel Bagley, were instrumental in bringing the college to Seattle. Denny persuaded the legislature to grant Seattle the rights to the territorial university and donated 10 acres of his own property as the original site. Bagley had convinced Denny that the college would be more of an asset to the city than the other available alternatives: the state capitol, prison, or customs house. Asa Mercer, the university's first president and teacher, is best known today as the man who went east and recruited single women to move to Seattle when it was still a primarily male logging community. His substantial academic and advisory contributions to the fledgling college are largely overlooked. In 1909, the Alaska-Yukon-Pacific Exposition was held on campus, marking a turning point for the young university. Originally intended to celebrate the 10th anniversary of the Klondike Gold Rush, the event was held two years late but drew nearly four million visitors to the area. As a result of the exposition, the university received several new permanent buildings and gained national attention. Since then, annual enrollment has passed the 40,000 mark and the university has gained a reputation as a premier medical research institution. While some critics claim that the university gives special preference to its graduate and research programs, particularly the sciences over the humanities, it remains an affordable way to receive a high-quality undergraduate education—if you're lucky enough to be admitted. As a result of state budget cuts to education, in 2011 the UW began accepting fewer in-state students in favor of out-of-state and international students, who pay nearly three times as much in tuition and fees.

Students, staff, and faculty of the university buzz about the campus and fill area coffeehouses at all hours of the day. On campus, be sure to visit the Burke

University District

Museum for, among other attractions, its marvelous exhibits on local Native American tribes, and the Graduate Reading Room, a beautiful cathedral-shaped room in the Suzzallo Library. For a look at one of Seattle's natural wonders, stop at "Frosh Pond" for a fabulous view of Mount Rainier over the Guggenheim Fountain.

In addition to its solid academic reputation, the University of Washington is nationally recognized for its football program. The Huskies routinely attract sold-out crowds for home games, even during disastrous seasons. Wealthy UW graduates and football fans are generous supporters of the program, and regularly generate more interest in the team than the current university students. The UW crew and basketball teams (particularly the women's) also receive local attention, although they are overshadowed by the fervent devotion of Husky football fans. All of the UW sports facilities are on the shore of Union Bay, an inlet of Lake Washington, along Montlake Avenue. Parking is scarce and traffic problems are common on football Saturdays; at other times two large parking lots north of the stadium are sufficient. City regulations benefit those who live near the stadium by assigning parking stickers and by limiting parking on most streets to neighborhood residents. Some lucky football fans come to the games by boat, tying up at the east side of the UW stadium. Others take advantage of the additional buses added to local routes on game days. For the fitness and environmentally minded, you can bike or walk to the games via the Burke-Gilman trail.

Locals and students refer to the university as the UW (pronounced "U-Dub") and to the area around it as the "U-District." Although the campus is the geographic focal point of the area, the center of the community is "the Ave." (University Way), running just a block west of the campus. A tad run-down, it's a great place to see movies, buy books and CDs, play video games, or eat at an international variety of restaurants. Additional landscaping and wider sidewalks were recently added along "the Ave.," in order to improve the street surface. The Ave. is also a central location for bus service to the University District and other parts of the city, with routes to neighborhoods throughout the north end of Seattle and to downtown and Capitol Hill. Just south of NE 45th Street on the Ave., the University Bookstore carries an array of books, gifts, and art supplies, as well as required materials for UW classes. During the school year, the Ave. is a favorite student hangout. In the summer it is the site for the University District Street Fair, which takes over several blocks of the street for an entire weekend. It's best to avoid the west side of University Way between 47th and 50th streets, where drug activity congregates.

Away from the Ave., you can commune with the ghosts of former Seattle-ites at the Blue Moon Tavern at NE 45th St and 8th Avenue, which has been serving up suds to thirsty poets and others since 1936. Film buffs can choose from five movie theaters within a five-block radius, including the Grand Illusion, the city's oldest continuously running film house, or rent from Scarecrow, the largest independent video store in the country. For serious crafters, Weaving Works offers an incredible collection of yarns and other materials for the fiber arts.

Beginning in 2016, the U District will be served by an extension of the city's expanding light rail service called the University Link, which will connect the neighborhood with Capitol Hill, downtown, Rainier Valley, and Sea-Tac Airport. Stations will be situated on Montlake Boulevard in front of Husky Stadium and on Brooklyn Ave.

As one would expect, the University District is predominantly a neighborhood of young people (the median age is 31), but plenty of families have set down roots here, too. Residents include undergraduate and graduate students and university faculty members, as well as young professionals, scholars, and artists. Some families own homes in the northeast corner of the district near Ravenna Boulevard, but the vast majority of U-District residents are renters. Just north of campus, 17th Avenue NE, a tree-lined avenue known informally as "Greek Row," is bordered by beautiful Colonial-style mansions. Many of these buildings, as well as those in the blocks east of 17th Avenue NE, have been converted into fraternities, sororities, and rooming houses. The north end of this area is popular with graduate students and visiting faculty, as well as longtime neighborhood residents.

West of campus you'll find apartment buildings and shared houses galore. Close to the campus there are several brick apartment buildings, offering small studios or one-bedrooms with hardwood floors and occasional views. Modern accommodations, built in the 1980s, are located near I-5 and offer multiple-bedroom apartments. Other rental opportunities are available near the University Village Mall, at the northeast corner of the UW campus. The mall includes an

Apple store and national chain stores such as H&M, Eddie Bauer, Juicy Couture, and Crate and Barrel. Apartment buildings and townhouses line NE 22nd Street, and other rentals are tucked into the base of the hill behind the retail stores and strip malls that line NE 25th Street. Rents here are comparable to those in Greenwood, and slightly less than those in the Wallingford neighborhood. The most affordable options here are rooms for rent in group houses—these are often listed in local papers such as *The Stranger* and the *Seattle Weekly*, and in the UW student paper *The Daily*. Rental houses are also readily available, particularly north of 50th Avenue NE. The best time for finding rentals of any kind is at the end of the school year when students head home for the summer. Many rentals are not listed in local papers, so it is generally a good idea to roam the neighborhood looking for "For Rent" signs. Additionally, the University of Washington Student Housing Affairs provides information to students and non-students alike about off-campus opportunities. Visit them in Room 218 of Condon Hall or call 206-543-8997.

The Roosevelt and Ravenna neighborhoods, located north of the University District, traditionally attract UW graduate students, faculty, and staff. In recent decades, professionals willing to commute to downtown or the Eastside have also moved to these areas. The center of the **Roosevelt** neighborhood is a small pedestrian-friendly retail district based around the intersection of Roosevelt Avenue NE and NE 65th Street, which boasts several small ethnic restaurants, coffee shops, and bookstores. An annual Bull Moose Street Festival brings the community together here each summer with live music and a pub crawl. Residents enjoy easy access to the University Village shopping center, Northgate Mall, and the pleasures of Green Lake. A light rail station is currently being built in the neighborhood, which will speed riders downtown in just seven minutes. On the first Wednesday of every month, vintage motorcycle enthusiasts flock to Teddy's Tavern, lining the street with bikes of all makes and models. Despite this "biker bar" tradition, the Roosevelt neighborhood is a tranquil residential community, with an excellent public high school boasting an award-winning jazz band. Most houses in the Roosevelt District are Arts-and-Crafts-style bungalows and Tudor-style cottages. There are a few apartment buildings and condominiums in the neighborhoods, mostly near I-5 and Ravenna Boulevard, but upzoning plans will bring more housing and businesses to the area.

The **Ravenna** neighborhood is named for the ravine that runs through the area, at one time connecting Green Lake with Union Bay and Lake Washington. Water still flows in the ravine, fed by underground streams and Seattle's ubiquitous rain. Ravenna Park follows the ravine, winding northwest toward the Green Lake area. It is a beautiful and lush city park with trails, tennis courts, and picnic areas. There are a variety of architectural styles in Ravenna, including modest Tudors, roomy Arts-and-Crafts homes, and 1960s bungalows. Home prices are on average higher here than in Roosevelt and the U District. There are occasional opportunities for renting houses here, and a few apartments and townhouses line 25th Avenue East.

The **University Park** neighborhood ranges from 16th Avenue NE in the west to 21st Avenue NE in the east. Its northern border is Ravenna Park, and NE 50th Street marks its southern edge. The tiny neighborhood is home to Park Drive, known as "Candy Cane Lane" during the Christmas holidays because of the profusion of lights and decorations that draw visitors from all over the city. The neighborhood consists primarily of well-preserved Arts-and-Crafts homes.

The **Bryant** neighborhood (sometimes called Ravenna-Bryant), east of University Village, has much in common with Ravenna. Houses here are mainly modest bungalows and Tudors, with a few scattered brick ranch houses. Ravenna and Bryant attract families, UW faculty and staff members, and professionals who work downtown or on the Eastside. Commuters to the Eastside have few choices on their route to the 520 bridge from here, so the drive at rush hour can be time-consuming. Beyond that, you can't beat its offer of quiet streets and friendly neighbors.

Website: www.seattle.gov
Area Code: 206
Zip Codes: 98105, 98115
Post Office: University Station, 4244 University Way NE, 206-675-8114
Library: 5009 Roosevelt Way NE, 206-684-4063, www.spl.org
Public Schools: Seattle Public Schools, 2445 3rd Ave S, 206-252-0010, www.seattleschools.org
Police: North Precinct, 10049 College Way N, 206-684-0850, www.seattle.gov/police
Emergency Hospital: University of Washington Medical Center, 1959 NE Pacific St, 206-598-3300, http://uwmedicine.washington.edu
Community Publications: *North Seattle Herald-Outlook*, 636 S Alaska St, 206-461-1300, www.northseattleherald-outlook.com; *The Daily* (UW paper), 206-543-2700, http://dailyuw.com; *The Roosie* (monthly newsletter of the Roosevelt Neighborhood Association); UDistrict daily (blog), www.udistrictdaily.com
Community Resources: Ravenna-Bryant Community Association, P.O. Box 51250, Seattle, WA 98115, www.scn.org/neighbors/rbca; Ravenna-Eckstein Community Center, 6535 Ravenna Ave NE, 206-684-7534, www.ci.seattle.wa.us; Ravenna P-Patch, 5200 Ravenna Ave NE, www.seattle.gov/neighborhoods; Roosevelt Neighbors' Alliance, 4534 University Way NE, 360-951-6291, www.rooseveltneighborsalliance.org; Roosevelt Neighborhood Association, 6910 Roosevelt Way NE #518, http://rooseveltseattle.org; Roosevelt P-Patch, 7012 12th Ave NE, www.seattle.gov/neighborhoods; University District P-Patch, 4009 8th Ave NE,

www.seattle.gov/neighborhoods; University Heights P-Patch, 5031 University Way NE, www.seattle.gov/neighborhoods; University Neighborhood Service Center, 4534 University Way NE, 206-684-7542, www.seattle.gov/neighborhoods/nsc; University Park Community Club, www.upcc.org

Public Transportation: Metro Transit, 206-553-3000, http://metro.kingcounty.gov: 25, 30, 31, 43– 46, 48, 49, 64–68, 70–76, 79, 83, 133, 167, 197, 205, 243, 271, 272, 277, 301, 316, 372, 373, 810, 812, 821, 851, 855, 860, 870, 871, 880, 885; Sound Transit, 206-398-5000, www.soundtransit.org: 510, 511, 540, 542, 556, 586

LAKE CITY

Cedar Park
Matthews Beach
Meadowbrook
Victory Heights
Olympic Hills

Boundaries: **North**: NE 145th Street; **West**: 5th Avenue NE; **South**: NE 95th Street; **East**: Lake Washington

Lake City is located near the north end of Lake Washington, just inside the city limits. When Seattle annexed Lake City in 1957, it was a quiet lakefront suburb with a small retail core along Lake City Way, a branch of the state highway system also known as Highway 522. Much of that small town character remains in Lake City, which attracts a mix of low- and middle-income families and professionals. The residential streets of Lake City are sheltered from the busy traffic of the highway, resulting in a slice of seclusion and a friendly, small-town atmosphere.

Those looking to live in Lake City will find affordable homes and ample rental apartments. Homes here are modest, predominantly bungalows or modern split-levels; many are on unusually large lots. Those east of Lake City Way may have views of Lake Washington and the Cascades. The Lake Washington waterfront in Lake City known as the **Cedar Park** neighborhood used to be lined with small weekend cottages, but as property values have soared many of those have been replaced with large, contemporary homes. The Burke-Gilman Trail bisects Cedar Park from NE 150th Street to NE 120th Street, paralleling the lakeshore. The residential communities of **Matthews Beach** and **Meadowbrook** are the southern neighborhoods of Lake City. Matthews Beach Park boasts Seattle's largest freshwater bathing beach. Thornton Creek, which flows through Meadowbrook, has been restored and daylighted, or redirected to flow aboveground. Above Lake City Way and the southern branch of the creek, **Victory Heights** stretches from NE 98th to NE 125th streets and from

Lake City Way to 15th Avenue NE. Speakeasies and taverns once clustered here during Prohibition, and the neighborhood had a rabble-rousing reputation. Today, Victory Heights is a community of single-family homes occupied by a youthful population that includes many UW students. North of here you'll find **Olympic Hills**, a peaceful neighborhood of many mid-century bungalows on large lots, surrounded by tall pine trees.

Because of the distance from downtown and the Eastside, real estate prices and rents are generally lower in Lake City than in other residential neighborhoods in Seattle. However, living here makes for an easy commute to the north end of Lake Washington, Bothell, and Kenmore. Most apartment buildings are located in the few blocks to either side of Lake City Way and along NE 125th Street. Nearly half of the residents of Lake City rent apartments or houses, though new, modern condominium complexes on Lake City Way—with retail spaces at street level—will alter the demographic.

Lake City Way has changed significantly since it became part of Seattle; a small, tree-lined and pedestrian-friendly section of the "old town" still exists, with restaurants and small, locally owned retail businesses, but a major part of the highway is crowded with strip malls, gas stations, and auto lots. Adult bookstores and strip clubs have given Lake City Way a slightly seedy reputation, although the businesses have had little impact on the residential areas of the neighborhood. The community has experienced some problems with criminal activity near the highway, but community watch groups and patrols have substantially reduced crime along Lake City Way and throughout the neighborhood.

This is a culturally diverse community, and the meld of cultures and languages is reflected in the assortment of new businesses that have sprouted up along Lake City Way, including international art shops and restaurants.

Lake City

Because of the affordable rents and homes, residents are primarily blue-collar workers and their families. More recently, the area has begun to attract artists and college-educated professionals, as well as retirees with modest incomes. The neighborhood particularly appeals to renters because of its wide variety of housing and affordability. In 2011, work was completed on Lake City Court, an 86-unit development located on 33rd Avenue NE, which is the greenest afford-able housing complex in Seattle.

Website: www.seattle.gov
Area Code: 206
Zip Code: 98125
Post Office: Lake City Station, 3019 NE 127th St, 206-364-0608
Library: 12501 28th Ave NE, 206-684-7518, www.spl.org
Public Schools: Seattle Public Schools, 2445 3rd Ave S, 206-252-0010, www.seattleschools.org
Police: North Precinct, 10049 College Way N, 206-684-0850, www.seattle.gov/police
Emergency Hospital: Northwest Hospital, 1550 N 115th St., 206-364-0500, www.nwhospital.org
Community Publications: Lake City Live (blog), http://lakecitylive.net; *North Seattle Herald-Outlook*, 636 S Alaska St, 206-461-1300, www.northseattleherald-outlook.com
Community Resources: Lake City Community Center, 12531 28th Ave NE, 206-362-4378; Lake City Neighborhood Service Center, 12525 28th Ave NE (2nd fl), 206-684-7526, www.seattle.gov/neighborhoods/nsc; Matthews Beach Park, 49th Ave NE and NE 93rd St, 206-684-4075, www.seattle.gov/parks; Meadowbrook Community Center, 10517 35th Ave NE, 206-684-7522, www.seattle.gov/parks;
Public Transportation: Metro Transit, 206-553-3000, http://metro.kingcounty.gov: 41, 64, 65, 72, 75, 79, 243, 306, 309, 312, 330, 372; Sound Transit, 206-398-5000, www.soundtransit.org; 522

NORTHGATE

Jackson Park
Haller Lake
Pinehurst
Licton Springs
Aurora

Boundaries: North: North 145th Street; **West:** Aurora Avenue North (Highway 99); **South:** NE 92nd Street; **East:** 5th Avenue NE

Northgate is a large neighborhood centered around the Northgate Mall, which opened in 1950 and claims to be the oldest shopping mall in North America. The mall itself is rather small by current standards, and the businesses located there tend to be scaled-down versions of their downtown or Bellevue Square counterparts. Nevertheless, ample parking around the mall, as well as its close proximity to I-5, makes it a popular shopping destination. The mall and surrounding areas underwent renovations in 2006–2007, expanding the mall and adding a large parking garage to accommodate increased traffic in the area. A new branch of the Seattle Public Library on Fifth Avenue NE facing the mall was completed in 2006, along with a new community center and park.

While the immediate area around the Northgate Mall is filled with small retail businesses that benefit from the mall traffic—restaurants, drugstores, banks, and sporting goods stores—the heart of Northgate's residential community is north of the mall, stretching as far as the **Jackson Park** neighborhood (named after the public park and golf course) at the city boundary. Houses in this area are 1950s brick ranch houses or modest split-levels on large lots, popular with first-time homebuyers. There are also a number of duplexes, townhouses, apartment buildings, and condominiums, as well as an increasing number of senior citizen residences. While real estate and rental prices are lower here than in other parts of the city, this is a close-knit community, complete with freshly painted houses, well-kept lawns, and friendly neighbors. Many contemporary apartments and condominiums are just off the main streets in the area surrounding Northgate Mall.

North and west of Jackson Park lies **Haller Lake**, a neighborhood short on sidewalks but long on peace and quiet. Properties directly on the lake for which the neighborhood is named run the risk of flooding. Despite drainage problems, homes here tend to be more slightly more expensive than those in nearby Bitter Lake and Lake City, but still a bargain compared to many other areas of the city. Access to I-5 and Highway 99 makes this area convenient for commuters. East of Haller Lake you'll find **Pinehurst**, similar to other Northgate neighborhoods in terms of appearance, amenities, and types of available housing. Bungalows here are packed closely together with small yards, but Pinehurst residents have

Northgate

access to two neighborhood parks, the Pinehurst Playground and the Pinehurst Pocket Park. A drainage project called the Pinehurst Green Grid, completed in 2006, eliminated spot flooding in the neighborhood and added new sidewalks and roadways to the area.

Licton Springs (sometimes called North College Park) is situated between Aurora Avenue and I-5, bounded by NE 85th Street and Northgate Way. Modest homes and brightly painted townhouses are spacious and plentiful in this quiet community. Nearby North Seattle Community College, an imposing concrete structure that resembles a small penitentiary, has a solid reputation, attracting students of all ages. The area around the college includes several small government agencies as well as the North Precinct for the Seattle Police Department. In addition to the community college, several other trade and vocational schools are located here, which makes this neighborhood popular with students. Nearby commercial districts include Aurora Avenue N, with plenty of shops and restaurants. The Oak Tree Village Shopping Center has a Starbucks, several good restaurants, a large multiplex theater, and a supermarket.

North of Licton Springs is **Aurora**, which includes the area north of Northgate Way (105th Street) between Aurora Avenue North and I-5. Aurora Avenue North is a major business district, with a seemingly endless series of strip malls, car dealerships, small hotels, taverns, and appliance stores. While Aurora Avenue North has a reputation for petty crime and prostitution, residents who live even a few blocks off this main street rarely encounter any problems. A block or two east of Aurora Avenue North is a selection of modest split-level and contemporary brick homes. Real estate and rental prices in this area tend to be slightly lower than in those neighborhoods closer to downtown.

Website: www.seattle.gov

Area Code: 206

Zip Codes: 98103, 98133, 98125

Post Office: Northgate Station, 11036 8th Ave NE, 206-364-9270

Library: Northgate Branch, 10548 5th Ave NE, 206-386-1980, www.spl.org

Public Schools: Seattle Public Schools, 2445 3rd Ave S, 206-252-0010, www.seattleschools.org

Police: North Precinct, 10049 College Way N, 206-684-0850, www.seattle.gov/police

Emergency Hospital: Northwest Hospital, 1550 N 115th St, 206-364-0500, www.nwhospital.org

Community Publications: *Currents* (Licton Springs Community Council newsletter), *North Seattle Herald-Outlook*, 636 S Alaska St, 206-461-1300, www.northseattleherald-outlook.com; Pinehurst Community Blog, www.pinehurstseattle.org

Community Resources: Haller Lake Community Club, www.hallerlake.info; Haller Lake P-Patch, 13045 1st Ave NE, www.seattle.gov/neighborhoods; Madison Pool, 13401 Meridian Ave N, 206-684-4979, www.seattle.gov/parks; Jackson Park Golf Course, 1000 NE 135th St, 206-363-4747; Licton Springs Community Council, www.lictonsprings.org; Licton Springs Park, 9536 Ashworth Ave N, 206-684-4075, www.seattle.gov/parks; Northgate Community Center, 10510 5th Ave NE, 206-386-4283, www.seattle.gov/parks; Pinehurst Community Council, 206-659-5814; Pinehurst Playground, 12029 14th Ave NE, 206-684-4075, www.seattle.gov/parks; Pinehurst Pocket Park, NE 117th St and 19th Ave NE

Public Transportation: Metro Transit, 206-553-3000, http://metro.kingcounty.gov: 5, 16, 41, 66, 67, 68, 72, 73, 75, 77, 242, 303, 304, 308, 345, 346, 347, 348, 373, 995; Sound Transit, 206-398-5000, www.soundtransit.org: 555, 556

BROADVIEW

Bitter Lake

The Highlands

Boundaries: **North**: NW 145th Street; **West**: Puget Sound; **South**: NW 110th Street; **East**: Aurora Avenue North (Highway 99)

Located in the northwest corner of Seattle, Broadview, with its quiet residential streets and unremarkable commercial district, is really more of a suburban community than an urban neighborhood. Most of the area bears a close similarity to the suburban Shoreline community located just north of the city.

Greenwood Avenue North, the commercial street in this neighborhood, is lined with a variety of retail businesses, restaurants, and several small strip malls. This avenue also serves as a dividing line down the center of the neighborhood, with more affluent residents to the west and working-class families to the east. **Bitter**

Broadview

Lake, just northeast of the intersection of 130th and Greenwood, is surrounded by single-family homes that attract middle-income professionals to this quiet community. First-time homebuyers can still find affordable properties in the neighborhood, which features an elementary school. The lake that gives the neighborhood its name has an adjoining park with tennis courts, a playfield, and a community center. A neighborhood P-Patch is also under construction. There are some apartments and new condominium complexes between Greenwood Avenue and Aurora Avenue North, particularly south of 130th Street. Because this area is not so close to downtown or I-5, these generally rent for less than comparable in-city units. Rental rates in Bitter Lake match those in the U District.

Houses in the Broadview neighborhood are mainly modern bungalows, ramblers, and split-levels, although the homes grow grander as you progress north along 3rd Avenue NW, especially on the west side of the street. Many of these homes have splendid views of the Puget Sound and the Olympic Mountains, similar to the more expensive homes just south in the North Beach area.

At the far north end of 3rd Avenue NW, the Seattle Golf Club and the entrance to **The Highlands** present a glimpse of one of the most exclusive developments in Seattle. The Highlands, designed in 1909 by the Olmsteds (who also designed Seattle's park system), remain an exclusive and private enclave for the very wealthy. Although the lots are smaller now than the original minimum of five acres, the winding wooded roads and gated entrance have preserved the quiet seclusion of this community.

Houses and apartments close to Aurora Avenue North offer the least expensive prices and rents, while still providing the comforts of a close-knit residential community. A variety of modest and affordable houses for young families and middle-income professionals can be found north of 130th Street between 3rd Avenue NW and Greenwood Avenue NW, and in the vicinity of Carkeek Park. While Broadview does not attract tourists, nor promise adventurous

living, it will satisfy those looking for a stable suburban-style community within
the city.

Website: www.seattle.gov
Area Code: 206
Zip Code: 98133, 98177
Post Office: Bitter Lake Station, 929 N 145th St, 206-364-0663
Library: Broadview Branch, 12755 Greenwood Ave N, 206-684-7519, www.spl.
  org
Public Schools: Seattle Public Schools, 2445 3rd Ave S, 206-252-0010, www.
  seattleschools.org
Police: North Precinct, 10049 College Way N, 206-684-0850, www.seattle.gov/
  police
Emergency Hospital: Northwest Hospital, 1550 N 115th St, 206-364-0500,
  www.nwhospital.org
Community Publications: *The Broaderview* (community council newslet-
  ter), www.broadviewcc.info; *North Seattle Herald-Outlook*, 636 S Alaska
  St, 206-461-1300, www.northseattleherald-outlook.com; Our Broadview
  Neighborhood (website), www.broadviewseattle.org
Community Resources: Bitter Lake Community Center, 13035 Linden Ave N,
  206-684-7524, www.seattle.gov/parks; Broadview Community Council, 206-
  283-2705, www.broadviewcc.info
Public Transportation: Metro Transit, 206-553-3000, http://metro.kingcounty.
  gov: 5, 28, 304, 345, 355, 358, 981, 982, 984, 986– 989, 994, 995

SAND POINT

Laurelhurst
Windermere
View Ridge
Wedgwood

Boundaries: **North**: NE 95th Street; **West**: 35th Avenue NE, Lake City Way;
South: Union Bay; **East**: Lake Washington

On the shore of Lake Washington, the Sand Point neighborhood is best known
as the location of the National Oceanic and Atmospheric Administration (NOAA)
and Children's Hospital & Regional Medical Center. NOAA, a federal research
facility that studies the weather and its impact upon the ocean and coastlines,
shares a base with the Sand Point Naval Station on Lake Washington. Children's
Hospital and Regional Medical Center, located on Sand Point Way, is a regional

pediatric referral center that serves the special health care needs of children and their families.

Sand Point also features two public parks, both with access to the Lake Washington waterfront. Matthews Beach, located north of NOAA, is a summer favorite of sunbathers, picnickers, and swimmers. The Burke-Gilman trail stops off at Matthews Beach as it follows the edge of Lake Washington, giving bicyclists and in-line skaters easy access to the park. South of NOAA, Magnuson Park offers visitors the use of several sports fields, a swimming beach, kite hill, off-leash dog park, trails, public art, and a boat launch. Magnuson Park is also the home of a new community garden and outdoor amphitheater.

Laurelhurst, on the southern hill of the Sand Point neighborhood, is a quiet and determinedly private neighborhood. Residents here tend to be affluent professionals and retirees living in homes with incredible views of Lake Washington and Union Bay, with Mount Rainier and the snow-capped Cascades providing a stunning backdrop. Laurelhurst, where Bill Gates grew up and where Bill Gates, Sr., still lives, is a neighborhood of some of the most expensive homes in the city, with appropriately manicured lawns and private waterfront access. Most houses are single-family residences, ranging in style from modest brick Tudors to palatial Georgians and Colonials. Members of the exclusive Laurelhurst Beach Club have access to 450 feet of lakefront and private swimming beach. The border of Laurelhurst, along Sand Point Way, includes a thriving upscale retail district, as well as Children's Hospital and other clinics. At the top of the hill, the Laurelhurst park and community center serves as a hub for neighborhood activities, including softball games, summer picnics, aerobics, and pottery classes. North of Laurelhurst along the water is the neighborhood of **Windermere**, with similarly high-end properties featuring excellent views of Wolf Bay and the lake. Only dues-paying members and their guests have access to the local park. The few rental opportunities to be found in these neighborhoods are in the handful of apartment buildings located along Sand Point Way.

View Ridge, north of Laurelhurst, tends to attract wealthy professionals, affluent retirees, and UW professors. Homes in this area are modest brick Tudors and 1950s ranch houses with well-kept lawns; many have panoramic views of the sun rising over Lake Washington and the Cascades. Near Matthews Beach are renovated beach cottages, a reminder of an earlier time when this area was an out-of-town destination for Seattle residents. There are several newer "view" condominiums in this area as well. As with Laurelhurst and Windermere, most rentals are limited to apartment buildings on busy Sand Point Way.

Located between Sand Point Way and 25th Avenue NE, **Wedgwood** offers a mix of affordable single-family homes, duplexes, townhouses, and apartment buildings with occasional views of the Cascade Mountains. Many old-growth trees were preserved when Wedgwood was built—a first in the history of Seattle development. Shaded by towering pines, the neighborhood also boasts the city's oldest and largest P-Patch. Though homes in Wedgwood can't be

Sandpoint

considered cheap, they are less expensive here than elsewhere in the Sand Point area. Most homes are Cape Cod and Saltbox-style cottages, or Craftsman bungalows. The rental market is dominated by Wedgewood [sic] Estates, a large, nicely tended complex owned by the City of Seattle to ensure that mid-range housing remains available in this increasingly expensive part of town. Residents tend to be middle-income professionals and young families, as well as UW faculty and staff. Wedgwood has a strong and active Jewish community, with two synagogues located in the neighborhood, and two more within walking distance. The retail district centers on two intersections along 35th Avenue NE, at NE 75th and NE 85th Streets, with grocery stores, medical offices, coffee shops and bakeries, restaurants, and a few locally owned businesses.

Websites: www.seattle.gov, www.northeastseattle.com
Area Code: 206
Zip Codes: 98105, 98115
Post Office: Wedgwood Station, 7724 35th Ave NE, 206-527-9825
Library: North East Library, 6801 35th Ave NE, 206-684-7539, www.spl.org
Public Schools: Seattle Public Schools, 2445 3rd Ave S, 206-252-0010, www.seattleschools.org
Police: North Precinct, 10049 College Way N, 206-684-0850, www.seattle.gov/police
Emergency Hospital: University of Washington Medical Center, 1959 NE Pacific St, 206-548-3300, http://uwmedicine.washington.edu
Community Publications: Laurelhurst Blog, http://thelaurelhurstblog.blogspot.com; *Laurelhurst Letter* (newsletter), www.laurelhurstcc.com; *North Seattle Herald-Outlook*, 636 S Alaska St, 206-461-1300, www.northseattleherald-outlook.com
Community Resources: Laurelhurst Community Center, 4554 NE 41st St, 206-684-7529, www.ci.seattle.wa.us/parks; Laurelhurst Community Club, www.laurelhurstcc.com; Laurelhurst Playfield, 4544 NE 41st St, 206-684-4075, www.seattle.gov/parks; Magnuson P-Patch, 7400 Sand Point Way NE, www.seattle.gov/magnusongarden; Picardo Farm P-Patch, 8040 25th Ave NE,

www.seattle.gov/neighborhoods; Sand Point Community Housing Association, 6940 62nd Ave NE, 206-517-5499; View Ridge Community Council, P.O. Box 15218, Seattle, WA 98115, www.scn.org/viewridge; Wedgwood Community Council, http://wedgewoodcc.org

Public Transportation: Metro Transit, 206-553-3000, http://metro.kingcounty. gov: 30, 64, 65, 68, 71, 74–76, 83, 243, 372, 982, 986–989, 994, 995

MADISON PARK

Washington Park
Denny-Blaine
Broadmoor

Boundaries: **North**: Union Bay; **West**: Lake Washington Boulevard; **South**: Lake Washington Boulevard; **East**: Lake Washington

On the shore of Lake Washington, the community of Madison Park lies just south of Union Bay and the 520 floating bridge. During the late 1800s, Madison Park was a beachfront resort town frequented by Seattle residents. Many took the cable car from downtown Seattle to the shore to spend the day or rented a nearby cottage for the week. Festivities in the summer included a carnival with food and games, and a Ferris wheel.

Today, Madison Park is an affluent community with a small-town feel. Shop owners know the names of their local customers, traffic is slow and leisurely, people stroll the sidewalks and smile at one another. It's one of the few Seattle neighborhoods that is not on a shortcut route to other parts of the city, so it is spared the traffic problems of other less fortunate neighborhoods.

One-of-a-kind restaurants and cafés, fashionable boutiques, and fragrant bakeries offering scrumptious goodies line East Madison Street, Madison Park's main thoroughfare. Nowhere will you find sprawling supermarkets, warehouse stores, chain restaurants, or fast food joints. Although First Hill and Capitol Hill, with their mainstream business districts, are only ten minutes away, many Madison Park residents do most of their shopping locally.

Near the east end of East Madison Street, Colonial and Northwest Modern homes intermingle with more modest Cape Cods, reminiscent of the beach cottages that lined the shore in early Madison Park. Two traditionally expensive and fashionable Madison Park neighborhoods, **Washington Park** and **Denny-Blaine**, lie farther south along the shore of Lake Washington and on the hill facing the lake. Homes in these areas are an interesting mix, primarily Colonials and Northwest Moderns, as well as a few Elizabethan or Tudor homes. Many of the stately homes here were built when Seattle's wealthiest migrated to this area and other posh neighborhoods, such as Queen Anne and Capitol Hill, away

Madison Park

from downtown and First Hill. Finally, the gated community of **Broadmoor** offers a variety of elegant homes in an ultra-exclusive golf and country club setting, tucked between Lake Washington and the Arboretum.

Just south of East Madison Street, high-rise condominiums face Lake Washington. Since these were completed, local zoning restrictions have changed, preventing other similar buildings from crowding out the homes that are the core of Madison Park. These condos offer the neighborly appeal of Madison Park and spectacular views of Lake Washington, the Cascades, and imposing Mount Rainier. On the north shore of the Madison Park peninsula, other contemporary and Colonial-style condominiums offer views of Lake Washington and the 520 Bridge.

Madison Park continues to be a neighborhood of wealthy and influential Seattle citizens. The community has a median income more than twice that of the rest of the city, and the homes here are some of the most expensive in Seattle; even modest Cape Cod cottages run in the several-hundred-thousand-dollar range. Though they rarely appear on the market, since turnover in the area is low, the grand residences in Broadmoor and Denny-Blaine often break the million-dollar mark.

Website: www.seattle.gov
Area Code: 206
Zip Codes: 98112, 98122
Post Office: East Union Station, 1110 23rd Ave, 206-328-9712
Library: Montlake Library, 2401 24th Ave E, 206-684-4720, www.spl.org
Public Schools: Seattle Public Schools, 2445 3rd Ave S, 206-252-0010, www.seattleschools.org
Police: East Precinct, 1519 12th Ave, 206-684-4300, www.seattle.gov/police

Emergency Hospital: Swedish Medical Center, 747 Broadway, 206-386-6000, www.swedish.org

Community Publication: Madison Park Blogger, http://madisonparkblogger.blogspot.com; *Madison Park Times*, 636 S Alaska St, 206-461-1300, www.madisonparktimes.com

Community Resources: Denny-Blaine Park, 200 Lake Washington Blvd E, 206-684-4075, www.seattle.gov/parks; Ida Mia Garden, alley near E Madison St and Lake Washington Blvd; Madison Park, E Madison St and E Howe St, www.seattle.gov/parks

Public Transportation: Metro Transit, 206-553-3000, http://metro.kingcounty.gov: 11, 84, 988

MADISON VALLEY

Boundaries: **North**: Washington Park Arboretum; **West**: 23rd Avenue East; **South**: East Howell Street; **East**: Lake Washington Boulevard and Dorffel Drive

Sandwiched between Madison Park and Capitol Hill, and centered around the intersection of East Madison Street and Martin Luther King Jr. Way East, is Madison Valley, a diverse neighborhood with a range of income, religion, race, and age groups. When you visit this thriving neighborhood, it's difficult to imagine that it was once a blighted area of abandoned houses and the occasional brothel, shunned by its affluent neighbors in nearby Madison Park and Denny-Blaine. A committed and well-organized community group now known as the Greater Madison Valley Community Council has been instrumental in making Madison Valley what it is today. Businesses that serve the neighborhood cluster along East Madison Street and include garden shops, wellness services, boutiques, and a bounty of excellent restaurants, including Luc, Nishino, the Spanish Table, and Café Flora, which is justifiably famous for its vegetarian food. The neighborhood is also home to the Bush School, one of the city's best private schools, and the nation's first AIDS hospice, the Bailey-Boushay House.

Residents of Madison Valley range from Seattle University students to families and singles, who live in Craftsman-style homes or newer properties with green territorial views. Condos and townhouses afford additional housing options, and rents here average about $500 less than you'll pay in Madison Park. Home prices are more affordable, too, though still spendy. Residents can easily access downtown, the nearby Arboretum, and Lake Washington, though the hilly terrain can make it a challenge to bike around here. The relative proximity of I-5 and the 520 bridge will serve those whose daily commute takes them north or to the East Side.

Madison Valley

In addition to various parks, Madison Valley has two greenbelts. The Harrison Ridge Greenbelt runs along 32nd Avenue between Denny Way and Harrison Street, providing drainage and a haven for birds and other animals. The greenbelt's retaining wall was a WPA project built with the community's help. Neighborhood activists banded together to create another greenbelt area and a P-Patch in 2001. The neighborhood's susceptibility to flooding has spurred another public works project, the Madison Valley Stormwater Project, scheduled for completion by the end of 2011. Those looking for a green enclave with an abundance of community spirit will find it in Madison Valley.

Website: www.seattle.gov; www.madisonvalley.org
Area Code: 206
Zip Codes: 98112, 98122
Post Office: East Union Station, 1110 23rd Ave, 206-328-9712
Library: Montlake Library, 2401 24th Ave E, 206-684-4720, www.spl.org
Public Schools: Seattle Public Schools, 2445 3rd Ave S, 206-252-0010, www.seattleschools.org
Police: East Precinct, 1519 12th Ave, 206-684-4300, www.seattle.gov/police
Emergency Hospital: Swedish Medical Center, 747 Broadway, 206-386-6000, www.swedish.org
Community Publication: *The Valley View* newsletter, www.madisonvalley.org
Community Resources: Denny-Blaine Park, 200 Lake Washington Blvd E, 206-684-4075, www.seattle.gov/parks; Greater Madison Valley Community Council, www.madisonvalley.org; Ida Mia Garden, alley near E Madison St and Lake Washington Blvd; Madison Park, E Madison St and

E Howe St, www.seattle.gov/parks; Mad-P (P-Patch), 3000 E Mercer St, www.seattle.gov/neighborhoods

Public Transportation: Metro Transit, 206-553-3000, http://metro.kingcounty. gov: 11, 84, 988

MONTLAKE

Portage Bay

Boundaries: **North**: Lake Washington Ship Canal; **West**: Fuhrman Avenue East; **South**: Boyer Avenue East; **East**: Lake Washington Boulevard

The Montlake Cut is a small, man-made waterway that connects Lake Union and Lake Washington. Each year on the first Saturday in May, the annual Opening Day celebration of boating season is celebrated here. Spectators, boating enthusiasts, and crew teams fill the cut for a day of races and boats on parade. The event's highlight is the Windermere Cup, the final race of the day that features the men's and women's Husky crew teams. Just south of the UW Husky Stadium, the Montlake Bridge crosses the cut, connecting Montlake Avenue to 24th Avenue East. The Montlake neighborhood includes all of the homes to the south side of this bridge and to either side of 24th Avenue East, which divides the community into east and west. Highway 520 further divides the area into north and south halves. Because it is located at the crossroads of two major thoroughfares, Montlake suffers from heavy traffic, particularly at rush hour. Despite this, the neighborhood feels tucked away from the cares of the city.

Homes in Montlake are a mix of imposing mansions, exquisite cottages, brick Tudors, and elaborate Colonials. Winding streets and culs-de-sac add to the feeling of privacy in the neighborhood, though navigating the streets can be confusing. With the Montlake Cut to the north and the Arboretum to the east, Montlake's only close neighbor is **Portage Bay**, itself a tiny residential offshoot of the Eastlake and Capitol Hill neighborhoods, with one of the few remaining communities of houseboats in Seattle. There are no shopping centers or malls, only a couple of small corner grocers and a freeway on-ramp gas station. University Village, an upscale outdoor shopping center located just north of Montlake on 25th Avenue NE, offers everything from an Anthropologie and Eddie Bauer to an Apple store and a huge QFC Grocery. The neighborhood is home to two of Seattle's premier yacht clubs, the Seattle Yacht Club and Queen City Yacht Club, giving members easy access to both Lake Union and Lake Washington. The beautiful Foster Island Park is a popular place to rent canoes, rowboats or sailboats and paddle or sail through the Arboretum.

On the south side of Highway 520 and west of 24th Avenue East, the Montlake Playfield is a center of activity for the neighborhood, with quiet tennis

Montlake

courts and a popular activity center. Just across 24th Avenue East, Montlake homes brush up against the Washington Park Arboretum, a 200-acre public park with 5,500 different trees and shrubs and a stunning Japanese Garden. A quick drive through the Arboretum brings you to the edge of the Madison Park neighborhood, and provides access to the heavenly bakeries, elegant salons, and excellent restaurants that line Madison Street.

Most Montlake residents are middle- or high-income professionals who work downtown or on the Eastside. When lucrative high-tech jobs on the Eastside, including those at Microsoft, increased in the late 1990s, Montlake became a popular neighborhood for successful software engineers and other technical workers. Other residents include current and retired UW professors and UW Medical Center doctors. Average rental prices in Montlake are similar to those in Green Lake, and less expensive than those in Ballard and Walling-ford. Convenient access to I-5 and the Highway 520 Bridge—as well as the secluded and quiet nature of the residential areas—makes Montlake an attractive and sought-after location. Many bus routes service this neighborhood, and a proposed Montlake Boulevard light rail station, next to Husky Stadium, is scheduled to open in 2016.

Websites: www.seattle.gov, http://montlake.net
Area Code: 206
Zip Code: 98112
Post Office: East Union Station, 1110 23rd Ave, 206-328-9712
Library: 2401 24th Ave E, 206-684-4720, www.spl.org
Public Schools: Seattle Public Schools, 2445 3rd Ave S, 206-252-0010, www.seattleschools.org
Police: East Precinct, 1519 12th Ave, 206-684-4300, wwwseattle.gov/police

Emergency Hospital: University of Washington Medical Center, 1959 NE Pacific St, 206-548-3300, http://uwmedicine.washington.edu

Community Publication: *The Montlake Flyer* (newsletter), http://montlake.net

Community Resources: Montlake Community Center, 1618 E Calhoun St, 206-684-4736, www.seattle.gov/parks; Montlake Playfield, 1618 E Calhoun St, 206-684-4075, www.seattle.gov/parks; University Neighborhood Service Center, 4534 University Way NE, 206-684-7542, www.seattle.gov; Washington Park Arboretum, 2300 Arboretum Dr, 206-543-8800, http://depts. washington.edu/uwbg

Public Transportation: Metro Transit, 206-553-3000, http://metro.kingcounty. gov: 25, 43, 44, 48, 167, 242, 243, 250, 252, 255–257, 260, 261, 265, 266, 268, 271, 272, 277, 280, 311, 424, 982, 986; Sound Transit, 206-398-5000, www.soundtransit.org: 540, 545, 555, 556

CENTRAL DISTRICT

JUDKINS PARK

Boundaries: North: East Madison Street, **West**: 12th Avenue East; **South**: I-90; **East**: Martin Luther King Jr. Way

The Central District or Central Area, referred to as "the CD" by most Seattle residents, cuts a long narrow swath through the center of Seattle. Most retail enterprises in the CD are located along 12th Avenue East and on 23rd Avenue East; many are family-owned restaurants and shops, including small African- or Asian-American groceries.

Sandwiched between Capitol Hill, First Hill, and the International District to the west, and Madison Valley, Madrona, and Leschi to the east, the CD has long had an uneasy relationship with the rest of Seattle. Homes here are not all that different from those at this end of Capitol Hill—most are charming turn-of-the-century Victorians, 1920s Colonials, and Craftsman bungalows. Nevertheless, housing prices in the Central District, especially the eastern portion, have historically lagged behind prices in the rest of Seattle, in part because of geography. Steep slopes in the area slowed development and served as dividers from the rest of the city; the CD was further cut off by the expansion of I-90. Between 1970 and 1990, many homes in the area were neglected or even abandoned as residents moved out to the suburbs.

Over the last decade, however, the Central District has changed dramatically. Housing prices in the CD have risen as more affluent residents have moved to the area, particularly in the north end of the neighborhood. Although many houses in the CD are still run-down from years of neglect, many are being refurbished by newcomers and longtime residents. Home prices in the central section of Seattle now approach those in the Ballard/Greenlake region. Condemned property has been replaced with multi-unit townhouses and condos. Millions of dollars of new construction, including a four- to six-story building at 2211 East Madison Street that now houses a Safeway supermarket, upper level residential units, and an underground parking garage, have contributed to the ongoing transformation of the CD.

Bordered by I-90 to the south, 20th Avenue South to the west, Yesler Way to the north, and Martin Luther King Jr. Way to the east, **Judkins Park** is a one-mile rectangle in the southeast corner of the Central Area. Once a neglected neighborhood decimated by the expansion of I-90 in the 1960s, Judkins Park, like much of the rest of the Central District, is now flourishing. Residents can buy freshly baked bread from Gai's Northwest Bakery Thrift on South Weller Street. At the corner of South Jackson Street and 23rd Avenue South, site of the Welch Plaza mixed-use development, there is a Walgreens drugstore, a Starbucks, and a Red Apple market.

At the center of the Central District is Garfield High School, which consistently produces National Merit Scholars, and boasts a number of famous former students, including Jimi Hendrix, Bruce Lee, Quincy Jones, and Ernestine Anderson. Other notable Central Area institutions include the Swedish Medical Center's Cherry Hill campus, Seattle University, and the Langston Hughes Performing Arts Center.

The Central District has undergone many revisions over the course of Seattle's history. In the early 1900s the neighborhood supported a predominantly Jewish population. Decades later, many Japanese-Americans lived here before they were forcibly relocated to internment camps during World War II. During the sixties and seventies the Central District was home to much

Central District

of Seattle's African-American population and the center of its civil-rights movement. Census data showed that in 1980 the area was more than 80% African-American and about 11% white. During the 1990s the area developed a reputation for crime and poverty. By 2000, *The Seattle Times*, reporting on the changing demographics of the CD, declared that the area had become home to fewer African-Americans than at any other time in the previous 30 years. The 2011 Census figures reveal that many minorities have been migrating out of the Central District and other parts of the city such as Beacon Hill and Rainier Valley and into the suburbs.

Prospective residents should be aware that racial tensions do exist in the Central District. The general target of the neighborhood's anger, however, is the city and its law enforcement, and steps have been taken to improve relations, including the formation of a civilian-led Office of Professional Accountability.

Websites: www.seattle.gov, www.centralarea.org
Area Code: 206
Zip Codes: 98122, 98144
Post Office: East Union Station, 1110 23rd Ave, 206-328-9712
Library: Douglass-Truth Library, 2300 E Yesler Way, 206-684-4704, www.spl.org
Public Schools: Seattle Public Schools, 2445 3rd Ave S, 206-252-0010, www.seattleschools.org
Police: East Precinct, 1519 12th Ave, 206-684-4300, www. seattle.gov/police
Emergency Hospital: Swedish Medical Center, Cherry Hill Campus, 540 16th Ave, 206-320-2000, www.swedish.org
Community Publications: *Central District News*, www.centraldistrictnews.com
Community Resources: Central Area Development Association, 320 17th Ave S, 206-328-2240, www.cada.org; Central Area Motivation Program, 722 18th Ave, 206-812-4940, www.campseattle.org; Central Area Senior Center, 500 30th Ave S, 206-726-4926, www.centralareaseniorcenter. org; Central Area Youth Association, 119 23rd Ave, 206-322-6640, www. seattle-caya.org; Central Neighborhood Service Center, 2301 S Jackson St, Ste 208, 206-684-4767, www.seattle.gov/neighborhoods/nsc; Garfield Community Center, 2323 E Cherry St, 206-684-4788, www.seattle.gov/ parks; Hawkins P-Patch, 504 Martin Luther King Jr. Way, www.seattle.gov/ neighborhoods; Immaculate P-Patch, 18th Ave and E Columbia St, www. seattle.gov/neighborhoods; Judkins P-Patch, 24th Ave S and S Norman St, www.seattle.gov/neighborhoods; Judkins Park and Playfield, 2150 S Norman St, 206-684-4075, www.seattle.gov/parks; Langston Hughes Performing Arts Center, 104 17th Ave S, 206-684-4757; Medgar Evers Pool, 500 23rd Ave, 206-684-4766, www.seattle.gov/parks; Spring Street P-Patch, 25th Ave and E Spring St, www.seattle.gov/neighborhoods; Squire Park Patch,

14th Ave and E Fir St, www.seattle.gov/neighborhoods; Yesler Community Center, 917 E Yesler Way, 206-386-1245, www.seattle.gov/parks

Public Transportation: Metro Transit, 206-553-3000, http://metro.kingcounty. gov: 2–4, 7–9, 11, 12, 14, 27, 34, 42, 43, 48, 60, 64, 193, 205, 211, 303, 984

MADRONA/LESCHI

Boundaries: **North**: Denny Way; **West**: Martin Luther King Jr. Way; **South**: I-90; **East**: Lake Washington

The Madrona and Leschi neighborhoods lie along Lake Washington, east of the Central District and the International District. While Madrona sits atop the hill facing west, Leschi, named for a Nisqually Indian executed for resisting the whites, faces east toward Lake Washington. Some consider Madrona and Leschi part of the Central District, but both neighborhoods are quite different from the CD. While the CD historically has been a neighborhood for those with moderate means, both Madrona and Leschi started out as affluent neighborhoods. It wasn't until after the 1960s when many of its wealthy residents moved to other areas of Seattle and outside Seattle that Madrona/Leschi declined. Fortunately for many, this shift made the area more affordable, and allowed for an influx of people from varied backgrounds. The result is that today these neighborhoods are a welcoming blend of various ethnic groups and income levels with both longtime residents and newcomers.

Madrona's center is the lively intersection of 34th Avenue East and East Union Street. Clustered here are the popular cafés and trendy shops, including

Madrona

Leschi

a branch of the wildly popular Molly Moon Ice Cream Shop. The few blocks surrounding this pedestrian-friendly intersection create an idyllic urban village, with people sitting on storefront steps and at restaurant tables along the sidewalks. There are several small eateries here that cater to a Sunday brunch crowd. In Leschi, most businesses are located on the lake, and are primarily view restaurants and boat-related ventures. The family-owned Leschi Market on Lakeside has been a part of this community since the 1950s. A condominium and retail complex, Lakeside at Leschi, is located on the shore of Lake Washington. To the south, Leschi Park features Victorian-style grounds, towering sequoias, and colorful tulip trees. Atop the hill, Frink Park offers lovely walking trails under grand maples.

Residents of Madrona and Leschi range from artists and artisans to young professionals, from retirees to families with young children. Homes also run the gamut in size and style, from opulent turn-of-the-century Victorians and Colonials to narrow abodes that were once corner groceries. Many of the splendid homes in Leschi have spectacular views of Lake Washington, the Cascade Mountains, and Mount Rainier. Other homes in both Madrona and Leschi share a view of downtown and the Olympics to the west.

Security concerns are evidenced by the bars on the windows on some businesses and houses in these neighborhoods. While there is a strong sense of community here, proximity to higher crime neighborhoods such as Rainier Valley and the Central District make both Madrona and Leschi more vulnerable than other Seattle neighborhoods. However, the crime rates are trending down in these areas and local neighborhood watch groups are organized and effective.

Website: www.seattle.gov

Area Code: 206

Zip Codes: 98122, 98144

Post Office: East Union Station, 1110 23rd Ave, 206-328-9712

Libraries: Douglass-Truth Library, 2300 E Yesler Way, 206 684-4705, www.spl.org; Madrona-Sally Goldmark Library, 1134 33rd Ave, 206-684-4705, www.spl.org

Public Schools: Seattle Public Schools, 2445 3rd Ave S, 206-252-0010, www.seattleschools.org

Police: East Precinct, 1519 12th Ave, 206-684-4300, www.seattle.gov/police

Emergency Hospital: Swedish Medical Center, Cherry Hill Campus, 540 16th Ave, 206-320-2000, www.swedish.org

Community Publication: *Madrona News* (newsletter), http://madrona. wetpaint.com

Community Resources: Central Area Motivation Program, 722 18th Ave, 206-812-4940, www.campseattle.org; Central Neighborhood Service Center, 2301 S Jackson St, Ste 208, 206-684-4767, www.seattle.gov/neighborhoods/ nsc; Garfield Community Center, 2323 E Cherry St, 206-684-4788, www.seattle.gov/parks; Madrona Community Council, 206-285-9166, http://madrona. wetpaint.com; Madrona Playfield, 3211 E Spring St, 206-684-4075, www.seattle.gov/parks

Public Transportation: Metro Transit, 206-553-3000, http://metro.kingcounty. gov: 2, 3, 27, 84, 988

BEACON HILL

South Beacon Hill
Newholly
Othello Station
Mount Baker

Boundaries: North: I-90; **West**: I-5; **South**: South Ryan Street (to Martin Luther King Jr. Way South), South Genesee Street; **East**: Lake Washington

From the top of Beacon Hill, the former Amazon.com Building looms over the city like a huge gothic castle. The Internet giant, headquartered in the building until its relocation to South Lake Union in 2011, helped to change the face of this south Seattle community. Beacon Hill is now a flourishing neighborhood with a strong sense of community and comfortable homes, which are among the most affordable in the city. According to the 2010 Census, the neighborhood's 98118 zip code is the most diverse in the country. Residents hope to retain the neighborhood's friendly character, despite present questions about

Beacon Hill

which tenants will replace the Amazonians. A new light rail station, opened in 2009, connects Beacon Hill to downtown and Sea-Tac Airport. With improved transit attracting commercial developers to the area, Beacon Hill is undoubtedly poised for new growth.

North of Spokane Street, quiet streets are lined with 1940s tract houses and modest bungalows on small but well-kept lots. Residents include middle-income families and young or retired couples. Apartment buildings in the area offer studio, one-, and two-bedroom units for rents slightly below the city average. Many streets have views of downtown, the Cascades, or the Olympics, and a small park on 12th Avenue South has provided memorable postcard pictures of Seattle and Elliot Bay.

South of Spokane Street, small bungalows and contemporary split-levels sell for slightly less than comparable homes at the north end of the hill. New townhomes have subdivided several of the larger lots in the neighborhood. Small family businesses such as Asian groceries and restaurants dot the neighborhood, and the beautiful Jefferson Park and Public Golf Course is located here.

Farther south, **NewHolly** (formerly the Holly Park public housing development) is an award-winning redevelopment featuring 1,400 units of affordable housing available to tenants from a range of income brackets. NewHolly has parks, playgrounds, a Neighborhood Campus featuring a branch of the Seattle public library and South Seattle Community College classrooms, and other neighborhood services. **Othello Station**, another pioneering mixed-income development, contains new single-family homes and townhomes interspersed with small parks. The area is racially and economically diverse and offers housing for low and middle-income families as well as market rate homes. Othello Station is a stop on the city's Link light rail line. The **South Beacon Hill** neighborhood, west of Beacon Ave S, is also changing as a result of the new light rail service, which has begun attracting commuters to the area and energized local businesses.

Clinging to the east slope of the hill, the **Mount Baker** neighborhood is the most affluent section of Beacon Hill. Most homes here have spectacular views of the south end of Lake Washington and the Cascades. Many wealthy professionals live in this area, and it is certainly one of the most racially diverse of Seattle's affluent neighborhoods. Mount Baker has a wealth of waterfront parks, but is hampered by a pedestrian-hostile business district at the busy intersection of Rainier Avenue and Martin Luther King Jr. Way S.

Crime may be a concern on some parts of Beacon Hill, particularly in the southeast section, as gang-related activities occasionally encroach from nearby Rainier Valley. Local crime prevention groups have been increasingly successful in mobilizing the community and in cleaning up public spaces, but newcomers should be aware of the neighborhood dynamics before choosing a home here.

Website: www.seattle.gov

Area Code: 206

Zip Codes: 98118, 98144, 98108

Post Offices: Columbia Station, 3727 S Alaska St; Terminal Finance Station, 2420 4th Ave S

Library: Beacon Hill, 2821 Beacon Ave S, 206-684-4711; NewHolly, 7058 32nd Ave S, 206-386-1905, www.spl.gov

Public Schools: Seattle Public Schools, 2445 3rd Ave S, 206-252-0010, www.seattleschools.org

Police: South Precinct, 3001 S Myrtle St, 206-684-4300, www.cityofseattle.net/police

Emergency Hospital: Harborview Medical Center, 325 9th Ave, 206-744-3000, www.uwmedicine.washington.edu

Community Publications: *South Seattle Beacon*, 636 S Alaska S, 206-461-1300; Beacon Hill Blog, http://beaconhill.seattle.wa.us

Community Resources: Beacon Bluff P-Patch, 1201 15th Ave S, www.seattle.gov/neighborhoods; Beacon Hill Alliance of Neighbors, www.seattle.gov/ban; Hillside Garden, MLK Jr Way S and S McClellan St, www.seattle.gov/neighborhoods; Jefferson Community Center, 3801 Beacon Ave S, 206-684-7483, www.seattle.gov/neighborhoods; New Holly Lucky Garden, S Holly and Shaffer Ave S, www.seattle.gov/neighborhoods; New Holly Power Garden, 7123 Holly Park Dr S, www.seattle.gov/neighborhoods; New Holly Rockery Community Garden and Market Garden, Holly Park Dr S and S 40th, www.seattle.gov/neighborhoods; New Holly 29 Ave Garden, 29th Ave S and S Brighton St, www.seattle.gov/neighborhoods; New Holly Youth and Family P-Patch, 32nd Ave S and S Brighton St, www.seattle.gov/neighborhoods; Snoqualmie P-Patch, 4549 13th Ave S, www.seattle.gov/neighborhoods

Public Transportation: Metro Transit, 206-553-3000, http://metro.kingcounty.gov: 14, 27, 36, 38, 39, 42, 48, 60, 106, 987

RAINIER VALLEY

Columbia City
Hillman City
Rainier Beach
Dunlap

Boundaries: **North**: South Genesee Street; **West**: Martin Luther King Jr. Way South; **South**: South Juniper Street, South 116th Street; **East**: 48th Avenue South, Lake Washington

Until the construction of I-90 through the Central District, what is now Rainier Valley was a southerly extension of the CD. Today, Rainier Valley is one of Seattle's most ethnically diverse neighborhoods, with a large minority and immigrant population. Unfortunately, it has a higher percentage of residents living in poverty than many other areas of the city. Residents believe the neighborhood is a better place to live in now than it was a decade ago, but they are still frustrated by the fact that while crime rates drop in other parts of the city, Rainier Valley continues to experiences spikes in criminal activity, especially in terms of robberies and gang activity. In 2009 between January and November, 600 violent crimes were reported in this area; in 2010 this number had risen to 700. Perhaps because of its physical isolation from the rest of Seattle, Rainier Valley has not received the attention that might have prevented or lessened many of its current socioeconomic problems.

Despite these statistics, there are still hopeful signs that this is a community on the mend. Seattle's new light rail service links Rainier Valley with downtown and other neighborhoods. Rainier Valley community groups regularly organize for graffiti paint-outs, the annual Bridge to Beach Makeover, and to celebrate Night Out Against Crime every August. New housing developments have sprung up, as well. The mixed-use Rainier Court development at 3700 Rainier Avenue South, which includes the Dakota and Courtland Place (for seniors) apartments, provides 500 housing units and retail space on a formerly contaminated industrial site. The city estimates that the valley's industrial north end will employ about 5,000 people by 2014.

The retail district is located along Rainier Avenue South, and is Rainier Valley's main thoroughfare. It is home to small, locally owned shops, delis, bakeries, and take-out restaurants. The renowned Borracchini's Bakery has been in the neighborhood for 90 years, and attracts people from all over Seattle with its delicious decorated-while-you-wait sheet cakes. It's one of the few reminders of Rainier Valley's Italian heritage—the area was settled almost a century ago by Italian immigrants, and was referred to as "Garlic Gulch." Once the exclusive province of ethnic shops and eateries, national chain retailers have recently come this way, allowing residents to meet almost all of their shopping needs without leaving the neighborhood. The Mutual Fish Company is one of the best places in the city for fresh seafood; for the alternative-minded, the neighborhood offers a PCC Natural Market (bordering the Seward Park neighborhood), specializing in organic produce, natural foods, and freshly baked treats. Overall, Rainier Valley

Rainier Valley

seems to be benefiting from both the hard work of committed community groups and the increased prosperity of the greater Seattle area.

Columbia City, In the heart of Rainier Valley, is also experiencing revitalization. Beginning in 1995, residents joined together to fight increasing crime through an innovative crime-stopping dog walk. Several nights a week, residents and their pets would stroll through the community. The idea was to get people out of their homes, allow them to meet their neighbors, and send a message to criminals that they were not welcome. This, combined with other efforts, including those by the Columbia City Revitalization Committee, worked. As crime decreased, the commercial district, centered at Rainier Avenue South and South Ferdinand Street, began to expand to include new restaurants, coffee shops, art galleries, and offices, attracting a hip mix of residents. A farmers' market at the corner of Rainier Avenue South and South Edmunds, and live-music walks are other popular attractions. Just 18 minutes from downtown via light rail, Columbia City has become one of Seattle's most appealing neighborhoods. The Rainier Valley Cultural Center offers a wide variety of performing arts in a classic building. Homes in Columbia City range from turn-of-the-century Victorians to modest bungalows. While homes here are slightly more expensive than those in the rest of Rainier Valley, the prices are still well below the city average. South of Columbia City, the adjacent neighborhood of **Hillman City** seems ready for a similar reawakening.

Rainier Beach and **Dunlap** (also known as Othello), located on the Lake Washington waterfront, offer lovely old homes, ranging from modest 1920s bungalows to stately turn-of-the-century mansions, most with spectacular views of Lake Washington and the Cascades. Crime rates in this part of the Rainier Valley are at or below the Seattle average. Seward Park Estates, once one of the most run-down apartment complexes in Seattle, now provides quality low-income housing just steps from Lake Washington. In general, real estate prices in this neighborhood remain slightly lower than they are for comparable view homes in other parts of the city.

Rainier Beach reflects the racial diversity of the entire Rainier Valley, with a mixture of whites, African-Americans, Asian/Pacific Islanders, and Hispanics. Such diversity is reflected in the tiny business district (characterized by the popular King Donut, at 9232 Rainier Avenue South, which also serves teriyaki), where you'll find a Filipino-owned, coin-operated laundry, a Vietnamese jewelry store, and a Mexican restaurant, among other establishments.

Newcomers to Seattle looking into Rainier Valley should keep in mind that gang-related activities and violent crimes are more common here than elsewhere in the city. Although most residents are respectable, hard-working folks, and there are many wonderful streets in Rainier Valley, pockets of criminal activity may be only a block or two away.

Website: www.seattle.gov
Area Code: 206
Zip Codes: 98118, 98178, 98144
Post Office: Columbia Station, 3727 S Alaska St, 206-721-2368
Libraries: Columbia Library, 4721 Rainier Ave S, 206-386-1908, www.spl.org; NewHolly Library, 7058 32nd Ave S, 206-386-1905, www.spl.org; Rainier Beach Library, 9125 Rainier Ave S, 206-386-1906, www.spl.org
Public Schools: Seattle Public Schools, 2445 3rd Ave S, 206-252-0010, www.seattleschools.org
Police: South Precinct, 3001 S Myrtle St, 206-684-4300, www.cityofseattle.net/police
Emergency Hospital: Harborview Medical Center, 325 9th Ave, 206-744-3000, www.uwmedicine.washington.edu
Community Publications: Columbia City Blog, www.columbiacityblog.com; *Rainier Valley Post*, www.rainiervalleypost.com
Community Resources: Southeast Neighborhood Service Center, 3815 S Othello St, Ste 105, 206-386-1931, www.seattle.gov/neighborhoods/nsc; Rainier Community Center, 4600 38th Ave S, 206-386-1919, www.seattle.gov/parks; Rainier Beach Community Center (scheduled to reopen 2013), 8825 Rainier Ave S, 206-386-1925, www.seattle.gov/parks; Van Asselt Community Center 2820 S Myrtle St, 206-386-1921, www.seattle.gov/parks; Rainier Valley Cultural Center, 3515 S Alaska St, 206-725-7517, www.seedseattle.org
Public Transportation: Metro Transit, 206-553-3000, http://metro.kingcounty.gov: 7– 9, 34, 36, 38, 39, 42, 48, 987

SEWARD PARK

Boundaries: **North**: South Genesee Street; **West**: 48th Avenue South; **South**: South Holly Street; **East**: Lake Washington

The Seward Park neighborhood is located just south of Mount Baker, on Lake Washington. The park from which this community takes its name is a 277-acre peninsula filled with lush vegetation, including cherry trees, lofty Douglas firs, and silvery madrona trees. Whether or not you choose to live here, Seward Park is always worth a visit: during the summer the park hosts jazz concerts and the annual Seafair celebration; and, in addition to nature trails and the lake, it is one of the best places in the city to savor breathtaking views of Mount Rainier. Residents take advantage of the Seward Park Clay Studio, located in the original 1927 bathhouse, which offers pottery classes for all levels of students and serves as a workshop for several professional artists. And, residents and visitors alike line the streets for the annual Danskin Triathlon for women, held at either Seward Park or nearby Stan Sayres Park.

Residents of Seward Park are mostly affluent professionals, including local politicians and judges, and plenty of seniors, some of whom reside in the Kline Galland nursing home. The neighborhood is best known for its strong Jewish community. Most of Seattle's Orthodox Jews live in or near Seward Park, attending one of the three synagogues located here. Bikur Cholim Machzikay Hadath, the oldest synagogue in Washington, is located at 5145 South Morgan Street. A small business district on Wilson Ave features restaurants, a pet supply store, and a PCC Natural Market. The neighborhood is not well served by public transportation, unfortunately.

The northern part of Seward Park is sometimes referred to as Lakewood, and the neighborhood is also known as Lakewood/Seward Park. Homes range from 1950s brick ranch houses to stately modern mansions. Most have views of Lake Washington and Mount Rainier; many have waterfront access. While homes here are expensive due to the panoramic views, the neighborhood's proximity to Rainier Valley has kept real estate prices slightly lower than other Seattle neighborhoods.

Seward Park

Website: www.seattle.gov
Area Code: 206
Zip Code: 98178, 98118
Post Office: Columbia Station, 3727 S Alaska St, 206-721-2368
Library: Rainier Beach Library, 9125 Rainier Ave S, 206-386-1906, www.spl.org
Public Schools: Seattle Public Schools, 2445 3rd Ave S, 206-252-0010, www.seattleschools.org
Police: South Precinct, 3001 S Myrtle St, 206-684-4300, www.cityofseattle.net/police
Emergency Hospital: Harborview Medical Center, 325 9th Ave, 206-744-3000, www.uwmedicine.washington.edu
Community Publication: *Rainier Valley Post,* www.rainiervalleypost.com
Community Resources: Southeast Neighborhood Service Center, 3815 S Othello St, 206-386-1931, www.seattle.gov/neighborhoods/nsc; Rainier Beach Community Center (scheduled to reopen 2013), 8825 Rainier Ave S, 206-386-1925, www.seattle.gov/parks; Seward Park, 5895 Lake Washington Blvd S (Environmental and Audubon Center, 206-652-2444, Clay Studio, 206-722-6342); Lakewood Seward Park Community Center, 4916 S Angeline St, 206-722-9696; Bikur Cholim Machzikay Hadath Congregation, 5145 S Morgan St, 206-721-0970, http://bcmhseattle.org
Public Transportation: Metro Transit, 206-553-3000, http://metro.kingcounty.gov: 34, 39

DUWAMISH DISTRICT

South Park
Georgetown
Sodo

Boundaries: North: South Royal Brougham Way, South Dearborn Street; **West**: Duwamish Waterway, Highway 509; **South**: South Barton Street; **East**: I-5

The Duwamish District is a primarily industrial area that starts just south of Safeco Field and follows the Duwamish River south to the city limits. Originally the land on either side of the river was fertile farmland, but eventually the farms were displaced by industries that used the river for shipping and, unfortunately, dumping. Over time, the waterway became a toxic stew of chemicals, heavy metals, and raw sewage. In 2001, the EPA designated the lower Duwamish River as a federal Superfund site. A cleanup is under way, but restoration will be a decades-long process. The 38,000 residents who live in the surrounding neighborhoods experience a disproportionate amount of health problems, such as asthma and low birth weights, in comparison to the rest of King County, something you should certainly bear in mind if you are considering moving to this area. Today, most of the district remains strictly industrial, although there are growing pockets of residential and retail activity in the South Park and Georgetown areas. Boeing Field is located in the vicinity, but most employees commute

Georgetown

to the area rather than live here. People from other parts of the city visit the Gai's Bakery outlet store and the nearby Museum of Flight at Boeing Field, or use the through streets in this neighborhood as shortcuts to the Sea-Tac Airport, Burien, and West Seattle.

South Park is a small community at the south end of this district, near the Duwamish River. This is a neighborhood of extremely modest bungalows, many of which are rentals, as well as a few well-tended cottages near the South Park Marina. Known to some as as "Little Tijuana," South Park is the only neighborhood in Seattle where Hispanic residents are heavily concentrated. Anchoring the neighborhood's four-block retail core on 14th Avenue South is the Mexi-Mart, a Mexican grocery, bakery, take-out restaurant, clothing, and music store. The residential face of the neighborhood is slowly changing, however, as more middle-class Seattle residents are finding South Park one of the most affordable areas in the city. One means of access to the community was lost when the aging South Park Bridge was closed in 2011. The new bridge will be completed late in 2013.

The **Georgetown** neighborhood, in the area around South Michigan Street, is also experiencing a kind of renaissance. Formerly an odd assortment of bungalows, Victorians, and ramblers, breakfast cafés, warehouses, and other industrial buildings, Georgetown has evolved into an offbeat and quirky community, home to a mix of artists, families, gardeners, and blue-collar workers who appreciate the lower housing prices. Georgetown is the oldest continually settled neighborhood in the city, and most of the homes were built before 1939, though some have been recently replaced with modern structures. New condo developments have opened here, as well. The retail core along Airport Way features a colorful mix of funky shops, bars, and hip restaurants, including Stella Pizza. Fantagraphic Books on South Vale Street is a mecca for comic book aficionados. The neighborhood hosts events, such as the Georgetown Art Attack, held monthly, and the annual Carnival, that draw visitors from all over the city to hear live music and watch bicycle jousting, among other diversions. A growing number of artists have discovered Georgetown's affordable studio space, including several who collaborate and share resources in the former Rainier Brewery on Airport Way South, now an official Seattle landmark and home to artist live/work spaces and Tully's Coffee headquarters. The Seattle Design Center, a 360,000-square-foot complex of 60 designer showrooms on 6th Avenue South, provides many of the city's contractors and homeowners with furnishings, fabrics, and accessories.

The **SODO** (South of the Dome/South of Downtown) area borders downtown at Royal Brougham Street, south of the former Kingdome area. It's an industrial area, filled with warehouses and small manufacturing plants. The historic Sears building—now headquarters to Starbucks Coffee—is located here, as well as a sprawling new Home Depot and a Costco. Few people actually live in SODO, but many of those who do are artists, residing in spacious lofts tucked inside converted warehouses. Rents tend to be much lower than in other Seattle neighborhoods. Though there are no grocery stores here except the Grocery Outlet Bargain Market, and the noise from passing cargo and passenger trains can be unbearable at times, creative types appreciate the lofts' high ceilings and plentiful elbowroom. Central Link light rail service now makes stops at the new SODO and Stadium stations in this area. City planners are considering new zoning laws that would allow higher buildings, which would pave the way for future development of condominiums and apartment buildings in a plan to remake the area into a mixed-use urban neighborhood.

Website: www.seattle.gov
Area Code: 206
Zip Codes: 98108, 98168, 98106, 98104, 98134
Post Office: Georgetown Station, 620 S Orcas St, 206-767-9473
Library: Delridge Library, 5423 Delridge Way SW, 206-733-9125, www.spl.org
Public Schools: Seattle Public Schools, 2445 3rd Ave S, 206-252-0010, www.seattleschools.org
Police: West Precinct, 810 Virginia St, 206-684-8917, www.seattle.gov/police
Emergency Hospital: Harborview Medical Center, 325 9th Ave, 206-744-3000, www.uwmedicine.washington.edu
Community Publications:
All About South Park (Website), www.allaboutsouthpark.com;
Blogging Georgetown, www.blogginggeorgetown.com
Community Resources: Duwamish River Cleanup Coalition, www.duwamishcleanup.org; Georgetown Crime Prevention and Community Council, P.O. Box 80021, Seattle, WA 98108, www.georgetownneighborhood. com; Delridge Neighborhood Service Center, 5405 Delridge Way SW, 206-684-7417, www.seattle.gov/neighborhoods/nsc; Marra Farm P-Patch, 9026 4th Ave S, www.seattle.gov/neighborhoods; Oxbow Park P-Patch, 6400 Corson Ave S, www.seattle.gov/neighborhoods; SODO Business Association,

2732 3rd Ave S, 206-292-7449, www.seattle.gov; South Park Business Association, 1408 South Cloverdale St, PMB #283, 206-763-8777, www.seattle.gov; South Park Community Center, 8319 8th Ave S, 206-684-7451, www.seattle.gov; South Park Neighborhood Association, 8201 10th Ave S, #7, Seattle, WA 98108

Public Transportation: Metro Transit, 206-553-3000, http://metro.kingcounty.gov: 21–23, 35, 39, 56, 57, 60, 85, 101, 106, 113, 116, 118, 119, 121 124, 131–134, 150, 152, 154, 173, 177, 190, 191, 194, 196, 280; Sound Transit, 206-398-5000, www.soundtransit.org: 590, 592– 595

WEST SEATTLE

Admiral
Alki
Fauntleroy
Delridge

Boundaries: **North**: Puget Sound, Elliott Bay; **West**: Puget Sound; **South**: Seola Beach Drive SW, SW Roxbury Street; **East**: Duwamish Waterway, Highway 509

In 1851, the schooner *Exact* landed on Alki Beach in what is now West Seattle, bringing the Denny party to the Puget Sound. Charles Terry, a member of the original party, remained behind while the rest of the group moved on to what is now the Seattle waterfront. By 1897, the peninsula had a large enough population to merit a ferry between downtown and West Seattle. Today, West Seattle is a comfortable residential hill connected to the rest of the city by the West Seattle Freeway, which bridges the Duwamish Waterway and the man-made Harbor Island.

In many respects, West Seattle seems self-contained, a world unto itself. In fact, over a century ago, West Seattle was a separate city, until its annexation by Seattle in 1907. Today, some residents rarely venture across the West Seattle Bridge, since the area supports plenty of services and shops, markets, and restaurants, as well as the West Village shopping center, for those who crave a mall-like experience. In fact, a small but vocal group of residents believe West Seattle should secede from Seattle proper and form its own city. Proponents of succession believe that West Seattle has historically been handed the short end of the stick in terms of city services like police protection, pothole filling, and libraries. They claim that West Seattle has been made a dumping ground for an unfair share of urban development. Nonetheless, in recent years many prospective homebuyers have set their sights on West Seattle, drawn here by the prospect of lower housing prices than in similar neighborhoods closer to the city. Homes can be found in the $300,000 to $400,000 range. Data from the

2010 Census show that West Seattle has become increasingly popular with gay couples, especially those raising children. Between 2000 and 2010 the percentage of gay couples living together in West Seattle (or "Capitol Hill West," as some have taken to calling it) increased by 55%.

West Seattle

West Seattle comprises dozens of neighborhoods—too many to profile individually here. In this book we concentrate on the principal districts of West Seattle, which include Admiral, Alki, Fauntleroy, and Delridge. If you are working with a real estate agent to view properties in this area, you will hear the names of neighborhoods such as Fairmont Park, Sunrise Heights, Morgan, Genesee, Seaview, and others. Areas in the south end near Fauntleroy include Fauntlee Hills, Westwood, Arbor Heights, Arroyo Heights, and Seola Beach.

The West Seattle Junction at SW Alaska Street and California Avenue SW is a commercial center for West Seattle. Clothing boutiques, bookstores, small diners, and drugstores fill the ground floor retail space around "the Junction." Young couples and singles rent the quaint apartments above the storefronts. East of the junction, auto dealerships and take-out restaurants cluster around the intersection of SW Alaska Street and Fauntleroy Way SW.

The intersection of SW Admiral Way and California Avenue SW is the second retail core on the hill. Here, the historic Admiral Theater presides over the intersection, which is lined with small shops, espresso joints, and restaurants. The **Admiral** district, which surrounds this intersection, is one of the more affluent areas in West Seattle. Homes at the top of the hill, mainly Craftsman bungalows and Northwest Moderns, have views of downtown to the northeast or of the Olympics to the west. Residents of the Admiral area tend to be middle- to upper-income professionals and their families.

The Admiral business district enjoys a Metropolitan Market, filled with gourmet cheeses, fresh flowers, and fine wines, but suffers from a shortage of parking. Residents here lobbied for a parking garage near the Admiral Theater, but the city council refused to approve funding. Instead, a local developer agreed to add an extra floor of parking to a condominium project. Nonetheless, parking on a Saturday night, when the district is filled with diners and moviegoers, continues to present a challenge.

Alki is a long, narrow beach neighborhood that stretches along the north and west sides of the peninsula and offers the atmosphere of an ocean resort town. In the summer, the beach is crowded with sunbathers, in-line skaters, bicyclists, and volleyball players. In the spring and fall, residents meet for breakfast at the Alki Café or dinner at Spud Fish & Chips. Although development has begun to change the face of this area, many 1960s condominiums and beach cottages are still located Just a short walk or bicycle ride from the beach. Condos here sell for a good deal more than they do in other West Seattle neighborhoods. Rents are currently comparable to those in the Capitol Hill neighborhood. Residents are generally middle-income service professionals, many of whom are longtime West Seattle residents. Alki has extraordinary views of both downtown Seattle and the Olympic peninsula. The most spectacular views of the Olympics come during early spring or late fall, when the sun is bright and the snow has not yet melted in the mountains. The Alki beachhead is a popular destination for couples watching the sunset during the summer, and many intrepid Seattle residents brave inclement winter weather to watch the waves crash against the shore. Salty's on Alki, at 1936 Harbor Avenue SW, is one of the city's favorite view restaurants and a popular spot for wedding receptions and Sunday brunch. If there is a downside to Alki, it is the waves of tourists, short-term renters, and sun-worshippers who crowd the neighborhood during the summer. The city's anti-cruising ordinance stopped most of the circling of cars and motorcycles, but traffic on sunny days still slows to a crawl on Harbor Avenue SW.

The **Fauntleroy** neighborhood lies along the southwest slope of the hill in West Seattle, facing the Puget Sound. Though Fauntleroy is best known throughout the rest of Seattle for its ferry dock, with services to Vashon Island and the Olympic Peninsula, it is also a comfortable, secluded neighborhood populated by affluent families and singles in their 30s and 40s. Beautiful brick Tudors, classic Northwest Modern homes, and modest bungalows line winding streets and quiet culs-de-sac. Renters make up only 25% of Fauntleroy residents. Fauntleroy was home to some of Seattle's original families, like the Colmans, who built the city's first brick building and its downtown ferry terminal. Another famous resident, Jim Whittaker, who was the first American to stand atop Mount Everest, grew up playing in the woods in Fauntleroy. Homes here are spacious and have unparalleled views of Puget Sound, Vashon Island, and the Olympics and go for more than similar properties do in Alki. Lincoln Park, at 8011 Fauntleroy Way SW, has grills for summer barbecuing, and a heated Olympic-size salt-water pool right on the edge of the sound for spectacular summer swimming. Fauntleroy's tiny commercial district, situated at what was formerly the end of the streetcar route, is comically called "Endolyne." It features a couple of restaurants—including Endolyne Joe's—a neighborhood bakery, gift shop, and beauty salon all concentrated in a single building at SW Wildwood Place and 45th Avenue SW.

As Fauntleroy's popularity grows, modest homes belonging to middle-income families are being sold to wealthy retirees and professionals, though turnover is occurring less quickly here than in other West Seattle neighborhoods. Interestingly, the transfer of property within families is not unusual, according to one local real estate agent.

In the southeast quarter of West Seattle, **Delridge** is a neighborhood of simple 1950s ramblers, contemporary split-levels, and tract houses. On its eastern edge near West Marginal Way, Delridge is primarily industrial. To the west, residential areas offer modest homes and modern apartment complexes. The median income in this neighborhood is lower than most of West Seattle; rents and real estate prices tend to be much lower as well. Community groups in Delridge work to improve the quality of life here. One such effort was the Delridge Neighborhoods Development Association's proposal to include affordable apartments on the top two floors of the new library. The impressive result is the full-service Delridge Public Library, 5423 Delridge Way SW, which opened in June 2002 and features 19 low-income housing units on the upper two floors. The High Point section of Delridge was formerly a sprawling low-income housing development that was razed to the ground and rebuilt as a mixed-income community, including market rate housing, rental units, a senior center, and retail space.

Though West Seattle is only a 20-minute drive from downtown, the neighborhood is not as convenient for those working on the Eastside. The commute covers the West Seattle Freeway, I-5, and I-90, all of which have heavy traffic during rush hour. During the spring and summer, a water taxi carries passengers between Seacrest Park in West Seattle and Pier 50 on the downtown Seattle waterfront. For people working downtown who would like to live in a neighborhood that feels utterly removed from the city, West Seattle may be the perfect spot.

Websites: www.seattle.gov, www.wschamber.com
Area Code: 206
Zip Codes: 98106, 98116, 98126, 98136, 98146
Post Office: West Seattle Station, 4412 California Ave SW, 206-937-7207
Libraries: Delridge Library, 5423 Delridge Way SW, 206-733-9125, www.spl.org; High Point Library, 6338 32nd Ave SW, 206-684-7454, www.spl.org; Southwest Library, 3411 SW Raymond St, 206-684-7454, www.spl.org; West Seattle Library, 2306 42nd Ave SW, 206-684-7444, www.spl.org
Public Schools: Seattle Public Schools, 2445 3rd Ave S, 206-252-0010, www.seattleschools.org
Police: South Precinct, 3001 S Myrtle St, 206-684-4300, www.cityofseattle.net/police
Emergency Hospital: Harborview Medical Center, 325 9th Ave, 206-744-3000, www.uwmedicine.washington.edu

Community Publication: Sustainable West Seattle (website), www. sustainablewestseattle.org; West Seattle Blog, http://westseattleblog.com; *West Seattle Herald/White Center News*, 14006 1st Ave S, Ste 8, Burien, WA 98168, 206-708-1378, www.westseattleherald.com

Community Resources: Alki Community Center, 5817 SW Stevens St, 206-684-7430, www.seattle.gov/parks; Colman Pool, 8603 Fauntleroy Ave SW, 206-684-7494, www.seattle.gov/parks; Delridge Community Center, 4501 Delridge Way SW, 206-684-7423, www.seattle.gov/parks; Delridge Neighborhood Service Center, 5405 Delridge Way SW, 206-684-7417, www. seattle.gov/neighborhoods/nsc; Delridge Neighborhoods Development Association, 4408 Delridge Way SW, 206-923-0917, www.dnda.org; Delridge P-Patch, 5078 25th Ave SW, www.seattle.gov/neighborhoods; Hiawatha Community Center, 2700 California Ave SW, 206-684-7441, www.seattle. gov/parks; High Point Community Center, 6920 34th Ave SW, 206-684-7422, www.seattle.gov/parks; High Point Juneau Community Garden, SW Juneau and 32nd Ave SW, www.seattle.gov/neighborhoods; Lincoln Park P-Patch, 7400 Fauntleroy Ave SW, www.seattle.gov/neighborhoods; Southwest Community Center, 2801 SW Thistle St, 206-684-7438, www.seattle.gov/ parks; West Genesee Garden, SW Genesee and 42nd Ave W, www.seattle. gov/neighborhoods; West Seattle Junction Association, 4210 SW Oregon St, Ste A, 206-935-0904, http://wsjunction.org

Public Transportation: Metro Transit, 206-553-3000, http://metro.kingcounty. gov: 21, 22, 37, 51, 53–57, 60, 85, 116, 118–120, 125, 128, 773, 775; Sound Transit, 206-398-5000, www.soundtransit.org; 560

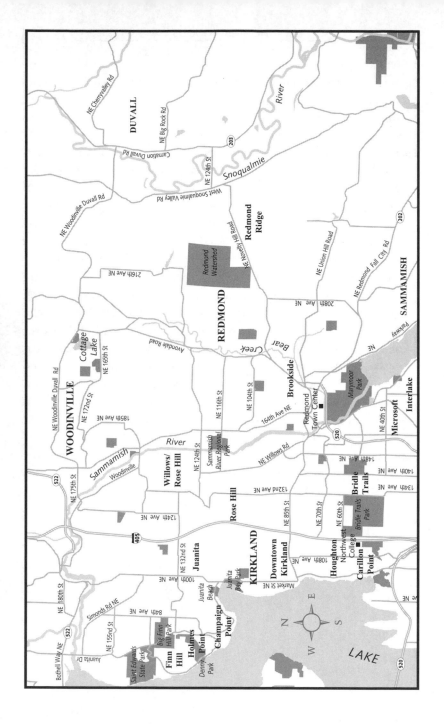

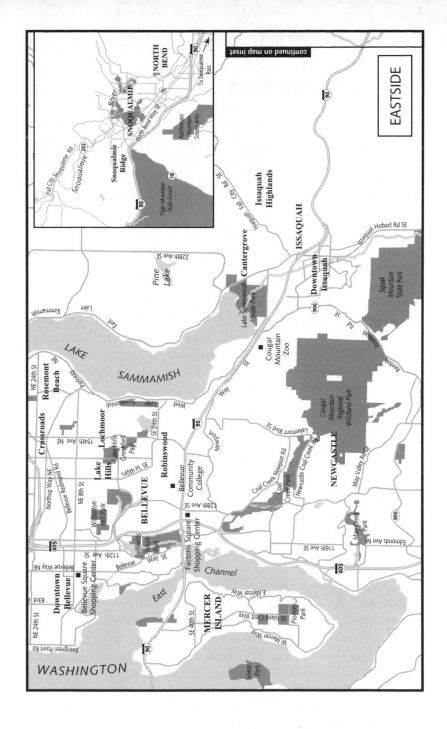

EASTSIDE

continued on map inset

WASHINGTON

99

SURROUNDING COMMUNITIES

Today, Seattle is composed of much more than simply the city itself. Beyond the city limits, many communities benefit from and contribute to Seattle's economy. A good number of Seattle residents go to work each day on the East-side, to communities such as Bellevue, Kirkland, or Redmond (where Microsoft is based). Both Seattle and Eastside residents commute to jobs in Tacoma to the south or Everett to the north. Many catch a ferry from Bainbridge Island west of downtown, or from towns and cities on the Olympic Peninsula.

According to local real estate agents, many newcomers arrive in Seattle with hopes of living in the city or very close to the city, only to find that housing prices are higher than they expected, or lot sizes smaller than they had hoped. Many choose to expand their search to include the Eastside, the north or south sides of greater Seattle, or along the I-5 corridor. When choosing a community outside Seattle, there are a few things to think about beyond housing prices. Consider if you want a suburban or rural environment—some make their homes in traditionally rural communities beyond the suburbs, including Duvall, Snoqualmie, and Woodinville. Do you want new construction in a planned com-munity, or an older home in a more established neighborhood? Do you prefer proximity to water or to mountains? Exclusive planned neighborhoods in some Eastside suburbs, particularly those with views of Lake Washington or Lake Sammamish, attract affluent residents looking for a suburban lifestyle. Com-munities like Issaquah and Redmond are filled with new developments, while mature communities like Burien or Shoreline offer established neighborhoods with spectacular views. And, perhaps most important, how much time do you want to spend in your car every day, commuting to work? Long commutes can negatively affect one's personal and professional life, not to mention harm done to the environment.

If you are considering relocating to one of Seattle's surrounding commu-nities to the east, north, south, or west of the city, you'll find useful contact information below for city services, school districts, post offices, and libraries as well as additional community resources and local publications. Each city pro-filed maintains its own website, with its current URL listed below: make this the first stop on your fact-finding tour. A wealth of additional information can be accessed here that is beyond the scope of this guide. (Be aware, too, that Web addresses are subject to frequent revision, and many King County communities are in the process of changing theirs. If you encounter a dead end with the URL provided in this guide, searching online for "City Name, Official Website" should reroute you to the correct site.)

EASTERN COMMUNITIES
(THE "EASTSIDE")—KING COUNTY

Mercer Island, Bellevue, Newcastle, Redmond, Kirkland, Woodinville, Duvall, Issaquah, Sammamish, North Bend/Snoqualmie

A decade ago, "The Eastside" consisted primarily of Bellevue, Redmond, and Kirkland. Today, just about any city east of Seattle to Snoqualmie Pass is referred to as being on the Eastside. With the exception of Mercer Island, which has a limited amount of land available for new construction, the Eastside is the place to turn if you're looking for a large new home in a planned or gated community. Many eastern cities also feature wooded or semi-rural areas—a rarity in Seattle. The Eastside has always been known as an upscale region, so it's not surprising that Bill Gates—one of the world's richest men—lives here, in the affluent suburb of Medina.

Mercer Island

Roanoke

Located at the south end of Lake Washington, Mercer Island is an established, upscale community. While only minutes away from downtown Seattle, it feels miles away from the urban hubbub. This insular city with beautiful view homes, plentiful opportunities for recreation, and a compact but comprehensive commercial district, attracts affluent professionals and entrepreneurs. Though small, the city boasts 400 acres of parks and open space, including Luther Burbank Park at the north end of the island. A popular summer recreation area, Luther Burbank offers swimming, boating, a playground, and an off-leash dog area. During the summer months, performances are held at its small outdoor amphitheater. Not surprisingly, Mercer Island's school district is well known for its academic accomplishments, and each year sends more than 90% of its seniors on to college. And, the cherry on the top, because Mercer Island is situated between Seattle and the Eastside, it's an easy commute for professionals in both regions—perfect for two-career couples. The island measures 5 miles long and 2 1/2 miles wide, and in 2011 reported a population of nearly 23,000 residents.

As you would expect, housing prices and rents on the island are high. Many of the homes here are sprawling estates and modern mansions, but there are a few modest houses around, mostly built between the 1950s and the 1980s. Houses in the $900,000 range are the norm, and rents are expensive, just a bit higher than those in downtown Seattle. While Mercer Island is known primarily as a single-family residential community, a number of new apartments and condos are being developed in Town Center on the island's north end.

Mercer Island

Mercer Island's primary artery is Mercer Way—East Mercer Way on the eastern half of the island and West Mercer Way on the western side. The winding road hugs the lakeshore, and seemingly is used as much by runners and bicyclists as by cars. (In fact, Mercer Island is a fantastic place to train for triathlons or races, because of its opportunities for swimming, running and biking.) Island Crest Way, running north/south, bisects the island. The community's commercial district is located adjacent to the freeway at the north end of the island, and is bounded by 27th and 32nd streets, Island Crest Way and 77th Avenue SE.

At the northern tip of Mercer Island is the **Roanoke** neighborhood. This is where you'll find two of Mercer Island's historic landmarks, the Roanoke Inn and the VFW Hall. The Roanoke Inn, at 72nd Avenue SE and North Mercer Way, is a homey little tavern and eatery smack-dab in the middle of a residential community. Established in 1914, "the Roanoke" served as a speakeasy during Prohibition. Today, the restaurant is popular with both islanders and city folk for its weeknight dinner specials, cozy atmosphere, and patio dining during the summer. The VFW Hall, which began its history as the Keewaydin ("the north wind") Club and later the Mercer Island Community Club, was built by Mercer Island residents in 1922 to host social events.

Website: www.mercergov.org
Area Code: 206
Zip Code: 98040
Post Office: 3040 78th Ave SE, 206-232-8834
Library: 4400 88th Ave SE, 206-236-3537, www.kcls.org
Public Schools: Mercer Island School District, 4160 86th Ave SE, 206-236-3330,
    www.misd.k12.wa.us
Police: City Hall, 9611 SE 36th St, 206-275-7610, www.mercergov.org

Emergency Hospitals: Harborview Medical Center, 325 9th Ave, 206-744-3000, www.uwmedicine.washington.edu; Overlake Hospital Medical Center, 1035 116th Ave NE, 425-688-5000, www.overlakehospital.org

Community Publication: *Mercer Island Reporter*, 7845 SE 30th St, 206-232-1215, www.pnwlocalnews.com

Community Resources: Community Center at Mercer View, 8236 SE 24th St, 206-275-7609, www.mercergov.org; Mercer Island Beach Club, 8326 Avalon Dr, 206-232-3125, www.mibeachclub.com; Mercer Island Boys' & Girls' Club, 4120 86th Ave SE, 206-232-4548, www.mi.positiveplace.org; Mercer Island Chamber of Commerce, 7605 SE 27th St, Ste 109, 206-232-3404, www.mercerislandchamber.org; Mercer Island Country Club, 8700 SE 71st St, 206-232-5600, www.mercerislandcc.com; Mercer Island Historical Society, 206-236-3274, www.mihistory.org; Mercerwood Shore Club, 4150 East Mercer Way, 206-232-1622, www.mercerwood.com; Stroum Jewish Community Center, 3801 East Mercer Way, 206-232-7115, www.sjcc.org

Public Transportation: Metro Transit, 206-553-3000, http://metro.kingcounty.gov: 201–205, 211, 213, 216, 891, 892, 942, 981, 989; Sound Transit, 206-398-5000, www.soundtransit.org: 550, 554

Bellevue

Downtown Bellevue
Newport Hills
Bridle Trails
Brookside
Crossroads
Rosemont Beach
Interlake
Lochmoor
Robinswood
Lake Hills

Bellevue was once a small city best known to Seattle residents as home to Bellevue Square, an upscale mall. Today, Bellevue is the state's fifth-largest city, and enjoys a thriving downtown, excellent schools, and abundant parks. While the area has a reputation of being home to wealthy residents (the cost of living here tops the national average by more than 55%, according to Bestplaces.net), you'll find people of various incomes living in Bellevue. Suburban housing developments filled with modest split-level and contemporary homes dot the area, and homes close to Lake Washington to the west or Lake Sammamish to the east are more elegant and expensive. Most houses to the east are on the newer side, and range in style from traditional brick ranch houses to angular art deco homes to lavish new brick Tudors. Home prices in Bellevue range from the $400,000s to the millions.

Bellevue

According to the City of Bellevue, the region's largest employers are Bellevue Community College, the Bellevue School District, the City of Bellevue, Boeing, Microsoft, Expedia, T-Mobile USA, Verizon Wireless, Puget Sound Energy, and Overlake Hospital. Along with Microsoft, many high-tech companies are located in the Eastside. In fact, high-tech jobs account for about 20% of all Eastside jobs. Bellevue is also a popular choice for professionals who work in Seattle, as evidenced by the heavy morning and evening traffic across both bridges.

The previous decade marked a significant shift in the city's demographics. Between 2000 and 2011, census figures show that Bellevue's Asian population increased by 77%, and minority groups currently make up over 40% of the city's population. Bellevue's thriving economy and excellent educational system attract people from all over the world, and 30% of the population is foreign born. Microsoft employs many individuals from China and India, in particular.

Though Bellevue is primarily a city of unassuming neighborhoods (only a sampling of which are profiled here), **Downtown Bellevue** has become a hip place to live, with 6,000 residents now calling it home. Several condominiums have been erected here, more are being constructed, and a host of new shops and restaurants have been added to the area near Bellevue Square. Lincoln Square is a soaring skyscraper with condos, retail and office space, restaurants, and the four-star Westin Bellevue Hotel. The city has a strong public art program and has worked to build a thriving arts community. The Bellevue Arts Museum, located at 510 Bellevue Way NE, is the site of the city's annual arts and crafts fair, and each spring the city hosts a jazz festival.

Most of Bellevue's neighborhoods offer a range of housing styles and prices, though properties near the water will generally cost more than those inland. Southeast of downtown, the **Newport Hills** neighborhood, one of King County's first planned residential areas, has a lively commercial area that includes the Factoria Square Mall, as well as single and multi-family housing options. Many new properties being built in Bellevue are larger and more expensive than the older homes they replace. If you're looking for seclusion and large lots, consider the **Bridle Trails** community in northern Bellevue. Most homes in the neighborhood rely on septic tanks instead of sewers, but property is at a premium, and there are some incredible new estates peeking through the pines. The median home price here is over $1,000,000. To the southeast are the **Brookside** and **Microsoft** neighborhoods, popular options for many Microsoft employees. Homes here are large and comfortable, and sell for prices comparable to Bridle Trails.

Crossroads is one of Bellevue's most culturally diverse neighborhoods and the location of some of its more affordable housing. About 9,000 people live here and you are just as likely to hear residents speaking Russian, Spanish, or Chinese as English. Crossroads Shopping Center, at NE 8th Street and 156th Avenue NE, is a popular meeting place for members of the East European, Hispanic, and Asian communities. The mall frequently hosts live music and community celebrations. Also at the mall is the Library Connection, a public library with multi-language programs and materials, and Internet access. In northeast Bellevue, near Lake Sammamish, are the **Rosemont Beach, Interlake,** and **Lochmoor** neighborhoods. Homes in these communities have risen sharply in value in recent years, with the median price at just over $490,000 in 2011, though those with views are considerably more expensive. Most houses are large ramblers built in the mid- to late-1970s.

The **Robinswood** and **Lake Hills** communities are located in southeast Bellevue, near Bellevue Community College. This area includes a variety of rentals, which are popular with students and employees of nearby Factoria Mall. Most homes here are generally more affordable than those in other areas of Bellevue. The exception is the area overlooking the Glendale Golf & Country Club, where newly constructed homes can cost up to a million. Robinswood Community Park, at 148th Avenue SE and SE 22nd Street, is a favorite local attraction. It features soccer and baseball fields, and a quaint cottage for party and banquet rentals.

Website: www.bellevuewa.gov
Area Code: 425
Zip Codes: 98004–9, 98015
Post Offices: 1171 Bellevue Way NE, 425-453-5655; 11405 NE 2nd Pl, 425-462-7508; 15731 NE 8th St, 425-401-0892
Libraries: 1111 110th Ave NE, 425-450-1765; 15590 Lake Hills Blvd, 425-747-3350; 14250 SE Newport Way, 425-747-2390, www.kcls.org
Public Schools: 12111 NE 1st St, 425-456-4000, www.bsd405.org
Police: City Hall, 450 110th Ave NE, 425-452-6917, 877-881-2731; Factoria Substation, 3915 Factoria Blvd SE, 425-452-2880; Crossroads Substation, 1336 156th Ave NE, 425-452-2891; www.bellevuewa.gov/contact-police.htm
Emergency Hospital: Overlake Hospital Medical Center, 1035 116th Ave NE, 425-688-5000, www.overlakehospital.org

Community Publications: *Bellevue Reporter*, 2700 Richards Rd, Ste 201, 425-453-4270, www.pnwlocalnews.com; *King County Journal*, 11400 SE 8th St, 425-455-2222, www.pnwlocalnews.com

Community Resources: Bellevue Chamber of Commerce, 302 Bellevue Square, 425-454-2464, www.bellevuechamber.org; Bellevue Community College, 3000 Landerholm Circle SE, 425-564-1000, http://bellevuecollege.edu; Bellevue Downtown Association, 400 108th Ave NE, Ste 110, 425-453-1223, www.bellevuedowntown.org; Crossroads Community Center, 16000 NE 10th St, 425-452-4874, www.bellevuewa.gov; Eastside Heritage Center, P.O. Box 40535, Bellevue, WA 98105, 425-450-1049, www.eastsideheritagecenter. org; Highland Park Community Center, 14224 NE Bel-Red Rd, 425-452-7686, www.bellevuewa.gov; North Bellevue Community Senior Center, 4063 148th Ave NE, 425-452-7681, www.bellevuewa.gov; Northwest Arts Center, 9825 NE 24th St, 425-452-4106, www.bellevuewa.gov

Public Transportation: Metro Transit, 206-553-3000, http://metro.kingcounty. gov: 167, 211, 212, 215– 217, 221, 222, 225, 229, 230, 232– 234, 237, 240, 243, 245, 247, 249, 253, 256, 261, 271, 272, 280, 342, 885, 886, 889, 890, 952, 981, 989; Sound Transit, 206-398-5000, www.soundtransit.org: 532, 535, 550, 554–556, 560, 566

Newcastle

China Creek

Situated between the cities of Bellevue, Renton, and Issaquah, Newcastle is a new community (incorporated as a city in 1994), with a population of about 10,000. Depending on whom you ask, Newcastle is either an Eastside neighborhood or a South End neighborhood. In fact, it is located southeast of Seattle, so both descriptions are accurate. But, Newcastle's numerous planned housing communities, like **China Creek**, and the public—but nonetheless swanky— Golf Club at Newcastle, give the city a distinctly Eastside feel. In general, homes in Newcastle are more expensive than in Renton to the south, ranging from $400,000 to $800,000. Many have views of the mountains, Lake Washington, or the golf course. Condos and townhouses can be found for just over $300,000.

Despite its proximity to the much larger city of Bellevue, Newcastle's leaders and residents take pride in the city's small-town feel and strong sense of community. Each year in September, the city hosts Newcastle Days. This two-day celebration is at Lake Boren Park, a 20-acre park located on SE 84th Avenue just off Coal Creek Parkway, one of Newcastle's major thoroughfares. Another impressive local treasure is Cougar Mountain Regional Wildland Park, the biggest park in King County, with more than 3,000 acres of trails and wildlife habitat.

Website: www.ci.newcastle.wa.us

Area Code: 425

Zip Codes: 98056, 98059

Post Office: Renton Highlands Station, 4301 NE 4th St, Renton, 425-227-6304

Libraries: 14250 SE Newport Way, Bellevue, 425-747-2390, www.kcls.orq; Bellevue Regional Library, 1111 110th Ave NE, Bellevue, 425-450-1765; Fairwood Library, 17009 140th SE, Renton, 425-226-0522

Public Schools: Issaquah School District, 565 NW Holly St, 425-837-7000, www.issaquah.wednet.edu; Renton School District, 300 SW 7th St, 425-204-2300, www.rentonschools.us

Police: 13020 Newcastle Way, 425-649-4444, www.ci.newcastle.wa.us/police

Emergency Hospital: Overlake Hospital Medical Center, 1035 116th Ave NE, 425-688-5000, www.overlakehospital.org

Community Publication: *The Newcastle News*, P.O. Box 1328, Issaquah, WA 98027, 425-392-6434, www.newcastle-news.com

Community Resources: China Creek Homeowner's Association, 325 118th Ave SE, Ste 204, Bellevue, WA 98005, 425-285-5858, www.chinacreek.org; Cougar Mountain Regional Wildland Park, 18201 SE Cougar Mountain Dr, 206-296-4145; http://www.kingcounty.gov/recreation; The Golf Club at Newcastle, 15500 Six Penny Ln, 425-793-5566, www.newcastlegolf.com; Newcastle Chamber of Commerce, 6947 Coal Creek Pkwy SE, #150, 425-462-3351, newcastlecc.com; Newcastle Historical Society, 425-226-4328

Public Transportation: Metro Transit, 206-553-3000, http://metro.kingcounty.gov: 114, 219, 240

Redmond

Downtown
Overlake
Bear Creek
Sammamish Valley
Southeast Redmond
Willows/Rose Hill
Education Hill
Grass Lawn
Idylwood
North Redmond
Redmond Ridge

Though it is known as the bicycle capital of the Pacific Northwest, Redmond certainly is best known as the home of technology powerhouse Microsoft and renowned game maker Nintendo. Once a sleepy farming community, Redmond today is a thriving city of more than 54,000 residents. Most are in the middle- to upper-income bracket; many are affiliated with Microsoft or Nintendo. According to Bestplaces.net, Redmond's cost of living is nearly 50% higher than the national average. Redmond increasingly attracts professionals and their families who seek larger homes and acreage that can't be found in the city. However, not everyone who works in Redmond can afford the price of housing in this area, where the median price for homes is around $510,000 though many reach well over a million. Approximately 41% of the city's residents are renters.

The city of Redmond consists of eleven neighborhoods. **Downtown** and **Overlake** contain Redmond's two urban centers. The **Bear Creek**, **Sammamish Valley**, **Southeast Redmond**, and **Willows/Rose Hill** neighborhoods include a variety of land uses such as business parks, industrial and manufacturing, and residential. **Education Hill**, **Grass Lawn**, **Idylwood**, and **North Redmond** are primarily residential.

Though much of it looks new, Redmond is one of the Eastside's oldest communities, and despite traffic and parking issues here, there is a lovely small-town feel. Perhaps that stems from its deep agricultural roots, or from efforts to preserve open spaces. In **Redmond Ridge**, a popular planned community in the northeast part of the city, developers preserved 600 acres of forest, wet-lands, and parks. The insular neighborhood has its own community center, parks, and elementary school. (Currently, Redmond schools are part of the Lake Washington school district, known for its strong academics and athletics.) In tune with the technology needs of Redmond's residents, the Ridge offers residents three Internet and two cable television options.

To the west of Redmond Ridge is the **Willows/Rose Hill** neighborhood, which borders Kirkland to the west and the Willows Run Golf Course to the

Redmond

east. Numerous high-tech offices are located along the community's eastern edge, including 3-Com, Nextel, and Metawave. Like many Eastside neighborhoods, old meets new here, with small ramblers on large lots perched next to contemporary planned communities. Along the neighborhood's outer edges are townhomes and apartment and condominium complexes, which are popular with students attending nearby Lake Washington Technical College.

Even before Redmond became a popular place to live, a variety of local attractions drew thousands of visitors to the city each year. Marymoor Park, along West Lake Sammamish Parkway, is one of the region's best parks. Along with the most popular off-leash dog area in Western Washington, the 640-acre park features a velodrome (hence the city's cycling moniker), numerous sports fields, tennis courts, a 35-foot freestanding climbing wall, and a venue designated specifically for remote-controlled airplanes. Numerous festivals, concerts, sporting, and community events take place here.

At the southern tip of Marymoor Park is Lake Sammamish, which covers almost 4,900 acres to touch the cities of Sammamish, Bellevue, and Issaquah. Idylwood Park, south of Marymoor on West Lake Sammamish Parkway NE, is a popular summertime recreation area on the western shore of the lake, and features picnic tables, outdoor grills, and a dock. The homes along the lakefront are a mix of summer cottages and large contemporary houses. Most have beach access and moorage. During the summer, the lake is busy with water skiers and boaters.

State Route 520 is the primary route in and out of Redmond, and ends at the city's southeastern border. Unfortunately, traffic jams on the highway are notorious, and Redmond residents can do little to avoid them. However, Redmond's explosive population growth over the past decade has delivered lots of new amenities and commercial endeavors to its confines, and unless you work in Seattle, you may never feel the need to leave. A modern new downtown has grown up around its original core, and stylish brick mixed-use buildings now surround the quaint city center. Residents no longer need trek to Bellevue Square now that the massive, open-air Redmond Town Center, comprised of 120 acres of stores, restaurants and offices, is right in their own backyards.

Website: www.ci.redmond.wa.us
Area Code: 425

Zip Codes: 98052, 98053, 98073, 98074
Post Office: 7241 185th Ave NE, 425-885-0207
Library: 15990 NE 85th, 425-885-1861, 425-895-7951 (TTY), www.kcls.org
Public Schools: Lake Washington School District, 16250 NE 74th St, 425-936-1200, www.lwsd.org
Police: 8701 160th Ave NE, 425-556-2500, www.redmond.gov
Emergency Hospital: The Eastside Hospital (Group Health Cooperative), 2700 152nd Ave NE, 425-888-5151, www.ghc.org
Community Publication: *King County Journal*, 11400 SE 8th St, 425-455-2222, www.pnwlocalnews.com
Community Resources: Friends of Marymoor Park, 6046 West Lake Sammamish Pkwy NE, 206-296-0673, www.marymoor.org; Old Firehouse Teen Center, 425-556-2370; Old Redmond Schoolhouse Community Center, 16600 NE 80th St, 425-556-2386, www.redmond.gov; Senior Center, 8703 160th Ave NE, 425-556-2314, 425-556-2906 (TTD), www.redmond.gov; Serve Our Dog Areas, 425-881-0148, www.soda.org
Public Transportation: Metro Transit, 206-553-3000, http://metro.kingcounty.gov: 216, 221, 224, 230, 232, 233, 244, 245, 247–251, 253, 265, 266, 268, 269, 441, 930; Sound Transit, 206-398-5000, www.soundtransit.org: 542, 545, 554, 566

Kirkland

Downtown
Houghton
Carillon Point
Juanita
Champagne Point
Homes Point
Finn Hill
Rose Hill

Formerly a small town on the shore of Lake Washington, in 2011 Kirkland nearly doubled in size to become the sixth largest city in King County, with a population of around 80,000. The annexation of an unincorporated area north of Kirkland near Bothell made the North Juanita, Kingsgate, and Finn Hill neighborhoods an official part of the city. Real estate prices in Kirkland are expensive, as many homes have views of the lake. In fact, some of the most spectacular views on the Eastside are found in Kirkland, with Lake Washington, the Seattle skyline, and Mount Rainier all visible from a few fortunate neighborhoods. The influx of nearby technology companies helped to fuel Kirkland's housing boom. Many choose to live here because of the short drive to Redmond, and because

Kirkland

Kirkland is close to Highway 520 and Interstate 405, some residents commute west to Seattle or north to Everett.

Housing styles in Kirkland are a mixed bag, from turn-of-the-century homes like those on Seattle's Queen Anne Hill to ultra-modern condominiums to 1960s ramblers. Because land is scarce in Kirkland, short-platting—the practice of building multiple homes on a piece of property that used to contain just one house—is increasingly common. Many neighborhoods offer an odd combination of homes; it's not uncommon to find quaint Craftsman bungalows rubbing elbows with massive, newly built houses.

The **Downtown** area is a sophisticated shopping district with a colorful marina, cozy cafés, trendy boutiques, and unique gift shops. This neighborhood also supports several bars that are popular with the early-20s crowd. Condos are the norm in downtown Kirkland, and can cost as little as $250,000 or as much as $2.5 million. Young professionals and empty-nesters alike live along the city's waterfront and in the **Houghton** area, just south of downtown. A handful of small beachfront parks cozy up to the lakeshore, and the upscale Woodmark Hotel perches on **Carillon Point**. If you're not ready to buy, or if you plan to rent until you find the perfect house, this area offers lots of rental properties, from apartments to condominiums to small houses. The eastern section of Houghton, near Northwest University, offers more affordable homes, but homes with views can still garner up to $3 million.

The **Juanita** neighborhood, north of downtown Kirkland, is an up-and-coming community anchored by the Juanita Village mixed-use property. Modeled after the village centers in northern Europe, the pedestrian-friendly project combines shops, banks, and restaurants with apartments, condominiums, and townhomes. West of Juanita, the **Champagne Point** and **Homes Point** neighborhoods are private, funky communities with incredible views of Lake Washington. Homes are anywhere from 60 years old to brand new, and prices are high. Residents here can just as easily go for a sheltered walk in the woods or take a leisurely stroll along the beach.

For affordable homes, newcomers should look to the Finn Hill and Rose Hill neighborhoods. **Finn Hill** is located northwest of downtown and **Rose Hill,** where you can still find some reasonably priced older homes, is situated to the northeast. Newcomers should be aware, however, that while most of Kirkland is free from traffic congestion except during rush hour, the area surrounding Rose Hill is frequently backed up along NE 85th Street.

Website: www.kirklandwa.gov
Area Code: 425
Zip Codes: 98033, 98034, 98083
Post Office: 721 4th Ave, 425-739-6727
Libraries: 308 Kirkland Ave, 425-822-2459; 12315 NE 143rd, 425-821-7686, www.kcls.org
Public Schools: Lake Washington School District, 16250 NE 74th St, 425-936-1200, www.lwsd.org
Police: 123 5th Ave, 425-577-5656, www.kirklandwa.gov
Emergency Hospital: Evergreen Hospital Medical Center, 12040 NE 128th St, 425-899-3000, www.evergreenhospital.org
Community Publication: *King County Journal*, 11400 SE 8th St, 425-455-2222, www.pnwlocalnews.com; *Kirkland Views*, www.kirklandviews.com
Community Resources: Greater Kirkland Chamber of Commerce, 401 Parkplace, Ste 102, 425-822-7066, www.kirklandchamber.org; Kirkland Arts Center, 620 Market St, 425-822-7161, www.kirklandartscenter.org; Kirkland Heritage Society, 203 Market St, 425-827-3446, www.kirklandheritage.org; North Kirkland Community Center, 12421 103rd Ave NE, 425-587-3350, www.kirklandwa.gov; Senior Center, 352 Kirkland Ave, 425-587-3360, www.kirklandwa.gov; Teen Center, 348 Kirkland Ave, 425-822-3088, www.kirklandwa.gov
Public Transportation: Metro Transit, 206-553-3000, http://metro.kingcounty.gov: 230, 234, 236–238, 245, 248, 249, 252, 255–257, 260, 265, 277, 311, 342, 930, 935, 952, 981, 986; Sound Transit, 206-398-5000, www.soundtransit.org: 532, 535, 540

Woodinville

Woodinville is a close neighbor of Redmond, attracting many Microsoft employees and their families. The city is located in the north central region of King County, just east of the intersection of State Route 522 and Interstate 405, with a population of just over 11,000. Most homes in Woodinville are large contemporary structures in suburban developments or modest farmhouses on acreage. The city epitomizes the goal of many formerly rural Eastside communities, which is to blend city living with a country attitude. With an excellent school system and a new sportsfield complex and skate park, this city is popular with young families.

Formerly a heavily forested region of King County, Woodinville became an incorporated city in 1993. The community is made up primarily of single-family homes, with about 40% of dwellings designated for multi-family use. Generally,

Woodinville

homes here cost less than they do in nearby Redmond. Older, modest homes dating from before Woodinville's housing boom of the late 1990s have a median price of $300,000. Most new properties sell for more than a half-million dollars, and larger palatial estates are priced in the millions.

Residents have access to the usual suburban shopping centers, grocery stores, fast food restaurants, and chain stores, plus the country's largest single-outlet garden center, Molbak's. This local gem serves as Woodinville's commercial hub, taking up 15 acres on NE 175th Street. The company also has a high-tech, 42-acre greenhouse complex near NE 124th Street and State Route 202.

In addition to being a beautiful place to live, Woodinville is now a popular tourist destination, something you should take into account if you're thinking of moving here. The Herbfarm, considered by some to be one of the top destination restaurants in the world, is located in Woodinville. At the heart of the Woodinville wine country, the city is home to more than 50 wineries, including two of the state's largest, Chateau St. Michelle and Columbia. If you're more partial to suds, you'll find the Redhook Brewery's restaurant and bottling facility here as well. The Sammamish River Trail, which runs through Woodinville, becomes the Burke-Gilman Trail and is used recreationally as well as by bicycle commuters to Seattle.

Website: www.ci.woodinville.wa.us
Area Code: 425
Zip Code: 98072, 98077
Post Office: 17610 Woodinville-Snohomish Rd NE, 425-487-0995
Libraries: Woodinville Library, 17105 Avondale Rd NE, 425-788-0733; Kingsgate Library, 12315 NE 143rd, 425-821-7686, www.kcls.org
Public Schools: Northshore School District, 3330 Monte Villa Pkwy, Bothell, WA 98021, 425-489-6000, www.nsd.org
Police: 17301 133rd Ave NE (City Hall), 425-877-2279, 425-489-2700, www.ci.woodinville.wa.us/CityHall
Emergency Hospital: Evergreen Hospital Medical Center, 12040 NE 128th St, 425-899-3000, www.evergreenhospital.org
Community Publication: *The Woodinville Weekly*, 13400 NE 175th St, Ste C, 425-483-0606, www.nwnews.com

Community Resources: Cottage Lake Community Service Center, 19145 NE Woodinville-Duvall Rd, 206-296-2733, www.kingcounty.gov; Rotary Community Park, 19518 136th Ave NE, 425-489-2700, www.myparksandrecretion.com; Woodinville Chamber of Commerce, 17401 133rd St NE, 425-481-8300, www.woodinvillechamber.org

Public Transportation: Metro Transit, 206-553-3000, http://metro.kingcounty.gov: 236, 237, 251, 311, 372; Sound Transit, 206-398-5000, www.soundtransit.org; 522

Duvall

Duvall is a farming community in the valley east of Redmond and Bothell. The city offers country homes and a half-hour commute to Redmond or Bellevue. Many of the houses are hidden in wooded hills; some have views of the Snoqualmie River, lush farmland or the Cascades.

Despite its proximity to the larger cities of the Eastside, Duvall is a rural community with a very low crime rate. At the height of the 1990s high-tech boom, families flocked to Duvall for its short commute to Microsoft, but that influx has now tapered off. Today Duvall has fewer than 7,000 residents, and the city's commercial district consists of about three blocks on Main Street, home to city hall, the public library, restaurants, grocery stores, and gas stations.

Short-platting—building multiple homes on a piece of property that used to contain just one house—is common in Duvall. As demand for housing in Duvall grew, property owners, many of them farmers, realized they could make more money by dividing and selling off pieces of land than by farming it. In some cases, this has resulted in a patchwork effect in the community, with small clusters of homes popping up next to large farms.

Duvall's demographics are diverse and reflect the area's home prices, which range from inexpensive mobile homes to several thousand dollars for new construction. The median price of a home in 2011 was $406,000, while the average price of a condominium was $211,000. Newcomers should be able to find a home for less than in other Eastside communities.

Website: www.duvallwa.gov
Area Code: 425
Zip Codes: 98019
Post Office: 26400 NE Valley St, 425-788-5645
Library: 15619 NE Main St, Duvall, 425-788-1173, www.kcls.org
Public Schools: Riverview School District, 32240 NE 50th St, 425-844-4500, www.riverview.wednet.edu
Police: 26225 NE Stephens St, 425-788-1519, www.duvallwa.gov

Emergency Hospital: Overlake Hospital Medical Center, 1035 116th Ave NE, 425-688-5000, www.overlakehospital.org

Community Publications: *River Current News*, 23515 NE Novelty Hill Rd, Redmond, WA 98053, 206-795-0989, www.rivercurrentnews.com; *The Valley View*, 13400 NE 175th St, Ste C, Woodinville, WA 98072, www.nwnews.com

Community Resources: Duvall Chamber of Commerce, 425-788-9182, www.duvallchamberofcommerce.com; Duvall Foundation for the Arts, P.O. Box 1043, 425-788-3928, www.duvallarts.org; Duvall Historical Society, 26526 NE Cherry Valley Rd, www.duvallhistoricalsociety.org; P-Patch, 26526 NE Cherry Valley Rd, 425-788-3434, www.duvallwa.gov/peapatch; Sno-Valley North Little League, P.O. Box 1166, 425-844-1991, www.svnll.org

Public Transportation: Metro Transit, 206-553-3000, http://metro.kingcounty.gov: 224, 232, 311

Issaquah

Cantergrove
Issaquah Highlands
Downtown

If location is the most important tenet in real estate, then it is no wonder Issaquah's housing market is booming. Nestled midway between Seattle and Snoqualmie Pass, the once-sleepy town is ideally located to take advantage of the best the city and the mountains have to offer. According to census data, between 2000 and 2010 the population of Issaquah swelled by nearly 150%. Unfortunately, the city's rapid growth has had a less-than-ideal side effect: some of the worst traffic on the Eastside.

During this period Issaquah saw more than a million square feet of commercial space added, and there is also a Costco, Lowe's Home Improvement Center, a movie theater, and numerous restaurants. The concentration of retail businesses just off the freeway results in frequent congestion in the downtown core. But, once you leave downtown, it is still possible to find the quieter rural atmosphere that attracted residents to Issaquah decades ago, although it's hard to look at the hills surrounding the city without seeing a housing development. Suburban neighborhoods are becoming more the norm.

Issaquah is the community of choice for many of Seattle's highly paid athletes. Former Mariners Ken Griffey Jr. and Jay Buhner lived here, and at least one Seahawk has been in residence. Planned communities like **Cantergrove** in eastern Issaquah offer million-dollar homes with huge, wooded lots and mountain views. Nearby, the **Issaquah Highlands** neighborhood resembles a movie set, rising above the city and surrounded by spectacular views that reach all the way to Bellevue. The Highlands community is a mix of new condos and homes

Issaquah

situated around a village green complete with its own cash machine and nearby shopping center. Homes start at about a half-million dollars, with townhomes selling for around $320,000 and up.

In **Downtown** Issaquah is a small collection of historic homes and buildings, and most of the city's apartments. On Front Street, quaint brick buildings house shops and theaters; also in downtown are the police department and library, and every year Front Street hosts the large and popular Issaquah Salmon Days Festival.

Website: www.ci.issaquah.wa.us
Area Code: 425
Zip Codes: 98027, 98029, 98075
Post Office: 400 NW Gilman Blvd, 425-837-8795
Library: 10 W Sunset Way, 425-392-5430, www.kcls.org
Public Schools: Issaquah School District, 565 NW Holly St, 425-837-7000, www.issaquah.wednet.edu
Police: 130 E Sunset Way, 425-837-3200, www.ci.issaquah.wa.us
Emergency Hospitals: Overlake Medical Center at Issaquah, 24-hour Urgent Care Clinic, 5708 E Lake Sammamish Pkwy SE, 425-688-5777, www.overlakehospital.org; Valley Medical Center, 400 S 43rd St, Renton, 425-228-3450, www.valleymed.org
Community Publication: *Issaquah Press*, P.O. Box 1328, Issaquah, 425-392-6434
Community Resources: Issaquah Community Center, 301 Rainier Blvd S, 425-837-3300, www.ci.issaquah.wa.us; Issaquah Historical Society, 425-392-3500, www.issaquahhistory.org; Issaquah Little League, www.issaquahlittleleague.org; Issaquah Valley Senior Center, 75 NE Creek Way, 425-392-2381, www.issaquahseniorcenter.org
Public Transportation: Metro Transit, 206-553-3000, http://metro.kingcounty.gov: 200, 209, 210, 214–218, 269, 271, 927; Sound Transit, 206-398-5000, www.soundtransit.org:554–556

Sammamish

Sammamish Plateau

With Redmond to the north and Issaquah to the south, the newest city in King County is ideally situated for commuters to those cities, though traffic can be very difficult during rush hour. Incorporated in 1999, Sammamish, with a population of over 45,000, hugs the shores and hills east of Lake Sammamish. The majority of the population lives on the **Sammamish Plateau** to the east of the lake. Rapid growth and numerous new housing developments cause traffic headaches, but the area still retains a rural feeling. *Money Magazine* ranked Sammamish 15th on its 2011 list of Best Small Towns in the United States. Homes here run between $400,000 and $1,300,000. Homes on the lake or with lake views can sell for considerably more.

Sammamish is a young city with many parts still in the planning stages. An area on the Plateau known as the Commons, adjacent to the newly built City Hall, now includes a civic plaza, parking, greenspaces, and a $16.3-million library that opened in 2010. The schools are split between the Lake Washington School District and the Issaquah School District. The pleasant and safe neighborhoods and good schools make the city popular with families.

Website: www.ci.sammamish.wa.us
Area Code: 425
Zip Codes: 98074, 98075
Post Offices: 400 NW Gilman Blvd, Issaquah, 425-837-8795; 15731 NE 8th St, Bellevue, 425-401-0892
Library: 825 228th Ave NE, 425-392-3130, www.kcls.org
Public Schools: Lake Washington School District, 16250 NE 74th St, Redmond, 425-936-1200, www.lwsd.org; Issaquah School District, 565 NW Holly St, 425-837-7000, www.issaquah.wednet.edu
Police: 801 228th Ave SE, 425-295-0770, www.ci.sammamish.wa.us
Emergency Hospitals: Overlake Medical Center at Issaquah, 24-hour Urgent Care Clinic, 5708 E Lake Sammamish Pkwy SE, 425-688-5777, www.overlakehospital.org; The Eastside Hospital (Group Health Cooperative), 2700 152nd Ave NE, 425-888-5151, www.ghc.org
Community Publication: *Sammamish Review*, P.O. Box 1328, Issaquah, 425-392-6434, http://sammamishreview.com
Community Resources: Sammamish Chamber of Commerce, 704 228th Ave NE #123, 425-681-4910, www.sammamishchamber.org; Sammamish Community Service Center, 801 228th Ave SE, 206-295-0750, www.kingcounty.gov; Sammamish Heritage Society, 704 228th Ave NE, 425-260-9804, www.

sammamishheritage.org; Sammamish Symphony Orchestra, 206-517-7777, www.sammamishsymphony.org

Public Transportation: Metro Transit, 206-553-3000, http://metro.kingcounty. gov: 216, 269, 927; Sound Transit, 206-398-5000, www.soundtransit.org: 554

North Bend/Snoqualmie

Snoqualmie Ridge

Located approximately 30 miles east of Seattle, the communities of North Bend and Snoqualmie are in the Snoqualmie Valley, surrounded by mountains and lush pasture. Before the area's high-tech boom in the 1990s, which brought tremendous growth here, the two towns were primarily a stop on the way to the mountain passes and to Eastern Washington.

It was in the early 1990s when the North Bend/Snoqualmie area was thrust into the limelight as the backdrop for David Lynch's groundbreaking television show, *Twin Peaks*. The show's introduction prominently featured the area's best-known natural wonder, the Snoqualmie Falls. (The region still hosts an annual Twin Peaks Festival each August.) At the time, the area was rural, and the pace of life here was slower than in established suburbs like Bellevue. For that reason, although these two towns certainly lie to Seattle's east, North Bend and Snoqualmie were not generally included in the blanket description of "Eastside." That changed in the late 1990s, when high-tech employees and first-time homebuyers began moving to the region in droves. Snoqualmie, in particular, has seen tremendous growth: between 2000 and 2010 its population ballooned by over 500%. Today, North Bend and Snoqualmie are known as much for their housing developments as they once were for winter recreation. The Snoqualmie Casino, run by the Snoqualmie tribe, attracts gamblers year-round from Seattle as well as from affluent communities such as Mercer Island and Snoqualmie Ridge along the I-90 corridor.

In theory, North Bend and Snoqualmie are about a half-hour drive from Seattle and 20 minutes from Bellevue, but heavy traffic on Interstate 90 usually makes for a much longer commute. A trip to downtown Seattle during rush hour will take at least 45 minutes.

Despite the drive, both North Bend and Snoqualmie are well on their way to becoming suburban bedroom communities, as developments like **Snoqualmie Ridge** continue to attract families looking to buy bigger houses and pay lower prices. Snoqualmie Ridge is a sprawling, 1,300-acre community that boasts its own golf course and more than 500 acres of preserved open space. Homes in the mixed-use development sell for between $350,000 and $1 million. A new city hall has opened in Snoqualmie's historic downtown district, where other revitalization projects are under way.

North Bend looks out on Mount Si, a 4,167-foot peak scored by one of Washington's most well-traveled hiking trails, which draws an estimated 350,000 visitors annually. The region serves as a base for rock climbers and whitewater rafters, as well. North Bend maintains eight public parks, including the historic Meadowbrook and Tollgate Farms. Downtown,

North Bend

Torguson Park features a climbing wall. Median home and condo prices in North Bend are at least $100,000 less than those in Snoqualmie.

Websites: http://ci.north-bend.wa.us; www.ci.snoqualmie.wa.us

Area Code: 425

Zip Codes: 98045, 98065, 98068

Post Offices: 451 E North Bend Way, North Bend, 425-831-7020; 8264 Olmstead Ln SE, Snoqualmie, 425-888-4317

Libraries: North Bend Library, 115 E 4th, 425-888-0554; Snoqualmie Library, 7824 Center Blvd NE, 425-888-1223, www.kcls.org

Public Schools: Snoqualmie Valley Public Schools, 8001 Silva Ave SE, 425-831-8000, www.svsd410.org

Police: 1550 Boalch Ave NW, North Bend, 425-888-4433, http://northbendwa.gov; 34825 SE Douglas St, Snoqualmie, 425-888-3333, www.ci.snoqualmie.wa.us

Emergency Hospital: Snoqualmie Valley Hospital, 9575 Ethan Wade Way SE, 425-831-2300, www.snoqualmiehospital.org

Community Publications: *Snoqualmie Valley Record*, P.O. Box 300, 425-888-2311, www.pnwlocalnews.com

Community Resources: Northwest Railway Museum, 38625 SE King St, Snoqualmie, 425-888-3030, www.trainmuseum.org; Snoqualmie Valley Chamber of Commerce, 425-888-4440, www.snovalley.org

Public Transportation: Metro Transit, 206-553-3000, http://metro.kingcounty.gov: 209, 215

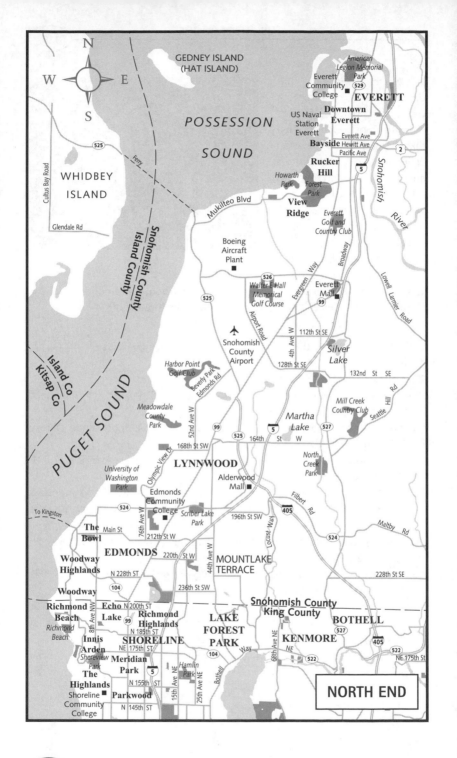

N
W E
S

GEDNEY ISLAND
(HAT ISLAND)

American Legion Memorial Park
Everett Community College
EVERETT
Downtown Everett
US Naval Station Everett
Bayside
Everett Ave
Hewitt Ave
Pacific Ave

POSSESSION

SOUND

Rucker Hill
Howarth Park
Forest Park

View Ridge

Everett Golf and Country Club

Mukilteo Blvd

WHIDBEY
ISLAND

Glendale Rd

Cultus Bay Road

Ferry

Snohomish County
Island County

Boeing Aircraft Plant

Walter E Hall Memorial Golf Course

Evergreen Way
Broadway

Everett Mall

PUGET SOUND

Island Co
Kitsap Co

To Kingston

Harbor Point Golf Club

Snohomish County Airport

Beverly Park
Edmonds Rd

112th St SE

128th St SE

Silver Lake

132nd St SE

Seattle Hill Rd

Lowell Larimer Road

Snohomish River

Mill Creek Country Club

Meadowdale County Park

University of Washington Park

Olympic View Dr

52nd Ave W

76th Ave W

168th St SW

LYNNWOOD

Alderwood Mall

Edmonds Community College

Scriber Lake Park

196th St SW

Martha Lake

164th St W

North Creek Park

Filbert Rd

Maltby Rd

EDMONDS

The Bowl

Main St

212th St W

220th St W

MOUNTLAKE TERRACE

44th Ave W

228th St SE

Woodway Highlands

N 228th ST

Woodway

236th SW

Richmond Beach

Echo Lake

N 200th ST

N 185th ST

Richmond Highlands

Richmond Beach

8th Ave NW

Innis Arden

NE 175th ST

SHORELINE

Shoreview Park

Meridian Park

N 155th ST

The Highlands

Shoreline Community College

N 145th ST

Parkwood

Hamlin Park

15th Ave NE

25th Ave NE

Snohomish County
King County

LAKE FOREST PARK

Bothell Way

68th Ave NE

KENMORE

BOTHELL

NE 175th St

NORTH END

120

NORTHERN COMMUNITIES—KING COUNTY

Shoreline, Lake Forest Park, Bothell, Kenmore

The communities north of Seattle are often collectively referred to as the "North End." For the most part, homes in these cities are more affordable than in Seattle or the Eastside. The North End is popular with Boeing employees who commute to Everett, and with first-time homebuyers looking for less expensive housing than what can be found in Seattle. The North End is varied; with charming seaside communities like Edmonds just a few miles away from high-tech suburbs like Lake Forest Park.

Shoreline

Richmond Beach
Innis Arden
The Highlands
Richmond Highlands
Echo Lake
Meridian Park
Parkwood

Shoreline, home to over 54,000, is a growing community just north of Seattle. Twice named Best Neighborhood by *Seattle* magazine, Shoreline is known for its excellent schools, abundant parks, and affordable contemporary homes. The community has become popular with young families increasingly priced out of Seattle and the Eastside. Before becoming a city in 1995, Shoreline was an unincorporated region of King County. It is surrounded by Edmonds and Woodway to the north, Lake Forest Park to the east, and Seattle to the south.

As its name implies, the city hugs the Puget Sound shoreline, offering spectacular sound and mountain views from expensive waterfront homes. Further inland, local architecture is best described as a mix of older split-levels, Colonials, mid-century ramblers, and modern new construction. As you travel east toward I-5, homes in Shoreline become even more affordable. Shoreline consists of fourteen distinct neighborhoods (a selection of which we've profiled here), offering a range of housing options for newcomers, from upscale properties with water views to more modest homes and condos. Neighborhoods east of Aurora Avenue offer smaller fixer-uppers and rental homes. Generally, home prices in Shoreline range from the low $200,000s to just over $400,000, depending on the neighborhood. Exceptions include **Richmond Beach**, in the northwest corner of the city, where most homes start at $500,000, with view properties costing even more. Lots here are larger than those in Seattle, and charm and privacy are abundant. Not surprisingly, there is little turnover. The

Shoreline

same is true for upscale **Innis Arden**, just south of Richmond Beach. Residents here are working and retired professionals who value the protections of covenant communities and the generous greenbelt. Lots are spacious and housing prices begin around the half-million-dollar mark. South of Innis Arden is **The Highlands**, where some of Seattle's wealthiest families have lived since the turn of the century. The gated waterfront/golf-course community is filled with multimillion-dollar mansions and sprawling estates. Some of the region's most incredible sound and mountain views are from the homes in this community that is so exclusive the houses don't have addresses.

A good bet for newcomers seeking moderately priced housing is the central Shoreline area, which includes the **Richmond Highlands**, **Echo Lake**, **Meridian Park**, and **Parkwood** neighborhoods. Situated between Aurora Avenue and I-5, these communities offer affordable homes typically built during the 1920s and 1930s, or during the post–World War II expansion of the 1950s and 1960s. Many have been painstakingly restored or remodeled, but others could use a little TLC.

Shoreline boasts one of the region's most popular two-year colleges: Shoreline Community College, at Greenwood Avenue North and Arden Way, just east of The Highlands. About 14,000 students attend the college, which also offers adult continuing education classes.

Shoreline doesn't really have a city center, but Aurora Avenue North's sprawling commercial district cuts through the city and offers ample opportunities for commerce, including Sears at North 155th Street, Fred Meyer and QFC at North 185th Street, and Home Depot and Costco at North 205th Street. Real estate in this area consists of small to medium-sized homes and apartment complexes, occupied by a mixture of owners and renters. Vacancy rates here and in other Shoreline neighborhoods are quite low.

Just 15 miles north of downtown Seattle, Shoreline offers a relatively easy commute to the city. Both I-5 and Highway 99 connect Shoreline and Seattle, so drivers have two options when traveling between the two cities. An average commute takes about 20 minutes.

Website: www.cityofshoreline.com

Area Code: 206

Zip Codes: 98133, 98155, 98177

Post Offices: Bitter Lake Station, 929 N 145th St, Seattle, 206-364-0663; North City Branch, 17233 15th Ave NE, 206-364-0656; Richmond Beach Contract Station, 1430 NW Richmond Beach Rd, 206-533-2345

Libraries: 19601 21st Ave NW, Shoreline, 206-546-3522; 345 NE 175th, 206-362-7550, Shoreline, www.kcls.org

Public Schools: Shoreline School District, 18560 1st Ave NE, 206-393-6111, www.shorelineschools.org

Police: Shoreline Police Station, 1206 N 185th St, 206-801-2710; Eastside Police Center, 521 NE 165th St, 206-363-8424; Westside Police Center, 624 NW Richmond Beach Rd, 206-546-3636, www.cityofshoreline.com

Emergency Hospital: Northwest Hospital, 1550 N 115th St, Seattle, 206-364-0500, www.nwhospital.org

Community Publication: Shoreline Area News (blog), www.shorelineareanews.com

Community Resources: Center for Human Services, 17018 15th Ave NE, 206-362-7282 (Voice/TDD), www.chs-nw.org; Richmond Highlands Recreation Center, 16554 Fremont Ave N, 206-542-6511; Shoreline Chamber of Commerce, 18560 1st Ave NE, 206-361-2260, www.shorelinechamber.com; Shoreline Community College, 16101 Greenwood Ave N, 206-546-4101, www.shoreline.edu; Shoreline–Lake Forest Park Arts Council, 18560 1st Ave NE, 206-417-4645, www.shorelinearts.net; Shoreline Pool, 19030 1st Ave NE, 206-801-2650, www.cityofshoreline.com; YMCA,19290 Aurora Ave N, 206-363-0446, www.seattleymca.org

Public Transportation: Metro Transit, 206-553-3000, http://metro.kingcounty.gov: 5, 77, 100, 101, 118, 130, 131, 242, 301, 303, 304, 308, 316, 330, 331, 342, 345–348, 355, 358, 373, 416, 510, 511; Sound Transit, 206-398-5000, www.soundtransit.org

Lake Forest Park

Lake Forest Park

Lake Forest Park, located north of Seattle and east of Shoreline, is a small community of fewer than 13,000 residents. It has a mix of contemporary single-family homes on large lots, with a median home price of under $400,000. Rentals account for only about 20% of the area's housing units. People choose Lake Forest Park as much for its lack of excitement as for its tree-covered hillsides. The Burke-Gilman Trail runs right through this quiet place, where kids play in the street and residents are surprised when they don't run into a friend or acquaintance at the grocery store. The city falls within the Shoreline School District, considered one of the best in the area. Thanks to the passing of a recent levy, both high schools in the district are currently being rebuilt.

One area of Lake Forest Park with a particularly strong sense of community is the Sheridan Heights/Beach neighborhood, thanks to the local Beach Club. Residents with a "deeded" lot gain automatic membership to a pool and Lake Washington Beach access. Each summer, many of the neighborhood kids join the swim team or spend most days splashing in the lake or the pool. The Beach Club also organizes seasonal holiday family activities, such as a Fourth of July field day and a Christmas ship bonfire.

Many residents work out of their residences, with home-based businesses accounting for more than half all registered businesses. The city's social and commercial center is the Town Center at Lake Forest Park, near the intersection of Bothell Way NE and Ballinger Way NE. The center includes Third Place Books, a huge retail space that combines books, food, and entertainment, as well as Third Place Commons, a large indoor park-like space where many community groups meet. The center is also home to a branch of Shoreline Community College. Foodies bemoan the lack of good restaurants, but there are plenty of great choices in Seattle just a short distance south. Residents have easy access to I-5 north, which makes this a good neighborhood for commuters working north of the city.

Website: www.cityoflfp.com
Area Code: 206

Zip Code: 98155
Post Office: Lake Forest Way Substation (open intermittently), 17425 Ballinger Way NE; North City Branch, 17233 15th Ave NE, Seattle, 206-364-0656
Library: 17171 Bothell Way NE, 206-362-8860, www.kcls.org
Public Schools: Shoreline School District, 18560 1st Ave NE, Shoreline, 206-343-6111, www.shorelineschools.org
Police: 17425 Ballinger Way NE, 206-364-8216, www.cityoflfp.com
Emergency Hospital: Northwest Hospital, 1550 N 115th St, 206-364-0500, www.nwhospital.org
Community Publication: *Shoreline Area News*, www.shorelineareanews.com
Community Resources: Lake Forest Park Garden Club, www.secretgardensoflakeforestpark.com; Lake Forest Park Stewardship Foundation, P.O. Box 82861, Kenmore, WA 98028th, www.lfpsf.org; Shoreline Community College at Lake Forest Park, 17171 Bothell Way NE, 206-533-6700, www.shoreline.edu; Shoreline–Lake Forest Park Senior Center, 18560 1st Ave NE, Shoreline, 206-365-1536, www.shorelinelfpseniorcenter.org; Third Place Commons, 17171 Bothell Way NE, 206-366-3302, www.thirdplacecommons.org; YMCA,19290 Aurora Ave N, 206-363-0446, www.seattleymca.org
Public Transportation: Metro Transit, 206-553-3000, http://metro.kingcounty.gov: 306, 308, 309, 312, 331, 342, 372; Sound Transit, 206-398-5000, www.soundtransit.org: 522

Bothell, Kenmore

Bothell

Bothell is no longer just a bedroom community for Seattle and Eastside employees. More than 20,000 people now work in Bothell, instead of commuting to jobs in other areas, and economic development is a high priority here. Major employers include high-tech, communications, medical equipment companies, a branch of the University of Washington, and the Cascadia Community College. Located just 12 miles north of Seattle, the city is home to about 34,000 residents. Ongoing efforts to annex unincorporated areas around Bothell will likely increase the current population. The city straddles both King and Snohomish counties, a geographic oddity that can confuse visitors. Most Bothell streets are numbered, rather than named, and the numbers change once one crosses the county line.

Kenmore

With median home prices of about $350,000, the city is a popular choice for young families and early career professionals. Though the city has grown considerably in the past decade, it retains a friendly downtown core that revolves around sleepy Main Street. Here you'll find cozy cafés and restaurants, plus furniture, retail, and antique stores, and more to come: Paul Allen's Vulcan Real Estate, the engine behind the transformation of Seattle's South Lake Union neighborhood, has invested in Bothell's plans to revitalize its downtown. Another popular spot with residents is the Park at Bothell Landing, at 9919 NE 180th Street, just south of the city center. The site features playground equipment, a pedestrian bridge to the Sammamish River Trail, fishing, and small-boat mooring. In the works for 2013 are an entry plaza with a water feature and facilities for renting bicycles and kayaks. Bothell Landing is also the site of the city's first schoolhouse and a log cabin.

West of Bothell is **Kenmore**, which *Seattle Magazine* gave the top slot in its 2009 selection of "Best Metropolitan Neighborhoods to Live." Incorporated in 1998, Kenmore is a growing city, with a population of nearly 21,000 residents who live in long-established, mostly single-family neighborhoods as well as condominiums and apartments. Kenmore is also the site of Bastyr University, an acclaimed college of natural medicine and one of the city's top employers. Housing options include spacious homes overlooking Lake Washington, as well as more modest dwellings, some along partially forested hills. Housing prices are slightly higher than those in Bothell, but over the years property values have shown more stability in Kenmore than in many other communities. Key to the city's future is a proposed development called Lakepointe, a 45-acre site at the northeast end of Lake Washington, which would include 1,200 condos, a marina, a lakefront park, pedestrian walkways, an amphitheater, and 650,000 square feet of commercial space.

Websites: www.ci.bothell.wa.us; www.cityofkenmore.com
Area Code: 425
Zip Codes: 98011, 98012, 98021, 98028, 98041, 98082

Post Offices: Bothell Main Office, 10500 Beardslee Blvd, Bothell, 425-482-9755; Kenmore Branch, 6700 NE 181st St, Kenmore, 425-482-9755

Libraries: Bothell Library, 18215 98th Ave NE, Bothell, 425-486-7811, 425-402-7071 (TTY); Kenmore Library, 6531 NE 181st St, Kenmore, 425-486-8747, www.kcls.org

Public Schools: Northshore School District, 3330 Monte Villa Pkwy, Bothell, 425-408-6000, www.nsd.org

Police: 18410 101st Ave NE, Bothell, 425-486-1254, www.ci.bothell.wa.us; 18118 73rd Ave NE, Kenmore, 206-296-5020, www.cityofkenmore.com

Emergency Hospital: Northwest Hospital, 1550 N 115th St, Seattle, 206-364-0500, www.nwhospital.org

Community Publications: *Bothell/Kenmore Reporter*, 11630 Slater Ave NE, Kirkland, WA 98034, 425-483-3732, www.pnwlocalnews.com

Community Resources: Bothell Historical Museum, P.O. Box 313, Bothell, 425-486-1889; Cascadia Community College, 18345 Campus Way NE, Bothell, 425-352-8000, www.cascadia.edu; Greater Bothell Chamber of Commerce, 10017 NE 185th St, Bothell, 425-485-4353, www.bothellchamber.com; Kenmore Heritage Society, P.O. Box 82027, Kenmore, www.scn. org/kenmoreheritage; Kenmore Senior Center, 6910 NE 170th St, Kenmore, 425-489-0707; Northshore Community Service Center, 10808 NE 145th St, Bothell, 206-296-9840, www.kingcounty.gov; South Snohomish County Chamber of Commerce, 723 134th St SW, Ste 128, Everett, 425-248-4224, www.s2c3.com

Public Transportation: Metro Transit, 206-553-3000, http://metro.kingcounty. gov: 105, 106, 120, 121, 234, 236, 238, 244, 251, 306, 309, 312, 331, 342, 372, 435, 441, 935; Sound Transit, 206-398-5000, www.soundtransit.org: 522, 532, 535

NORTHERN COMMUNITIES—SNOHOMISH COUNTY

Edmonds, Mountlake Terrace, Lynnwood, Everett

Edmonds

The Bowl
Woodway
Woodway Highlands

Edmonds, overlooking Puget Sound just north of Seattle, is a peaceful village with a quaint shopping district. The Edmonds-Kingston Ferry Terminal, once the central attraction of the city, is now overshadowed by the popular downtown waterfront amenities, including restaurants, chic clothing boutiques, and gift shops. While there is tremendous wealth in Edmonds, you have to look hard to find it. This is a decidedly low-key community where residents are friendly and unpretentious and consider Edmonds the gem of Puget Sound. Recognized as an artists' community, Edmonds displays an impressive collection of public art and sponsors monthly Art Walks.

The neighborhood that encompasses downtown and the surrounding hillside is **The Bowl**. The architecture here is varied, with a mix of Victorian homes, small bungalows, new condominiums, and older apartment buildings. Houses are staggered along the hillside for optimal views, and housing prices often depend on how much of the mountains and water you can glimpse—median price in 2011 was $360,000. Most city services are located right in downtown Edmonds, including the police and fire stations, civic center, city hall, and museum. Condos are abundant in downtown Edmonds. Many are occupied by snowbirds who spend the spring and summer in the Northwest, and fly to warmer climes for fall and winter. Many year-round residents travel to Seattle or Bothell for work, with an average commute of about 30 minutes.

South of downtown is the community of **Woodway**, a secluded, woodsy neighborhood of expensive homes on large lots—one to five acres, due to the restrictions on short-platting here. Home prices range from $800,000 to over two million, and you won't find any condos here. Also in Woodway is one of Edmonds' only planned communities, **Woodway**

Edmonds

Highlands, which is similar to new developments on the Eastside: large homes nestled close together.

Website: www.ci.edmonds.wa.us
Area Code: 425
Zip Codes: 98020, 98026
Post Office: 201 Main St, 425-670-8407
Library: 650 Main St, 425-771-1933, www.sno-isle.org
Public Schools: Edmonds School District, 20420 68th Ave W, Lynnwood, 425-431-7000, www.edmonds.wednet.edu
Police: 250 5th Ave N, 425-771-0200, www.ci.edmonds.wa.us
Emergency Hospital: Swedish/Edmonds, 21601 76th Ave W, Edmonds, 425-640-4000, www.swedish.org/edmonds
Community Publication: *The Weekly Herald*, 4303 198th St SW, Lynnwood, WA 98036, 425-339-3415, www.weeklyherald.com
Community Resources: Edmonds Art Commission, 650 Main St, 425-771-0228, www.ci.edmonds.wa.us/artscommission; Edmonds Chamber of Commerce, 121 5th Ave N, 425-776-6711, www.edmondswa.com; Edmonds Community College, 20000 68th Ave W, Lynnwood, WA 98036, 425-640-1459, www.edcc.edu; Edmonds Senior Center, 220 Railroad Ave, 425-774-5555, http://southcountyseniorcenter.org; Frances Anderson Cultural and Leisure Center, 700 Main St, 425-771-0230, www.ci.edmonds.wa.us
Public Transportation: Community Transit, 425-353-RIDE, 800-562-1375, www.commtrans.org: 404–406, 416; Washington State Ferry, 206-464-6400, www.wsdot.wa.gov/ferries

Mountlake Terrace

Mountlake Terrace

Like Lake Forest Park in King County, Mountlake Terrace, situated in south Snohomish County, fifteen miles north of downtown Seattle, has a mix of contemporary single-family homes on large lots. This is a family-oriented community of nearly 21,000, with some of the city's most popular attractions revolving around children and recreation: Lake Ballinger is flanked by golf courses, and features a boat ramp and fishing pier; the city's public pavilion includes a swimming pool, racquetball courts, a weight room, and a preschool facility; next to the pavilion are outdoor playing fields, tennis courts, and a park. There are even a few casinos in the city for adult entertainment. The city's downtown core supports an increasing number of businesses, but growth is managed here with an emphasis on sustainability, green building, and conservation. The recently completed Mountlake Terrace Freeway Station is expected to more than triple the number of buses operating between Mountlake Terrace and Seattle.

When you consider the city's kid-friendly attitude it's easy to understand why Mountlake Terrace is a good choice for young families. *Seattle Magazine* has twice named it among the top five Best Neighborhoods for affordability, low crime rate, student test scores, abundant parks, and short commute times. Tthe median price of a home in 2011 was $250,000, with condos averaging $178,000, considerably less than housing prices in neighboring Lake Forest Park. Major employers include Blue Cross of Washington and Alaska, and the Edmonds School District.

Website: www.cityofmlt.com

Area Code: 425

Zip Code: 98043

Post Office: 23210 57th Ave W, 425-778-0429

Library: 23300 58th Ave W, 425-776-8722, www.sno-isle.org

Public Schools: Edmonds School District, 20420 68th Ave W, Lynnwood, 425-431-7000, www.edmonds.wednet.edu

Police: 5906 232nd St SW, 425-670-8260, www.cityofmlt.com

Emergency Hospital: Swedish/Edmonds, 21601 76th Ave W, Edmonds, 425-640-4000, www.swedish.org/edmonds

Community Publications: *MLT News*, http://mltnews.com; *The Weekly Herald*, 4303 198th St SW, Lynnwood, WA 98036, 425-339-3415, www.weeklyherald.com

Community Resources: Edmonds Community College, 20000 68th Ave W, Lynnwood, WA 98036, 425-640-1459, www.edcc.edu; Mountlake Terrace Recreation Pavilion and Community Center, 5303 228th St SW, 425-776-9173, www.cityofmlt.com; South Snohomish County Chamber of Commerce, 728 134th St SW, Ste 128, Everett, WA 98204, 425-248-4224, www.s2c3.com

Public Transportation: Community Transit, 425-353-RIDE, 800-562-1375, www.commtrans.org: 110–112, 130, 413, 415, 810, 871; Sound Transit, 206-398-5000, www.soundtransit.org: 511, 512

Lynnwood

Lynnwood

For those who live outside it, Lynnwood is best known as the home of Alderwood Mall. But, if you can get beyond the sprawling shopping center and surrounding strip malls, you may find a gem of a home in the residential areas of Lynnwood. Tranquil suburban streets with modest affordable homes make Lynnwood the choice of many middle-income families and first-time homebuyers. Most of the city's nearly 36,000 residents either work in one of the community's numerous retail outlets, or commute south to Seattle or north to Everett. Lynnwood's proximity to major thoroughfares, including I-5 and Highway 99, is advantageous for commuters, and the community is well served by bus routes. A light rail station is due to open at the Lynnwood Transit Center by 2023.

Though about midway between Seattle and Everett, Lynnwood's residents generally turn to Seattle for attractions not found in their community. Future plans for Lynnwood's city center include new retail, office, and residential space, along with open-air plazas and promenades. Situated in wooded surroundings, Lynnwood does boast the Interurban Trail, which offers 4 miles of trails for biking and walking, as well as hundreds of park acres in the city limits.

In Lynnwood, home prices are comparable to those in Mountlake Terrace to the south, though properties don't linger on the market. There is a pleasant mix of older construction and new developments, plus numerous condominiums and apartments, particularly near Edmonds Community College, which is actually located in Lynnwood.

Website: www.ci.lynnwood.wa.us
Area Code: 425
Zip Codes: 98036, 98037, 98046, 98087
Post Offices: Alderwood Manor Station, 3715 196th St SW, Ste 101, 425-778-3447; Lynnwood Station, 6817 208th St SW, 425-778-3447
Library: 19200 44th Ave W, 425-778-2148, www.sno-isle.org
Public Schools: Edmonds School District, 20420 68th Ave W, Lynnwood, 425-431-7000, www.edmonds.wednet.edu
Police: 19321 44th Ave W, 425-670-5600, www.ci.lynnwood.wa.us

Emergency Hospital: Swedish/Edmonds, 21601 76th Ave W, Edmonds, 425-640-4000, www.swedish.org/edmonds

Community Publications: *Inside Lynnwood* (newsletter), www.ci.lynnwood.wa.us; *The Weekly Herald*, 4303 198th St SW, Lynnwood, WA 98036, 425-339-3415, www.weeklyherald.com

Community Resources: Lynnwood Municipal Golf Course, 20200 68th Ave W, 425-672-4653, www.ci.lynnwood.wa.us; Recreation Center, 18900 44th Ave W, 425-670-5732, www.ci.lynnwood.wa.us; Senior Center, 19000 44th Ave W, 425-670-5050, www.ci.lynnwood.wa.us; South Snohomish County Chamber of Commerce, 728 134th St SW, Ste 128, Everett, WA 98204, 425-248-4224, www.s2c3.com

Public Transportation: Community Transit, 425-353-RIDE, 800-562-1375, www.commtrans.org: 101–113, 115, 116, 118–120, 130, 131, 190, 201/202, 401/402, 413–415, 421, 422, 425, 810, 821, 855, 860, 880/885; Sound Transit, 206-398-5000, www.soundtransit.org: 511, 512, 532/535

Everett

Bayside
Downtown
Rucker Hill
View Ridge–Madison
The Preserve

Everett, a large city about forty minutes north of Seattle, was established in the late 1800s to support the infamous Monte Cristo gold mines. Although the mines never produced the expected amount of gold, the city continued as an industrial center. Today, Boeing and Naval Station Everett are the primary employers in Everett, although many other companies, including a sawmill, are also located here. The Port of Everett connects the community to international shipping from around the world. As with Seattle, many distinct neighborhoods exist in Everett (only a selection of these are profiled here), each worth exploring if you are considering making your home here. For those who prefer properties with a history, Everett contains many well-built older residences featuring unique architectural details.

Everett, with a population of approximately 104,000, according to the 2010 Census, is the seat of Snohomish County, one of the fastest growing counties in the state. Broadway divides Everett into western and eastern halves, and is the city's major north-south thoroughfare. In the northern end of the city, west of Broadway, you'll find **Bayside**, a classic Everett neighborhood of turn-of-the-century homes, some with fantastic views of Possession Sound, the naval station, and the largest public marina on the West Coast. Many of the houses here are handed down from generation to generation but when they do come on the market, they are usually more affordable than the Craftsman and Victorian homes for sale in Seattle's view neighborhoods. Average rents in Everett are also considerably less expensive than those in Seattle. As you travel south along

Everett

Marine View Drive toward downtown Everett, you'll find that many of these historic homes have been turned into multi-family rental units.

To fill Everett's growing need for affordable housing, a number of developers built new condominiums in **Downtown Everett** and apartment buildings are still being converted to condominiums. These new dwellings offer proximity to law firms, banks, and government buildings, some shops and restaurants, historic theatres, and the city's performing arts center. City planners worked hard to transform a less-than-exciting reputation by overhauling Everett's sleepy downtown. Hewitt Avenue was made more pedestrian-friendly, and, in 2003, the new $71.5 million Comcast Arena at Everett provided a concert venue and ice skating rink, the home of the Silvertips hockey team. While the city's waterfront district lacks housing options, it does feature a small shopping center, a hotel, a marina, and the Everett Yacht Club.

Though Everett certainly claims its share of view properties and esteemed neighborhoods, newcomers will find a good selection of quiet, comfortable areas with affordable houses. **Rucker Hill** and **View Ridge–Madison** are attractive neighborhoods with many view homes and nearby parks. The Rucker Hill historic district includes over 80 single-family homes, well-preserved examples of early 20th century architecture. In the current housing market, properties can be found here for less than $200,000. **The Preserve** is a new community, complete with sidewalks and underground power lines; prices start at around $300,000.

It is unlikely that you will choose to commute from Everett to Seattle each day, especially since traffic on I-5 invariably snarls around the city, but if your job takes you north of Seattle or if you plan to work from home and want a little more bang for your buck, Everett is worth considering. The city offers many of the same attractions as Seattle, including performing arts, sporting events (the city is home to 2010 Northwest League champions the Everett AquaSox, a minor league ball club), a shopping mall, and popular city parks.

Website: www.everettwa.org
Area Code: 425
Zip Codes: 98201, 98203–8, 98213
Post Office: 3102 Hoyt Ave, 425-257-3208; Paine Field Station, 2201 100th St SW, 425-514-8063
Libraries: 2702 Hoyt Ave, 425-257-8000; 9512 Evergreen Way, 425-257-8250, www.epls.org
Public Schools: Everett Public Schools, 4730 Colby Ave, 425-385-4000, www.everett.k12.wa.us
Police: 3002 Wetmore Ave, 425-257-8400, www.everettwa.org
Emergency Hospital: Providence Regional Center Everett, 1700 13th St, 425-261-2000, www2.providence.org
Community Publication: The Herald, P.O. Box 930, 425-339-3000, http://herald.net
Community Resources: Boeing Everett Tour Center, 800-464-1476, www.boeing.com; Downtown Everett Association, P.O. Box 748, Everett, 98206, 425-258-0700, www.downtowneverett.com; Everett Area Chamber of Commerce, 2000 Hewitt Ave, Ste 205, 425-257-3222, www.everettchamber.com; Everett Community College, 2000 Tower St, 425-388-9100, www.everettcc.edu; Everett Performing Arts Center, 2710 Wetmore Ave, 425-257-8600, www.villagetheatre.org; Evergreen Arboretum and Gardens, 145 Alverson Blvd, 425-257-8300, www.evergreenarboretum.com; Port of Everett, P.O. Box 538, Everett, 98206, 800-729-7678, www.portofeverett.com; Imagine Children's Museum, 1502 Wall St, 425-258-1006, www.imaginecm.org; Schack Art Center, 2921 Hoyt Ave, 425-259-5050, www.schack.org
Public Transportation: Community Transit, 425-353-RIDE, 800-562-1375, www.commtrans.org: 101, 105, 210/202, 227, 247, 270/271, 277, 280, 410, 414, 860; Everett Transit (bus service within the city), 425-257-7777, www.everettwa.org; Sound Transit, 206-398-5000, www.soundtransit.org: 510, 512, 513, 532/535

WESTERN COMMUNITIES—KITSAP COUNTY

Bainbridge Island, Bremerton

Bainbridge Island

Winslow

In the decade between 1990 and 2000, Bainbridge Island's population jumped from approximately 3,000 to 20,000—an increase of over 560%—as Seattle residents sought out alternatives to the bustle of living in the city. Growth has slowed considerably since then. A 35-minute ferry ride from the Seattle waterfront, Bainbridge Island is currently a community of around 23,000 residents, including lawyers, doctors, successful artisans, architects, and others, many of them ex-Seattleites.

At just under 28 square miles, the island, which is linked to the Kitsap Peninsula by the Agate Pass Bridge, is comparable in size to Manhattan, but residents and real estate agents say it more closely resembles the idyllic California seaside communities of Sausalito or La Jolla. Many homes on Bainbridge have stunning views of Puget Sound or the distant Seattle skyline, and as in any community with a good location and spectacular views, housing prices can be steep. The median home price in 2011 was $550,000, with the housing market beginning to show signs of recovery from its 2009 nadir. Rentals are scarce, except for seasonal accommodations during the summer months.

The **Winslow** neighborhood, adjacent to the ferry terminal, offers shops, restaurants, and the island's few condominiums. The community resembles Seattle's Madison Park neighborhood, with its spectacular water views and upscale boutiques. The neighborhood is popular with young professionals, who commute to the city and appreciate the short walk to the ferry terminal.

As many an avid reader of David Guterson's best-selling 1994 novel *Snow Falling on Cedars* can tell you, Bainbridge Island was once covered with strawberry farms. Prior to World War II, a community of Japanese-Americans called Bainbridge Island their home, until Executive Order 9066 required their forced relocation. The newly built Japanese-American Exclusion Memorial commemorates the event.

Despite its explosive growth, Bainbridge Island has managed to hang on to its rural feel, with abundant trees, parks, ponds, and beaches. Equestrian trails wind through the community, and many of the island's kids take riding lessons in addition to golf and swimming instruction. Like Mercer Island to the east of Seattle, Bainbridge is known for its excellent schools. The island also offers golf and country clubs, quaint restaurants, seven wineries, and homey bed and breakfast inns.

So what are the drawbacks? Cell phone reception can be iffy on Bainbridge, island kids may suffer from a bit of pre-adolescent claustrophobia,

Bainbridge Island

some people find the lack of diversity a drawback, and residents are dependent on the state ferry system for access to the big city. But, with metro area's heavy traffic, Bainbridge Islanders are happy to forgo the messy daily grind of the Seattle expressways. In emergency situations, island patients are airlifted to Seattle's Harborview Medical Center in minutes.

Website: www.ci.bainbridge-isl.wa.us
Area Code: 206
Zip Code: 98110
Post Office: 271 Winslow Way E, 206-855-9571
Library: 1270 Madison Ave N, 206-842-4162, www.bainbridgepubliclibrary.org
Public Schools: Bainbridge Island School District, 8489 Madison Ave NE, 206-842-4714, www.bainbridge.wednet.edu
Police: 625 Winslow Way E, 206-842-5211, www.ci.bainbridge-isl.wa.us
Emergency Hospital: Harborview Medical Center, 325 9th Ave, 206-744-3000, www.uwmedicine.washington.edu
Community Publications: *Bainbridge Island Review*, P.O. Box 10817, 206-842-6613, www.pnwlocalnews.com; *The Kitsap Sun*, 545 5th St, Bremerton, WA 98337, 360-377-3711, www.kitsapsun.com
Community Resources: Bainbridge Island Chamber of Commerce, 395 Winslow Way E, 206-842-3700, www.bainbridgechamber.com; Bainbridge Island Community Network, 206-842-0236, www.bainbridgeisland.org; Bainbridge Island Downtown Association, 120 Madrone Ln N, Ste 203, 206-842-2982, www.bainbridgedowntown.org; Bainbridge Island Japanese American Community, 1298 Grow Ave NW, 206-842-4772. www.bijac.org; Bainbridge Island Senior Center, 370 Brien Dr, 206-842-1616, www.biseniorcenter.org; Helpline House, 282 Knechtel Way NE, 206-842-7621, http://helplinehouse.org

Public Transportation: Washington State Ferries, 206-464-6400, 888-8\
www.wsdot.wa.gov/ferries; Kitsap Transit, 360-377-2877, 800-501-7433,
www.kitsaptransit.org: 33, 90, 91, 93–99, 106

Bremerton

Manette
Charleston
Rocky Point

The largest city on the west side of Puget Sound, Bremerton has a population of about 36,000 anchoring the Kitsap Peninsula. An hour's ferry ride away from Seattle, and a half hour drive to Tacoma, puts Bremerton within easy reach of Puget Sound's other largest cities. Best known as the home of the Puget Sound Naval Shipyard, which employs 8,000 civilians and the same amount of military, Bremerton long had a slightly dingy, navy town reputation. The city has worked hard to change that, with continuing efforts to revitalize the downtown core. Restaurants, art galleries, art walks, and shops lure residents to downtown, while historic ships, a Naval Museum, festivals, and the beautiful Harborside waterfront park lure tourists. A 60-minute ferry ride to the Seattle waterfront is daunting to some, but more and more people are finding the lower home prices in Bremerton a sufficient reason to endure the commute to jobs in Seattle.

The city of Bremerton is divided by the Port Washington Narrows and connected by two bridges that help to create distinct neighborhoods within this diverse city. The **Manette** neighborhood, in East Bremerton, is a tight-knit community with quirky appeal, where a new mixed-use housing, community center, and retail development is planned. Quaint, older bungalows can be

Manette

found in the **Charleston** section of the city, and **Rocky Point** features rows of waterfront homes. Median home prices are half of what they are in Seattle, and homes with water views, or even waterfront property, sell for less than they do on the east side of the Sound. New waterfront condominiums with spectacular views are comparable in price to Tacoma and Seattle, starting around $350,000 (though the median price for a condo is over half that amount) and can run over a million. As in most towns with a military base, rentals are plentiful, from older apartment buildings to spacious houses. A one-bedroom apartment averages around $870 a month.

Website: www.ci.bremerton.wa.us

Area Code: 360

Zip Codes: 98310–12, 98314, 98337

Post Offices: 602 Pacific Ave, 360-475-0248; Sheridan Park Station, 1281 Sylvan Way, 360-377-0738; West Hills Station, 200 National Ave S, 360-377-2722

Libraries: 612 5th St, 360-377-3955; 1301 Sylvan Way, 360-405-9100, www.krl. org

Public Schools: Bremerton School District, 134 N Marion Ave, 360-473-1000, www.bremertonschools.org

Police: 1025 Burwell St, 360-473-5220, www.ci.bremerton.wa.us

Emergency Hospital: Harrison Medical Center, 2520 Cherry Ave, 866-844-WELL, www.harrisonmedical.org

Community Publication: *The Kitsap Sun*, 545 5th St, 360-377-3711, www.kitsapsun.com

Community Resources: Aquatic Center, 2270 Schley Blvd, 360-337-3741, www.ci.bremerton.wa.us; Bremerton Senior Center, 1140 Nipsic Ave, 360-473-5357, www.ci.bremerton.wa.us; Chamber of Commerce, 286 4th St, 360-479-3579, www.bremertonchamber.org; Gold Mountain Golf Complex, 7263 W Belfair Valley Rd, 360-415-5432, www.goldmt.com; Kitsap Historical Society and Museum, 280 4th St, 360-479-6226, www.kitsaphistory. org; Olympic College, 1600 Chester Ave, 360-792-6050, www.olympic.edu; Puget Sound Navy Museum, 251 1st St, 360-479-7447, www.museumsusa. org; Sheridan Park Recreation Center, 680 Lebo Blvd, 360-473-4305, www. ci.bremerton.wa.us; Sustainable Bremerton, www.sustainablebremerton. org

Public Transportation: Washington State Ferries, 206-464-6400, 888-808-7977, www.wsdot.wa.gov/ferries; Kitsap Transit, 360-377-2877, 800-501-7433, www.kitsaptransit.org: 11–13, 15, 17, 19, 20–26, 29, 34–37

SOUTHERN COMMUNITIES—KING COUNTY

Renton, Kent, Auburn, Burien, Sea-Tac, Tukwila, Normandy Park, Des Moines, Federal Way, Vashon Island

The communities south of Seattle are often collectively referred to as the "South End." For the most part, homes in these cities are more affordable than in Seattle or the Eastside. Many years ago, the common perception was that these areas were less desirable because they were farther away from big city attractions like professional sports, theater, museums, and fine dining. Today, however, many of these communities are energetically coming into their own, with revitalized downtown cores, improved infrastructures, and expanding public transit systems. Inspired municipal planning and public and private investment has increased the quality of life and attracted businesses. (For instance, you won't need to drive into Seattle for your Uwajimaya fix, since a branch of the Asian specialty store opened in Renton 2009.) A choice of good restaurants and evening entertainment are increasingly attracting singles, couples, and young professionals and their families to these cities. Many neighborhoods to the west offer fantastic views of the sound and mountains, and most have thriving shopping centers. The 2010 Census confirmed that, over the previous decade, a tremendous influx of people has moved into the southern "exurbs" of Auburn and Renton, in particular. One negative consequence of all this explosive growth has been an increase in gang violence in the South End. While the vast majority of communities are safe places to live, certain hot spots have become the locus of turf battles. Money has been allocated and task forces created to aggressively address this problem. Another drawback to the South End is airplane noise from nearby Sea-Tac Airport.

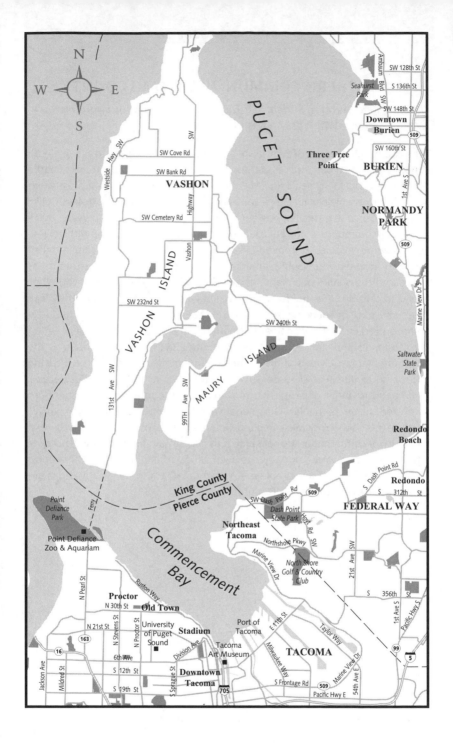

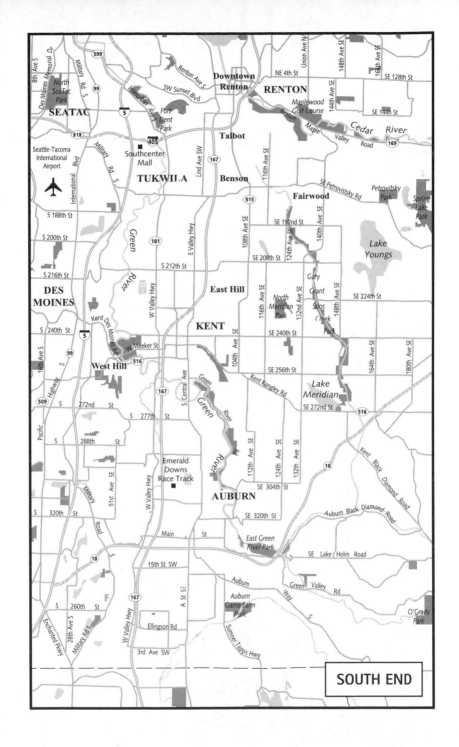

SOUTH END

Renton

Downtown
Talbot
Benson
Fairwood
Renton Highlands

Renton has always been best known as the home of Boeing's commercial airplane factory. However, a series of major public and private projects have shaken up the heavily industrial perception of this town on the south end of Lake Washington and dramatically revitalized Renton's downtown core. Recent developments include the Virginia Mason Athletic Center, the Seattle Seahawks' new headquarters and training facility; and The Landing, a new urban village style shopping center and residential development on 46 acres just across from the Boeing factory.

In the last decade Renton's population swelled more than 72%, partly as a result of the 2008 annexation of adjacent unincorporated areas of King County. Three more potential annexation areas have been identified, which will increase the population from approximately 83,000 to 130,000—as many residents as the city of Bellevue. Traditionally home to middle-income Boeing employees and a healthy working class population, Renton has already been attracting a crowd of young professionals. For the price of a small Seattle home on a tiny lot, prospective homeowners can buy a large, modern home in Renton, although that is changing in certain neighborhoods.

This swiftly growing community has 74 officially recognized neighborhoods, only a handful of which are profiled below. Shopping centers or small business districts anchor most of Renton's mature neighborhoods. **Downtown**, mom-and-pop stores and restaurants occupy historic brick structures, while large chain stores like IKEA and Fry's Electronics dominate vast parking lots and

Renton

strip malls. Housing here is limited to small bungalows, ramblers, and rental houses, and home prices are low. Fixer-uppers can be had for less than in any other area in Renton. Downtown residents are close to the city's main library, a popular walking trail along the Cedar River, which flows though the heart of the city, and the sport stadium shared by all three city high schools.

Above downtown is the **Talbot** or **Benson** area, which is popular with employees of Valley Medical Center. There is a good selection of condominiums and apartments in this neighborhood, as well as affordable homes built in the 1980s. New developments here are

Talbot

small because they are limited by the hillside and I-405, and some have views of downtown. This is a good area for entry-level homebuyers.

Fairwood is an established, upscale community that revolves around the Fairwood Golf and Country Club. Built in the late 1960s and early 1970s, the neighborhood features a mix of Colonials, brick ramblers, and contemporary homes. In most of the neighborhood, power lines are hidden underground, and many of the houses abut the golf course.

On the city's east side, the **Renton Highlands**, especially east of 156th Avenue, is a neighborhood of quiet suburban-type streets and good schools. The Issaquah School District, which serves the eastern portion of the neighborhood, rates 9 out of 10 on greatschool.org. Large newly constructed homes are available here for prices in the low $400,000s.

New housing developments began to spring up around Renton in the early 1990s. With names like Summerwind, The Orchards, Windwood, and Stonegate, they feature large homes in safe communities. There are houses in just about every price range, from the $300,000s to half a million dollars, depending on construction, views, and lot size. Once the housing market recovers, watch for more luxury lakefront homes ($800,000 – $3 million) in keeping with Renton's large-scale economic development. The city has its own housing authority, which means that Renton property owners have some of the smallest average tax increases in King County.

Website: www.ci.renton.wa.us
Area Code: 425
Zip Codes: 98055–9
Post Offices: 17200 116th Ave SE, 425-255-4278; 314 Williams Ave S, 425-227-6304; 4301 NE 4th St, 425-227-6304
Libraries: 17009 140th SE, 425-226-0522; 100 Mill Ave S, 425-226-6043; www.kcls.org

Public Schools: Renton School District, 300 SW 7th St, 425-204-2300, www.rentonschools.us

Police: 1055 S Grady Way, 425-430-7500, www.rentonwa.gov

Emergency Hospital: Valley Medical Center, 400 S 43rd St, Renton, 425-228-3440, www.valleymed.org

Community Publication: *Renton Reporter*, 19426 68th Ave S, 425-255-3484, pnwlocalnews.com

Community Resources: Black River Community Service Center, 919 Grady Way SW, 206-296-7810, www.kingcounty.gov; Renton Chamber of Commerce, 300 Rainier Ave N, 425-226-4560, www.gorenton.com; Renton Community Center, 1715 Maple Valley Hwy, 425-430-6700, www.rentonwa.gov; Renton Community Foundation, 1101 Bronson Way N, 425-282-5199, www.rentonfoundation.org; Renton History Museum, 235 Mill Ave S, 425-255-2330, www.rentonwa.gov; Renton Senior Activity Center, 211 Burnett Ave N, 425-430-6633, www.rentonwa.gov; Renton Technical College, 3000 NE 4th St, 425-235-2352, www.rtc.edu

Public Transportation: Metro Transit, 206-553-3000, http://metro.kingcounty.gov: 101, 102, 105–107, 110, 111, 114, 140, 143, 148, 149, 153, 155, 161, 167, 169, 240, 247, 280, 342, 908, 909, 952; Sound Transit, 206-398-5000, www.soundtransit.org: 560, 566

Kent

East Hill
West Hill

Formerly a rich agricultural valley, Kent today is one of the country's busiest distribution centers, with the second largest warehouse area in the United States. Kent is the third-largest city in King County, and it's growing. As a result of the King County Annexation Initiative, in 2010 the city annexed parts of unincorporated King County, adding 5 square miles of area and 24,000 additional residents. Like many exurbs in the South End, Kent has been busy rebranding itself. The city has funneled both energy and funding into the revitalization of its historic downtown and the $100-million Kent Station project, a new event center, as well as other major retail developments and road improvements.

The city is comprised of three distinct areas: East Hill, the Valley, and West Hill. Kent's downtown area is located on the east side of the Valley; the rest is covered almost entirely by warehouses. Boeing has a plant here with over 5,000 employees, and the Kent School District is the second largest employer in town.

In Kent, renters used to outnumber homeowners, nearly two to one. Today, almost half of Kent residents own their homes. There are dozens of multiple-family housing units, particularly on **East Hill**, the site of many strip malls and

Kent

fast-food restaurants. Traffic in the teeming East Hill area is a constant challenge, as commuters headed toward Tacoma, Seattle, and Everett converge on the arterials and freeways. Despite the congestion, Kent enjoys an abundance of designated parks and greenspace, ranging in size from the one-tenth of an acre Gowe Street Mini Park (Kennebeck Avenue and Titus Street) to the 310-acre Green River Natural Resources Area, a wetland and wildlife refuge at 22000 Russell Road, in the Kent Valley. The Green River Trail, a popular path for walking, running and biking, follows the east bank of the river from south Seattle through downtown Kent and on into Auburn.

This is a popular community for first-time homebuyers. Affordable older homes can be found in established neighborhoods, and new properties are plentiful in the East and **West Hill** districts. The median home price in 2011 was just under $260,000, making Kent one of the more affordable cities in the greater Seattle area. Likewise, apartments here are reasonably priced, averaging approximately $655 per month, less than comparable rentals in nearby communities such as Renton, Auburn, and Sea-Tac.

Website: www.kentwa.gov

Area Code: 253

Zip Codes: 98030–2, 98035, 98042, 98064, 98089

Post Office: Downtown Station, 216 W Gowe St, 253-520-7576; Midway Station, 23418 Pacific Hwy S, 253-856-2406; 10612 SE 240th, 253-850-8379

Library: 212 2nd Ave N, 253-859-3330, 253-854-1050 (TTY), www.kcls.org

Public Schools: Kent School District, 12033 SE 256th St, 253-373-7000, www.kent.k12.wa.us

Police: 232 4th Ave S, 253-856-5800, www.kentwa.gov

Emergency Hospital: Valley Medical Center, 400 S 43rd St, Renton, 425-228-3440, www.valleymed.org

Community Publications: *Kent Reporter*, 19426 68th Ave S, Ste A, 253-872-6600, www.pnwlocalnews.com

Community Resources: Kent Chamber of Commerce, 524 W Meeker St, Ste 1, 253-854-1770, www.kentchamber.com; Kent Commons, 525 4th Ave N, 253-856-5000, www.kentwa.gov; Maleng Regional Justice Center, 401 4th Ave N, 206-205-2501, 206-205-2655 (TTY), www.kingcounty.gov; P-Patch, 220 4th Ave S, 253-856-5110, www.kentwa.gov; Resource Center, 315 E Meeker St, 253-856-5030, www.kentwa.gov; Senior Activity Center, 600 E Smith St, 253-856-5161, www.kentwa.gov

Public Transportation: Metro Transit, 206-553-3000, http://metro.kingcounty.gov: 150, 153, 157–159, 161, 162, 164, 166, 168, 169, 173, 175, 180, 183, 190–194, 197, 247, 912, 914, 916, 918, 952; Sound Transit, 206-398-5000, www.soundtransit.org: 566, 574

Auburn

Auburn

South of Kent, the city of Auburn is located on the Green and White rivers with grand views of Mt. Rainier. Billing itself as "the world's biggest small town," Auburn boasts a population of more than 70,000 people. Now more of an industrial town, the area has a long history as a farming center and has preserved many of its historic sites, including the Neely Mansion, which is listed on the National Register of Historic Places.

The Mary Olson Farm is the only intact family farm in King County, and offers tours of its 60 acres and historic buildings, which were newly restored in 2011.

Downtown Auburn still has a picturesque, small town feeling, with much of its original architecture remaining intact, but this city is also the home of the Auburn SuperMall, an enormous hybrid (outlet, discount, and traditional retailers) mall in the Northwest, as well as four golf courses. The Muckleshoot Casino, run by the Muckleshoot Indian tribe, is a major entertainment draw, as are the Emerald Downs horse racing track, the White River Amphitheatre, and the Auburn Performing Arts Center. For families with children, Auburn offers

90 public play spaces and numerous parks, including the 32,000-square-foot Discovery Playground, which opened in 2010. The small town character of Auburn draws families, as do lower average home prices than those to be found in Renton, Kent, and Burien. Despite the rural feeling of much of the area, and the sense of being far from the "big city," the Sounder train travels to both Seattle and Tacoma, a convenience for commuters. For those who prefer to fly, there's the Auburn Municipal Airport, the third largest in the state.

Website: www.auburnwa.gov

Area Code: 253

Zip Codes: 98001–3, 98023, 98047, 98063, 98071, 98092, 98093

Post Offices: 120 Cross St SE, 253-735-5112; Pacific Station, 11 3rd St NW, 253-333-1377; Shona Gift Gallery Station, 223 Auburn Way N, 253-735-5112

Library: 1102 Auburn Way S, 253-931-3018, www.kcls.org

Public Schools: Auburn School District, 915 4th St NE, 253-931 4900, www.auburn.wednet.edu

Police: 340 E Main St, 253-931-3080, www.auburnwa.gov

Emergency Hospital: Auburn Regional Medical Center, 202 N Division St, 253-833-7711, www.auburnregional.com

Community Publication: *Auburn Reporter*, 3702 West Valley Hwy N, Ste 112, 253-833-0218, www.pnwlocalnews.com

Community Resources: Auburn Performing Arts Center, 700 E Main St, 253-931-4827; Chamber of Commerce, 108 S Division St, 253-833-0700, www.auburnareawa.org; Green River Community College, 12401 SE 320th St, 253-833-9111, www.greenriver.edu; Auburn Senior Activity Center, 808 9th St SE, 253-931-3016, www.auburnwa.gov

Public Transportation: Metro Transit, 206-553-3000, http://metro.kingcounty.gov: 152, 164, 180, 181, 186, 497, 910, 917, 919, 952; Pierce Transit, 253-581-8000, wwwpiercetransit.org; Sound Transit, 206-398-5000, www.soundtransit.org: 566, 578

Burien

Downtown
Three Tree Point
White Center

Like many south-end cities, Burien often hides its charms among strip malls and busy intersections. But a closer look at this diverse community reveals sound and mountain views, saltwater beaches, affordable housing, and easy commutes to Seattle and Sea-Tac Airport. Burien is popular with medical professionals who work at Highline Community Hospital, pilots and flight attendants, and Weyerhaeuser employees. A 2011 annexation of the North Highline area, which includes White Center and Boulevard Park, increased Burien's population to approximately 46,000.

The quickest route to Burien from downtown Seattle is Highway 509, a road much less traveled than the better-known I-5. Unfortunately, the route ends at the intersection of 1st Avenue South and Highway 518, a conglomeration of fast food restaurants and auto dealerships that doesn't give visitors a terribly good first impression of Burien. City planners have worked to change that impression by renovating the downtown core and adding the large, pedestrian-friendly Town Square complex that includes over 400 new condominiums and townhomes, stores, restaurants, a new park, and library.

Rentals are plentiful in and around **Downtown**, with a mix of old and new apartment buildings, condominiums, and senior housing units. First-time homebuyers may be interested in areas east of downtown, like Chelsea Park, where post–World War II homes go for less than $300,000.

Burien

Three Tree Point is the jewel of Burien, an entirely residential neighborhood of artists, writers, doctors, and lawyers, among others, who seek privacy and spectacular Puget Sound views. The homes perched along the bluff and waterfront are varied, ranging from beach bungalows to turn-of-the-century farmhouses. The neighborhood is also popular with scuba divers, who come to explore underwater shipwrecks, and hikers and history buffs, who climb the old Indian trail that winds up the hillside from the beach.

White Center, part of the newly annexed portion of Burien, is an economically disadvantaged area that has suffered from neglect over the years, but seems ripe for revitalization. The King County Housing Authority has invested about $300 million in public and private funds to build new housing and expand community services in White Center. The Greenbridge project, launched in 2005, added 478 rental homes, community facilities and services, twelve new parks, and an elementary school to the neighborhood. In 2011, the decrepit Park Lake housing projects were reborn as Seola Gardens. This development, scheduled for completion in 2018, will include 177 units of subsidized rental housing and a variety of 107 for-sale homes for a range of income levels. Interesting new businesses have sprung up along White Center's dusty commercial strip on 16th Avenue SW, where you can lunch on pho or carnitas tacos, or satisfy your sweet tooth at Full Tilt Ice Cream, a neighborhood favorite that wins accolades for its bacon ice cream, among other highly original flavors. Older properties in White Center tend to be very modest single-family homes on narrow lots, still affordable for the artists, musicians, and others who have begun to set down roots in this diverse neighborhood. Socioeconomic problems still persist, however. While crime rates in Seattle have been trending downward, White Center has experienced a spike, especially in terms of public drunkenness and family disturbances. The corner of Roxbury and 15th Avenue SW seems like a magnet for violence and should be avoided.

Website: www.burienwa.gov

Area Code: 206

Zip Codes: 98146, 98148, 98166, 98168

Post Offices: Burien Station, 609 SW 150th, 206-248-0398; Seahurst Main Office, 2116 SW 52nd St, 206-244-6947

Library: Burien Branch, 400 SW 152nd St, 206-243-3490th; White Center Branch, 11220 16th Ave SW, 206-243-0233; www.kcls.org

Public Schools: Highline School District, 15675 Ambaum Blvd SW, 206-433-2331, www.hsd401.org

Police: 14905 6th Ave SW, 206-296-3311, www.burienwa.gov

Emergency Hospital: Highline Medical Center, 16251 Sylvester Rd SW, 206-244-9970, www.highlinemedicalcenter.org

Community Publications: The B-Town Blog, www.b-townblog.com; *Highline Times, West Seattle Herald/White Center News*, 206-708-1378, www.highlinetimes.com

Community Resources: Burien Community Center, 14700 6th Ave SW, 206-988-3700, www.burienwa.gov; Burien Community Computer Center, 653 SW 152nd St, 206-241-3551, www.burien.org; Burien Little Theatre, SW 146th and 4th Ave S, 206-242-5180, www.burienlittletheatre.com; Burien Senior Center, 425 SW 144th St, 206-244-3686, www.burienwa.gov; Evergreen Community Aquatic Center, 606 SW 116th St, 206-588-2297, www.teamunify.com; Southwest King County Chamber of Commerce, 14220 Interurban Ave S, Ste 134th, Tukwila, 206-575-1633, www.swkcc.org; White Center Community Development Association, 1615 SW Cambridge St, Seattle, WA 98106, 206-694-1082, www.wccda.org

Public Transportation: Metro Transit, 206-553-3000, http://metro.kingcounty.gov: 22, 23, 54, 60, 85, 113, 120, 121, 122, 123, 125, 128, 131, 132, 133, 134, 139, 140, 180; Sound Transit, 206-398-5000, www.soundtransit.org; 560

Sea-Tac, Tukwila

Sea-Tac (named for the Seattle-Tacoma International Airport) is primarily a modest middle-class suburb with pleasant and inexpensive contemporary homes and close to 26,000 residents. Airline and Boeing employees live in this area, but other local businesses employ many residents as well. Sea-Tac's largest industry sectors include hotel, passenger airline, air cargo, and food services, and Horizon and Alaska airlines have their headquarters here. Sea-Tac, and its neighbor, Tukwila, are subject to heavy airport noise. In fact, many homes have been vacated or torn down to make way for the airport's third runway. But,

Sea-Tac

Tukwila

both communities enjoy a wealth of starter homes and apartments, some of the least expensive housing prices in the South End, and easy access to shopping and banking. Some larger, luxury properties are also available in Sea-Tac, in the Angle Lake and McMicken Heights neighborhoods. Condo prices tend to be higher here than in other South End communities.

One of King County's most diverse cities, Tukwila is best known as the site of Southcenter Mall (now officially known as the Westfield Southcenter Shopping Mall), a popular shopping center anchored by Nordstrom and Macy's, as well as other big-name department stores. There are numerous restaurants and strip malls surrounding Southcenter, and many industrial buildings. Major road projects can be expected to disrupt traffic around the mall until the spring of 2012. Tukwila is also home to the region's first major league soccer team, the Seattle Sounders FC, based at the Starfire Sports Center. Because of the wealth of retail and industry, taxes in Tukwila are low, making the community attractive to young families and first-time homebuyers. Most houses here are slightly more expensive on average than in neighboring Sea-Tac, though still affordable. Properties in new subdivisions can set you back $600,000 and up.

Websites: www.ci.seatac.wa.us; www.ci.tukwila.wa.us
Area Code: 206
Zip Codes: 98108, 98138, 98148, 98158, 98168, 98178, 98188, 98198
Post Offices: Riverton Heights Station, 15250 32nd Ave S, 206-241-7061; Tukwila Station, 225 Andover Park W, 206-244-9592
Libraries: Foster Library, 4060 S 144th, Tukwila, 206-242-1640; Library Connection @ South Center, 1386 Southcenter Mall, Tukwila, 206-242-6044; 14475 59th S, 206-244-5140; Valley View Library, 17850 Military Rd S, 206-242-6044, 206-242-4335 (TTY); www.kcls.org

Public Schools: Highline School District, 15675 Ambaum Blvd SW, 206-433-2311, www.hsd401.org; Tukwila School District, 4640 S 144th St, 206-901-8000, www.tukwila.wednet.edu

Police: 4800 S 188th St, Sea-Tac, 206-296-3311, www.ci.seatac.wa.us; 6200 Southcenter Blvd, Yukwila, 206-433-1808, www.tukwilawa.gov

Emergency Hospital: Highline Medical Center, 16251 Sylvester Rd SW, 206-244-9970, www.highlinemedicalcenter.org

Community Publication: *Sea-Tac News*, 206-708-1378, 14006 1st Ave S, Ste B, Burien, WA 98168, www.highlinetimes.com; *Tukwila Reporter*, www.pnwlocalnews.com

Community Resources: Foster Golf Links, 12424 Interurban Ave S, Tukwila, 206-768-2822, www.ci.tukwil.wa.us; Sea-Tac Community Center and Senior Program, 13735 24th Ave S, 206-973-4680, www.ci.seatac.wa.us; Southwest King County Chamber of Commerce, 14220 Interurban Ave S, Ste 134, Tukwila, 206-575-1633, www.swkcc.org; Tukwila Community Center and Senior Program, 12424 42nd Ave S, 206-768-2822, www.ci.tukwila.wa.us; Tukwila Pool, 4414 S 144th St, 206-267-2350

Public Transportation: Metro Transit, 206-553-3000, http://metro.kingcounty.gov: 124, 126, 128, 140, 150, 154–156, 161, 180, 193, 280, 600; Sound Transit, 206-398-5000, www.soundtransit.org: 560, 574, 599

Normandy Park

Normandy Park

About 20 miles south of Seattle is Normandy Park, a timeless Sound-side community between Burien and Des Moines. The city's location, small size (the 2010 Census counted just over 6,500 residents), and reputable police force make it a popular choice with middle- to upper-income families and older residents. It lacks the suburban sprawl of other South End communities, and enjoys over 100 acres of parkland and water views. The community is primarily residential, with two main retail areas: Normandy Park Town Center and Manhattan Plaza. Residents rely on the commercial districts of nearby Burien or Des Moines when they can't find what they need in town.

As with any city situated on the water, Normandy Park offers a range of housing, from multimillion-dollar estates with commanding views to large ramblers that sell for less than half a million. Because lot and home sizes are larger here than in most Seattle suburbs, affording residents much treasured privacy, you won't find much for less than $350,000. Those lucky enough to land a beachfront home have access to The Cove, a parcel of jointly owned property that includes the beach, a playground, tennis and volleyball courts, and a community center. Beachfront property owners pay a small annual fee and split the property taxes for the privilege.

Normandy Park is known for its speeding restrictions, so if you come looking here, be sure to keep it to 25 miles per hour. The speed limit is in effect throughout the city, not just in the residential areas.

Website: www.normandyparkwa.gov

Area Code: 206

Zip Codes: 98148, 98166, 98198

Post Offices: 609 SW 150th St, Burien, 206-248-8647; 2003 S 216th St, Des Moines, 206-824-3647

Library: Burien Library, 400 SW 152nd St, 206-243-3490; Des Moines Library, 21620 11th Ave S, 206-824-6066; www.kcls.org

Public Schools: Highline School District, 15675 Ambaum Blvd SW, Burien, 206-433-2311, www.hsd401.org

Police: 801 SW 174th St, 206-248-7600, www.normandyparkwa.gov

Emergency Hospital: Highline Medical Center, 16251 Sylvester Rd SW, 206-244-9970, www.highlinemedicalcenter.org

Community Publications: City Scene Newsletters, 206-248-8256, www.normandyparkwa.gov; The Normandy Park Blog, www.normandyparkblog.com

Community Resources: Des Moines Activity Center, 2045 S 216th St, Des Moines, 206-878-1642, www.desmoineswa.gov; Normandy Park Community Club, 1500 NW Shorebrook Dr, 206-242-3778, www.npcove.org; Normandy Park Swim Club, 17655 12th Ave SW, 206-244-0700, www.normandyparksharks.com

Public Transportation: Metro Transit, 206-553-3000, http://metro.kingcounty.gov: 121, 122, 131, 132

Des Moines

Des Moines

Des Moines (pronounced "da MOINZ,") is a peaceful town with a population of about 29,000, located midway between Seattle and Tacoma. Highline Community College and a satellite campus of Central Washington University are situated here, as well as Aviation High School. Marine View Drive, the primary artery through town, hugs the shoreline and meanders through the city's small commercial district.

Commerce revolves around the marina and waterfront, where a handful of seafood restaurants attract diners from all over the South End. The waterfront promenade is a safe and popular spot for walkers and runners and the pier is usually full of people fishing and crabbing. There is a dense concentration of condominiums near the Des Moines waterfront, many with gorgeous views. Like Edmonds to the north, Des Moines is popular with retirees who spend summers in the Northwest and escape to warmer climates during the winter.

Most homes in Des Moines are mature, comfortable ramblers and split levels built in the 1950s and later. There are small pockets of newer construction, but development is limited by geography. Median home prices here match those in Burien and Kent, though rents tend to be slightly higher than in those South End communities.

Website: www.desmoineswa.gov
Area Code: 206
Zip Codes: 98148, 98198
Post Office: 2003 S 216th St, 206-824-3647
Libraries: 21620 11th Ave S, 206-824-6066; Woodmont Branch, 26809 Pacific Hwy S, 253-839-0121; www.kcls.org
Public Schools: Highline School District, 15675 Ambaum Blvd SW, Burien, 206-433-2311, www.hsd401.org
Police: 21900 11th Ave S, 206-878-3301, www.desmoineswa.gov
Emergency Hospital: Highline Medical Center, 16251 Sylvester Rd SW, 206-244-9970, www.highlinemedicalcenter.org
Community Publications: *Des Moines News*, 14006 1st Ave S, Ste B, Burien, WA 98168, 206-708-1378, www.highlinetimes.com

Community Resources: Des Moines Activity Center, 2045 S 216th St, Des Moines, 206-878-1642, www.desmoineswa.gov; Des Moines Historical Society Museum, 730 S 125th St, 206-824-5226, www.dmhs. org; Des Moines Legacy Foundation, P.O. Box 13582, 206-870-6527, http://desmoineslegacy.com; Greater Des Moines Chamber of Commerce, P.O. Box 98672, 206-878-7000; Mt. Rainier Pool, 22722 19th Ave S, 206-824-2722, http://mountrainierpool.com

Public Transportation: Metro Transit, 206-553-3000, http://metro.kingcounty.gov: 121, 122, 131, 132, 166, 173, 175

Federal Way

Redondo Beach
Redondo

Federal Way is a modest middle-class suburb with pleasant and inexpensive (compared to Seattle) contemporary homes. Airline, Boeing, and Weyerhaeuser employees live in this area, but other area businesses employ many of the city's approximately 89,000 residents as well. Median house prices in Federal Way are less than those in Auburn and Kent, making it one of the area's more affordable communities. You'll find plenty of nice starter homes here, many of them older ramblers and/or fixer-uppers that sell for less than a quarter of a million. There are also many pockets of planned communities, like Steel Lake and Twin Lakes, with gorgeous homes on large lots. Adding to the city's diversity is a variety of apartments, condominiums, and rental homes. The location, between Seattle and Tacoma, makes sense for couples needing easy access to both communities, although congestion on I-5 can considerably lengthen the average 35-minute commute.

As with many of the region's communities that hug Puget Sound, Federal Way also has a handful of waterfront communities that offer panoramic views. **Redondo Beach** is one such neighborhood. Formerly a vacation spot, the community is now a mix of beach bungalows, contemporary new homes, and condominiums. In **Redondo**, the community above the beach, you'll find large homes with partial views that sell in the half-million dollar range.

Like Lynnwood to the north of Seattle, Federal Way serves as a retail center for residents of many South End communities. The Commons at Federal Way, the city's only indoor shopping center, is located here, along with numerous chain stores and restaurants. Other sources of local pride are the King County Aquatic Center, which was built for the 1990 Goodwill Games, and the rhododendron and bonsai garden, owned by Weyerhaeuser Co.

Website: www.cityoffederalway.com
Area Code: 253

Federal Way

Zip Codes: 98001, 98003, 98023, 98063, 98093

Post Office: 32829 Pacific Hwy S, 253-924-1692

Libraries: 34200 1st Way S, 253-838-3668; 848 S 320th St, 253-839-0257, 206-296-5203 (TTY), www.kcls.org

Public Schools: Federal Way Public Schools, 31405 18th Ave S, 253-945-2000, www.fwps.org

Police: 33325 8th Ave S, 253-835-6700, www.cityoffederalway.com

Emergency Hospital: St. Francis Hospital, 34515 9th Ave S, 253-835-8100 (King County), 253-944-8100 (Pierce County), www.fhshealth.org

Community Publication: *Federal Way Mirror*, 31919 1st Ave S, Ste 101, 253-925-5565, www.pnwlocalnews.com

Community Resources: Federal Way Chamber of Commerce, P.O. Box 3440, 253-838-2605, www.federalwaychamber.com; Federal Way Community Center, 876 S 333rd St, 253-835-6900, http://itallhappenshere.org; Federal Way Senior Center, 4016 S 352nd St, Auburn, WA 98001, 253-838-3404, wwwfederalwayseniorcenter.org; Federal Way Symphony, 32020 1st Ave S, 253-529-9857, http://federalwaysymphony.org; King County Aquatic Center, 650 SW Campus Dr, 206-296-4444, www.kingcounty.gov

Public Transportation: Metro Transit, 206-553-3000, http://metro.kingcounty.gov: 173, 175, 177, 179, 181–183, 187, 190, 192, 196, 197, 901, 903; Sound Transit, 206-398-5000, www.soundtransit.org; 574, 577, 578; Pierce Transit, 253-581-8000, www.piercetransit.org: 061, 402, 500, 501

Vashon Island

A mere 15 minutes by ferry from the West Seattle dock, Vashon Island feels like it's a world away. Situated in the heart of southern Puget Sound between Seattle and Tacoma, Vashon Island is approximately 13 miles long and 8 miles at its widest point and connects to the much smaller Maury Island via a paved road. With 45 miles of shoreline, Vashon boasts the majority of waterfront property in King County, with views from Mount Baker to Rainier. Because of development restrictions, virtually no vacant waterfront lots remain, so would-be homebuilders must purchase existing properties and remodel them. Most of the island's beaches are private, and from here residents can watch orcas and pilot whales breach the chilly waters of the Sound. Maury Island teems with birdlife and features the historic Point Robinson Lighthouse.

The year-round population of about 11,000 features an eclectic mix of artists, writers, composers, and entrepreneurs. The island has a reputation for being a counterculture haven where people wear tie-dyed T-shirts and refuse to vaccinate their children. During the last decade, as affordable housing became increasingly scarce, the demographic skewed toward a wealthier population. Rental properties are rare, and most residents own their own homes. Between 2009 and 2010, the average price of a home on Vashon dropped by 12% to $422,000, though property taxes increased by 14% during the same period. A 1,500-square-foot beach cabin on the island will set you back about $500,000 to $600,000.

Some of the island's newest residents have relocated to Vashon after years of living in Seattle. On the island, they become part of a cliquish and insular community that embraces its independence and the relaxed pace of life in this rural setting. No bridges connect Vashon with the mainland (and residents don't seem to be clamoring for them, either), which contributes to its feeling of remoteness and isolation. There is no full-service hospital, either, and residents must be airlifted to Seattle hospitals in emergencies. Neighbors watch out for one another, and many people feel safe enough to leave their doors unlocked at night. As in any small community where everyone knows your business, privacy can be an issue here. If you're single, there's a limited pool of local people to date, and if things turn sour, you're bound to keep running into your ex, possibly in the company of your ex–best friend.

You won't find any restaurant chains on this island. Disembarking from the Fauntleroy ferry at the north of the island and cresting a steep incline that bicyclists call "the hill of death," you'll eventually encounter a mix of quaint shops, art galleries, and small restaurants with an emphasis on organic, local foods. The Vashon Highway takes you out of town past second-growth forests of fir, maple, and madrona trees that have filled in areas once cleared for farmland. Dense stands of fir trees were logged during the 1880s to make way for strawberry

Vashon Island

farms, though few of these remain. At roadside produce stands known as honor farms, customers are invited to help themselves to local produce and cheeses and leave payment in a box.

Green values are conspicuous on Vashon. At the center of the island, a former NIKE missile site was converted into a 43-acre park called Paradise Ridge. A majority of the island's residents demonstrated their commitment to environmental sustainability when 77% agreed with a recent proposal to make Vashon self-sufficient in energy use by generating power entirely from solar and wind sources. In 2010, the City Council approved a proposal to buy a 250-acre Maury Island gravel mine for $36 million and turn it into a park.

The island has the highest number of same-sex households per capita of any community in the state. If you're looking for racial diversity, however, this is not the place for you (in 2006, the population of Vashon was approximately 94% white). Vashon's highly rated public schools include Chautauqua Elementary, McMurray Middle School, and Vashon High. Parents can send their preschoolers to what might be the only all-outdoor preschool in the region, Cedarsong Nature Preschool, where kids play outside regardless of temperature and weather and learn firsthand about the natural world.

Vashon Island's main attractions are outdoors. If you are an avid hiker, cyclist, or birdwatcher you'll find plenty of opportunities here to pursue your interests. The whole island has been designated an equestrian community, and the majority of roads are designed to be horse-friendly.

In recent years, Vashon lost two of its major employers when K2 Sports outsourced its manufacturing to China and the Seattle's Best Coffee company was bought by Starbucks. Currently, the largest manufacturer on Vashon is Pacific Research Laboratories, a leading producer of artificial bone. Most full-time residents of Vashon Island telecommute or commute to Seattle or Tacoma. At peak times, that short ferry ride can turn into hours of waiting in line in your car to board. The ferries that service the island are old and prone to breaking down. A passenger ferry takes commuters directly to downtown Seattle in just thirty minutes, though it runs less frequently.

For those who can afford it, Vashon offers the creative stimulation of an artists' colony thriving in a peaceful rural environment just a ferry ride away from downtown.

Website: www.vmicc.org
Area Code: 206
Zip Codes: 98013, 98070
Post Office: Vashon Post Office, 10005 SW 178th St
Library: Vashon Library, 17210 Vashon Hwy SW, 206-463-2069, www.kcls.org
Public Schools: Vashon School District, 9309 SW Cemetery Rd, 206-463-2121, www.vashonsd.wednet.edu
Police: Vashon Police Department, P.O. Box 233, Vashon, WA, 98070, 206-463-3618
Emergency Care: Harborview Medical Center, 325 9th Ave, 206-744-3000, www.uwmedicine.washington.edu; Island Emergency Care, Vashon, WA, 98013, 206-463-9673
Community Publication: *Vashon-Maury Island Beachcomber*, 17141 Vashon Hwy SW, Suite B, Vashon, WA 98070, www.pnwlocalnews.com
Community Resources: Maury Island/Vashon Chamber of Commerce, P.O. Box 1035, Vashon, WA 98070, 206-463-6217, www.vashonchamber.com; Vashon-Maury Island Community Council; Vashon Community Pool, 9600 SW 204th St, 206-463-9602, http://vashonparkdistrict.org; Voice of Vashon, the Island's Community Internet Radio and Public Access Television station; Vashon Allied Arts, 19704 Vashon Hwy SW, 206-463-5131, www.vashonalliedarts.org; Vashon-Maury Senior Center, 10004 Bank Rd, 206-463-5173, www.seniorservices.org/sc/vashon/asp
Public Transportation: Washington State Ferries, 206-464-6400, 888-808-7977, www.wsdot.wa.gov/ferries. Vashon has one public airport, Vashon Municipal Airport, on Cove Road about 2 miles from the main town intersection. Metro Transit, 206-553-3000, http://metro.kingcounty.gov: 54, 118, 119; Pierce County Transit, 253-581-8000, www.piercetransit.org: 10, 11 (to Defiance Ferry Terminal, Tacoma)

SOUTHERN COMMUNITIES—PIERCE COUNTY

Tacoma

Northeast Tacoma
Downtown
Stadium District
Old Town
Proctor

As the third largest city in western Washington (population 204,200), Tacoma doesn't quite count as a suburb, although some residents do commute to Seattle for work. An industrial and port city, Tacoma remains a less expensive alternative to Seattle. To truly appreciate Tacoma, you must get off I-5. Otherwise, it's easy to assume that the city's only attractions are the famous Tacoma Dome, the only dome remaining in western Washington, and the Emerald Queen Casino, whose enormous electrified billboard looms over the freeway.

A decade ago, parts of Tacoma were troubled by gang activity, but efforts by the city and local community action groups have done much to contain and improve the situation. Today, home and personal security concerns for Tacoma residents are comparable to those in Seattle.

Tacoma has its own $100-million fiber optics network under the city, making it the most wired city in the country—according to its economic development director. So, it's not surprising that the city has been able to lure high-tech companies from other parts of the United States, including Seattle. Other major employers in Tacoma include the Tacoma School District, the Frank Russell Company, University of Washington at Tacoma, Regence Blue Shield, DaVita Inc., and local hospitals. Cultural attractions include the Museum of Glass and the Tacoma Art Museum next to Union Station. Free light rail service links the museum and theater districts to the nearby Dome. In addition, the city zoned warehouse district space for artists, and boasts a fine arts high school (grades 10–12), the Tacoma School of the Arts, located at 1950 Pacific Avenue.

There are many distinct neighborhoods in Tacoma. If you're looking for new construction and a neighborhood of young, professional families, check out **Northeast Tacoma**, a conglomeration of planned developments staggered along the hillside. Homes started going up in the early 1980s, and construction continues; prices range from $250,000 to $400,000. There is no real commercial center here, but the conveniences of Federal Way and downtown Tacoma are just a short drive away.

Downtown Tacoma is experiencing a major revitalization. You will find hundreds of refurbished and new apartments, condominiums and artists' lofts, quaint pubs, historic theaters, a gorgeous new art museum, the Washington State History Museum and a burgeoning nightlife. Similar to Seattle's Belltown neighborhood, downtown Tacoma has become a hip spot to live, particularly for employees of the city's growing banking and finance community.

Tacoma

Some of Tacoma's most attractive neighborhoods are located in the city's northern sector. The **Stadium District** is home to the astonishing Stadium High School and a nearly century-old French Renaissance castle, originally intended as a luxury hotel. The Stadium neighborhood is an eclectic mix of condominiums, turn-of-the-century Victorians, Craftsman bungalows, and mansions. Lively and diverse, the Stadium District is home to Tacoma's gay community, young professionals, and longtime residents. The neighborhood boasts spectacular views, good schools and wide, tree-lined streets. Except for the occasional mansion, homes here cost less than $700,000, and many go for under $400,000.

Old Town, above the city's bustling waterfront, is a former fishing village that offers modest homes at affordable prices. Tacoma's waterfront is a popular recreation area, with numerous docks and walkways, restaurants, and a new hotel. In the works is a planned community at the site of the former ASARCO smelter at the end of Ruston Way. The plan includes a mix of housing, parks, and retail space, and is sure to raise property values in the area. **Proctor**, again in North Tacoma, is also popular with young professionals. With a quaint commercial district, Proctor offers the convenience of a small downtown with the charm of a residential neighborhood. Well-kept Craftsman homes line the quiet streets. Prices begin at around $200,000.

Tacoma has an expansive parks system, including a series of greenspaces and trails along the Commencement Bay waterfront. On sunny days, the area resembles Seattle's Alki shorefront, with walkers, runners, and rollerbladers jostling for position on the sidewalks—there's no place better for people-watching during the summer. Also in Tacoma are Point Defiance Park and Point Defiance Zoo & Aquarium, two of the South End's premier weekend destinations. At 698 acres, Point Defiance Park is among the 20 largest urban parks in the United States. It includes a replica of Fort Nisqually, a logging museum, rose and Japanese gardens, and 14 miles of hiking trails.

Website: www.cityoftacoma.org

Area Code: 253

Zip Codes: 98401–9, 98411–13, 98415–19, 98421, 98422, 98424, 98431, 98433, 98443–48, 98450, 98455, 98460, 98464–66, 98471, 98477, 98481, 98490, 98493, 98498

Post Offices: Downtown Tacoma Station, 1102 A St, 253-627-4026; Evergreen Station, 4001 S Pine St, 253-471-5384; Lincoln Station, 3705 S "G" St, 253-476-1251; Martin Luther King Jr Station, 1220 Martin Luther King Jr Way, 253-272-3082; Proctor Station, 3801 N 27th St, 253-759-7701; South Tacoma Station, 3503 S 56th St, 253-474-7791; University Place Station, 6817 27th St W, 253-566-7133

Libraries: Main Library, 1102 Tacoma Ave S, 253-591-5666; Fern Hill Library, 765 S 84th St, 253-591-5620; Kobetich Library, 212 Brown's Point Blvd NE, 253-591-5630; Moore Library, 215 S 56th St, 253-591-5650; Mottet Library, 3523 E "G" St, 253-591-5660; South Tacoma Library, 3411 S 56th St, 253-591-5670; Swasey Library, 7001 6th Ave, 253-591-5680; Wheelock Library, 3722 N 26th St, 253-591-5640, www.tpl.lib.wa.us; Parkland/Spanaway Branch, 13718 Pacific Ave S, 253-531-4656; Summit Branch, 5107 112th St E, 253-536-6500; Tillicum Branch, 14916 Washington Ave SW, Lakewood, 253-588-1014; www.piercecountylibrary.org

Public Schools: Tacoma School District, 601 S 8th St, 253-571-1000, www.tacoma.k12.wa.us

Police: 3701 S Pine St, 253-798-4721, www.cityoftacoma.org

Emergency Hospital: Tacoma General Hospital, 315 Martin Luther King Jr Way, 253-403-1000, www.multicare.org

Community Publications: *The News Tribune*, 1950 S State St, 253-597-8742, www.thenewstribune.com; *Tacoma Daily Index*, 1019 Pacific Ave, Ste 1216, 253-627-4853, www.tacomadailyindex.com

Community Resources: Beacon Senior Center, 415 S 13th St, 253-591-5083; Lighthouse Senior Center, 5016 A St, 253-591-5080; Point Defiance/Ruston Senior Center, 4761 N Baltimore, 253-756-0601; Point Defiance Zoo & Aquarium, 5400 N Pearl St, 253-591-5337, www.pdza.org; Port of Tacoma, One Sitcum Plaza, 253-383-5841, www.portoftacoma.com; Spana-Park Senior Center, 325 152nd St E, 253-537-4854; Tacoma Art Museum, 1701 Pacific Ave, 253-272-4258, http://tacomaartmuseum.org; University of Washington at Tacoma, 1900 Commerce St, 253-692-4000, www.tacoma.uw.edu; YMCA of Tacoma-Pierce County, 1002 S Pearl St, 253-564-9622; 9715 Lakewood Dr SW, 253-584-9622; 1144 Market St, 253-597-6444, www.ymcapkc.org

Public Transportation: Pierce Transit, 3701 96th St SW, 253-581-8000, 800-562-8109, www.piercetransit.org

O NCE UPON A TIME, FINDING A PLACE TO LIVE IN SEATTLE WAS easy. Today, it will take persistence and some luck to find what you want. Situated between two bodies of water, with only narrow bridges and ferries to connect it to surrounding communities, Seattle faces the challenges of a growing population—over 600,000 in 2010—and substantial geographical constraints. Although Seattle was once a city primarily of single-family homes, the creation of duplexes and triplexes from older homes is now common. City planners want to encourage urban density, and condominiums and apartment buildings account for a large portion of current building projects, as do townhouses and multi-family houses. Beginning in the mid 1990s, housing prices in Seattle began to rise, accounting for Seattle's listing by the National Association of Realtors and the Washington Center for Real Estate Research as being among the country's most expensive places to buy residential real estate. Though the national and regional economies slowed after 2000, home prices in King County continued to climb. As a result, during the first decade of the new millennium, most of the growth in the Puget Sound region occurred beyond the city limits, in communities that lie to the east, north, and south.

In the wake of the 2008–2009 financial crisis, the Seattle housing bubble burst, and homes in the city began steadily losing value, with many properties returning to their pre-2007 price levels. According to Zillow.com, as of April 2011, the median sale price for a single-family home in Seattle was $379,100, down from $501,000 in September 2007. What that means for a newcomer to the city is that, for the first time in more than two decades, housing prices in Seattle may be within reach of the average homebuyer. However, the average homebuyer has been hit hard by economic woes, and likely may not be in a financial position to take advantage of this opportunity, especially since most lenders have become more cautious.

In fact, many prospective buyers have been hesitant to purchase a home or a condo, for fear that its value will continue to tank. Rental units, especially houses, are more in demand, meaning they are harder to find, and landlords offer fewer incentives to new renters. A landlord-hosted open house often attracts numerous applicants, and the event takes on the air of a job interview, with well-dressed renters vying for the landlord's attention. To get an edge over the competition, bring a prepared rental application with you, along with a list of references, and be ready to write a check for first and last month's rent and a damage deposit. If you are moving from out of state, you may be required to get a cashier's check or money order. In the spring of 2011, the average cost of renting a two-bedroom, two-bath apartment in Seattle was $1,913. Dupre + Scott Apartment Advisors forecast that rents in the city will continue to rise, with a projected increase of 4.6% in 2012 and 5.1% in 2013. (More about Seattle's cost of living can be found at www.BestPlaces.net, a non–ad-driven site with information and statistics for 3,000 U.S. cities and towns.)

APARTMENT HUNTING

DIRECT ACTION

To find an apartment in Seattle on your own, consider a strategy using several methods. Searching the local classifieds, either online or in print, is the best way to begin. An early edition of the *Sunday Seattle Times* arrives in stores on Friday night, allowing you to call landlords first thing Saturday morning. The listings should give you a good sense of prices in various neighborhoods. Since many local landlords don't run advertisements in the paper it's also a good idea to drive through the neighborhoods you're interested in, looking for posted rental notices. Many rentals offered by owners can also be found on http://seattle.craigslist.com, where you can filter your search by apartment size, neighborhood, price, furnished vs. unfurnished rentals, and other factors. You might also consider posting your own ad on craigslist, since many landlords search for tenants on this site. Always exercise caution and common sense when you meet up with prospective landlords or roommates, however.

If you'd like to be near a local university or college, late spring is the best time to look for vacancies. These neighborhoods include Fremont, Wallingford, or North Queen Anne near Seattle Pacific University; the University District, Green Lake and Ravenna near the University of Washington; or Capitol Hill and the Central Area, which border the Seattle University campus.

Wherever you set your sights, check out www.seattlerentals.com, which lists vacancies in Seattle and surrounding communities. The site also includes neighborhood descriptions, pictures, and maps, as well as moving resources. You can find listings for apartments, condos, and houses offered through landlords and property management firms, and use tools to save your favorites and get e-mail listing updates.

Also, don't forget **word of mouth**. Some of the best apartments are found through the grapevine. Even if you are new to the area and haven't yet established such connections, you can still put the word out. Check college/ university, coffee shop, and grocery bulletin boards (see below). When you call about vacancies, ask about any others that may be opening up in the neighborhood. Chances are, even if the apartment you are calling about has been taken, someone knows someone up the street who is moving on. In addition, the neighborhood profiles include a list of neighborhood organizations, which may be a good resource for finding out about available apartments, as well as area safety and neighborhood events.

CLASSIFIED ADVERTISEMENTS

In **Seattle**, check out these news sources for the best selection of classified ads:

- **Seattle Classifieds;** this online portal consolidates classified ads from thirteen different Seattle neighborhoods at www.seattleclassifieds.com
- **The Seattle Times;** get the Sunday edition, which has the most comprehensive rental and real estate listings for Seattle and surrounding communities. Rentals and home sales are posted in the "NW Homes" section, and can be filtered by location, type of housing, price, etc. Houses for sale are listed in the "NW Homes" section, too, also organized by location. The newspaper's online classifieds section can be accessed at http://nwsource.kaango.com. New listings appear daily in both the print and online versions.
- **Seattle Weekly;** a free newspaper, the *Weekly* is distributed on Wednesdays and is available in newspaper vending boxes, cafés, bars, and convenience and grocery stores. The paper often lists rental opportunities not found in the larger publications. To view ads online, visit www.seattleweekly.backpage. com. New ads are posted to the website every day.
- **The Stranger;** a free weekly newspaper that can be found in restaurants and bars throughout Seattle. *The Stranger* is distributed on Thursdays, and contains rental and real estate classifieds. Online ads, which are updated daily, can be found at www.thestranger.com.

Community newspapers are excellent avenues for finding an apartment; many run local classifieds that will give you first crack at vacancies that may not appear in the citywide papers. These papers are usually available free of charge at neighborhood businesses and cafés.

- **Ballard News Tribune**, www.ballardnewstribune.com
- **Capitol Hill Times**, www.capitolhilltimes.com
- **Madison Park Times**, www.madisonparktimes.com

- **North Seattle Herald-Outlook**, www.northseattleherald-outlook.com
- **Queen Anne & Magnolia News**, www.queenannenews.com
- **South Seattle Beacon**, www.southseattlebeacon.com
- **West Seattle Herald/White Center News**, www.westseattleherald.com

To find housing in Seattle's surrounding communities, check out the classified ads in these major newspapers:

- **Federal Way News**, www.federalwaynews.net
- **The Herald** (Everett), www.heraldnet.com
- **Highline Times** (Des Moines–Sea-Tac), www.highlinetimes.com
- **Issaquah Press**, www.issaquahpress.com
- **Kirkland Reporter**, www.pnwlocalnews.com/east_king/kir
- **Mercer Island Reporter**, www.pnwlocalnews.com/east_king/mir
- **The News Tribune** (Tacoma-Seattle), www.thenewstribune.com
- **PNWLocalNews.com**, www.pnwlocalnews.com
- **Seattle Post-Intelligencer**, www.seattlepi.kaango.com

Some of the newspapers listed above have "roommate wanted" or "room available" sections, worth a look if you're on a limited budget. Shared houses are common in some areas of Seattle, particularly in the University District and the southeast side of Capitol Hill. These can be a good option if you plan to move again in several months, as many do not require a long-term lease.

OTHER RENTAL PUBLICATIONS

Several companies publish free rental guides. Most list newer apartment complexes or apartments that are maintained by large property management companies. You can pick up rental guides at most grocery or convenience stores.

- **Apartment Guide**, www.apartmentguide.com
- **For Rent**, www.forrent.com

BULLETIN BOARDS

Check out bulletin boards on college campuses, or in laundromats, coffee shops, and convenience stores in the neighborhoods that interest you.

- **Bellevue College**: housing opportunities are posted in the college cafeteria.
- **North Seattle Community College**: housing information can be found on campus at Baxter Center.
- **Seattle Central Community College**: two community bulletin boards are available in the Broadway Edison Building.

- **Seattle Pacific University**: bulletin boards can be found on campus at Weter Hall and in the Student Union Building. You can also search online at **http://spu.uloop.com/housing**.
- **Seattle University**: a classifieds ads bulletin board is located on the second floor of the Student Union Building. The university housing office also recommends you visit **Places4Students.com**.
- **South Seattle Community College**: a student bulletin board is located in the Jerry Brockey Center (or JMB).
- **University of Washington**: off-campus housing information is available in Room 218 Condon Hall, 206-543-8997. You can also visit online listings for off-campus housing at **http://housing.asuw.org**.

ONLINE RESOURCES

These local and national apartment-listing and roommate referral sites may be worth a look. Each lists vacancies in the Seattle area.

- **Apartment Rental Guide.com**, www.apartmentrentalguide.com
- **Apartments.com,** www.apartments.com
- **MyNewPlace.com**, www.mynewplace.com
- **Rent.com**, www.rent.com
- **Rentals.com**, www.rentals.com
- **Roommate Express**, www.e-roommate.com
- **Roommates.com**, www.roommates.com
- **Seattle Apartment Finders**, www.seattleapartmentfinders.com
- **Seattle Rentals**, www.seattlerentals.com

APARTMENT SEARCH FIRMS

One way to find an apartment, particularly if your time is limited, is to use an apartment search firm. These can be especially helpful if you want to set up your rental before arriving in town, as most agents will do a lot of the legwork for you. When speaking to an apartment search firm agent, be specific about your needs and budget. The following firms offer free search services.

- **Apartment Finders of Seattle**, 425-455-3733, 800-473-3733, www.seattleapartmentfinder.com
- **Apartment Hunters**, 206-770-0111, 888-400-4177, www.apthunters.com

CHECKING IT OUT

You're on your way to the day's first rental appointment, you haven't had breakfast, the old college friends you're staying with are getting restless, your back is aching from a bad night's sleep on their sofa-bed, and twenty other people are waiting outside the prospective apartment when you drive up. You panic, take a quick glance around, like what you see, and grab an application. Three months later you're wondering how you landed in such a dump.

To avoid this scenario, tour each apartment with a clear idea of what you want. Beyond personal likes and dislikes, there are some specific things to check for as you look:

- Is the apartment on the first floor? If so, does it have burglar bars? First floor apartments are easy targets for burglary.

- Are the appliances clean and in good working order? Test all of the stove's burners. Does the kitchen sink have one or two basins? Is there sufficient counter space? Is the freezer compartment of the refrigerator a frost-free variety?

- Check the windows to make sure they open, close, and lock. Do the windows, especially the bedroom windows, open onto a busy street or alley? Alleys are especially notorious for late-night car horns and loud early morning trash removal.

- Are there enough closets? Are the closets big enough to accommodate your belongings?

- Is there private storage space in a secure area?

- Is there adequate water pressure for the shower, the sink, and the toilet? Turn them on and check.

- Flush all toilets and check for leaks or unusual noises.

- Check the number of electrical outlets. In older buildings it is common to have one or two outlets per room. Are there enough outlets for all your plug-in appliances?

- Are there laundry facilities in the building? Is there a laundromat within walking distance?

- How close is the building to public transportation and grocery stores?

- If you are looking at a basement apartment, check to see if there are any water stains along the walls. They're a sure sign of flooding.

- Does it smell funny? They may have sprayed the apartment for bugs. You should think twice before taking it.

- Is there a smoke and/or carbon monoxide detector in the apartment?

Ed Sacks' *Savvy Renter's Kit* contains a thorough renter's checklist for those interested in augmenting theirs.

If it all passes muster, be prepared to stake your claim without delay!

STAKING A CLAIM

When you view a unit, come prepared. Bring your checkbook and a picture ID. If you are moving from out of state, you may be required to provide a cashier's check or money order instead of a personal check. Have cash on hand in case you cannot get to the bank and need to purchase a money order from a convenience store or check-cashing outlet. Also bring money for a non-refundable screening fee ($25 to $55) and a copy of your credit report for the building manager. Prepare a renter's resume with addresses of your last three residences, including the names, phone numbers, fax numbers, and e-mail addresses of your previous landlords, building managers, and roommates. Better yet, before you come to the Seattle area, bring letters of recommendation from the aforementioned that vouch for your sterling qualities. Employment information may also be helpful. If you have secured a job, ask your employer to write a letter on company stationery that verifies your start date and salary.

It won't hurt to mention casually that you don't have a dog, cat or monkey, and that you don't smoke or play the drums. Feel free to rave about the unit and how great it feels (after all, a landlord is human, too). If there is a garden, mention that you love gardening and have a very green thumb. If you do have a pet, ask former landlords to write letters praising its good behavior. If your dog is well behaved, you may want to bring him with you to show how well trained he is (if, of course, he actually is well trained).

When applying for a place, consider that landlords will want your monthly earnings to be equal to at least three times the monthly rent. They can request only non-smokers, they can prohibit pets other than a working dog, and they can bar you from having overnight guests for more than a certain number of nights per year. (If you think you'll have lots of visitors, watch out for a lease containing such a clause, as this may not bode well for your tenant/landlord relationship.)

In Seattle's competitive job market, it isn't just the early bird that gets the worm, it can also be the polite worm, the well-dressed worm, and the worm with the highest bid. Treat the open house or appointment like a job interview. If competition is particularly stiff, you may want to offer to sign a lease for longer than the required time period.

According to The Tenants Union (see below), the renter's most powerful moment is right before the rental agreement is signed. Once you sign an agreement, you will be bound by its terms, except for provisions that are illegal under the Landlord-Tenant Act. The union says these issues should be discussed before you agree to move in:

- How much is the rent, and when is it to be paid?
- Are there any rate charges for delinquent payments?
- Who will pay for the utilities?
- Is the tenancy for a fixed period, like one year, or is it for an indefinite period?

- What are the rules on guests, pets, parking, etc.?
- What repairs or cleaning has your landlord agreed to complete before you move in? (Get all promises in writing.)
- Is there a deposit? If so, how much, and when will it be refunded? (A non-refundable fee may not be called a deposit.

TENANT/LANDLORD RELATIONS

LEASES/RENTAL AGREEMENTS AND SECURITY DEPOSITS

Most landlords in Seattle require your first month's rent, a security or "damage" deposit, and a signed lease agreement prior to moving in. Many also require the last month's rent to be paid either prior to renting or within the first three months of tenancy. Make sure that you read your lease agreement before signing, and before paying anything. Check to see how and when the rent can be increased and by how much; don't assume that it can't be increased during the initial term of your lease. Such details should be negotiated before you sign the lease.

In Washington, the type of your tenancy (month-to-month or fixed period) will determine your rights and duties under the Landlord-Tenant Act, according to The Tenants Union. If you have an agreement with your landlord to stay for a fixed period at the same rent, you have a lease. To be valid, it must be in writing. If it is to be in effect for more than one year, it must not only be in writing, but it must also be signed by the landlord before a notary public. Rent cannot be increased during the fixed period, and the tenancy rules cannot be changed, unless both you and your landlord agree about it. At that time, says The Tenants Union, you must initial any changes that are made.

In the city of Seattle, month-to-month rental agreements are legal but a minimum stay requirement or penalties for not fulfilling a minimum stay on a month-to-month agreement are illegal. (These agreements usually state that if the tenant does not stay for a minimum number of months, usually six, he/she forfeits the deposit.) If a tenant loses a deposit because of such illegal provisions, the tenant is entitled to collect from the landlord double the deposit, plus actual damages incurred and attorney's fees and costs. Before a tenant sues in small claims court, he/she must request that the landlord return the deposit. For more information, contact **The Tenants Union** at 206-723-0500 or visit www.tenantsunion.org.

If a landlord charges a deposit, the lease or rental agreement must be in writing, and must include the terms under which any of the deposit will be returned. A deposit cannot be withheld for normal wear and tear, according to the Washington State Bar Association. If a tenant pays a deposit, the landlord must provide a written document describing the condition of the rental unit, and keep the deposit in a trust account. The landlord has 14 days after a tenant moves out to return a deposit, or give a written explanation why it was not refunded.

RENT AND EVICTION CONTROL

There is no rent control in Washington State. In fact, a state law prohibits cities and counties from passing any kind of rent control measure. According to The Tenants Union, a tenant's only protection against a rent increase is a lease. In a month-to-month agreement, a landlord can raise the rent as often as he/she pleases, but must give 30 days' written notice. Landlords are prohibited from raising rent as a means of either discrimination or retaliation.

In Seattle, landlords are required to give tenants a minimum of 60 days' written notice when rent is to be increased by 10% or more during a 12-month period. The same rule applies to other housing costs like water or sewage. The notice must coincide with the beginning of the rental period, usually the first day of the month.

The landlord-tenant rules in Washington tend to favor landlords. A landlord can issue a three-day notice to pay rent or vacate to a tenant who is only one day late with the rent. If the tenant pays rent after the three days given on the notice, the landlord is not obliged to accept payment. Landlords are also not obligated to accept partial payments. Many landlords will accept rent within five days of the date it is due, but may charge a late fee. Emergencies that prevent a tenant from paying rent on time should be discussed with the landlord, who may agree to accept partial payment or to set up a payment plan. If alternate terms are agreed upon, tenants should be sure to get them in writing, and ask the landlord to sign and date them. If additional assistance is necessary, contact The Tenants Union.

In 1996, Seattle passed a Just Cause Eviction Ordinance that prohibits landlords from evicting tenants without a court order. For the full text of the law, visit The Tenants Union website at www.tenantsunion.org.

LANDLORD/TENANT RIGHTS AND RESPONSIBILITIES

Washington landlords have a list of obligations that they must fulfill, including being accessible to their tenants and obeying the rules of the rental agreement. In addition, they must keep the rental property up to code, maintain the roof, walls, and structural components of the building, keep common areas safe and clean, provide a pest-control program, and provide the facilities necessary to supply heat, electricity, and hot and cold water. They must also provide adequate locks and maintain the appliances that come with the rental unit.

Contrary to what some believe, a landlord may not enter your apartment whenever he/she wishes. A landlord must have tenant consent to inspect the premises, make repairs, supply necessary services, or show the unit to a prospective renter. The time of entry must be reasonable, and he/she must notify you two days in advance. Of course, in an emergency, your landlord can enter your apartment without notice or permission.

A tenant must also meet a series of legal responsibilities. He/she must pay rent, keep his/her dwelling clean and sanitary, dispose of garbage, and properly use fixtures and appliances. He/she must not damage or permit damage to the property, and property must be restored to its original condition, except for normal wear and tear, before moving out. He/she must also comply with the rental agreement.

The Federal Fair Housing Act of 1968 makes it illegal for a landlord to discriminate based on a person's race, sex, national origin or religion. In addition, various local laws forbid discrimination against unmarried persons, children, gays, and disabled persons.

If you have any problems with your landlord while you're renting, or if you feel that you were discriminated against while you were hunting for an apartment or house, the resources listed below may help:

- **City of Seattle Office for Civil Rights**, 206-684-4500, 206-684-4503 (TTY), www.seattle.gov/civilrights
- **City of Seattle Office of Housing**, 206-684-0721, www.seattle.gov/housing
- **The Tenants Union**, 206-723-0500, www.tenantsunion.org
- **Washington State Attorney General's Office**, 206-464-6684, 800-551-4636, www.atg.wa.gov
- **Washington State Bar Association**, 206-443-WSBA (-9722), 800-945-WSBA, www.wsba.org

RENTER'S/HOMEOWNER'S INSURANCE

You've moved into your new apartment, and the last boxes have been cleared away. Take a look around and ask yourself, "How much would it cost to start over if everything I own was destroyed by fire?" Probably more than you might think. Imagine having to replace your clothing, television, stereo, furniture, computer and other accumulations of a lifetime. No small bill.

Typically, with renter's insurance you are protected against fire, hail, lightning, explosion, aircraft, smoke, vandalism, theft, building collapse, frozen plumbing, defective appliances, and sudden electrical damage. Renter's insurance also may cover personal liability as well as damage done (by you) to the property of others.

By now you should be convinced that renter's insurance is a good idea, especially because your belongings would not be insured under your landlord's policy. The good news about renter's insurance is that it is not a huge expense. For $20,000 in coverage your annual rate may run between $150 to $200 if you live in an apartment, and $200 to $250 if you live in a house.

When shopping for renter's insurance, be sure to ask whether the insurance company pays as soon as the claim is filed and whether it pays cash-value or replacement value. If you have a cash-value policy, you will only be paid what your five-year-old television is worth, not what it costs to replace it. Some big-ticket items, such as computers or jewelry, are insured only to a certain amount. Find out what these limits are. A higher deductible usually gives you a lower premium. You can purchase renter's insurance through almost any insurance agency.

Websites worth investigating as you search for renter's insurance are Insure.com, www.insure.com, which offers instant quotes from more than 300 insurance companies; Insweb, www.insweb.com, which is good for finding competitive insurance rates online; and InsureMe, www.insureme.com, which offers online quotes from several companies for you to choose from.

Whether you get renter's insurance or not, it's a good idea to keep an inventory of all items of value and record their serial numbers. You may also want to take photographs of your belongings, or walk through your apartment with a video camera and record them on tape. Make a copy of these records and keep one at a friend's house or in a safe deposit box.

Below is a list of some of the major insurers in the Seattle area:

- **Allstate**, www.allstate.com
- **Farmers Insurance Group**, www.farmersinsurance.com
- **Liberty Mutual**, www.libertymutual.com
- **MetLife**, www.metlife.com
- **Pemco**, www.pemco.com
- **Safeco**, www.safeco.com
- **State Farm Insurance**, www.statefarm.com
- **Unigard**, www.unigard.com

BUYING

Many people come to Seattle intending to buy a house in the city, but find that the cost of a home is just too high. Newcomers can avoid sticker shock by thoroughly researching home prices and neighborhoods before they arrive, and by keeping an open mind about the types of housing and the locations they are willing to consider. For instance, you will get more bang for your buck in Renton or Snoqualmie, but your commute to the city will be longer. Or, maybe you had your heart set on living in Queen Anne or Magnolia, but you find a really wonderful Craftsman home in Madrona that's in your price range. It's important to determine your priorities ahead of time, but to be flexible when possible.

Most streets in Seattle are lined with single-family homes on roomy lots. After a period of steady growth that mirrored the economic growth of the region, the Seattle housing market exploded in the late 1990s. Homes were on the market for just days before selling, and bidding wars were common. Affordable housing became increasingly rare, and even million-dollar (and upward) homes were snapped up quickly. The Seattle real estate bubble burst in 2008, as it did in most other parts of the country, as a result of the U.S. recession. Between 2008 and 2011, housing prices in Seattle declined steadily. When this guide went to press, a single-family home in Seattle was worth 13.5% less than it was in 2007.

While Seattle property values have declined, unfortunately property taxes have not. In some areas of the city they have actually increased. In 2011, a total of 44 tax ballot measures, the majority of which were school district levies, were approved by voters. Washington State has a "budget-based" tax system that allows cities and other taxing districts to boost tax collections without voter approval by 1% a year plus tax on the value of new construction. As a result, that year property taxes went up in 17 out of 20 King County school districts. The **King County Department of Assessments** is responsible for collecting property taxes in Seattle and most surrounding communities. You can estimate your annual property taxes if you know the assessed value of your property and your tax levy rate. Divide the value of your home by 1,000 and multiply by the tax levy rate. In Seattle in 2011, the tax levy rate was $9.65. Thus, for a home valued at $300,000, property taxes would be about $2,895. The tax levy rate varies by city; to find the rate in the city of your choice, visit the Department of Assessments website at www.kingcounty.gov/Assessor.

Before buying a house, it's a good idea to hire an independent building inspector or engineer to examine the foundation and overall structure, heating and plumbing systems, and the roof. Also request that the inspector check for mold, particularly if the roof has been replaced recently or if there are signs of water damage in the basement. Your lender will appraise the house, but only to determine if its value will safely secure the loan. If possible, you should include language in your purchase offer that allows you to take back the offer if your inspection uncovers a serious problem. At the very least, your real estate agent should be willing to negotiate with the seller on any major flaws turned up during the inspection. For more see below under **Purchase Agreements**.

How should you go about finding a home to buy in Seattle? Any good real estate agent will tell you there are three things to consider when purchasing a house: location, location, location. The **Neighborhoods** chapter of this book will give you a good overview of the neighborhoods in Seattle, as well as profiles of many of the city's suburbs. On Fridays, the *Seattle Times* publishes a "Neighborhood of the Week" feature in its Real Estate section that profiles different parts of the city and its surrounding communities. You'll find these archived on their website at www.seattletimes.nwsource.com. From there, visit the neighborhood(s) you're considering. Get a general feel for the area; visit the schools and parks; drive to or from the neighborhood during rush hour to evaluate traffic flow and freeway noise. Attend a few open houses to find a realtor that knows the area. The *Seattle Times* Sunday edition has a Real Estate section that lists many of the open houses in Seattle and surrounding communities. The paper is available on Friday evenings, so you can get a drive-by preview. On Saturdays the *Times* also features a New Homes section, showcasing new construction around the region, and a NW Homes section. Or, visit the classifieds' website at http://marketplace.nwsource.com/realestate; new open house announcements are added daily. Additional newspaper sites are listed previously in this chapter under **Classified Advertisements**. Seattle Met (www.seattlemet.com), the website for *Seattle Metropolitan* magazine, is another useful online resource for local real estate information. The site includes a "Neighborhoods by the Numbers" section that compares data—such as median home prices, number of markets, crime rates, miles of bike lanes, average commute time, median age of residents, and many other factors—from different neighborhoods in Seattle and its surrounding communities.

The **Washington State Housing Finance Commission** offers free home ownership programs and homebuyer education seminars (see below under **Additional Resources**). For more information, visit the agency's website at www.wshfc.org or call 206-464-7139 (in Seattle) or 800-767-4663. You can also find information on buying or selling a home at the **National Association of Realtors** website, www.realtor.com.

CONDOMINIUMS, CO-OPS, AND CO-HOUSING

Buying a home in Seattle doesn't necessarily mean buying a traditional single-family house. Condominiums, co-ops, and co-housing projects are all options, depending on your needs. All three are usually less expensive than traditional houses, and may be a good first step for first-time homeowners. Condominiums in particular have become a popular housing choice in places like Downtown and Ballard, where many new buildings are going up, and units are often sold before construction is complete.

A **condominium** is a type of joint ownership. Each housing unit is individually owned and residents collectively own the common areas—grounds, lobbies, elevators, hallways, surrounding property, and recreational facilities. You own the apartment outright, so you can usually make improvements to it, rent it out, or resell it as you see fit. However, some restrictions apply to condo ownership. Generally, a condo association oversees the rules of the complex, making decisions about building repairs, external improvements, and landscaping. Some condo associations impose rules on subletting. Be sure to review, with your real estate lawyer, the association rules and regulations, and the current operating budget. Consider any major improvements or repairs that will be required in the next few years, and see if the budget will be able to cover most of the cost.

If your building has jointly owned amenities, such as a hot tub, rooftop deck, or pool, the association coordinates maintenance on those facilities as well. All of these services come at a cost; expect to pay anywhere between $100 to several hundred dollars (or more) in monthly association dues, as well as a one-time fee for capital improvements or emergency repairs, such as a new roof. While these dues may add up over time to little more than the maintenance on your own house, you'll need to factor them in when evaluating your monthly house payments. Condo associations can foreclose on your unit if you fall behind on payments, so be sure to include these fees in your housing budget.

A **co-op** (cooperative apartment) is another option for home ownership in Seattle. When you buy a co-op, you are buying shares in the ownership of a building. Co-ops tend to be much less expensive than comparable condominiums, but there are some important trade-offs. Co-ops are tightly controlled by the shareholders in the building—in other words by all of the co-op owners. This can make it difficult to buy a cooperative apartment, since the co-op board will interview you, consider both your financial status and neighborly qualities, and may require several letters of reference. You may not have the option to remodel your unit, rent it out, or even sell it quickly, should you need to (as the co-op board must approve prospective buyers). If you're short on cash, buying into a co-op can be challenging because many lenders will not approve mortgages for them. Unfortunately, many co-ops do not accept anything but a full cash payment at the time of purchase. Co-ops are most common in the Capitol Hill and Queen Anne neighborhoods.

Those thinking about buying a condominium or co-op should seriously consider that owning a condo or co-op obligates you socially a bit more than does a freestanding house. While your co-op or condo neighbors could turn out to be great friends and neighbors, the opposite could also be true.

Co-housing projects are catching on in Seattle as residents seek to recapture the aura of a close-knit neighborhood in a rapidly growing city. Also called "intentional communities," co-housing projects offer communal living with affordable condo-style ownership opportunities. Each household owns its own unit, but shares communal space such as a "common house." Co-housing residents often prepare and eat meals together, share gardening responsibilities, and promote environmental initiatives like recycling and composting. For more information on co-housing, visit The Co-housing Association of the United States at www.cohousing.org, or contact one of the co-housing communities listed here:

- **Capitol Hill Urban Cohousing,** Seattle, 206-285-1589, www.capitolhillurbancohousing.org

- **Duwamish Cohousing**, Seattle, 206-767-7726, www.duwamish.net
- **Jackson Place Cohousing**, 206-522-3099, www.seattlecohousing.org
- **Puget Ridge Cohousing**, 206-763-3450, www.pugetridge.net
- **Sharingwood Co-housing**, Snohomish County, 360-668-1439, http://sharingwood.org
- **Songaia Cohousing Community**, Snohomish County, www.songaia.com
- **Vashon Co-housing**, Vashon Island, 206-463-4053, www.vashoncohousing.org
- **Winslow Cohousing Group**, Bainbridge Island, 206-780-1323, www.winslowcohousing.org

WORKING WITH REALTORS

If you are unfamiliar with the city, it may be helpful to find a real estate agent or broker to help you with your search. Friends or co-workers may be able to recommend someone, or consider the agents who host open houses in your neighborhood of choice. The agent should be someone you trust, who listens to you, knows the city and the neighborhoods you like, and understands the market. A good realtor will not expect you to pay more than you can afford, although you may find that the house you can afford and the house you want are very different things.

Generally, homebuyers in Seattle do not use a real estate lawyer. Often the only lawyer involved is an employee of the escrow company. Nevertheless, it is a good idea to have the name of a real estate attorney available just in case. Ask friends or co-workers for recommendations, or ask your agent to suggest a reputable attorney.

The major national and regional real estate companies offer online lists of agents. To begin your search you may want to visit one of those national or regional realtor websites, or go to HomeGain (www.homegain.com), a company that offers free tools for estimating the value of a home; finding a real estate agent or a home; and getting a mortgage.

PURCHASE AGREEMENTS, CREDIT, MORTGAGES, INSURANCE

The purchase agreement is a legally binding document signed by the buyer and seller that states the price and all the terms of the sale. It is the most negotiable, variable, and important document produced in the home-buying process. The purchase agreement is the document to which a buyer may attach contingencies. Such contingencies can protect you, the buyer, from being legally bound by the purchase agreement if, for example, you cannot sell the house you live in now, the house you are buying does not pass mechanical and structural inspection, the seller is not able to give you possession by a certain date, or you cannot qualify for a loan.

Washington does not regulate purchase agreements, but it does require Form 22J, the disclosure of lead-based paint. If a seller does not give a buyer this form, the buyer can rescind the sale up until the closing date. The state also requires the seller to deliver to the buyer a property disclosure statement (Form 17). The statement provides the buyer with information about the condition of the property, and may outline known or potential problems, like a leaky roof or drainage problems.

It's a good idea to get pre-approved for a loan before looking for houses in earnest. Most sellers will not seriously consider an offer from a buyer who is not pre-approved. The pre-approval process should not commit you to a particular lender or interest rate. It is simply a document that indicates to the seller that when you formally apply for a loan, you will most likely qualify to purchase the home. Most banks or mortgage brokers will process a pre-approval application without a fee. In addition to making your offer more attractive to the seller, the pre-approval process gives you, the buyer, an accurate idea of how much you can spend on a house.

A key factor when seeking a loan is your credit history. Check your credit report to make sure it is accurate before meeting with a loan officer. You can check your credit report with all three national credit bureaus listed here. You will need to provide your name, address, previous address, and Social Security number with your request. Check with each company for specific instructions. Reports are free if you have been denied credit based on your credit report within the last 30 days; otherwise, expect to pay a fee. You can also request a free credit report from each of the three national credit bureaus once every year at www.annualcreditreport.com. The national credit bureaus are:

- **Equifax**, P.O. Box740241, Atlanta, GA 30347, 800-685-1111, www.equifax.com
- **Experian**, P.O. Box 9554, Allen, TX 75002-2104, 888-397-3742, www.experian.com
- **TransUnion Corporation**, 2 Baldwin Pl, P.O. Box 1000, Chester, PA 19022, 800-493-2392, www.transunion.com

When contemplating buying a house, you'll want to evaluate your personal finances. How much can you afford to pay up front, and how much will you then be able to pay per month? Generally, you will be able to qualify for a loan of about three or four times your yearly income, depending on your credit record and other debts. The loan won't cover your down payment and closing costs, however. In most cases closing costs, which are in addition to the down payment, run 3% to 7% of the purchase price. These can include loan origination fees, attorney's fees, title search, title insurance, inspections, and tax and insurance premiums held in escrow. As a buyer you will probably not be expected to pay the broker's fees, which are commonly paid by the seller. Expect your down payment to be from 5% to 20% of the price of the home. Additional fees, such as mortgage insurance or higher loan origination fees, are often required if the down payment is less than 20%.

Finally, a few words about getting a loan: it may be most convenient to get your pre-approval from a local bank, but shop around before you sign for your loan. While many banks offer competitive interest rates, mortgage brokers can often match or beat their best offers. Make sure you ask about loan origination fees (points) when requesting interest rate quotes. Usually the lowest interest rate includes a hefty one-time fee, one that may not be mentioned until you're ready to sign the papers. The Bankrate website (www.bankrate.com) provides mortgage and interest rate data on over 4,800 lending institutions.

Major banks and mortgage-lending institutions usually have websites, and most now allow you to get pre-approved online. See **Mortgages** below for a list.

Once your loan is approved, your lender will require you to buy **homeowner's insurance** to protect their investment (your home). Be sure the policy you choose covers the house, its contents, and any outbuildings. Seattle is located in the Cascadia region, which is vulnerable to earthquakes and tsunamis. Standard homeowner's policies in Washington State do not cover earthquake damage; coverage must be purchased as a separate endorsement. Depending on where your new home is located, you may want to explore the option of flood insurance as well. You'll also want to protect yourself in case of liability. Policies vary, so check restrictions and exclusions carefully to make sure you have the coverage you need. A basic homeowner's policy includes liability insurance to protect you if someone is injured on your property; property protection, which insures your house and personal belongings against damage or loss; and living expense coverage that will pay for you to live elsewhere while repairs are being made.

You may also need mortgage insurance, which is required by many lenders as well as the FHA to cover them if you default on your loan, and title insurance, which protects the lender in case the legal title to the property isn't clear. It doesn't protect you though, so, in addition, you may want to buy an owner's title insurance policy, or get an attorney's opinion on your title. If the seller has purchased title insurance in recent years, you may be able to get the same title company to issue you a new policy at a lower cost, so be sure to ask for a reissue credit. See **Renter's Insurance** above for a list of insurance companies.

ONLINE RESOURCES—HOUSE HUNTING

You can start your search on the Internet before you arrive in Seattle. Surfing the Web will give you a good idea about what's on the market, where you should look once you get here, and about how much you can expect to pay. Not every site lists every home in the Seattle area, but most homes will be listed on at least one site. Also, don't forget the newspaper classifieds (see above under **Apartment Hunting**).

- **Cyberhomes**, www.cyberhomes.com
- **Homes.com,** www.homes.com
- **HomeSeekers.com**, www.homeseekers.com
- **Move.com,** www.move.com
- **National Association of Realtors**, www.realtor.com
- **Real Estate.com**, www.realestate.com
- **Trulia**, www.trulia.com
- **Yahoo! Real Estate**, http://realestate.yahoo.com
- **Zillow,** www.zillow.com
- **ZipRealty**, www.ziprealty.com

House hunting has gone high tech. Today's smart phones and PDAs often come with real estate apps that are a real boon to homebuyers. You can download mobile apps (many are free) that enable you to search for nearby properties for sale whenever you find yourself in a neighborhood that appeals to you. Online real estate giants Zillow, Trulia, and Realtor.com offer apps that let you view color pictures of homes by street view or satellite, and filter your results by the features you're looking for in a home. If you see a property you like, you can e-mail your agent about it on the spot.

FOR SALE BY OWNER

If you prefer to buy or sell a home without an agent, check out the sites below; they specialize in home listings by owners:

- **ByOwner.com**, www.byowner.com
- **ForSaleByOwner.com**, www.forsalebyowner.com
- **HomesByOwner.com**, www.homesbyowner.com
- **Owners.com**, www.owners.com

MORTGAGES

The following sites might be useful:

- **CitiMortgage**, www.citimortgage.com; CitiMortgage's site lets visitors pre-qualify for loans, shop and compare rates, and apply for loans online.
- **E-Loan**, www.eloan.com; find loans with low rates and low origination fees.
- **Freddie Mac**, www.freddiemac.com; offers information on current mortgage averages.
- **Home Finance of America**, www.bestrateloans.com; offers competitive home financing rates.

- **Interest.com**, www.interest.com; includes suggestions on how to find a lender close to home, and mortgage rate comparisons.
- **Mortgage 101,** www.mortgage101.com; offers a lender directory, mortgage calculators, and mortgage "snapshots" for different states.
- **Mortgage-calc.com**, www.mortgage-calc.com; find several simple, free online calculators for mortgages, amortization, refinancing and more.
- **Quicken Loans**, www.quickenloans.com; includes information for first-time homebuyers, plus easy-to-use calculators that help expedite and clarify the finance process.

ADDITIONAL RESOURCES

If you want to buy a house, especially if you are a first-time homebuyer, consider taking a real estate class, often available at area colleges. The **Washington State Housing Finance Commission** offers free home ownership programs and homebuyer education seminars. For more information, visit the agency's website at www.wshfc.org or call 206-464-7139 (in Seattle) or 800-767-HOME. Another good resource for classes is the **Washington Homeownership Resource Center**, at www.homeownership-wa.org, or call 206-542-1243. If you don't have the time or inclination for a class, but are willing to conduct your own research, look for a book on homebuying how-tos. An invaluable resource is the **Washington Center for Real Estate Research (WCRER)**, 800-835-9683 or www.wcrer.wsu.edu. The WCRER, a division of the Washington State University College of Business, provides research and education materials to consumers.

The following resources may be of interest for those in the market for a new home:

- *100 Questions Every First-Time Homebuyer Should Ask* by Ilyce R. Glink
- **Environmental Protection Agency,** www.epa.gov/epahome; the EPA maintains a website that lets you search your environment by zip code if you are concerned about toxic waste issues or chemical releases in or near your prospective neighborhood.
- *How to Buy Your Own Home*, a pamphlet published by the Fannie Mae Foundation for first-time homebuyers, can be accessed at http://literacyworks. org/fmfhome/index.html.
- **Rain City Guide**, www.raincityguide.com, a Seattle real estate blog with helpful, relevant and constantly updated information on the local real estate market.
- **Seattle Office of Housing,** www.seattle.gov/housing/buying/resources. htm; in addition to links to resources, this city government website contains information about affordable housing and down payment assistance.
- **The U.S. Department of Housing and Urban Development** offers an online tutorial on the homebuying process at www.hud.gov/buying.

- ***Your New House: The Alert Consumer's Guide to Buying and Building a Quality New Home***; in its fourth edition, a very helpful resource, especially for those building a new home. While the book is unfortunately out of print, you can find both new and used copies at Amazon.com and other online booksellers' sites, or check out a copy from the library.
- **Zillow.com**, www.zillow.com, offers estimates of what your home is worth, as well as comparisons with comparable homes in your neighborhood. Search for any address, for free, and get aerial maps, home info, charts, graphs and more.

BEFORE YOU CAN START YOUR NEW LIFE IN SEATTLE, YOU AND YOUR worldly possessions have to get here. How difficult that will be depends on how much stuff you've accumulated, how much money you're willing or able to spend on the move, and where you're coming from.

TRUCK RENTALS

The first question you need to answer: am I going to move myself or will I have someone else do it for me? If you're used to doing everything yourself, you can rent a vehicle and head for the open road. Look in the Yellow Pages or online under "Truck Rental," and call around and compare; also ask about any specials. Below we list four national truck rental firms and their toll-free numbers and websites. For the best information, you should call a local office. Note: most truck rental companies now offer "one-way" rentals (don't forget to ask whether they have a drop-off/return location in or near your destination), as well as packing accessories and storage facilities. Of course, these extras are not free. If you're cost-conscious you may want to scavenge boxes in advance of your move and, if you haven't yet found your new residence, make sure you have a place to store your belongings upon arrival. Also, if you're planning to move during the peak moving months of May through September, call or reserve a truck online well in advance of when you'll need the vehicle—a month at least.

Once you're on the road, keep in mind that your rental truck may be a tempting target for thieves. If you must park it overnight or for an extended period (more than a couple of hours), try to find a safe spot, preferably a well-lit place you can easily observe.

- **Budget**, 800-527-0700, www.budget.com
- **Penske**, 888-996-5415, www.gopenske.com

- **Ryder**, 800-297-9337, www.ryder.com
- **U-HAUL**, 800-468-4285, www.uhaul.com

COMMERCIAL FREIGHT CARRIERS AND CONTAINER-BASED MOVERS

Not sure if you want to drive the truck yourself? Commercial freight carriers, such as ABF U-Pack, offer an in-between service: they deliver an empty 28-foot trailer to your home, you pack and load as much of it as you need, and they drive the vehicle to your destination (usually with some commercial freight filling up the empty space). Information is available through their website at www.upack.com.

Another increasingly popular (though not inexpensive) option is to hire a container-based moving service, such as **Seattle Storage and Moving Company**, (888-366-7222, www.doortodoor.com,), **Smartbox** (877-627-8269, www.smartboxusa.com), **PODS** (877-770-PODS, www.pods.com), and **1-800-Pack-Rat** (www.1800packrat.com, 800-722-5728). These carriers will deliver sturdy containers (often called storage pods), usually made of metal, fiberglass or treated plywood, to your home. At your own pace, you load the containers with the items you need to move, and the company delivers the loaded containers to your destination or to a storage facility, if you're not ready to unpack yet. Some containers are compact enough to fit in a parking space or a driveway adjacent to your property, where you can temporarily store and access them easily. The container system allows you to compartmentalize your move, keeping the contents of a certain room in one place. Having control over the packing process may limit damage to your possessions (don't skimp on the bubble wrap!). Containers are also a sensible option when the sale of your property doesn't coincide with the move-in date for your new home, or if you are planning to paint or remodel the property before moving in. When pricing this option, which often costs more than hiring a conventional moving company, be sure you take careful measurements of the items you're planning to move, since certain pieces may be too large for the dimensions of the available containers. You should also find out the maximum weight that a container can handle.

MOVERS

You can search for a mover in the Yellow Pages, but the best way to find a reliable mover is through a personal recommendation. Absent a friend or relative who can point you to a trusted moving company, try some of the online personal recommendation sites like www.citysearch.com, www.yelp.com, and www.judysbook.com. It's not a good idea to merely do an Internet search for movers, as you'll likely be taken to websites for online moving brokers, who do not have a good track record for steering customers to reputable movers. For long distance or interstate moves, the **American Moving and Storage Association's** site (www.moving.org) identifies member movers both in Washington and across the country. In the past, *Consumer Reports* (www.consumerreports. org) has published useful information on moving. Members of **AAA** can call their local office and receive discounted rates and service through AAA's Consumers Relocation Service.

Disagreeable moving experiences, while common, aren't obligatory. To aid you in your search for a hassle-free mover, we offer a few general recommendations. First and foremost, make sure any moving company you consider hiring is **licensed by the appropriate authority**:

- **The Washington Utilities and Transportation Commission (WUTC) regulates intrastate moves**. All movers operating within the state of Washington are required to have a valid state UTC permit. The permit number must appear on the mover's vehicles, advertisements, correspondence, business cards, and website. A licensed mover must comply with UTC safety, insurance, and service standards, and must perform its services at reasonable rates and within a reasonable time. Visit the WUTC website (www.utc.wa.gov) for a list of registered movers. To check on your mover by phone, call the WUTC consumer help-line at 888-333-9882 (toll-free in Washington), or 360-664-1234. When you call, you will be informed if the moving company is registered, and whether there have been complaints lodged against it.

- **Interstate moves** are regulated by the U.S. Department of Transportation's **Federal Motor Carrier Safety Administration (FMCSA)**. When reviewing prospective carriers, make sure the carrier has a Department of Transportation MC ("Motor Carrier") or ICC MC number that should be displayed on all advertising and promotional material as well as on the truck. With the MC number in hand, you can contact the Washington office of FMCSA at 360-753-9875 or check www.fmcsa.dot.gov to see if the carrier is licensed and insured. You can also learn how to protect yourself from scams by downloading brochures from the website https://www.protectyourmove.gov. Before a move takes place, federal regulations require interstate movers to furnish customers with a copy of "Your Rights and Responsibilities When You Move." If they don't give you a copy, ask for one. FMCSA's role in the regulation of interstate carriers concerns safety issues, not consumer issues. To find out if any complaints have been filed against a prospective mover, check with the Better Business Bureau (www.bbb.org) in the state where the moving company is licensed, as well as with that state's Consumer Protection Office.

ADDITIONAL RECOMMENDATIONS

- If someone recommends a mover to you, get names (the salesperson or estimator, the drivers, the loaders). To paraphrase the NRA, moving companies don't move people, people do.

- Once you've narrowed your search down to two or three companies, ask a mover for references, particularly from customers who recently did moves similar to yours. If a mover is unable or unwilling to provide such information or tells you that it can't give out names because their customers are all in the federal Witness Protection Program…perhaps you should consider another company.

- Even though movers will put numbered labels on your possessions, you should make a numbered list of every box and item that is going in the truck. Detail box contents and photograph anything of particular value. Once the truck arrives on the other end, you can check off every piece and know for sure what did (or did not) make it. In case of claims, this list can be invaluable. Even after the move, keep the list; it can be surprisingly useful.

- Be aware that during the busy season (May through September), demand can exceed supply and moving may be more difficult and more expensive than during the rest of the year. If you must relocate during the peak moving months, call and book service well in advance, a month, at least, ahead of your moving date. If you can reserve service way in advance, say four to six months early, you may be able to lock in a lower winter rate for your summer move. Keep in mind that Saturdays are usually busy moving days and you might have better luck moving on a less busy day of the week.

- Whatever you do, do *not* mislead a salesperson about how much and what you are moving. And make sure you tell a prospective mover how far they'll have to transport your stuff to and from the truck as well as any stairs, driveways, obstacles or difficult vegetation, long paths or sidewalks, etc. The clearer you are with your mover, the better he or she will be able to serve you.

- You should ask for and receive a written estimate of the probable cost of your move. The estimate should clearly and accurately describe all charges. In Washington, there are two types of estimates: A **non-binding estimate** is an educated guess of what your move would cost based on the mover's survey of your belongings. In this scenario your final cost can exceed the non-binding estimate—though there is a limit on how much over the estimate the company can charge. A **binding estimate** is a written agreement that guarantees the price you pay based on the items to be moved and the services listed on the estimate, inventory or tally sheet.

- Remember that price, while important, isn't everything, especially when you're entrusting all of your worldly possessions to strangers. Choose a mover you feel comfortable with.

- Think about packing. Depending on the size of your move and whether or not you do the packing yourself, you may need a lot of boxes, tape, and packing material. Boxes provided by the mover, while not cheap, are usually sturdy and the right size. Sometimes a mover will give a customer free used boxes. It doesn't hurt to ask. Liquor stores and grocery stores are also good places to ask for boxes. Also, *don't* wait to pack until the last minute. If you're doing the packing, give yourself at least a week to do the job, two is better. Keep in mind that moving companies will usually not accept liability for "owner-packed" boxes, however, so you might want to stock up on the bubble wrap.
- Listen to what the movers say; they are professionals and can give you expert advice about packing and preparing. Also, be ready for the truck on both ends—don't make them wait. Not only will it irritate your movers, but it may cost you. Understand, too, that things can happen on the road that are beyond a carrier's control (weather, accidents, etc.) and your belongings may not get to you at the time or on the day promised. (See note about insurance below.)
- Treat your movers well, especially the ones loading your stuff on and off the truck. Offer to buy them lunch, and tip them if they do a good job.
- Ask about insurance; the "basic" 60 cents per pound industry standard coverage is not enough. If you have homeowner's or renter's insurance, check to see if it will cover your belongings during transit. If not, consider purchasing "full replacement" or "full value" coverage from the carrier for the estimated value of your shipment. Though it's the most expensive type of coverage offered, it's probably worth it. Trucks get into accidents, they catch fire, they get stolen—if such insurance seems pricey to you, ask about a $250 or $500 deductible. This can reduce your cost substantially but still give you much better protection in the event of a catastrophic loss. Transport irreplaceable items, such as jewelry, photographs or key work documents, yourself.
- Be prepared to pay the full moving bill upon delivery. Cash or bank/cashier's check may be required. Some carriers will take VISA and MasterCard but it is a good idea to get it in writing that you will be permitted to pay with a credit card since the delivering driver may not be aware of this and may demand cash. Unless you routinely keep thousands of dollars of greenbacks on you, you could have a problem getting your stuff off the truck.
- Above all, ask questions, and if you're concerned about something, ask for an explanation in writing.
- Finally, before moving pets, attach a tag to your pet's collar with your new address and phone number in case your pet accidentally wanders off in the confusion of moving.

Those **moving within the Seattle area** with minimal belongings probably won't need a huge truck to complete the task. If you (and your friends) are not interested in loading and unloading a rented truck, you may consider hiring one of the following local movers. All were registered with the WUTC and held current permits at the time of publication:

- **Crown Moving Company**, 1071 Andover Park W, 206-336-2500, 800-824-7769, www.crownmoving.com
- **Hansen Bros. Moving & Storage**, 10750 Aurora Ave N, 206-365-4454, 888-300-7222, www.hansenbros.com
- **Neighbors Moving & Storage**, 253-872-9400, 800-940-1939, www.neighborsmoving.com
- **Puget Sound Moving,** 206-568-0600, www.psmoving.com
- **University Moving & Storage**, 905 N 128th, 206-362-0508, www.universitymovingandstorage.com

According to the WUTC, moving costs in Washington are calculated in one of two ways, depending on the distance. For moves of 55 miles or more, rates are based on the weight of your goods and the distance hauled. For moves of fewer than 55 miles, rates are based on the number of workers used, the amount of time necessary to load, move, and unload your goods, and the mover's hourly rate. The UTC sets maximum rates that a mover can charge, but it can be worth your while to shop around among legitimate, trustworthy movers, as many will charge less than the maximum rates to get your business.

CONSUMER COMPLAINTS—MOVERS

If you have a problem with your mover that you haven't been able to resolve directly, you can file a complaint about an intrastate move with the **Washington Utilities and Transportation Commission**. Call the Consumer Complaints section at 888-333-9882, or use the online complaint form at www.utc.wa.gov. If yours was an interstate move, your options for government intervention or assistance are limited. Years ago the now-defunct Interstate Commerce Commission (ICC) would log complaints against interstate movers. Today, you're pretty much on your own. The Federal Motor Carrier Safety Administration recommends that you call 888-368-7238 to lodge a complaint against a moving company. You can also contact the Better Business Bureau in the licensing state, as well as that state's consumer protection office to register a complaint. If satisfaction still eludes you, begin a letter writing campaign: to the state Attorney General, to your congressional representative, to the newspaper, the sky's the limit. Of course, if the dispute is worth it, you can hire a lawyer and seek redress the all-American way.

STORAGE

If you and your belongings are going to arrive at your destination at different times, you have a few options. Many movers have their own warehouses for storage, or contract out with other warehouse companies. If your mover is going to handle storage for you for up to 90 days, it is considered **storage in transit** and is regulated by the WUTC. Any storage after 90 days is considered **permanent storage** and is no longer regulated. The WUTC website provides more information at www.utc.wa.gov.

If you discover that your new abode is too small for all of your stuff, or it's taking longer than expected to get permanently settled and you need storage beyond 90 days, you'll want to explore a couple of options. You can go the **Self Storage** route (see below) or rent a container from a portable storage company. These companies will deliver as many 5' by 8' wooden containers as you need to your home, where you will pack them. When you're finished packing, the company will come to pick the containers up and store them in their secured facilities until you need them. A good rule of thumb is that two containers will generally store the contents of a studio or one-bedroom home or apartment. Five containers will hold the contents of a two- or three-bedroom home. Some companies offer their services nationally, so you can pack your belongings in one state and have them delivered to your new home for less than hiring a traditional mover. Other companies only service local regions so this may be an alternative to traditional self-service storage.

- **Door to Door Storage & Moving**, several locations in the Puget Sound area, 888-366-7222, www.doortodoorst.com
- **PODS**, Portable On Demand Storage, 888-776-PODS, www.pods.com
- **PortaBox Storage**, multiple locations, 888-269-8646, www.portabox.com

SELF STORAGE

If you prefer a do-it-yourself approach and need a temporary place to store your stuff while you find a new home, self-storage is the answer. Most units are clean, secure, insured, and inexpensive, and you can rent anything from a locker to your own mini-warehouse. You'll need to bring your own padlock and be prepared to pay first and last month's rent up front. Many will offer special deals to entice you, such as second month free. Probably the easiest way to find storage is to look in the Yellow Pages under "Storage—Household & Commercial." To conduct your search online, visit the site of local Yellow Pages provider www.dexknows.com.

Keep in mind that demand for storage surges in the prime moving months (May through September), so try not to wait until the last minute to rent storage. If you don't care about convenience, your cheapest storage options may be out in the boonies. You just have to figure out how to get your stuff there and back.

A word of warning: unless you no longer want your stored belongings, pay your storage bill and pay it on time. Storage companies may auction the contents of delinquent customers' lockers.

- **12th & Madison Self Storage**, 1111 E Madison St, 206-973-2459, www.urbanstorage.com
- **Belltown Self Storage**, 1915 3rd Ave, 206-973-3680, www.urbanstorage.com
- **Extra Space Storage**, 1430 N 130th St, 888-609-8483, www.extraspace.com
- **Market Street Self Storage**, 2811 NW Market St, 206-789-8080, www.marketstreetstorage.com
- **Nickerson Self Storage,** 130 W Nickerson St, 206-274-5525, www.nickersonstreetstorage.com
- **Northgate Self Storage**, 10805 Roosevelt Way NE, 206-364-8777, www.northgateselfstorage.com
- **Peoples Storage,** 4213 Leary Way NE, 206-452-1366, www.iarbiz.com
- **Public Storage**, 800-688-8057, www.publicstorage.com
- **Vine Street Storage**, 11 Vine St, 206-443-3500, www.vinestreetstorage.com

CHILDREN

Studies show that moving can be hard on children. According to an American Medical Association study, children who move often are more likely to suffer from such problems as depression, worthlessness, and aggression. Often their academic performance suffers as well. If you must move, there are a few things you can do to help your children through this stressful time:

- Talk about the move with your kids. Be honest but positive. Listen to their concerns. To the extent possible, involve them in the process.
- Make sure the child has his/her favorite possessions on the trip; don't pack "blankey" in the moving van.
- Make sure you have some social life planned on the other end. Your child may feel lonely in your new home and such activities can ease the transition.
- Keep in touch with family and loved ones as much as possible. Photos and phone calls are important ways of maintaining links to the important people you have left behind.
- If your child is of school age, take the time to involve yourself in his/her new school.

There are many good books and resources to help children adjust to moving. First Books (www.shopfirstbooks.com) offers *The Moving Book: A Kids' Survival Guide* by Gabriel Davis; *Max's Moving Adventure: A Coloring Book for Kids on the Move*, by Danelle Till; and a Kid's Moving Kit—a colorful backpack filled with fun activities. Other good publications include *Alexander, Who's Not (Do You Hear Me? I Mean It!) Going to Move* by Judith Viorst; *Moving with Kids: 25 Ways to Ease Your Family's Transition to a New Home* by Lori Collins Burgan, and *Smart Moves: Your Guide through the Emotional Maze of Relocation* by Nadia Jensen, Audrey McCollum, and Stuart Copans.

TAXES

If your move is work-related, some or all of your moving expenses may be tax-deductible—so you will want to keep those receipts. Though eligibility varies, depending, for example, on whether you have a job or are self-employed, the cost of moving yourself, your family, and your belongings is generally tax deductible, even if you don't itemize. The criteria: in order to take the deduction your move must be employment-related, your new job must be more than 50 miles away from your current residence, and you must be at your new location for at least 39 weeks during the first 12 months after your arrival. If you take the deduction and then fail to meet the requirements, you will have to pay the IRS back, unless you were laid off through no fault of your own, or transferred again by your employer. It's probably a good idea to consult a tax expert regarding IRS rules related to moving. If you're a confident soul, get a copy of IRS Form 3903 and Publication 521 (www.irs.gov) and do it yourself!

ONLINE RESOURCES—RELOCATION

- **www.shopfirstbooks.com**: relocation resources and information on moving to Atlanta, Austin, Boston, Chicago, Dallas–Ft. Worth, Houston, Los Angeles, Minneapolis-St. Paul, New York City, Portland, OR, the San Francisco Bay Area, and Washington, D.C., as well as China and London, England. The *Newcomer's Handbook for Moving to and Living in the USA* is also available.
- **www.homefair.com**: realty listings, school reports, cost-of living calculators, moving tips, and more.
- **www.moving.com**: comprehensive Web portal featuring a tool that lets you compare movers' rate quotes online.
- **www.moving.org**: American Moving and Storage Association site; referrals to interstate movers, local movers, storage companies, and packing and moving consultants.
- **www.movingscam.com**: provides helpful articles, volunteer-staffed message boards, and a list of "blacklisted" movers.

BANKING

A S SOON AS YOU FIND A PLACE TO HANG YOUR HAT, YOU WILL WANT to find a home for your money. For major deposits, shop around for interest rates, but for routine checking and savings, you'll be more interested in ATM fees, online banking options, and direct deposit services—an increasingly common alternative to getting a paycheck in the mail or on your desk. Although opening an account is fairly simple, it's a good idea to keep your old checking account current until you've completed the task of setting up a new one here. This can be particularly important if you're going to try to rent a home or apartment before opening a local account; many landlords won't accept a tenant who doesn't have a bank account.

You'll probably want to call around to find out about special promotions; many banks offer special deals or extra perks for opening a checking account. But be sure to find out when the promotion ends and what the normal rates are. Debit cards, often displaying a VISA or MasterCard symbol, take the place of a written check, deducting the amount of your purchase directly from your checking account, usually at no charge. They can be used as an ATM card for cash withdrawals and deposits, but be aware that using ATM machines that are not owned by your bank can often incur fees. Most banks in the Seattle area charge non-members a fee to use their ATM machines. This charge can range from $3.00 to $5.00.

To open a checking account, you'll need to apply at the bank's website, or visit a local branch office and bring the minimum deposit required (this amount varies from bank to bank, so call ahead). You will also need photo ID and proof of address (a letter or utility bill mailed to your new address, or your rental contract).

You may also want to open a savings account in addition to your checking account. With some banks, you will save on fees by having two accounts at the same location. Other services offered by banks include credit cards, loans, mortgages, lines of credit, and online bill paying. The largest Seattle banks offer the convenience of branches throughout the Puget Sound area. There are also many smaller community banks offering competitive rates and services. You may find membership in a credit union more appealing, with better interest rates, lower loan fees, and low-fee checking. Most of the following area banks have several branch offices in the city and surrounding communities:

- **Bank of America**, 800-442-6680, www.bankofamerica.com
- **Banner Bank**, 800-272-9933, www.bannerbank.com
- **Cascade Bank**, 800-326-8787, www.cascadebank.com
- **Chase**, 800-935-9935, www.chase.com
- **Citibank**, 800-374-9700, www.citibank.com
- **Columbia Bank**, 877-272-3678, www.columbiabank.com
- **East West Bank**, 888-895-5650, www.eastwestbank.com
- **HomeStreet Bank**, 800-719-8080, www.homestreet.com
- **KeyBank**, 800-539-2968, www.key.com
- **Peoples Bank**, 800-584-8859, www.peoplesbank-wa.com
- **Seattle Bank**, 888-500-2265, www.seattlebank.com
- **Sound Community Bank**, 800-458-5585, www.soundcb.com
- **Sterling Savings Bank**, 800-772-7791, www.sterlingsavingsbank.com
- **Umpqua Bank**, 866-486-7782, www.umpquabank.com
- **US Bank**, 800-685-5065, www.usbank.com
- **Viking Bank**, 206-784-2200 (Ballard, one of multiple locations), www.vikingbank.com
- **Washington Federal**, 800-324-9375, www.washingtonfederal.com
- **Wells Fargo**, 800-869-3557, www.wellsfargo.com

CREDIT UNIONS

A low-cost alternative to a bank checking account is a similar type of account at a credit union, where rates are often higher and fees lower. Formerly, you had to belong to a union or an employee organization to have access to these consumer-friendly nonprofits, but recent rule changes have relaxed membership requirements to allow wider access to credit unions. In many cases, all you need is to be a state or county resident. Contact information for local credit unions is listed here:

- **Alaska USA Federal Credit Union**, 800-525-9094, www.alaskausa.org
- **Boeing Employees Credit Union**, 800-233-2328, www.becu.org
- **Cascade Federal Credit Union**, 800-562-2853, www.cascadefcu.org

- **Prevail Credit Union**, 800-248-6928, www.prevailcu.com
- **Qualstar Credit Union**, 800-848-0018, www.qualstarcu.com
- **Salal Credit Union**, 800-562-5515, www.salalcu.org
- **School Employees Credit Union of Washington**, 888-628-4010, www.secuwa.org
- **Seattle Metropolitan Credit Union**, 800-334-2489, www.smcu.com
- **Verity Credit Union**, 800-444-4589, www.veritycu.com
- **Washington State Employees Credit Union**, 800-562-0999, www.wsecu.org

INTERNET AND ONLINE BANKING

While online banking has been provided by traditional brick-and-mortar banks for years, there is a new breed of institutions, the Internet-only banks. These are banks without brick-and-mortar counterparts, and while some believe they are the future of banking, traditional institutions don't seem to be in immediate danger. While many people still like knowing that their bank has a branch in their neighborhood or city, an increasing number take advantage of the online banking services provided by their bank.

Even if you choose to do most of your banking at a traditional bank, it might be worth your while to investigate an Internet bank for high interest rate products like CDs, though be sure to read the fine print carefully. Most offer introductory rates that will change after your account has been established for a specified time. Also be aware that Internet banking can be convenient if you have payroll direct deposit, but if you need to deposit checks you will have to send them in by mail in prepaid envelopes and wait for your funds to be available. The following are some of the institutions that offer interest-bearing checking and savings accounts:

- **Ally**, 877-247-2559, www.ally.com
- **Bank of Internet USA**, 877-541-2634, www.bankofinternet.com
- **EverBank**, 888-882-3837, www.everbank.com
- **HSBC**, 800-875-4722, www.us.hsbc.com
- **ING Direct**, 800-464-3473, www.ingdirect.com
- **NetBank**, 888-256-6932, www.netbank.com

CONSUMER PROTECTION

If you have a problem with your financial institution, first try to resolve the issue through their customer service department or with a bank officer. If the matter concerns a discrepancy on your statement, time is usually important. Find out how long you have to resolve the situation, and file a written complaint with the bank as soon as possible. If attempts to resolve the issue are unsuccessful, call the Washington State Attorney General's Office, Consumer Protection Division complaints hotline at 800-551-4636, or visit www.atg.wa.gov. Another good resource for banking regulations and how to protect yourself from fraud is the Washington State Department of Financial Institutions, which regulates banks, credit unions, mortgage lenders and other financial services providers. You can also file a complaint about a company by calling 877-746-4334 or visiting www. dfi.wa.gov.

CREDIT CARDS

As soon as you've established a new address in Seattle, chances are you'll start receiving plenty of credit card offers in the mail. In the unlikely event they don't find you, here are credit card companies you can contact:

- **American Express**, 800-528-4800, www.americanexpress.com
- **Department store credit cards**, check at the customer service counter or at the checkout counter, or apply online. Many stores offer a discount on your first purchase, with some restrictions. Department store cards are sometimes easier to qualify for than traditional credit cards, and can be used to establish a credit history if you have none. Seattle-area department stores that offer credit cards include Macy's (www.macys.com), Nordstrom (www.nordstrom. com), JC Penney (www.jcpenney.net), Sears (www.sears.com), and Target (www.target.com).
- **Diner's Club International**, 800-234-6377, www.dinersclubinternational. com
- **Discover Card**, 800-347-2683, www.discovercard.com
- **MasterCard and VISA**, www.mastercard.com, www.usa.visa.com; most banks offer one or both of these two major credit cards, and you can sign up for the card when opening your bank account. However, you may be able to find a more competitive interest rate by shopping around. See **Additional Credit Card Resources** below.

A word of warning to credit card users: the biggest revenue sources for credit card issuers are penalty charges for late credit card payments. If you want to avoid high finance charges, determine your grace period—the period between the end of a billing cycle and the payment due date—and pay off your balance within this period. For some cards, grace periods have been eliminated (often the case for cards issued with rewards programs, such as university cards or frequent-flyer cards). Another method to calculate finance charges compounds interest daily instead of monthly. Called "daily periodic rate" billing, this may only squeeze a few extra pennies out of you, but they're still your pennies. Since credit card issuers are always coming up with new ways to improve their profits, be sure to read the fine print in your contract. For additional consumer information, access **CardWeb**, 239-325-5300, www.cardweb.com, or the **Consumer Action** organization, www.consumer-action.org.

ADDITIONAL CREDIT CARD RESOURCES

A list of low-rate card issuers can be found on the Internet at **CardWeb**, the **Consumer Action** site, **Bankrate.com** (www.bankrate.com), and **iMoneynet.com** (www.imoneynet.com).

To see your personal credit report, go to **www.annualcreditreport.com**. At this site, you can receive a free copy of your credit report from the three main credit bureaus once a year. You can also visit each credit bureau individually:

* **Equifax**, 800-685-1111, www.equifax.com
* **Experian**, 888-397-3742, www.experian.com
* **TransUnion Corporation**, 800-493-2392, www.transunion.com

PREPAID DEBIT CARDS

An alternative to credit cards, and the fastest growing payment method in the United States, is prepaid debit cards. These are cards with a MasterCard or Visa logo that are bought online, at banks, or at retailers like Rite-Aid or Walgreens, and are also called "stored value" cards. You load money on the card, depending on the limits set by the issuer, and use the card the same way you would any debit or credit card. You can reload money at any time, but shop around for the best fees as most cards have a monthly charge, as well as fees, to reload money. For the credit challenged, most of these cards don't require credit checks. However, because prepaid card use is not reported to major credit card bureaus, they won't help establish a user's credit history or credit score, which can make it difficult to get a loan later on. The major advantage of a prepaid debit card is not being able to spend what you don't have, and some issuers target parents of teens, touting the advantage of using a prepaid card over handing out a cash allowance. The following are some of the better-known prepaid cards:

* **Green Dot**, 866-795-7597, www.greendotonline.com
* **Mango Financial**, 877-896-2646, www.mangomoney.com
* **NetSpend**, 86NETSPEND (866-387-7363), www.netspend.com
* **SmartyPig**, 888-567-6278, www.smartypig.com
* **Western Union PrePaid MasterCard,** 800-325-6000, www.westernunion.com

TAXES

SALES TAX

Washington state residents do not pay a state income tax. Instead, there is a high sales tax (6.5% to 9.5%) that is charged on all purchases other than food and most prescription drugs. The sales tax is a combination of state and local taxes, so the rate varies by municipality and region, but is among the highest in the nation. In Seattle, the combined sales tax rate is 9.5% (6.5% for the state, and 3% for the city and the Regional Transit Authority). After you've lived here for a while, you'll get used to paying more than the listed price for most items.

FEDERAL INCOME TAX

The IRS's Live Telephone Assistance, 800-829-1040, is available for consumers with questions and/or in need of forms or help with forms. For free publications about IRS tax services, call 800-829-3676. During tax season, IRS forms are available at local libraries and post offices. You can also find forms online at www.irs.gov. When filing federal tax forms, the following numbers may be useful:

- Where's My Refund?, 800-829-1040
- Washington State Department of Revenue, 800-647-7706

If you need more help than you think you can get online or over the phone, you can go to a local Taxpayer Assistance Center. While you can call ahead for an appointment, taxpayers are welcome to drop in any time during business hours, from 8:30 a.m. to 4:30 p.m. Centers in the Puget Sound area:

- **Seattle**, 915 2nd Ave, 206-220-6015
- **Bellevue**, 520 112th Ave NE, 425-456-9637
- **Everett**, 3020 Rucker Ave, 425-304-1656
- **Tacoma,** 1201 Pacific Ave, 253-428-3518

ELECTRONIC INCOME TAX FILING

Record numbers of taxpayers took advantage of e-filing in 2010, according to the IRS. Nearly 99 million people filed their taxes electronically. With tax software, such as TurboTax, widely available, and many online options for filing, e-filing has never been more convenient, or so heavily encouraged by the IRS. The IRS website offers links to authorized providers, payment and direct deposit options, calculators, and more. You can even check the status of your refund online. Telephone filing is no longer available, but in its place is a service called Free File. Companies listed on the IRS site offer free online filing for taxpayers with an adjusted gross income (AGI) of $58,000 or less. Eligibility and services vary from company to company, so be sure to read their guidelines carefully to find out if you qualify and if the services are right for you. Visit www.irs.gov for more information.

STARTING OR MOVING A BUSINESS

When Boeing decided to move its corporate headquarters from Seattle to Chicago in 2001, the company cited traffic, education, and taxes as its top complaints. However, according to the Small Business Survival Index released by the Small Business Survival Committee in 2010, Washington was the fifth most entrepreneur-friendly state, and the Small Business Tax Climate Index ranked Washington 11th best in the United States in 2011. That year, the Seattle-Bellevue-Everett area was 32nd on Inc.com's national list of Best Large Cities for Doing Business.

Business owners in Washington are subject to a business and occupation (B&O) tax and/or a public utility tax. These are based on the gross receipts of the business and the rates vary depending on the type of business. The tax can be manageable for established companies, but hard on start-up companies that have yet to show a profit. The Washington Alliance for a Competitive Economy notes that business taxes are high, and a 2010 study for the Council on State Taxation found that "state and local business taxes in Washington amount to 5.4 percent of Gross State Product, significantly higher than the U.S. average of 5.0%." One bright note is that the state lacks a corporate and a personal income tax. An amnesty period between February 1 and April 18, 2011, helped ease the strain on business owners by allowing them to pay their taxes late without incurring penalties or interest.

If you do choose to start a business in Washington, the state has created a simple, one-stop system called the Business Licensing Service that will walk you through the process, with all of the checklists, forms, and resources you'll need. For details, visit the Department of Revenue at http://dor.wa.gov, or call 800-647-7706. Other good resources for starting, operating, expanding, or relocating a business within Washington include:

- **Access Washington**, http://access.wa.gov
- Washington Small Business Development Center, 509-358-7765, www.wsbdc.org
- **Washington State Department of Commerce**, 206-256-6100, www.choosewashington.com

NCE YOU'VE FOUND A PLACE TO CALL HOME, YOU'LL NEED TO arrange phone service, electric and/or gas accounts, trash pick-up, and so on. Most of your utilities can be hooked up with a phone call, although in some cases you may be required to mail or fax documents. Other services in this chapter, such as auto registration or photo ID, will require a visit to an office but you can probably live without these for a few days or even weeks. Also included in this chapter: a list of broadcast media; passport, voter, and library registration details; assistance with finding a doctor and/or vet; and consumer protection and safety information.

UTILITIES

ELECTRICITY

Seattle City Light (206-684-3000, 206-684-3225 [TTY], www.seattle.gov/light) supplies electricity for all residences within the city limits. Seattle City Light offers four ways to open a new account. You can handle it by phone using one of the following numbers: 206-684-3000, 800-862-1181, 206-684-3225 (TTY); or download a form online and fax it to 206-684-3347 or mail it to Seattle City Light Customer Service Center, 700 5th Ave, Ste 3300, Seattle 98124-4023. You can also set up your new account completely online, where you can transfer service and close accounts as well. You will also need to get a meter reading at your new address. You can do this by reading the meter yourself, paying a fee to have Seattle City Light do it for you, or let them estimate the reading for free.

Outside the Seattle city limits, **Puget Sound Energy** (888-225-5773, 800-962-9498 [TTY], www.pse.com) provides electrical service for the remainder of King County and much of Pierce County. Customer service is accessible any time of day at the above numbers. Multilingual representatives are available.

In Tacoma, electric service is provided by **Tacoma Power** (253-502-8600, www.mytpu.org). Tacoma Power also covers Fircrest, University Place, Fife, and parts of Steilacoom, Lakewood, and unincorporated Pierce County. In **Snohomish County**, including Everett, contact the Snohomish County Public Utility District (www.snopud.com, 425-783-1000; 425-783-8660 [TTY], or toll free in western Washington at 877-783-1000), Monday through Friday, 8 a.m. to 5:30 p.m.

NATURAL GAS OR OIL HEAT

In Seattle, heating options are electric, natural gas, or oil. Most likely you will go with whatever is already at your new house, apartment, or condominium. Unless the cost is included in your rent or condominium dues, you will be responsible for setting up a new account and for filling the existing tank (if using oil). If you decide to install a new furnace, water heater, or stove, you must be home for the line hook-up. If you choose the same fuel as the previous resident, just call for service; the gas or oil company will handle the rest. Natural gas is supplied to Seattle and Seattle suburbs by **Puget Sound Energy**, 888-225-5773, www.pse.com.

Heating oil may be purchased from any of several local companies; a few are listed here. Check the Yellow Pages or online for additional companies.

- **Ballard Oil Co.**, 206-783-0241, www.ballardoil.com
- **Cascade Oil Company**, 206-323-6050, 800-823-6050, www.cascadeoil.com
- **Glendale Heating**, 800-392-7687, www.glendaleheating.com
- **Laurelhurst Oil**, 206-523-4500, www.laurelhurstoil.com
- **Olson Energy Service**, 206-782-5522, www.olsonenergy.com
- **Rossoe,** 206-725-7555, www.rossoe.com

TELEPHONE

With the prevalence of mobile phone service today, fewer people have or need landlines in their homes. Residential telephone service is often bundled with access to high-speed and wireless Internet and cable TV. For those who want a designated residential line, the following companies provide local telephone service:

- **CenturyLink (formerly Qwest),** 800-475-7526, 800-223-3131 (Voice and TTY); call 8 a.m. to 6 p.m., weekdays to set up your account, or go to www.qwest.com, to order service online.
- **Comcast,** 800-266-2278; call anytime, or visit www.comcast.com

- **Verizon,** 800-922-0204; call Monday through Sunday, 6 a.m. to 11 p.m., or order online at www22.verizon.com.
- **Vonage,** 888-692-8078; call anytime or visit www.vonage-promotions.com

Be prepared with the following information: home address, preferred long distance company, and information on your previous phone account (including your former address and telephone number). A deposit may be required when you set up service depending on your credit status and previous telephone service history.

AREA CODES

The area code in Seattle, and just north and south of the city limits, is 206. A large group of cities located to the north, east, and south of Seattle uses the 425 area code. In cities farther south, like Kent and Tacoma, the area code is 253. Other areas in western Washington use 360 (both north and south of Seattle). East of the Cascades the area code is 509. Long distance calls require 11 digits (1 + area code + number).

The following area codes represent the Seattle local calling area and surrounding communities:

- **206**: Bainbridge Island, Des Moines, Kirkland, Redmond, Richmond Beach, Seattle, Vashon
- **253**: Auburn, Des Moines, Kent, Tacoma
- **425**: Ames Lake, Bellevue, Bothell, Duvall, Everett, Issaquah, Kent, Kirkland, Lynnwood, Maple Valley, North Bend, Redmond, Renton, Snoqualmie

LONG DISTANCE

Long distance service providers frequently advertise very low per-minute rates, but be sure to read the fine print. If you have to pay $5.95 a month to get the five-cents-per-minute deal, and you don't make many long distance calls, it may make more sense for you to use a prepaid calling card—or even your cell phone for long distance. For help comparing long distance and wireless calling plans, visit the *Consumer Reports* website at www.consumerreportst.org. Major long distance service providers include:

- **AT&T**, 800-222-0300, www.att.com
- **Comcast,** 800-266-2278
- **MCI/Verizon**, 800-444-3333, www.mci.com
- **Skype,** www.skype.com
- **Sprint**, 866-866-7509, www.sprint.com

CELLULAR PHONES

There are many choices for cellular service in Seattle. Shop around, as rates and telephone prices can vary widely, and always ask about current promotions or discounts before committing yourself to a contract. If you will be working for a large company or government agency, ask your employer whether there is a company service plan. Often these offer much lower rates than you could get on your own. Listed here are some cellular companies that serve the Seattle area:

- **AT&T Wireless**, 800-222-0300, www.att.com
- **Cricket,** 800-922-5159, www.mycricket.com
- **Sprint**, 866-866-7509, www.sprint.com
- **T-Mobile**, 800-T-MOBILE, www.t-mobile.com
- **Verizon Wireless**, 855-234-5724, www.verizonwireless.com

PREPAID CELLULAR PHONE SERVICE

With only slightly higher rates and no yearly contracts, prepaid cellular phone service is catching on with those who need mobile phone service. Simply purchase a phone that comes with prepaid service and activate the service online or with a phone call. When minutes run out the service is easily replenished with a payment. Some of the bigger cellular companies like Verizon (www.verizonwireless.com) and T-Mobile (www.t-mobile.com) offer prepaid plans, and other companies like TracFone (www.tracfone.com) are exclusively prepaid. Phones may be bought online or at hundreds of retail stores like drugstores and grocery stores.

DIRECTORY ASSISTANCE

In today's Web-oriented world, directory assistance need no longer be fee-laden. An online Yellow Pages directory is available from Dex (www.dexknows.com) and numerous sites are dedicated to providing telephone listings and websites, including the following:

- www.411.com
- www.anywho.com
- www.superpages.com
- www.switchboard.com
- www.whitepages.com
- www.yellowbook.com

Of course, you can still pay to access a local or national number by dialing 411. In Washington, a directory assistance call can cost you $1.99 for two listings, for both local and national numbers.

ONLINE SERVICE PROVIDERS

There are many online service providers that offer basic Internet access and e-mail service via existing phone lines. Some of these provide free service but often bombard you with advertisements. For a complete list of Internet service providers located near you, check the Yellow Pages under "Internet Access Providers."

For high-speed Internet (aka broadband) access, consider signing up for service on a digital subscriber line (known as DSL), or via cable modem access. DSL runs over copper wires like those used for telephone calls, but on a separate line. Unlike a dial-up option, a DSL connection is always on, so logging onto the Internet is nearly instantaneous. Cable Internet access is available from cable TV providers. Like DSL, the cable modem is always on. One possible disadvantage with cable modem is that your access speed may decrease if your neighbors also use cable. Before you sign up for cable modem, ask the provider what speed they guarantee.

Whatever type of connection you select, here are a few questions you may want to ask:

- What must the provider do to your home when installing the system?
- Does the provider offer technical support?
- What are the tech support hours?
- What is the average wait on the telephone for technical support? How long is it before tech support e-mail is answered?
- Does the provider offer e-mail accounts?
- Will the provider host your website?
- What is the monthly fee?

Here are some Internet providers that offer dial-up access, DSL, and/or cable modem:

- **America Online**, 888-265-8005, www.aol.com
- **AT&T Worldnet Service**, 800-524-8500, www.att.com
- **Comcast**, 800-COMCAST, www.comcast.com
- **Drizzle,** 206-447-2702, 877-255-4767, www.drizzle.com
- **Earthlink**, 866-383-3080, www.earthlink.net
- **CenturyLink (formerly Qwest) Internet Services**, 800-475-7526, www.centurylink.com
- **Juno,** 800-879-5866, www.juno.com
- **Seanet**, 800-973-2638, www.seanet.com
- **Verizon**, 888-588-0875, www.verizon.net

WATER

Seattle Public Utilities supplies drinking water to more than 1.4 million people in the Seattle/King County area. If you are renting, the property owner must notify the utility of changes in occupancy, but it's likely you will be responsible for the monthly bill. If you have purchased a home, you must change the current service to your name. Call 206-684-3000, Monday through Friday, 7:30 a.m. to 6 p.m., or visit www.seattle.gov/util. The charge for water usage can amount to a significant portion of your utilities bill. For suggestions about how to conserve water, see the **Green Living** chapter of this guide.

According to Seattle Public Utilities, the water it provides—which is supplied by the Cedar River and Tolt River watersheds—meets or exceeds all federal drinking water quality standards. The Cedar River Watershed, 143 square miles in size, at an elevation ranging from 538 feet to 5,447 feet, collects between 57 and 140 inches of precipitation each year and supplies over 65% of the area's drinking water. The South Fork Tolt River in the foothills of the Cascades east of Carnation, at an elevation ranging between 760 and 5,535 feet, collects between 90 and 160 inches of precipitation each year and supplies about 30% of Seattle's drinking water.

Like electricity, water service outside Seattle is provided by local public utility districts or private companies. If you live outside the Seattle Public Utilities district, the Department of Ecology recommends that you call the city nearest you to determine your supplier. See the **Useful Phone Numbers and Websites** chapter to contact your local government office.

If you have questions or concerns about water quality, call King County **Environmental Health Services** (206-205-4394) or the state **Department of Ecology** (425-649-7000). For current reports on water quality and legislative activity related to the state's water supply, visit the Department of Health's Office of Drinking Water website at www.doh.wa.gov/ehp/dw.

GARBAGE AND RECYCLING

Seattle Public Utilities provides trash and recycling services. The Seattle Municipal Code requires that all residents have garbage containers and pay for garbage collection. Charges appear every other month on a combined utility bill, along with water and sewer fees. Garbage is collected once a week on an assigned day. The cost of the service depends on the number and size of garbage containers. It is important to note that recycling is mandatory in Seattle and the city will provide recycling containers and pickup at no charge. You can be fined for putting recyclables in your regular garbage. Call 206-684-3000 for customer service or recorded information on rates and services. To view a rate table, visit www.seattle.gov/util/services.

For most apartments and condominiums, sanitation and recycling fees are included in your monthly rent or dues. For single-family residences, you must buy a garbage can from the city or from a hardware store, and you must set up service with the city. Charges vary from $16.55 to $79.20 depending on the size of your container. Backyard collection is available at higher rates. There are also charges for additional garbage collected beyond your usual level of service. Yard waste is collected every week, on your regular garbage day. The city requires that yard waste be contained in rigid cans, placed in compostable bags, or bundled with twine. A monthly charge of $8.35 covers the 96-gallon container provided by the city; smaller containers cost less. Food scraps, including meat, fish, eggshells, and bones, as well as food-soiled paper such as napkins and greasy pizza boxes is allowed in yard waste containers.

The city also offers recycling pick-ups every other week at both houses and apartments in the city, scheduled on the same day as your garbage collection day. One recycling container is provided for newspapers, mixed papers, aluminum, plastic, tin, and glass. Recycling is free in Seattle, and should go a long way toward reducing what you pay for garbage. Again, call 206-684-3000 for customer service or recorded information on services. If you live in an apartment or condominium, these services should be provided for all tenants. If you are renting or have purchased a house, the recycling containers should be with the house.

The City of Seattle runs two recycling and disposal stations. Both transfer stations are open seven days a week, except for Thanksgiving, Christmas, and New Year's Day. Each site features a web cam, so you can see how long the wait is before you go. Go to www.ci.seattle.wa.us/util for hours or directions or to access the web cams.

- **North Recycling and Disposal Station**, 1350 N 34th St
- **South Recycling and Disposal Station**, 8105 Fifth Ave S (south of First Ave South Bridge)

Residents outside Seattle should check with their local municipality regarding trash pick-up and recycling.

HAZARDOUS WASTE DISPOSAL

Hazardous waste materials, such as fluorescent light bulbs and tubes, oil-based paint, and cleaning products, should not be tossed in with your regular garbage but must be taken to one of the following designated facilities for disposal:

- **North Hazardous Waste Facility**, 12550 Stone Ave N; open Sunday, Monday, Tuesday, from 9:30 a.m. to 4:30 p.m.
- **South Hazardous Waste Facility,** 8105 Fifth Ave S; open Thursday, Friday, and Saturday, from 9:30 a.m. to 4:30 p.m. Both sites are closed on July 4th, Thanksgiving, Christmas, and New Year's Day.

There is no fee for disposing of these items. For more information call 206-296-4692 or visit the website of the King County Hazardous Waste Management Program at www.lhwmp.org. A roving **Wastemobile** makes regular visits to surrounding communities such as Bothell, Kirkland, Sea-Tac, and Vashon. To find out about the schedule, call 206-296-4692, 888-869-4233, or go to the website above.

CONSUMER PROTECTION—UTILITY COMPLAINTS

It's always a good idea to try to resolve billing or other disputes directly with the utility company. If that fails you can file a formal complaint with the appropriate consumer complaint office. A division of the Department of Neighborhoods, the **Customer Service Bureau** fields all complaints about city departments. Call the Customer Service Bureau at 206-684-8811, or fill out an online service request/complaint form at www.seattle.gov/customerservice/request.htm.

To file a complaint about a state department or independent company, contact the state **Consumer Protection Division** (800-551-4636). You may also file a complaint online, or download a complaint form at www.atg.wa.gov/consumer.

AUTOMOBILES

Details about licensing, operating and parking a car in Seattle, auto insurance, and seatbelt laws are covered here. For information about auto repair and consumer protection related to automobiles, check the **Helpful Services** chapter. Additional auto-related listings, such as auto impound numbers, parking tickets and traffic violations line, and who to call about illegally parked and/or abandoned vehicles are in the **Useful Phone Numbers and Websites** chapter.

DRIVER'S LICENSE, STATE IDENTIFICATION

You must apply for a Washington State driver's license within 30 days of becoming a resident. You are considered a resident when you establish a permanent home in the state, register to vote, receive state benefits, apply for any state license, or seek in-state tuition fees. To obtain a license for the first time, you must pass a written exam, a vision test, and a driving skills test. The fee is $45. If you have a valid driver's license from another state, bring proof of identification, fill out an application, and pay a fee to receive a Washington license. You will have to surrender your out-of-state license. If you currently live out of state, you can order a *Washington State Driver's Guide* by phone, or find it on the **Department of Licensing** website (www.dol.wa.gov; click on "Driver License," then "Getting a License," then "Driver License Testing"). The cost of a state photo ID is $20. Given the proximity of Washington State to Canada (Seattle is just a three-hour drive from Vancouver), if you don't already have a passport, you might also want to consider getting an enhanced driver license (EDL) or enhanced ID card (EID), which confirms your identity and citizenship. An EDL/ EID is an alternative to a passport, allowing reentry to the United States at land and sea border crossings. The fee for a new EDL is $60 and an EID costs $35. For more information, call 866-520-4365.

You must visit a department of licensing to obtain your license, temporary permit, EDL/EID, or photo ID card. Recent customer service improvements have greatly increased the efficiency of these offices, but you're still better off going on a weekday rather than a Saturday when the lines are longer. Bring your current (valid or expired) license, other proof of identification, and proof of state residence, such as a utility bill or rental agreement. If you've recently been married and need your name changed on your driver's license, bring your marriage certificate. Finally, don't forget to bring cash or a personal check. The Department of Licensing accepts credit cards, personal checks, and cash as payment. Most offices are open Tuesday, Wednesday, Friday, and Saturday from 8:30 a.m. to 4:30 p.m. and Thursday from 9:30 a.m. to 4:30 p.m., but office hours vary by location. Call to confirm hours of operation before you visit, or check their website (www.dol.wa.gov).

- **Bellevue/Bel-Red**, 13133 Bel-Red Rd, 425-649-4281
- **Bremerton**, 1550 NE Riddell Rd, 360-478-6975
- **Downtown Seattle (renewals only)**, 205 Spring St, 206-464-6845
- **Downtown Seattle (EDL/EIDs only)**, 1000 2nd Ave, 866-520-4365
- **Everett**, 5313 Evergreen Way, 425-356-2966
- **Federal Way**, 1617 324th St, 253-661-5001
- **Kent**, 25410 74th Ave S, 253-872-2782
- **Lynnwood**, 18023 Hwy 99, Ste E, 425-672-3406
- **North Bend**, 402 Main Ave S, 425-888-4040
- **Renton**, 1314 Union Ave NE, Ste 4, 425-277-7231
- **Shoreline (limited services)**, 18551 Aurora Ave N, Ste 100, 425-670-8375
- **Tacoma South**, 6402 S Yakima Ave, Ste C, 253-593-2990
- **West Seattle**, 8830 25th Ave SW, 206-764-4143

Seniors and disabled persons may apply for a City of Seattle identification card, entitling them to discounts in the Seattle area. Call the **Mayor's Office for Senior Citizens** (206-684-0500) for more information about the Gold Card for Healthy Aging (for residents age 60 and above) and the FLASH card (for disabled adults).

AUTO REGISTRATION

You must license your automobile or motorcycle within 30 days of becoming a Washington resident, even if the tabs from your previous state of residence are still valid. The fine for driving an unregistered vehicle is a minimum of $330.

The cost of licensing your vehicle in Washington is a basic license fee of $30. In addition, you will pay various filing, county, and state fees totaling approximately $30. You may pay a $10 surcharge if you get your registration from a sub-agent (often worth the additional charge for the added efficiency; see below), and a $15 emissions test charge (for vehicles manufactured after 1967; see below). The **State of Washington Department of Licensing** web-page (www.dol.wa.gov) offers tips on vehicle, vessel, and driver's licensing; contact them at P.O. Box 9030, Olympia, 98507-9030, 360-902-3600, 360-664-0116 (TTY). For more information on vehicle licensing in Washington, contact the **King County License and Regulatory Service Division** (500 4th Avenue, Room 401, 206-296-4000, www.metrokc.gov/lars/autoboat).

VEHICLE/VESSEL LICENSE SUB-AGENTS

- **Bellevue: Bel-Red Auto License**, 15600 NE 8th Ste O-14, 425-747-0444
- **Bothell: Canyon Park Vehicle Licensing Agency**, 20631-D Bothell-Everett Hwy, 425-481-7113; Worthington Licensing, 10035 NE 183rd St, 425-481-1644
- **Edmonds: Edmonds Auto License Agency**, 550 5th Ave S, 425-774-6657
- **Everett: Bev's Auto Licensing Inc.**, 9111 Evergreen Way, 425-353-5333; Julie's Licensing Service, 1001 N Broadway, Ste A-7, 425-252-3518; Snohomish County Auditor Auto License, 3000 Rockefeller Ave, 425-388-3371; Village Licensing, 9327 4th St NE, Ste 7, 425-334-7311
- **Federal Way: Federal Way Auto License Agency**, 32610 17th Ave S, Ste C4, 253-874-8375
- **Kent: Kent License Inc.**, 331 Washington Ave S, 253-852-3110
- **Kirkland: Eastside Auto License**, 12006 NE 85th St, 425-828-4661
- **Lakewood: Active Military/Civilian Agency**, 12500 Bridgeport Way SW, 253-588-7786; Military Retired Bureau, 10644 Bridgeport Way SW, 253-588-9049; Lakewood Vehicle/Vessel Licensing, 10102 Bristol Ave SW, 253-588-7786
- **Lynnwood: Lynnwood Auto License Agency**, Fred Meyer, 4615 196th St SW, Ste 150, 425-774-7662
- **Mountlake Terrace: McMahan License Agency**, 22911 56th Ave W, 425-670-3874
- **Renton: Renton License Agency**, 329 Williams Ave S, 425-228-5640
- **Seattle: Ballard Licensing Agency**, 2232 NW Market St, 206-781-0199; Bill Pierre License Agency, 12531 30th Ave NE, 206-361-5505; Georgetown License Agency, 5963 Corson Ave S, Ste 162, 206-767-7782; Puget Sound License Agency, 3820 Rainier Ave S, Ste C, 206-723-9370; University License Agency, 5615 Roosevelt Way NE, 206-522-4090; Wendel's License and Service, 13201 Aurora Ave N, St206-362-6161; West Seattle License, 5048 California Ave SW, 206-938-3111; White Center License Agency, 10250 16th Ave SW, 206-763-7979
- **Snoqualmie: Sno-Falls Licensing**, 9025 Meadow Brook Way SE, 425-888-8705

- **Tacoma: Parkland Licensing Agency**, 215 Garfield St S, 253-537-3112; Pierce County Auditor Auto License, 2401 S 35th St, Ste 200, 253-798-3649; Quik Stop Licensing II, 6722 W 19th St (University Place), 253-564-6555
- **Vashon Island: Vashon Island Vehicle Licensing Agency**, Island Mall Building, 206-463-9170
- **Woodinville: Woodinville License Agency**, 17403 139th Ave NE, 425-486-0289

EMISSIONS TEST INFORMATION

In Clark, King, Pierce, Snohomish, and Spokane counties, most vehicles must pass an emissions test every other year, even if the vehicle is certified in another state. The fee for testing is $15 and can be paid in cash, or with a check, credit, or debit card. Testing station hours are Monday through Friday, 9 a.m. to 5 p.m., and Saturday, 9 a.m. to 1 p.m. The list below is for testing stations in King County. For additional sites and more information, call the state **Department of Ecology** at 425-649-7000, or visit the agency's website: www.ecy.wa.gov

- **Auburn**, 3002 "A" St SE, 253-939-1225
- **Bellevue**: 15313 SE 37th St, 425-644-1803
- **Redmond**: 18610 NE 67th Ct, 425-882-3317
- **Renton**: 805 SW 10th St, 425-228-6453
- **Seattle**: 12040 Aurora Ave N, 206-362-5173; 3820 6th Ave S, 206-624-1254

AUTOMOBILE INSURANCE

The State of Washington requires drivers to have automobile insurance for all owned or leased vehicles, providing liability coverage for damage to the other driver's vehicle, as well as bodily damage to the driver and passengers of the other car. Minimum requirements are $25,000 for bodily injury to the other driver; $50,000 for total bodily injury to driver and all passengers; and $10,000 for property damage to the other driver's car. The fine for not carrying automobile insurance is steep, at $450. You are required to show proof of insurance if stopped for a moving violation or if involved in an automobile accident. Coverage is available from area and national insurance companies. Contact your homeowners' insurance agent first, and ask about a possible discount for carrying multiple policies with the same company. Check the Yellow Pages under "Insurance" or search online for listings of area companies. The **Washington State Insurance Commissioner** provides a free online consumer guide to auto insurance at www.insurance.wa.gov.

AUTOMOBILE SAFETY

Washington is a pretty safe place for drivers. In 2010, traffic fatalities reached an all-time low, after the state established a plan called Target Zero, aiming to eliminate all traffic fatalities by 2030. According to the state Traffic Safety Commission, the declining number of deaths on Washington roads is the result of public education campaigns, highway safety projects, and strenuous enforcement of traffic laws.

When highway accidents do occur, they are often caused by the combination of drinking and driving. In 2009, alcohol-related deaths accounted for 42% of the state's traffic fatalities. In comparison, the national percentage for alcohol-related fatalities was 32%. While dropping the legal blood alcohol level for drivers to 0.08% in 1999 and enacting new laws slowed the rate of deaths, driving under the influence remains a problem.

According to the Washington State Patrol, the new laws give police more power when arresting people charged with DUI (Driving Under the Influence), allowing them to suspend driver's licenses, impound vehicles, and pursue drivers across state lines. The rules also require breath-triggered ignition locks, for at least a year, for those drivers convicted of DUI with alcohol levels above 0.15%, and limit to once in a lifetime the opportunity to avoid DUI prosecution by entering an alcohol-treatment program.

Distracted driving is a new and growing problem. A recent study by the National Safety Council determined that 28% of traffic accidents occur while people talk on cell phones or send text messages while driving. State legislation passed in 2010 made it a primary offense to talk or text on a wireless device that is not hands-free while driving, which means that the police can pull you over for that reason alone. If an officer sees you holding your phone or PDA, you can be pulled over and ticketed to the tune of $124.

Washington also regulates the use of seat belts and child restraints. Every person riding in a motor vehicle must wear a seat belt. Driving without a seat belt is considered a primary offense. The fine for driving without a seat belt is $124. Child guidelines are: kids under one year or less than 20 pounds must ride in a rear-facing infant seat; kids between one and four years, or up to 40 pounds, must be in a forward-facing safety seat; and kids between four and six, or up to 60 pounds, must ride in a booster seat. For tips on properly installing car seats check with your local fire department or go to www.safekids.org.

PARKING

Parking in Seattle can be challenging at times. Leaving your vehicle for a few hours in the business district can be very expensive, with the average lot charging $7.50 for two hours. Street parking is also available throughout downtown, at a cost of $4.00 per hour, but be sure to read the signs carefully. Some streets restrict parking during the busiest traffic hours; other parking meters have special time restrictions or fees. Parking fines are not insignificant: $42 for a street parking infraction. (See below for more about parking tickets.) The good news on street parking downtown is that you only need to pay between 8 a.m. and 8 p.m. Monday–Saturday, and 8 a.m. to 6 p.m. in other areas of the city. Meters are free on Sundays and holidays. Outside of the city's commercial core, on-street parking is more affordable, starting at $1.00 per hour in neighborhoods such as Greenlake and Roosevelt.

If you'll be commuting to downtown Seattle, your least expensive—and possibly most convenient—option may be to take the bus. Metro transit's online Trip Planner will help you tailor your route (http://tripplanner.kingcounty. gov). If that's not practical, consider setting up or joining a carpool and take advantage of reduced parking fees. Call **City of Seattle Commuter Services** (206-386-4648) to arrange for a carpool parking permit. Downtown carpool parking costs range from $300 to $600 per quarter (three months); vanpool parking, which costs just $5 a quarter, is far more popular. (See **Transportation** for more information.) Your employer may offer discounts at nearby parking lots or offer incentives to carpool or ride mass transit. You can also research your options on Rideshare (www.rideshareonline.com, 888-814-1300), an excellent resource for commuting options in the Northwest, which provides free carpool and vanpool ride-matching services, as well as bus/rail options.

If you prefer to drive to work by yourself, arrange to rent a space in a parking lot or garage. Street parking is too expensive and inconvenient for all-day parking. Here is a partial list of downtown parking garages.

- **1111 3rd Avenue Garage,** 1111 3rd Ave, 206-623-0226
- **4th & Columbia Parking,** 723 4th Ave, 206-622-7373
- **Broadway Market Garage,** 806 E Harrison, 206-324-0107
- **Grand Hyatt Self Parking,** 1508 7th Ave, 206-652-1451
- **IBM Building Garage,** 1200 5th Ave, 206-623-2675
- **Impark,** 2020 5th Ave, 206-448-9992
- **Key Tower Garage,** 700 5th Ave, 206-628-9042
- **Parking at Pacific Place,** 600 Pine St, 206-652-0416
- **Public Market Parking,** 1531 Western St, 206-621-0469
- **Russell Investment Parking Garage,** 1301 2nd Ave, 206-261-8444
- **Seattle Tower Garage,** 3rd Ave at University St, 206-624-2473
- **Securities Building Garage,** 1922 3rd Ave, 206-623-9937; 1913 4th Ave, 206-269-0762
- **Third Avenue Building Garage,** 1111 Third Ave, 206-623-0226
- **U-Park: Tower Lot,** 1825 7th Ave; 7th Ave & Marion St; 100 4th Ave S, 206-284-9797
- **Union Square Garage,** 601 Union St, 206-447-5664
- **Union Station Parking Garage,** 550 4th Ave S, 206-652-4602

RESIDENTIAL PARKING PERMITS

In Seattle proper, residential neighborhood parking can be a problem in some areas. Although there is still free street parking in residential neighborhoods, restrictions are common. Restricting parking on busy streets is done to keep traffic flowing, and parking time limits keep spaces available for shoppers. Other restrictions that limit parking on residential streets during certain hours of the day target habitual long-term parking by people who do not live in the area. For instance, neighborhoods with popular theaters and restaurants may have evening parking restrictions; areas with office buildings or hospitals nearby may have daytime parking restrictions. If your neighborhood has restricted parking, you'll want to get a residential parking zone permit. These RPZ permits cost $65 and are usually good for two years. Call **Seattle Transportation** at 206-684-5086 for more information, or visit www.seattle.gov/transportation/parking.

PARKING TICKETS

If you get a parking ticket, you must pay it within 15 days, or you'll be charged a penalty. If you have four or more unpaid tickets, a Scofflaw Ordinance allows your car to be "booted," or immobilized with a device that locks onto the wheel. The city will also notify the state Department of Licensing and a collection agency. To pay in person, visit the Municipal Court of Seattle in the Public Safety Building, 600 5th Avenue: 8 a.m. to 5 p.m. Monday–Friday. The court will accept cash, cashier's check, money order, VISA or MasterCard. If you can't get away during business hours, there is a green deposit box in front of the building, but only cashier's checks or money orders are accepted. You can also pay your ticket at one of seven neighborhood service centers around the city. Online ticket payments are accepted, too, but you will be charged an extra $3 for that convenience. Finally, you can mail payments to the Municipal Court of Seattle, 600 5th Avenue, Room 100, Seattle, WA 98104. For more information about parking tickets, call 206-684-5600 or visit www.seattle.gov/courts.

TOWED OR STOLEN CARS

There are tow-away zones and red curbs throughout the city where you may not park, even temporarily, or you will be subject to immediate towing. There are three towing companies that provide towing service and impound lots in Seattle. If you believe that your vehicle has been impounded by order of the police department, call 206-684-5444 (have your license number ready) and you will be directed to the appropriate lot. Sometimes it can take several hours for information to reach the police department, so if you want to take immediate action you can try calling the towing companies to discover which has your vehicle.

- **ABC Towing**, 206-682-2869
- **E T Towing**, 206-622-9188
- **Lincoln Towing**, 206-364-2000

Towing fees vary, but they start at a minimum of $65 and can go much higher. If your car was towed while on private property, call the owner or manager of that property or the posted towing company number. To report a stolen vehicle, call the Seattle Police Department non-emergency line at 206-625-5011.

SOCIAL SECURITY

It is the rare American citizen who does not have a Social Security number. Non-citizens who are working or studying here will also need a number. This can be done by mail, by first calling 800-772-1213 and answering five automated questions, then mailing a completed application form with the necessary documents (the form will be sent after the initial telephone interview); or go online to www.ssa.gov. You may also visit the nearest Social Security office (see the telephone book or get the address from the 800 number above or at www.ssa.gov), no appointment necessary.

- Bring with you a certified birth certificate and two other pieces of identification: passport, driver's license, school or government ID, health insurance card, military records, an insurance policy. A Social Security employee will complete the application, and you should receive a card with your number within several weeks.
- Non-citizens need a birth certificate and/or a passport and a green card or student documentation, as well as whatever immigration documents you have. It may take a month or more to receive a card.
- If you already have a number but have lost your card, call the number above to apply for a new card.

VOTER REGISTRATION

To register to vote in Seattle, you must be at least 18 years old, a citizen of the United States, and a legal resident of the state of Washington. To vote in an upcoming election, you must register at least 29 days prior. You may register to vote online, at government offices, fire stations, neighborhood service centers, schools, and public libraries. You can also register through the mail or through the "Motor Voter" program. "Motor Voter" registration is completed when you apply for or renew your driver's license. It takes only an extra minute or two. You need not declare your political affiliation or party membership when you register. In 2011, Washington was the second U.S. state, after Oregon, to begin conducting all elections by mail. Registered voters receive ballots in the mail prior to every election. Completed ballots can be mailed back or deposited at ballot drop boxes. For more information, or to register by mail, call the Secretary of State's **Voter Information and Elections Hotline** (800-448-4881) or go to www.secstate.wa.gov/elections/register.aspx.

LIBRARY CARDS

The Seattle metropolitan area has two overlapping library systems, the Seattle Public Library and the King County Library System. Both libraries offer an extensive selection of books and other materials and, upon request, will reserve books at other libraries in their system for your use.

The **Seattle Public Library** free service area includes the City of Seattle, the City of Bothell, and most of King County. The exceptions are the cities of Enumclaw, Yarrow Point, and Hunts Point. Anyone who lives, works, attends school, or owns property within the service area qualifies for a free library card. Seattle Public Library cards are available at any neighborhood library. Check the **Neighborhoods** chapter for listings of Seattle libraries near you. You must show identification, such as a driver's license or passport. If you live outside the library's free service area, you can purchase a non-resident library card for an annual fee of $85. For more information, call Borrower Services at 206-386-4190.

To borrow books from the **King County Library System (KCLS)**, you must apply for a King County Library card, which is available to anyone who lives in the KCLS service area, or in the service area of another library system that has a reciprocal borrowing agreement. This includes residents of Seattle, Renton, and Enumclaw. The KCLS service area consists of unincorporated King County and just about every city in the county. For the complete list, visit www.kcls.org. You can apply for a card at any King County Library branch or online at www.kcls.org. You must provide ID and verification of your address. Call the following for more information:

- **Seattle Public Library, Central Library**, 800 Pike St, 206-386-4636, www.spl.org
- **King County Library System**, Main Office, 960 NW Newport Way, Issaquah, WA, 800-462-9600, www.kcls.org

Seattle residents also benefit from proximity to the University of Washington and its libraries. Free services to visitors include in-library use of most materials, limited access to library computers, reference assistance, tours, and classes. Call 206-543-0242 or visit www.lib.washington.edu for more information. See the **Literary Life** section of the **Cultural Life** chapter for a list of UW libraries.

PASSPORTS

In Seattle, passports are processed at the **Seattle Passport Agency**, located downtown at the U.S. Department of State, Jackson Federal Building, 915 2nd Avenue, Suite 992, 877-487-2778 (appointment line). This office serves only those customers who are traveling within two weeks or who need foreign visas, and is by appointment only. Hours are Monday–Friday, 8 a.m. to 3 p.m. Travelers not meeting those criteria may pick up passport applications at the Lake City, University District, Ballard, Delridge, West Seattle, Southeast, or Central neighborhood service centers. Check the **Neighborhoods** chapter for locations. Bring two standard passport photos, a picture ID, and proof of U.S. citizenship, such as a previous U.S. passport, certified birth certificate, naturalization certificate or certificate of citizenship. The cost is $135 for a new passport for those 16 and older, $105 for those under 16, and $110 to renew a passport issued less than 15 years earlier. The standard turnaround time for a new passport is 25 days, but an expedited three-day passport can be requested for an additional $60 fee. For appointments and recorded information, call the Seattle Passport Agency office. To use the Internet for your passport application, go to the website for the **Bureau of Consular Affairs** (www.travel.state.gov).

TELEVISION

CABLE

Comcast, whose various services have been rebranded as XFINITY, provides cable television service to all of Seattle except for some parts of the Central District and Beacon Hill, where residents are served by **Broadstripe** (800-829-2225, www.broadstripe.com). Broadstripe also serves Duvall, the Sammamish Plateau (east of Redmond and north of Issaquah), Redmond, Issaquah, and Bellevue. Comcast/XFINITY currently offers hundreds of digital cable channels in Seattle, with similar lineups in King, Pierce, and Whatcom counties. The company also offers high-speed cable Internet access and digital phone service. Installation fees and monthly rates vary depending on which package you choose, but the company frequently offers special packages to new customers. Prices can vary widely depending on service, and the company offers discounts when you "bundle" services, such as having your cable TV, high speed Internet, and phone service all through Comcast/XFINITY. To order new service, call 800-COMCAST, or visit www.comcast.com. The website has a list of locations where you can pay your cable bill. Comcast/XFINITY office locations are listed here:

- **Auburn**, 4020 Auburn Way N
- **North Seattle,** 12645 Stone Ave N
- **Redmond**, 14870 NE 95th St
- **South Seattle**, 15241 Pacific Hwy S

LOCAL STATIONS

If you signed up for cable or satellite service, the local broadcast stations listed here may differ:

- Channel 4, KOMO-TV, ABC
- Channel 5, KING-TV, NBC
- Channel 6, KONG-TV, NBC
- Channel 7, KIRO-TV, CBS
- Channel 9, KCTS-TV, PBS
- Channel 11, KSTW-TV, CW
- Channel 13, KCPQ-TV, FOX

RADIO STATIONS

Seattle area residents love their music! The evolution of Internet radio means you can find anything you want to hear online. Here's a guide to local radio stations:

ADULT CONTEMPORARY

- KLCK, 98.9 FM
- KLSY, 92.5 FM
- KMIH, 88.9 FM
- KMTT, 103.7 FM
- KPLZ, 101.5 FM
- KRWM, 106.9 FM
- KSGX, 104.9 FM

ALTERNATIVE/MODERN ROCK

- KEXP, 90.3 FM
- KGRG, 89.9 FM
- KNDD, 107.7 FM

CHRISTIAN

- KBLE, 1050 AM
- KCIS, 630 AM
- KCMS, 105.3 FM
- KGNW, 820 AM
- KLFE, 1590 AM

CLASSICAL

- KING, 98.1 FM

COUNTRY

- KKWF, 100.7 FM
- KMPS, 94.1 FM

JAZZ, BLUES

- KBCS, 91.3 FM
- KPLU, 88.5 FM

KIDS

- KKDZ, 1250 AM

KOREAN

- KSUH, 1450 AM
- KWYZ, 1230 AM

NEWS, NPR

- KIRO, 97.3 FM, 710 AM
- KPLU, 88.5 FM
- KOMO, 1000 AM
- KSER, 90.7 FM
- KUOW, 94.9 FM

OLDIES

- KBSG, 1210 AM
- KJAQ, 96.5 FM
- KJR, 95.7 FM
- KMCQ, 104.5 FM
- KVI, 570 AM

PUBLIC AFFAIRS

- KSER, 90.7 FM

ROCK

- KISW, 99.9 FM
- KIXI, 880 AM
- KRWM, 106.9 FM
- KZOK, 102.5 FM

SPANISH

- KBRO, 1490 AM
- KKMO, 1360 AM
- KNTS, 1680 AM

- KTBK, 1210 AM

SPORTS

- KIRO, 710 AM
- KJR, 950 AM
- KRKO, 1380 AM
- KTTH, 770 AM

TALK RADIO

- KJR, 950 AM
- KKNW, 1150 AM
- KKOL, 1300 AM
- KLFE, 1590 AM
- KPTK, 1090 AM
- KTTH, 770 AM

TOP 40/DANCE

- KBKS, 106.1 FM
- KNHC, 89.5 FM

URBAN CONTEMPORARY

- KRIZ, 1420 AM
- KUBE, 93.3 FM
- KYIZ, 1620 AM

WORLD MUSIC AND FOLK

- KBCS, 91.3 FM

LOCAL NEWSPAPERS AND MAGAZINES

Once upon a time, Seattle could boast two metropolitan daily newspapers. The Seattle *Post-Intelligencer*, founded in 1863, and *The Seattle Times*, locally owned by the Blethen family since 1896, brought generations of Seattleites their news until March 17, 2009, when the last print edition of the *P-I* rolled off the presses and the paper converted to an online format. Years later, the city still mourns its passing. A beloved Seattle landmark, the giant eagle-topped globe that proclaims "It's in the P-I" still spins slowly over the paper's former headquarters on Elliott Avenue.

The following newspapers and magazines serve Seattle and surrounding communities:

- **The Herald**, 1213 California Ave, Everett, 425-339-3000, www.heraldnet.com

- *International Examiner*, www.iexaminer.org
- *Issaquah Press*, 45 Front St S, P.O. Box 1328, Issaquah, 98027, 425-392-6434, www.issaquahpress.com
- *The Kitsap Sun*, 545 5th St, Bremerton, 888-377-3711, www.kitsapsun.com
- *Mercer Island Reporter*, 7845 SE 30th St, 206-232-1215, www.mi-reporter. com
- *Newcastle News*, P.O. Box 1328, Issaquah, 98027, 425-392-6434, www. newcastle-news.com
- *Puget Sound Business Journal*, 801 2nd Ave, Ste 210, 206-876-5500, www. bizjournals.com/seattle
- *Real Change,* 96 S Main St, 206-441-3247, www.realchangenews.org
- *Seattle Daily Journal of Commerce*, 83 Columbia St, 206-622-8272, www.djc. com
- *Seattle Homes and Lifestyles*, 3240 Eastlake Ave E, Ste 200, 206-322-6699, www.seattlehomesmag.com
- *Seattle Magazine*, 1518 1st Ave S, Ste 500, 206-284-1750, www.seattlemag. com
- *The Seattle Medium,* 2600 S Jackson St, 206-323-3070, www.seattlemedium. com
- *Seattle Metropolitan Magazine*, 1201 Western Ave, Ste 425, 206-957-2234, www.seattlemet.com
- *Seattle Post-Intelligencer (online edition only)*, 101 Elliott Ave W, Ste 540, 206-448-8030, www.seattlepi.com
- *The Seattle Times*, 1120 John St, 206-464-2111, www.seattletimes.com
- *Seattle Weekly*, 1008 Western Ave, Ste 300, 206-623 0500, www. seattleweekly.com
- *Snoqualmie Valley Record*, P.O. Box 300, Snoqualmie, 425-888-2311, www. valleyrecord.com
- *The Stranger*, 1535 11th Ave, 3rd Flr, Seattle, 206-323-7101, www. thestranger.com
- *Tacoma News Tribune*, 1950 S State St, 253-597-8742, www.thenewstribune. com
- *Vashon-Maury Island Beachcomber*, 17141 Vashon Hwy SW, Ste B, 206-463-9195, http://www.vashonbeachcomber.com

FINDING A PHYSICIAN

When searching for a doctor in Seattle you will find plenty of options. Begin by determining your needs: are you looking for a general family practitioner or a specialist? An MD or a naturopath? Do you prefer the comforts of a small clinic or the more extensive services of a large hospital? And perhaps most importantly, does your health plan limit who you can see? Many new residents rely on recommendations from friends or co-workers when looking for a doctor.

Another option is to contact the **King County Medical Society** at 206-621-9396 or www.kcmsociety.org. Their website allows you to search by physician's last name, zip code, specialty, or language. Or, you can call a physician referral line or local hospital. Here is a list of local referral lines, many of which are affiliated with major area hospitals:

- **Children's Hospital and Regional Medical Center**, 866-987-2500, www.seattlechildrens.org
- **King County Medical Society**, 206-621-9396, www.kcmsociety.org
- **Northwest Hospital Physician Referral**, 206-633-4636, www.nwhospital.org
- **Overlake Hospital Medical Center**, 425-688-5211, www.overlakehospital.org
- **Pacific Medical Centers**, 888-472-2633, www.pacificmedicalcenters.org
- **Swedish Medical Center**, 800-833-8879, www.swedish.org
- **UW Medicine**, 800-852-8546, www.uwmedicine.washington.edu
- **Valley Medical Center**, 425-656-4636, www.valleymed.org
- **Virginia Mason**, 206-223-6881, www.virginiamason.org
- **Washington Association of Naturopathic Physicians**, 206-547-2130, www.wanp.org
- **Washington Osteopathic Medical Association**, 206-937-5358, www.woma.org

Should you have a **serious complaint** about a medical provider, which you cannot resolve directly with your provider, contact the **Washington Medical Quality Assurance Commission**, P.O. Box 47865, Olympia, WA 98504, 360-236-2762, or the **Washington State Board of Osteopathic Medicine and Surgery** (same address, 360-236-4700).

The Office of the Washington State Insurance Commissioner assists consumers with questions about health insurance concerns, from Medicare to HMOs to long-term care, through their **Statewide Health Insurance Benefits Advisors (SHIBA)**. Call their 24-hour consumer hotline, 800-562-6900.

PET LAWS & SERVICES

Pets in Seattle must be licensed annually, even those that generally are kept inside. A dog license costs $47.00 ($27.00 if the dog is spayed or neutered); cats are $30.00 ($20.00 if the cat is spayed or neutered). Two-year licenses are available for a discount. To qualify your pet for a license, you must provide proof that your pet has received a current rabies vaccination. The reduced license fee for a spayed or neutered pet requires a copy of a veterinarian's spay or neuter certificate. Low-income senior citizens and disabled persons with a City of Seattle ID card qualify for a 50% discount on all fees. (See the **Driver's License, State Identification** section of this chapter for more information about ID cards.)

Seattle is a very dog-friendly city—many people regularly bring their pet to work with them, and some establishments keep a full water bowl outside in case customers' dogs get thirsty. Nonetheless, all four-legged pets (except cats) must be on a leash or held by the owner when in public places in Seattle, including sidewalks. In addition, Seattle has strict "scoop laws" that require the person in charge of the animal to clean up after the pet.

Eleven city parks have "off-leash" areas where pets are allowed to roam freely, but there are a few rules. Owners must have voice control over their pets, dogs must be licensed, and poop must be scooped.

- **Dr. Jose Rizal Park**, 1008 12th Ave S
- **Genesee Park**, 4316 S Genesee St
- **Golden Gardens Park**, 8498 Seaview Place NW
- **I-5 Colonnade**, beneath I-5, south of E Howe St, between Lakeview Blvd and Franklin Ave E
- **Magnuson Park**, 7400 Sandpoint Way NE
- **Northacres Park**, 12718 1st Ave NE
- **Plymouth Pillars Park**, Boren Ave between Pike and Pine sts
- **Regrade Park**, 2251 3rd Ave
- **Sam Smith Park,** 1400 Martin Luther King Jr Way S
- **Westcrest Park**, 9000 8th Ave SW
- **Woodland Park**, 100 N 50th St

Luther Burbank Park on Mercer Island also has a popular off-leash area at 2040 84th Ave SE. One of the area's most popular dog parks is located outside the city limits in Redmond. This off-leash area at **Marymoor Park** covers over 40 acres and provides dogs with swimming and fetching opportunities. A nonprofit group, **Serve Our Dog Areas**, is dedicated to its maintenance and preservation. To volunteer, call 425-881-0148 or visit www.soda.org.

If you're interested in adopting an animal, you can visit the **Seattle Animal Shelter** at 2061 15th Avenue West (in the Interbay area), 206-386-7387. Fees range from $5 (for hamsters, birds, and snakes) to $200 depending on the size, gender, and type of animal. You must provide current photo ID, and your landlord's name and phone number if you live in a rental property. For more information about Seattle Shelter and pets available for adoption, visit the website at www.seattle.gov/animalshelter.

Organizations that may prove useful for those who have lost a pet or have found a stray are:

- **Humane Society for Seattle/King County**, 13212 SE Eastgate Way, Bellevue, 425-641-0080, www.seattlehumane.org
- **King County Animal Control Enforcement**, 206-296-7387

- **King County Animal Control Shelter**, 21615 64th Ave S, Kent, 206-296-7387, www.kingcounty.gov
- **Progressive Animal Welfare Society (PAWS)**, 15305 44th Ave W, Lynnwood, 425-787-2500, www.paws.org
- **Seattle Animal Control Hotline (Lost Pets)**, 206-386-7387, www.seattle.gov/animalshelter
- **Seattle Animal Shelter**, 2061 15th Ave W, 206-386-7387, www.seattle.gov/animalshelter

PET CARE SERVICES

If the off-leash areas in the city's parks aren't enough to convince you that Seattle has gone to the dogs in recent years, consider the rise in the canine comfort industry, and the increase in pet-sitting and dog-walking providers. If you must leave your dog or cat home alone for the day—or for weeks—consider hiring a surrogate or sending your pet to daycare.

- **2 Dogs & a Cat,** 425-379-6136, www.2dogsandacat.net
- **Adventures in Sitting Kitties**, 206-595-7473, www.sittingkitties.com
- **Bone-A-Fide Dog Ranch**, 206-501-9247, www.bone-a-fide.com
- **Central Bark**, 206-325-3525, www.central-bark.com
- **Downtown Dog Lounge**, 206-282-3647, www.downtowndoglounge.com
- **Great Dog Daycare**, 206-526-1101, www.gogreatdog.com
- **Happy Camper Pet Service**, 206-784-5291, www.happycamperpets.com
- **Hillrose Pet Resort**, 206-241-0880, www.petresort.com
- **The Pet Au Pair**, 206-200-5357, www.mypetaupair.com
- **Pet Sitters of Puget Sound**, 425-487-1697, www.petsittersofpugetsound.org
- **Raintown Pet Care,** 206-650-5228, www.raintownpetcare.com
- **While You Were Out Pet Care**, 206-297-1834, www.whileyouwereoutpetcare.com

Does your dog or cat need a ride to daycare, the vet, or a groomer? One service in town offers pet transport for a variety of needs. Try **Seattle Dog Taxi**, 425-780-9241, www.seattledogtaxi.com.

SAFETY AND CRIME

According to statistics compiled by the Seattle Police Department, in 2010, 36,706 major crimes were reported in Seattle, a 6% decrease from the previous year. Of these, 3,517 were violent crimes, with aggravated assault leading the way with 1,973. The murder rate saw a significant decrease in the 2000–2010 period, with 19 homicides reported in 2010, the lowest murder rate recorded since 1956. Property crimes—burglary, larceny, and auto theft—decreased 15% over the same ten-year period. Mere numbers don't tell the whole picture, of course. While Seattle is a relatively safe place to live (in 2009 *Forbes* magazine rated it the fourth safest large U.S. city), there are places you'd be wise to avoid after dark, such as the area surrounding Pike and Pine streets downtown. Auto theft is a crime of opportunity, so your best defense is to deny a thief the opportunity to take your automobile. Also protect yourself from car prowls or smash and grabs by not leaving anything in the car. Valuable or not, items left in cars are tempting to thieves. The Seattle Police Department Car Prowl Task Force recommends the following preventive measures:

• Always lock your car, and remove valuables when parking.
• Park in well-lighted areas, even at home.
• Park in areas of busy pedestrian traffic.
• Install an anti-theft device.
• Call 911 to report suspicious activity.

Auto thefts and car prowls notwithstanding, most Seattle neighborhoods are safe. Take precautions, however, especially in unfamiliar areas. The following safety tips may be helpful: walk quickly and with a purpose, especially at night; don't dawdle or slow your pace, even when approached, and keep clear of alleyways, deserted areas, and dead ends. If riding in a bus, stay close to the front, near the driver. Most of all, trust your instincts. If you feel uneasy about a person or situation, there may be a good reason for it. For more personal safety tips, visit the Seattle Police Department's crime page at www.seattle.gov/police.

Many neighborhoods participate in **Block Watch**, a free crime prevention and emergency preparedness program sponsored by the Seattle Police Department. Overseen by precinct coordinators, there are currently over 3,800 registered "block watches" operating throughout the city. To participate, or for more information, go to http://www.seattle.gov/police/blockwatch/default. htm.

NOW THAT YOU HAVE A PLACE TO CALL HOME, AND HAVE TAKEN care of the basics like setting up electricity and gas accounts, you might have time to investigate and benefit from some of the area's helpful services. Services such as Housecleaning, Pest Control or Automobile Repair can make your life a bit simpler. Other sections in this chapter include Postal and Shipping Services, Consumer Protection, Services for People with Disabilities, Gay and Lesbian Life and help for International Newcomers.

DOMESTIC SERVICES

For those who need a little extra help around the house, the following services might be of interest. Check the Yellow Pages for more listings.

DIAPER SERVICES

- **Baby Diaper Service**, 206-634-2229, www.babydiaperservice.net
- **Sunflower Diaper Service**, 206-782-4199

DRY CLEANING DELIVERY

- **Blue Sky Cleaners**, 1111 Elliott Ave W (one of multiple locations), 206-838-8433, www.blueskycleaners.com
- **Helena's Dry Cleaners**, 537 Warren Ave N, 206-282-0873, www.helenascleaners.com
- **Stadium Cleaners**, 3307 NE 65th St, 206-522-9125, www.stadiumcleaners.com
- **Valet Dry Cleaning to Your Door,** 4425 Fauntleroy Way SW, 206-932-2242
- **Village Cleaners**, 2929 NE Blakeley St, 206-522-1033, www.stadiumcleaners.com

HOUSECLEANING

You may decide to use a housecleaning service before you move into your new home or for routine chores on an ongoing basis. A few housecleaning businesses are listed below. As with all lists in this guide, inclusion does not indicate endorsement. If you are not satisfied with the service you receive from a company during the initial cleaning, request that they clean again at no charge.

- **April Lane's Home Cleaning**, Seattle: 206-527-4290; Eastside: 425-649-8610, www.aprillanescleaning.com
- **Attention to Detail**, 425-353-2850, www.attentiontodetailnw.com
- **Dana's Housekeeping–Housekeeper Referral Service**,866-826-3262; www.housecleaning.com
- **Maid Brigade**, 866-800-7470, www.maidbrigade.com
- **Maid in the Northwest**, Seattle: 206-527-3593th; Tacoma/Puyallup/Federal Way/Kent: 425-455-0655; Bellevue/Eastside: 425-455-0655;Everett / Edmonds/Bothell 425-337-7889; www.maidinthenw.com
- **Merry Maids**, Seattle/University District: 206-527-2984; West Seattle: 206-937-7083; North Seattle/South Snohomish County: 425-778-3355; Eastside: 425-881-6243; South King County: 253-833-6171; www.merrymaids.com
- **Mighty Maids**, West Seattle: 206-938-9662; Eastside/Renton: 425-226-1614; South King County: 253-630-2799, www.mightymaidswa.com
- **Rent-A-Yenta House Cleaning Service**, Seattle: 206-325-8902; Eastside: 425-454-1512; www.renta-yenta.com
- **Seattle Green Cleaner**, 206-499-3046, www.seattlegreencleaner.com

PEST CONTROL

Rats have long been a problem in Seattle, especially around greenbelt areas, and the pesky rodents are an increasing nuisance in the suburbs as well. If setting traps yourself hasn't worked or is not an option, consider calling an exterminator, or visit www.pestweb.com to find tips for dealing with unwelcome house "guests." These local pest control experts can also help you with carpenter ants (another local problem), as well as hornets, termites, and other pests that might be bugging you.

- **Aard Pest Control**, 206-575-3319, 425-776-3662, 425-353-5961, 800-359-6860, www.aardpestcontrol.net
- **Able Pest Control**, 206-575-9877, www.ablepestcontrol.net
- **Cascade Pest Control**, 888-989-8979, www.cascadepest.com
- **Eden Advanced Pest Technologies**, 800-401-9935, www.edenpest.com
- **Orkin**, 866-949-6097, www.orkin.com
- **Redi National Pest Eliminators**, 800-454-7334, www.redinational.net
- **Terminix**, 866-319-6528, www.terminix.com

- **United Pest Solutions,** Seattle: 206-632-1270, Eastside: 425-747-1003, www. unitedpestsolutions.com

POSTAL AND SHIPPING SERVICES

If you are between addresses and in need of a place to receive mail, you can rent a box at a local post office or choose a private receiving service. Many of the private services allow call-in mail checks and mail forwarding, but they are often more expensive than the post office.

MAIL RECEIVING SERVICES

- **Queen Anne Dispatch,** 2212 Queen Anne Ave N, 206-286-1024, www. queenannedispatch.com
- **The Mailbox**, Seattle: Ballard, 2400 NW 80th St, 206-789-7007; Magnolia, 3213 W Wheeler St, 206-285-4843
- **The UPS Store**, multiple locations include: 815 1st Ave, 206-624-3313; 1700 7th Ave, 206-624-1550; 4616 25th Ave NE, 206-524-2558; 4742 42nd Ave SW, 206-933-8038; 1037 NE 65th, 206-528-7447; 2311 N 45th St, 206-522-1970; 10002 Aurora Ave N, 206-527-5065; 410 Broadway Ave E, 206-860-0818; 1425 Broadway, 206-324-5600; 3518 Fremont Ave N, 206-547-4410; 24 Roy St, 206-282-2288, www.theupsstore.com

PACKAGE DELIVERY SERVICES

- **DHL**, 800-225-5345, www.dhl-usa.com
- **FedEx**, 800-463-3339, www.fedex.com/us
- **United Parcel Service (UPS)**, 800-742-5877, www.ups.com
- **U.S. Postal Service Express Mail**, 800-275-8777, www.usps.com

JUNK MAIL

To curtail the deluge of mail you surely will receive after relocating, register online with the **Direct Marketing Association's Mail Preference Service**. There is a $1 fee for having your name removed from marketing lists and you can also print out a form and mail it in. Visit the website at www.dmachoice.org. This should help, but you will have to contact some catalog companies directly with a purge request, and it won't affect companies who are not members of the DMA. (Keep in mind: you might actually appreciate some of the mass-market mail, as many retailers and household service providers welcome new residents with coupons and special offers.)

AUTOMOBILE REPAIR

Finding a mechanic you can trust is often difficult. The most popular way to find a shop is to ask around—co-workers, neighbors, and friends. You can also check websites such as Yelp, Judy's Book, and Angie's List for consumer reviews and recommendations. Though often pricey, auto dealers are generally reliable, and will have the right equipment and parts to work on your car. Check the Yellow Pages and online for listings.

Those considering an independent mechanic shop may want to check with the **Better Business Bureau** to determine if any complaints have been filed against it. The local chapter serves Alaska, Oregon, and Western Washington, and is located at 1000 Station Drive, Suite 222, in DuPont. Call 206-431-2222 or visit www.thebbb.org.

If it's just "advice" you need, consider tuning your radio to NPR's wildly entertaining call-in show "Car Talk." Locally, the program can be heard on KUOW, 94.9 FM, on Saturday from 9 to 10 a.m. You can also visit the show's website at www.cartalk.com.

If the question isn't who will repair your car, but rather who to call to have it towed, your best resource may be an automobile club like the **American Automobile Association**. For information about membership benefits and services, visit www.aaawa.com, or call 800-562-2582. There are three Seattle offices, located at: 4554 9th Avenue NE, 206-633-4222; 1523 15th Avenue West, 206-218-1222; and 4701 42nd Avenue SW, 206-937-8222. Additional locations are Bellevue, Bremerton, Everett, Federal Way, Issaquah, Kent, Lynnwood, Redmond, Renton, and Tacoma.

CONSUMER PROTECTION—AUTOMOBILES

If you are looking for a new car, Washington has a Lemon Law to protect owners who have "substantial or continuing problems with warranty repairs." A lemon is defined as a vehicle that has one or more substantial defects, which has been subject to a "reasonable number of attempts" to diagnose or repair the problem(s) under the manufacturer's warranty. The law does not cover problems caused by owner abuse or negligence, or any unauthorized modifications made to the vehicle. Nor does it cover some motorcycles and large commercial trucks, motor homes used as homes, office or commercial space, or vehicles purchased as part of a fleet of 10 or more. The law allows the owner to request an arbitration hearing through the office of the **Washington Attorney General** within 30 months of the vehicle's original retail delivery date. If you are not the original owner, you can still apply the lemon law if the vehicle was purchased within two years of delivery to the original retail consumer, and within the first 24,000 miles of operation. For more details, visit the Attorney General's Consumer Protection website at www.atg.wa.gov/consumer, or call 800-551-4636.

Information about vehicle recalls and crash tests can be found at the **U.S. Department of Transportation's Auto Safety Hotline**, 888-327-4236, or visit www.nhtsa.gov.

CONSUMER PROTECTION—RIP-OFF RECOURSE

Got a beef with a merchant or company? There are a number of agencies that monitor consumer-related businesses and will take action when necessary. The best defense against fraud and consumer victimization is to avoid it—read the contracts down to the smallest print, save all receipts and canceled checks, get the name of telephone sales and service people with whom you deal, check a contractor's license number with the state's Consumer Protection Division for complaints. Despite such attention to details, sometimes you still get stung. A dry cleaner returns your blue suit, but now it's purple and he shrugs. A shop refuses to refund, as promised, on the expensive gift that didn't suit your mother. After $898 in repairs to your engine, your car now vibrates wildly, and the mechanic claims innocence. Negotiations, documents in hand, fail. You're angry, and embarrassed because you've been had. There is something you can do.

- **Attorney General's Office**, Consumer Protection Division, 800 5th Ave, Ste 2000, 800-551-4636, www.atg.wa.gov/consumer; in 2010, problems with collection agencies, broadband service providers, telecommunications, retail and auto sales companies topped the list of consumer complaints received by the Attorney General's Office. The Consumer Protection Division website outlines how to resolve and file complaints. Seven neighborhood consumer resource centers are also available throughout the state.
- **Better Business Bureau**, 1000 Station Dr, Ste 222, DuPont, 206-431-2222, www.thebbb.org; the local chapter serves Western Washington, Oregon, and Alaska. The BBB can supply you with a reliability report for a business. The agency also accepts complaints when a breakdown in communication occurs between you and a business.
- **City of Seattle Department of Neighborhoods, Customer Service Bureau**, 600 4th Ave, Fl 1, 206-684-2489; www.seattle.gov/citizenservice; the Customer Service Bureau employs three complaint investigators who provide investigation, mediation, and assistance for questions and complaints about city services.
- **King County Office of Citizen Complaints**, 516 3rd Ave, Rm W1039, 206-205-6338, www.kingcounty.gov/operations/Ombudsman.aspx ; if your dispute is with a county agency, contact the county Ombudsman's Office. Though the office cannot take legal action on your behalf, they can generally resolve the matter through a fact-finding effort with the agency involved.
- **King County Small Claims Court**, King County Courthouse, 516 3rd Ave, Rm W-1034, 206-205-9200, www.kingcounty.gov/courts; with some exceptions,

an individual, business, partnership or organization can bring a small claims suit for the recovery of money only, up to $5,000. The filing fee is $35.

• **The Tenants Union**, 5425B Rainier Ave S, 206-723-0500, www.tenantsunion. org; their website provides a series of online brochures to answer renters' commonly asked questions. Phone calls are taken on Monday, Tuesday, and Wednesday from 10 a.m. to 12:30 p.m.; walk-ins to the office are taken on Monday, Tuesday, and Wednesday between 1:30 p.m. and 4 p.m.

MEDIA-SPONSORED CONSUMER ADVOCACY PROGRAMS

The following consumer advocacy and assistance programs are operated by Seattle area television stations.

• **KOMO 4 Problem Solvers**, 206-404-4799, 140 4th Ave N, http://www.ko-monews.com/news/content/5200077.html
• **KING 5 Get Jesse Jones**, 877-515-3773, 333 Dexter Ave N, www.king5.com
• **KIRO 7 Consumer Investigators**, 206-728-7777, 2807 3rd Ave, www.kirotv. com/consumer

LEGAL RESOURCES

• **Columbia Legal Services**, 101 Yesler Way, 206-464-1122, 800-542-0794, www.columbialegal.org
• **King County Lawyer Referral Service**, 206-267-7100, www.kcba.org
• **Northwest Justice Project**, 401 Second Ave S, 206-464-1519, 888-201-1012, www.nwjustice.org
• **Senior Services**, 2208 2nd Ave, Ste 100; 206-448-5720; www.seniorservices. org
• **Washington State Bar Association**, 206-443-9722, 800-945-9722; 1325 4th Ave, Ste 600; www.wsba.org
• **Washington LawHelp,** www.washingtonlawhelp.org

SERVICES FOR PEOPLE WITH DISABILITIES

There are a number of organizations in the Seattle area that serve as resources for disabled persons. The Alliance of People **with DisAbilities** offers legal services concerning civil rights violations; an employment program, which provides assistance in finding a job; a travel training program, to help disabled persons use the Metro bus system; a technical assistance program, providing job training; and a self-advocacy program, to teach disabled persons how to speak up for their rights. The **Disability and Business Technical Assistance Center (DBTAC) Northwest** supports the integration of all persons with disabilities into the community and provides publications on workplace accessibility and other topics. The **Washington Assistive Technology Alliance (WATA)** increases access to and awareness of technologies that provide assistance and accessibility for people with disabilities. The **University of Washington's Assistive Technology Resource Center (ATRC)** provides information, referral services, training, and consultation regarding assistive technology devices, services, and funding. The **Easter Seal Society of Washington** provides housing assistance programs and vocational rehabilitation, including interview skills training, job search techniques, and on-the-job support. They also publish pamphlets listing accessible sites in the Seattle area.

Metro Transit issues Regional Reduced Fare Permits (RRFPs) to individuals with disabilities. The permit costs $3 and is valid for Metro transportation, Washington State Ferries, Community Transit, Pierce Transit, and most other bus agencies in the region. Buses are equipped with wheelchair lifts and special seating. For those individuals who require assistance in riding the bus, a special Personal Care Attendant permit allows the disabled person's escort to ride free. Depending on the nature of the disability, a letter of certification from a physician, psychiatrist, psychologist or audiologist is required. Call the Metro Transit RRFP Helpline at 206-205-9185, 206-684-2029 (TTY) for more information and to receive a copy of the certification form. If you are a frequent rider, you should register for an ORCA card, which works like cash or a credit card and eliminates the need for exact change. Some regional transit systems accept the ORCA card for paratransit services (curb-to-curb transportation service for people with disabilities who can't ride fixed-route public transportation), as well.

Here's a list of addresses and phone numbers for the above centers and some other national and local organizations:

- **Alliance of People with DisAbilities**, 1120 E Terrace St, Ste 100, 206-545-7055, 206-632-3456 (TTY), www.disabilitypride.org
- **Center for Technology and Disability Studies**, University of Washington, 206-685-4181 (Voice), 206-616-1396 or 866-0162 (TTY), http://uwctds.washington.edu
- **Deaf–Blind Service Center**, 1620 18th Ave, Ste 200, 206-323-9178 (TTY), 866-238-8216 (Voice), www.seattledbsc.org
- **Disability Rights Washington**, 315 5th Ave S, Ste 850, 800-562-2702, 800-905-0209 (TTY), www.disabilityrightswa.org
- **Easter Seals Washington**, 220 W Mercer St, Ste 120-W, 206-281-5700 (Voice/TTY), www.wa.easterseals.com
- **Hearing Loss Association of Washington**, 4820 156th Pl SW, Edmonds, WA 98026-4846, 301-657-2248 (Voice), 301-657-2249 (TTY), www.hearingloss-wa.org
- **Hearing, Speech and Deafness Center**, 1625 19th Ave, 206-323-5770 (Voice), 206-388-1275 (TTY) www.hsdc.org

- **Learning Disabilities Association of Washington**, 16315 NE 87th St, Ste B-11, Redmond, WA 98052, 425-882-0820, www.ldawa.org
- **Metro Transit**, 206-553-3000, TTY relay 711, http://metro.kingcounty.gov
- **Northwest ADA Center**, 6912 220th St SW, 800-949-4232, 425-771-7426 (TTY), www.dbtacnorthwest.org
- **SightConnection**, 9709 3rd Ave NE, Ste 100, 206-525-5556, 800-458-4888, www.csbps.com
- **Washington Assistive Technology Act Program (WATAP)**, University of Washington, P.O. Box 357920, 800-214-8731, 866-866-0162 (TTY), http://watap.org
- **Washington State Department of Social and Health Services, Office of the Deaf and Hard of Hearing**, P.O. Box 45301, Olympia, WA 98504-5301, 360-902-8000 (Voice/TTY), 800-422-7930 (Voice/TTY), www.dshs.wa.gov
- **Washington Telecommunications Relay Services**, dial 711, or 800-676-3777 (TTY/Voice), 800-676-4290 (TTY/Voz [Spanish])), www.washingtonrelay.com

GAY AND LESBIAN LIFE

When the census counted same-sex partners for the first time in 2000, figures indicated that Seattle has one of the nation's highest percentages of gay households. According to the 2010 Census, one out of every 18 couples living together in Seattle are same-sex. While this may be news to some, it is not news to Seattle's thriving and well-established gay community. There are numerous organizations, businesses, and publications that address the concerns and interests of Seattle's lesbian, gay, bisexual, and transgender community—too many to detail here. We mention the following as starting points.

- **Dignity Seattle**, 206-659-5519, www.dignityseattle.org, is a local chapter of the country's largest and most progressive organization of gay, lesbian, bisexual and transgender Catholics.
- **Gay City Health Project,** 511 E Pike St, 206-860-6969, www.gaycity.org; Gay City is a multicultural gay men's health organization and the leading provider of HIV and STI testing in King County.
- **Gay Fathers Association of Seattle**, P.O. Box 1270, 1122 E Pike St, www.gfas.org; every Thursday evening GFAS sponsors a safe and anonymous support group for gay and bisexual men and their families.
- **Greater Seattle Business Association**, 400 E Pine St, Ste 322, 206-363-9188, www.thegsba.org; GSBA's goal is to strengthen and expand business and career opportunities in the gay and lesbian community.
- **Lambert House Gay Youth Center**, 1818 15th Ave, 206-322-2515, www.lamberthouse.org; an activities and resource center for lesbian, gay, bisexual, transgender, and questioning youth ages 22 and under.

- **Lesbian Resource Center**, 227 S Orcas St, 206-322-3953, www.lrc.net; established in Seattle in 1974, LRC promotes empowerment, visibility, and social change.
- **Parents, Families and Friends of Lesbians and Gays (PFLAG)**, Seattle Chapter, 1122 E Pike St, 206-325-7724, www.seattle-pflag.org, promotes the health and well-being of sexual minorities through support, education, and advocacy.
- **Rainbow Families of Puget Sound**, P.O. Box 70115, www.rainbowfamiliesps.org, helps GLBT families in the region to form strong community ties and spend time with families like their own.
- **Seattle LGBT Commission**, 810 3rd Ave, Ste 750, 206-684-4500, 206-684-4503 (TTY), www.seattle.gov/lgbt; the commission presents the concerns of lesbian, gay, bisexual, and transgendered citizens to the Mayor, City Council, and all city departments.
- **Seattle Out and Proud**, 1605 12th Ave, Ste 2, 206-322-9561, www.seattlepride.org, SO&P organizes and promotes the annual Seattle Pride parade and march.

NEWSPAPERS

- *Seattle Gay News*, 1605 12th Ave, Ste 31, 206-324-4297, www.sgn.org
- *The Stranger*, 1535 11th Ave, 206-323-7101, www.thestranger.com; while not strictly a gay paper, *The Stranger* is gay-friendly, produces an annual Queer Issue, and features Dan Savage's weekly advice column "Savage Love."

ENTERTAINMENT

Most of Seattle's gay bars and restaurants are located in the Capitol Hill neighborhood.

- **C.C. Attle's**, 1701 E Olive Way, 206-726-0565, www.ccattles.net
- **Changes**, 2103 N 45th, 206-545-8363.www.changesinwallingford.com
- **The Cuff**, 1533 13th Ave, 206-323-1525, www.cuffcomplex.com
- **Elite**, 1520 Olive Way, 206-860-0999, www.theeliteseattle.com
- **The Lobby,** 206-328-6703, 916 E Pike St, www.thelobbybar.seattle,com
- **Madison Pub**, 1315 E Madison, 206-325-6537, www.madisonpub.com
- **Neighbours Disco**, 1509 Broadway, 206-324-5358, www.neighboursnightclub.com
- **Pony,** 1221 E Madison St, 206-324-2854, www.ponyseattle.com
- **Purr Cocktail Lounge**, 1518 11th Ave, 206-325-3112, www.purrseattle.com
- **R Place**, 619 E Pine, 206-322-8828, www.rplaceseattle.com
- **Re-Bar**, 1114 Howell St, 206-233-9873, www.rebarseattle.com
- **The Seattle Eagle,** 314 E Pike St, 206-621-7591, www.seattleeagle.com
- **Wild Rose**, 1021 E Pike St, 206-324-9210, www.thewildrosebar.com

INTERNATIONAL NEWCOMERS

According to the 2010 Census, foreign-born people make up nearly 20% of Seattle's population—a 3% increase since the previous census. While the city is a desirable place to live, since 9/11 government regulations have made it a little more difficult to relocate here from abroad. Visit the U.S. consulate in your home country to learn the steps you will need to take depending on your relocation status. Rules are different for permanent residency, students, guest workers, etc. You can find comprehensive information and help on the **U.S. Citizen and Immigration Services** website at http://uscis.gov. There you can learn about the different types of immigrant and visa classifications, regulations, and the forms you will need. The USCIS strongly urges people to download forms from their website, but if you need to have forms mailed to you, call 800-870-3676. For more general questions and help, call 800-375-5283 or 800-767-1833 (TTY).

If you are already in Seattle and need to contact the USCIS, the local office is at 12500 Tukwila International Blvd. To make an appointment to speak with an Immigration Information Officer you must use an online service called INFO-PASS, www.infopass.uscis.gov. Call 800-375-5283 for details.

Contacting the consulate of your home country can be a good starting point for adjusting to your new home in Seattle. The area is home to five official consulates and many honorary consulates. While honorary consulates may not be able to handle issues like visas and passports, they often provide resources for newcomers, and can connect you with local organizations.

OFFICIAL CONSULATES

- **Consulate General of Canada**, 1501 4th Ave, Ste 600, 206-443-1777, www.canadainternational.gc.ca
- **Consulate General of Japan**, 601 Union St, Ste 500, 206-682-9107, www.seattle.us.enb-japan.go.jp
- **Consulate General of the Republic of Korea**, 2033 6th Ave, Ste 1125, 206-441-1011, http://usa-seattle.mofat.go.kr/eng/am/usa-seattle/main/index.jsp
- **Consulate of Mexico**, 2132 3rd Ave, 206-448-3526
- **Consulate General of the Russian Federation**, 2001 6th Ave, Ste 2323, 206-728-1910, www.netconsul.org

HONORARY CONSULATES

- **Consulate of Austria**, 310-444-9310, www.austrianconsulateseattle.org
- **Consulate of Belgium**, 2200 Alaskan Way, Ste 470, 206-728-5145
- **Consulate of Brazil,** 4559 Stanford Ave NE, 425-235-0724
- **Consulate of Cambodia**, 1818 Westlake Ave N, Ste 315, 206-217-0830, www.consulateofcambodia.com
- **Consul of the Republic of Croatia**, 7547 S Laurel St, 206-772-2968

- **Consulate of Cyprus**, 5555 Lakeview Dr, Ste 200, Kirkland, 425-827-1700
- **Consulate of Denmark**, 6204 E Mercer Way, Mercer Island, 206-230-0888
- **Consulate of Estonia**, 9133 View Ave NW, 206-310-2153
- **Consul General of Ethiopia**, P.O. Box 77447, 206-364-6401
- **Consulate of Finland**, 17102 NE 37th Pl, Bellevue, 425-885-7320
- **Consulate of France**, 2200 Alaskan Way, Ste 490, 206-256-6184
- **Consulate of Germany**, 7853 SE 27th St, Ste 180, 206-230-5138
- **Consul of Hungary**, 2901 NE Blakely St, #500, 206-432-9767
- **Consulate of Iceland**, 5610 20th Ave NW, 206-783-4100
- **Consulate of Italy**, 23718 7th Ave SE, Bothell, 206-851-8023
- **Consulate of Jamaica**, 8223 S 222nd St, Kirkland, 253-872-8950
- **Consulate of Latvia**, 13517 69th Ave SE, Snohomish, 425-773-0103
- **Consulate of Lithuania**, 5919 Wilson Ave S, 206-725-4576
- **Consulate of Luxembourg**, 812 Warren Ave N, 206-724-7598
- **Consulate of Malta**, P.O. Box 1104, Duvall, 425-788-3120
- **Consulate of New Zealand**, P.O. Box 51059, 206-527-1896
- **Consulate of Norway**, 7301 5th Ave NE, 206-284-2323
- **Consulate of Peru**, 3717 NE 157th St, Ste 100, 206-714-9037
- **Consulate General of the Seychelles**, 3620 SW 309th St, Federal Way, 253-874-4579
- **Consulate of Spain**, 4709 139th Ave SE, 425-237-9373
- **Consulate of Sweden**, 520 Pike St, Ste 2200, 206-467-8200
- **Consulate of Switzerland**, 6920 94th Ave SE, 206-228-8110
- **Consulate of The Netherlands**, 40 Lake Bellevue, Ste 100, Bellevue, 425-637-3050
- **Consulate General of Turkey**, 12328 NE 97th St, Kirkland, 425-739-6722
- **Consulate of Uganda**, 3226 Rosedale St, Gig Harbor, 206-571-9798
- **Consulate of the United Kingdom**, 500 108th Ave NE, Ste 1500, 425-453-9400
- **Consulate General of Uzbekistan**, 800 5th Ave, Ste 4000, 206-625-1199

PUBLICATIONS

- The USCIS has a free, online brochure called **Welcome to the United States: A Guide for New Immigrants** that can help you get settled, find resources, and learn about your rights and responsibilities. You can find it at www.welcometousa.gov.
- **Newcomer's Handbook for Moving to and Living in the USA**, by Mike Livingston, published by **First Books**, 503-968-6777, www.shopfirstbooks.com

MOVING PETS TO THE USA

- *The Pet-Moving Handbook*, by Carrie Straub, published by **First Books**, 503-968-6777, www.shopfirstbooks.com
- **Air Animal Pet Movers**, 800-635-3448, www.airanimal.com
- **Cosmopolitan Canine Carriers**, 800-243-9105, www.caninecarriers.com
- **Petrelocation.com,** 877-738-6683, www.petrelocation.com

O NE OF THE MOST CHALLENGING AND OVERWHELMING TASKS PARents face when moving to a new area is finding good childcare and/ or schools for their kids. While the process is not an easy one, with time and effort it is possible to find what is best for your children, whether it be in-home or on-site daycare, an after-school program, or a good public or private school. In addition, the possibilities presented by homeschooling and online schools are addressed in this chapter. The wide variety of opportunities available for higher education is also presented. Of course the keys to success in all of these areas are research and persistence.Note: mention in this book of a particular childcare organization or business is not an endorsement. We recommend that you scrutinize any persons or organizations before entrusting your youngster(s) to them.

CHILDCARE

DAYCARE

Often, the best advice when looking for childcare is to ask for referrals from friends or co-workers. For newcomers who may be lacking such resources, a good place to start is the **Washington State Child Care Resource & Referral Network**, 800-446-1114, www.childcarenet.org. This private, nonprofit agency will send you a packet of age-specific childcare, health, and parenting information, and tell you about a local referral program in your area. In the city of Seattle, that program is **Child Care Resources**, 206-329-5544, www.childcare. org. Based on your criteria, Child Care Resources will give you a list of providers from its database of more than 2,000 facilities in King County. While referrals are for state-licensed facilities, be sure to visit prospective sites and interview caregivers, regardless of any recommendations you may receive about an organization. Many local employers offer a benefits package that includes a similar service; check with your place of work for details.

Childcare in Washington is regulated by the state **Department of Early Learning (DEL)** (formerly the Division of Child Care & Early Learning), www.del. wa.gov. The agency offers several helpful publications on its website, including "You Have a Choice! A Guide to Finding Quality Child Care." The DEL is responsible for licensing more than 7,400 childcare homes and centers in King County. Licensers process background checks, inspect and monitor facilities, investigate complaints, and take corrective action when necessary. A bill passed in 2007 requires the DEL website to list the names of facilities under investigation for licensing violations. Parents can visit the DEL's online Licensed Care Information System (LCIS) to learn about the licensing history of a childcare provider. Despite such improvements, a shortage of trained teachers and aides in King County means that diligent and thorough research is in order when looking for childcare.

In Washington, a license is required for anyone paid to care for children on a regular basis (unless the children are related to the caregiver). The state imposes minimum licensing requirements for three different types of childcare facilities: licensed childcare centers; licensed school age centers; and licensed family homes.

- A **childcare center** is a facility that provides regularly scheduled care for a group of children age one month through age 12.
- A **school age center** is a program operating in a facility other than a private residence, accountable for school age children when school is not in session. The program must provide adult-supervised care and a variety of developmentally appropriate activities.
- A **licensed family home** is a facility in the family residence of the licensee that provides regularly scheduled care for 12 or fewer children from birth to age 11.

Before receiving a license from the DEL, a prospective daycare provider must have a business license, undergo a criminal history background check, attend a first aid/CPR class that includes infant/child CPR and pediatric first aid, attend an HIV/AIDS/bloodborne pathogens training class, and pass a state licensing inspection at the place of business. A law passed in 2005 requires all licensed childcare providers to purchase liability insurance. Family home providers can opt out of this requirement, but they must notify parents in writing that they do not have insurance. You can check the license status of your childcare provider through the DEL website at www.del.wa.gov, or call 866-48-CHECK.

The **Service Employees International (SEIU)** Local #925, the local union for childcare workers, may be able to offer some help in your search for good childcare. The SEIU district office is located at 1914 N 34th St, Ste 100. Call 206-322-3010 or go to www.seiu925.org for more information.

- **Child Care Resources**, 206-329-1011st, www.childcare.org
- **City of Seattle/North King County Child Care Information and Referral**, 206-329-5544, 206-461-4571 (TTY)
- **East King County Child Care Referral Line**, 206-329-5544
- **South King County Child Care Referral Line**, 206-329-5544

WHAT TO LOOK FOR IN DAYCARE

When searching for the best place for your child, be sure to visit prospective daycare providers—preferably unannounced. In general, look for a safe environment and caring attitude. Check that the kitchen, toys, and furniture are clean and safe. Observe the other kids at the center. Do they seem happy? Are they well behaved? Are the teacher/child ratios acceptable? Ask for the telephone numbers of other parents who use the service and talk to them before committing. It's a good idea to request a daily schedule—look for both active and quiet time, and age-appropriate activities. In the winter months, weather in Seattle doesn't allow for a lot of outdoor activities, but make sure that sports, games, and field trips are still included in the curriculum.

Keep in mind that a license does not guarantee the service of the quality you may want. If you think a provider might be acceptable, call the Licensed Child Care Information System at 866-48-CHECK to determine their licensing status, and call on parent referrals.

ONLINE RESOURCES—DAYCARE

The state Department of Early Learning suggests the following child-related online resources:

- **Consumer Product Safety Commission**, www.cpsc.gov
- **DSHS Children's Administration**, www.dshs.wa.gov/ca
- **National Association of Childcare Professionals**, www.naccp.org
- **Office of the Superintendent of Public Instruction**, www.k12.wa.us

NANNIES

A number of agencies match families with nannies. Although these services tend to be pricey, some include background checks or psychological testing during the applicant screening process. Nannies are not licensed by the state, and screening processes vary among agencies, so you may want to ask for interview specifics at the various agencies. That said, a nanny can be a wonderful addition to your family. Whether you're employed outside your home or simply need some assistance while working at home, a considerate and hard-working nanny may be the best option for your childcare needs. Area nanny services include:

- **A Nanny for U**, 206-525-1510, www.anannyforu.com
- **Annie's Nannies**, 206-784-8462, www.anihouseholdstaffing.com
- **CareWorks**, 206-325-9985, www.careworkseattle.com
- **Judi Julin, RN, Nannybroker Inc.**, Seattle, 206-624-1213, Eastside, 425-392-5681, www.nannybroker.com
- **Keepsake Nannies**, 253-845-2202, www.keepsakenannies.com
- **The Seattle Nanny Network Inc.**, st425-803-9511, www.seattlenanny.com
- **West Coast Nannies,** 206-910-9140, www.wcnannies.com

Be sure to check all references before hiring a nanny. These companies offer pre-employment screening services, and can provide criminal background checks, driving records, and credit reports:

- **Alliance 2020**, 800-289-8065, www.alliance2020.com
- **Background Investigations Inc.**, 888-338-1550, www.wedobackground-checks.com
- **eFindOutTheTruth.com,** www.efindoutthetruth.com
- **iDentityPi.com,** 888-366-5029, www.identitypi.com
- **TalentWise,** 866-338-6739, www.talentwise.com

For those hiring a nanny without an agency, there are certain taxes that must be paid: Social Security and Medicare, and possibly unemployment. For assistance with such issues, check the **Nanitax** website, www.4nannytaxes.com, or call them at 800-NANITAX.

AU PAIRS

If you'd like the convenience of a nanny at a considerably lower cost, or if you're simply interested in a cultural exchange, consider the services of an au pair. Young women (and a few men), usually from Europe, provide a year of childcare and light housekeeping in exchange for airfare, room and board, and a small stipend. Au pairs work up to 45 hours a week, and often go to school or sightsee during their time off.

It is a good program for those families and au pairs who understand the trade-offs of the system. Nevertheless, you may want to confirm that you and the au pair have mutual expectations for your year together. The au pair will be in a foreign country and interested in traveling and meeting people her age. While most agencies outline specific responsibilities, make sure the au pair understands what is expected during her year of employment; your au pair may not have fully considered how restricted her free time will be. Additionally, some parents may have unrealistic expectations of an au pair, assuming that she will be a combination nanny, babysitter, and full-time housekeeper, with few social interests. That said, if you and your au pair come to an agreement early in the relationship, and follow the guidelines detailed by the agency, most likely you will be very pleased with the au pair experience.

The U.S. Department of State **Bureau of Educational and Cultural Affairs** is responsible for authorizing the organizations that conduct au pair exchange programs. For answers to frequently asked questions, visit http://exchanges. state.gov/education. The following organizations administer the au pair program:

- **American Institute for Foreign Study**, Au Pair in America, 800-928-7247, www.aifs.org
- **AuPairCare**, 800-428-7247, www.aupaircare.com
- **Cultural Care Au Pair,** 800-333-6056, www.culturalcare.com
- **Euraupair Intercultural Child Care Programs**, 800-333-3804, www.euraupair.com
- **Go Au Pair**, 888-287-2471, www.goaupair.com
- **InterExchange Au Pair**, 800-287-2477, www.interexchange.org

BABYSITTERS

If you haven't found a reliable babysitter in your neighborhood, or the one you found just called and cancelled, the following companies offer babysitting services. Be prepared to pay more for immediate response.

- **Annie's Nannies**, 206-784-8462, www.anihouseholdstaffing.com
- **Best Sitters, Inc.**, 206-682-2556, 425-837-8200, www.bestsittersinc.com
- **Judi Julin, RN, Nannybroker Inc.**, Seattle, 206-624-1213, Eastside, 425-392-5681, www.nannybroker.com
- **The Seattle Nanny Network Inc.**, 425-803-9511, www.seattlenanny.com
- **Seeking Sitters,** 206-714-2222, www.seekingsitters.com
- **Sitter City,** 888-748-2489, www.sittercity.com

CHILD SAFETY

Numerous public agencies, private organizations, and hospitals offer resources to help keep your kids safe. The **Seattle Public Library** provides parents and teachers with a list of Internet safety organizations on its website (search: Internet safety). **Public Health of Seattle & King County** will deliver health and safety news alerts via e-mail; to subscribe, visit www.kingcounty.gov/healthservices/health.aspx. The **Seattle Fire Department** offers a program for children called Fire Stoppers—call 206-386-1338 for details. Several hospitals offer infant and child CPR programs, including **Children's Hospital & Regional Medical Center**, 206-987-2000, www.seattlechildrens.org, and **Swedish Medical Center**, 206-215-3338, www.swedish.org.

SCHOOLS

SEATTLE PUBLIC SCHOOLS (K–12)

Over the years, public schools in Seattle have faced a series of serious problems, approaching crisis level, including a huge budget deficit, low enrollment and graduation rates, and high dropout rates. The most recent upheaval in the school district was the 2011 financial scandal that led to the ousting of Superintendent Maria Goodloe-Johnson. During what some called "the worst state budget crisis in 40 years," $32 million in funding to the District had to be cut during the 2009–2010 academic year, and in 2011 the District faced a gap of $35 million more. These deficits necessitated school closures, reductions in staffing and school programs, mandatory work furloughs for teachers, and other painful cost-cutting measures.

Although the news is grim, there are a few bright spots. The graduation rate (according to the Washington State Report Card) has improved considerably in recent years, and is currently at 73.5%, slightly higher than the national rate of 72%, and the dropout rate has dropped to 5.1%; the Washington Assessment of Student Learning (WASL), a legacy of the Bush-era No Child Left Behind education policy, was replaced in 2009 with the more efficient Measurements of Student Progress (MSP), issued to public students in grades 3–8, and the High School Proficiency Exam (HSPE). (Private school students and those who have been homeschooled are exempt from state testing.) The MSP exams measure students' progress in reading, writing, math, and science. Online versions of these tests are being phased in. High school students who do not take and pass a state assessment in reading and writing will not graduate.

In 1995 Seattle voters approved a levy called Building Excellence, or BEX, to modernize or replace Seattle's aging school buildings, a third of which were more than a half-century old. Among the first schools to benefit from the initial phase of this ambitious project, the K–8 African American Academy moved into a new $24-million facility on Beacon Hill in the fall of 2000. The three-story building houses a science lab, photo darkroom, art room, music room, gymnasium, and 90-seat lecture hall.

Another development was the addition of the Center School (www.seattleschools.org/schools/thecenterschool), the district's newest high school, and the only school located in downtown Seattle. The small high school enjoys a home on the grounds of the Seattle Center, where seniors can take advantage of internships. While core academics are strong and technology is used throughout the curriculum, the school's focus is on the arts. All electives are based on the arts, and portfolios are a graduation requirement.

The BEX project has three phases, with BEX III, a $490-million project, scheduled for completion in 2012. As a result of BEX III, the newly renovated

Hamilton International Middle School and Chief Sealth High School opened their doors to students in the fall of 2010.

Other notable public school programs include **TOPS** (www.topsk8.org), a K–8 program known for its strong parent involvement and state-of-the-art school building, and **Summit** (www.seattleschools.org/schools/summitk-12), Seattle's only K–12 school, which prides itself on utilizing the cross-age learning opportunities that arise from having kids of all ages in the same building.

For younger students, Seattle Public Schools offers both half-day and full-day kindergarten. There is a huge demand for full-day programs, and some are fee-based. Check with area schools for more information. The Seattle school district also offers Montessori programs at three schools—**Graham Hill Elementary** (www.seattleschools.org/area/main/ShowSchool?sid=220), **Daniel Bagley Elementary** (www.seattleschools.org/area/cac/schoolprofiles/bagley.pdf), and **Leschi Elementary** (www.leschischool.com). (See below for a list of private Montessori programs.)

For more information about these schools and to see which schools are being closed or moved, go to www.seattleschools.org.

ENROLLMENT—SEATTLE PUBLIC SCHOOLS

The Seattle Public Schools enrollment process has a complicated and controversial history. The old system did not allow voluntary school selection and involved busing large numbers of students throughout the city to improve the racial balance at each school. While busing successfully integrated the schools, it also took its toll on the overall well-being of the public school community. With bus rides as much as 90 minutes each way, many students found it difficult to get to and from school, let alone participate in after-school sports and activities. With such inconveniences, many who could afford to chose private schools instead.

The current selection process, which the school district began phasing in during the 2011–2012 school year, has the advantage of simplicity. According to the New Student Assignment Plan (NSAP) adopted in 2009, each student shall have the opportunity to attend elementary, middle, or high school in a designated attendance area, determined by the student's home address. "Feeder patterns" channel elementary students toward middle schools in the same general geographic area; no feeder patterns exist from middle to high school, however. If the school in student's attendance area is not equipped to address her or his needs (for special education, bilingual, or advanced learning), as determined by the school district, the student will be assigned to another school with the appropriate services. Families may apply to a school in a different attendance area, or to one that does not have an attendance area (called an "option" school), with no guarantee of admission. Assignment to these schools is based on an open application process; if there are more applicants than available spaces, certain tiebreakers apply, such as having a sibling who attends that school. Students who apply to a different school of choice will be added to a waiting list if no space is available.

To enroll your child in Seattle Public Schools, you must obtain a registration form by visiting one of the enrollment service centers or by calling 206-252-0760. You can also download the application from the district's website at www.district.seattleschools.org. The centers can provide you with your child's designated attendance area. The Open Enrollment period for school registration varies according to school year: generally it's some time in February for elementary, and in March for middle and high schools. Families can avoid long lines during the spring and summer enrollment periods, and receive their school assignment notification early in the year, by enrolling prior to January 31. Early Enrollment is only for students registering at their attendance area school. Students who wish to attend another school of choice must apply during the Open Enrollment period.

To complete the registration process, you must bring a parent or guardian's photo ID, plus two proofs of address, such as a rent receipt, driver's license, or preprinted check, and your child's immunization records, called a Certificate of Immunization Status (CIS).

- **Bilingual Family Center**, Aki Kurose Middle School, 3928 S Graham St, Rm 104, 206-252-7750
- **John Stanford Center,** 2445 3rd Ave S, 206-252-0760
- **North Enrollment Service Center**, Wilson Pacific Bldg, 1330 N 90th St, 206-252-4765
- **South Enrollment Service Center,** Columbia Annex Bldg, 3100 S Alaska St, 206-252-6800

All applications received before the period deadline are processed together and each carries equal weight. After the regular enrollment period ends, applications are processed on a "first-come, first-served" basis. Some schools fill up quickly based on special programs or popularity; others simply have smaller buildings and cannot accommodate as many students. Alternative schools and classes, such as honors, special education, multicultural or bilingual programs, often have additional requirements that restrict enrollment.

An important element of the registration program is the appeals process. If your child does not receive his/her first-choice school, you may appeal to the school district and, if necessary, request a hearing before the Student Assignment Appeals Board. It is always worth taking this step if you are truly dissatisfied with your child's school assignment. Grounds for appeal include medical or psychological concerns, extreme hardship, and district failure to follow district guidelines.

While the Enrollment Service Centers can provide information on any of the Seattle Public Schools, another excellent resource for statistics and information on schools and programs is the State Report Card of the Office of the Superintendent of Public Instruction (http://reportcard.ospi.k12.wa.us). Other websites with useful school information and comparisons include www.greatschools.org and www.schooldigger.com. In addition, you may want to contact SchoolMatch in Westerville, Ohio, to request its report on Seattle schools. The report, which costs $34, will include information on student-teacher ratios, test scores, and even property values in your chosen neighborhood.

All of the abovementioned resources, as well as some other Seattle Public Schools resources, are listed here.

- **Advanced Learning**, 206-252-0130
- **Appeals**, 206-252-0586
- **Automated Enrollment Services Line**, 206-252-0410
- **Bilingual Services**, 206-252-7750
- **SchoolMatch**, 800-992-5323, 614-890-1573, www.schoolmatch.com
- **Seattle Public Schools**, P.O. Box 34165, Seattle, WA 98124-1165, 206-252-0010, www.seattleschools.org
- **Special Education Services**, 206-252-0055
- **Transportation Services**, 206-252-0900
- **Wait List Automated Info Line**, 206-252-0212

SURROUNDING COMMUNITIES

For information on public schools outside the city of Seattle, contact your local school district, or visit its website. A selection of districts is listed here:

- **Auburn School District**, 915 4th St NE, Auburn, WA 98002, 253-931-4900, www.auburn.wednet.edu
- **Bellevue Public Schools**, 12111 NE 1st St, Bellevue, WA 98005, 425-456-4000, www.bsd405.org
- **Bremerton School District**, 134 N Marion Ave, Bremerton, WA 98132, 360-473-1000, www.bremertonschools.org
- **Edmonds School District**, 20420 68th Ave W, Lynnwood, WA 98036, 425-431-7000, www.edmonds.wednet.edu
- **Everett Public Schools**, 4730 Colby Ave, Everett, WA 98203, 425-385-4000, www.everett.k12.wa.us
- **Federal Way Public Schools**, 31405 18th Ave S, Federal Way, WA 98003, 253-945-2000, www.fwps.org
- **Highline Public Schools**, 15675 Ambaum Blvd SW, Burien, WA 98166, 206-433-0111, www.hsd401.org
- **Issaquah School District**, 565 NW Holly St, Issaquah, WA 98027, 425-837-7000, www.issaquah.wednet.edu
- **Kent School District**, 12033 SE 256th St, Kent, WA 98030, 253-373-7000, www.kent.k12.wa.us

- **Lake Washington School District**, 16250 NE 74th St, Redmond, WA 98052, 425-938-1200, www.lwsd.org
- **Mercer Island School District**, 4160 86th Ave SE, Mercer Island, WA 98040, 206-236-3330, www.misd.k12.wa.us
- **Northshore School District**, 3330 Monte Villa Pkwy, Bothell, WA 98021, 425-408-6000, www.nsd.org
- **Renton School District**, 300 SW 7th St, Renton, WA 98057, 425-204-2300, www.rentonschools.us
- **Shoreline Public Schools**, 18560 1st Ave NE, Shoreline, WA 98155, 206-393-6111, www.shorelineschools.org
- **Tacoma Public Schools**, P.O. Box 1357, Tacoma, WA 98401-1357, 253-571-1000, www.tacoma.k12.wa.us
- **Tahoma School District**, 25720 Maple Valley-Black Diamond Rd SE, Maple Valley, WA 98038, 425-413-3400, www.tahomasd.us
- **Tukwila School District**, 4640 S 144th St, Tukwila, WA 98168, 206-901-8000, www.tukwila.wednet.edu
- **Vashon Island School District**, P.O. Box 547, Vashon, WA 98070-0547, 206-463-2121, www.vashonsd.wednet.edu

PRIVATE SCHOOLS

If you are considering a private school, the greater Seattle area offers a wide variety of options, many of which provide bus service. A few of the private schools in Seattle and its surrounding communities are listed here; check the Yellow Pages for more. Entrance requirements vary widely. Be sure to call or visit the school for more information.

- **Annie Wright School (P–12)**, 827 N Tacoma Ave, Tacoma, 253-272-2216, www.aw.org; situated on Commencement Bay, Annie Wright is a co-ed day school through grade 8 and an all-girls' boarding/day school grades 9 through 12.
- **Bellevue Christian School (P–12)**, 1601 98th Ave NE, Clyde Hill, 425-454-4402, www.bellevuechristian.org; with a comprehensive program that serves preschool through 12th-grade students, Bellevue Christian educates close to 1,200 children, and emphasizes academics with a Christ-centered curriculum.
- **Billings Middle School (6-8)**, 7217 Woodlawn Ave NE, 206-547-4614, www.billingsmiddleschool.org; this independent middle school, which fosters independent thinking and public mindedness, has fewer than 100 students and a student-to-teacher ratio of 5 to 1.
- **Bishop Blanchet High School (9–12)**, 8200 Wallingford Ave N, 206-527-7711, www.blanchet.k12.wa.us; a Catholic college preparatory school, Bishop Blanchet sends approximately 99% of its graduates on to higher education.

The north Seattle high school is a member of the Class AAA division of the Seattle Metro League.

- **Bush School (K–12)**, 3400 E Harrison St, 206-322-7978, www.bush.edu; the oldest K–12 independent coed school in Seattle commands nine acres in the Madison Valley neighborhood. Emphasis is placed on experiential learning, with students working in groups to reach common goals.
- **Cascade Christian Schools (P–12)**, 815 21st St SE, Puyallup, 253-841-1776, www.cascadechristianschool.org, support early childhood centers and elementary schools in Puyallup and Tacoma, as well as Cascade Christian Junior/Senior High School in Puyallup.
- **Charles Wright Academy (K–12)**, 7723 Chambers Creek Rd W, Tacoma, 253-620-8300, www.charleswright.org, is located on 90 acres in suburban Tacoma. The school provides a challenging college-prep curriculum at all grade levels.
- **The Clearwater School (ages 4–19)**, 1510 196th St SE, Bothell, 425-489-2050, www.clearwaterschool.com, is part of a national network of Sudbury Schools, modeled after the Sudbury Valley School in Massachusetts. Students direct their own activities and engage in a participatory democracy.
- **Concordia Lutheran School (P–8)**, 7040 36th Ave NE, 206-525-7407, http://concordia.seattle.wa.us; owned and operated by the Lutheran School Association of Greater Seattle, Concordia offers a strong Christian atmosphere where children develop academically, socially, and physically.
- **Giddens School (P–5)**, 620 20th Ave S, 206-324-4847, www.giddensschool.org, one of the most ethnically, economically, and socially diverse independent schools in the Northwest, combines its commitment to academic excellence with a focus on social justice.
- **Holy Family School (P–8)**, 505 17th St SE, Auburn, 253-833-8688; the philosophy of this Catholic school is that parents have the primary responsibility for their child's education, and that the church, school, and community complement this role.
- **Holy Names Academy (9–12)**, 728 21st Ave E, 206-323-4272, www.holynames-sea.org, a Catholic college preparatory school for girls, is a four-time winner of the U.S. Department of Education's blue ribbon of excellence. Athletes compete in the Class AAA division of the Seattle Metro League.
- **Islamic School of Seattle (P–6)**, 720 25th Ave, 206-329-5735, www.islamicschoolofseattle.com; founded in 1980, the Islamic School has since added an accredited Montessori preschool and a full-immersion Arabic program.
- **The Jewish Day School of Metropolitan Seattle (P–8)**, 15749 NE 4th St, Bellevue, 425-460-0200, www.jds.org; the Jewish Day School provides a challenging curriculum of general and Jewish studies, along with enrichment opportunities.

- **King's Schools (P–12)**, 19303 Fremont Ave N, Seattle, 206-289-7700; Crosspoint Academy (formerly King's West) (P–12), 4012 Chico Way NW, Bremerton, 360-377-7700, www.kingsschools.org; these schools serve Seattle and Kitsap families seeking a college preparatory program that emphasizes strong academics, positive discipline, and Christian faith.
- **Lakeside School (5–12)**, Middle School, 13510 1st Ave NE; Upper School, 14050 1st Ave NE, 206-368-3600, www.lakesideschool.org; this co-ed school enrolls about 800 students, with an average student to teacher ratio of 9 to 1, and an average class size of just 16 students. The school's most famous alumni are Microsoft co-founders and Seattle residents Bill Gates and Paul Allen.
- **Meridian School (K–5)**, 4649 Sunnyside Ave N, 206-632-7154, www.meridianschool.edu; located in the Wallingford neighborhood, Meridian School combines its academic curriculum with thematic studies like raising salmon or recreating a pioneer encampment.
- **The Northwest School (6–12)**, 1415 Summit Ave, 206-682-7309, www.northwestschool.org, is a college preparatory day and boarding school that offers cross-disciplinary study in the humanities, sciences, and performing and fine arts.
- **O'Dea High School (9–12)**, 802 Terry Ave, 206-622-6596, www.odea.org, a Catholic college preparatory high school for boys situated on Seattle's First Hill.
- **St. Edward (K–8)**, 4200 S Mead St, 206-725-1774, www.saintedwardseattle. org; Catholic values and church teachings permeate all aspects of the school community at St. Edward, where students are trained for leadership in the church and society.
- **St. Joseph School (K–8)**, 700 18th Ave E, 206-329-3260, www.stjosephsea. org, located on Seattle's Capitol Hill, the school's mission is to create a faith-centered community that educates and inspires students to their God-given potential.
- **Seattle Academy of Arts and Sciences (SAAS)**, (6–12), 1201 Union St, 206-323-6600, www.seattleacademy.org; a preparatory school in an urban environment that integrates the arts in its curriculum and emphasizes a global perspective.
- **Seattle Country Day School (K–8)**, 2619 4th Ave N, 206-284-6220, www.seattlecountryday.org; this private school for gifted children on Queen Anne stresses student-centered, interdisciplinary learning.
- **Seattle Girls' School (5–8)**, 2706 S Jackson St, 206-709-2228, www.seattlegirlsschool.org; a middle school committed to racial and socioeconomic equality, which helps prepare girls to be community leaders through a challenging academic program that emphasizes real-world problem solving.
- **Seattle Jewish Community School (K–5)**, 12351 8th Ave NE, 206-522-5212, www.sjcs.net; at SJCS, girls and boys participate equally in all areas of aca-

demics and Jewish ritual. The school stresses parental involvement and a non-competitive environment.

- **Seattle Lutheran Schools, Hope Lutheran School (P–12), 4456 42nd Ave SW, 206-935-8500; and Seattle Lutheran High School** (9–12), 4100 SW Genesee St, 206-937-7722; www.seattlelutheran.org; in 2009 these two West Seattle Lutheran schools joined forces to better accomplish their mission of preparing students for a lifetime of learning, service, and leadership.
- **Seattle Preparatory School (9–12)**, 2400 11th Ave E, 206-324-0400, www.seaprep.org, provides college preparatory instruction in the Jesuit tradition. Known for its athletic success, the school is a member of the Class AAA division of the Seattle Metro League.
- **Seattle Urban Academy (9–12)**, 3800 S Othello Ave, 206-723-0333, www.seattleurbanacademy.org; this small Christian school specializes in meeting the needs of at-risk students, helping them earn full or partial credit toward their high school diploma. Ninety percent of SUA graduates go on to pursue a two- or four-year college degree.
- **Shoreline Christian School (P–12)**, 2400 NE 147th St, Shoreline, 206-364-7777, www.shorelinechristian.org, is a multi-denominational Christian school that works in partnership with students' families and their church.
- **Soundview School (P–8)**, 6515 196th St SW, Lynnwood, 425-778-8572, www.soundview.org; an independent private school offering an International Baccalaureate (IB) Primary and Middle Years Program. In 2001 Soundview added five acres to its campus, and built a separate middle school to accommodate the upper grades.
- **University Preparatory Academy (6–12)**, 8000 25th Ave NE, 206-525-2714, www.universityprep.org; with approximately 500 students, University Prep stresses small classes, a commitment to diversity, and a balanced curriculum. One hundred percent of the class of 2010 went on to attend college.

MONTESSORI SCHOOLS

Dr. Maria Montessori developed the Montessori theory of education in the early 1900s. The Montessori Foundation estimates that there are more than 4,000 schools in the United States that follow her strategies. For information about the Montessori philosophy, visit the Pacific Northwest Montessori Association's website at www.pnma.org, or call 800-550-PNMA. The following is a partial list of Montessori schools in Seattle:

- **Chelsea House Montessori**, 13742 30th Ave NE, 206-363-5212, http://chelseahouse.tripod.com
- **Discovery Montessori School,** 2836 34th Ave W, 206-282-3848, http://discoverymontessorischool.org

- **Learning Tree Montessori**, 1721 15th Ave, 206-324-4788, www.learningtreemontessori.com
- **Montessori Garden**, 6615 Dayton Ave N, 206-524-8307, www.montessorigarden.net
- **Montessori School of Seattle**, 720 18th Ave E, 206-325-0497, www.montessorischoolofseattle.com
- **Northwest Montessori School**, 7400 25th Ave NE, 206-524-4244; 4910 Phinney Ave N, 206-634-1347; 7344 35th Ave SW, 206-933-8557;4025 86th Ave SE, Mercer Island, 206-232-4595, www.northwestmontessori.org
- **Pacific Crest Middle School,** 600 NW Bright St, 206-789-7889, http://pacificcrestmiddleschool.org
- **Pacific First Montessori**, 1420 5th Ave, #300, 206-682-6878, www.pacific firstmontessori.com
- **Sunnyside Montessori**, 3939 S Americus St, 206-725-5756, http://sunny sidemontessori.com
- **Veranda Montessori School**, 10417 3rd Ave NW, 206-782-5250, www.verandamontessori.com
- **Wedgewood Montessori Preschool**, 6556 35th Ave NE, 206-525-4432, http://wedgwoodmontessori.com
- **West Seattle Montessori (K-8)**, 4536 38th Ave SW, 206-935-0427, www.westseattlemontessori.com

WALDORF SCHOOLS

Waldorf education is based on the philosophy of Austrian philosopher Rudolf Steiner. For more information on the Waldorf method, visit the Association of Waldorf Schools of North America at www.whywaldorfworks.org. The following is a list of Waldorf schools in Western Washington:

- **Bright Water School (P-8)**, 1501 10th Ave E, 206-624-6176, www.brightwaterschool.org
- **Madrona School (P-8)**, 219 Madison Ave S, Bainbridge Island, 206-855-8041, www.madronaschool.org
- **Seattle Waldorf School (P-12)**, 2728 NE 100th St (kindergarten and grade school), 4919 Woodlawn Ave N (kindergarten), 160 John St (high school), 206-524-5320, www.seattlewaldorf.org
- **Tacoma Waldorf School (P-5) 2710 N Madison St**, Tacoma, 253-383-8711, www.tacomawaldorf.org; a middle school will be added in fall 2012.
- **Three Cedars School (P-8)**, 556 124th Ave NE, Bellevue, 425-401-9874, www.threecedars.org

HOMESCHOOLING

For a variety of reasons, homeschooling is attractive to many parents, and the state of Washington makes it fairly easy to choose that option. All you'll need to do is file a Declaration of Intent with your local school district and be sure you meet the qualifications for homeschooling. To qualify you must teach only your own child(ren) and have completed one year, or 45 credits, of college. If you don't have the college education you can be supervised by a qualified teacher for an hour a week, or complete a course in home-based instruction or be deemed qualified by your local school district superintendent. You will be required to have your children tested or assessed once a year and to meet the minimum hours for instruction, though how you construct those hours is up to you. You can request information and a forms packet from the Seattle School District's **Homeschool Resource Center** by calling 206-252-4720, or download the Declaration of Intent from the website at www.seattleschools.org/schools/hrc. The center also provides classes that homeschoolers can attend, a computer lab, library, gym and many other resources for support, encouragement and guidance for homeschooling families.

There are many homeschool support groups in the area with many different philosophies, as well as online sources of information. A few of these are listed here:

- **Washington Homeschool Organization (WHO)**, 6627 S 191st Pl, Ste F-109, Kent, 425-251-0439, www.washhomeschool.org
- **Homeschool Resource Center**, 1330 N 90th St, Bldg 200, 206-252-4720, www.seattleschools.org/schools/hrc
- **Home Education Magazine**, 800-236-3278, www.homeedmag.com
- **Homeschoolers' Support Association**, www.hsawa.org
- **Seattle Homeschool Group**, www.seattlehsg.org

ONLINE SCHOOLS

Once the sole domain of higher learning, online schools are slowly gaining ground at the high school, middle school, and even elementary school level. Some offer courses designed to supplement enrollment in a traditional school, or for homeschoolers, and some are completely online public schools offering valid high school diplomas. Depending on enrollment status and type of school, fees may be charged. There are no fees to attend public schools, even virtually.

- **Digital Learning Commons**, 4507 University Way NE, Ste 204, Seattle, 206-616-9940, http://digitallearning.k12.wa.us, grades K–12
- **Insight School of Washington**, 12011 Bel-Red Rd, Bellevue, 866-800-0017, http://wa.insightschools.net; grades 9–12

- **Internet Academy**, 31455 28th Ave S, Federal Way, 253-945-2230, www.iacademy.org; grades K–12
- **iQ Academy Washington,** Evergreen Public Schools, P.O. Box 8910, Vancouver, WA 98668-8910, 888-899-4792, http://iqacademywa.com, grades 6–12
- **Washington Virtual Academies,** 1584 McNeil St, Ste 200, DuPont, 253-964-1068, www.k12.com/wava; grades K–12

HIGHER EDUCATION

In some ways, Seattle is one big college town. It is the site of the state's largest public university, the University of Washington, and home to many other well-known private and community colleges. You can become a doctor, a diver, a lawyer, or a massage therapist without ever leaving the city limits. Educational programs abound outside the city as well.

The state's Direct Transfer Agreement makes it convenient for students to transfer from any Washington community college to one of the state's six four-year universities. The system works well for students who prefer to earn an Associate's degree before choosing a university, or who need to improve their grades a bit before applying to a four-year school. The agreement isn't a guarantee of admission, however, so it's best to check with the four-year college of your choice to discover any additional admission requirements.

In addition to traditional colleges, there are many special interest, vocational, and technical programs. Here is a partial list of schools located in the Seattle area.

SEATTLE

- **Antioch University**, 2326 6th Ave, 206-441-5352, www.antiochsea.edu, is a five-campus system that emphasizes an interdisciplinary curriculum. In addition to undergraduate courses, the college offers graduate programs in environment and community, management, whole systems design, and psychology.
- **Art Institute of Seattle**, 2323 Elliott Ave, 206-448-6600, 800-275-2471, www. artinstitute.edu/seattle; students here learn from artists and professionals in a hands-on environment. AIS offers either Associate of Applied Arts degrees or diploma certificates through the schools of design, fashion, culinary arts, and media arts.
- **City University**, 2150 N 107th St, 206-365-4228, www.cityu.edu, serves working adults who want to continue their education without interrupting their careers. CU offers more than 50 undergraduate and graduate programs and has campuses in Bellevue, Everett, Renton, and Tacoma.
- **Cornish College of the Arts**, 1000 Lenora St, 206-726-5016, www.cornish.edu, offers Bachelor of Fine Arts and Bachelor of Music degrees

in art, dance, design, music, theater, performance production, and humanities and sciences.

- **Everest College**, 2111 N Northgate Way, 206-440-3090, www.everest.edu/campus/seattle, provides instruction in massage therapy, medical assisting, and medical insurance billing and coding. Everest College campuses offering different programs of study are located in Everett, Tacoma, and Vancouver.
- **North Seattle Community College**, 9600 College Way N, 206-527-3600, www.northseattle.edu; located in a pleasant concrete building near Northgate Mall, NSCC is a versatile community college that offers day and evening classes for undergraduates and professionals. NSCC provides college transfer, career training, and pre-college programs in a range of subjects. The school's continuing education program offers a variety of computer courses for all levels of users, as well as cooking, business, and online courses.
- **Seattle Central Community College**, 1701 Broadway, 206-587-3800, http://seattlecentral.edu; a school of 10,000 students, SCCC is located in the Capitol Hill neighborhood, offering both undergraduate and professional education classes. In 2001, *TIME* magazine named SCCC as one of its four "Colleges of the Year" for its success in helping first-year students make the transition into college life.
- **Seattle Pacific University**, 3307 3rd Ave W, 206-281-2000, www.spu.edu; located at the north end of Queen Anne, SPU is a private Christian university with a picturesque campus, offering degrees in liberal arts, fine arts, business, and education, among others.
- **Seattle University**, 901 12th Ave, 206-296-6000, www.seattleu.edu; an independent Jesuit university located on First Hill, SU offers courses in a wide variety of subjects, including graduate programs in law, nursing, and software engineering, as well as undergraduate degrees in philosophy, theology, and the sciences. *U.S. News and World Report's* "Best Colleges of 2011" ranked SU among the top ten universities in the West that offer both master's and undergraduate programs.
- **South Seattle Community College**, 6000 16th Ave SW, 206-764-5300, www.southseattle.edu; located in West Seattle, SSCC offers both vocational and academic classes. The college's Georgetown Campus provides health and safety and apprentice-related training as well as labor education.
- **University of Washington**, 17th Ave NE and NE 45th St, 206-543-2100, www.washington.edu; founded in 1861, the University of Washington is a public research university attended by about 48,000 students. With campuses in Seattle, Tacoma, and Bothell, the UW (or "You Dub," as locals call it) is known internationally for its biomedical research. It also has outstanding graduate programs in business and law, and is a respected undergraduate institution. The university hosts guest speakers, dance troupes, and musicians throughout the year. In the fall, the Husky football team attracts alumni and sports fans from across the state.

EASTSIDE

- **Bastyr University**, 14500 Juanita Dr N, Kenmore, 425-823-1300, www.bastyr.edu; a renowned natural medicine university offering undergraduate and graduate degrees in fields ranging from naturopathic medicine and nutrition to acupuncture and Oriental medicine and exercise science.
- **Bellevue College**, 3000 Landerholm Circle SE, Bellevue, 425-564-1000, www.bellevuecollege.edu; one of western Washington's most popular two-year colleges, BCC offers A.A., A.S., and A.A.S. as well as bachelor's degrees in a variety of academic programs.
- **Lake Washington Technical College**, 11605 132nd Ave NE, Kirkland, 425-739-8100, www.lwtc.ctc.edu, offers job-training and professional development programs, and serves as a community resource, featuring a job placement center, library, dental clinic, and arboretum. The college has branch campuses in Redmond and Duvall.

NORTH

- **Cascadia Community College**, 18345 Campus Way NE, Bothell, 425-352-8000, www.cascadia.edu, is the state's newest community college, offering two-year degrees, certificate programs, and continuing education. In 2007, *Washington Monthly* ranked Cascadia as the second best community college in the United States.
- **Edmonds Community College**, 20000 68th Ave W, Lynnwood, 425-640-1459, www.edcc.edu; ECC's 50-acre campus is located just 15 miles north of Seattle. The college allows students the opportunity to combine weekend, online, and evening classes to fit busy schedules.
- **Everett Community College**, 2000 Tower St, Everett, 425-388-9100, www.everettcc.edu; in 1999, ECC offers a variety of university transfer, professional, technical, vocational, job skills, basic skills and personal enrichment courses and programs.
- **Shoreline Community College**, 16101 Greenwood Ave N, Shoreline, 206-546-4101, www.shoreline.edu; boasts a gorgeous, 83-acre campus just 10 miles north of downtown Seattle. More than 13,000 full- and part-time students benefit from small classes and the surrounding recreational and cultural opportunities.
- **Western Washington University**, 516 High St, Bellingham, 360-650-3000, www.wwu.edu; just 90 miles north of Seattle, WWU commands 200 acres in scenic Bellingham, a bayside city of 75,000. The university consistently ranks at the top of *U.S. News & World Report's* list of regional public universities.

SOUTH

- **Evergreen State College**, 2700 Evergreen Pkwy NW, Olympia, 360-867-6000, www.evergreen.edu; with a reputation as the state's most liberal and laid-back college, Evergreen State offers team-taught, multi-disciplinary programs that draw from many areas of study.
- **Green River Community College**, 12401 SE 320th St, Auburn, 253-833-9111, www.greenriver.edu; situated on over 180 acres of forested land, with branches in downtown Auburn, Enumclaw, and Kent, this two-year public college offers certificates and associate degrees in a variety of disciplines, from accounting to welding technology.
- **Highline Community College**, 2400 S 240th St, Des Moines, 206-878-3710, www.highline.edu; Highline's courses of study are divided into academic transfer, professional/technical, pre-college study, and extended learning.
- **Pacific Lutheran University**, 12180 Park Ave S, Tacoma, 253-531-6900, www.plu.edu; located in Tacoma's suburban Parkland neighborhood, PLU includes a College of Arts and Sciences, professional schools of the arts, business, education, natural and social sciences, nursing and physical education, and both graduate and continuing education programs.
- **Tacoma Community College**, 6501 S 19th St, 253-566-5000, www.tacomacc.edu, offers a range of academic and occupational degrees, worker retraining programs, and continuing education classes.
- **University of Puget Sound**, 1500 N Warner St, Tacoma, 253-879-3211, www.pugetsound.edu; Puget Sound is a private liberal arts college with fewer than 3,000 students, mostly undergraduates. The school offers graduate programs in education, occupational therapy, and physical therapy.

CONTINUING EDUCATION

Seattle boasts a highly educated population, according to the Census Bureau, but the learning doesn't stop here with a college degree. Non-degree continuing education classes are very popular and offered by most of the community colleges, as well as individuals and studios all over the city. You can take a class on everything from biodiesel basics and bookkeeping to Thai cooking and tying knots. Two good sources of continuing education classes are:

- **ASUW Experimental College**, University of Washington Husky Union Building, G-10, 206-543-4375, http://depts.washington.edu/asuwxpcl
- **Seattle Community Colleges (Central**, North, and South), 206-587-4100, www.seattlecolleges.com

S HOPPING IS GOOD IN SEATTLE AND MADE EVEN BETTER IN RECENT years with the addition of upscale stores to newly remodeled malls and shopping squares. Bellevue Square and University Village in particular have become destinations for the fashionable and affluent. Seattle's downtown shopping core also has been made more cosmopolitan with the arrival of stores like AllSaints Spitalfields, Coach, and Tiffany & Co. Heady espresso stands, swank cocktail lounges, and trendy eateries complete the day out. Most of the shopping locations listed in this chapter are found in Seattle or in nearby towns such as Lynnwood, Tukwila or the Eastside, but some may be in surrounding communities just a bit farther away, like the bargain-filled outlet malls in North Bend and Mount Vernon. Unless otherwise noted, all of the following are Seattle addresses.

SHOPPING DISTRICTS

While nearly every neighborhood in Seattle has its own small retail core, the following **Seattle districts** are well known for their shopping opportunities.

- If you are in a spending mood, some of the best shopping **downtown** can be found in and around the soaring Pacific Place mall at the intersection of 6th Avenue and Pine Street, and just west is the equally impressive Nordstrom flagship store. Westlake Center at 4th Avenue and Pine Street offers four floors of shopping and dining as well as a popular outdoor plaza. For over a decade this area of downtown has been undergoing a concerted and expensive retail makeover as many upscale, locally owned retailers, as well as big names in international fashion and entertainment, have located here.

- Originally a simple farmers' market, the popular and famous **Pike Place Market** is located downtown at 1st Avenue and Pike Street. In addition to the traditional fish, meats, fruits and vegetables, stalls are filled with local arts, crafts, flowers, teas, and clothing. Surrounding the marketplace, unique clothing shops, gardening and home decorating stores, antique malls and importers share space with tiny restaurants and fragrant bakeries.

• Located at the north end of Fremont Bridge, the **Fremont** shopping district is known for unique boutiques, vintage clothing stores, funky bakeries, and the Theo Chocolate factory. Fremont is a great location to visit for a strong cup of coffee and enjoyable windowshopping. Every Sunday the Fremont Market offers a European-style flea market that attracts treasure hunters from all over the city.

• Capitol Hill's busy **Broadway** shopping district runs along Broadway, from East Roy Street to Madison Street. Usually crowded until late at night, the district has almost as many restaurants, cafés, and bakeries as retail stores. Shops cater to a young crowd, with several new and used music stores, bookstores such as the popular Half-Price Books, costume jewelry and bead shops, tattoo and body-piercing parlors, movie theaters, and funky clothing stores.

MALLS

Most Seattle-area malls offer a combination of shopping options, from reasonably priced, practical stops, to high-end department stores, to one-of-a-kind boutiques—though not much in the way of discount stores. In the last decade, specialty retailers and popular national chains replaced many of the malls' bargain-oriented shops and dollar stores, which are now often located outside the malls.

• **Alderwood Mall**, I-5 and Alderwood Mall Blvd; 184th St SW, Lynnwood, 425-771-1121, www.alderwoodmall.com
• **Bellevue Square**, NE 8th St and Bellevue Way; 302 Bellevue Square, Bellevue, 425-454-8096, www.bellevuesquare.com
• **Crossroads Shopping Center**, NE 8th St and 156th Ave NE; 15600 NE 8th St, Bellevue, 425-644-1111, www.crossroadsbellevue.com
• **Everett Mall**, I-5 and Everett Mall Way; 1402 SE Everett Mall Way, Everett, 425-355-1771, www.everettmall.org
• **Lakewood Towne Center**, 5731 Main St SW, Lakewood, 253-584-6191, www.shoplakewoodtownceter.com
• **Marketplace @ Factoria**, I-405 and I-90; 4055 Factoria Mall SE, Bellevue, 425-641-8282, www.factoriamall.com
• **Northgate Mall**, I-5 and Northgate Way; 401 NE Northgate Way, Seattle, 206-362-4778, www.northgateshoppingctr.com
• **Pacific Place**, 6th Ave and Pine St; 600 Pine St, Seattle, 206-405-2655, www.pacificplaceseattle.com
• **Redmond Town Center**, NE 74th St and 164th Ave NE; 7525 166th Ave NE, Redmond, 425-867-0808, www.shopredmondtowncenter.com
• **Tacoma Mall,** 4502 S Steele St, 253-475-4566, www.simon.com

- **The Commons at Federal Way (formerly Sea-Tac Mall)**, S 320th St and Pacific Highway S; 1928 S Commons, Federal Way, 253-839-6156, www.tcafw. com
- **University Village**, 25th Ave NE and Montlake Ave NE; 2673 NE University Village St, Seattle, 206-523-0622, www.uvillage.com
- **Westfield Shoppingtown Southcenter (formerly named and still referred to as the Southcenter Mall)**, I-5 and I-405; 2800 Southcenter Mall, Tukwila, 206-246-7400, www.westfield.com/southcenter
- **Westlake Center**, 4th Ave and Pine St; 400 Pine St, Seattle, 206-467-1600, www.westlakecenter.com

FACTORY DISCOUNT STORES AND OUTLET MALLS

Great bargains can be found in factory discount stores, which often stock overruns and imperfect goods. Pay attention to price and merchandise quality. Most of these malls are quite a drive from Seattle, so check the locations on a map or call ahead for directions before you leave the city.

- **Birch Bay Square**, 3400 Birch Bay–Lynden Rd, Custer, 360-366-3127, www. birchbaysquare.com
- **Centralia Factory Outlet Center**, 1342 Lum Rd, Centralia, 360-736-3900, www.centraliafactoryoutlet.com
- **North Bend Premium Outlets**, 461 South Fork Ave SW, North Bend, 425-888-4505. www.premiumoutlets.com
- **The Outlet Shoppes at Burlington**, 448 Fashion Way, Burlington, 360-757-3548, www.horizongroup.com
- **SuperMall**, Hwy 18 and Hwy 167, Auburn, 800-SAY-VALU, www.supermall. com

WAREHOUSE STORES

Warehouse stores now offer good deals on just about anything, from clothing and groceries to furniture and appliances. One caveat: you have to buy many items in bulk, so unless you have room for 36 rolls of toilet paper… Both of the warehouse chains listed here have membership requirements; call for more details.

- **Costco**, 4401 4th Ave S, 206-674-1220; 1175 N 205th St, 206-546-0480; 10200 19th Ave SE, Everett, 425-379-7451; 35100 Enchanted Parkway S, Federal Way, 253-874-3652; 3900 20th St E, Fife, 253-719-1950; 1801 10th Ave NW, Issaquah, 425-313-0965; 8629 120th Ave NE, Kirkland, 425-827-1693; 19105 Hwy 99, Lynnwood, 425-640-7700; 1201 39th SW, Puyallup, 253-445-7543; 10000 Mickelberry Rd NW, Silverdale, 360-692-1140; 2219 S 37th St, Tacoma,

253-475-5595; 400 Costco Dr, Tukwila, 206-575-9191; 24008 Snohomish-Woodinville Rd SE, Woodinville, 425-806-7700, www.costco.com

- **Sam's Club**, 13550 Aurora Ave N, 206-362-6700; 1101 Super Mall Way, Auburn, 253-333-1026; 901 S Grady Way, Renton, 425-793-7443, www.samsclub.com

DEPARTMENT STORES

Nordstrom (not Nordstrom's) originated in Seattle, and still dominates the local market for high-end clothing and shoes. However, Seattle offers many alternatives for both home and personal shopping. A few of the largest stores are here:

- **Macy's**, 1601 3rd Ave, 206-506-6000; 7400 166th Ave NE, Redmond, 425-498-6000; Alderwood Mall, 425-712-6000; Bellevue Square, 425-688-6000; Northgate Mall, 206-440-6000; Westfield Shoppingtown Southcenter, 425-656-6000, www.macys.com
- **Nordstrom**, 500 Pine St, 206-628-2111; Alderwood Mall, 425-771-5755; Bellevue Square, 425-455-5800; Northgate Shopping Center, 206-364-8800; Westfield Shoppingtown Southcenter, 206-246-0400; Tacoma Mall 253-475-3630; www.nordstrom.com
- **JC Penney**, Alderwood Mall, 425-771-9555; Bellevue Square, 425-454-8599; Northgate Shopping Center, 206-361-2500; Puyallup, 253-845-6669; Westfield Shoppingtown Southcenter, 206-246-0850; Tacoma Mall, 253-475-4510; www.jcpenney.com
- **Sears Roebuck & Co.**, 76 S Lander, 206-344-4830; 15711 Aurora Ave N, 206-364-9000; Everett, 425-355-7070; Federal Way, 253-529-8200; Lynnwood, 425-771-2212; Puyallup, 253-770-5700; Redmond, 425-644-6749; Tukwila, 206-241-3400, www.sears.com

DISCOUNT DEPARTMENT STORES

Discount chains, such as Kmart, Target, and Walmart, do business throughout the Seattle area. Check the Yellow Pages or online for the nearest location of your favorite. Below are a few of the discount department stores in the region.

- **Fred Meyer**, 18325 Aurora Ave N, Shoreline, 206-546-0720; 100 NW 85th St, 206-784-9600; 915 NW 45th St, 206-297-4300; 13000 Lake City Way NE, 206-440-2400; 2041 148th Ave NE, Bellevue, 425-865-8560; 14300 1st Ave S, Burien, 206-433-6411; 12221 120th Ave NE, Kirkland, 425-820-3200, www.fredmeyer.com
- **Kmart**, 13200 Aurora Ave N, 206-363-6319; Everett, 425-353-8103; Kent, 253-852-9071; Tacoma, 253-752-3584, 253-531-6824; www.kmart.com
- **Marshalls**, 15801 Westminster Way N, 206-367-8520; 2600 SW Barton St, 206-933-3055; Lynnwood, 425-771-6045; Redmond, 425-644-2429; Renton, 425-203-9177; www.marshallsonline.com

- **Ross Dress for Less**, 301 Pike St, 206-623-6781; 13201 Aurora Ave N, 206-367-6030; 330 NE Northgate Way, 206-364-2111; Bellevue, 425-644-2433; Everett, 425-356-9970; Federal Way, 253-941-2122; Kent, 253-852-6442; Kirkland, 425-814-9798; Issaquah, 425-313-9616; Tukwila, 206-575-0110, www.rossstores.com
- **Sears,** multiple locations, www.sears.com
- **Target,** 302 NE Northgate Way, 206-494-0897; 2800 SW Barton, 206-932-1153; Bellevue, 425-562-0830; Everett, 425-353-3167; Federal Way, 253-733-7520; Issaquah, 425-392-3357; Kent, 253-850-9710; Lynnwood, 425-670-1435; Redmond, 425-556-9533; Renton, 425-207-0067; Tukwila, 206-575-0682; Woodinville, 425-482-6410, www.target.com
- **T.J Maxx,** 11029 Roosevelt Way NE, 206-363-9511; Bellevue, 425-373-0071; Edmonds, 425-774-5001; Woodinville, 425-398-0714; Everett, 425-348-5939; Kent, 253-852-8100; Federal Way, 253-946-2887; Tacoma, 253-272-4422; tjmaxx.com
- **Walmart,** Auburn, 253-735-1855; Bremerton, 360-698-2889; Everett, 425-923-1740; Federal Way, 253-835-4965; Lynnwood, 425-741-9445; Renton, 425-227-0407, www.walmartstores.com

HOUSEHOLD SHOPPING

APPLIANCES/ELECTRONICS/COMPUTERS & SOFTWARE

For your stereo, television, cellular phone, home theater, and technology purchases, there are a wide variety of electronics and computer stores in Seattle. Large department and warehouse stores such as Sears and Costco are worth a visit when shopping for home audio or video options and major appliances. All of the big box chain stores are represented, such as **Best Buy** (www.bestbuy.com), **Radio Shack** (www.radioshack.com), **Magnolia Audio Video** (www.magnoliaav.com), and **Fry's Electronics** (www.frys.com). One Seattle location well known for its concentration of electronics stores is just north of the University District on Roosevelt Way NE, between NE Ravenna Boulevard and NE 65th Street. The following list is a sampling of specialty electronics and appliance stores in the area:

- **Albert Lee Appliances**, 1476 Elliott Ave W, 206-282-2110; 1038 166th Ave NE, Bellevue, 425-451-1110; 404 Strander Blvd, Tukwila, 433-1110; 18620 33rd Ave W, Lynnwood, 425-670-1110; 4124 Tacoma Mall Blvd, 253-471-1110, www.albertleeappliance.com
- **The Apple Store,** 2656 NE University Village St, 206-892-0433, www.apple.com
- **The Audio Connection**, 5621-A University Way NE, 206-524-7251, www.audioconnectionseattle.com

- **Car Toys,** 307 Broad St, 206-443-2726; 12815 Aurora Ave N, 206-364-5534; check website for many other locations
- **Definitive Audio,** 6206 Roosevelt Way NE, 206-524-6633; 14405 NE 20th, Bellevue, 425-746-3188; 6450 Tacoma Mall Blvd, Tacoma, 253-472-3133; www. definitive.com
- **Hawthorne Stereo,** 6303 Roosevelt Way NE, 206-522-9608, www.hawthornestereo.com
- **The Mac Store,** 815 NE 45th St, 800-689-8191; 7501 166th Ave NE, 800-689-8191; www.themacstore.com
- **Metropolitan Appliance,** 1749 1st Ave S, 206-623-8811, www.directbuyingservice.com
- **Re-PC,** 1565 6th Ave S, 206-623-9151, www.repc.com
- **Resolution Audio Video,** 5459 Leary Ave NW, 206-784-4434, www.resolutionaudiovideoseattle.com
- **SpeakerLab,** 6220 Roosevelt Way NE, 206-523-2269, www.speakerlab.com
- **Stereo Warehouse,** 13728 Aurora Ave N, 206-365-5622, www.superstereowarehouse.com
- **Wiseman's Appliance & TV,** 2619 California Ave SW, 206-937-7400, www.wisemanappliance.com

BEDS, BEDDING & BATH

Some area department stores sell bedding as well as beds. For their names, locations and phone numbers, see the previous entries under **Department Stores**.

- **All About Down,** 352 N 78th St, 206-784-3444, www.allaboutdown.com
- **Bed Bath & Beyond,** multiple locations, www.bedbathandbeyond.com
- **Bedrooms and More,** 300 NE 45th St, 206-633-4494, www.bedroomsandmore.com
- **Feathered Friends,** 119 Yale Ave N, 206-292-2210, www.featheredfriends.com
- **Mattress Depot USA,** multiple locations, www.mattressdepotusa.com
- **Seattle Mattress Company,** 6019 15th Ave NW, 206-632-2240, www.seattlemattress.net
- **Sleep Country USA,** multiple locations, www.sleepcountry.com
- **Soaring Heart Natural Bed Company,** 101 Nickerson St, Ste 400, 206-282-1717, www.soaringheart.com
- **Yves Delorme,** 4608 25th Ave NE, 206-523-8407; 990 122nd Ave NE, Bellevue, 425-455-3508; www.yvesdelorme.com

CARPETS & RUGS

Carpet and flooring companies abound. Check the Yellow Pages or online for a complete listing. If it's an Oriental rug you need, a fun place to begin your search is in the many galleries and shops in the Pioneer Square area of downtown.

- **Abbey Carpet,** 2418 1st Ave S, 206-623-3550, http://seattle.abbeycarpet.com
- **Caravan Carpets,** 3500 Fremont Ave N, 206-547-6666, www.caravancarpetsseattle.com
- **Consolidated Carpets,** 200 N 85th St, 206-789-7737, www.consolidatedcarpets.com
- **Driscoll Robbins Oriental Carpets,** 1002 Western Ave, 206-292-1115, www.driscollrobbins.com
- **Great Floors,** multiple locations, www.greatfloors.com
- **Palace Rug Gallery,** 323 1st Ave S, 206-382-7401; 10644 NE 8th St, 425-454-7879; www.palacerug.com
- **Pande Cameron,** 333 Westlake Ave N, 206-624-6263; 13013 NE 20th, Bellevue, 425-885-1816, www.pande-cameron.com
- **Ravenna Interiors,** 2251 NE 65th St, 206-525-5794, http://ravennainteriors.com
- **Turabi Rug Gallery,** 113 1st Ave S, 206-624-7726; 7220 Greenwood Ave N, 206-782-9205; www.turabiruggallery.com

FURNITURE

A home furnishings store may be one of the first places you visit as you try to fill your new home or apartment. For a huge selection of reasonably priced contemporary furnishings, check out the IKEA store in Renton, south of Seattle. Many department stores offer good selections of traditional home furnishings. Call ahead for details, or check the newspaper for sales and special promotions. Catalog favorites, such as Pottery Barn, Restoration Hardware, and Crate and Barrel, allow consumers to shop in-person, by mail, or online.

- **Area 51,** 401 E Pine St, 206-568-4782, www.area51seattle.com
- **BoConcept,** 901 Western Ave, 206-464-9999, www.boconcept.us
- **Capers Home,** 4525 California Ave SW, 206-932-0371, http://caperscapers.blogspot.com
- **Dania Home and Office,** 825 Western, 206-262-1001; 6416 Roosevelt Way NE, 206-524-9611; 12230 NE 116th St, Kirkland, 425-823-9160; 19801 40th Ave W, Lynnwood, 425-673-1588; 1251 Andover Park W, Tukwila, 206-575-1918; www.daniafurniture.com
- **Design Within Reach,** 1918 1st Ave, 206-443-9900, www.dwr.com

- **Ethan Allen Home Interiors**, 2209 NE Bel-Red Rd, Redmond, 425-641-3133; 4029 Alderwood Mall Blvd, Lynnwood, 425-775-1901; 17333 Southcenter Pkwy, Tukwila, 206-575-4366, www.ethanallen.com
- **IKEA Home Furnishings**, 601 SW 41st St, Renton, 425-656-2980, www.ikea.com
- **Kasala,** 1505 Western Ave, 206-623-7795; 1018 116th Ave NE, Bellevue, 425-453-2823; 17275 Southcenter Pkwy, Tukwila, 206-436-8553; http://kasala.com
- **Ligne Roset,** 112 Westlake Ave N, 206-341-9990, www.ligne-roset-usa.com
- **Masins Furniture**, 220 2nd Ave S, 206-622-5606; 10708 Main St, Bellevue, 425-450-9999, www.masins.com
- **McKinnon Furniture**, 1201 Western Ave, Ste 100, 206-622-6474, www.mckinnonfurniture.com
- **Norwalk Furniture**, 304 Puyallup Ave, Tacoma, 253-284-3150, www.norwalkfurniture.com
- **Pottery Barn**, 4627 University Village, 206-522-6860; 212 Bellevue Square, Bellevue, 425-451-0097; 3000 184th St SW, Lynnwood, 425-774-5441; www.potterybarn.com
- **Restoration Hardware (at University Village)**, 4619 26th Ave NE, 206-522-2775, www.restorationhardware.com
- **SKARBOS Furniture,** 5354 Ballard Ave, 206-529-3830; 16705 Southcenter Pkwy, Tukwila, 206-575-3730

HOUSEWARES

- **Bed Bath & Beyond,** multiple locations, www.bedbathandbeyond.com
- **City Kitchens,** 1527 4th Ave, 206-382-1138, www.citykitchensseattle.com
- **The Container Store**, 700 Bellevue Way NE, Bellevue, 425-453-7120, www.containerstore.com
- **Cost Plus Imports**, 2103 Western Ave, 206-443-1055; 10300 NE 8th St, Bellevue, 425-453-1310; 4036 Tacoma Mall Blvd, 253-475-3500; 7214 170th St NE, Redmond, 425-883-8863; 13990 NE Mill Pl, Woodinville, 425-424-3214; www.worldmarket.com
- **Crate and Barrel**, 2680 NE 49th St, 206-937-9939; 555 Bellevue Square NE, Bellevue, 425-646-8900, www.crateandbarrel.com
- **Mrs. Cooks**, 2685 NE Village Ln, 206-525-5008, www.mrscooks.com
- **Pier 1 Imports**, multiple locations, www.pier1.com
- **Pottery Barn**, 4627 University Village, 206-522-6860; 212 Bellevue Square, Bellevue, 425-451-0097; 3000 184th St SW, Lynnwood, 425-774-5441, www.potterybarn.com
- **Restoration Hardware (at University Village)**, 4619 26th Ave NE, 206-522-2775, www.restorationhardware.com

- **Sur La Table**, 84 Pine St, 206-448-2244; 90 Central Way, Kirkland, 425-827-1311; 11111 NE 8th St, Bellevue, 425-450-4010; www.surlatable.com
- **Williams Sonoma**, 600 Pine St, 206-624-1422; 2530 NE University Village, 206-523-3733; 216 Bellevue Square, Bellevue, 425-454-7007; www.williams-sonoma.com

LAMPS & LIGHTING

- **Antique Lighting Company**, 8214 Greenwood Ave N, 206-622-8298, www.antiquelighting.com
- **Hansen Lamp and Shades**, 10706 Lake City Way NE, 206-363-1635, www.hansenlamp.com
- **Harold's Lighting**, 1912 N 45th St, 206-219-4341, www.haroldslighting.com
- **Lamps Plus**, 196th St SW, Lynnwood, 425-775-4320; 16839 Southcenter Pkwy, Tukwila, 206-575-9110, www.lampsplus.com
- **Lighting Supply Inc.**, 2729 2nd Ave, 206-441-5075, www.lightingsupply.net
- **Light Matters**, 905 Western Ave, 206-382-9667, www.lmatters.com
- **Rejuvenation**, 2910 1st Ave S, 206-382-1901, www.rejuvenation.com
- **Seattle Lighting**, 222 2nd Ave S, 206-622-4736; 14505 NE 20th St, Bellevue, 425-455-2110; 1811 Hewitt Ave, Everett, 425-252-4151; 6710 Tacoma Mall Blvd, Tacoma, 253-475-8730; 300 Andover Park W, Tukwila, 206-575-6224; www.seattlelighting.com

HARDWARE & GARDEN CENTERS

For paint and wallpaper, light fixtures, landscaping supplies, and anything else you might need for your Saturday projects, the following list might be useful.

- **Ballard Hardware & Supply Company,** 4749 Ballard Ave NW, 206-783-6626, www.ballardhardware.com
- **City People's**, 5440 Sand Point Way NE, 206-524-1200; 2939 E Madison St, 206-324-0737 (garden store); www.citypeoples.com
- **Crown Hill Hardware,** 7759 15th Ave NW, 206-784-0016, www.acehardware.com
- **Five Corners Hardware**, 305 W McGraw St, 206-282-5000, www.truevalue.com
- **Hardwick's**, 4214 Roosevelt Way NE, 206-632-1203, www.ehardwicks.com
- **Home Builders Center**, 1110 W Nickerson St, 206-283-6060, www.tweedypopp.net
- **The Home Depot**, multiple locations, www.homedepot.com
- **Junction True Value Hardware**, 4747 44th Ave SW, 206-932-0450, www.junctiontruevalue.com
- **Lowe's,** multiple locations, www.lowes.com

- **Madison Park Hardware**, 1837 42nd Ave E, 206-322-5331, www.madison-parkseattle.com
- **Magnolia Ace Hardware**, 2420 32nd Ave W, 206-282-1916, www.acehardware.com
- **Magnolia Garden Center**, 3213 W Smith St, 206-284-1161, www.magnoliagarden.com
- **Molbak's**, 13625 NE 175th St, Woodinville, 425-483-5000, www.molbaks.com
- **RE Store**, 1440 NW 52nd St, 206-297-9119, www.re-store.org
- **Sky Nursery**, 18528 Aurora Ave N, 206-546-4851, www.skynursery.com
- **Stewart Lumber & Hardware**, 1761 Rainier Ave S, 206-324-5000, www.acehardware.com
- **Swansons**, 9701 15th Ave NW, 206-782-2543, www.swansonsnursery.com
- **Stoneway Hardware & Supply**, 4318 Stone Way N, 206-545-6910, www.stonewayhardware.com
- **Tacoma Screw**, multiple locations, www.tacomascrew.com
- **Tweedy & Popp Ace Hardware**, 1815 N 45th St, 206-632-2290, www.tweedypopp.net
- **University Hardware**, 4731 University Way NE, 206-523-5353, www.truevalue.com

SECONDHAND SHOPPING

Secondhand shopping is a favorite pastime of many Seattle residents. What better way to spend a drizzly afternoon than digging for treasures that cost so little? There are many antique and vintage stores in Seattle, particularly near the Pike Place Market and in the Greenwood, Ballard, and Fremont neighborhoods. Several towns beyond the city limits, most notably Duvall, Issaquah, and Snohomish, are known for their many antique stores. Also, check the Sunday newspapers and on craigslist for estate sales or auctions. Most are open to the public, and some also hold previews so you can judge whether to arrive early.

- **Area 51**, 401 E Pine St, 206-568-4782, www.area51seattle.com
- **Antika**, 8421 Greenwood Ave N, 206-789-6393, www.antikaantiques.com
- **Antique Mall of West Seattle**, 4516 California Ave SW, 206-935-9774
- **Antiques at Pike Place**, 92 Stewart St, 206-441-9643, www.antiquesatpikeplace.com
- **Aurora Antique Pavilion**, 24111 Hwy 99, Edmonds, 425-744-0566
- **Bell'Occhio**, 1435 Elliott Ave W, 206-323-8833, www.bellocchiohome.com
- **Children's Hospital Thrift Stores**, 15835 Westminster Way N, 206-448-7609; 215 W Meeker, Kent, 253-850-8216; 15137 NE 24th, Redmond, 425-746-3092; www.seattlechildrens.org
- **Classic Consignment,** 5514 24th Ave NW, 206-781-7061, www.classicconsignmentseattle.com

- **Goodwill**, multiple locations, www.seattlegoodwill.org
- **Fremont Vintage Mall**, 3419 Fremont Place N, 206-548-9140, www.fremont-vintagemall.com
- **Gilman Antique Gallery**, 625 NW Gilman Blvd, Issaquah, 425-391-6640
- **Pacific Galleries Antique Mall**, 241 S Lander St, 206-292-3999, www.pacgal.com
- **Seattle Antique Market**, 1400 Alaskan Way, 206-623-6115, www.seattleantiquesmarket.com
- **Value Village**, multiple locations, www.valuevillage.com

FOOD

Now comes the fun part, eating! Seattle has a great selection of eateries, ranging from greasy spoons to elegant seafood restaurants. Almost every neighborhood in Seattle has at least one espresso stand, a café or bakery, and a local pub or micro-brewery. Ask your neighbors for recommendations, check the newspapers for restaurant write-ups, or visit one of the websites offering reviews by locals, such as **Yelp** (www.yelp.com), **Judy's Book** (www.judysbook.com), or **Citysearch** (www.seattle.citysearch.com).

At-home chefs are in luck too. In addition to the well-stocked supermarkets common in any city, Seattle has a nice selection of specialty grocers, food co-ops, farmers' markets, and fresh seafood markets.

GROCERY STORES

Many of the large grocery stores in the city are open 24 hours, and most feature well-stocked delis and on-site bakeries. The current trend in the new and remodeled stores is to offer an in-house floral department, espresso stand, and a take-out food counter with sandwiches, salads, sushi, and hot entrees. Many have adjoining businesses such as bakery, bagel or coffee shops, and small bank branches. **Trader Joe's** (www.traderjoes.com), **Thriftway** (www.thriftway.com), and **Albertsons** (www.albertsons.com), each have several locations throughout the city, but the predominant chains are **QFC** (www.qfconline.com) and **Fred Meyer** (www.fredmeyer.com), both owned by food giant Kroger, and **Safeway** (www.safeway.com). Selection, good sales, and convenience are consumers' oft-cited reasons for shopping at large chains; some even have in-store pharmacies. But don't miss out on the unique offerings at the smaller grocers. **Ballard Market** and **Greenwood Market** (http://townandcountrymarkets.com), both owned by Town and Country Markets, Inc., are popular for their large bulk selections, organic goods, and great weekly specials.

Two warehouse stores in the Seattle area offer good deals on bulk foods and other household items. These are **Costco** (www.costco.com) and **Sam's**

Club (www.samsclub.com). See above under **Warehouse Stores** for locations. Both have membership requirements. Call ahead for details.

SPECIALTY/HEALTH FOOD GROCERS

- **Central Co-op (formerly Madison Market)**, 1600 E Madison St, 206-329-1545, www.madisonmarket.com
- **Central Market,** 15505 Westminster Way N, Shoreline, 206-363-9226, http://shoreline.central-market.com
- **Metropolitan Market**, 1908 Queen Anne Ave N, 206-284-2530; 2320 42nd Ave SW, 206-937-0551; 5250 40th Ave NE, 206-938-6600, 100 Mercer St, 206-213-0778; 2420 N Proctor St, Tacoma, 253-761-3663; 10611 NE 68th St, Kirkland, 425-454-0085; www.metropolitan-market.com
- **Small Potatoes Urban Delivery**, 8 S Idaho St, 206-621-7783, www.spud.com
- **Whole Foods**, 2001 15th Ave W, 206-352-5440; 2210 Westlake Ave, 206-621-9700; 1026 NE 64th St, 206-985-1500; 888 116th Ave NE, Bellevue, 425-462-1400; 17991 Redmond Way, Redmond, 425-881-2600; www.whole-foods.com

Another grocery shopping option is the food cooperative. With nine neighborhood stores, Seattle's largest is **PCC (Puget Consumers Co-Op)**, which offers a wide selection of natural and organic foods. Visit www.pccnaturalmarkets.com or call your nearest store for membership information.

- **PCC Edmonds,** 9803 Edmonds Way, 425-275-9036
- **PCC Fremont**, 600 N 34th St, 206-632-6811
- **PCC Greenlake**, 7504 Aurora Ave N, 206-525-3586
- **PCC Issaquah**, 1810 12th Ave NW, 425-369-1222
- **PCC Kirkland**, 10718 NE 68th St, 425-828-4622
- **PCC Redmond**, 11435 Avondale Rd NE, 425-285-1400
- **PCC Seward Park**, 5041 Wilson Ave S, 206-723-2720
- **PCC View Ridge**, 6514 40th Ave NE, 206-526-7661
- **PCC West Seattle**, 2749 California Ave SW, 206-937-8481

INTERNATIONAL DISTRICTS AND MARKETS

Small grocery stores specializing in delicacies from other parts of the world are scattered throughout the Seattle area and surrounding communities. Immigrants and natives alike are attracted to these unique stores.

AFRICAN

- **J&B African Market,** 10327 3rd Ave S, 206-915-5178
- **Kilimanjaro Market**, 12515 Lake City Way NE, 206-440-1440

- **Superior Import Market,** 12528 Lake City Way NE, 206-397-3519, www.superiorim.com
- **West African Market,** 5997 Rainier Ave S, 206-723-6218
- **Zuma Grocery & Deli,** 129 NW 85th St, Ste A, 206-781-8600

ASIAN

There are numerous Asian markets in Seattle's International District, also known as Chinatown. Start at the intersection of 4th Avenue South and Jackson Street and head east. Don't miss Uwajimaya, the biggest Asian store in the West. You will also find a collection of Asian groceries along Aurora Avenue in North Seattle and on Beacon Hill.

- **Center Oriental Grocery,** 9641 15th Ave SW, 206-762-5620
- **Foulee Market,** 2050 S Columbian Way, 206-764-9607
- **Hau Hau Market,** 412 12th Ave S, 206-329-1688
- **Hop Thanh Supermarket,** 1043 S Jackson St, 206-322-7473
- **HT Oaktree Market,** 10008 Aurora, 206-527-5333
- **Hung Long Asian Market,** 9988 15th Ave S
- **Lam's Seafood Market,** 1221 S King St, 206-720-0969, www.lamsseafood. com
- **Mekong Rainier,** 3400 Rainier Ave S, 206-723-9641
- **Phnom Khiev Super Market,** 9841 16th Ave SW, 206-764-1009
- **Phnom Penh Market,** 7123 Martin Luther King Jr Way S, 206-723-4341
- **Uwajimaya,** 4601 6th Ave S, Seattle, 206-624-3215; 15555 NE 24th, Bellevue, 425-747-9012; 501 S Grady Way, Renton, 425-277-1635; www.uwajimaya.com
- **Vientian Asian Grocery,** 6059 Martin Luther King Jr Way S, 206-723-3160
- **Viet Wah Super Foods,** 1032 S Jackson St, 206-329-1399; 6040 Martin Luther King Jr Way S, 206-760-8895; 2820 NE Sunset Blvd, Renton, 425-336-6888; www.vietwah.com
- **Vina Supermarket,** 6951 Martin Luther King Jr Way S, 206-722-3918

GREEK-MIDDLE EASTERN

- **Byblos Deli,** 14220 NE 20th St, Bellevue, 425-455-4355, www.simplymedi. com
- **Pacific Market,** 132332 Lake City Way NE, 206-363-8639
- **Persepolis Specialties,** 13112 NE 20th St, Bellevue, 425-462-8987
- **The Shop Agora,** 6417-A Phinney Ave N, 206-782-5551, www.theshopagora. com
- **The Souk,** 1916 Pike Place #11, 206-441-1666

INDIAN-PAKISTANI

- **Apna Bazar,** 2245 148th Ave NE, Bellevue, 425-644-6887; 20710 Bothell Everett Highway, Bothell, 425-485-9900
- **Bharat Groceries**, 14340 NE 20th St, Bellevue, 425-746-0857
- **Imran's Market,** 11501 Highway 99, Everett, 425-610-4215
- **K. K. Market,** 23805 SE 104th Ave, 253-854-5236
- **Mayuri Food & Video**, 2560 152nd Ave NE, Redmond, 425-881-6284
- **Pakistani and Indian Grocery**, 12325 Roosevelt Way NE, 206-368-7323
- **R&M Videos and Grocery**, 5501 University Way NE, 206-526-1793
- **Ravi Sweet and Snacks**, 23609 104th Ave SE, Ste 102, Kent, 253-850-3333
- **Ravi Video and Grocery,** 23613 104th Ave SE, Kent, 253-850-6885
- **Sunny Supermarket,** 25414 SE 104th Ave, Kent, 253-373-0028

ITALIAN

- **Big John's PFI,** 1001 6th Ave S, level B, 206-682-2022, www.bigjohnspfiseattle.com
- **Borracchini's Bakery & Market**, 2307 Rainier Ave S, 206-325-1550, www.nowcake.com
- **De Laurenti Specialty Food and Wine**, 1435 1st Ave, 206-622-0141, www.delaurenti.com
- **Salumi**, 309 3rd Ave S, 206-621-8772, www.salumicuredmeats.com

SPANISH–MEXICAN–LATIN AMERICAN

Many local supermarkets such as QFC and Metropolitan Market carry a sizeable selection of ingredients and fresh produce used in Mexican and Latin American cooking, as do many of the Asian markets listed above. In addition, you can check the following sources:

- **ABC Supermarket,** 2500 Beacon Ave S, 206-323-2050
- **Carniceria Azteca,** 1265 S Main St #108, 206-323-1267
- **Carniceria El Paisano,** 9629 15th Ave SW, 206-767-5526
- **Castillos Supermarkets,** 10426 16th Ave SW, 206-988-4903
- **El Habanero Products,** 14830 1st Ave S, Burien, 206-244-3443
- **El Mercado Latino**, 1514 Pike Pl #6, 206-623-3240, www.latinmerchant.com
- **Guadalupe Market,** 1111 SW 128th St, Burien, 206-901-1529
- **La Benedicion Tienda Mexicana,** 2544 Beacon Ave S, 206-329-1039
- **La Conasupo**, 8532 Greenwood Ave N, 206-782-0533
- **Mendoza's Mexican Mercado,** 7811 Aurora Ave N, 206-245-1089
- **Mexican Grocery**, 1914 Pike Pl, 206-441-1147
- **Plaza Latina,** 17034 Aurora Ave S, 206-533-9440
- **Salvadoran Bakery,** 1719 SW Roxbury St, 206-762-4064

- **The Spanish Table,** 1426 Western Ave, 206-682-2827, www. spanishtable.com
- **Tienda Mi Ranchita,** 7636 Rainier Ave S, 206-725-9582

SCANDINAVIAN

As Seattle's demographic shifts, many Scandinavian specialty shops have closed their doors. Here are some of the survivors.

- **Larsen's Bakery,** 8000 24th Ave NW, 206-782-8285
- **Nielsen's Pastries,** 520 2nd Ave W, 206-284-3004, www.nielsenspastries.com
- **Scandinavian Specialties,** 6719 15th Ave NW, 206-784-7020, www.scanspecialties.com
- **Svedala Bakery (by appointment)**, 501 2nd Ave W, 206-407-4092, www. svedalabakery.com

FARMERS' MARKETS

If you're searching for the highest quality in fruits and vegetables, your best bet is to buy right from the growers. During the summer, you can often find corn, cherries, raspberries, strawberries, apples, and peaches sold from truck beds on city street corners. For a bigger selection, try one of the many farmers' markets in Seattle. The largest is Pike Place Market, in downtown Seattle at the west end of Pike Street. Don't be fooled by the fact that Pike Place is a popular tourist attraction; it is also a year-round destination for locals in search of fresh produce—succulent nectarines, perfect tomatoes, or flavorful Walla Walla sweet onions. You can also find fresh fish and shellfish, homemade jams, jellies and honey, and brilliantly colored tulips, daffodils, and dahlias. Neighborhood farmers' markets are open either on weekends or on an assigned weekday, and offerings include fresh produce from local farmers, and arts and crafts. The Pike Place Market, Fremont Market, Ballard Market, West Seattle Market, University District Market, and the Vashon Island Market are all open year-round; most of the other markets here are open from late spring to early fall.

SEATTLE

- **Ballard Farmers' Market**, Ballard Ave, Sundays, 10 a.m. to 3 p.m.
- **Broadway Farmers' Market**, Broadway and Pine St, Sundays, 11 a.m. to 3 p.m.
- **Cascade Farmers' Market,** Minor Ave between Thomas and Harrison St, Thursdays, 3 p.m. to 7 p.m.
- **Columbia City Farmers' Market**, Edmunds St and 37th St, Wednesdays, 3 to 7 p.m.
- **Fremont Sunday Market**, 400 N 34th St, Sundays, 10 a.m. to 5 p.m.

- **Georgetown Farmers' and Flea Market,** 6000 Airport Way S, Saturdays, 10 p.m. to 4 p.m.
- **Interbay Farmers' Market,** 2001 15th Ave W (Whole Foods parking lot), Thursdays, 3 p.m. to 7 p.m.
- **Lake City Farmers' Market,** NE 125th and 28th NE, Thursdays, 3 p.m. to 7 p.m.
- **Madrona Farmers' Market,** Martin Luther King Way and Union St, Fridays, 3 p.m. to 7 p.m.
- **Magnolia Farmers' Market,** 33rd Ave W and W Smith St, Saturdays, 10 a.m. to 2 p.m.
- **Mercer Island Farmers' Market,** 77th Ave S and SE 32nd, Sundays, 10 p.m. to 3 p.m.
- **Pike Place Market,** 1st Ave and Pike St, Monday–Saturday, 9 a.m. to 6 p.m.; Sunday 10 a.m. to 5 p.m.
- **Queen Anne Farmers' Market,** W Crocket St and Queen Anne Ave, Thursdays, 3 p.m. to 7:30 p.m.
- **University District Farmers' Market,** NE 50th St and University Way NE, Saturdays, 9 a.m. to 2 p.m.
- **Wallingford Farmers' Market,** Meridian Ave N and N 50th St, Wednesdays, 3:30 p.m. to 7 p.m.
- **West Seattle Farmers' Market,** 44th Ave SW and SW Alaska St, Sundays, 10 a.m. to 2 p.m.

SURROUNDING COMMUNITIES

- **Bellevue Farmers' Market,** 1717 Bellevue Way NE, Thursdays, 3 p.m. to 7 p.m.
- **Bothell Country Village Farmers' Market,** 23718 Bothell-Everett Hwy, Fridays, noon to 3 p.m.
- **Crossroads Farmers' Market (Bellevue),** NE 8th St and 156th Ave NE, Tuesdays, noon to 6:30 p.m.
- **Edmonds Museum Summer Market,** Bell St at 5th Ave N, Saturdays, 9 a.m. to 3 p.m.
- **Everett Farmers' Market,** Everett Marina at Port Gardner Landing, Sundays, 11 a.m. to 4 p.m.
- **Issaquah Public Market,** 1730 10th Ave NW, Saturdays, 9 a.m. to 2 p.m.
- **Juanita Friday Market (Kirkland),** 9703 NE Juanita Dr, Fridays, 3 p.m. to 7 p.m.
- **Kirkland Farmers' Market,** Park Ln E, between 3rd and Main, Wednesdays, 2 to 7 p.m.
- **North Bend Farmers' Market,** Main and Park at State Route 202, Saturdays, 9 a.m. to 1 p.m.
- **Redmond Saturday Market,** 7730 Leary Way NE, Saturdays, 9 a.m. to 3 p.m.

- **Sammamish Farmers' Market,** 801 220th Ave SE, Wednesdays, 4 p.m. to 8 p.m.
- **Vashon Island Growers Association Farmers' Market**, 1/2 block north of Bank Rd on Vashon Hwy SW, Saturdays, 10 a.m. to 2 p.m.
- **Woodinville Farmers' Market**, 17301 133rd Ave NE, Saturdays, 9 a.m. to 3 p.m.

COMMUNITY GARDENS

For the ultimate in freshness you could grow your own herbs and veggies. It doesn't take much space; a window box will do for many herbs. If you prefer a little more growing room when you garden, but don't have the space in your own backyard, consider a community garden. In Seattle, residents of 75 neighborhoods share "P-Patches," community gardens that boast more than 4,400 plots on 23 acres of land. **P-Patch** gardeners supply more than twelve tons of fresh organic vegetables to Seattle food banks each year. Many gardens have waiting lists—some up to three years long. According to the Seattle Department of Neighborhoods, only 10% to 20% of plots turn over each year, so you might want to get on the list as soon as you are settled into your new neighborhood. To sign up, or for more information, call the P-Patch Program at 206-684-0464, or visit www.seattle.gov/neighborhoods/ppatch.

RESTAURANTS

Depending on your degree of interest in food, dining out here can be a convenience, a diversion, a hobby, a sport, a religion, or a vocation. The city's dynamic restaurant scene offers diners every cuisine imaginable. Award-winning chefs such as Tom Douglas, Ethan Stowell, Maria Hines, and Matt Dillon have helped transform Seattle into a food mecca with restaurants such as the Dahlia Lounge, How to Cook a Wolf, Tilth, and Sitka & Spruce. The Herbfarm, widely considered one of the best restaurants in America, is in nearby Woodinville. To find popular eateries in your neighborhood, visit www.seattle. citysearch.com, www.yelp.com, or www.zagat.com. For helpful printed guides, consider buying the *Zagat Survey, Seattle/Portland Restaurants* or the *Food Lovers' Guide to Seattle* by Keren Brown.

Thanks to a cookbook from authors Cynthia Nims and Kathy Casey, Seattle's cooks can reproduce their favorite restaurant meals at home: *Best Places Seattle Cookbook: Recipes from the City's Outstanding Restaurants and Bars* features 125 recipes and 24 essays about local food and drink.

If you're tired after a long day of work and prefer to eat in without the hassle of cooking, consider picking up some food to go. Nearly all restaurants and most local grocery stores and specialty food shops offer take-out. If you can't even muster the energy to pick up a meal, a company called **Restaurants**

on the Run (www.rotr.com) will pick up a meal you order online from area restaurants and deliver it to you. Minimum orders and delivery fees apply, but it can be convenient, especially if you're craving food from a restaurant clear across town. Call 800-510-3663 for more information, or visit the website to place your order.

FOOD TRUCKS

Another grab-and-go alternative for busy Seattleites are the food trucks that have recently become a fixture of the street scene, where you can pick up everything from a gourmet hamburger (Skillet) to a shrimp po' boy (Where Ya At Matt). The website For Truck's Sake (www.facebook.com/fortruckssake) may be able to help you find out which trucks frequent your neighborhood, or where to go for the chow you're craving.

MAKE-AND-TAKE MEAL ASSEMBLY

An option that might be more of a bargain than you'd expect is make-and-take meal assembly, where the store does the prep and all you do is the assembly. The now popular national concept actually originated in Seattle in 2002. A few of the more popular companies, all with multiple Seattle-area locations, follow. You can also go to the Easy Meal Prep Association's website, www.easymeal-prep.com, for updated lists and locations.

- **Dinners Done Right**, www.dinnersdoneright.com
- **Dinners Ready**, www.dinnersready.com
- **Dish D'lish**, www.kathycasey.com
- **Dream Dinners**, www.dreamdinners.com
- **Kitchen 2 Kitchen**, www.kitchen2kitchen.com
- **Savory Moment**, www.savorymoment.com

DRINKING WATER

Many Seattle residents drink plain tap water, though some use a simple home filtering system, such as a Brita water pitcher. Less trusting souls can find companies that will deliver drinking water to a home or business:

- **Allwater Corp**, 206-624-3266, 425-451-0610, www.allwatercorp.com
- **Crystal Springs**, 800-201-6218, www.crystal-springs.com
- **Culligan**, 847-430-2800, www.culligan.com
- **Mountain Mist**, 800-232-7332, www.mountainmist.com

WINES

If you want to experience a wine country tour without traveling to California, you're in luck: the cup of Washington's wine industry overfloweth, with more than 700 licensed wineries, and counting. Just north of Seattle, the Woodinville area is home to more than 50 wineries and tasting rooms, including **Chateau Ste. Michelle** (www.ste-michelle.com), voted 2004 American Winery of the Year by *Wine Enthusiast* magazine. To arrange for tours or tastings, visit www.woodinvillewinecountry.com. Eastern Washington has its own wine country, as well, with a multitude of nationally and internationally known wineries. Visit the website of **Wines Northwest** (www.winesnw.com) to plan your trip.

Most grocery stores in the city carry an extensive selection of wine (and now liquor as well, following the success of a 2011 ballot measure to privatize liquor sales). Some, such as Metropolitan Market, make selections that are sold under the store's label for a limited time. If you prefer to buy your wines from a specialty store staffed with knowledgeable merchants who can offer suggestions about which wines pair best with salmon, visit one of Seattle's many wine stores. The following list offers just a taste:

- **Champion Wine Cellars**, 108 Denny Way, 206-284-8306, www.championwinecellars.com
- **City Cellars Fine Wines**, 1710 N 45th St, 206-632-7238, www.citycellar.com
- **Esquin Wine Merchants**, 2700 4th Ave S, 206-682-7374, www.esquin.com
- **Fremont Wine Warehouse**, 3601 Fremont Ave N, 206-632-1110, www.fremontwines.com
- **Madison Park Cellars**, 4227 E Madison, 206-323-9333
- **McCarthy & Schiering,** 2401 Queen Anne Ave N, 206-282-8500; 6500 Ravenna Ave NE, 206- 524-9500; www.mccarthyandschiering
- **Pete's Wine Shop,** 58 E Lynn St, 206-322-2660; 134 105th St NE, Bellevue, 425-454-1100; www.peteswineshop.com
- **Pike and Western Wine Merchants**, 1934 Pike Pl, 206-441-1307, www.pikeandwestern.com
- **Portalis Wine Shop**, 5205 Ballard Ave NW, 206-783-2007, www.portaliswines.com
- **Seattle Cellars Ltd.**, 2505 2nd Ave, #102, 206-256-0850, www.seattlecellars.com
- **University Wine/La Cantina Wine Merchants**, 5436 Sandpoint Way NE, 206-525-4340
- **West Seattle Cellars**, 6026 California Ave SW, 206-937-2868, www.wscellars.com

THOUGH SEATTLE LANDED ON THE WORLD MUSIC MAP AS THE BIRTH-place of grunge, it is not just a music mecca for alternative rock and its fans. Seattle is home to big and small arts venues that offer top-notch live performances in classical music, opera, comedy, and theater. Area residents flock to film openings, improvisational theater, traveling Broadway shows, art walks and galleries, and readings by visiting authors. The months of inclement winter weather guarantee large audiences for most performances. In the summer, entertainers simply move to the enticing outdoors. Music concerts are held in local parks, on the waterfront, and in concert halls. Another concert venue about two and a half hours east of Seattle is "The Gorge," a huge amphi-theater with a stunning view of the Columbia River that attracts big names in contemporary and classic rock, blues, and jazz. Located in George, Washington, it has been called the best outdoor concert venue in the country. Several summer festivals feature fabulous musical and theatrical performances; see **A Seattle Year** for more details. Also covered in this chapter: **Museums, Literary Life**, and **Culture for Kids**. Unless otherwise noted, the following establish-ments are in Seattle.

TICKETS

As in nearly every major city in the United States, tickets to most shows in Seattle can be bought through **Ticketmaster**: 800-745-3000 or online at www.ticketmaster.com. For especially popular events, such as rock concerts and pro-fessional sports playoffs, you may have no choice but to buy from Ticketmaster. However, for many events and performances you can avoid paying the extra Ticketmaster fees by purchasing tickets directly at the event venue's box office. Many area Fred Meyer stores have a Ticketmaster outlet, but check the website for retail locations.

Several local live entertainment venues, including the Crocodile Café, Comedy Underground, and Tractor Tavern, use the online ticket service **TicketWeb**, www.ticketweb.com. Still other attractions, like the Showbox Theater, use **TicketsWest**; go to ticketswest.rdln.com or call 800-992-8499 for a list of venues using this service. An increasing number of local events issue tickets through locally based **Brown Paper Tickets,** which charges small processing and delivery fees, donates part of its profits back to the community, and allows customers to designate which charities should benefit. You can reach them online at www.brownpapertickets.com, or by phone at 800-838-3006. Those ages 13–18 can sign up for **Teen Tix** (206-233-3959, www.seattlecenter.com/teentix), a free access pass that allows teenagers to buy $5 rush tickets to theater, dance, music, film, and visual art events.

If you have your heart set on a sold-out performance, try searching for tickets on fan-to-fan ticket reselling site such as stubhub.com, or search the listings on eBay or craigslist. Licensed ticket brokers such as Tickets Now (www.ticketsnow.com) and Admit One (www.admitone.com) can usually provide a ticket, but expect to pay dearly for the opportunity. Look in the Yellow Pages under "Ticket Sales—Entertainment & Sports."

CLASSICAL MUSIC AND DANCE

PROFESSIONAL—SYMPHONIC, CHORAL, OPERA, CHAMBER MUSIC

- **Seattle Choral Company**, 1516 NE 143rd St, 206-363-1100, www.seattlechoralcompany.org; performances are held November through May at various venues.
- **Seattle Men's Chorus**, 319 12th Ave, 206-388-1400, www.flyinghouse.org/smc; the largest community chorus in North America and the largest gay men's choir in the world, the Seattle Men's Chorus offers lavish performances, often with nationally famous guest artists. Under the same production umbrella is the **Seattle Women's Chorus**, formed in 2002, www.flyinghouse.org/swc; both groups offer five concerts per season.
- **Seattle Opera**, 1020 John St, 206-389-7676, www.seattleopera.org; world renowned, the Seattle Opera features five productions from August to May, as well as a summer presentation of "The Ring" cycle by Wagner every four years. A typical season includes several traditional performances of popular operas, as well as contemporary works and fresh takes on old standards. The opera routinely attracts international stars for lead roles, and longtime patrons recognize the local performers filling out each performance, held in the Marion Oliver McCall Hall.

- **Seattle Musical Theatre**, 7400 Sand Point Way NE #101N, 206-363-4807, www.seattlemusicaltheatre.org; for 33 years this group has provided local audiences with professional musical theater. Performances are from September through May at the Magnuson Park Recreation/Theatre.
- **Seattle Pro Musica**, 1770 NW 56th St #124, 206-781-2766, www.seattlepromusica.org; this award-winning group performs a four-concert season that ranges from medieval chant to the works of living composers.
- **Seattle Symphony**, 200 University St, 206-215-4700, www.seattlesymphony.org; presents weekly performances, September through June, in Benaroya Hall, an acoustic masterpiece with seating for 2,500.
- **Seattle Baroque Orchestra**, 911 Pine St, 206-322-3118, www.earlymusic-guild.org; this popular orchestra performs 17th- and 18th-century music from October through April in Benaroya Hall and the Kirkland Performance Center, using historical—or replicas of historical—instruments.
- **Northwest Sinfonietta**, P.O. Box 1154, Tacoma, WA 98401, 253-383-5344, www.nwsinfonietta.org; Tacoma's classical chamber orchestra performs in the Rialto Theater in Tacoma as well as Town Hall in Seattle.
- **Tacoma Opera**, 917 Pacific Ave, Ste 407, Tacoma, WA 98402, 253-627-7789, www.tacomaopera.com; performances are held at the Pantages Theater in downtown Tacoma.
- **Bellevue Opera**, 8726 NE 11th St, Bellevue, WA 98004, 425-454-1906, www.bellevueopera.org; offers two productions per year in Bellevue's Meydenbauer Center.

COMMUNITY—SYMPHONIC, CHORAL, OPERA, CHAMBER MUSIC

For a list of all Puget Sound choral groups, from small neighborhood groups to large-scale community choruses, visit the website of **Open Harmony**, www.openharmony.org.

- **Choral Arts**, P.O. Box 9009, 877-404-2269, www.choral-arts.org; this 30-member choir presents concerts in Seattle and Tacoma.
- **Federal Way Symphony**, P.O. Box 4513, Federal Way, WA 98063, 253-529-9857, www.federalwaysymphony.org; performances take place at St. Luke's Church, 515 S 312th St, in Federal Way.
- **Lake Union Civic Orchestra**, P.O. Box 75387, Seattle, WA 98175, 206-343-5826, www.luco.org; made up of all volunteers, this chamber orchestra offers four performances from November to June in Seattle's Town Hall.
- **Masterworks Choral Ensemble**, P.O. Box 1091, Olympia, WA 98507, 360-491-3305, www.mce.org; presents five concerts from October to June at the Washington Center for the Performing Arts in Olympia.

- **Northwest Symphony Orchestra**, P.O. Box 16231, Seattle, WA 98116, 206-242-6321, www.northwestsymphonyorchestra.org; performs works by Pacific Northwest composers, as well as classical pieces.
- **Rainier Symphony**, P.O. Box 58182, Seattle, WA 98138, 206-781-5618, www.rainiersymphony.org; serving up classical and pops to South King County audiences in the Foster Performing Arts Center in Tukwila and the Renton IKEA Performing Arts Center.
- **Seattle Modern Orchestra,** www.seattlemodernorchestra.org; this chamber orchestra performs underrepresented works from the 20th and 21st centuries in both traditional and unconventional venues.
- **Thalia Symphony**, P.O. Box 31117, Seattle, WA 98103, 253-642-7657, www.thaliasymphony.org; the orchestra primarily performs tonal music from the mid-19th century to the present. Performances take place in November through June.

DANCE

- **ARC Dance Company**, P.O. Box 9997, Seattle, WA 98109, 206-352-0798, www.arcdance.org; the resident dance company of the ARC School of Ballet presents a repertoire of contemporary ballets.
- **Evergreen City Ballet**, 2230 Lind Ave SW, Renton, WA 98057, 425-228-6800, www.evergreencityballet.org; performances are held October through June in various venues in Renton, Auburn, and Bellevue.
- **On the Boards**, 100 W Roy St, 206-217-9888, www.ontheboards.org; approximately 200 experimental and contemporary performances are presented October through December in two theaters at the Behnke Center for Contemporary Performance, and at theaters throughout Seattle.
- **Pacific Northwest Ballet (PNB)**, 301 Mercer St, Seattle, WA 98109, 206-441-2424, www.pnb.org; presents nine programs, September through June, including several performances of short contemporary works and longer traditional pieces. Also offers lectures and community outreach events. The annual Christmas show is a beloved version of *The Nutcracker*, featuring sets designed by author and illustrator Maurice Sendak. Performances are in the Marion Oliver McCaw Hall.
- **Spectrum Dance Theater**, 800 Lake Washington Blvd, Seattle, WA 98122, 206-325-4161, www.spectrumdance.org; Seattle's premier contemporary dance company draws on influences from swing to scat and tango to blues. Performances are held at a variety of venues throughout Seattle and the Eastside.
- **UW World Dance Series**, 3901 University Way NE, 206-543-4882, www.uw-worldseries.org; as part of the UW World Series, Meany Theater presents a selection of dance performances from around the globe. The series runs from

October to May. Meany Theater is located on the UW campus, at 15th Ave NE and Campus Parkway.

CONTEMPORARY MUSIC

Seattle burst onto the national music scene in the early 1990s as the home of "grunge" rock. While bands like Pearl Jam, Soundgarden, Alice in Chains, and Nirvana put the city on the map for alternative music, other musical genres likewise thrive in Seattle. The following bars, clubs, and concert halls are best known for the category under which they are listed, but many book a variety of acts. Check out the *Seattle Weekly* (www.seattleweekly.com) or *The Stranger* (www.thestranger.com)—both free local newspapers found in bars, cafés, and music stores—to find out each venue's schedule.

CONCERT VENUES

- **Benaroya Hall**, S. Mark Taper Auditorium, 200 University St, 206-215-4747, www.seattlesymphony.org/benaroya
- **Chateau Ste. Michelle Winery**, 14111 NE 145th St, Woodinville, WA 98072, 425-415-3300, www.ste-michelle.com
- **Comcast Arena at Everett**, 2000 Hewitt Ave, Everett, WA 98201, 425-322-2600, www.comcastarenaeverett.com
- **Gorge Amphitheatre**, 754 Silica Rd NW, George, WA 98848, 206-628-0888, http://www.livenation.com
- **Key Arena**, Seattle Center, 206-684-7200, www.keyarena.com
- **Memorial Stadium**, Seattle Center, 206-252-1800, www.seattlecenter.com
- **Paramount Theatre**, 911 Pine St, 206-467-5510, www.stgpresents.org
- **Tacoma Dome**, 2727 East D St, Tacoma, WA 98421, 253-272-3663, www.tacomadome.org

BARS AND NIGHTCLUBS

ALL AGES

- **El Corazon,** 109 Eastlake Ave. E. 206-381-3094, www.elcorazonseattle.com
- **Gallery 1412,** 1412 18th Ave, www.gallery1412.org
- **Ground Zero,** 209 100th Ave NE, Bellevue, WA 98004, 425-452-6118, www.bgcbellevue.org
- **Old Firehouse Teen Center,** 16510 NE 79th St, Redmond, WA 98052, 425-556-2389, www.theoldfirehouse.org
- **Studio Seven**, 110 S Horton St, 206-286-1312, www.studioseven.us
- **The Vera Project**, 305 Harrison St, 206-956-8372, www.theveraproject.org

ALTERNATIVE, INDUSTRIAL, ROCK

- **Central Saloon**, 207 1st Ave S, 206-622-0209, www.centralsaloon.com
- **Chop Suey**, 1325 E Madison St, 206-324-8005, www.chopsuey.com
- **The Crocodile**, 2200 2nd Ave, 206-441-4618, www.thecrocodile.com
- **El Corazon**, 109 Eastlake Ave E, 206-381-3094, www.elcorazonseattle.com
- **FunHouse**, 206 5th Ave N, 206-374-8400, www.thefunhouse.com
- **Hard Rock Café**, 116 Pike St, 206-204-2233, www.hardrock.com
- **Heaven Nightclub**, 172 S Washington St, 206-622-1863, www.heavenseattle.com
- **High Dive**, 513 N 36th St, 206-632-0212, www.highdiveseattle.com
- **King Cat Theater**, 2130 6th Ave, 206-448-2829, www.kingcattheater.com
- **Moore Theatre**, 1932 2nd Ave, 206-467-5510, www.stgpresents.org
- **Neumos**, 925 E Pike St, 206-709-9467, www.neumos.com
- **Rocksport**, 4209 SW Alaska St, 206-935-5838, www.rocksport.net
- **Showbox**, 1426 1st Ave, 206-628-3151, and 1700 1st Ave S, 206-652-0444, www.showboxonline.com
- **Sunset Tavern**, 5433 Ballard Ave, 206-784-4880, www.sunsettavern.com
- **Tractor Tavern**, 5213 Ballard Ave NW, 206-789-3599, www.tractortavern.com

BLUES, JAZZ

- **Bad Albert's**, 5100 Ballard Ave NW, 206-782-9623, www.badalberts.com
- **Dimitriou's Jazz Alley**, 2033 6th Ave, 206-441-9729, www.jazzalley.com
- **Egan's Ballard Jam House**, 1707 NW Market St, 206-789-1621, www.ballardjamhouse.com
- **Highway 99 Blues Club**, 1414 Alaskan Way, 206-382-2171, www.highway99blues.com
- **Larry's Greenfront Restaurant and Lounge**, 209 1st Ave S, 206-624-7665
- **Lucid Jazz Lounge**, 5241 University Ave NE, 206-402-3042, www.lucidseattle.com
- **New Orleans Creole Restaurant**, 114 1st Ave S, 206-622-2563, www.neworleanscreolerestaurant.com
- **Old Timer's Café**, 620 1st Ave S, 206-623-9800
- **Seamonster Lounge**, 2202 N 45th St, 206-992-1120, www.seamonsterlounge.com
- **The Triple Door**, 216 Union St, 206-838-4333, www.thetripledoor.net
- **Tula's Restaurant and Jazz Club**, 2214 2nd Ave, 206-443-4221, www.tulas.com

COUNTRY

- **Cowgirls, Inc.**, 421 1st Ave S, 206-340-0777, www.cowgirlsinc.com
- **Little Red Hen**, 7115 Woodlawn Ave NE, 206-522-1168, www.littleredhen.com
- **McCabe's American Music Café**, 3120 Hewitt Ave, Everett, 425-252-3082
- **Dance**, DJs
- **Baltic Room**, 1207 Pine St, 206-625-4444, www.thebalticroom.net
- **Belltown Billiards**, 90 Blanchard St, 206-420-3146, www.belltownseattle.com
- **Club Noc Noc**, 1516 2nd Ave, 206-223-1333, www.clubnocnoc.com
- **Contour**, 807 1st Ave, 206-447-7704, ww.clubcontour.com
- **Down Under**, 2407 1st Ave, 206-728-4053, www.downundernightclub.com
- **Element**, 332 5th Ave N, 206-441-7479, www.elementseattle.com
- **Last Supper Club**, 124 S Washington St, 206-748-9975, www.lastsupperclub.com
- **Neighbours**, 1509 Broadway, 206-324-5358, www.neighboursnightclub.com
- **Paragon Restaurant and Bar**, 2125 Queen Anne Ave N, 206-283-4548, www.paragonseattle.com
- **Re-bar**, 1114 Howell St, 206-233-9873, www.rebarseattle.com
- **The Ballroom**, 456 N 36th St, 206-634-2575, www.ballroomfremont.com
- **Trinity**, 111 Yesler Way, 206-447-4140, www.trinitynightclub.com
- **Venom**, 2218 Western Ave, 206-448-8887, www.venomseattle.com
- **Vogue**, 1516 11th Ave, 206-324-5778, www.vogueseattle.com

FOLK, ROCKABILLY, SWING

- **Fiddler's Inn**, 9219 35th Ave NE, 206-525-0752, www.3pubs.com
- **Tractor Tavern**, 5213 Ballard Ave NW, 206-789-3599, www.tractortavern.com

FUNK, HIP HOP, R&B, SOUL

- **The Baltic Room**, 1207 Pine St, 206-625-4444, www.thebalticroom.net
- **Club Noc Noc**, 1516 2nd Ave, 206-223-1333, www.clubnocnoc.com
- **Highway 99 Blues Club**, 1414 Alaskan Way, 206-382-2171, www.highway99blues.com
- **Last Supper Club**, 124 S Washington St, 206-748-9975, www.lastsupperclub.com
- **Republiq**, 2946 1st Ave S, 206-552-8730, 222.republiqofseattle.com
- **Seamonster Lounge,** 2202 N 45th St, 206-992-1120, www.seamonsterlounge.com
- **Trinity**, 111 Yesler Way, 206-447-4140, www.trinitynightclub.com
- **Vito's**, 927 9th Ave, 206-682-6959, www.vitosseattle.com

IRISH AND CELTIC

- **Celtic Bayou,** 7281 West Lake Sammamish Parkway NE, Redmond, WA 98052, 425-869-5933, www.celticbayou.com
- **The Celtic Swell**, 2722 Alki Ave SW, 206-932-7935, www.celticswell.com
- **Conor Byrne Pub**, 5140 Ballard Ave NW, 206-784-3640, www.conorbyrnepub.com
- **The Dubliner Pub**, 3517 Fremont Ave N, 206-548-1508, www.dublinerseattle.com
- **Fadó Irish Pub**, 801 1st Ave, 206-264-2700, www.fadoirishpub.com
- **Kells**, 1916 Post Alley, 206-768-728-1916, www.kellsirish.com
- **Mulleady's Irish Pub**, 3055 21st Ave W, 206-283-8843, www.mulleadyspub.com
- **Murphy's Irish Pub**, 1928 N 45th St, 206-634-2110, www.murphyseattle.com
- **The Owl 'n' Thistle**, 808 Post Ave, 206-621-7777, www.owlnthistle.com
- **Paddy Coyne's,** 1190 Thomas St, 206-405-1548 (also Tacoma and Bellevue locations), www.paddycoynes.net

LATIN

- **Babalu,** 1723 N 45th, 206-547-1515, www.babaluseattle.com
- **Century Ballroom**, 915 E Pine St, 206-324-7263, www.centuryballroom.com
- **HaLo, 500 E Pike St, 206-324-7263,** www.centuryballroom.com/html/halo.html
- **Rock Salt,** 1232 Westlake Ave N, 206-284-1047, www.rocksaltlakeunion.com
- **See-Sound Lounge,** 115 Blanchard St, 206-736-5009, www.seesoundlounge.com

THEATER AND FILM

While many residents become season ticket subscribers, you'll find this is a city of last-minute ticket buyers. Even the most popular shows may not sell out until the day of the performance, though it's always good to call ahead and check availability.

PROFESSIONAL THEATER

- **A Contemporary Theater (ACT)**, 700 Union St, 206-292-7676, www.acttheatre.org; referred to as "ACT theater" or "the ACT," presents contemporary works by both established and little-known playwrights.
- **ArtsWest Theatre,** 4711 California Ave SW, 206-938-0339, www.artswest.org; the theatrical arm of this West Seattle nonprofit multidisciplinary arts organi-

zation is committed to the production of theatrical experiences that inspire ideas and debate.

- **Centerstage Theater Arts**, 3200 SW Dash Point Rd, Federal Way, 98023, 253-661-1444, www.centerstagetheatre.com; this award-winning South Sound theater company, founded in 1977, has a reputation for staging innovative productions of new and popular works that appeal to all ages.
- **Eclectic Theater,** 1214 10th Ave, 206-679-3271, www.eclectictheatercompany.org, formed in 2006, this is the resident company at the Odd Duck Studio, where it produces and presents original, new, contemporary and re-envisioned classics for the stage and screen.
- **The 5th Avenue Theatre**, 1308 5th Ave, 206-625-1900, www.5thavenue.org; the opulent and Chinese inspired 5th Avenue produces musical theater and hosts traveling productions of major Broadway shows, as well as concerts, lectures, and films.
- **Intiman Theatre**, Playhouse, Seattle Center, 201 Mercer St, 206-269-1900, www.intiman.org; this outstanding theater won the 2006 Tony Award for the best U.S. regional theater. Presenting a variety of modern and classic works, the Intiman addresses contemporary issues with ambitious and dynamic interpretations of new and established plays.
- **Neptune**, 1303 NE 45th St, 206-682-1414, www.stgpresents.org; after its recent facelift, this historic U District movie palace, dating from 1921, has been reborn as a live performance multi-arts venue. The newly burnished glass eyes of Neptune, whose image is imbedded in the theater's ceiling, gaze down upon audience members.
- **Paramount Theater**, 911 Pine St, 206-682-1414, www.stgpresents.org; the magnificent Paramount Theater hosts traveling productions of Broadway shows, as well as concerts, dance performances, and outreach programs. The plush lobby and ornate performance hall, which can be converted into a dinner theater, make this an elegant venue for any play or musical.
- **Seattle Public Theater**, 7312 W Green Lake Dr N, 206-524-1300, www.seattlepublictheater.org; the company performs at the Greenlake Bathhouse, a cozy brick building which used to serve as the lake's bathhouse. The theater produces classic shows with a good dose of humor.
- **Seattle Repertory Theatre**, Bagley Wright Theater, Seattle Center, 155 Mercer St, 206-443-2222, www.seattlerep.org; perhaps Seattle's best-known theater, "The Rep" presents a mix of classical and contemporary plays each season, from October to May. The theater often performs plays that have recently completed successful Broadway runs, but never hosts touring shows.
- **Seattle Shakespeare Company**, Center House Theater, Seattle Center, 206-733-8222, www.seattleshakespeare.org; professional theater company highlighting the works of Shakespeare, often with a contemporary twist. Occasionally offers a non-Shakespearean classic play.

- **SecondStory Repertory**, Redmond Town Center, 16587 NE 74th St, Redmond, 98052, 425-881-6777, www.secondstoryrep.org; a nonprofit, professional ensemble, SecondStory presents comedies, revues, dramas, and musicals year-round. The company also offers musicals for children through the Children's Theater series.
- **Taproot Theatre Company**, 204 N 85th St, 206-781-9707, www.taproottheatre.org; celebrating their 35th anniversary in 2011, the popular Taproot produces musicals, comedies, and dramas that celebrate theater and reflect their values of faith and respect.
- **Teatro Zinzanni**, 3rd Ave N and Mercer Street, 206-802-0015, www.zinzanni.org; part dinner theater, part circus, part cabaret, Teatro Zinzanni spins improv comedy, vaudeville revue, music, dance, cirque, and sensuality into a three-hour whirlwind of entertainment. Audience members watch the show from restaurant-style tables inside an antique mirrored wooden tent, while eating an excellent five-course meal. The company produces at least three new shows a year.
- **Woodinville Repertory Theatre**, at the Denali Stone Slab Studio, 16120 Woodinville Redmond Rd NE, Ste 15, Woodinville, 206-203-4168, www.woodinvillerep.org; this company, founded in 1998 by the late Peg Phillips of TV's *Northern Exposure*, is dedicated to producing quality theater in order to inspire and engage the local youth and community in theatrical arts.

COMMUNITY THEATER

- **Annex Theatre**, 1100 E Pike St, 206-728-0933, www.annextheatre.org
- **Bellevue Civic Theatre**, Meydenbauer Center, 11100 NE 6th St, Bellevue, 98004, 425-235-5087, http://www.bellevuecivic.org
- **Book-It Repertory Theatre**, 305 Harrison St, 206-216-0833, www.book-it.org
- **Driftwood Players**, Wade James Theatre, 950 Main St, Edmonds, 98020, 425-774-9600, www.driftwoodplayers.com
- **Freehold Theatre**, 2222 2nd Ave, Ste 200, 206-323-7499, www.freeholdtheatre.org
- **Lakewood Playhouse**, 5729 Lakewood Towne Center Blvd, Lakewood, 98499, 253-588-0042, www.lakewoodplayhouse.org
- **Renton Civic Theatre**, 507 S Third St, Renton, 98055, 425-226-5529, www.rentoncivictheater.org
- **Theater Schmeater**, 1500 Summit Ave, 206-324-5801, www.schmeater.org
- **Village Theatre**, Francis J. Gaudette Theatre, 303 Front St N, Issaquah, 98027, 425-392-2202; Everett Performing Arts Center, 2710 Wetmore Ave, Everett, 98201, 425-257-8600, www.villagetheatre.org

IMPROV

A combination of stand-up comedy and acting, improvisational theater uses audience suggestions to create a scene, which is then played for laughs. Most improv groups perform only on the weekends; make sure you call ahead as times and locations change.

- **Jet City Improv**, 5510 University Way NE, 206-352-8291, www.jetcityimprov. com
- **TheatreSports**, 1428 Post Alley, 206-587-2414, www.unexpectedproductions.org

COMEDY

- **Comedy Underground**, 109 S Washington St, 206-628-0303, www.comedyunderground.com
- **Laughs,** 12099 124th Ave NE, Kirkland, 98034, 425-823-6306, www.laughscomedy.com
- **Parlor Live,** 3rd fl Lincoln Square, 700 Bellevue Way NE, 98004, 425-289-7000, www.parlorlive.com

FILM

There are numerous movie theaters in Seattle, and multi-screen outlets continue to rise in developing areas outside of Seattle. For general multi-screen movie complexes, visit www.movies.com or check the Yellow Pages under "Theatres-Movies." The following is a list of alternative and fine art movie houses.

- **Central Cinema**, 1411 21st Ave W, 206-686-6684, www.central-cinema.com
- **Crest Cinema Center**, 16505 5th Ave NE, 206-781-5755, www.landmarktheatres.com
- **Egyptian Theatre**, 805 E Pine St, 206-781-5755, www.landmarktheatres.com
- **Grand Illusion Cinema**, 1403 NE 50th St, 206-523-3935, www.grandillusioncinema.org
- **Guild 45th Theatre**, 2115 N 45th, 206-781-5755, www.landmarktheatres. com
- **Harvard Exit**, 807 E Roy, 206-781-5755, www.landmarktheatres.com
- **Metro, 4500 9th Ave NE,** 206-781-5755, www.landmarktheatres.com
- **Northwest Film Forum**, 1515 12th Ave S, 206-829-7863, www.nwfilmforum.org
- **Seven Gables Theater**, 911 NE 50th St, 206-781-5755, www.landmarktheatres.com
- **Uptown Theater,** 511 Queen Anne Ave N, www.siff.net
- **Varsity Theatre**, 4329 University Way NE, 206-781-5755, www.landmarktheatres.com

FILM FESTIVALS

- **Children's Film Festival,** 1515 12th Ave, 206-329-2629, www.nwfilmforum. org
- **Independent South Asian Film Festival,** www.issaff.tasveer.org
- **Irish Reels Film Festival,** www.irishreels.org
- **The Langston Hughes African American Film Festival,** 104 17th Ave S, 206-684-4758, www.langstonblackfilmfest.org
- **National Film Festival for Talented Youth,** 1319 Dexter Ave N Ste 250, 206-905-8400, www.nffty.org
- **Northwest Asian American Film Festival,** 409 7th Ave S, 206-340-1445, www.nwaaff.org
- **Post Alley Film Festival,** 1216 10th Ave, 206-447-1537, www.postalleyfilm-festival.com
- **Seattle Arab & Iranian Film Festival,** 206-322-0882, www.saiff.com
- **Seattle International Film Festival,** 321 Mercer St, 206-633-7151, www.siff. net
- **Seattle Jewish Film Festival,** 206-324-9996, www.seattlejewishfilmfestival. org
- **Seattle Lesbian and Gay Film Festival,** 1122 E Pike St, #1313, 206-323-4274, www.seattlequeerfilm.org
- **Seattle Polish Film Festival,** www.polishfilms.org
- **Seattle's True Independent Film Festival,** 2311 N 45th St #194, 206-650-7470, www.trueindependent.org

MUSEUMS

Rainy days are perfect for strolling through the quiet (and dry) halls of fine museums—and Seattle has plenty of both! From art and science to culture and history, area museums offer interesting and diverse exhibitions, and many host traveling exhibits. Be sure to call ahead or go online to find out about the latest offerings and to check on days and hours of operation (several museums are closed on Monday and most have free admission days).

ART

- **Bellevue Arts Museum,** 510 Bellevue Way NE, 425-519-0770, www.bellev-uearts.org; located across the street from Bellevue Square, the Eastside's most popular shopping mall. A 2005 building renovation and a change in the museum's mission statement resulted in a cutting edge museum focused on crafts and design. Offering lectures, workshops and demonstration, it also sponsors the yearly Bellevue Arts and Crafts Fair. Hours are Tuesday–Sunday,

11 a.m. to 5 p.m. Admission is $10 for adults, $7 for seniors and students. Kids under 6 are free.

- **Frye Art Museum**, 704 Terry Ave, 206-622-9250, www.fryemuseum.org; located on First Hill in an International Style building designed in 1952 by Paul Thiry, the Frye Art Museum houses a collection of 19th-century paintings by European artists, as well as a large collection of works by 18th-century German artists. It also offers art classes and art history courses. Open Tuesday–Sunday, 11 a.m. to 5 p.m., until 7 p.m. on Thursday. Free admission.
- **Henry Art Gallery**, University of Washington, 15th Ave NE and NE 41st St, 206-543-2280, www.henryart.org; the 19th-century and early 20th-century American and European works originally donated by local businessman Horace C. Henry are still the backbone of this museum's collection, but the museum also offers modern and multidisciplinary art and design and innovative programs. Open Wednesday, 11 a.m. to 4 p.m., Thursday–Friday 11 a.m. to 9 p.m., Saturday–Sunday, 11 a.m. to 4 p.m. General admission is $10. No charge for high school and college students, UW faculty and staff, and kids 13 and younger. Thursdays are free.
- **Museum of Glass**, 1801 Dock St, Tacoma, 253-284-4750, 866-468-7386, www.museumofglass.org; devoted to the exhibition and interpretation of contemporary art with a focus on the medium of glass. A 500-foot pedestrian tunnel crafted by legendary glass artist Dale Chihuly links the museum to downtown Tacoma. Check the website or call for hours. Admission is $12 for adults, $10 for seniors, $5 for children, 6–12. Free every third Thursday of the month.
- **Museum of Northwest Art (MoNA)**, 121 S 1st St, LaConner, 98257, 360-466-4446, www.museumofnwart.org; the Skagit Valley, north of Seattle, has long been a haven for Northwest artists. MoNA opened in 1981 to present the works of these artists, and to serve as a source of education. The museum's small permanent collection consists of paintings, sculpture, glass and works on paper. Open daily, Sunday–Monday, noon to 5 p.m., Tuesday–Saturday 10 a.m. to 5 p.m. Admission is $5 for adults, $4 for seniors, $2 for students, and free for children 12 and under.
- **Seattle Art Museum (SAM)**, 1300 First Ave, 206-654-3100, www.seattleartmuseum.org; located near the Pike Place Market, the Seattle Art Museum houses an exceptional collection, which includes a variety of African, Chinese, and Native American pieces, as well as European and American art. SAM is Seattle's preeminent art museum, showcasing international traveling exhibits of photography, painting, and sculpture. Closed in 2005 for major renovation and expansion, SAM reopened with a dramatic new space in May 2007. Open Wednesday–Sunday, 10 a.m. to 5 p.m., Thursday–Friday 10 a.m. to 9 p.m. Free admission every first Thursday, and free for seniors every first Friday. Suggested admission is $15 for adults, $12 for seniors and members of the military, $9 for students and teens. Kids under 12 are free. Broadening the museum's scope, the **Olympic Sculpture Park** at 2910 Western Ave opened

in January 2007. This waterfront park, a transformed nine-acre industrial site, features over 20 sculptures along with a series of gardens as well as spectacular views of Puget Sound and the Olympic Mountains. Free admission.

- **Seattle Asian Art Museum**, Volunteer Park, 1400 E Prospect St, 206-654-3100, www.seattleartmuseum.org; housed in a 1933 Art Deco building flanked by two popular replicas of Ming Dynasty camels, this gallery presents art from all over Asia. The museum is a focal point of Volunteer Park, located at the northeast corner of Capitol Hill. Open Wednesday–Sunday, 10 a.m. to 5 p.m., Thursday 10 a.m. to 9 p.m. Admission for adults is $7; $5 for seniors, youths 13–17, and students with ID; those 12 and under are admitted free. Admission on the first Saturday of the month is free.
- **Tacoma Art Museum (TAM)**, 1701 Pacific Ave, Tacoma, 98402, 253-272-4258, www.tacomaartmuseum.org; TAM's exhibits emphasize art and artists from the Northwest. A permanent fixture of TAM is the most comprehensive public collection of Tacoma native Dale Chihuly's glass works. Every other summer the museum hosts the Northwest Biennial, a juried competition for artists from Washington, Oregon, Idaho, and Montana. Hours are Wednesday–Sunday, 10 a.m. to 5 p.m., every third Thursday, 10 a.m. to 8 p.m. Admission is $9 for adults, $8 for seniors, members of the military, and students, and free for kids 5 and under. Admission on the third Thursday of each month is free.

ART GALLERIES

A vibrant art scene thrives in Seattle, with many galleries receiving national and international attention and acclaim. Dozens of galleries showcase everything from traditional to cutting edge art by both local artists and those outside the Northwest. Check the Art Guide Northwest website for listings of galleries, artists, and events around Puget Sound, www.artguidenw.com. Listed below are just some of the galleries to be found in Seattle.

- **Azuma Gallery**, 530 1st Ave S, 206-622-5599, www.azumagallery.com
- **Benham Gallery**, 1216 1st Ave, 206-622-2480, www.benhamgallery.com
- **Patricia Cameron Gallery**, 234 Dexter Ave N, 206-343-9647, www.patricia-camerongallery.com
- **Center on Contemporary Art**, 6413 Seaview Ave NW; 2721 1st Ave, 206-728-1980, www.cocaseattle.org
- **Davidson Galleries**, 313 Occidental Ave S, 206-624-7684, www.davidsongalleries.com
- **Foster/White Gallery**, 220 3rd Ave S, 206-622-2833, www.fosterwhite.com
- **Friesen Gallery**, 1200 2nd Ave, 206-628-9501, www.friesengallery.com
- **G. Gibson Gallery**, 300 S Washington St, 206-587-4033, www.ggibsongallery.com

- **Grover/Thurston Gallery**, 309 Occidental Ave S, 206-223-0816, www.groverthurston.com
- **James Harris Gallery**, 309A 3rd Ave S, 206-903-6220, www.jamesharrisgallery.com
- **Lisa Harris Gallery**, 1922 Pike Pl, 206-443-3315, www.lisaharrisgallery.com
- **Linda Hodges Gallery**, 316 1st S, 206-624-3034, www.lindahodgesgallery.com
- **Howard House**, 604 2nd Ave, 206-256-6399, www.howardhouse.net
- **Greg Kucera Gallery**, 212 3rd Ave S, 206-624-4031, www.gregkucera.com
- **Jeffrey Moose Gallery**, 1333 5th Ave, 206-467-6951, www.jeffreymoosegallery.com
- **Bryan Ohno Gallery**, 519 S Main St, 206-459-6857, www.bryanohno.com
- **Pacini Lubel Gallery**, 207 2nd Ave S, 206-326-5555, pacinilubel.com
- **Catherine Person Gallery**, 319 3rd Ave S, 206-763-5565, www.catherinepersongallery.com
- **Platform Gallery**, 114 3rd Ave S, 206-323-2808, www.platformgallery.com
- **Roq La Rue Gallery**, 2312 2nd Ave, 206-374-8977, www.roqlarue.com
- **Francine Seders Gallery**, 6701 Greenwood Ave N, 206-782-0355, www.sedersgallery.com
- **Soil Art Gallery**, 112 3rd Ave S, 206-264-8061, www.soilart.org
- **Stonington Gallery**, 119 S Jackson St, 206-405-4485, www.stoningtongallery.com
- **William Traver Gallery**, 110 Union St, Ste 200, 206-587-6501; 1821 E Dock St, Ste 100, 253-383-3685, www.travergallery.com

ART WALKS

Each month, various communities in the Puget Sound region host monthly "art walks," where neighborhood galleries stay open late and often provide food and live music. This is a great way to see the exhibits without fighting daytime traffic and crowds. Look in weekly newspapers for information or call participating galleries.

FIRST WEDNESDAY

- **Wallingford Art Walk**, 206-547-5177, 6 p.m.–9 p.m.

FIRST THURSDAY

- **Pioneer Square**, 6 p.m.–8 p.m.

FIRST FRIDAY

- **Fremont Art Walk**, 6 p.m.–9 p.m.
- **Anacortes Gallery Walk**, Anacortes, 360-293-6938, 6 p.m.–9 p.m.

- **Artwalk Issaquah**, 5 p.m.–9 p.m.
- **Bainbridge Island Galleries**, Bainbridge Island, 5 p.m.–8 p.m.
- **Bremerton Gallery Walk**, Bremerton, 5 p.m.–8 p.m.
- **Vashon Island Gallery Cruise**, Vashon Island, 206-463-1722, 6 p.m.–9 p.m.

SECOND THURSDAY

- **Capitol Hill Art Blitz**, 5 p.m.–8 p.m.
- **West Seattle Art Walk**, 6 p.m.–9 p.m.

SECOND FRIDAY

- **Art Up Phinneywood**, Phinney and Greenwood neighborhoods, 6 p.m.–9 p.m.
- **Kirkland Art Walk**, Kirkland, 6 p.m.–9 p.m.

SECOND SATURDAY

- **Ballard Art Walk**, 206-784-9705, 6 p.m.–9 p.m.

THIRD THURSDAY

- **Edmonds Art Walk**, Edmonds, 425-776-6711, 5 p.m.–8 p.m.
- **Tacoma Art Walk**, Tacoma, 253-272-4258, 5 p.m.–8 p.m.

CULTURE, HISTORY

- **Burke Museum of Natural History and Culture**, University of Washington, NE 45th St and 17th Ave NE, 206-543-5590, www.washington.edu/burkemuseum; the Burke Museum houses fascinating exhibits on Pacific Rim geology, natural history, and anthropology. Native American artifacts—including masks, beads, and totem poles—and displays of dinosaur skeletons and fossils, are especially popular with children. Open seven days a week, 10 a.m. to 5 p.m., the first Thursday of the month until 8 p.m. General admission for adults is $9.50, $7.50 for seniors, $6 for students and youths over 4, and free for children 4 and under. Free for UW staff, faculty, and students.
- **Coast Guard Museum Northwest**, Pier 36, 1519 Alaskan Way S, 206-217-6993, *www.rexmwess.com/cgpatchs/cogardmuseum.html*; Coast Guard memorabilia, photographs, model ships and other nautical items are on display at this museum. Tours of Coast Guard cutters are available on weekends. Open Monday, Wednesday, and Friday, 9 a.m. to 3 p.m. Free admission.
- **Experience Music Project/Science Fiction Museum (EMP)**, 325 5th Ave N, 206-770-2700, www.empsfm.org; Microsoft co-founder Paul Allen first envisioned EMP as a place for music enthusiasts to explore and celebrate the history and diversity of popular music. In 2004, the museum morphed into the hybrid it is today, home to both innovative musical exhibits and

the world's first science fiction museum. The 140,000-square-foot building (either a masterpiece or an eyesore, depending on whom you ask), offers interactive exhibits, unique artifacts, performance spaces, and the Science Fiction Hall of Fame. Open daily, 10 a.m. to 8 p.m. Admission is $15 for adults 18 to 64, $12 for seniors, members of the military, and youths 5–17, and free for children 4 and under.

- **History House of Greater Seattle**, 790 N 34th St, 206-675-8875, www.historyhouse.org; through photographs and documents, History House displays the pictorial history of Seattle and its neighborhoods. Open Thursday–Sunday, noon to 5 p.m. Admission is $1.
- **Museum of History and Industry**, 2700 24th Ave E, 206-324-1126, www.seattlehistory.org; local Northwest history is presented in this museum, which will open in its new site at the Armory in South Lake Union in late 2012. Past exhibits of the museum, which is popular with children, have included old-fashioned fire engines, model ships, and figureheads. History buffs will enjoy the large collection of archival photographs and the many artifacts of Seattle's fishing, lumber, and shipping industries. Amazon's founder Jeff Bezos recently donated $10 million to create a "Center for Innovation" at MOHAI. Hours are daily, 10 a.m. to 5 p.m., first Thursday of the month from 10 a.m. to 8 p.m. Admission is $8 for adults, $7 for seniors, students, and members of the military, $6 for kids 5–17, and free for children under 5. No admission fee on first Thursday.
- **Nordic Heritage Museum**, 3014 NW 67th St, 206-789-5707, www.nordicmuseum.org; this museum chronicles the history of the Scandinavian immigrants who settled in the Ballard neighborhood and other areas of the Pacific Northwest. The museum offers Nordic dance and language classes, Scandinavian films, and lectures. Hours are Tuesday–Saturday, 10 a.m. to 4 p.m., Sunday, noon to 4 p.m. Admission is $6 for adults, $5 for seniors and college students, $4 for youths over 5, and free for children under 5.
- **Science Fiction Museum and Hall of Fame**, 325 5th Ave N, 206-724-3428, www.empmuseum.org; housed in the same building as the EMP, this is the first museum devoted to the genre of science fiction and its creators. Interactive exhibits explore literature, movies, and art, and this is now the permanent physical home of the Sci-Fi Hall of Fame. Open Monday–Thursday, 10 a.m. to 5 p.m., Friday–Sunday 10 a.m. to 6 p.m. Admission is $12.95 for adults 18–64, $8.95 for seniors and youths 7–17, $10.95 for military, and free to kids 6 and under.
- **Seattle Metropolitan Police Museum**, 317 3rd Ave S, 206-748-9991, www.seametropolicemuseum.org; located in Pioneer Square, the museum is the largest police museum in the western United States, combining historical displays with an interactive learning area for children and adults. The museum is open Tuesday–Saturday, 11 a.m. to 4 p.m. Admission is $4 for adults and $2 for kids under 12 and the disabled.

- **Wing Luke Asian Museum**, 719 S King St, 206-623-5124, www.wingluke. org; in the historic International District, the nationally recognized Wing Luke Asian Museum showcases pan-Asian culture, history, and art. Open Tuesday–Sunday, 11 a.m. to 4:30 p.m. Admission is $12.95 for adults, $9.95 for seniors and students (age 13–18 or with ID), $8.95 for kids 5–12, children 4 and under free.

SCIENCE

- **Museum of Flight**, 9404 E Marginal Way S, 206-764-5720, www.museumof-flight.org; located on the original site of the Boeing Company, the museum presents a complete history of flight and aviation technology. This is a great museum for kids and adults alike, with interactive exhibits, flight simulators, archival film footage, and colorful full-scale reproductions of some of Boeing's first airplanes—early bi-planes and military jets among them—hanging from the ceiling. The Red Barn, which housed the first Boeing airplane factory, is also part of the exhibit. Across the road from the main building, you can board an actual Concorde jet and a plane from Airforce One. Open daily from 10 a.m. to 5 p.m., first Thursdays until 9 p.m. General admission is $16, $14 for seniors, $9 for children ages 5–17, and free for those 4 and under.
- **Pacific Science Center**, Seattle Center, 200 2nd Ave N, 206-443-2001, www. pacsci.org; not your traditional museum by any means, the Pacific Science Center has more than 200 interactive exhibits on science and nature. Children in particular enjoy the hands-on activities, which approach learning in fun and creative ways. Open Monday–Friday, 10 a.m. to 5 p.m., weekends and holidays, 10 a.m. to 6 p.m. General admission ranges from $14 for adults to free admission for those under 3.

LITERARY LIFE

With its rainy days and coffee worship, Seattle is a great bookstore town, and in 2009 was named, for the third time, America's most literate city. Area residents flock to fiction and poetry readings, book groups, and book-signings. Seattle is even home to that bookstore without shelves, Amazon.com. While the city has chain stores like Barnes & Noble, many residents are fiercely loyal to Seattle's independent booksellers. Twice a year the Friends of the Seattle Public Library hold a popular book sale in a huge warehouse at Magnuson Park. Despite this support, tough economic times forced the closure of many beloved bookstores in recent years, and the famed Elliott Bay Books relocated from its longtime site in Pioneer Square to Capitol Hill in 2010. See the *Seattle Weekly*, the *Seattle Post-Intelligencer* online, and the *Seattle Times* for listings of upcoming readings and author signings, or contact your local bookstore for its calendar of events.

BOOKSTORES

GENERAL INTEREST

- **B. Dalton Bookseller**, Northgate Mall, 206-364-5810
- **Barnes & Noble Booksellers**, 2675 NE University Village St, 206-517-4107; 600 Pine St, 206-264-0156; 2600 SW Barton St, 206-932-0328, www.barnesandnoble.com
- **Elliott Bay Book Company**, 1521 10th Ave, 206-624-6600, www.elliottbaybook.com
- **Island Books**, 3014 78th Ave SE, Mercer Island, 206-232-6920, www.mercerislandbooks.com
- **Magnolia's Book Store**, 3206 West McGraw St, 206-283-1062
- **Queen Anne Books**, 1811 Queen Anne Ave N, 206-283-5624, www.queenannebooks.com
- **Santoro's Books**, 7405 Greenwood Ave N, 206-784-2113
- **Seattle University Book Store**, Seattle University, 823 12th Ave, 206-296-5820, www.seattleubookstore.com
- **Secret Garden Bookshop**, 2214 NW Market St, 206-789-5006, www.secretgardenbooks.com
- **Third Place Books**, 17171 Bothell Way NE, Lake Forest Park, 206-366-3333, www.thirdplacebooks.com; **Ravenna Third Place Books**, 6504 20th Ave NE, 206-525-2347, www.ravenna.thirdplace.com
- **University Bookstore**, 4326 University Way NE, 206-634-3400; 990 102nd Ave NE, Bellevue, 425-462-4500; 18325 Campus Way NE, Ste 102, Bothell, 425-352-3344; 15311 Main St, Mill Creek, 425-385-3530; 1754 Pacific Ave, Tacoma, 253-692-4300, www.bookstore.washington.edu

SPECIAL INTEREST

- **Alphabet Soup,** 1406 N 45th St, 206-547-4555
- **Armchair Sailor,** 2110 Westlake Ave N, 206-283-0858
- **Art Books & Press,** 5418 20th Ave NW, 206-285-2665, www.artbookspress.com
- **Arundel Books,** 1001 1st Ave, 206-624-4442
- **Aviation Book Company**, 7201 Perimeter Rd S, Ste C, Boeing Field, 206-767-5232, www.aviationbook.com
- **Cinema Books**, 4753 Roosevelt Way NE, 206-547-7667, www.cinemabooks.net
- **East West Bookshop**, 6500 Roosevelt Way NE, 206-523-3726, 800-587-6002, www.eastwestbookshop.com

- **Edge of the Circle Books**, 701 E Pike St, 206-PAN-1999, www. edgeofthecircle.com
- **Flora & Fauna Books**, 3212 W Government Way, 206-623-4727, www. ffbooks.net
- **Kinokunyia Book Store,** 525 S Weller St, 206-587-2477
- **Left Bank Books**, 92 Pike St, 206-622-0195, www.leftbankbooks.com
- **Lion Heart Books and Records**, 1501 Pike Pl #432, 206-903-6511
- **Mockingbird Books,** 7220 Woodlawn Ave NE, 206-518-5886
- **Mountaineers Bookstore**, 1001 SW Klickitat Way, West Seattle, 206-223-6303, www.mountaineersbooks.org
- **Open Books: A Poem Emporium**, 2414 N 45th St, 206-633-0811, www. openpoetrybooks.com
- **SeaOcean Book Berth**, 3534 Stone Way N, 206-675-9020, www. seaoceanbooks.com
- **Seattle Mystery Bookshop**, 117 Cherry St, 206-587-5737, www. seattlemystery.com
- **Wessel and Lieberman Booksellers,** 208 1st Ave S, 206-682-3545, www. wlbooks.com
- **Wide World Books & Maps**, 4411 Wallingford Ave N, 206-634-3453, www. wideworldtravelstore.com

USED BOOKSTORES

- **Couth Buzzard Used Books**, 8310 Greenwood Ave N, 206-436-2960, www. buonobuzzard.com
- **Epilogue Books**, 2005 NW Market St, 206-297-2665, www.epiloguebooks. com
- **Globe Bookstore**, 218 1st Ave S, 206-682-6882
- **Half Price Books**, 115 Belmont Ave E. 206-267-7777; 4709 Roosevelt Way NE, 206-547-7859, www.hpb.com (see website for other locations)
- **Horizon Books and Recollection Books**, 1423 10th, Studio A, 206-523-4217
- **Lamplight Books,** 1514 Pike Pl, 206-652-5554
- **Magus Bookstore**, 1408 NE 42nd St, 206-633-1800, www.abebooks.com
- **Ophelia's Books**, 3504 Fremont Ave, 206-632-3759, www.opheliasbooks. com
- **Seattle Book Center**, 3530 Stone Way N, 206-547-7870, www. seattlebookcenter.com
- **Spine & Crown,** 315 E. Pine St, 206-322-1227
- **Twice Sold Tales**, 905 E John St, 206-324-2421; 1311 NE 45th St, 206-545-4226; 3504 Fremont Ave N, 206-632-3759; 7 Mercer St, 206-282-7687, www. twicesoldtales.com

LIBRARIES

In addition to the bookstores mentioned above, the Seattle area is fortunate to have two strong public library systems—Seattle Public and King County—an extensive university library network, and a handful of specialty collections. In 1998, Seattle voters approved a $196.4 million bond measure for building new libraries, and to improve or replace existing branches.

PUBLIC LIBRARIES

In Seattle, most residents borrow their books from the Seattle Public Library system, a network of 26 neighborhood branches, plus the Washington Talking Book and Braille Library, and the central downtown branch. The Central Library, designed by renowned architect Rem Koolhaas and completed in 2004, is a modern architectural masterpiece that receives 8,000 visitors a day. For a public library branch near you, see the community resources listed at the end of each neighborhood profile.

The King County Library System (KCLS) complements the Seattle network and is the second largest library system in the United States. It is composed of 48 community branches from Kenmore to Muckleshoot, and Vashon Island to North Bend. KCLS also offers a number of traveling library services that allow trained library staff to visit senior centers, social service agencies, community centers, and childcare centers to bring books and computer training to those who can't always get to a library. For a list of neighborhood branches, visit www.kcls.org.

- **King County Library System**, 960 Newport Way NW, Issaquah, 425-369-3200, www.kcls.org
- **Seattle Public Library**, 1000 4th Ave, 206-386-4636, www.spl.org
- **Washington Talking Book and Braille Library**, 2021 9th Ave, 206-615-0400, TTY 206-615-0418, www.wtbbl.org

SPECIALTY

- **Chaya Mushka Jewish Public Library**, 3502 NE 65th St, 206-290-6301, www.chaiseattle.com
- **Gordon Ekvall Tracie Music Library,** 3014 NW 67th St, 206-789-5707, www.nordicmuseum.org
- **Karpeles Manuscript Library**, Tacoma Museum, 407 S "G" St, Tacoma, 206-383-2575, www.rain.org/~karpeles
- **The Mountaineers Library**, The Mountaineers Program Center, 7700 Sandpoint Way NE, 206-521-6000, www.mountaineers.org/library/
- **Pacific West Regional Library,** 168 S Jackson St, Ste 315, 206-220-4154, www.nps.gov/ccso/library/library.htm

- **Railway Library**, Northwest Railway Museum, 38625 SE King St, Snoqualmie, 425-888-3030, www.trainmuseum.org
- **Seattle Metaphysical Library**, 2220 NE Market St, L-05, 206-329-1794, www. seattlemetaphysicallibrary.org
- **Walter Johnson Memorial Library (currently in storage)**, Nordic Heritage Museum, 3014 NW 67th St, 206-789-5707, www.nordicmuseum.org

UNIVERSITY OF WASHINGTON LIBRARIES

The University of Washington maintains 20 libraries, from general undergraduate to specialized academic. Below is a list of available libraries. For more information, call or visit the website, 206-543-0242, www.lib.washington. edu: Art, Built Environments, Drama, East Asia, Engineering, Foster Business Library, Friday Harbor Library, Gallagher Law Library, Government Publications, Health Sciences, K. K. Sherwood Library, Mathematics Research, Miller Horticultural Library, Music, Odegaard Undergraduate Library, Preservation, Physics-Astronomy Reading Room, Southeast Asia, Suzzallo & Allen Library, Special Collections, UW Bothell/Cascadia Community College Library, UW Tacoma Library.

CULTURE FOR KIDS

In Seattle, there are so many cultural opportunities for kids they may grow up before they can see or do everything. Besides numerous musical and outdoor opportunities, there are museums, dance and theatre performances, and puppet shows all aimed at or containing children. Several print and online publications offer calendars of events for family and kids' events. In print, check the calendar listings in the Thursday editions of the *Seattle Times* (www.seattletimes.com) and the *Seattle Post-Intelligencer* online (www.seattle-pi.com). *ParentMap Magazine* is issued for free monthly and offers a complete calendar of events and activities on its website at www.parentmap.com. *Seattle's Child* (www.seattleschild.com), another free monthly newsmagazine for parents, contains features, reviews, lists of classes, and guides to events and outings for kids. The Seattle Center, a popular family venue, hosts a variety of colorful festivals and cultural events throughout the year, www.seattlecenter.com.

The following child-oriented listing of events and places represents only a part of what the Emerald City has to offer. For more ideas on how to entertain the kids, including a cornucopia of family and holiday festivals, see **A Seattle Year**.

MUSIC

- **Bellevue Youth Symphony Orchestra**, 400 108th Ave NE, #204, Bellevue, 425-467-5604, www.byso.org; there are no age requirements for the four main orchestras and flute and small group ensembles, just one year of school or private instruction. Students come from over 20 communities in King, Snohomish, and Pierce counties and offer several performances throughout the school year.
- **Columbia Choirs**, 425-486-1987, 866-486-1987, www.columbiachoirs.com; the Columbia Choirs program trains preschoolers through adult singers. The organization operates several choirs for different youth levels, as well as women's and men's choirs. Performances are held throughout the Puget Sound region.
- **Northwest Boychoir,** 5031 University Way NE, 206-524-3234, www.north-westchoirs.org; the choir is made up of 150 boys ages 6–13, from 115 different public and private schools in the region; beginning in first grade, boys advance through four levels of vocal training. The year-round program includes a rigorous concert schedule, a residential summer camp, and biennial international touring.
- **Northwest Girlchoir**, 520 NE Ravenna Blvd, 206-527-2900, www.northwest-girlchoir.org; offering five choir divisions for girls ages 4–18. Five mainstage concerts are produced each year, as well as several community performances and national and international tours.
- **Pacifica Children's Chorus**, 11342 17th Ave NE, 206-527-9095, www.paci-ficachoirs.org; over 70 young singers are given music education and the opportunity to join one of four performing choirs. Two or three concerts are offered each year from a repertoire of predominantly world folk music, and at least one performance is multi-disciplinary, combining music, dance, poetry, prose, and drama.
- **Seattle Children's Chorus,** 17544 Midvale Ave N, Ste 200; 206-542-5998; www.seattlechildrenschorus.org; offers four levels of instructions for over 200 choristers ages 7–20; the chorus performs a wide range of sacred, classical, and folk music, and tours to compete domestically and internationally.
- **Seattle Girls' Choir**, P.O. Box 22388, Seattle, WA 98122, 206-526-1900, www.seattlegirlschoir.org; performances include an annual SGC concert series, collaborative events with the Seattle Opera and Seattle Symphony, and tours, festivals, and competitions across the country and internationally. Students ages 6 to 18, from 35 communities around Puget Sound, participate in six different choirs, and receive instruction in vocal technique, music theory, and composition.
- **Seattle Youth Symphony Orchestras (SYSO)**, 11065 5th Ave NE, Ste A, 206-362-2300, www.syso.org; the largest youth symphony organization in the United States operates four full orchestras during the school year, three sum-

mer programs, and extensive outreach programs, including the Endangered Instruments Program. Each of the four orchestras performs three concerts during the academic year.

- **Vocalpoint!**, 5031 University Way NE, 206-524-3234,www.northwestchoirs. org; an ensemble vocal group for young adults with a busy performance schedule, specializing in musical revues built around themes in rock and roll; members receive professional-level training as singers, dancers, and actors. Male members are graduates of Northwest Boychoir, and female members earn a spot after a two-year training program (Girls Prep).

MUSEUMS

- **The Children's Museum**, 305 Harrison St, Seattle Center, 206-441-1768, www.thechildrensmuseum.org; a 22,000-square-foot play space intended for children ages 10 months to 10 years, this delightful interactive museum also presents special multicultural programs in the lower level of the Center House. Open Monday–Friday, 10 a.m. to 5 p.m., Saturday and Sunday, 10 a.m. to 6 p.m. Hands-on exhibits designed for children age 8 and under. General admission is $7.50, $6.50 for grandparents, and $6 for members of the military and large groups. Children under 1 year are free.
- **Children's Museum of Tacoma,** 936 Broadway Ave, Tacoma; 253-627- 6031; www.childrensmuseumoftacoma.org; open Monday–Saturday 10 a.m. to 5 p.m., Sunday noon to 5 p.m. Free admission; donations welcome.
- **Imagine Children's Museum,** 1502 Wall St, Everett, WA 98201, www.imag- inecm.org; open Tuesday and Wednesday from 9 a.m. to 5 p.m., Thursday, Friday, Saturday from 10 a.m. to 5 p.m., and Sunday from 11 a.m. to 5 p.m. General admission is $7.75; Thursday from 5 p.m. to 8 p.m. is half price. Kids younger than 1 are free.
- **KidsQuest,** 4091 Factoria Mall SE, Bellevue 98006, 425-637-8100; a hands-on, interactive children's museum with an emphasis on science, art, and technol- ogy. Designed for kids from birth to age 10. Open Tuesday, Wednesday, and Saturday 10 a.m. to 5 p.m., Thursday and Friday 10 a.m. to 8 p.m., and Sunday 12 p.m. to 5 p.m. First Fridays from 5 p.m. to 8 p.m. are free. General admission is $7.50. Seniors pay $6.50, and children under 1 are free.
- **Northwest Railway Museum**, 38625 SE King St, Snoqualmie, 425-888-3030, www.trainmuseum.org; the Snoqualmie Depot, the centerpiece of the North- west Railway Museum, is on the National Register of Historic Places. The museum's collection includes steam locomotives, passenger and freight cars, and railway artifacts. This is the largest railway museum in Washington. Open Thursday–Monday, 10 a.m. to 5 p.m. No charge for admission.
- **Rosalie Whyel Museum of Doll Art**, 1116 108th Ave NE, Bellevue, 425-455- 1116, www.dollart.com; a premier collection of over 1,200 dolls, from antique

to modern, as well as dollhouses, miniatures, and teddy bears, and exhibits on the history of doll making. Open Monday–Saturday, 10 a.m. to 5 p.m., Sunday, 1 p.m. to 5 p.m. Admission is $10 for adults, $9 for seniors, $5 for kids 5–17, and free for children 4 and under.

OUTDOOR

- **Cougar Mountain Zoo**, 19525 SE 54th, Issaquah, WA 98027; 425-391-5508; www.cougarmountainzoo.org; this unique zoo has the largest herd of Siberian reindeer in the country, places in the top three for cougar facilities in the country, and offers the world's only wildlife tracks library. Open January through November, Wednesday through Sunday from 9:30 a.m. to 5 p.m. Also open in December for the Reindeer Festival (check website for times). General admission is $11 for those ages 13 and up, $10 for seniors, and $8 for children 2–12; kids under 2 are free.
- **Northwest Trek**, 11610 Trek Dr E, Eatonville, 360-832-6117, www.nwtrek.org; located in Eatonville, southeast of Seattle, the Northwest Trek 723-acre wildlife park features up-close views of cougars, eagles, bighorn sheep, grizzly and black bears, and wolves, among other creatures. A tram tour is included in the admission price. Park hours vary depending on the time of year, so call or visit their website before you visit. Admission is $17 for adults, $15.50 for seniors, $12 for kids 5–12, $9 for 3- and 4-year-olds, and free for kids 2 and under. Admission is less for Pierce County residents and members of the military.
- **Point Defiance Zoo & Aquarium**, 5400 N Pearl St, Tacoma, 253-591-5337, www.pdza.org; a favorite among residents south of Seattle, Point Defiance Zoo & Aquarium puts kids eye-to-eye with beluga whales, pachyderms, sharks, and reptiles. The zoo opens at 9:30 a.m. year-round except between July 1 and September 5, when it opens at 8:30 a.m.; closing time varies from 4 p.m. in winter to 6 p.m. in summer. Admission is $13.75 for adults, $12.75 for seniors, $11.75 for kids 5–12, $7.75 for children ages 3–4, and free for kids under 3. Admission is lower for residents of Pierce County.
- **Seattle Aquarium**, Pier 59, 1483 Alaskan Way, 206-386-4300, www.seattleaquarium.org; the star attractions at the Seattle Aquarium are the adorable sea otters and the underwater viewing dome, but kids also love the jellyfish tank and the giant octopus. A major expansion is scheduled to open in spring 2008, but the aquarium remains open during construction. Open daily, 10 a.m. to 5 p.m. in the fall and winter; 9:30 a.m. to 5 p.m. in the spring; 9:30 a.m. to 7 p.m. in the summer. Admission is $12.50 for adults, $8.50 for kids 6–12, $5.50 for children 3–5, and free for kids 2 and under.
- **Woodland Park Zoo**, 5500 Phinney Ave N, 206-548-2500, www.zoo.org; the zoo's 92 acres are divided into biomorphic zones, with popular exhibits like

the Tropical Asian Zone, Bug World, the African Village, and Williwong Station. Scheduled feeding times around the zoo are also a big hit. Hours vary, depending on the season, but the zoo is open every day of the year except on Christmas. Call or visit the website for specifics. Admission costs vary according to time of year; high season (May 1–September 30) rates are $17.50 for adults, $15.50 for seniors and disabled persons, $11.50 for kids 3–12, and free for kids 2 and under.

THEATER AND DANCE

- **Kaleidoscope Dance Company**, 12577 Densmore Ave N, 206-363-7281, www.creativedance.org/kaleidoscope; the only modern dance company in the world composed of 8- to 14-year-olds. Offers two performances a year in winter and spring.
- **Northwest Puppet Center**, 9123 15th Ave NE, 206-523-2579, www.nwpuppet.org; the only permanent puppet theater in the region features the Carter Family Marionettes and hosts guest artists from around the world. Also offers a museum and archival library.
- **Seattle Children's Theatre**, Charlotte Martin Theater, 201 Thomas St, Seattle Center, 206-441-3322, www.sct.org, the second largest resident theater for young audiences in North America, SCT offers seven productions each season (September through June) geared to audiences of different ages, plus school matinees, two school touring productions, drama classes, and outreach programs. SCT occupies a state-of-the-art facility that includes paint, costume, prop, and scene shops as well as rehearsal and classroom spaces.
- **Youth Theatre Northwest**, 8805 SE 40th St, Mercer Island, 206-232-4145, www.youththeatre.org; teaches theater skills to kids 3–18 and presents twelve productions during the school year, including three summer stock performances.

S EATTLE HAS MUCH TO OFFER IN THE WAY OF SPORTS AND RECRE-
ation. For weekend warriors who enjoy playing games as much as they
like watching them, there are plenty of indoor and outdoor activities
available, from a recreational pick-up game at one of Seattle's many parks to
participation in an organized league. For avid spectators, there is professional
and college action galore. Health clubs are listed at the end of this chapter.

These **sports publications** offer in-depth coverage of local sporting events and
activities:

- *48 Degrees North (Sailing)*, 6327 Seaview Ave NW, 206-789-7350,
  www.48north.com
- *Northwest Runner*, 206-527-5301, www.nwrunner.com
- *Northwest Sportsman,* 1201 1st Ave S, Ste 309, 206-382-9220, www.nws-
  portsmanmag.com
- *Northwest Yachting Magazine*, 7342 15th Ave NW, 206-789-8116, www.nwy-
  achting.com
- *Outdoors NW*, 10002 Aurora Ave N #36rd, 206-418-0747, www.outdoorsnw.
  com

TICKETS

If you follow sports at all, you already know that Seattle has professional basketball, baseball, and football teams. What you may not realize until you live here
is that fans in the Pacific Northwest tend to be of the fair-weather variety, both
figuratively and literally. While that can be upsetting to the players, it is often
good news for die-hard fans, because during mediocre seasons, tickets generally can be purchased without much advance notice. In boom years, however,
like the Seattle Seahawks' 2005 season leading up to their appearance in Super-
Bowl XL, tickets are hard to come by.

Tickets for all Seattle professional sporting events can be purchased by phone or online at **Ticketmaster** (206-628-0888, www.ticketmaster.com) or in person at Ticketmaster outlets at most Fred Meyer stores. Or, you can visit the venue's box office. The Seattle SuperSonics left the city in 2008 to become the Oklahoma City Thunder, and the city currently hosts no men's pro basketball team. Fans of women's basketball cheer on the 2010 WNBA Champions the Seattle Storm at Key Arena. The Seattle Mariners play at Safeco Field, and the Seattle Seahawks play at CenturyLink Field. See below under **Professional Sports** for web addresses and contact information for each team.

Tickets to sold-out events are a little easier to come by than in years past, when your only recourse would be a high-priced ticket broker. Tickets for sporting and cultural events may be purchased through the website stubhub.com (a subsidiary of eBay), where fans resell tickets to other fans for a preset price, which may be more or less than the tickets' original face value. Tickets purchased on Stubhub are guaranteed by the sponsoring website, which earns a 25% commission (10% from buyer and 15% from the seller) for each sale. You can also try purchasing secondhand tickets online directly from individuals via websites such as eBay.com and craigslist.com. If you're wary of such transactions and price is no object, traditional online ticket brokers are still an option. You can find brokers in the Yellow Pages under "Ticket Sales—Entertainment & Sports," or typing the search phrase "online ticket broker" into Google.com will result in pages of online brokers. While ticket scalping in Seattle was declared legal in 2005, tickets can't be resold on event property. As a last resort you can usually find people selling tickets near event venues, though you may be limited in availability and price. It's a seller's market.

PROFESSIONAL AND COLLEGE SPORTS

PROFESSIONAL SPORTS

BASEBALL

Seattle is home to the Seattle Mariners, which after many years of being a sub-500 team, earned fan love and loyalty through a series of winning streaks and playoff berths. Nonetheless, the M's hold the dubious honor of being the only team in the American League never to have gained a berth in the World Series, and in recent seasons have ranged from better than average to abysmal. Also in the Seattle area are two minor league teams, the Tacoma Rainiers and the Everett AquaSox.

- The American League's **Seattle Mariners** play 81 home games. They play in the highly touted Safeco Field, a ballpark admired for its easy viewing of baseball and a retractable roof for those notorious Seattle rain showers. You can order tickets by calling 800-SEA-HITS or online, where you can also print your tickets after purchasing. Visiting one of the Mariner stores, located in most area malls, is another option for ticket purchase. For a Mariners schedule and more information, go to http://seattle.mariners.mlb.com.

- The **Tacoma Rainiers** are a Triple-A club in the Pacific Coast league. A farm team for the Mariners, the Rainiers play during the spring and summer in Cheney Stadium. There are usually several fun theme nights throughout the season with extra entertainment and prizes. For a schedule or tickets call 253-752-7707, or visit tacoma.rainiers.milb.com.
- The **Everett AquaSox** host their home games at Everett Memorial Stadium in downtown Everett. The AquaSox are a Single-A farm team for the Seattle Mariners, and offer many exciting games during the summer. Contact their office at 425-258-3673, or visit www.aquasox.com.

BASKETBALL

The **Seattle Storm,** named after the rainy weather in their home city, joined the Women's National Basketball Association for the 2000 season. Like most expansion teams, the Storm struggled in their first season, but rapidly improved, and in 2004 they won the WNBA Championship and the continued adoration of fans. In 2006 the Storm was sold along with the Seattle SuperSonics (now the Oklahoma City Thunder), and it looked like the team might also be Oklahoma bound. However, the Storm was bought by a Seattle group of Women called Force 10 Hoops, in a deal that disconnected the team from the Sonics and kept it in Seattle, much to the fans' relief. During the 2010 season, the Storm was virtually unstoppable, winning a record of 17–0 games at the Key to grab their second WNBA championship. Storm games are family-friendly and feature an all-kid dance troupe that performs at home games. For tickets and information, call 206-217-WNBA or visit www.wnba.com/storm.

FOOTBALL

In 2002, the National Football League's **Seattle Seahawks** moved into their new, state-of-the-art stadium at Qwest Field (now called CenturyLink Field)—and into a new division, the NFC West. The team went on to a championship 2005 season and an appearance in Super Bowl XL, where they suffered a heartbreaking loss to the Steelers. Disappointed fans all over the city rallied around the cry "next year." For more about the Seahawks, go to www.seahawks.com. For tickets, call 888-NFL-HAWK.

HOCKEY

- Key Arena is also home to the **Seattle Thunderbirds**, a Western Hockey League team. The Thunderbirds always draw a large and enthusiastic crowd for competitive games and the occasional brawl. Tickets and information are at 206-448-PUCK or www.seattlethunderbirds.com.
- The **Everett Silvertips** made their Western Hockey League debut in the 2003–2004 season and two years later reached the final 4 in the WHL Play-offs. They play before enthusiastic fans in the Everett Events Center. For more information call 425-252-5100 or visit www.everettsilvertips.com.

HORSE RACING

Northwest thoroughbred racing enthusiasts trek to Auburn to catch the action at **Emerald Downs**. For more information call 253-288-7000 or visit www.emeralddowns.com.

SOCCER

- The **Seattle Sounders** are Seattle's professional soccer team. Part of the Western Conference of Major League Soccer, they play their home games at CenturyLink Field and have a loyal following of boisterous fans. Their loyalty has been rewarded by three consecutive U.S. Open Cup wins in 2009, 2010, and 2011, as well as MLS playoff appearances. Call 800-745-3000 for tickets, or visit www.soundersfc.com.
- Women's soccer in Seattle is represented by the **Seattle Sounders Women**, a member of the USL W-League founded in 2003. They play at the Starfire Sports complex in Tukwila. For information call 206-431-3232 or visit www.starfiresports.com.

COLLEGE SPORTS

Many sports fans prefer college games to professional contests. For reasons of convenience, cost, or alum loyalty, it's true that the frenzied fans and the youthful energy found at college events make for an exciting experience. The area's largest draw for college sports is the University of Washington, which offers many first-class sporting events. The ticket office is at 101 Graves Building on the UW campus. For more information about UW athletics see below or visit http://gohuskies.com. To find out more about the sports programs of other nearby colleges or universities, call their information desk. (See **Childcare and Education** for a list of area schools.)

UW BASEBALL

The Huskies have a men's baseball team and a women's softball team. Both play at Husky Ballpark. Call 206-543-2200 or go to http://gohuskies.com for more information.

UW BASKETBALL

The Husky Women's Basketball team, once a frequent contender in the NCAA championship tournament, has foundered of late. Recent coaching changes may improve the team's performance. The Husky Men's team made the NCAA championship tournament in 2005 and 2006. Both teams play their home games at Alaska Airlines Arena at the Hec Edmundson Pavilion (aka Hec Ed) on the UW campus. In the 2011, the University announced plans to build a new multimillion-dollar training facility near the arena. Check http://gohuskies.com on the web or call 206-543-2200 for tickets and information.

UW FOOTBALL

The University of Washington's Husky Football team has a long list of national championships. On game days a steady stream of purple and gold clad fans makes its way into Husky Stadium, one of the best college football venues in the nation. Currently undergoing a $250-million renovation, the stadium is scheduled to reopen by the start of the 2013 football season (2012 home games will be played at CenturyLink Field). Husky Stadium offers great seating for the game, and provides fans with a panoramic view of Lake Washington and snow-capped Mount Rainier. Football games are popular with students, and many alumni are season ticket holders, so it's often difficult to get tickets. Call 206-543-2200 or go to http://gohuskies.com for more information.

PARTICIPANT SPORTS AND ACTIVITIES

Ask residents what they love most about the Puget Sound area, and a common response will be the great selection of outdoor recreation opportunities. From watching the sunset over the Olympics in a nearby neighborhood park to climbing to the summit of Mount Rainier, there are hundreds of activities for every level of athlete throughout the four seasons.

If you're looking for general information on local parks, kiddie pools, tennis courts or community programs, start with the **Seattle Parks and Recreation Department** (206-684-4075, www.seattle.gov/parks) or your local community center (listed after the neighborhood profiles). In addition to playgrounds, ball fields, swimming pools, and basketball and tennis courts, neighborhood community centers offer fitness classes, dance lessons, pottery and art classes, and other activities. **King County Parks** can be reached at 206-296-8687 or www. kingcounty.gov/recreation/parks.aspx, and the **Kitsap County Department of Facilities, Parks and Recreation** can be reached at 360-337-5350 or www.kitsapgov.com/parks.

PARKS AND RECREATION DEPARTMENTS

- **Auburn**, 910 9th St SE, 253-931-3043, www.auburnwa.gov
- **Bainbridge Island**, 7666 NE High School Rd, 206-842-2306, www.biparks.org
- **Bellevue**, 450 110th Ave NE, 425-452-6885, www.ci.bellevue.wa.us
- **Bothell**, 9929 NE 180th St, 425-486-7430, www.ci.bothell.wa.us
- **Bremerton**, 680 Lebo Blvd, 360-473-5305, www.ci.bremerton.wa.us
- **Burien**, 14700 6th Ave SW, 206-988-3700, www.burienparks.net
- **Des Moines**, 1000 S 220th St, 206-870-6527, www.desmoineswa.gov
- **Duvall**, 14525 Main St, 425-788-3434, www.duvallwa.gov
- **Edmonds**, 700 Main St, 425-771-0230, www.ci.edmonds.wa.us
- **Everett**, 802 E Mukilteo Blvd, 425-257-8300 ex. 2, www.ci.everett.wa.us
- **Federal Way**, 33325 8th Ave S, 253-835-6901, www.cityoffederalway.com
- **Issaquah**, 301 Rainier Blvd S, 425-837-3300, www.ci.issaquah.wa.us
- **Kenmore**, 18120 68th Ave NE, 425-398-8900, www.cityofkenmore.com
- **Kent**, 220 4th Ave S, 253-856-5000, www.ci.kent.wa.us
- **Kirkland**, 505 Market St, Ste A, 425-587-3300, www.kirkland.gov/depart/parks.htm
- **Lake Forest Park**, 17425 Ballinger Way NE, 206-368-5440, www.cityoflfp.com
- **Lynnwood**, 18900 44th Ave W, 425-670-5732, www.ci.lynnwood.wa.us
- **Mercer Island**, 2040 84th Ave SW, 206-275-7609, www.mercergov.org
- **Mountlake Terrace**, 6100 219th St SW, 425-776-9173, www.cityofmlt.com
- **Newcastle**, 13020 Newcastle Way, 425-649-4444, www.ci.newcastle.wa.us
- **North Bend**, 211 Main Ave N, 425-888-0486 ex. 3, www.ci.north-bend.wa.us
- **Redmond**, 15670 NE 85th St, 425-556-2300, www.ci.redmond.wa.us
- **Renton**, 1055 S Grady Way, 425-430-6600, www.rentonwa.gov
- **Sammamish,** 801 228th Ave SE, 425-295-0500, www.ci.sammamish.wa.us
- **Sea-Tac**, 13735 24th Ave S, 206-973-4680, www.ci.seatac.wa.us
- **Seattle**, 100 Dexter Ave N, 206-684-4075, www.cityofseattle.net/parks
- **Shoreline**, 17500 Midvale Ave N, 206-801-2630, www.cityofshoreline.com
- **Snoqualmie**, 38194 SE Stearns Rd, 425-831-5784, www.ci.snoqualmie.wa.us
- **Tacoma**, 4702 S 19th St, 253-305-1000, www.metroparkstacoma.org
- **Tukwila**, 12424 42nd Ave S, 206-768-2822, www.ci.tukwila.wa.us
- **Vashon Island**, 17130 Vashon Hwy SW, 206-463-9602, www.vashonparkdistrict.org
- **Woodinville**, 17301 133rd Ave NE, 425-489-2700, www.ci.woodinville.wa.us

ADVENTURE RACING/ORIENTEERING

- Adventure racing is a multi-discipline sport that usually involves paddling, mountain biking, and trekking, as well as navigating a course through wilderness, and can take anywhere from hours to days. Sometimes other disciplines like horseback riding and fixed rope are involved. Some teams offer training to those new to the sport, but you may have to find other like-minded individuals and form your own team. The **Pacific Northwest Adventure Racing Community** offers links to teams, events, and a forum, and can be reached at www.pnwar.com.

- Orienteering is a fast-growing sport in the area involving navigating a course through sometimes difficult terrain with a map and compass. The **Cascade Orienteering Club** offers events, training, and maps, as well as permanent orienteering courses around the area. They can be reached at 425-778-7202 or www.cascadeoc.org.

BASEBALL/SOFTBALL

Every spring, as the cherry trees blossom, Seattle residents flock to local fields to play baseball or softball. If you're simply in the mood for an impromptu game with friends or for some casual batting practice, ball fields are available. To reserve a field, call the **Seattle Parks and Recreation Individual Field Reservation Line** at 206-684-4077. For parks in surrounding communities, contact the city parks and recreation departments listed previously in this chapter.

If you'd like to put together your own team and/or participate in a league, most leagues are organized privately or through local community centers (listed after the neighborhood profiles). The following resources may also be helpful:

ADULT LEAGUES

- **Bellevue Baseball/Softball Athletic Association**, 425-746-4592, www.bbsaa.org
- **Puget Sound Senior Baseball League**, 425-957-1430, www.pssbl.com

YOUTH LEAGUES

- **Little League,** www.littleleague.org; every city and town in the Puget Sound region offers Little League baseball and softball. Larger cities like Seattle and Bellevue have several leagues. To find a league near you visit the official website.
- **United States Amateur Baseball Association**, 425-776-7130, www.usaba.com

BASKETBALL

Considering Seattle's unpredictable weather, you might think that basketball would be near the bottom of the list as a favorite sport. That's definitely not the case. Lively pick-up games are common in Seattle's playgrounds and community centers, and there are many organized leagues at gyms and athletic clubs. If you're interested in league play or workshops, consider the health clubs listed later in this chapter, or call one of the area's parks and recreation departments (see above). For a casual but competitive pick-up game in Seattle call your local community center (see **Community Resources** following each neighborhood write-up in the **Seattle Neighborhoods** chapter) or call the **Seattle Parks and Recreation Department** at 206-684-4075.

BICYCLING

In Seattle, cycling is popular as both a sport and a means of transportation. Despite the unpredictable weather and hilly topography, many residents bike to work and school, and to do errands. Bicycle lanes have become more common on major thoroughfares throughout the city and its surrounding communities. Seattle is also home to the World Naked Bike Ride (aka the WNBR Seattle) and other events when riders can cycle in the buff, if they are so inclined. (For more information on commuting by bike, naked or fully clothed, see the **Transportation** chapter.)

Green Lake is a popular destination for recreational cyclists, as are many locations along the **Burke-Gilman Trail**. For a fun and scenic ride, bike the Burke-Gilman Trail from Gasworks Park on Lake Union to Kenmore on Lake Washington. This trail is also used as a shortcut for many UW students riding to school each morning.

Cascade Bicycle Club (CBC), the largest cycling club in the United States, is based in Seattle. With more than 13,000 members, CBC sponsors several rides each day, for riders of all skill levels, as well as several annual events. Contact CBC at 206-522-BIKE, or check out their comprehensive website at www. cascade.org. Those interested in track racing should contact the **Marymoor Velodrome Association** at 206-957-4555, or go to www.velodrome.org/mva/node/19. Racing events are held regularly at Marymoor Park in Redmond.

The following are a few of the most popular annual street rides in the Seattle area:

- **The Cannonball**, held in late June and organized by the Redmond Cycling Club, is a one-day trek from Seattle to Spokane along I-90. Call 425-739-8609 or visit www.redmondcyclingclub.org.
- **Chilly Hilly**, held in late February and sponsored by CBC, is a 33-mile bicycle tour around Bainbridge Island. It marks the official opening of bicycle season in the Pacific Northwest.

- **The Daffodil Classic**, an annual ride sponsored by the **Tacoma Wheelmen's Bicycle Club**, is held in mid-April. There are several routes, ranging from 40 to 100 miles. Call 253-759-2800 or visit www.twbc.org.
- **The Kitsap Color Classic**, a ride through Kitsap County on the Olympic Peninsula, is held in late September when the leaves begin to turn. CBC sponsors this ride, with features a variety of loop options for variously skilled riders.
- **PROS (Perimeter Ride of Seattle),** sponsored by Cyclists of Greater Seattle (COGS) and held annually on Labor Day, is a hilly ride around the city's perimeter, with options of a 60- and 80-mile route.
- **The RAMROD (Ride Around Mount Rainier in One Day) is sponsored by the Redmond Cycling Club and takes place in late July. It is a 150+ mile race around Mount Rainier**, and is perhaps the most challenging in the area, with 10,000 feet of climbing during the race.
- **RAPSody (Ride Around Puget Sound),** held in late August, is a 170-mile weekend ride organized by five bike clubs in support of the Bicycle Alliance of Washington (BAW). This challenging event is known for live music and great food along the route.
- **STP (Seattle-to-Portland) is a two-day non-competitive bike ride from Seattle to Portland**, sponsored by the CBC. Riders can choose to participate for one or two days; those riding for two days stay overnight midway. The STP takes place in mid-July and is the best-known bicycling event in the area.

Just as popular as traditional bicycling, mountain biking is a favorite recreational activity for many Seattle residents. Seattle's hills provide great practice routes, and there are several scenic and challenging mountain-bike trails just a short drive out of the city. An excellent resource for local mountain-biking information is the **Evergreen Mountain Bike Alliance** (206-524-2900, www. evergreenmtb.org). If you're new to the sport, the club offers a "boot camp" for first-time trail riders. For information on nearby trails, check out a copy of the *King County Bicycling Guidemap*, available at King County Public Libraries; it can also be ordered by phone at 206-263-4741, or downloaded from www.kingcounty.gov/transportation/kcdot/Roads/Bicycling.aspx.

BIRD WATCHING

Though bird watching may not rank high on Seattle's list of popular pursuits, the region does include its fair share of birders. In Seattle, the **National Audubon Society** recommends Discovery and Green Lake parks, the Montlake Wetlands, Washington Park Arboretum, and in West Seattle, Alki Beach and Lincoln Park. The Great Washington State Birding Trail, a series of detailed maps completed in 2011, describes the best sites for observing birds in nature around the region. To find bird watching spots in surrounding communities, visit http://wa.audubon.org.

- **Audubon Washington**, 5902 Lake Washington Blvd S, Seattle, 206-652-2444, http://wa.audubon.org
- **Eastside Audubon**, P.O. Box 3115, Kirkland, WA 98083, 425-576-8805, www.eastsideaudubon.org
- **Pilchuck Audubon Society**, 1429 Ave D, PMB 198, Snohomish, WA 98290, 425-252-0926, www.pilchuckaudubon.org
- **Seattle Audubon Society**, 8050 35th Ave NE, 206-523-4483, www.seattle audubon.org
- **Washington Ornithological Society**, 12345 Lake City Way NE #215, www.wos.org

BOATING

It's no surprise that Seattle residents love their watercraft. Even on cloudy days, you'll see several boats out on the lakes or in Puget Sound. Colorful spinnakers dot the Sound each weekend, as sailing races are held near Shilshole Bay. On sunny days, floatplanes arriving at Lake Union dodge the many sailboats that crowd the lake, and the early-morning calm of Lake Washington entices crowds of skiers, kayakers, and stand-up paddle boarders.

ELECTRIC BOATS

- **The Electric Boat Company**, 2046 Westlake Ave N, 206-223-7476, www.the-electricboatco.com

ROWING, CANOEING, KAYAKING, AND STAND-UP PADDLE BOARDING (SUP)

- **Everett Rowing Association**, 300 Smith Island Rd, Everett, 98205, 425-345-5138, www.everettrowing.com
- **Green Lake Boat Rentals,** Green Lake Boat House, 206-527-0171, www.greenlakeboatrentals.com (this facility rents paddle boards)
- **Green Lake Small Craft Center**, 5900 W Green Lake Way N, 206-684-4074, www.seattle.gov/parks/boats/Grnlake.htm
- **Lake Union Crew Rowing Club**, 11 E Allison St, 206-860-4199, www.lakeunioncrew.com
- **Lake Washington Rowing Club**, 910 N Northlake Way, 206-547-1583, http://lakewashingtonrowing.com
- **Moss Bay Row**, Kayak, Paddle Board, and Sail Center, 1001 Fairview Ave N #1900, 206-682-2031, www.mossbay.net
- **Mount Baker Rowing and Sailing Center**, 3800 Lake Washington Blvd S, 206-386-1913, www.seattle.gov/parks/boats/Mtbaker.htm

- **Northwest Outdoor Center**, 2100 Westlake Ave N Ste #1, 206-281-9694, www.nwoc.com
- **Sammamish Rowing Association**, 5022 W Lake Sammamish Pkwy, Redmond, WA 98052, 425-653-2583, www.sammamishrowing.com
- **Seattle Canoe and Kayak Club**, 5900 W Green Lake Way N, 206-684-4074, www.seattlecanoeclub.org
- **Washington Kayak Club**, P.O. Box 24264, Seattle, WA 98124, www.washingtonkayakclub.org

SAILING

- **Mount Baker Rowing and Sailing Center**, 3800 Lake Washington Blvd S, 206-386-1913, www.seattle.gov/parks/boats/Mtbaker.htm
- **Renton Sailing Club**, 425-235-0952, www.rentonsailing.org
- **Sail Sand Point**, 7777 62nd Ave NE, #101, 206-525-8782, www.sailsandpoint.org
- **Seattle Sailing Club**, 7001 Seaview Ave NW, Ste 130, 206-782-5100, www.seattlesailing.com
- **Wind Works Sailing Center**, 7001 Seaview Ave NW, Ste 110, 206-784-9386, www.windworkssailing.com

YACHT CLUBS

- **Bellevue Yacht Club,** 3911 Lake Washington Blvd SE, Bellevue, WA 90006, 206-910-2203, www.bellevueyachtclub.com
- **Corinthian Yacht Club of Seattle**, 7755 Seaview Ave NW, 206-789-1919, http://cycseattle.org
- **Edmonds Yacht Club**, 326 Admiral Way Ste 100, Edmonds, WA 98020, 425-778-5499, www.edmondsyachtclub.com
- **Everett Yacht Club,** 404 14th St, Everett, WA 98201, 425-210-0830, www.everettyachtclub.com
- **Meydenbauer Bay Yacht Club**, 9927 Meydenbauer Way SE, Bellevue, WA 98009, 425-454-8880, www.mbycwa.org
- **Port Madison Yacht Club**, www.portmadisonyc.org
- **Puget Sound Yacht Club,** 2321 N Northlake Way, 206-634, 3733, www.pugetsoundyc.org
- **Queen City Yacht Club**, 2608 Boyer Ave E, 206-709-2000, www.queencity.org
- **Rainier Yacht Club**, 9094 Seward Park Ave S, 206-722-9576, www.rainieryachtclub.com
- **Seattle Yacht Club**, 1807 E Hamlin St, 206-325-1000, www.seattleyachtclub.org

- **Shilshole Bay Yacht Club,** 2242 NW Market St, Box 98, www.shilshole-bayyc. org
- **Tyee Yacht Club**, 3229 Fairview Ave E, 425-408-0239, www.tyeeyachtclub.org
- **Washington Yacht Club**, University of Washington, 206-543-2219, www. washingtonyachtclub.org

OTHER BOATING RESOURCES

- **Boating Safety Classes,** 800-336-BOAT
- **Seattle Police Harbor Patrol Unit,** 206-684-4071
- **Seattle Boat Ramp Supervisor,** 206-684-7249
- **U.S. Coast Guard 24-hour Emergency,** 206-217-6001 or 800-424-8802

BOWLING

Bowling is most popular during Seattle's wet, gray winter months. The following bowling alleys organize leagues regularly, but also welcome amateur and first-time bowlers.

- **Garage,** 1130 Broadway Ave, 206-322-2296, www.garagebilliards.com
- **Imperial Lanes,** 2101 22nd Ave S, 206-325-2525, www.amf.com/imperiallanes
- **Hi-Line Lanes**, 15733 Ambaum Blvd SW, Burien, 206-244-2272, www. hilinelanes.com
- **Magic Lanes**, 10612 15th Ave SW, 206-244-5060, www.magiclanesbowl.com
- **Roxbury Lanes**, 2823 SW Roxbury St, 206-935-7400, http://roxburylanes. com
- **Skyway Park Bowl,** 11819 Renton Ave S, 206-772-1220, www.skywaypark bowl.com
- **Sun Villa Lanes**, 3080 148th SE, Bellevue, 425-455-8155, www.amf.com/ sunvillalanes
- **West Seattle Bowl**, 4505 39th Ave SW, 206-932-3731, www.wsbowl.com

CHESS

- **America's Foundation for Chess**, 11120 NE 33rd Pl, Ste 105, Bellevue, WA 98004, 425-629-4000, www.af4c.org
- **Seattle Chess Club**, 2150 N 107th St, 206-417-5405, www.seattlechess.org
- **Seattle Chess Foundation,** www.seattlechessfoundation.org

DANCE

- **All That Dance,** 8507 35th Ave NE, 206-524-8944, www.all-that-dance.com
- **Arthur Murray Dance Studios**, 530 Dexter Ave N, Ste 1B, 206-447-2701, www.washingtondancesport.com
- **Century Ballroom**, 915 E Pine St, 206-324-7263, www.centuryballroom.com

- **Dance Fremont!,** 4015 Stone Way N, 206-633-0812, www.dancefremont.com
- **DanceSport International**, 12535 Lake City Way NE, 206-361-8239, www.dancesportseattle.com
- **Dance Underground,** 340 15th St E, 206-328-1500, www.dance-under ground.com
- **eXit Space,** 414 NE 72nd St, 206-949-8643, www.exitspacedance.com
- **Fifth Avenue Dance Studio**, 222 Wall St #100A, 206-621-9824, www.fifthavenuedancestudio.com
- **Velocity Dance Center,** 1621 12th Ave, 206-325-8773, www.velocitydance center.org
- **Washington Dance Club**, 1017 Stewart St, 206-628-8939, www.washington dance.com
- **Westlake Dance Center,** 10703 8th Ave, 206-621-7378, www.westlakedance. com

FENCING

- **Fleur de Lys Fencing Club**, 2550 34th Ave W, 206-782-1165, www.fleurdelysfencing.org
- **Rain City Fencing Center**, 1776 136th Pl NEth, Bellevue, WA 98005, 425-747-6300, www.raincityfencing.com
- **Salle Auriol Seattle**, 760 Harrison St, 206-623-8357, www.salleauriol.com
- **Washington Fencing Academy,** 1470 19th Ave NW, Issaquah, WA 98027, 425-657-0110, www.washingtonfencing.com

FIELD HOCKEY/LACROSSE

- **Coopers Lacrosse Club**, 8065 Lake City Way NE, 206-522-2923, www.cooperslacrosse.com
- **Seattle Lacrosse Club**, www.seattlelacrosseclub.com
- **Seattle Women's Field Hockey Club**, www.seattlefieldhockey.org

FISHING AND SHELLFISH GATHERING

The fishing and shellfishing opportunities in Washington are nothing short of amazing. Although the area is famous for salmon and Dungeness crab, you'll also find clams, mussels, oysters, trout, and steelhead. If you're gathering shellfish with a local, you may even get a glimpse of a geoduck. Geoducks, pronounced "gooey-ducks," are huge razor clams indigenous to Washington's ocean beaches. Like clams, you'll need to dig for geoducks, but they're fast and a lot tougher to catch! There are two things to be aware of before heading to a beach with bucket and shovel in hand— beaches are periodically closed due to algae blooms and/or pollution, and you need a license.

The summers of 2009 and 2010 saw some of the worst red tides in a decade and many Puget Sound beaches were closed to shellfish harvesting. Some of the toxins affecting shellfish can cause paralytic shellfish poisoning in humans and can't be cooked out, so it's always a good idea to check with the **Washington Department of Fish and Wildlife** first. You can reach their shellfish hotline at 800-562-5632 or visit their website (see below) or that of the Washington State Department of Health at http://www.doh.wa.gov/shellfishsafety.htm.

The **Washington Department of Fish and Wildlife (WDFW)** regulates fishing and shellfish gathering throughout the state, acting as both conservation and licensing entity. The agency provides many helpful publications on a variety of fish and wildlife subjects, which can be ordered by phone or downloaded from the department's website (see below). Recreational fishing licenses are required for all state residents 15 and over, and for all non-residents, regardless of age. Licenses are divided into three categories: freshwater, saltwater, and shellfish/seaweed. Licenses are valid for a variety of time periods, from one day to one year, and must be displayed at all times while fishing or gathering shellfish. License fees and restrictions vary according to the fish or shellfish collected; fees range from $5.40 to $46.20 for residents. Licenses may be purchased from most sporting goods stores, or online at http://fishhunt.dfw.wa.gov.

- **Washington State Department of Fish and Wildlife**, 1111 Washington St SE, Olympia, WA 98501, 360-902-2200, http://wdfw.wa.gov

Several types of salmon and trout migrate through the waters of western Washington. Chinook are the largest of the Pacific salmon and spawn in the Columbia and Snake rivers, as well as other small rivers and streams. Coho or silver salmon are a popular sport fish in the Puget Sound, and can also be found in coastal tributaries. Sockeye salmon are a flavorful salmon, found in Lake Washington, Baker Lake, Quinault Lake, Ozette Lake, and Lake Wenatchee. Pink salmon, or humpback salmon, spawn only every other year, so they appear in Washington waters during odd-numbered years only. Chum salmon can be found in small coastal streams, but are not particularly tasty and so are not popular as a sport fish. Steelhead and cutthroat trout, named for the red markings just below the head of the fish, live in freshwater streams and Puget Sound bays. Although cutthroats are common throughout North America, those in Washington are the only ones that spend the warm summer months in saltwater.

Lakes and rivers in Washington yield an unusual catch of fish, including many non-native species. When settlers arrived here in the mid-1800s, they caught trout, char, whitefish and a few other small fish in the freshwater lakes and streams. As more people moved to the area and the trout population began to dwindle, additional species of fish were imported. While trout (including rainbow, cutthroat, steelhead, brook, and brown trout) are still the most popular fish in Washington's many rivers, the state's lakes and rivers are now stocked with a variety of fish, from sunfish and catfish, to perch and pike. Favorite locations for trout fishing near the Puget Sound are the Skagit, Snoqualmie, Skykomish, and Green rivers. Other plentiful rivers in the state include the Columbia, Cowlitz, Kalama, and Hoh. Bottomfish such as halibut, cod, and rockfish are common in Neah Bay, the Hood Canal, and around the San Juan Islands. Lake Washington and the Puget Sound have limited numbers of sturgeon, which are more numerous in the Columbia and Snake Rivers. If you're looking for largemouth bass, try Moses Lake, Silver Lake, Long Lake, Sprague Lake or the Columbia River. Smallmouth bass are commonly found in the Columbia, Snake, and Yakima rivers, and in Lake Washington, Lake Sammamish, and Lake Stevens. You may catch yellow perch in Lake Washington, Lake Sammamish or Lake Stevens. You're more likely to find walleye in eastern Washington lakes such as Moses Lake, Lake Roosevelt or Soda Lake. If you're a fan of catfish, you'll find brown bullheads in Lake Washington, Moses Lake or Liberty Lake, and channel catfish in Fazon Lake and Sprague Lake. Tiger muskies (pike) are commonly found in Mayfield Lake in Lewis County, while northern pikes swim in Long Lake near Spokane.

FRISBEE

While many Seattle parks have adequate open spaces for a game of frisbee, a few parks are especially popular with enthusiasts. Gasworks Park, at the north end of Lake Union, combines a wide expanse of green lawn with pleasant breezes off the lake. Discovery Park in Magnolia has a good-sized grassy meadow in which to play, and Woodland Park near Green Lake offers a quiet shady expanse. The Seattle area also features several disc golf courses, including Lakewood King County Park, North Park (Mineral Springs), Juel Community Park, and Lake Fenwick. For more information, go to www.pdga.com.

If ultimate frisbee is your game of choice, you may want to try one of several regular pick-up games in the area. Common locations are Volunteer Park, Lincoln Park in West Seattle, and Marymoor Park in Redmond. League play is organized privately or through the **Northwest Ultimate Association**, P.O. Box 85112, Seattle, WA 98145, 206-781-5840, www.discnw.org.

GEOCACHING

This high-tech worldwide treasure hunting game is played using GPS devices to locate hidden containers, called geocaches, filled with trinkets, toys, or trackable items. Players log in to share their experiences online at sites such as www.geocaching.com. Whether you call it a sport, a game, or a hobby, geocaching originated in the Northwest and is the site of the Triad—three sought-after caches hidden around the region. The geocaching community has an environmental agenda, and many geocachers participate in Cache In Trash Out (CITO), a global environmental cleanup effort. In 2010, GeoWoodstock, the largest annual geocaching event in the world, was held in Carnation, Washington, and drew thousands of enthusiasts from around the globe. The Groundspeak "lackeys," considered the stewards of the sport, are based in Fremont. For more information, visit www.groundspeak.com.

GOLF

Three public golf courses, run by the City of Seattle Parks and Recreation Department, are listed below, along with public courses in surrounding communities. In addition, the parks department offers a short course near Green Lake, the **Green Lake Pitch and Putt** (walk-ons only), and near Queen Anne, the **Interbay Golf Center**, with miniature golf course and driving range (reservations taken up to seven days in advance). While there are many other golf courses in the greater Seattle area, most are private or semi-private courses. Check the local Yellow Pages or online for more information.

- **Classic Country Club**, 4908 208th St E, Spanaway, WA 98387, 253-847-4440, www.classicgolfclub.net
- **The Golf Club at Newcastle**, 15500 Six Penny Ln, Newcastle, WA 98059, 425-793-5566, www.newcastlegolf.com
- **Green Lake Pitch and Putt**, 5701 W Green Lake Way N, 206-632-2280, www.seattle.gov/athletics/golfcrse.htm
- **Harbour Pointe Golf Club**, 11817 Harbour Pointe Blvd, Mukilteo, 206-355-6060, www.harbourpointegolf.com
- **Interbay Golf Center**, 2501 15th Ave W, 206-285-2200, www.seattlegolf.com/interbay.php
- **Jackson Park Golf Club**, 1000 NE 135th St, 206-363-4747, www.seattlegolf.com/jackson.php
- **Jefferson Park Golf Club**, 4101 Beacon Ave S, 206-762-4513, www.seattlegolf.com/jefferson-park.php
- **Kayak Point Golf Course**, 15711 Marine Dr, Stanwood, 360-652-9676, www.golfkayak.com
- **Meadow Park Golf Course**, 7108 Lakewood Dr W, Tacoma, 253-473-3033, www.metroparkstacoma.org
- **West Seattle Golf Club**, 4470 35th Ave SW, 206-935-5187, www.seattlegolf.com/west-seattle.php

GYMNASTICS

Most community centers and YMCAs offer gymnastics and tumbling classes, but there are various gyms in the area devoted exclusively to the sport:

- **Cascade Elite Gymnastics,** 23101 56th Ave W, Mountlake Terrace, WA 98043, 425-672-6887, www.cascadeelite.com
- **Emerald City Gymnastics Academy,** 17735 NE 65th St, Ste 110, and 17969 NE 65th, Redmond, 425-861-8772, www.emeraldcitygymnasticsacademy. com
- **Gymnastics East,** 13425 SE 30th St, Ste 2A, Bellevue, 425-644-8117, www. gymeast.com
- **Gymnastics Unlimited,** 34016 9th Ave S, D-5, Federal Way, 253-815-0998, www.gymnasticsunlimitedus.com
- **Metropolitan Gymnastics,** 6822 S 190th St, Kent 98032, 425-282-5010, www.metropolitangym.com
- **Northshore Gymnastics Center,** 19460 144th Ave NE, Woodinville 98072, 425-402-6602, www.northshoregymnastics.com
- **Northwest Aerials,** 12440 128th Ln NE, Kirkland 98034, 425-823-2665, www. nwaerials.com
- **Seattle Gymnastics Academy,** 12535 26th Ave NE, 206-362-7447; 5313 Shilshole Ave NW, 206-782-1496; 5035 37th Ave S, Ste 200, 206-708-7497; wwwseattlegymnastics.com

HANG GLIDING/PARAGLIDING/PARASAILING

On sunny days in downtown Seattle, the billowing parachutes of parasailers are a familiar sight on Elliott Bay. Most of the Puget Sound region is an hour or less from the foothills of the Cascade Mountains, which are an ideal place for hang gliding and paragliding, offering spectacular scenery on long, slow descents.

- **AAAA Hang Gliding School,** 11345 Sand Point Way NE, 206-363-3680
- **Cloudbase Country Club,** P.O. Box 629, Issaquah, 98027, 425-703-2382, www.cloudbase.org
- **The Northwest Paragliding Club,** P.O. Box 2265, Issaquah, 98027, www.nw paragliding.com
- **Pacific Parasail,** 821 Dock St, Ste 407, Tacoma 98402, 253-272-3883, www. pacificparasail.net
- **Parafly Paragliding,** 10534 157th Ave NE, Redmond 98052, 425-605-0433, www.paraflyparagliding.com
- **Paraglide Washington,** 206-679-1002, www.paraglidewashington.com
- **Pier 66 Parasail,** 2203 Alaskan Way, 206-622-5757
- **Seattle Paragliding,** 11206 Issaquah-Hobart Rd SE, Issaquah 98027, 206-387-3477, www.seattleparagliding.com

HIKING

If you like to hike, you'll love living in Seattle. Not only are there several short hikes in local parks, such as Discovery Park and Seward Park, but just outside of the city there are hundreds of trails for hikers of all fitness levels. Mountaineers Books publishes a series of useful books that describe nearly every trail in Washington. The following resources may be helpful when choosing a trail.

- **LocalHikes,** www.localhikes.com/MSA/MSA_7602.asp
- **Mountaineers Books**, 1001 SW Klickitat Way, Ste 201, 206-223-6303, www.mountaineersbooks.org
- **National Park Service**, 909 1st Ave, 206-220-4000, www.nps.gov
- **The Mountaineers Club**, 7700 Sand Point Way NE, 206-521-6000, www.mountaineers.org
- **WashingtonHikes.com**, www.washingtonhikes.com
- **Washington Hiking Advisor,** www.washington-hiking-advisor.com
- **Washington Trails Association**, 705 2nd Ave, Ste 300, 206-625-1367, www.wta.org

HORSEBACK RIDING

Horseback rides and lessons are available in many of Seattle's surrounding rural communities. Check with the following, search online, or look in the Yellow Pages under "Horse Rentals & Riding" for more listings.

- **Creekside Stables**, 17513 51st Ave SE, Bothell, 98011, 425-485-6040, www.creeksideriding.com
- **Elk Run Stables**, 45004 SE 161st Pl, North Bend, 98045, 425-888-4341
- **Gold Creek Equestrian Center**, 16528 148th Ave NE, Woodinville 98072, 425-806-4653, www.gold-creek.com
- **Parkside Stables,** 13020 N 39th St, Bellevue, 98005, 425-885-5025, www.parksidestables.com
- **Phoenix Farm**, 8832 222nd St SE, Woodinville, 98077, 425-486-9395, www.phoenixfarm.com
- **Tiger Mountain Stables**, 24508 SE 133rd, Issaquah, 98027, 425-392-5090

ICE SKATING/HOCKEY

Most bodies of water in Seattle never freeze, but there are plenty of ice skating opportunities available, albeit the indoor kind. Most rinks offer skate rentals, lessons, hockey leagues and open ice sessions. During the holiday season, an ice rink at **Seattle Center** is open to the public. Call 206-684-7200 for details. Year-round rinks include:

- **Castle Ice Arena**, 12620 164th SE, Renton, 425-254-8750, www.castleice.com
- **Highland Ice Arena,** 18005 Aurora Ave N, Shoreline, 206-546-2431, www. highlandice.com
- **Kingsgate Ice Arena**, 14326 124th Ave NE, Kirkland, 98024, 425-821-7133 ext. 104, www.kingsgateskatingclub.org
- **Lynnwood Ice Center**, 19803 68th Ave W, Lynnwood, 98036, 425-640-9999, www.lynnwoodicecenter.com
- **Olympic View Arena**, 22202 70th Ave W, Mountlake Terrace, 98043, 425-672-9012, www.olyview.com

IN-LINE/ROLLER SKATING AND SKATEBOARDING

In-line skating is a popular activity on Seattle's paved paths, particularly at Green Lake, Alki Beach, and on the Burke-Gilman Trail. Some skaters even turn vacant parking lots into impromptu rinks for trick skating or pick-up hockey games. Several sporting goods stores offer in-line skating rentals. **Gregg's Greenlake Cycle**, 7007 Woodlawn Ave NE (one of three locations in the area), 206-523-1822, www.greggscycles.com, offers easy access to a paved path.

For in-line skating lessons, try **the Lynnwood Bowl & Skate**, 6210 200th St SW, Lynnwood, 425-778-3133, www.bowlandskate.com, or Skate Journeys, 206-276-9328, www.skatejourneys.com. For in-line hockey leagues and drop-ins, go to **Arena Sports** at Magnuson Park, 7727 63rd Ave NE, Ste 101, 206-985-8990, www.arenasports.net. You can also connect with the Greater Seattle Hockey League at www.gshockey.com. A good roller rink for family skating is the **Skate King**, 2301 140th Ave NE, Bellevue 98005, 425-641-2047, www.bellevueskateking.homestead.com.

If skateboarding is your thing, plenty of new skate parks have sprung up around the city. Head for the SkatePark at the Seattle Center (dubbed "Sea Sk8" by local skaters), or the outdoor skate park at **Ballard Commons Park**, 5701 22nd Ave NW. If the weather is lousy, try the recently remodeled **Inner Space Skatepark** at 3506-1/2 Stone Way N, 206-634-9090. www.innerspaceskateboarding.com.

MARTIAL ARTS

Every style of martial arts is represented by dozens of schools and dojos in the Seattle area and surrounding communities. The martial arts have a long history in Seattle, where the first U.S. judo dojo was founded in 1907. Bruce Lee, who attended the University of Washington, developed his style of kung-fu here and is buried in Lake View Cemetery on Capitol Hill. Whether you're looking for simple self- defense instruction or advanced karate moves, you're sure to find a sensei (instructor) to suit your needs. Many community centers offer classes, and the following are just a sampling of the martial arts schools in the area. For a complete listing, search online or check the Yellow Pages under "Martial Arts Instruction."

- **Aikido of West Seattle**, 4421 Fauntleroy Way SW, 206-938-5222, www.aiki dows.com
- **Chinese Wushu and Tai Chi Academy**, 709-1/2 S King St, 206-749-9513, www.yijiaowushu.com
- **Greenlake Martial Arts**, 319 NE 72nd St, 206 522-2457, www.newkungfu. com
- **Minakami Karate Dojo**, 9871 Aurora Ave N, 206-525-6100, www.minakami karate.com
- **MKG Martial Arts International**, 10722 5th Ave NE, 206-789-2411, www. mkgseattle.com
- **Two Cranes Aikido**, 8512 20th Ave NE, 206-523-5503, www.twocranesaikido. com
- **Washington Karate Association**, 8618 3rd Ave NW, 206-784-3171, www. washingtonkarate.com
- **World Martial Arts & Health**, 2002 NW Market St, 206-782-7000

RACQUET SPORTS

TENNIS

Outdoor public tennis courts dot the city and are generally open on a first-come, first-served basis, although reservations may be requested through the Seattle Parks and Recreation Department. The Amy Yee Tennis Center in the Mount Baker neighborhood, also run by the Seattle Parks and Recreation Department, offers lessons and indoor and outdoor courts. For tennis courts in surrounding communities, contact one of the parks and recreation departments listed previously in this chapter.

- **Seattle Parks and Recreation Department**, Outdoor Court Information/ Reservations, 206-684-4062, www.seattle.gov/parks/athletics/tennis.asp
- **Amy Yee Tennis Center**, 2000 Martin Luther King Jr Way S, 206-684-4764, www.seattle.gov/parks/athletics/tennisct.htm

RACQUETBALL

A few racquetball courts in the greater Seattle area are open to the public:

- **Kent Commons**, 525 4th Ave N, Kent 98032, 253-856-5030, www.ci.kent. wa.us
- **Lynnwood Recreation Center,** 18900 44th Ave W, Lynnwood 98046, 425-771-4030, www.playlynnwood.com

- **Mountlake Terrace Recreation Pavilion**, 5303 228th St SW, Mountlake Terrace 98043, 425-776-9173, www.cityofmlt.com
- **Steve Cox Memorial Park**, 1321 SW 102nd St, Seattle, 206-205-5275, www.kingcounty.gov

CLUBS

Private racquet clubs and health clubs offer lessons and court rentals for a variety of games, including tennis, racquetball, and squash. Call for details, as activities and services vary.

- **Central Park Tennis Club**, 12630 NE 59th, Kirkland 98033, 425-822-2206, www.centralparktennisclub.com
- **Edgebrook Club**, 13454 SE Newport Way, Bellevue 98006, 425-746-2786, www.edgebrookclub.org
- **Forest Crest Tennis Club**, 4901 238th St SW, Mountlake Terrace 98043, 425-774-0014, www.forestcrest.com
- **Gold Creek Tennis & Sports Club**, 15327 140th Pl NE, Woodinville 98072, 425-487-1090, www.goldcreektennis.com
- **LA Fitness,** 1416 NW Ballard Way (one of many locations), 206-508-5030, www.lafitness.com
- **Mercer Island Country Club**, 8700 SE 71st St, Mercer Island, 206-232-5600, www.mercerislandcc.com
- **Olympic Athletic Club**, 5301 Leary Way NW, 206-789-5010, www.olympicathleticclub.com
- **Pro Sports Club,** 501 Eastlake Ave E, 2nd fl, 206-332-1873; 4455 148th Ave NE, Bellevue 98002, 425-885-5566; 9911Willows Rd, #100, Redmond 98052, 425-869-4760; www.proclub.com
- **Seattle Athletic Club Downtown,** 2020 Western Ave, 206-443-111, www.sacdt.com
- **Seattle Tennis Club**, 922 McGilvra Blvd E, 206-324-3200, www.seattletennisclub.org
- **Silver Lake Tennis & Fitness Club**, 505 128th St SE, Everett, 425-745-1617, www.columbiaathletic.com

ROCK CLIMBING

Rock climbing is a popular sport in Washington, with several local climbing clubs and walls, as well as many nearby outdoor destinations. Closest perhaps is Little Si, near North Bend along I-90. Leavenworth, a Bavarian-style village on Highway 2, attracts a variety of climbers. If you're new to the sport, visit the Leavenworth area and start with the boulders near Icicle Creek; many of them have bars embedded in the rock for easy top-roping. More difficult climbs near

Leavenworth can be found at Castle Rock and the Peshastin Pinnacles. Near Stevens Pass, the Index Town Wall provides challenging routes for climbers of all levels. Close to the town of Vantage, basalt columns near the Columbia River offer good climbing for experienced climbers only. Nearby, an area known as The Feathers is appropriate for beginners. In the Olympics, Flapjack Lakes Trail leads to challenging rock-climbing.

If you've never tried rock-climbing before, or if you're an experienced climber who wants to stay in practice without leaving the city, the following climbing walls and clubs offer a variety of rock-climbing experiences. Most of the clubs offer rock-climbing lessons, as do those organizations listed under "Lessons and Guide Resources" below.

CLIMBING WALLS

- **The Center at Norpoint, Climbing Wall** (indoor), 4818 Nassau Ave NE, Tacoma 98422, 253-591-5504, www.metroparkstacoma.org
- **REI Pinnacle (indoor)**, 222 Yale Ave N, 206-223-1944, www.rei.com
- **University of Washington Climbing Rock (outdoor)**, south of Husky Stadium on Montlake Ave NE, 206-543-9433
- **Schurman Rock (outdoor)**, Camp Long, 5200 35th Ave SW, 206-684-7434, www.ci.seattle.wa.us
- **Marymoor Climbing Structure (outdoor)**, east end of Marymoor Park, Redmond, 206-296-2964, www.freemarymoor.com
- **The Crag at South Bellevue Community Center,** 14509 SE Newport Way, Bellevue 98009, 425-452-4240, www.ci.bellevue.wa.us/sbcc_crag.htm
- **The Mountaineers' Climbing Wall at Magnuson Park,** 7400 Sand Point Way NE, 206-684-4946, www.seattle.gov/parks/magnuson/mountaineers.htm

ROCK-CLIMBING CLUBS

- **Edgeworks Climbing,** 6102 NE 9th St, Ste 200, Tacoma 98406, 253-564-4899
- **Stone Gardens**, 2839 NW Market St, 206-781-9828, www.stonegardens.com
- **Vertical World**, 2123 W Elmore St, Seattle, 206-283-4497; 15036-B NE 95th Street, Redmond 98052, 425-881-8826; 5934 State Hwy 303 NE, Bremerton 98311, 360-373-6676; 2820 Rucker Ave, Everett 98201, 425-258-3431; 102 S 24th St, Tacoma 98402, 253-683-4791; www.verticalworld.com

LESSONS AND GUIDE RESOURCES

- **Alpine Ascents International**, 109 W Mercer St, 206-378-1927, www.alpineascents.com
- **KAF Adventures,** 8512 122nd Ave NE, Kirkland 98034, 206-713-2149, www.kafadventures.com

- **Mountain Madness**, 3018 SW Charlestown St, 206-937-8389, www.moun
tainmadness.com
- **The Mountaineers**, 7700 Sand Point Way NErd, 206-521-6000, www.moun
taineers.org
- **REI**, 222 Yale Ave N, 206-223-1944; 7500 166th Ave NE, Redmond 98052, 425-
882-1158; 3000 184th St SW, Lynnwood 98037, 425-640-6200; 240 Andover
Park W, Tukwila 98188, 206-248-1938; 3825 S Steele St, Tacoma 98409, 253-
671-1938, www.rei.com

RUGBY/GAELIC FOOTBALL

- **Eastside Rugby Football Club**, 206-409-0134, www.eastsiderugby.org
- **The Seattle Gaels**, www.seattlegaels.com
- **The Seattle Quake Rugby Football Club**, 1122 E Pike St, #1124, 206-337-
1346, www.quakerugby.org
- **Seattle Rugby Club**, www.seattlerfc.org
- **Tacoma Nomads Rugby Football Club**, www.tacomarugby.com
- **Valley Rugby Football Club**, P.O. Box 58551, Tukwila, 98138, 206-382-7299,
www.valleyrugby.com

RUNNING

Considering the weather in Seattle, you might think that running wouldn't
be a favorite sport in the city. For some reason, though, the rain just seems to
make area runners more determined. The most popular running locations in
Seattle are Green Lake (the inner loop is 2.8 miles, the outer loop is slightly over
3 miles), the Burke-Gilman Trail, Myrtle Edwards Park, and Alki Beach in West
Seattle. Listed below are several running clubs in Seattle, which sponsor weekly
club runs and annual events:

- **Club Northwest**, www.clubnorthwest.org
- **Eastside Runners**, www.eastsiderunners.com
- **Seattle Frontrunners (Gay/Lesbian)**, P.O. Box 31952, Seattle, WA 98103,
www.seattlefrontrunners.org
- **Seattle Running Club**, 747 N 77th St, Seattle 98103, www.seattlerunning-
club.org
- **West Seattle Runners**, 206-938-2416, www.westseattlerunners.org

Many races are held annually throughout Seattle, some of the most popular of
which are the St. Patrick's Day Dash (4 miles) held in March, the Jingle Bell Run/
Walk (5K) held in early December, and the Komen Race for the Cure (5K). The
Torchlight Run (8K), held in August as part of the Seafair celebration, is both a

run and a parade event, with prizes given for best costume and group theme. The Beat the Bridge Run (8K) is a favorite local run, so named because the object is to cross the University Bridge before the bridge goes up. Comedians and musicians entertain those runners who get stuck behind the bridge until the bridge is lowered again. The Seattle Marathon and Half-Marathon are held each year in November. The best option for getting information on upcoming races is to contact a local running club or running store. In addition, the following stores advertise races and also sponsor weekly group runs:

- **Seattle Running Company**, 919 E Pine St, 206-329-1466, 206-325-4800, www.fleetfeetseattle.com
- **Super Jock 'n Jill**, 7210 E Greenlake Dr N, 206-522-7711, www.superjocknjill.com

SCUBA DIVING

If you think that scuba diving is a purely tropical pastime, think again! Puget Sound may be cold and a bit murky, but with the proper equipment it can be a diver's paradise. Depending on the time of year, you'll probably want a drysuit and gloves, but once you're in the water, with the abundance of fish and sights, you won't mind the extra weight. You can find octopus, wolf eels and the occasional sixgill shark among many other natural wonders. There are plenty of dive schools and supply shops in the area.

- **A2Z Scuba**, 1109 River Rd, Puyallup 98371, 253-840-DIVE, www.a2zscuba.com
- **Bubbles Below Diving**, 17315 140th Ave NE, Woodinville 98072, 425-424-3483, www.bubblesbelow.com
- **Exotic Aquatics,** 146 Winslow Way W, Bainbridge Island 98110, 206-842-1980, www.exoticaquaticsscuba.com
- **GirlDiver,** 625C S Landers St, 253-217-8204, www.girldiver.com
- **Lighthouse Diving Center**, 8215 Lake City Way, 206-524-1633; 5421 196th St SW, #6, Lynnwood 98036, 425-771-2679; 2502 Pacific Ave, Tacoma 98402, 253-627-7617, www.lighthousediving.com
- **Northwest Sports Divers**, 1233 164th St SW #N, Lynnwood 98037th, 425-361-7696, www.nwsportsdivers.com
- **Seattle Scuba Schools,** 2000 Westlake Ave N, #210, 206-284-2350; in Tacoma call 253-256-1759; www.seattlescuba.com
- **Silent World Scuba Diving**, 13433 NE 20th St, Ste V/W, Bellevue 98005, 425-747-8842, www.silent-world.com
- **Sound Dive Center**, 5000 Burwell St, Bremerton 98312, 360-373-6141, www.sounddivecenter.com
- **Tacoma Scuba**, 1602 Center St, Ste C, Tacoma 98409, 253-238-1754, www.tacomascubacenter.com

- **TL Sea Diving**, 23405 Pacific Hwy S, 206-824-4100, www.tlsea.com
- **Underwater Sports**, 10545 Aurora Ave N, 206-362-3310; 264 Railroad Ave, Edmonds 98020, 425-771-6322; 205 E Casino Rd, Everett, 425-355-3338; 11743 124th Ave NE, Kirkland, 425-821-7200; 12003 NE 12th, #59 Brierwood Center, Bellevue 98005, 425-454-5168; 34428 Pacific Hwy S, Federal Way 98003, 253-874-9387; 9608 40th Ave SW, Lakewood 98499, 253-588-6634; www.underwatersports.com

SKIING AND SNOWBOARDING

The highways over the Cascade Mountains lead to several ski resorts that are not too far. Whistler, a few hours' drive north of Vancouver, BC, is considered one of the best ski resorts in North America. Skiing and snowboarding are both popular activities at nearby resorts, which usually offer lessons for all levels of skiers. Call ahead for details and lodging reservations.

WASHINGTON STATE SKI AREAS

- **Crystal Mountain**, near Mount Rainier, 33 miles east of Enumclaw on Highway 410, 360-663-2265, snow-line 888-754-6199, www.crystalmoun tainresort.com
- **Mission Ridge**, 12 miles east of Wenatchee on Highway 2, 509-663-6543, snow-line 509-663-3200, www.missionridge.com
- **Mount Baker**, 56 miles east of Bellingham on Highway 542, snow phone 360-671-0211, www.mtbakerskiarea.com
- **Stevens Pass**, 65 miles east of Everett on Highway 2, 206-812-4510, snow-line 206-634-1645, www.stevenspass.com
- **The Summit at Snoqualmie**, (includes Alpental, Hyak, Ski Acres and Snoqualmie ski areas), 60 miles east of Seattle on I-90, 425-434-7669, snow-line 206-236-1600, www.summit-at-snoqualmie.com
- **White Pass**, near Mount Rainier, 50 miles west of Yakima on Highway 12, 509-672-3101, snow-line, 509-672-3100, www.skiwhitepass.com

OUT-OF-STATE SKI AREAS

- **Mount Bachelor**, 22 miles southwest of Bend, OR, 541-382-7888 or 800-829-2442, www.mtbachelor.com
- **Mount Hood Meadows**, 80 miles east of Portland near Hood River, OR, 503-337-2222 or 503-659-1256, www.skihood.com
- **Mount Washington**, located 80 miles north of Nanaimo on Vancouver Island, BC, 888-231-1499, www.mtwashington.bc.ca

- **Silver Mountain**, located 70 miles east of Spokane in Kellogg, ID, 866-344-2675, www.silvermt.com
- **Schweitzer**, located 86 miles northeast of Spokane near Sandpoint, ID, 208-263-9555, snow phone 208-263-9562, www.schweitzer.com.
- **Whistler (includes Whistler and Blackcomb ski areas)**, 75 miles north of Vancouver, BC, 866-218-9690, www.whistler-blackcomb.com

SKI/SNOWBOARD RENTALS

- **All About Bike and Ski**, 3615 NE 45th St, 206-524-2642, www.allaboutbike andski.com
- **Alpine Hut,** 2215 15th Ave W, 206-284-3575, www.alpinehut.com
- **Bob's Bike & Board,** 3605 NE 45th St, 206-524-2642, www.bobsbikenboard. com
- **Eastside Ski & Sport**, 15606 Woodinville Duvall Rd, Woodinville 98072, 425-485-7547; West Commons Campus, 1 Microsoft Way, Bldg 98, Redmond 98052, 425-885-3000, www.eastsideskiandsport.com
- **REI**, 222 Yale Ave N, 206-223-1944; 7500 166th Ave NE, Redmond 98052, 425-882-1158; 3000 184th St SW, Lynnwood 98037, 425-640-6200; 240 Andover Park W, Tukwila 98188, 206-248-1938; 3825 S Steele St, Tacoma 98409, 253-671-1938, www.rei.com
- **Seattle Ski and Snowboard**, 14915 Aurora Ave N, 206-548-1000, www.se attleski.com
- **Seattle Snowboard Connection (Sno Con),** 263 Yale Ave N, 206-467-8545, www.snowboardconnection.com

SNOWMOBILING

In Washington, snowmobiling is allowed on many forest and park trails. Snow-mobiles are available for rent near most ski areas and in other wilderness areas throughout the state. Check the Yellow Pages. Rentals generally include a short lesson that covers riding techniques and safety tips. The following resources may be helpful if you're planning a day of snowmobiling:

- **Washington State Parks and Recreation Commission**, 360-902-8844, www.parks.wa.gov
- **Washington State Snowmobile Association**, 800-783-9772, www.wssa.us

WASHINGTON STATE SNOWMOBILE SNO-PARK INFORMATION

- **Apple Country Snowmobile Club**, 509-667-0550
- **Chelan Ranger District**, 509-682-4900
- **Cle Elum Ranger District**, 509-852-1100

- **Colville National Forest**, 509-684-7000
- **Cowlitz Valley Ranger District**, 360-497-1100
- **Entiat Ranger District**, 509-784-1511
- **Lake Wenatchee Ranger District**, 509-763-3103
- **Mount Adams Ranger District**, 509-395-3400
- **Mount Baker Ranger District**, 360-856-5700
- **Mount St. Helens Ranger District**, 360-449-7800
- **Okanogan County**, 509-422-7324
- **Naches Ranger District**, 509-653-1401
- **Pomeroy Ranger District**, 509-843-1891
- **Snoqualmie Ranger District**, 360-825-6585, 360-888-1421
- **Spokane County Parks and Recreation**, 509-477-4730, www.spokanecoun ty.org/parks
- **Tonasket Ranger District**, 509-486-2186
- **Wenatchee River Ranger District**, 509-548-2550
- **White River Ranger District**, 360-825-6585

SOCCER

While a few high schools have teams, most children and adults play competitive soccer in private leagues. The following soccer resources are in the greater Seattle area:

- **Ballard Youth Soccer**, 1752 NW Market St #224th, www.ballardsoccer.org
- **Beacon Hill Soccer Club**, 2811 14th Ave S, 206-853-9935
- **Capitol Hill Soccer Club**, www.capitolhillsoccer.org
- **Co-Rec Soccer Association**, P.O. Box 22064, Seattle 98122, 206-329-1548, www.co-recsoccer.com
- **Eastside Youth Soccer Association**, 15600 NE 8th St, Ste B1, Bellevue 98008, 425-454-7224, www.eysa.org
- **Emerald City Football Club**, P.O. Box 85505, Seattle 98145, 206-629-8860, www.emeraldcityfc.org
- **Greater Seattle Soccer League (GSSL)**, 9750 Greenwood Ave N, 206-782-6831, www.gssl.org
- **Hillwood Soccer Club**, P.O. Box 60226, Shoreline 98160, 206-542-3353, www.hillwoodsoccer.com
- **Lake City Soccer Club**, 12345 Lake City Way NE, #401, 206-365-7684, www.lkcitysoccer.org
- **LVR Youth Soccer Club (Laurelhurst**, View Ridge, Ravenna), www.lvr-soccer.org
- **Lake Washington Youth Soccer Association**, 12525 Willows Rd NE, Ste 100, Kirkland 98034, 425-821-1741, www.lwysa.org

- **Liga Hispana del Noroeste**, 11401 Rainier Ave S, 206-772-3785, www.ligahispana.com
- **Liga Hispana Rainier Youth Soccer Club**, 11401 Rainier Ave S, 206-772-3785, www.laligayouthsoccerclub.org
- **Magnolia Soccer Club**, 3213 W Wheeler St, P.O. Box 188, www.magnoliasoccerclub.com
- **McGilvra Youth Soccer Club**, 4111 E Madison St #144, Seattle 98122, www.mcgilvrasoccer.org
- **Mount Baker/Lakewood Youth Soccer Club**, 2945 36th Ave S, www.mblsoccer.org
- **Queen Anne Soccer Club**, 2212 Queen Anne Ave N, www.qasoccer.org
- **Seattle Youth Soccer Association**, 520 NE Ravenna Blvd, 206-274-1318, www.sysa.org
- **Shorelake Soccer Club**, P.O. Box 55472, Shoreline, 98155, 206-362-3594, www.shorelake.org
- **Silver Lake Soccer Club**, P.O. Box 12543, Mill Creek, 98082, 425-481-2665, www.silverlakesoccerclub.com
- **Washington State Adult Soccer Association**, 7800 NE Bothell Way, Kenmore 98028, 425-485-7855, www.wssa.org
- **Washington State Women's Soccer Association**, P.O. Box 7505, Covington 98042, 206-626-6750, www.wswsa.org
- **Washington State Youth Soccer Association**, 500 S 336th St, Ste 100, Federal Way 98003, 253-4-SOCCER, www.wsysa.com
- **Woodinville Indoor Soccer Center**, P.O. Box 871, Woodinville 98072, 425-481-5099, www.woodinvilleindoor.com
- **Woodland Soccer Club**, www.woodlandsoccer.org

SWIMMING

When hot weather hits Seattle, folks head in droves to the few swimming beaches in the city. Lifeguards are generally on duty at Seattle beaches 11 a.m. to 8 p.m., from June 20 through Labor Day (except in inclement weather). To find beaches in communities outside Seattle, contact one of the parks and recreation departments listed previously in this chapter. The following are Seattle parks with swimming areas (call Seattle Parks and Recreation's general information line at 206-684-4075 for more information):

- **Green Lake Park**, 7201 E Green Lake Dr and 7312 W Green Lake Dr
- **Madison Park**, E Madison and E Howe St
- **Madrona Park**, 853 Lake Washington Blvd
- **Magnuson Park**, 7400 Sand Point Way NE
- **Matthews Beach Park**, 49th Ave NE and NE 93rd St
- **Mount Baker Park**, 2521 Lake Park Dr S

- **Pritchard Island Beach**, 8400 55th Ave S
- **Seward Park**, 5895 Lake Washington Blvd S

Wading pools are open for the little ones in many parks, playgrounds, and community centers in Seattle. Park wading pools are open daily (provided the temperature is over 70 degrees), from 11 a.m. to 8 p.m. Community center and playground wading pools are open weekdays only, and hours vary. Call the city's Wading Pool **Hotline** at 206-684-7796 for more information. Here are the city's three biggest wading pools:

- **Green Lake Park,** 7312 W Green Lake Dr
- **Lincoln Park**, 8600 Fauntleroy Way SW
- **Volunteer Park**, 1400 E Galer St

For those interested in year-round swimming, Seattle city pools offer a variety of open swim sessions, lessons and lap-swimming options. Many host swim club practices for Masters and all-ages programs. To find pools in communities outside Seattle, contact one of the parks and recreation departments listed previously in this chapter.

- **Ballard Pool**, 1471 NW 67th St, 206-684-4094
- **Colman Pool (outdoor)**, 8603 Fauntleroy Way SW, 206-684-7494
- **Evans Pool**, 7201 E Green Lake Dr N, 206-684-4961
- **Madison Pool**, 13401 Meridian Ave N, 206-684-4979
- **Meadowbrook Pool**, 10515 35th Ave NE, 206-684-4989
- **Medgar Evers Pool**, 500 23rd Ave, 206-684-4766
- **Mounger Pool (outdoor)**, 2535 32nd Ave W, 206-684-4708
- **Queen Anne Pool**, 1920 1st Ave W, 206-386-4282
- **Rainier Beach Pool**, 8825 Rainier Ave S, 206-386-1944
- **Southwest Pool**, 2801 SW Thistle St, 206-684-7440

Several swim clubs hold regular practices at pools around Seattle, many offering a variety of practices for all levels of experience. Call for details, as prices and entrance requirements vary widely. An excellent resource for competitive swimming information in Washington is **Pacific Northwest Swimming (PNS)**, 501 30th St NE, Ste E, Auburn, WA 98002, 1-888-300-SWIM. The organization maintains a comprehensive website at www.pns.org that includes swim club directories. Some local swim clubs are listed below. Because many practice at multiple locations, business office addresses are given for some clubs.

- **Cascade Swim Club**, 20127 183rd Pl NE, Woodinville, WA 98077, 425-788-6860, www.cascadeswimclub.org
- **Chinook Aquatic Club**, 54 Skagit Key, Bellevue 98006, 206-230-5812, www.chinookaquaticclub.org

- **Salmon Bay Aquatics**, P.O. Box 17442, Seattle 98127, 206-362-3277 (message machine)

VIDEO ARCADES

- **Chuck E. Cheese's**, 2239 148th Ave NE, Bellevue, 425-746-5000; 25817 104th Ave SE, Kent, 253-813-9000; 3717 196th St, Lynnwood, 425-771-1195; 4911 Tacoma Mall Blvd, Tacoma, 253-473-3078, www.chuckecheese.com
- **Gameworks**, 1511 7th Ave, 206-521-0952, www.gameworks.com
- **Seattle Waterfront Arcade**, Pier 57, 1301 Alaskan Way, 206-906-1081, www.seattlewaterfrontarcade.com
- **Shorty's (21 and over)**, 2222 2nd Ave, 206-441-5449, www.shortydog.com

VOLLEYBALL

You might think that volleyball would be a purely indoor sport in western Washington, and while there are many indoor leagues, summertime finds players on the sands of Alki Beach and Golden Gardens Park enjoying beach volleyball. North Beach Volleyball even offers indoor beach volleyball in a spacious warehouse at Magnuson Park. Many local community centers offer drop-in volleyball, and a good place to find resources is the website of **Seattle Volleyball.Net**, www.seattlevolleyball.net, a site devoted to connecting people to all things volleyball. The following organizations offer league play for different ages and skill levels nearly year round.

- **A/E Volleyball Association**, 6724 2nd Ave NW, 206-782-8030, www.aevolleyball@comcast.net
- **Jet City Sports**, info@jetcitysports.com
- **Moxie Volleyball**, 770 122nd Ave NE, Bellevue, 98005, 425-985-0540
- **North Beach Volleyball Seattle**, 7727 63rd Ave NE, Bldg #2, 206-624-2899, seattle@northbeachvolleyball.com
- **Northwest Volleyball**, 15821 NE 8th St, Ste W-200, Bellevue, 98008, 425-497-1051, www.volleyballnw.com
- **Seattle Volleyball Club**, 9501 Evanston Ave N, www.seattlevolleyballclub.com
- **Strike Force Volleyball**, P.O. Box 3073, Redmond, 98052, 425-867-0489, www.sfvbclub.org
- **Underdog Sports Leagues Volleyball**, 206-320-8326, www.underdogseattle.com

WATER-SKIING

During the summer, there are hundreds of people water-skiing on Lake Washington. Many skiers launch their boats early in the morning from Magnuson Park in Sand Point and head out to the middle of the lake. Other lakes in Washington popular with water-skiers are Lake Sammamish in Bellevue and Lake Chelan, north of Wenatchee. For equipment and supplies, try the following resources:

- **Adrenaline Water Sports**, 13433 NE 20th Ave, Ste C, Bellevue, 425-746-9253, www.adrenalinewatersports.com
- **Bakes ProShop**, 6424 E Lake Sammamish Pkwy SE, Issaquah 98029, 425-392-7599, www.bakesmarine.com
- **Connelly Skis (online store based in Lynnwood)**, 425-775-5416, http://store.connellyskis.com
- **Seattle Watersports**, 6820 NE 175th St, Kenmore 98028th, 888-481-2754, www.seattlewatersports.com
- **Sturtevant's Sports**, 1100 Bellevue Way NE, Bellevue 98004, 425-454-6465 or 888-454-7669; Ski Mart Bellevue, 13219 NE 20th St, Bellevue 98005, 425-637-8958; Ski Mart Tacoma, 2220 S 37th St, Tacoma 98409, 253-473-1134; Ski Mart Alderwood, 18920 28th Ave W #N, Lynnwood 98036, 425-778-3616, www.sturtevants.com
- **Wiley's Ski Shop**, 1417 S Trenton St, 206-762-1300, www.wileyski.com

WINDSURFING

While Green Lake, Lake Union, Puget Sound, and Lake Washington are all popular destinations for windsurfing enthusiasts, the Columbia River Gorge is the ultimate thrill for experienced windsurfers. Located on the southern border of Washington near Hood River, Oregon, the gorge is challenging and exciting for veteran surfers, but can be rough and even dangerous for beginners. The following resources provide information and lessons for both experienced windsurfers and beginners:

- **Columbia Gorge Windsurfing Association**, 202 Oak St, Ste 150, Hood River, OR, 541-386-9225, www.gorgewindsurfing.org
- **Urban Surf**, 2100 N Northlake Way, 206-545-9463, www.urbansurf.com

YOGA

Yoga has become enormously popular in Seattle, with studios popping up all over the city, and health clubs rushing to add classes. Here are a few Seattle yoga studios:

- **8 Limbs Yoga Centers**, 6801 Greenwood Ave N, 206-432-9609; 500 E Pike St, 206-325-8221; 7345 35th Ave NE, 206-523-9722; 4546-1/2 California Ave SW, 206-933-YOGA, www.8limbsyoga.com
- **Bikram Yoga Seattle**, 1054 N 34th St, 206-547-0188; 4747 California Ave SW, 206-937-3900; www.bikramyogaseattle.com
- **The Center for Yoga in Seattle**, 2261 NE 65th St, 206-526-9642, www.yoga seattle.com
- **Hatha Yoga Center**, 4550 11th Ave NE, 206-632-1443, www.hathayogacen ter.com
- **Inside Out Yoga**, 8016 Dayton Ave N, 206-992-4808, www.kimtrimmer.com
- **Lila Yoga**, 2812 E Madison St, 206-323-7138, www.lilayogaseattle.com
- **Lotus Yoga**, 4860 Rainier Ave S, 206-760-1917, www.lotusyoga.biz
- **Planet Earth Yoga Center**, 418 N 35th St, 206-365-1997, www.planetearthyo ga.com
- **Red Square Yoga**, 1911 10th Ave W, 206-999-6274, www.redsquareyoga. com
- **The Samarya Center**, 1806 E Yesler Way, 206-568-8335, www.samaryacenter. org
- **Seattle Holistic Center**, Good Shepherd Center, 4649 Sunnyside Ave N, Room 302, 206-525-9035, www.seattleholisticcenter.com
- **Seattle Yoga Arts**, 1540 15th Ave, 206-440-3191, www.seattleyogaarts.com
- **Sound Yoga**, 5639 California Ave SW, 206-938-8195, www.soundyoga.com
- **Two Dog Yoga Studio**, 12549 28th Ave NE, 206-367-9608, www.twodogyo ga.com
- **Whole Life Yoga**, 8551 Greenwood Ave N, Ste 2, 206-784-2882, www. wholelifeyoga.com
- **The Yoga Tree**, 4250 Fremont Ave N, 206-545-0316, www.yogatree.com

HEALTH CLUBS

Whether you're trying to stay in shape during the off-season, get in shape for spring break, or simply prefer group fitness or weight-lifting to outdoor sports, Seattle is full of health clubs and gyms. Most offer conditioning classes, as well as personal training programs. Some clubs also offer yoga, spinning, Pilates, Zumba classes, swimming workouts, and nutrition and health classes. Call or visit the club you're interested in to get details on their programs.

- **24 Hour Fitness**, multiple locations, 800-224-0240, www.24hourfitness.com
- **Allstar Fitness**, 511 Olive Way, Ste 213, 206-292-0900; 2629 SW Andover St, 206-932-9999; 700 5th Ave, 14th floor, 206-343-4692, 31 Montana Ave, Ta-coma, 253-475-7000; www.allstarfitness.com

- **Ballard Health Club**, 2208 NW Market St, 206-706-4882, www.ballardhealth club.com
- **Bally Total Fitness**, multiple locations, 800-515-2582, www.ballyfitness.com
- **Community Fitness,** 6108 Roosevelt Way NE, 206-523-3363; 2113 NE 65th St, 206-523-1534; www.communityfitness.com
- **Curves**, multiple locations, 800-848-1096, www.curves.com
- **Gold's Gym**, multiple locations, www.goldsgym.com
- **LA Fitness,** 1416 NW Ballard Way, 206-508-5030; 13244 Aurora Ave, 206-973-0232; 350 Baker Blvd, Tukwila 98188, 206-331-4071; www.lafitness.com
- **Mieko's Fitness**, 1629 220th St SE, Bothell, 425-483-3330, 206-286-9070; 12015 31st Ave NE, 206-417-4715; 8401 Main St, Edmonds, 425-712-0363, 13018 39th Ave SE, Everett, 425-385-8038, www.miekosfitness.com
- **Olympic Athletic Club**, 5301 Leary Ave NW, 206-789-5010, www.olympic athleticclub.com
- **Pro-Robics**, 1530 Queen Anne Ave N, 206-283-2303; 3811 NE 45th St, 206-524-9246, www.prorobics.com
- **Pro Sports Club**, 501 Eastlake Ave, 2nd Flr, 206-332-1873; 4455 148th Ave NE, Bellevue 98007, 425-885-5566; 9911 Willows Rd #100, Redmond 98052, 425-869-4760; www.proclub.com
- **Seattle Athletic Club**, 2020 Western Ave, 206-443-1111; 333 NE 97th St, 206-522-9400, www.sacdt.com
- **Seattle Fitness Club**, 83 S King St, 206-467-1800, http://seattlefitness.com
- **Snap Fitness,** multiple locations, 877-474-5422, www.snapfitness.com
- **Sound Mind & Body**, 437 N 34th St, 206-547-3470, www.smbgym.com
- **Washington Athletic Club**, 1325 6th Ave, 206-622-7900, www.wac.net
- **X GYM**, 11 Vine St #B, 206-728-XGYM; 3213 Harbor Ave SW, 206-938-XGYM; 126 Central Way, Ste 150, Kirkland, 425-822-XGYM, www.xgym.com

ACTIVITY CLUBS

- **Events and Adventures (for singles)**, 325 118th Ave SE, Ste 200, Bellevue 98005, 800-386-0866, www.eventsandadventures.com
- **The Mountaineers**, 7700 Sand Point Way NE, 206-521-6000, www.mountain eers.org
- **Sierra Club**, Washington State Chapter, 180 Nickerson St, Ste 202, 206-378-0114, http://cascade.sierraclub.org

SPORTING GOODS AND OUTDOOR WEAR

Whether you're heading out of town for a rugged hike or spending an hour at the park with a Frisbee, you may need to go shopping first. Seattle is the birthplace of sporting goods giant REI, and residents take their sports and recreational activities seriously, so there are dozens of places to find just the right equipment. Check the Yellow Pages under "Sporting Goods—Retail" or search online for everything from boots and bicycling to fleece and fishing. Some of the best-known retailers are listed here:

- **Big 5 Sporting Goods,** multiple locations, 800-898-2994, www.big5sporting goods.com
- **Columbia Sportswear,** 290 Pine St, 206-443-7639, www.columbia.com
- **Filson,** 1555 4th Ave S, 206-622-3147, www.filson.com
- **Mountain to Sound Outfitters,** 3602 SW Alaska St, 206-935-7669, www. m2soutfitters.com
- **The North Face,** 1023 1st Ave, 206-622-4111, www.thenorthface.com
- **Outdoor Emporium,** 1701 4th Ave S, 206-624-6550, www.sportco.com
- **REI Flagship store,** 222 Yale Ave N, 206-223-1944, www.rei.com
- **Second Ascent,** 5209 Ballard Ave NW, 206-545-8810, http://secondascent. com

S EATTLE'S LANDSCAPE IS THE RESULT OF VARIOUS GEOLOGIC FORCES: the hills and mountains created by shifting plates far beneath the earth's surface, the lakes and waterways carved out by a great system of glaciers and several ice ages. Add to this a rainy climate broken by bright sunlight, throw in lush indigenous evergreens and colorful rhododendrons, and it is no wonder that Seattle residents spend so much time outdoors. The city's park system, which includes many lakes and beaches, provides abundant opportunities for enjoying the area's natural beauty.

In 1903, J. C. Olmsted designed most of Seattle's park system. The Seattle park board hired Olmsted to design a boulevard system that would link much of the city's parkland, which had been purchased between 1897 and 1903. The result is impressive, with approximately 20 miles of winding parkway connecting many of Seattle's major greenspaces. The following is a brief description of Seattle's most popular parks, although in addition to those listed here, many neighborhoods also have small parks, athletic fields, and playgrounds. To get more information on any of the parks listed here, call the **Seattle Parks and Recreation Department** at 206-684-4075 or visit www.cityofseattle.net/parks.

NORTHWEST SEATTLE PARKS

INLAND PARKS

- **Green Lake** is perhaps Seattle's most popular public park. It is surrounded by almost three miles of paved walkway, attracting bicyclists, in-line skaters, runners, and strolling couples. In Seattle, where locals are undaunted by drizzle and early winter darkness, Green Lake has become a year-round mecca for early-morning and late-evening walkers and joggers. During the summer, fields at the east side of the lake fill with volleyball teams, the basketball courts host informal but competitive pick-up games, and in the evenings, in-line skaters can be found playing hockey in the drained kiddie pool. The Seattle Parks Department's Green Lake Small Craft Center, 206-684-4074, sponsors rowing classes as well as novice sailing classes at the south end of the lake, and beginning wind-surfers set sail from the eastern shore. Another Seattle tradition, the annual Seafair Milk Carton Derby, launches from the shore each July, and there are many other events held on Green Lake throughout the year.

- **Kerry Park**, on the southwest corner of Queen Anne Hill, overlooks Elliott Bay and the downtown skyline, providing a spectacular view of the city.

- **Woodland Park**, at the south end of Green Lake, offers tennis courts, lawn bowling, and grassy picnic areas, as well as the Woodland Park Zoo, a seasonal favorite of adults and kids alike. One particularly popular program is the Bird of Prey program, where kids delight in watching trained raptors in flight. Small children enjoy the petting zoo and pony rides in the summer. The zoo is located in the Phinney Ridge neighborhood, at Phinney Avenue North and North 50th Street. Call 206-548-2500 for hours. Also worth a visit is the spectacular Rose Garden, just outside the zoo's south gate. Call 206-548-2500 for details and special events information.

PARKS WITH BEACHES

- **Carkeek Park,** north of Golden Gardens, offers stunning vistas of Puget Sound from bluff trails, an Environmental Learning Center and, at the right time of year, glimpses of salmon in Piper Creek, which runs through the park. A trail through wetlands leads to the beach, accessed by a footbridge over the railroad tracks.

- **Discovery Park**, on the western point of Magnolia, is the largest of the Olmsted-designed parks. Its over-500 acres of wooded trails and flowery meadows, towering sea cliffs, and windy beaches provide everyone with something to do. Visit in the evening to watch the sun set over the Olympics, or come during the day for a pleasant hike down to the beach. Clay cliffs overhang the rocky beach, furnishing hours of fun for kids. Nearby quiet meadows are great places for picnics or impromptu bird watching. You may see bald eagles, hawks, falcons or even an osprey. From the beach you may catch sight of migrating seabirds and views of the West Point Lighthouse. The Daybreak Star Cultural Center, in the center of the park, celebrates Native American culture with art exhibits and special programs. Call 206-285-4425 for details.

- **Gasworks Park**, at the north end of Lake Union, is built around the dramatic skeleton of the old gasworks factory and offers stunning views of the downtown skyline. The park attracts kite-flyers and Frisbee players, and is a starting point for the Burke-Gilman Trail, a paved walkway that heads east from Gasworks to Lake Washington, then along the lake shore to the Eastside. The giant sundial atop the park's central hill is always worth a visit. Gasworks Park hosts an annual Independence Day celebration, complete with a spectacular fireworks display over Lake Union.

- **Golden Gardens Park**, which is not a part of the Olmsted plan, is located at the north end of Ballard. The park features one of Seattle's few truly sandy beaches, luring swimmers, picnickers, and volleyball players through the summer months, and is one of the few public parks in the city that allow bonfires.

NORTHEAST SEATTLE PARKS

INLAND PARKS

- **Ravenna Park**, north of the University of Washington, follows a steep ravine northwest to Cowen Park. It features a wading pool and wooded trails and is a favorite for picnics.

PARKS WITH BEACHES

- **Magnuson Park is the second largest park in the city**, with sports fields and a boat launch to Lake Washington. It features Kite Hill, for, you guessed it, kite flying, as well as outdoor art installations, an outdoor amphitheater hosting theater productions in the summer, a community garden, a swimming beach with lifeguard on duty during the summer, plenty of trails, and one of the best off-leash dog parks. The site of a former naval station, many of the large, old buildings are now used as headquarters for community organizations, and sizeable events like the Friends of the Seattle Public Library Book Sale and a popular plant sale are held here.
- **Matthews Beach Park**, on the Lake Washington waterfront near Sand Point, is a popular summer destination for sunbathers and swimmers, and is also a stop on the Burke-Gilman Trail.

SOUTHEAST SEATTLE PARKS

INLAND PARKS

- **Volunteer Park**, on the northeast corner of Capitol Hill, also provides incredible views of downtown, as well as Puget Sound and the Olympic Mountains. For an even more dazzling view, climb to the top of the 75-foot water tower. In Volunteer Park you'll also find the Seattle Asian Art Museum, and a 1912 conservatory filled with orchids and other tropical plants. Just north of the park, the Lake View Cemetery contains the graves of several prominent Seattle citizens, including "Doc" Maynard and Bruce Lee.

- **Jefferson Park on Beacon Hill**, with sweeping views of the city, is also home to the Jefferson Park Golf Course. The initial phases of a planned expansion to the park, which will eventually include sports courts, a skateboard park, community center, large lawns, gardens, and meadows, were completed in 2010.

PARKS WITH BEACHES

- **Madison Park** is located on Lake Washington at the far east end of Madison Street. Although not part of the Olmsted plan, it originated in the 1890s as the site of a summer amusement park. Today it is a popular sunny-day hangout, offering the perennial summer favorites of picnicking, swimming, and sunbathing.
- **Mount Baker Park** is north of Seward Park, near the site of the Seafair hydroplane races that take place each August. The Mount Baker Rowing and Sailing Center hosts beginning rowing and sailing classes, and is home to both an adult and a high school crew team. Call the center at 206-386-1913 for details.
- **Seward Park**, in the southeast corner of Seattle, is located on the 277-acre Bailey Peninsula. In addition to a beach, the park has a system of nature trails perfect for solitary walks or bird-watching (bald eagles are occasionally sighted here). Also enticing, the 1920s bathhouse now serves as an artists' studio, offering a variety of ceramics classes for adults and children; call 206-722-6342 for class availability.
- **The Washington Park Arboretum**, along Madison Avenue, picks up the Olmsted planned parkway in Madrona. The Arboretum is a 255-acre woodland managed by the University of Washington. Though it was a part of the Seattle park system as early as 1904, it was developed by the university as an arboretum in 1936. Originally filled with native Northwest plants and trees, today the Washington Park Arboretum is home to more than 5,500 flowers, trees, and shrubs from all over the world. It includes the beautifully sculptured Japanese Tea Garden, designed in 1960 by Japanese architect Juki Iida.

SOUTHWEST SEATTLE PARKS

INLAND PARKS

- **Schmitz Preserve Park** in West Seattle is a 53-acre haven of old-growth forest and hiking trails lovingly tended by neighborhood groups, with very little change over the last century.

- **Westcrest Park** is a large park wrapped around the West Seattle Reservoir with a great view of the city, paths, a playground, and an off-leash dog park.

PARKS WITH BEACHES

- **Alki Beach Park** in West Seattle is a great place to watch sunsets over the Olympics or enjoy a spectacular view of downtown Seattle. During the summer, in-line skaters, bicyclists, and serious beach volleyball players flock to this park. The beach resort atmosphere adds to the charm of this narrow strip of land along the northwest shore of West Seattle.
- **Lincoln Park,** in West Seattle's Fauntleroy neighborhood, is one of Seattle's most popular parks, with bluffs overlooking Puget Sound, miles of trails through dense woods, and a paved walking path along the beach. There's a large wading pool, and the city's only saltwater swimming pool. Colman pool is an outdoor heated pool on the beach, only open in the summer and popular with generations of Seattleites. With ball fields, picnic shelters, beachcombing, and watching ferries plying the waters just south of the park, this is easily a daylong destination.

SURROUNDING COMMUNITIES

Several Seattle-area parks are owned or maintained by the **King County Park System**, a vast network of lakes and greenspaces. They operate 180 parks, 175 miles of trails, and pools and sports fields all over the county. To find a county park in your neck of the woods, call 206-296-0100 or visit www.kingcounty.gov/recreation/parks.aspx.

MERCER ISLAND

- **Luther Burbank Park**, on the northeast end of Mercer Island, commands 77 acres and a three-quarters-of-a-mile stretch of Lake Washington waterfront. Nearly three miles of trails provide opportunities for walks and bird watching. Other amenities include tennis courts, a group picnic area, a grassy amphitheater, and daily moorage. Luther Burbank's off-leash dog area offers pets the rare opportunity to swim legally in a public park. 206-275-7609, www.mercergov.org. Plans currently in development aim to improve the park's infrastructure and add new features and amenities.

BELLEVUE

- **Cougar Mountain Regional Wildland Park** is surrounded by the cities of Bellevue, Newcastle, and Issaquah, just minutes from downtown Seattle. The park covers more than 3,000 acres, making it the largest park in the King County system. More than 36 miles of trails are for hikers, and 12 miles are devoted to equestrians. Fourteen creeks originate within the park, including three salmon-spawning creeks: Coal Creek, May Creek, and Tibbett's Creek. 206-296-0100, www.kingcounty.gov/recreation/parks.aspx

- **Kelsey Creek Park** consists of 150 acres of wetland and forest habitat. The park boasts numerous hiking and jogging trails, including a gravel loop trail that circles picturesque barns and pastures. The highlight of the park is Kelsey Creek Farm, which is home to a variety of animals, and offers several children's programs. 425-452-7688, www.ci.bellevue.wa.us
- **Robinswood Community Park** is the setting for Robinswood House, one of the area's most popular wedding reception and private-party sites. For rental information, call 425-452-7850. The park also features four indoor and four outdoor tennis courts, a pond and playground, and a fully equipped baseball field with scoreboard. 425-452-7850, www.ci.bellevue.wa.us
- **Wilburton Hill Park**, which includes the Bellevue Botanical Garden, features ball fields, hiking trails, and a children's play area. The Botanical Garden contains 36 acres of lush flower gardens and landscaping. Guided tours of the grounds are available. 425-452-6914, www.ci.bellevue.wa.us

KIRKLAND

- **Juanita Bay Park** offers numerous opportunities to view a variety of wildlife, including songbirds, waterfowl, raptors, shorebirds, turtles, and beavers. The 144-acre park's paved trails and boardwalks make self-guided tours easy, but volunteer park rangers also offer interpretive tours on the first Sunday of the month at 1 p.m. 425-828-2237, www.kirklandwa.gov

REDMOND

- **Marymoor Park** is the crown jewel of the King County Park System and one of the most popular parks in the entire Puget Sound region, particularly among dog owners, soccer players, bicycle racers, rock climbers, and model airplane enthusiasts. Covering 640 acres, the park is visited by more than a million people each year. Annual events at Marymoor include King County's Heritage Festival and several music events. Notable attractions at Marymoor include a 40-acre off-leash dog area, the Marymoor Velodrome, Willowmoor Farm, and the Marymoor Climbing Rock. 206-205-3661, www.kingcounty.gov/recreation/parks

RENTON

- **Gene Coulon Memorial Beach Park** was originally named Lake Washington Beach Park because of its location on the southeast shore of the region's most popular recreational lake. The park consists of 57 acres of land and water, and encourages several aquatic activities, including swimming, boating, water-skiing and windsurfing. Gene Coulon is home to two commercial quick-service restaurants, Kidd Valley and Ivar's, a rarity at area parks. 425-430-6700, www.rentonwa.gov

TUKWILA

- **Fort Dent Park** is best known for its plentiful softball fields. The park hosts dozens of tournaments each year, including state and national competition. Fort Dent also features soccer fields and a kids' play area, along with a variety of birds and animals that flock to the park's wetlands. The 54-acre park is located adjacent to the Green River Trail, a regional pathway that winds 14 miles through South King County. 206-768-2822, www.ci.tukwila.wa.us

BURIEN

- **Seahurst Park** is popular with divers and beachcombers. The 185-acre park was owned by the King County Park System, until it was given to the new city of Burien in 1994. The park's main attraction is the 2,000-foot-long saltwater beach, undergoing a series of restoration efforts. Other highlights include picnic shelters and tables, a play area, and numerous trails. 206-988-3700, www.burienparks.net

TACOMA

- **Point Defiance Park** is among the 20 largest urban parks in the United States, and is the setting for one of Tacoma's most popular destinations, the Point Defiance Zoo and Aquarium. About two million people visit the 702-acre park each year to stroll through gardens and old-growth forests, travel back in time at Fort Nisqually, ride behind an authentic locomotive at Camp 6 Logging Museum, or bike along Five Mile Drive. 253-305-1000, www.metroparkstacoma.org
- **Wright Park**, just north of Tacoma's city center, is one of the few Washington parks listed on the National Register of Historic Places. The park's centerpiece is the glass-domed W. W. Seymour Botanical Conservatory, which was built in 1908. The conservatory presents seasonal floral displays in addition to its permanent collection of exotic tropical plants. Other attractions include walking and jogging paths, a children's play area and wading pool, lawn bowling, horseshoes and a community center. 253-305-1000, www.metroparkstacoma.org

BAINBRIDGE ISLAND

- **Gazzam Lake Park and Wildlife Preserve**, on the southwest corner of the island, is Bainbridge's second-biggest area of undeveloped land. The 445-acre park includes 13 acres of freshwater wetlands, home to a variety of wildlife, including deer and birds. An interpretive center is planned for the park, as well as a trail to Puget Sound. 206-842-2306, www.biparks.org

- **Grand Forest** consists of 240 acres spread over three plots on central Bainbridge Island. The property includes second-growth forests plus wetlands and wildlife habitat. Thanks to the Eagle Scouts, the former Department of Natural Resources land now features trails and trail signs. 206-842-2306, www.biparks.org

- **Manzanita Park**, at the north end of Bainbridge Island, is popular with hikers and horseback riders because its 120 acres are ribboned with hiking and equestrian trails. 206-842-2306, www.biparks.org

MOUNTLAKE TERRACE

- **Terrace Creek Park** (known to local kids as Candy Cane Park, due to its red-and-white-striped playground equipment) is Mountlake Terrace's largest park, occupying 60 acres in the center of the city. Amenities include barbecues, picnic areas, trails, play equipment, and playfields. 425-776-9173, www.cityofmlt.com

EDMONDS

- **Underwater Park** is located just north of the ferry dock, at the foot of Main Street in downtown Edmonds. One of the first underwater parks on the West Coast, Underwater Park is 27 acres of tide and bottom lands with artificial reefs and an abundance of marine life. Designated as a marine preserve and sanctuary in 1970, the park attracts scuba divers from across the state. 425-771-0227, www.ci.edmonds.wa.us/parks.stm

VASHON ISLAND

- **Dockton Park**, sheltered by Quartermaster Harbor, offers boat moorage, a swimming beach, picnic areas and playground, and hiking trails. 206-463-9602, www.vashonparkdistrict.org

- **Ober Park** in downtown Vashon is popular for outdoor concerts, picnics, its playground and meeting spaces. The park district headquarters are located here, as is the library, and the grassy lawns and earthen berms play host to the annual Strawberry Festival. 206-463-9602, www.vashonparkdistrict.org

- **Pt. Robinson Park** on the eastern tip of Maury Island is home to the historic Pt. Robinson Lighthouse, which offers free tours, as well as trails, picnic areas and beachcombing. 206-463-9602, www.vashonparkdistrict.org

STATE AND NATIONAL PARKS

Ii y.. the mood for something slightly more adventurous than a city outing, consider a trip to one of Washington's many state or national parks. Visitors to the parks can rent a cabin or a yurt for overnight stays, and engage in activities that range from hiking and bird watching to ATV riding, scuba diving, geocaching, and clam digging. Certain pursuits, such as metal detecting and paragliding, require a registration procedure and permit, so check the parks website (www.parks.wa.gov/activities) before you go.

In order to keep Washington state recreation lands open to the public, the 2011 Legislature instituted a pass system to generate much-needed revenue. You will need to display the **Discover Pass** (www.discoverpass.wa.gov) on your vehicle when visiting state recreation lands managed by the Washington State Parks and Recreation Commission, the Washington State Department of Natural Resources (DNR), and the Washington Department of Fish and Wildlife (WDFW), or risk a hefty $99 fine. The Discover Pass costs $35 annually ($30, if you purchase one when renewing your vehicle license), and $11.50 (with fees) for a one-day permit. Certain exemptions to the pass do exist; for instance, you may camp in any Washington State park without a Discover Pass, and Sno-Park seasonal permit holders are not required to display one. Be sure to check the website listed above for a list of current exemptions.

The Discover Pass may be purchased:
- In person from nearly 600 recreational license vendors where state fishing and hunting licenses are sold
- Online through the WDFW's online recreation licensing system.
- By phone at 866-320-9933
- When you renew your vehicle license

Pass holders gain access to nearly 7 million acres of Washington state-managed recreation lands, including state parks, water-access points, heritage sites, wildlife and natural areas, trails and trailheads. To receive information about any of Washington's 125 state parks, call the Washington State Parks and Recreation Commission at 360-902-8844, or visit their website at www.parks.wa.gov.

A few of the most popular National Park destinations are listed below:
- **Mount Rainier National Park** activities include skiing, hiking, camping, and mountain climbing. For more information, see the **Quick Getaways** chapter, call 360-569-2211 for more information, or visit www.nps.gov/mora.
- **Olympic National Park** on the Olympic Peninsula (about two hours northwest of Seattle) also offers hiking, camping, and mountain-climbing opportunities. For an up-close look at the mountains without the hike, visit Hurricane Ridge near Port Angeles. You can drive to the ridge and view the

mountains from the comfort of the visitors' center. Also worth a visit is Sol Duc Hot Springs, in the center of the park. For more information on the Olympic National Park, see the **Quick Getaways** chapter, call 360-565-3130, or visit www.nps.gov/olym.

* **North Cascades National Park** offers stunning views, hundreds of hikes and an outstanding museum; 360-854-7200, www.nps.gov/noca.

FORESTS

Surrounding Olympic National Park, on the Olympic Peninsula, is the **Olympic National Forest**. Its 633,600 acres are shared by outdoor enthusiasts and wildlife, and are managed for timber, mining, grazing, oil and gas, watershed, and wilderness. Twenty campgrounds pepper the land, and 266 miles of trails wind through the area. For more information, call 360-956-2402 or visit www.fs.fed.us/r6/olympic.

ADDITIONAL RESOURCES

For comprehensive recreation information for the entire state, visit **Washington State Tourism** at www.experiencewa.com or call a state travel counselor, 800-544-1800, Monday through Friday, from 8 a.m. to 5 p.m. If you're heading for one of the region's mountain passes, call the **Washington State Department of Transportation** highway information line at 511, or check the pass report online at www.wsdot.wa.gov/traffic. For additional outdoor recreation ideas, read the **Quick Getaways** and **Sports and Recreation** chapters of this book.

"THE BLUEST SKIES YOU'VE EVER SEEN ARE IN SEATTLE," SANG Perry Como, "and the hills the greenest green…" The late crooner was right. On a sunny summer day, the city is wrapped in aquamarine and the landscape glows green. Such brilliantly lush environs led in part to the city's nickname of the Emerald City. But Como forgot to mention the rain, and the accompanying mudslides, the frequent windstorms, occasional earthquakes and, every now and then, a drought; such are some of the challenges that Gore-Tex–clad residents contend with every year. In Seattle, jokes about the perpetual precipitation are as constant as the rain. One holds that residents of Seattle don't tan—they rust. Then there's the one that asks, "What do you call two straight days of rain in Seattle?" A weekend. The soggiest time in Seattle is November through February, with an average rainfall of nearly 22 inches during those four months. In November 2006 nearly 16 inches of rain fell on the region, dousing the previous record set back in 1933. While waterlogged years like 2006 (when it rained for 27 days in a row, not quite beating the 1953 record of 33 straight days of rain) stand out because they are extraordinary, Seattle is, generally, a soggy city throughout the winter, though stories of nine months of solid rain should be discounted.

When heavy rains do arrive, they are sometimes accompanied by damaging mudslides and floods. The same hills that offer residents spectacular views render homes, trees, and roads vulnerable in extreme weather. In the aftermath of heavy rains and snowstorms residents face mudslides and sinkholes that damage houses and wash out roads, a fact that new residents should keep in mind when searching for a new home. Though mudslides certainly aren't an everyday occurrence during the rainy months, they happen often enough to cause concern. Geologists recommend that homeowners try to determine if they are at risk for a slide by understanding how water causes damage and what triggers slides. According to experts, steep bluffs and hillsides where earth movement has occurred in the past or where the geology favors such movement are most at risk. That includes the bluffs that encircle Puget Sound and parts of Lake Washington, like West and North Seattle, Magnolia, and Bainbridge Island. With this in mind, folks should search a prospective property for signs of earth movement or signs that the property is getting a lot of water. Indicators include leaning or bent trees, and cracks in the yard, the foundation, driveway or patio. A property that is getting a lot of water may have spots on the lawn that stay greener or that are continually wet, and/or mossy. If you find potential problems, you may want to hire a civil or geo-technical engineer to analyze the drainage situation and make recommendations. Both can be found in the Yellow Pages or by searching online.

Despite its proximity to both the Cascade and Olympic mountain ranges, Seattle is not a snowy city, receiving on average only 8.1 inches per year, though years without any measurable snowfall in the urban areas are common. Communities to the east, like Issaquah, North Bend, and Snoqualmie, get a little more snowfall. Of course, there are exceptions, like the winter of 1999, when record snow levels were recorded in the Northwest and more than 300 inches piled up at the base of the Mount Baker Ski Area. Thing is, it doesn't take much snow to bring Seattle to a screeching halt. In 2010, a mere 2.5 inches virtually crippled the city, and many people believe the city's haphazard response to the winter storms of 2008–2009 cost Greg Nickels his third term as mayor.

If you are looking for sun, you may have to drive to find it in abundance. According to the Western Regional Climate Center, Seattle enjoys only 71 days of clear skies a year. In comparison, Yakima, about two and a half hours east of the city, experiences 109 clear days. The WRCC defines a clear day as one that sees zero to 3/10 average cloud cover. The clearest months here are July, with 12 days, August, with 10 days, and September, with nine days. November through February average just three clear days each month. The mixed blessing is that there are also 93 partly cloudy days a year, defined by the WRCC as days with 4/10 to 7/10 cloud cover. Breaks in the clouds can send people racing outdoors to enjoy a couple of hours of sun, regardless of the time of year.

Because sunshine is not a daily occurrence, and weeks can pass without a break in the clouds, about 10% of the region's residents suffer from **Seasonal Affective Disorder (SAD)**, according to David Avery, a professor of psychiatry and behavioral sciences at the University of Washington. Another 10% experience milder forms of depression. The National Mental Health Association says that as the seasons change, a shift occurs in our internal biological clocks that can cause us to be out of step with our daily schedules. Symptoms include sadness, sluggishness, change in appetite, and excessive sleeping. If you are moving from a sunny state like California or Florida, you should be aware of possible seasonal depression. Many people affected by the disorder have found relief using portable light boxes, like the ones sold by The SunBox Company (www.sunbox.com).

Washington does occasionally experience drought conditions, which in turn set the stage for dangerous wildfires. During drought years, local governments usually ask residents to limit yard watering, and farming communities may impose rolling dry-outs to conserve irrigation water. Wildfires generally are confined to the eastern part of the state, though forested neighborhoods like those in southeast King County also can be at risk. At its website, www.firewise.org, the National Fire Protection Association offers tips on protecting your home from wildfire.

Climatologists predict that we'll see an increase in extreme weather around the world as a result of global warming, and their fears seemed realized when 2010 turned out to be the wettest and hottest year on record. It's likely that, overall, Seattle will be a wetter and a warmer city in years to come, but it will be more difficult to predict the weather in any given season. In 2011, for instance, the temperature at Sea-Tac airport did not crack 75 degrees until June 23rd—the latest date ever recorded.

Though Seattle's weather picture can seem bleak, its bane—the rain—is also its blessing. If it weren't for the rain the hills wouldn't grow nearly as green and the deep blue skies wouldn't be so revered.

WEATHER STATISTICS

Despite the clouds, a reputation for rain and occasional extreme weather, Seattle has a mild, temperate climate, receiving 38.06 average inches of rain in a year, far less than some other areas of the country. According to the **Western Regional Climate Center** (www.wrcc.dri.edu), the average minimum and maximum temperatures at Sea-Tac Airport are as follows: **January** 37–46° F; **February** 37–49° F; **March** 40–52° F; **April** 42–58° F; **May** 48–64° F; **June** 52–69° F; **July** 56–76° F; **August** 56–76° F; **September** 52–70° F; **October** 46–59° F; **November** 40–51° F; **December** 36–46° F.

AIR POLLUTION

Gazing out at the Sound on a crystal-clear, rain-washed afternoon, it might be hard to believe that Seattle has an air pollution problem. However, the American Lung Association's 2011 air quality report ranked the city the 18th most polluted in the country for fine particles such as soot. In winter, particles associated with smoke from wood stoves and fireplaces build up. In summer, the region's traffic congestion, and the emissions from gas engines on boats, jet skis, and lawnmowers creates smog or ozone problems. High ozone levels place Seattle 180th of 220 metro areas for this public health hazard. To help combat the problem, vehicle emission tests are required every other year in King, Pierce, and Snohomish counties. Recent programs to scrap or retrofit the exhausts on older diesel trucks and to reduce school bus emissions are among the efforts to improve air quality in the region. In 2011, the city pledged to become a climate-neutral city, setting the goal of reaching zero net greenhouse gas emissions per capita by 2030.

The **Puget Sound Clean Air Agency**, which is charged with enforcing federal, state, and local air quality laws, provides current air quality reports and forecasts at its website, www.pscleanair.org. You can also view images from its Seattle visibility camera and receive information about local burn bans. The agency recommends the following tips for improving air quality:

- Use an efficient EPA-certified pellet or wood stove. Uncertified wood stoves are illegal to use during a burn ban.
- Burn manufactured logs or pellets.
- Dry firewood at least six months before using it.
- Give your fire lots of air for optimum heat and minimum smoke.
- Drive less. Take public transportation, bike, or walk whenever possible.
- When the weather is hot, refuel your vehicle during cooler evening hours.
- Make sure your gas cap seals properly.
- Wait until temperatures decrease and breezes pick up before mowing the lawn or using gas-powered garden equipment.
- Consider using non–gasoline-powered equipment, like a sailboat instead of a motorboat or a manual push mower instead of a gas-powered lawn mower.

DISASTER PREPAREDNESS

A federal study released in 2000 found that Washington is the nation's second-most-vulnerable state to costly damage from earthquakes. Seattle ranks seventh in the nation among major cities that could expect severe quake damage. Knowing this, it was nonetheless shocking when the 6.8-magnitude Nisqually Earthquake struck the Puget Sound region on February 28, 2001. It was the biggest quake to rattle the area in more than half a century. It caused 410 injuries, and damage statewide was estimated at $2 billion. Experts agree that Seattle was lucky. The quake was buried 32 miles deep, so its effects were muted. Experts also agree that the Nisqually Earthquake was not the "Big One" that the region can expect. The Seattle Fault Line, which runs east-west through the heart of downtown Seattle, Bellevue, and Bainbridge Island, is a shallow fault that would cause severe damage if it's the cause of the next big earthquake. Such a seismic event is overdue, but experts can't predict if it will happen tomorrow or a hundred years from now. Seattle's tsunami risk has not been fully studied, but most tsunamis damage open coastlines and not enclosed bodies of water such as Puget Sound.

Aside from luck, the secret to surviving a major earthquake, or any other major disaster, is found in the time-proven Boy Scout adage, "Be prepared." There are dozens of good books about how to get ready for a seismic onslaught, and plenty of free information available from local, state, and federal agencies. You should prepare to be on your own for three to seven days, as it may take that long for emergency crews to restore power, water, and telephone service to affected areas.

The **King County Office of Emergency Management** maintains a 3 Days 3 Ways website (www.3days3ways.org) that provides links to disaster preparedness resources and recommends a simple three-step approach to any disaster: make a plan; build a kit; get involved. You can get in-depth information about local hazards, learn how to develop communication and evacuation plans and what kind of supplies to keep in a disaster kit. The basic rule of thumb is to keep enough water and food on hand to supply your family for three days. For a major disaster, however, supplies for seven days are strongly urged. You'll want supplies like flashlights, a battery-operated radio, and a first aid kit as well. Don't forget about medications and providing for your pets.

The **Red Cross of Seattle King County** (www.seattleredcross.org) also offers plans and resources for disaster preparation. Both sites urge people to get training in CPR and basic first aid, and outline ways to get involved with helping your neighbors and community. The **City of Seattle** sponsors SNAP (Seattle Neighborhoods Actively Prepare), a program in which the city trains groups of local people to respond to the needs of their neighbors and coordinate with officials during a crisis. To get more information or to find a SNAP group near you, call 206-233-5076 or visit www.seattle.gov/emergency/programs/snap/.

Here are a few additional resources for disaster preparedness:

- **American Red Cross**, Seattle King County Chapter, 206-323-2345, www.seattleredcross.org
- **Cascadia Region Earthquake Workgroup**, 360-725-7244, www.crew.org
- **City of Seattle Office of Seattle Emergency Management**, 206-233-5076, www.seattle.gov/emergency
- **Federal Emergency Management Agency**, 800-621-FEMA (3362), www.fema.gov
- **King County Office of Emergency Management**, 206-296-3830, www.kingcounty.gov/safety/prepare
- **Pierce County Department of Emergency Management**, 253-798-7470, www.co.pierce.wa.us
- **Snohomish County Department of Emergency Management**, 425-388-5060, www1.co.snohomish.wa.us
- **USGS Geologic Hazards Science Center**, 888-275-8747, https://geohazards.usgs.gov

One final note: be sure to purchase a homeowner's insurance policy that covers quake damage. Generally, earthquake coverage is not part of a standard policy. See **Finding a Place to Live** for a list of area insurers.

N OW THAT THE ELECTRICITY IS ON, YOUR INTERNET SERVICE IS UP and running, and most of your boxes are unpacked, it's time to meet the locals. This chapter lists a number of ways you can begin to make connections with people in your community, from volunteering, to social clubs, to places of worship.

VOLUNTEER MATCHING AND PLACEMENT

When you're new in town, volunteering may provide the perfect opportunity to get acquainted with the community and to make new friends in the process. In addition to meeting people with similar interests, you'll be helping organizations that are often short on cash and resources. Seattle has many charitable and philanthropic organizations that offer a variety of services, from the basics of food and clothing, to counseling, to funding education or medical research.

If you're not sure where to begin, the following volunteer placement services can point you in the right direction:

- **Seattle Works**, 1625 19th Ave, 206-324-0808, www.seattleworks.org
- **United Way of King County**, 720 2nd Ave, 206-461-3700, www.uwkc.org
- **Volunteers of America**, 2802 Broadway Ave, Everett, 425-259-3191, www. voa.org
- **VolunteerMatch**, www.volunteermatch.org

AREA CAUSES

Volunteer opportunities also can be found in the Yellow Pages, in newspaper advertisements, and online at craigslist.org. The following is a sample of possibilities, listed by category:

AIDS AND HIV

- **Bailey-Boushay House**, 2720 E Madison St, 206-322-5300, www.baileyboushay.org
- **Gay City Health Project**, 511 E Pike, 206-860-6969, www.gaycity.org
- **Lifelong AIDS Alliance**, 1002 E Seneca, 206-328-8979, www.lifelongaidsalliance.org
- **People of Color Against AIDS Network**, Seattle office: 1609 19th Ave, 206-322-7061; South Seattle office: 4437 Rainier Ave S, 206-760-5588, www.pocaan.org
- **Rosehedge/Multifaith Works**, 115 16th Ave, 206-324-1520, www.rosehedge.org
- **Seattle Area Support Groups & Community Center (SASGCC)**, 303 17th Ave E, 206-322-2437, http://sasgcc.org

ALCOHOL AND DRUG DEPENDENCY

- **Alcohol/Drug Help Line**, 206-722-3703, http://adhl.org
- **Prevention Works**, 206-987-7612, www.preventionworksinseattle.org
- **Recovery Café**, 2022 Boren Ave, 206-374-8731, www.recoverycafe.org
- **Salvation Army Adult Rehabilitation Center**, 1010 4th Ave S, 206-587-0503, www.seattle.satruck.org

ANIMALS

- **The Humane Society for Seattle/King County**, 13212 SE Eastgate Way, Bellevue, 425-641-0080, www.seattlehumane.org
- **Pasado's Safe Haven**, P.O. Box 171, Sultan, 98294, 360-793-9393, www.pasadosafehaven.org
- **Progressive Animal Welfare Society (PAWS)**, 15305 44th Ave W, Lynnwood, 425-787-2500, www.paws.org
- **Seattle Animal Control**, 2061 15th Ave W, 206-386-PETS, www.cityofseattle.net/animalshelter

ATHLETICS

- **Northwest Senior Games**, 206-755-3588, www.northwestseniorgames.org
- **Rat City Rollergirls**, www.ratcityrollergirls.com
- **Seattle Youth Soccer Association (SYSA)**, 520 NE Ravenna Blvd, 206-274-1318, www.sysa.org
- **Special Olympics Washington,** 1809 7th Ave, 206-362-4949, www.specialolympicswashington.org

CHILDREN

- **Big Brothers Big Sisters of King County**, 1600 S Graham St, 206-763-9060, 877-700-2447, www.bbbsps.org
- **Big Brothers Big Sisters of Pierce and Kitsap Counties**, 2107 S 12th St, Tacoma, 253-396-9630, www.bbbsps.org
- **Boys and Girls Clubs of King County**, 603 Stewart, #300, 206-436-1800, www.positiveplace.org
- **Catholic Community Services**, 100 23rd Ave S, 206-328-5696, www.ccsww.org
- **Childhaven**, 316 Broadway, 206-464-3923 ex 4911, www.childhaven.org
- **Children's Home Society of Washington**, 3300 NE 65th St, 206-695-3200, www.chs-wa.org
- **Seattle Children's Hospital**, 4800 Sand Point Way NE, 206-987-2155, www.seattlechildrens.org

CRIME PREVENTION

- **Seattle Police Department Victim Support Team**, 206-615-0892, www.cityofseattle.net/police
- **Volunteers in Police Service (VIPS)**, 206-615-0890, www.policevolunteers.org

CULTURAL IDENTITY

- **Asian Counseling and Referral Service**, 3639 Martin Luther King Jr Way S, 206-695-7600, www.acrs.org
- **Casa Latina**, 317 17th Ave S, 206-956-0779, www.casa-latina.org
- **Chinese Information and Service Center**, 611 S Lane St, 206-624-5633, www.cisc-seattle.org
- **El Centro de la Raza**, 2524 16th Ave S, 206-957-4634, www.elcentrodelaraza.com
- **Japanese American Citizens League**, 805-225-3169, www.jaclseattle.org
- **Jewish Family Service**, 1601 16th Ave, 206-461-3240; 15821 NE 8th St, Ste 210, Bellevue, 425-643-2221; 1209 Central Ave S, Ste 134, Kent, 253-850-4065; www.jfsseattle.org
- **Jewish Federation of Greater Seattle**, 2031 3rd Ave, 206-443-5400, www.jewishinseattle.org
- **Korean Community Counseling Center**, 23830 Hwy 99 #206, Edmonds, 425-776-2400
- **Seattle Indian Center**, 611 12th Ave S, 206-329-8700, http://seattleindiancenter.us
- **United Indians of All Tribes Foundation**, Daybreak Star Art & Cultural Center, Discovery Park, 206-285-4425, www.unitedindians.com

- **Urban League of Metropolitan Seattle**, 105 14th Ave, 206-461-3792, www. urbanleague.org

CULTURE AND THE ARTS

- **Arts Corps,** 4408 Delridge Way SW, Ste 110, 206-722-5440, www.artcorps.org
- **ArtWorks,** 923 S Bayview, 206-292-4141, www.urbanartworks.org
- **Frye Art Museum**, 704 Terry Ave, 206-622-9250, http://fryemuseum.org
- **911 Media Arts Center**, 909 NE 43rd St, Ste 206, 206-682-6552, www.911media.org
- **Seattle Arts & Lectures**, 105 S Main St #201, 206-621-2230, www.lectures. org
- **Seattle Center for the Book Arts**, 206-659-1055, www.seattlebookarts. org
- **Youngstown Cultural Arts Center**, 4408 Delridge Way SW, 206-935-2999, www.youngstownarts.org

DISABILITY ASSISTANCE

- **Catholic Community Services**, 100 23rd Ave S, 206-328-5696, www.ccsww. org
- **Deaf-Blind Service Center**, 1620 18th Ave, Ste 200, 206-323-9178, www. seattledbsc.org
- **Easter Seals Washington**, 220 W Mercer St, 206-281-5700, http:// wa.easterseals.com
- **Hearing, Speech, and Deafness Center**, 1625 19th Ave, 206-323-5770, www.hsdc.org
- **Outdoors for All Foundation**, 6344 NE 74th St, Ste 102, 206-838-6030, www. outdoorsforall.org
- **Sight Connection**, 9709 3rd Ave NE, 206-525-5556, www.csbps.com

ENVIRONMENT

- **EarthCorps**, 6310 NE 74th St, Ste 201E, 206-322-9296, www.earthcorps.org
- **Earth Ministry**, 6512 23rd Ave NW, Ste 317, 206-632-2426, http:// earthministry.org
- **Earth Share of Washington**, 1402 3rd Ave, 206-622-9840, www.esw.org
- **National Wildlife Federation,** 6 Nickerson St., Ste 200, 206-285-8707, www. nwf.org/pacific
- **People for Puget Sound**, 911 Western Ave, Ste 580, 206-382-7007, http:// pugetsound.org
- **Seattle Audubon Society**, 8050 35th Ave NE, 206-523-4483, www. seattleaudubon.org

- **Seattle Inner City Outings**, 117 E Louisa #315, http://seattle.ico.sierraclub.org
- **Volunteers for Outdoor Washington (VOW)**, 12345 NE 30th Ave, Ste I, 206-517-3019, www.trailvolunteers.org
- **Washington Wilderness Coalition**, 305 N 83rd St, 206-633-1992, www.wawild.org

FOOD DISTRIBUTION

- **Auburn Food Bank**, 930 18th Pl NE, Auburn, 253-833-8925, www.theauburn foodbank.org
- **Ballard Food Bank**, 5130 Leary Ave NW, 206-789-7800, www.ballardfood bank.org
- **Beacon Avenue Food Bank**, 6230 Beacon Ave S, 206-722-5105
- **Des Moines Area Food Bank**, 22225 9th Ave S, Des Moines, 206-878-2660, www.myfoodbank.org
- **Downtown Food Bank**, 1531 Western Ave, 206-626-6462, www.pikemarket seniorcenter.org
- **Edmonds Food Bank**, 828 Caspers St, Edmonds, 425-778-5833, www.edmondsumc.org/carol_rowe_memorial.htm
- **Federal Way Food Bank**, 1200 S 336th St, Federal Way, 253-838-6810, www.multi-servicecenter.com
- **Food Lifeline**, 1702 NE 150th St, Shoreline, 206-545-6600, www.foodlifeline.org
- **Highline Food Bank**, 18300 4th Ave S, 206-433-9900, http://skcfc.org/highline
- **Hopelink (operating five food banks in greater Seattle area)**, 425-869-6066, www.hope-link.org
- **Issaquah Food Bank**, 179 1st Ave SE, Issaquah, 425-392-4123, http://issaquahfoodbank.org
- **Kent Food Bank**, 515 W Harrison St, Kent, 253-520-3550, http://dwp.big planet.com/foodbanks/kentfoodbank
- **Lynnwood Food Bank**, 5320 176th St SW, Lynnwood, 425-745-1635, www.lynnwoodfoodbank.org
- **Northwest Harvest**, P.O. Box 12272, Seattle 98102, 206-625-0755, www.northwestharvest.org
- **Rainier Valley Food Bank**, 4205 Rainier Ave S, 206-723-4105, www.rvfb.org
- **Tukwila Food Pantry**, 3118 S 140th St, Tukwila, 206-431-8293, www.tukwila pantry.org
- **University District Food Bank**, 1413 NE 50th St, 206-523-7060, www.udis trictfoodbank.org
- **Vashon Maury Community Food Bank**, 206-463-6332, www.vashonfood bank.org

- **West Seattle Food Bank**, 3419 SW Morgan St, 206-932-9023, www.westseattlefoodbank.org
- **White Center Food Bank**, 10829 8th SW, 206-762-2848, www.skcfc.org/whitecenterfoodbank

GAY AND LESBIAN

- **Seattle Out and Proud**, 1605 12th Ave, Ste 2, 206-322-9561, www.seattlepride.org
- **Lambert House**, 1818 15th Ave, 206-322-2515, www.lamberthouse.org
- **Lesbian Resource Center**, 227 S Orcas St, 206-322-3953, www.lrc.net
- **OUT for Sustainability**, 1122 E Pike St, #1015, 206-395-6884, http://outsustainability.org
- **The Pride Foundation**, 1122 E Pike St, PMB 1001, 206-323-3318, www.pridefoundation.org

HEALTH AND HOSPITALS

Most hospitals welcome volunteers—just give the nearest one a call. For specific health issues, contact one of the following organizations:

- **Alzheimer's Association**, Western and Central Washington State Chapter, North Tower, 100 W Harrison St, N200, 206-363-5500, www.alz.org/alzwa
- **American Cancer Society**, 728 134th St SW, Ste 101, Everett, 425-741-8949, www.cancer.org
- **American Heart Association**, 710 2nd Ave, Ste 900, 206-632-6881, www.heart.org
- **American Lung Association**, 2625 3rd Ave, 206-441-5100, www.alaw.org
- **Gilda's Club**, 1400 Broadway, 206-709-1400, www.gildasclubseattle.com
- **Make-A-Wish Foundation**, 811 1st Ave, 206-623-5300, www.northwestwishes.org
- **March of Dimes Birth Defects Foundation**, 1904 3rd Ave, Ste 230, 206-624-1373, www.marchofdimes.org/washington
- **National Multiple Sclerosis Society**, Greater Washington Chapter, 192 Nickerson St, Ste 100, 206-284-4254, www.nationalmssociety.org

HOMELESS SERVICES

- **DESC**, 515 3rd Ave, 206-464-1570, www.desc.org
- **Jubilee Women's Center**, 620 18th Ave E, 206-324-1244, www.jwcenter.org
- **Millionair Club**, 2515 Western Ave, 206-728-5600, www.millionairclub.org
- **Real Change**, 96 S Main St, 206-441-3247, www.realchangenews.org
- **Sacred Heart Shelter**, 232 Warren Ave N, 206-285-7489, www.ccsww.org
- **Salvation Army**, 811 Maynard Ave S, 206-621-0145, www1.usw.salvationarmy.org

- **Union Gospel Mission**, Department of Volunteer Efforts, 3800 S Othello, 206-723-0767, www.ugm.org
- **Wellspring Family Services**, 206-826-3050, www.family-services.org
- **YouthCare**, 2500 NE 54th St, 206-694-4500, www.youthcare.org

HUMAN SERVICES

- **American Red Cross**, 1900 25th Ave S, 206-323-2345; 811 Pacific Ave, Bremerton, 360-377-3761; www.seattleredcross.org
- **Catholic Community Services**, 100 23rd Ave S, 206-328-5696, www.ccsww.org
- **Habitat for Humanity**, 560 Naches Ave SW, Ste 110, Renton, 206-292-5240, www.seattle-habitat.org
- **Salvation Army**, 811 Maynard Ave S, 206-621-0145, www1.usw.salvationarmy.org
- **Seattle Goodwill**, 1765 6th Ave S, 206-329-1000, www.seattlegoodwill.org

INTERNATIONAL RELIEF AND DEVELOPMENT

- **Architects Without Borders**, 1205 E Pike St, http://awb-seattle.org
- **Global Partnerships**, 1932 1st Ave, Ste 400, 206-652-8773
- **Medical Teams International**, 9680 153rd Ave NE, 425-454-8326, www.medicalteams.org
- **Mercy Corps**, 509 Fairview N, Ste 200, 206-547-5212, www.mercycorps.org

LEGAL AID

- **American Civil Liberties Union of Washington**, 901 5th Ave, Ste 630, 206-624-2184, www.aclu-wa.org
- **Catholic Community Services**, 100 23rd Ave S, 206-328-5696, www.ccsww.org
- **LegalVoice**, 907 Pine St, Ste 500, 206-682-9552, www.legalvoice.org
- **Northwest Immigrant Rights Project**, 206-587-4009, www.nwirp.org
- **Volunteer Legal Services**, 206-623-0281
- **Washington State Bar Association**, 1325 4th Ave, Ste 600, 800-945-9722, 206-443-9722, www.wsba.org

LITERACY

- **Friends of the Seattle Public Library**, 1000 4th Ave, 206-523-4053
- **King County Library System**, 960 Newport Way NW, Issaquah, 425-369-3200, www.kcls.org
- **Literacy Council of Seattle**, 8500 14th Ave NW, 206-233-9720, www.literacyseattle.org

- **Literacy Source**, 206-782-2050, www.literacy-source.org
- **Page Ahead Children's Literacy Program,** 1130 NW 85th St, 206-461-0123, www.pageahead.org

MEN'S SERVICES

- **Northwest Men's Project**, 1419 S Jackson St, Ste 103, 206-718-6177, www.northwestmensproject.org

MENTORING AND CAREER DEVELOPMENT

- **Community for Youth**, 999 3rd Ave, Ste 1570, 206-325-8480, www.communityforyouth.org
- **Dress for Success**, 1118 5th Ave, 206-325-3453, www.dressforsuccess.org
- **Washington State Mentors**, 1605 NW Sammamish Rd, Ste 200, 425-416-2030, www.wamentors.org

POLITICS—ELECTORAL

- **Freedom Socialist Party**, New Freeway Hall, 5018 Rainier Ave S, 206-722-2453, www.socialism.com
- **Green Party of Seattle**, www.seattlegreens.wordpress.com
- **International Socialist Organization**, 206-309-7274, http://isoseattle.blogspot.com
- **King County Democrats**, 425-255-2679, www.kcdems.org
- **League of Women Voters of Washington**, 4710 University Way NE, Ste 720, 206-622-8961, www.lwvwa.org
- **Libertarian Party of Washington State**, 10522 Lake City Way NE, Ste C-103, www.lpwa.org
- **King County Republican Party**, 845 106th Ave NE, Ste 110, Bellevue, 425-990-0404, www.kcgop.org

POLITICS—SOCIAL

- **American Veterans Association**, 5717 S Tyler St, Tacoma, 253-472-2552, www.amvetswa.org
- **Amnesty International Seattle**, 206-622-2741, http://amnestyseattle.org
- **Blacks in Government**, 206-624-4870, www.bignet.org/regional/southeast
- **League of Education Voters**, 2734 Westlake Ave N. 206-728-6448, www.educationvoters.org
- **Washington Ceasefire**, 206-972-1952, http://washingtonceasefire.org

MEETING PEOPLE

Transplants to Seattle seeking to make connections in the community have a common complaint: the natives are friendly—they're just not terribly sociable. Seattleites have a reputation for being socially standoffish, and getting beyond surface pleasantries can take some work. As with any new job, it helps to have references. Before you move, ask your friends for the names and contact information of people they know in the area. Sometimes just one friendly person can open up a whole social scene for you. Seek out fellow transplants, who may be more socially welcoming. Other good places to meet people are volunteer groups (see "Volunteer Matching and Placement," above), cultural events (see "Cultural Life"), recreational groups or sports clubs (see "Sports and Recreation"), and religious or spiritual groups (see "Places of Worship," below). Free local papers such as *The Stranger* and *Seattle Weekly* as well as *The Seattle Times* are chock full of event listings in their arts and entertainment sections. Get out and circulate! These days there are a multitude of location-based apps for smart phones and PDAs that can put you in touch with likeminded people in your immediate vicinity. Dating and matchmaking services, as well as social networking sites such as Facebook and LinkedIn, are beyond the scope of this guide, but the following suggestions may help you connect with people who share your interests:

ALUMNI GROUPS

Most colleges and universities have alumni groups in Seattle that host social and networking events for former students. Check with the alumni or development office at your alma mater about alumni groups in your area. Be sure your old school has your current contact information, so they can let you know about any upcoming alumni events planned in your area. Armed with an alumni directory, you might consider initiating an event yourself and inviting fellow alumni in your area.

BUSINESS GROUPS

People (especially those who are single and in their 20s or 30s) often make important social connections at work, at informal gatherings of coworkers. But depending on your field, you might want to consider joining a professional networking group, since these organizations frequently schedule social events for members. Two useful websites for finding such groups include the **Seattle Networking Guide** (www.iloveseattle.org) and **Women's Resource** (253-572-9108, www.womensresourcedirectory.com). If you're working from home, seek out groups that organize social and networking events for freelancers, such as

MediaBistro (www.mediabistro.com) and the **Northwest Freelancers Association** (www.nwfreelancers.org).

POLITICAL GROUPS

Waving a soggy placard in the rain and waiting for the speeches to begin (or end) can be a good opportunity to chat it up with your fellow protestors and maybe make a connection or two. Whatever your political persuasion, joining a political group (some are listed above under "Area Causes") can put you in touch with individuals who share many of your values and beliefs.

THE OUTDOORS

The Puget Sound region is a magnet for outdoors enthusiasts, with innumerable organized groups, clubs, and societies devoted to every imaginable type of recreation Newcomers to the area can join groups that organize long-distance cycling trips, kayak on Lake Union, schedule urban scavenger hunts, or go foraging for wild foods. Bulletin boards at local climbing gyms are often papered with notices of people looking for climbing partners, outdoor clubs such as **The Mountaineers** (206-521-6000, www.themountaineers.org) sponsor a gazillion different activities at a range of skill levels and ages, and there is even an informal social networking group for environmentalists, **Greendrinks**, www.greendrinks.org.

PARENTS' GROUPS AND SCHOOL FUNCTIONS

If you are moving to the city with kids, you have a social advantage, at least in terms of meeting other parents. Many Seattle parents with very young children join a local organization called **PEPS** (Program for Early Parent Support, 206-547-8570, www.peps.org), and the people they meet in their PEPS groups often become lifelong friends. Once your children are school age, you'll have plenty of opportunities to meet and chat up other parents at school functions or just while waiting outside the building to collect your charges. Public schools, in particular, depend upon the help of parent volunteers—if you advertise your willingness to help out, you'll get a flood of invitations.

SPECIAL INTERESTS

Join a poker league, meet up with fellow falconers, confer with other beading enthusiasts, or practice your conversational Portuguese—start searching and you'll find there's a group for nearly every interest. A good website to investigate is **Meetup** (www.meetup.com), which lists scheduled gathering of various groups in your area. Type in your zip code and the subjects you're interested in, and you'll be rewarded with a wealth of options.

There's even an organization called Seattle Anti-Freeze, devoted to thawing out the city's social scene one theme party at a time (www.seattleantifreeze. com). And there's the city's largest social club, Space City Mixer, www.spacecity-mixer.com, with over 20,000 members.

In the chapter of this book entitled **A Seattle Year**, you'll find listings of festivals and events occurring each month that rely on an army of volunteers to run smoothly. Choose one that appeals to you and sign up. For newcomers with a literary bent, libraries and bookstores around the city sponsor book groups that anyone can join.

PLACES OF WORSHIP

Finding a place of worship can be as simple as soliciting the suggestion of a co-worker or neighbor, or as intensely personal and complex as choosing a spouse. If you belong to a congregation in your old hometown, your religious leader might be able to refer you to a kindred congregation in Seattle. If you don't have a referral, search online, or in the Yellow Pages under "Churches," "Synagogues" and "Mosques." The phone book listings are arranged by denomination and include sections for nondenominational, interdenominational, and independent churches, as well as metaphysical centers.

These interfaith agencies, representing congregations working together to address hunger, homelessness, and other urban problems, might be able to refer you to a congregation:

- **The Church Council of Greater Seattle**, 2701 1st Ave, Ste , 206-525-1213, www.thechurchcouncil.org
- **The Interfaith Council of Washington**, P.O. Box 31005, Seattle 98103, www. interfaithcouncil.com
- **Washington Association of Churches**, 1415 NE 43rd St, 206-625-9790, http://thewac.org

Online directories—generally limited to Christian denominations—include **Net Ministries**, http://netministries.org, **Churches Dot Net**, http://churches.net, **USA Church**, www.usachurch.com, and **For Ministry**, www.forministry.com. Synagogues serving all branches of Judaism are listed at **Maven Search**, www. mavensearch.com.

While Seattle may consistently rank among the least religious cities in the nation, there are plenty of places of worship to accommodate individuals of every faith and spiritual persuasion. The following list consists primarily of useful websites to help you locate facilities in your area.

ALTERNATIVE WORSHIP

GAY & LESBIAN SPIRITUAL GROUPS

For information regarding gay-friendly churches, visit the website of **Gay Church** at www.gaychurch.org. Notable LGBT-friendly congregations of different faiths include:

- **All Pilgrims Christian Church, Lambda Ministries,** 509 10th E, 206-322-0487, www.allpilgrims.org. A huge rainbow sign proclaiming "Come As You Are" adorns the brick tower of this church on Capitol Hill.
- **Central Lutheran Church,** 1710 11th Ave, 206-322-7500, www.loveiscentral. org
- **Congregation Tikvah Chadasha**, 1122 E Pike St, 206-353-1414, www. tikvachadasha.org
- **Dharma Buddies**, 400 Broadway, www.dharmabuddies.org
- **Dignity Seattle**, 5751 33rd Ave NE, 206-659-5519, www.dignityseattle.org, is the country's largest and most progressive organization of gay, lesbian, bisexual and transgender Catholics.
- **Edmonds Unitarian Universalist Church,** 8109 224th St SW, Edmonds, 425-778-0373, http://euuc.org
- **Grace Gospel Chapel**, 2052 NW 64th St, 206-784-8495, www. gracegospelwa.org
- **Kol HaNeshamah**, 6115 SW Hinds St, 206-935-1590, www.kol-haneshamah. org
- **Lotus Sisters,** 303 17th Ave E, 206-323-5505, http://lotussisters.org
- **Metropolitan Community Church Seattle**, 1415 NE 43rd St, 206-325-2421, www.mccseattle.org
- **St. Mark's Episcopal Cathedral**, 1245 10th Ave E, 206-323-0300, www. saintmarks.org

NEW AGE SPIRITUALITY, PAGANISM, AND MORE

- **Center for Spiritual Living,** 206-527-8801, www.spiritualliving.org
- **Eagle Wings Ministries**, 206-235-8340, http://eaglewingsministries.net
- **Native American Tribal Spirituality**, 206-324-9360 ex. 2202
- **New Connexion,** website for Pacific Northwest's Journal of Conscious Living, www.newconnexion.net
- **Pagan Resources**, www.widdershins.org
- **The Witches' Voice**, www.witchvox.com

SPIRITUALITY/ETHICS

- **Ethical Culture Society of Puget Sound**, 425-562-8740, http://ethical culturesociety.orq
- **Theosophical Society in Seattle**, 717 Broadway Ave E, 206-323-4281, http://seattle-ts.org

BAHA'I

- **Bahá'á Faith**, website of the Bahá'ís of the United States, www.bahai.us
- **Seattle Bahá'í Center**, 206-329-2564, http://seattlebahais.org

BUDDHIST

The non-sectarian **Northwest Dharma Association** publishes the *Northwest Dharma News* and organizes multi-tradition events. The organization's website provides a calendar of Buddhist retreats, classes and events, and links to other Buddhist sites. For more information visit their office at 305 Thomas St, 206-441-6811, or visit www.northwestdharma.org.

- **Sakya Monastery of Tibetan Buddhism**, 108 NW 83rd St, 206-789-2573, www.sakya.org
- The **Seattle Buddhist Center**, 12056 15th Ave NE, is affiliated with the international movement known as the Friends of the Western Buddhist Order. The center offers shrine rooms for meditation, Dharma book sales and merchandise, a lending library, and conversation areas. Call 206-726-0051 or visit www.seattlebuddhistcenter.org.
- **Seattle Buddhist Church**, 1427 S Main St, 206-329-0800, www.seattlebetsuin.com

CHRISTIAN

If you are looking for a church that is convenient to where you live, start your search at one of the online directories listed above. The **National Council of the Churches of Christ in the USA**, 212-870-2228, www.ncccusa.org, publishes the *Yearbook of American & Canadian Churches*, a directory that lists thousands of Christian churches in North America. Order one for $55 at 888-870-3325.

AFRICAN METHODIST EPISCOPAL

- **The African Methodist Episcopal Church's official website**, 615-254-0911, www.ame-church.com
- **The First African Methodist Episcopal Church (1522 14th Ave**, 206-324-3664, www.fameseattle.org) is the oldest congregation in the Pacific Northwest to be established by African Americans. Founded in 1886, First

AME Church Seattle is a historical landmark. In August 2001, the church welcomed Bishop Vashti McKenzie, the first woman ever appointed bishop in the AME Church.

ANGLICAN

• **Northwest Anglican**, www.nwanglican.org

APOSTOLIC

• **Apostolic Faith Church**, 503-777-1741, www.apostolicfaith.org

ASSEMBLIES OF GOD

• **Northwest Ministry Network**, 425-888-4848, www.northwestministry.com

BAPTIST

• **Baptist 411**, www.baptist411.com
• **Baptistinfo Directory of Independent Baptist Churches**, www.baptistinfo.com
• Founded in 1890, **Mount Zion Baptist Church** (1634 19th Ave, 206-322-6500, www.mountzion.net) in Seattle's Central District is one of the city's oldest continuously active places of worship. Mount Zion is perhaps best known to those outside its congregation for its annual Martin Luther King, Jr. celebration. The church is also active in community outreach, and serves as a meeting place for a variety of local organizations and committees.

CATHOLIC

ROMAN CATHOLIC

The **Archdiocese of Seattle** encompasses all of western Washington, and includes more than 178 parishes and missions that serve over half a million Catholics. In addition to managing the many ministries and programs that serve the Catholic community, the Archdiocese runs a library/media center and publishes the *Catholic Northwest Progress*. The Archdiocese offices are located at 710 9th Ave. For more information, call 206-382-4560, or visit www.seattlearchdiocese.org.

• The century-old **St. James Cathedral** (804 9th Ave, 206-622-3559, www.stjames-cathedral.org) is the cathedral for the Catholic Archdiocese of Seattle, as well as an active parish church for the Capitol Hill community. Check the schedule for outstanding classical musical events throughout the year, including a popular New Year's Eve gala.

ORTHODOX

See separate listing under **Orthodox**, below.

CHRISTIAN SCIENCE

- **Christian Science**, http://christianscience.com
- **CS Directory**, www.csdirectory.com

CHURCH OF CHRIST

- **The Churches of Christ in Washington**, www.churches-of-christ.net/usa/wa_churches.html
- **Churches of Christ Online in Washington**, www.cocn.org/wa.html

CHURCH OF GOD

- Pacific Northwest Association of the Church of God, 509-457-1941, www.pnacog.org

CHURCH OF JESUS CHRIST OF LATTER-DAY SAINTS (MORMONS)

- **Mormon.org,** http://mormon.org
- **The Temple of The Church of Jesus Christ of Latter-day Saints** (2808 148th Ave SE, Bellevue, 425-643-5144) was the first Mormon temple built in the Pacific Northwest. The 110,000-square-foot temple attracted its share of controversy when it was built in the late 1970s, from environmentalists who balked at its size and location, to women's rights activists who opposed the church's stand on the Equal Rights Amendment. Today, the temple's lofty gold leaf statue of the angel Moroni is a familiar local beacon.

COVENANT

- **Northern Pacific Conference of the Evangelical Covenant Church**, 206-275-3903, www.covchurch-npc.org

EMERGING CHURCHES

Generally speaking, "emerging churches" are nondenominational, non-hierarchical congregations of Christians seeking, in postmodern society, to identify with the life of Jesus. Members often express their disillusionment with institutionalized Christianity and place a high value on social activism, communal values, and acceptance of outsiders. Emerging churches in Seattle include the **Church of the Apostles** (4272 Fremont Ave N, www.apostleschurch.org) and **Quest Church** (3233 15th Ave W, 206-352-3796, www.seattlequest.org).

- **Emergingchurch.info**, www.emergingchurch.info

- **Emerging Church Meetups**, http://emerging-church.meetup.com

EPISCOPAL

- **St. Clement of Rome Episcopal Church**, established in 1891, 1501 32nd Ave S, 206-324-3072, http://stclementseattle.org
- **Trinity Parish**, established in 1865, 609 8th Ave, 206-624-5337, www.trinityseattle.org

FOURSQUARE GOSPEL

- The Foursquare Church—Northwest District, 253-284-1674, www.foursquare.org

FRIENDS (QUAKERS)

- **Friends General Conference**, 215-561-1700, ww.fgcquaker.org
- **Quakerfinder.org**, www.quakerfinder.org

JEHOVAH'S WITNESSES

You can download a list of **Kingdom Halls** in Washington State at www.jehovah-witnesses.org/downloads/locat/us/WA.pdf

- **The Watchtower**, www.watchtower.org

LUTHERAN

- Northwest District of the Lutheran Church-Missouri Synod, 888-693-5267, www.lcms.org
- Northwest Washington Synod of the Evangelical Lutheran Church in America, 5519 Phinney Ave N, 206-783-9292, www.lutheransnw.org

MENNONITE

- Pacific Northwest Mennonite Conference, 888-492-4216, www.pnmc.org

METHODIST

- The **First United Methodist Church** was established in 1853, making it the oldest congregation in Seattle. The church's first services were held in a log cabin. The congregation moved to its current location at 180 Denny Way in 2010 (206-622-7278, www.firstchurchseattle.org).
- **Pacific Northwest Conference of the United Methodist Church**, 206-870-6820, www.pnwumc.org

NAZARENE

- **Church of the Nazarene**, www.nazarene.org
- **Washington Pacific District Church of the Nazarene**, 360-489-1060, www. wapacnaz.org

NON-DENOMINATIONAL

- **Mars Hill Church** (206-816-3500, www.marshillchurch.org) appeals to a youthful congregation with live rock bands and a theologically conservative message. Founded in 1996, this mega-church now has ten campuses in the Pacific Northwest, where 10,000 people attend weekly services.
- Other non-denominational churches in the region are listed on the **USA-Church** website (www.usachurch.com).

ORTHODOX

- **Saint Spiridon Orthodox Cathedral**, 400 Yale St N, 206-624-5341, www. saintspiridon.org. The parish maintains a conscious policy of welcome to newcomers.
- **Washington Orthodox Clergy Association,** 425-391-2240, www.orthodox washington.org

PENTECOSTAL

- **Apostolic Pentecostal Church Directory**, www.apostolicpentecostal churches.org

PRESBYTERIAN

- **Seattle Presbytery**, 1625 S Columbian Way, 206-762-1991, www.seattle presbytery.org
- **Synod of Alaska-Northwest**, 1544 S Snoqualmie St, 206-448-6403, www. synodnw.org

SEVENTH-DAY ADVENTIST

- **Adventist Churches Online**, http://mcdonaldroad.org/churches/nwusa. html
- **Washington Conference of Seventh-Day Adventists**, 253-681-6008, www. washingtonconference.org

UNITARIAN UNIVERSALIST

- **Pacific Northwest District of the Unitarian Universalist Association**, 425-957-9116, www.pnwd.org

UNITED CHURCH OF CHRIST

- **Plymouth Congregational Church**, founded in 1869 by early settlers, is the second oldest congregation in Seattle. The church is located in downtown Seattle at 1217 6th Ave (206-622-4865, www.plymouthchurchseattle.org).
- **United Church of Christ**, 216-736-2100, www.ucc.org

UNITY

- **Western Region Association of Unity Churches**, Washington-Puget Sound, www.websyte.com/unity/western/wanw.html

WESLEYAN

- **Northwest District of the Wesleyan Church**, 360-693-1677, www. nwwesleyan.org

HINDU

- The **Vedanta Society of Western Washington** is a branch of the Ramakrishna Order of India, which was established by Swami Vivekananda in 1894. The main temple and bookshop are located at 2716 Broadway East, on Capitol Hill, and the Tapovan Retreat is at 23217 27th Avenue NE, in Arlington, north of Seattle. For more information, call 206-323-1228 or visit www.vedanta-seattle.org.
- **Hindu Temple and Cultural Center**, 3818 212th St SE, Bothell, 425-483-7115, www.htccwa.org

ISLAM

- The **Islamic Educational Center** of Seattle is located in Mountlake Terrace at 23204 55th Ave W. The center offers religious, educational and cultural services, and a library. For details, call 206-428-1970 or visit http://iecseattle.org.
- **The Islamic (Idriss) Mosque**, at 1420 NE Northgate Way (206-363-3013, www.idrismosque.com) is Seattle's first mosque and the first built west of the Mississippi in a Middle Eastern style. The mosque is also home to the **Islamic Center of Washington**.
- **Islamic Center of Eastside**, 14700 Main St, Bellevue, 425-746-0398, www. eastsidemosque.com. The center is currently planning a major expansion.

JAIN

- **Jaina, Federation of Jain Associations in North America,** 718-606-2885, www.jaina.org
- **Jain Society of Seattle**, http://jainsocietyofseattle.org

JEWISH

- You'll find a listing of Seattle area synagogues at **Maven.com** (www.maven. com).
- The **Jewish Federation of Greater Seattle**, 2031 3rd Avenue, which coordinates and funds Jewish projects, provides leadership, and supports educational programs, is a substantial resource for the Jewish community. The organization's comprehensive website, www.jewishinseattle.org, provides links to Jewish resources, lists holidays and Shabbat candle-lighting occasions, and offers reprints of the *Guide to Jewish Washington*, which is published each year by Seattle's only Jewish newspaper, the *JT News* (formerly the *Jewish Transcript)*. For more information, call 206-443-5400 or visit www.jtnews.net.
- The **Stroum Jewish Community Center** promotes intergenerational Jewish events, informal education programs and activities, and social services, including a childcare center and senior adult programs. The JCC's primary facility on Mercer Island, 3801 East Mercer Way, features a state-of-the-art fitness center. Call 206-232-7115 or visit www.sjcc.org. The Center also has a facility at 2618 NE 80th St (206-526-8073).
- Seattle's oldest Jewish congregation is **Bikur Cholim Machzikay Hadath**, located at 5145 S Morgan St (206-721-0970, http://bcmhseattle.org) in the Seward Park neighborhood.

RELIGIOUS STUDIES

The following colleges and universities offer graduate degree programs in religious studies:

- **Northwest Baptist Seminary**, 4301 N Stevens St, Tacoma, 253-759-6104
- **Seattle Pacific Seminary, Seattle Pacific University,** 206-281-2342, http:// www.spu.edu/depts/theology/grad/index.asp
- **The Seattle School of Theology and Psychology**, (formerly Mars Hill Graduate School; the school is not affiliated with Mars Hill Church), 2525 220th St SE, Bothell, 425-415-0505, http://theseattleschool.edu
- **Seattle University**, Theology and Ministry, 206-296-5330, www.seattleu.edu
- **University of Washington**, Jackson School of International Studies, Comparative Religion Program, 206-543-4370, www.washington.edu
- **Western Reformed Seminaries**, Pastoral Studies, 5 S "G" St, Tacoma, 253-272-0417, www.wrs.edu

GETTING AROUND BY CAR

SEATTLE'S TRAFFIC HAS BECOME AS LEGENDARY AS LA'S, AND FOR A good reason—it's actually worse. The metro area's major interstate highways, I-5, I-405, and both bridges to the Eastside are invariably crowded during rush hour. According to the 2000 census, between 1990 and 2000, the number of people in the state of Washington commuting an hour or more to work increased 73%. Despite the frustration of getting behind the wheel, many Seattle residents still persist in driving everywhere—to work, to church, and to the grocery store.

King County and the city of Seattle have sponsored a number of initiatives designed to reduce the number of single-occupancy vehicles on the road, including the One Less Car study conducted between 2000 and 2002, in which 86 Seattle households agreed to give up one vehicle for a limited period. The program demonstrated that all kinds of families, including those with and without children, can save money and reduce stress by limiting car trips. Beginning in 2008, the Department of Transportation initiated the Car Free Days campaign, urging residents to combat global warming by driving their cars 1,000 fewer miles per year. Seattle also sponsors an ongoing Walk Bike Ride challenge that awards prizes for converting car trips to alternative forms of transportation, and businesses offer incentives to employees who take public transit to work. The city's website (www.seattle.gov) includes resources to encourage fewer car trips, including calculators that allow you to determine the cost of your commute and the bite that your car takes out of your annual budget. As a result, there have been some signs of progress. **Commute Seattle** (www.commuteseattle.com), an online resource for Seattle and King County commuters, reports that, according to a 2010 survey, 65% of people who work in downtown Seattle are finding alternative ways to get there, rather than driving alone. Buses, carpools, and ride-sharing programs are viable options for many residents. If you must drive, here are a few tips for making your commute a little easier.

- **Metered ramps** are freeway on-ramps equipped with traffic lights to control the flow of traffic. Most in-city ramps to I-5 are now metered, although the lights operate only during high-volume hours. Metered ramps usually have an H.O.V. (high occupancy vehicle) on-ramp lane, which allows carpool vehicles on without stopping.

- **H.O.T. lanes,** or high occupancy toll lanes, allow solo drivers to use carpool lanes if they pay a toll. The state's first H.O.T lane, established in 2008, extends from Auburn to Renton on State Route 167. If the pilot program proves successful, you may see additional H.O.T. lanes on highways in the metro area.

- **Traffic reports** are available on all major radio and television stations during rush hour, and on news radio station KOMO 1000 AM every 10 minutes weekday mornings and afternoons. These reports can be invaluable once you've identified a few routes to your usual destinations. Or call the **Washington State Department of Transportation (WSDOT)** traffic line at 511 to get information on current traffic conditions, including traffic flow statistics and accident and construction reports. Transportation trouble spots are listed on the *Seattle Post-Intelligencer's* website at www.seattlepi.com/local/transportation. This is also the site to visit for more information about local transportation issues and concerns, including a link to help you locate the lowest gas prices in the region.

- **Traffic webcams** and traffic flow maps for freeways and major highways are available from the WSDOT and are updated every few minutes at www.wsdot.wa.gov/traffic/seattle. You can also access ferry webcams and webcams in the mountain passes and at the Canadian border crossing. The City of Seattle also maintains webcams of city streets and traffic hotspots at www.seattle.gov/trafficcams, and the City of Bellevue does the same at www.cityofbellevue.org/trafficcam. King County offers cameras in outlying communities at http://gismaps.kingcounty.gov/MyCommute.

- **Electronic signs** placed over freeways alert drivers to accidents and, during rush hours, will give point-to-point commute times. This may not help you plan in advance, but if you're late for a meeting it's helpful to know that it will take 21 minutes to drive from downtown Seattle to Lynnwood.

- **Travel times** for 46 different commute routes around Puget Sound are updated every five minutes on the DOT website at www.wsdot.wa.gov/traffic/seattle/traveltimes. The table shows distance, average commute time, and current commute time.

MAJOR EXPRESSWAYS

As you get to know Seattle, you'll establish alternatives to the major freeways, highways, and thoroughfares. Until then, here are some of the main arteries:

- The main north-south freeway is **Interstate 5**. Running smack through the middle of the city, this freeway is both a blessing and a curse for those living near it. If you're running errands, and if I-5 is moving at all, it is usually the quickest way to other neighborhoods in the city. However, if you're more than ten minutes from the freeway, it's often quicker to take local streets across town.
- Another north-south thoroughfare in the city is **Highway 99** (Aurora Avenue), which parallels I-5 as far as the Seattle Center, then cuts under the city and follows the waterfront. The section of Highway 99 along the waterfront is a stacked freeway known as "the viaduct." In 2010, demolition began on the southern part of the viaduct, since the aging freeway and the adjacent seawall have deteriorated and are at risk of failure during an earthquake. The thoroughfare will eventually be replaced by a deep-bore tunnel. Until then, this stretch of Highway 99 will continue to be subject to closures. North of the Green Lake area, Highway 99 can be fairly slow because of the traffic lights. South of the lake and through the downtown area, Highway 99 is a reliable alternative to I-5, especially for those coming from the Greenwood, Phinney Ridge, Fremont or Wallingford neighborhoods. If you travel to the airport often from any of these neighborhoods, there is a shortcut to the airport, which includes Highway 99, Highway 509, and then Highway 518. This can save you 30 minutes during rush hour.
- The main east-west freeway is **Interstate 90**. The I-90 bridge is usually the better of the two Lake Washington bridges, because it has several lanes in each direction as well as a reversible H.O.V. lane. Because it begins near Safeco Field and CenturyLink Field, I-90 does back up before and after games, so give yourself extra time when traveling on those days.
- The other east-west thoroughfare, **Highway 520**, runs from I-5 just north of Capitol Hill to the Eastside. The 520 Floating Bridge is one of the worst stretches of road during rush hour. Even if there is no accident on the bridge, the amazing view of the lake and Mount Rainier, as well as bright sunlight, slows traffic on the bridge decks. The "high rises" (the high portions of the bridge) at the west end also cause traffic backups because drivers have to slow for the curves and accelerate for the incline. If you can't use I-90 as your regular route over the lake, set up a carpool and take advantage of the H.O.V. lanes or try to use an on-ramp as close to the bridge as possible. The 520 Bridge is subject to ongoing closures because of work on a major construction project designed to ease traffic along this route. The SR 520 High Capacity Transit Plan, which will add bus rapid transit lines and eventually light rail over Lake Washington, is scheduled for completion by 2014.

- Another route from Seattle to the Eastside is **Interstate 405,** which generally runs north-south on the east side of Lake Washington. Interstate 405 goes through Renton, Bellevue, Kirkland, and Bothell, connecting with I-5 south of Seattle near Southcenter Mall, and north of Seattle in Lynnwood. Depending on your destination and the time of day, an I-5 to I-405 route might be the quickest way around the lake.
- The **West Seattle Freeway** starts at I-5 near Beacon Hill and heads west to the West Seattle peninsula, crossing Highway 99 on the way. This is the main thoroughfare in and out of the north end of West Seattle.

CARPOOLING

High Occupancy Vehicle (H.O.V.) lanes or "diamond lanes" are located on Interstates 5, 405, and 90. These lanes are reserved for carpools (minimum two or three passengers, depending on the lane), buses, and motorcycles. If you must travel over one of the Lake Washington bridges (I-90 or Highway 520) during rush hour, these lanes are the way to go. You'll be able to pass the rest of the traffic and cut to the front of the line at the bridge deck. For information on carpool parking permits, which can be used for discounted or free parking in downtown Seattle, call the city's **Carpool Parking/Permits** line at 206-684-0816.

If you don't have a carpool partner, Metro Transit offers **Rideshare,** a regional ride-sharing program that matches commuters with carpools. Visit www.rideshareonline.com to find a commuting partner in just minutes. Another option available through Metro and most other public transit services is a vanpool. **Vanpools** require 5 to 15 passengers and monthly fares vary depending on origin, destination, and number of riders. The advantages are that Metro provides the van, insurance, and gasoline. In addition, the carpool parking permit is just $5 for vanpools. Another program called VanShare is designed to help groups of five or more passengers reach other forms of mass transit without having to drive. For more information on the Ridematch, VanPool, and VanShare programs, call 206-625-4500 or 800-427-8249, or visit Metro's website, http:// metro.kingcounty.gov.

Free online services that match carpoolers are also an option. You can browse driver and passenger options and post your own offers and requests. Try www.AlterNetRides.com; www.Carpoolworld.com; and eRideShare.com.

PARK & RIDES

Many drive to Park & Ride lots and then commute by bus to Seattle. For a complete and current listing of lots, go to www.wsdot.wa.gov/choices/parkride.cfm.

AUBURN

- **All Saints Lutheran Church,** 27225 Military Rd S
- **Auburn Park & Ride,** "A" Street SW and 1st St SW

- **Auburn Station Garage,** "A" Street SW and 1st St SW
- **Auburn Station Surface Lot,** "A" Street SW and 1st St SW
- **Peasley Canyon Park & Ride,** W Valley Rd and Peasley Canyon Rd

BELLEVUE

- **Bellevue Christian Reformed Church,** 1221 148th Ave NE
- **Bellevue Foursquare Church,** Richards Rd and 128th, west side, near 20th Pl
- **Eastgate Congregational Church,** 15318 SE Newport Way
- **Grace Lutheran Church,** NE 8th St and 96th Ave NE
- **Newport Covenant Church,** Coal Creek Pkwy and Factoria Blvd
- **Newport Hills Community Church,** 119th Ave SE and SE 58th St
- **Newport Hills Park & Ride,** I-405 and 112th Pl SE
- **South Bellevue Park & Ride,** Bellevue Way SE and 112th Ave SE
- **St. Andrew's Lutheran Church,** 2650 148th Ave SE
- **St. Luke's Lutheran Church,** Bellevue Way NE and NE 30th Pl
- **St. Margaret's Episcopal Church,** 4228 Factoria Blvd
- **Wilburton Park & Ride,** I-405 and SE 8th St

BOTHELL

- **Bothell Park & Ride,** Woodinville Dr and Kaysner Way
- **Brickyard Road,** I-405 and NE 160th St

BURIEN

- **Burien Church of God,** 1st Ave S and SW 166th St
- **Burien Transit Center,** SW 150th St and 4th Ave SW

DUVALL

- **Duvall Park & Ride,** State Route 203 and Woodinville-Duvall Rd

FEDERAL WAY

- **Federal Way Park & Ride,** 23rd Ave S and S 323rd St
- **Federal Way Transit Center,** S 317th St and 23rd Ave S
- **Our Saviour's Baptist Church,** S 320th St and 8th Ave S
- **Redondo Heights Park & Ride,** Pacific Hwy S at S 276th St
- **South Federal Way Park & Ride,** 9th Ave S and S 348th St
- **St. Luke's Lutheran Church,** 515 S 312th St
- **Sunrise United Methodist Church,** 150 S 356th St
- **Twin Lakes Park & Ride,** 21st Ave SW and SW 344th St

ISSAQUAH

- **Issaquah Highlands Park & Ride,** Highlands Dr NE and NE High St
- **Issaquah Park & Ride,** 1740 NW Maple St

- **Issaquah Transit Center,** State Route 900 and Newport Way
- **Klahanie #1 Park & Ride,** SE Klahanie Blvd and 244th Pl SE
- **Klahanie # 3 Park & Ride,** SE Klahanie Dr and SE 40th St
- **Tibbetts Lot,** 1675 Newport Way NW
- **Tibbetts Valley Park Park & Ride,** 12th NW and Newport Way

KENMORE

- **Bethany Bible Church,** NE 181st St and 62nd Ave NE
- **Kenmore Park & Ride,** Bothell Way NE and 73rd Ave NE
- **Kenmore Community Church,** Bothell Way NE & 75th Ave NE

KENT

- **East Hill Friends Church,** 22600 116th Ave SE
- **Kent Covenant Church,** 12010 SE 240th St
- **Kent-Des Moines Park & Ride,** I-5 and Kent-Des Moines Rd
- **Kent/James Street Park & Ride,** N Lincoln Ave & W James St
- **Kent Station Transit Center,** 301 Railroad Ave N
- **Kent United Methodist Church,** SE 248th St and 110th Ave SE
- **Lake Meridian Park & Ride,** 132nd Ave SE and SE 272nd St
- **St. Columba's Episcopal Church,** 26715 Military Rd S
- **Star Lake Park & Ride,** I-5 and 272nd St
- **Valley View Christian Church,** 124th Ave SE and SE 256th St

KIRKLAND

- **Holy Spirit Lutheran Church,** NE 124th St and 100th Ave NE
- **Houghton Park & Ride,** I-405 and NE 70th Pl
- **Korean Covenant Church of Kirkland,** 14220 Juanita/Woodinville Way NE
- **Kingsgate Park & Ride,** I-405 and NE 132nd St
- **South Kirkland Park & Ride,** NE 38th Pl and NE 37th Circle
- **SR-908/Kirkland Way Park & Ride,** NE 85th St and Kirkland Way

MEDINA

- **Evergreen Point Bridge,** State Rte 520 and Evergreen Point Rd
- **St. Thomas Episcopal Church,** 84th Ave NE and NE 12th St

MERCER ISLAND

- **Mercer Island Presbyterian Church,** 84th Ave SE and SE 36th St
- **Mercer Island United Methodist Church,** SE 24th St and 70th Ave SE
- **Mercer Island Park & Ride,** 80th Ave SE and N Mercer Way
- **QFC Village,** SE 68th St and 84th Ave SE

REDMOND

- **Bear Creek Park & Ride**, 178th Pl NE and NE Union Hill Rd
- **Overlake Park & Ride**, 152nd Ave NE and NE 24th St
- **Overlake Transit Center**, NE 40th St and 156th Ave NE
- **Redmond Home Depot**, 17777 NE 76th St
- **Redmond Park & Ride**, 161st Ave NE and NE 83rd St
- **Redwood Family Church,** 11500 Redmond-Woodinville Rd NE

RENTON

- **Fairwood Assembly of God**, 131st Ave SE and SE 192nd St
- **First Baptist Church**, Hardie Ave SW and SW Langston Rd
- **Fred Meyer**, near 3rd Pl, south of Sunset Blvd
- **Kennydale United Methodist Church**, Park Ave N and N 30th St
- **Nativity Lutheran Church**, 140th Ave SE and SE 177th St
- **New Life Church**, 152nd and Renton-Maple Valley Hwy
- **Renton Boeing Lot 12**, N 6th St and Park Ave N
- **Renton City Municipal Garage**, 655 S 2nd St, Flrs 4-7
- **Renton Highlands Park & Ride**, NE 16th St and Edmonds Ave NE
- **Renton Transit Center Park & Ride Garage**, S 2nd St and Burnett Ave
- **South Renton Park & Ride**, S Grady Way and Shattuck Ave S

SEATTLE—CENTRAL

- **Calvary Christian Assembly Church**, NE 68th St and 8th Ave NE
- **Green Lake Park & Ride**, I-5 and NE 65th St

SEATTLE—NORTH

- **South Jackson Park Park & Ride**, 5th Ave NE and NE 133rd St
- **North Jackson Park Park & Ride**, 5th Ave NE and NE 145th St
- **North Seattle Park & Ride,** 1st Ave NE and NE 100th St
- **Northgate Mall Park & Ride**, just north of Northgate Transit Center, floors 1 and 2
- **Northgate Park & Ride**, NE 112th St and 5th Ave NE
- **Northgate Transit Center**, NE 103rd St and 1st Ave NE
- **Our Savior Lutheran Church**, NE 125th St and 27th Ave NE
- **Prince of Peace Lutheran Church**, 14514 20th Ave NE

SEATTLE—SOUTH

- **Airport and Spokane Park & Ride**, Airport Way S and S Spokane St
- **Beverly Park First Baptist Church**, 11659 1st Ave S
- **Community Bible Fellowship**, 11227 Renton Ave S
- **Holy Family Church**, SW Roxbury St and 20th Ave SW
- **Sonrise Evangelical Free Church**, 610 SW Roxbury

- **Southwest Spokane Street Park & Ride**, 26th Ave SW and SW Spokane St

SHORELINE

- **Aurora Church of the Nazarene**, 175th St and Meridian Ave N
- **Aurora Village Transit Center**, N 200th St and Meridian Ave N
- **Bethel Lutheran Church**, NE 175th St and 10th Ave NE
- **Korean Zion Presbyterian Church**, 17920 Meridian Ave N
- **Prince of Peace Lutheran Church**, 14514 20th Ave NE
- **Shoreline United Methodist Church**, NE 145th St and 25th Ave NE
- **Shoreline Park & Ride**, Aurora Ave N and N 192nd St

TUKWILA

- **Church by the Side of the Road**, S 148th St and Pacific Hwy S
- **Olson Place and Myers Way Park & Ride**, Olson Pl SW and Myers Way S

VASHON ISLAND

- **Episcopal Church of the Holy Spirit**, 15420 Vashon Hwy SW
- **Ober Park Annex**, 17130 Vashon Hwy SW
- **Ober Park Park & Ride**, Vashon Hwy SW and SW 171st St
- **Tahlequah Park & Ride**, Vashon Hwy SW and SW Tahlequah Rd
- **Valley Center Park & Ride**, Vashon Hwy SW and SW 204th St

WOODINVILLE

- **Cottage Lake Assembly of God**, 15737 Avondale Rd
- **Woodinville Park & Ride**, 140th Ave NE and NE 179th St
- **Woodinville Unitarian Universalist Church**, 19020 NE Woodinville-Duvall Rd

CAR SHARING

Seattle and Eastside residents now have a car-sharing option, good for out-of-the-way errands or appointments. Car-sharing services such as Zipcar offer the freedom of driving a car without the expense of owning one. Drivers pay for the time they use the car, and the company pays for gas, insurance, and maintenance. Members determine their monthly driving needs and then choose one of several plans, which start at about $7 per hour. An application fee and yearly membership apply and some plans have monthly fees. For more information call Zipcar at 206-682-0107, or visit the website at www.zipcar.com.

CAR RENTAL

Those who need a weekend rental should reserve at least a week in advance.
- **Advantage**, 800-777-5500, www.advantagerentacar.com

- **Alamo**, 877-222-9075, www.alamo.com
- **Avis**, 800-230-4898, www.avis.com
- **Budget**, 800-527-7000, www.budget.com
- **Dollar**, 800-800-3665, www.dollar.com
- **Enterprise**, 800-261-7331, www.enterprise.com
- **Fox,** 800-225-4369, ex. 1, www.foxrentacar.com
- **Hertz**, 800-654-3131, www.hertz.com
- **National**, 877-9058, www.nationalcar.com
- **Thrifty**, 800-847-4389, www.thrifty.com

TAXIS

Unless you are downtown, on Capitol Hill, or at the airport, you'll probably need to call ahead to arrange for a taxi. A few of Seattle's many taxicab companies are listed here; others can be found in the Yellow Pages and online.

- **Farwest Taxi**, 206-622-1717, www.farwesttaxi.net
- **Orange Cab**, 206-522-8800, www.orangecab.net
- **Stita Taxi,** 206-246-9999, wwwstitataxi.com
- **Yellow Cab**, 206-622-6500, www.yellowtaxi.net

BY BIKE

Despite the hilly terrain and the wet, chilly fall and winter weather, a surprisingly large number of Seattle residents use bikes for recreation or transportation. An estimated 4,000 to 8,000 people commute by bicycle each day, and the city government is committed to making Seattle as bike-friendly as possible. To assist bicycle commuters, the **Seattle Department of Transportation Bicycle Program** has created about 45 miles of shared use paths, 120 miles of on-street, striped bike lanes and sharrows (shared lane pavement markings), and about 120 miles of signed bike routes. In addition, "bike boxes" are being installed to create safety zones for cyclists at intersections, in order to minimize car-bicycle collisions.

During the summer months, Seattle's Lake Washington Boulevard becomes a long, winding playground for the city's bike enthusiasts. On Bicycle Sundays, between 10 a.m. and 6 p.m., the city shuts down the lakeside thoroughfare to automobile traffic. For more information about the Seattle Bicycle & Pedestrian Program or to order a free Seattle bicycling guide map, call 206-684-7583 or visit www.seattle.gov/transportation/bikeprogram.htm.

Bicyclists can "bike and ride" at no extra cost, thanks to a Metro Transit program that allows riders to load their bikes onto racks installed on Metro buses. For details on the **Bike + Bus program**, visit Metro's website at http://metro. kingcounty.gov or call 206-553-3000. Bicyclists can also travel for free across

Lake Washington on the 520 floating bridge (which currently has no bicycle or pedestrian access) on any Metro or Sound Transit bus.

Bicycle helmets are mandatory in Seattle and all of King County. You will be ticketed if you're caught riding without one. King County maintains a list of organizations that offer free or low-cost helmets. Visit www.kingcounty.gov/healthservices/health/injury/traffic/bicycles.aspx. For more information on helmets, visit the **Bicycle Helmet Safety Institute** website (www.helmets.org).

BY PUBLIC TRANSPORTATION

Traffic and public transportation issues have taken center stage in local elections for many years, as Seattle residents have struggled with some of the worst traffic in the country. Major transportation issues affecting the Puget Sound region include replacing the aging 520 bridge and the Alaskan Way Viaduct, widening I-405, connecting Highway 509 to I-5, and creating some type of regional transit. As the wealth of public transportation options listed below—as well as the many projects currently in the works—will attest, the region is fully committed to solving its transportation woes.

LIGHT RAIL

Light rail service is relatively new to Seattle (if you don't count the Monorail) and is overseen by the **Sound Transit** agency. **Central Link** light rail travels between Westlake Station in downtown Seattle and Sea-Tac Airport, making 11 stops along the way. Link trains run every 7.5, 10, or 15 minutes depending on the time of day. Service is available from 5 a.m. to 1 a.m. Monday through Saturday and from 6 a.m. to midnight on Sunday and holidays. Adult fares range from $2.00 to $2.75 depending on how far you travel. Scheduled to open in 2016, **University Link** is a 3.15-mile light rail extension that will run in tunnels from downtown Seattle north to the University of Washington. Also in the planning stages is an Eastlink line, designed to eventually (watch for it in 2022!) connect downtown Seattle and Mercer Island, and link the Bellevue, Bel-Red, and Overlake areas. For more information, construction updates, and depot locations, visit www.soundtransit.org.

The city of Tacoma already has a short light rail line called **Tacoma Link**, running from the Tacoma Dome Station to the Theater District, with stops at Union Station and the Convention Center. Link trains run every 12 to 24 minutes, depending on the time of day. Service is available from 5:30 a.m. to 10 p.m. Monday to Friday, from 8 a.m. to 10 p.m. Saturdays, and from 10 a.m. to 6 p.m. on Sundays and holidays. Riding on Tacoma Link is free and more information can be found at www.soundtransit.org.

For the time being, until additional light rail is completed, buses are the primary means of mass transit in Seattle.

BUSES

Metro Transit provides buses that are generally clean and on time, although they make frequent, time-consuming stops as they traverse the city. Express buses are much faster but go to fewer destinations. Crosstown buses are limited and transfers are often necessary when traveling between neighborhoods. Bus fares have increased sharply in recent years: adult fares are $2.25/off-peak, $2.50/one-zone peak, $3/two-zone peak; the fare for youths, seniors, and persons with disabilities is $.75. Fortunately, most of downtown is part of a Ride Free Area, meaning that passengers can use the bus for free in the downtown area as long as they disembark before crossing Battery Street or South Jackson Street—most bus drivers announce the end of the Ride Free Area. The Ride Free area in downtown is possible since fares are collected at the beginning of the ride if you're traveling toward downtown, or at the end of the ride if you're traveling away from downtown. A sign at the front of the bus will let you know when to pay your fare. Another freebie is the Route 99 bus, which connects the Seattle downtown waterfront with the International District, Pioneer Square, the downtown retail area, Pike Place Market, and Belltown. Northbound service runs on 1st Avenue; southbound travels along Alaskan Way from Broad Street to Yesler Way.

RapidRide is a new express bus service being phased in through 2013. These red, yellow, and black hybrid low-emission buses make limited stops at designated stations and arrive with greater frequency than regular Metro buses. The A and B lines are already in service; ultimately lines C through F will be added. RapidRide bus maps and information can be found at www.metro. kingcounty.gov.

Another option is **Dial-a-Ride Transit (DART)**, which is available in some areas of King County for the price of a regular Metro Transit ticket. DART vans can go off regular routes to pick up and drop off passengers, but you must arrange for this service in advance by calling 866-261-DART(3278) (voice), or 1-800-246-1646 (TTY), or by reserving a place online at www.hope-link.org/programs/dart.htm. DART vans do not go door-to-door and operate on a fixed schedule, but have more flexibility than regular Metro bus service. DART service areas include West Seattle, Redmond, Renton Highlands, Kent, Federal Way, and other areas beyond Seattle. More information is available at the King County website listed above.

Bus passes and ticket books are available and can save a lot of money for regular passengers. Some employers, institutions, and community organizations provide free or discounted passes for employees and members, as part of the Employer Commute Services sponsored by King County Metro. Metro Transit offers a variety of bus passes, including PugetPass, Access Pass, and a Vanpool pass. Passes are available at over 100 locations in the city, including some drugstores and cash machines, or you can call Metro at 206-624-PASS or visit http://metro.kingcounty.gov/tops/bus/fare/tickets.html, and purchase online with a credit or debit card. Tickets can also be paid for on the bus with cash (exact change). Metro Transit's latest payment system is the **ORCA** card, a value-added payment card that also carries your pass information electronically. Visit www.orcacard.com for information.

Bus schedules are posted at all bus stops (but only for the buses that use that route), or you can call Metro's Automated Schedule Information Line at 206-BUS-TIME. Metro's 24-hour Rider Information Line at 206-553-3000 connects you to a Metro employee who can assist you with schedule and route information, as long as you can provide your starting point and destination. A public-safety service called **Night Stop**, in effect between 8 p.m. and 5 a.m., allows bus drivers to let you off anywhere along a route, even if it is not a regular bus stop—just come to the front of the bus at least a block ahead of where you want to get off and request your stop. The online **Trip Planner** is a handy tool that lets you input your starting and ending destinations, and date and time of trip to get a customized route that will provide bus numbers and bus stop locations, and can be sorted by fastest trip, fewest transfers or least amount of walking. You can use the service for trips within King, Pierce, and Snohomish counties. It's located at http://tripplanner.kingcounty.gov. **OneBusAway.org** lets you get real-time transit information texted to your regular phone, or you can call in for audio bus info. You can also download an app on your smart phone. Metro Transit also has an informative and comprehensive website at http://metro.kingcounty.gov.

Apps and mobile tools that are useful for bus riders include Google Maps, Walk Score, and SeattleBus (for Metro Transit only).

In addition to buses, Metro Transit runs the **Monorail**. This relic of the 1962 Seattle World's Fair runs the 1-mile route between Westlake Center in the downtown shopping district and the Seattle Center, where it passes through the dazzling titanium curves of the Experience Music Project. Numerous problems with the aging system make it mostly a tourist attraction with a doubtful future. Another public transportation mini-trip you can take is on the **South Lake Union Trolley** (or, as some locals call it, the S.L.U.T.), part of the planned Seattle Streetcar network. The trolley makes the 1.3-mile trip between the new South Lake Union neighborhood and downtown Seattle.

Express buses travel between major cities in King, Pierce, and Snohomish counties, making limited stops along the way. The buses operate on a three-zone fare system. The cost depends on the number of fare zones you traverse and your fare type (youth, adult, or senior/disabled). Fares range from $2.50 to $3.50 for adults, $1.25 to $2.50 for youth, and $.75 to $1.50 for senior/disabled passengers. For more information, call 888-889-6368 or visit www.soundtransit.org.

Outside Seattle, Community Transit covers most of Seattle's neighboring communities; Everett Transit covers the greater Everett area north of Seattle; Pierce Transit provides bus service in Tacoma.

- **Community Transit**, 425-353-RIDE or 800-562-1375, www.commtrans.org
- **Everett Transit**, 425-257-7777, www.everettwa.org/transit
- **Pierce Transit**, 253-581-8000, 800-562-8109, www.piercetransit.org

COMMUTER TRAINS

The **Sounder** commuter trains offer rail service between Tacoma and downtown Seattle, with stops in Puyallup, Sumner, Auburn, Kent, and Tukwila. The north route serves Everett, Mukilteo, Edmonds, and downtown Seattle. The trains offer service in peak directions only, so trains leave Tacoma at seven different times of the morning, and twice in the early evening, heading for Seattle, and return to Tacoma twice in the morning and seven times in the afternoon and evening. Sounder trains leave Everett for Seattle twice every morning and return twice in the afternoon. In a partnership with Amtrak, two more trains are offered on the Everett-Seattle route each morning and afternoon, although you must use one of the Sounder train passes for your fare, or pay full price Amtrak fares. Some Sounder trains are equipped with free wireless Internet—look for the WiFi icon near the vehicle doors. For the schedule and more information about Sounder trains, call 888-889-6368 or visit www.soundtransit.org.

FERRIES

Because there are no bridges connecting Seattle with the Olympic Peninsula, many area residents commute to and from work by ferry. The **Washington State Ferries** system is the largest in the United States, and the third largest in the world, and includes nine routes that serve the Puget Sound area. To commute to the city, residents ride the **Seattle-Bremerton**, **Seattle-Bainbridge Island** routes or the **Seattle-Vashon Island** passenger-only route, which all dock at the Seattle waterfront terminal at Colman Dock. The **Fauntleroy-Vashon-Southworth** route serves West Seattle, Vashon Island, and the Olympic Peninsula, and the **Edmonds-Kingston** route departs from a terminal in Edmonds, 20 minutes north of Seattle. The **Anacortes–San Juan Islands** and **Anacortes-Sidney, BC,** routes originate in Anacortes, about an hour north of Seattle.

Those routes used for commuting to Seattle can be very busy in the morning and evening hours. If you're walking on, you probably won't have any problem, even if you arrive just a few minutes before departure. If you're driving, however, you'll need to arrive early or be prepared to take a later ferry. This is also true for weekends or holidays. The wait time for those who want to ferry their vehicles on the San Juan Islands routes can be several hours on summer holiday weekends.

Schedules and fares vary according to season and route. The peak season is May through September when fares will be higher, and non-peak is October through April. Some routes only charge fares one way, generally westbound, like the Fauntleroy-Vashon route. Others charge vehicle/driver fares both ways, but passenger fares only one way. Fares also vary depending on size and type of vehicle. Discounted passes are available for frequent passengers, children, disabled persons, and senior citizens. WiFi is available on board the ferries, but you have to pay for it.

Ferry information pamphlets are available at all ferry terminals, as well as at some transit information booths in the city. For more information, call the Washington State Ferries' information line at 206-464-6400 or 888-808-7977 or visit www.wsdot.wa.gov/ferries, where you can also view webcams of the ferry docks, learn wait times, and use a fare calculator to find out how much your trip will cost. Mobile apps, such as iFerry, can bring you up-to-the-minute information.

WATER TAXIS

Two water taxi routes operate in King County for foot passengers and bicyclists. The Vashon Island/Downtown Seattle route provides commute-hour weekday service between Vashon Island's north end ferry terminal and Pier 50. The West Seattle route connects Seacrest Park in West Seattle with Pier 50 on the downtown waterfront, operating seven days a week in spring and summer. Metro transit buses connect with both routes. Passengers board on a first-come, first-served basis, and animals (with the exception of service animals) are not allowed. For information about water taxi schedules and fares, visit http://www.kingcounty.gov/transportation/kcdot/WaterTaxi.aspx or call 206-684-1551.

REGIONAL/NATIONAL TRANSPORT

AMTRAK

Recently restored to its original grandeur, the King Street Station, which serves as Seattle's **Amtrak** station, borders the historic International District and Pioneer Square, near the CenturyLink Field at the south end of downtown. The station is served by the Cascades (Eugene, Portland, Seattle, Vancouver, BC), Coast Starlight (Seattle, Portland, Oakland, Los Angeles), and Empire Builder (Chicago, Seattle or Portland) trains. Free WiFi is available to riders on the Cascades line.

- **Amtrak National Route Information**, 800-USA-RAIL, www.amtrak.com
- **Amtrak Seattle Station**, 303 S Jackson St, 206-382-4125

BUSES

The **Greyhound Lines** bus terminal is located at 8th Avenue and Stewart Street in downtown Seattle. For reservation information call the terminal directly at 206-628-5526, Greyhound's national reservation number at 800-231-2222, or visit www.greyhound.com. Another option for bus trips to some eastern Washington cities is **Northwestern Trailways**. Call 800-366-3830 for reservations and information, or visit www.northwesterntrailways.com.

AIRPORTS/AIRLINES

The **Seattle-Tacoma International Airport**, known locally as Sea-Tac, is located south of Seattle at 17801 Pacific Highway South. For parking rates and information, airport weather conditions, and general information, call 206-787-5388 or visit www.portseattle.org/seatac.

Sea-Tac offers plenty of amenities for passengers, such as shops and restaurants where you can buy food to take on the plane, since in-flight meal service has become a rarity. A USO offers assistance to military personnel and their families, and there is a Meditation Room in the Main Terminal and places to get a massage or a manicure. Passengers can charge their cell phones at designated spots, and "Send It Home" kiosks allow you to mail any items you packed inadvertently that can't pass through security, such as Aunt Minnie's pickled onions. In addition, there is free WiFi throughout the airport. If you're not racing to catch a plane, you can enjoy some of the art on display throughout the airport, which features a permanent collection of 20th-century works as well as a rotating collection of installations.

Recent improvements at Sea-Tac earned the airport an award for on-time departures, and its security procedures have been streamlined, as well. Despite some controversy regarding their implementation, AIT (Advanced Imaging Technology) scanners are now used to screen incoming passengers. If you prefer not to submit to a full body scan, you can request a patdown from a TSA agent. (Give yourself extra time to clear security if you opt for the patdown.) Express security lines are available at security checkpoints for those in wheelchairs, passengers with no carry-on luggage, and for some frequent fliers and first- or business-class passengers, depending on the airline. Contact your airline to see if you qualify. Security regulations change frequently; one day you're allowed an item in your carry-on luggage and the next it is only allowed in checked baggage. The best ways to keep up with the changes and rules are to contact your airline, check the Sea-Tac airport website for updates, or contact the **Transportation Security Administration** at 866-289-9673 or visit their website at www.tsa.gov for the latest news and updates on security and travel-related issues.

Passengers who check in online before they arrive will be able to avoid some of the lines inside the terminal. Curbside check-in is available for domestic passengers only on the upper airport drive, but stopping your car is allowed only for picking up or dropping off passengers, and loading or unloading luggage. Passengers are not permitted to leave their cars while they check their bags curbside. Vehicles left unattended are ticketed even if the driver is nearby. At Sea-Tac, the upper drive is for departures, and baggage claim and pick-up are located on the lower drive. Note: when the upper drive is congested, passengers with few or no bags should consider being dropped-off on the lower drive.

A cell phone waiting lot, where you can wait until you get a call that someone is ready to be picked up, is available just a couple of minutes away from the baggage claim area. It has space for 40 vehicles to wait at one time.

When flight delays happen, rain, fog, and clouds are often to blame, since they reduce visibility on the airport's three runways. Be sure to call your airline or check the status of your flight online before you head to the airport.

These major airlines serve passengers at Sea-Tac:

- **Air Canada**, 800-247-2262, www.aircanada.ca
- **Alaska Airlines**, 800-252-7522, www.alaskaair.com
- **American Airlines**, 800-433-7300, www.aa.com
- **Asiana Airlines**, 800-227-4262, http://us.flyasiana.com
- **British Airways**, 800-247-9297, www.britishairways.com
- **China Airlines**, 800-227-5118, www.china-airlines.com
- **Condor,** 866-960-7915, www.condor.com
- **Continental Airlines**, 800-523-5273, www.continental.com
- **Delta Airlines**, 800-221-1212, www.delta.com
- **EVA Air**, 800-695-1188, www.evaair.com.
- **Frontier Airlines**, 800-432-1359,
- **Hainan Airlines,** 888-688-8813, http://www.hainanair.us
- **Hawaiian Airlines**, 800-367-5320, www.hawaiianair.com
- **Icelandair,** 800-223-5500, www.icelandair.com
- **JetBlue Airways**, 800-JETBLUE, www.jetblue.com
- **Korean Air**, 800-438-5000, www.koreanair.com
- **Lufthansa,** 800-645-3880, www.lufthansa.com
- **Scandinavian Airlines**, 800-221-2350, www.flysas.com
- **Southwest Airlines**, 800-435-9792, www.southwest.com
- **Sun Country Airlines**, 800-359-6786, www.suncountry.com
- **United Airlines**, 800-864-8331, www.united.com
- **US Airways**, 800-428-4322, www.usairways.com
- **Virgin America,** 877-359-8474, www.virginamerica.com

TRAVELING TO SEA-TAC AIRPORT BY CAR

When traveling to the airport by car, use the following directions: from Seattle take I-5 south to the Southcenter/Sea-Tac Airport exit and follow the signs to get on Highway 518. From Highway 518 take the Sea-Tac Airport exit and stay to the left as you exit. This will put you on the main road into the airport, which is clearly marked with signs to baggage claim, airline counters, and parking.

Alternate directions from downtown Seattle, Ballard, Phinney Ridge, Greenwood, Fremont, and Broadview (these are just a little faster during rush hour): take Highway 99 south until it forces you left onto 1st Avenue South. Stay in the right lane and follow directions to the 1st Avenue South Bridge (only a few blocks). After you cross the bridge, the road you are on becomes Highway 509. Stay on Highway 509 to the Sea-Tac Airport and Highway 518 exit. Take Highway 518 east, then, from Highway 518, take the Sea-Tac exit. This exit puts you on the main road into the airport.

The parking garage at Sea-Tac is connected to the main terminal by sky-bridges on the 4th floor. To get a complete list of parking rates, visit the airport website or call the Public Parking Office at 206-433-5308. The following **parking options** are available:

- Terminal Direct Parking, the shortest route from car to plane, is available on the fourth floor, skybridge level. Both short- and long-term parking is possible here. Rates start at $4 an hour with a daily maximum of $35 for up to 24 hours.
- General Parking, available on five floors of the garage (levels 3 and 5–8) for both short- and long-term parking. The rate is $3 an hour with a maximum of up to $28 for up to 24 hours, and a special weekly rate of $130. Six spaces that provide free charging for electric cars are available on the fifth floor of the garage.
- Accessible Parking: ADA-designated parking spaces are located on the fourth and fifth floors of the airport garage; hourly parking rates apply. If you need wheelchair and/or luggage assistance from the garage to the terminal, call 206-433-5287 four to six hours in advance of your arrival.

Sea-Tac uses an automated parking payment system to help travelers get out of the airport quickly. Automated pay kiosks on the 4th floor of the garage allow visitors to pay for both long- and short-term parking before they reach their cars. Simply take a ticket as you enter the parking garage, and keep it with you. When you're ready to retrieve your car, you can pay at the kiosks with a credit or a debit card and then feed your validated ticket into the machine at the garage exit as you are leaving. Cash is accepted at the toll plazas, or at the black-and-yellow "pay on foot" machines on the fourth floor. For additional parking details, call 206-433-5308 or visit the Port of Seattle's website at www.portseattle.org/seatac.

Finally, there are several discount parking lots near Sea-Tac Airport that cost much less than the airport parking garage and offer quick shuttle service to and from their lots and the airport. Many have security services so your vehicle will be monitored while you are gone. Reservations can generally be made over the phone or online. The following will get you started, but check the Yellow Pages under "Parking Facilities" for a comprehensive list.

- **Doug Fox Parking**, 2626 S 120th St, 206-248-2956; this off-site lot has shuttles equipped with wheelchair lifts for disabled passengers.
- **Extra Car Airport Parking**, 16300 S International Blvd, 206-248-3452, 800-227-5397, www.extracar.com
- **Park N Fly**, 17400 International Blvd, 206-433-6767, www.parknflyseattle. com
- **Sea-Tac Park**, 2701 S 200th St, 206-824-2544, www.seatacpark.com
- **Thrifty Airport Parking**, 18836 International Blvd, 888-634-7275, www. thriftyparking.com

TRAVELING TO SEA-TAC AIRPORT BY LIGHT RAIL

Central Link light rail, which began service in 2009, is a new and convenient way to get the airport. Starting at 5 a.m. until just after midnight (6 a.m. to 11 p.m. on Sundays), trains run between Westlake Station in downtown Seattle and the airport, making 11 stops along the way. Tickets are available from the machines at the base of the escalators when you descend Westlake Station in the Downtown Transit Tunnel on Pine Street between 3rd and 4th streets. Train frequency varies, but the longest wait time is 15 minutes. The trip takes approximately 35 minutes and costs $2.75 if you travel the full distance. Travelers with a lot of luggage should bear in mind that, once you disembark at the airport, it's a bit of a hike down a long breezeway until you reach the terminal. For information visit the Sound Transit website at www.soundtransit.org or call 888-889-6368.

TRAVELING TO SEA-TAC AIRPORT BY BUS & SHUTTLE VAN

The following public transportation bus routes provide airport service to and from Seattle and surrounding communities. Buses arrive at and leave from the far south end of the baggage claim area, outside Door 2. Departure times are posted at the bus stop and bus timetables can be picked up near Door 16 on the baggage claim level. For bus departure and arrival times, and route maps, check the website at http://metro.kingcounty.gov/tops/bus/destinations/flymetro.html.

- **Metro Route 124**: daily early morning service to and from downtown Seattle. Travel time is 30 minutes.

- **Metro Route 180**: service to and from Burien, Kent, and Auburn, weekdays, Saturday, and Sunday, from early mornings to early evenings. Includes "Night Owl" service from Auburn and Kent nightly.
- **RapidRide A Line**: service to and from Federal Way Transit Center, weekdays, Saturday, and Sunday.
- **Sound Transit Route 560**: daily service to and from Bellevue, Renton, Burien, and West Seattle. Travel time is 45 minutes to and from Bellevue, 15 minutes to and from Renton, and 40 minutes to and from West Seattle.
- **Sound Transit Route 574**: daily service to and from Lakewood, Tacoma, and Sea-Tac Airport.

Shuttle van or **bus**: most downtown hotels offer shuttle service to the airport; call ahead for times and costs (it may be free if you are a hotel guest). For door-to-door shuttle service, try one of the following:

- **Airporter Shuttle**, 360-380-8800, 866-235-5247, www.airporter.com
- **Bremerton-Kitsap Airporter**, 360-876-1737, www.kitsapairporter.com
- **Capital Aeroporter**, Olympia: 360-754-7113, Tacoma: 253-927-6179, Sea-Tac Airport: 206-244-0011, outside Washington: 800-962-3579, www.capair.com
- **Olympic Bus Lines**, 360-417-0700, 800-457-0700, www.olympicbuslines. com
- **Quick Shuttle**, 604-940-4428, 800-665-2122, www.quickcoach.com
- **Shuttle Express**, 425-981-7000, 800-487-7433, www.shuttleexpress.com
- **Vashon Shuttle**, 206-463-2664
- **Whidbey–Sea-Tac Shuttle,** 360-679-4003, 877-679-4003, www.seatac shuttle.com

There are two other airports in the Seattle area. **Renton Municipal Airport** (425-430-7471, www.rentonwa.gov), owned by the City of Renton, is located about 25 miles south of downtown Seattle. The airport is used primarily by single and twin-engine planes, a few corporate jets, and some private flying clubs. There is no commercial flight activity. **King County International Airport**, also known as Boeing Field, serves air cargo companies, recreational fliers, charter and commercial services, flight schools, and emergency services. **Kenmore Air** offers passenger service to the San Juan Islands, Oak Harbor, Port Angeles, Victoria and the Gulf Islands and Campbell River Airport in Canada, among other destinations. Call 866-435-9524 or visit www.kenmoreair.com for more information. Boeing Field is also a major center for Boeing operations. For more information, visit www.kingcounty.gov/airport.

TRAVEL RESOURCES

There are a number of online travel sites where you can sometimes find good deals. They include, among others, **Travelocity.com**, **Expedia.com**, **Orbitz. com**, **Lowestfare.com**, **Hotwire.com** and **Cheaptickets.com**. If cost far outweighs convenience, check **Priceline** (www.priceline.com), where you may be able to pin down an inexpensive fare at inconvenient hours (often in the middle of the night). Their motto, "Name Your Price and Save" says it all. KAYAK**.com** is a travel search engine that offers comparison shopping—listing comparable routes, services, and prices from all the major sites like Expedia and Orbitz. Their search results also include listings directly from suppliers and cover some services the major sites don't offer, like JetBlue.

Many airlines post last-minute seats at reduced rates, usually on Wednesdays. In fact, booking with the airline of your choice, either online or by phone, often proves less expensive than booking with some so-called discount travel sites.

Have you ever wondered where the best seats are on a plane? **Seatguru. com** can tell you. On this website you can choose the airline and the plane you'll be flying on and view a diagram of the plane with seats marked as good, be aware, or poor, and use that information when making a seat request with your airline. New mobile apps, many of which are free, can help travelers navigate the airport. **GateGuru** puts 86 U.S. airport maps at your fingertips and features user reviews of airport restaurants and shops. **USA Today AutoPilot** stores travel information for your trips, such as flight confirmation numbers, and gives you updates on flight status and weather for your destination.

To register a complaint against an airline, the Department of Transportation is the place to call or write: 202-366-2220, Aviation Consumer Protection Division, C-75, U.S. Department of Transportation, 1200 New Jersey Ave SE, Washington, DC 20590. You can also use e-mail to lodge complaints or concerns using this address: airconsumer@dot.gov.

Information about airport conditions, including weather and air traffic congestion, which could create flight delays, can be checked online at www. fly.faa.gov.

APTLY NICKNAMED, THE "EMERALD CITY" HAS A LOT RIDING ON ITS reputation as one of the greenest cities in the nation. With the support of mayors Greg Nickels (2002–2010) and Mike McGinn (2010–present), Seattle has worked hard to distinguish itself as an environmental leader, and in some important respects it has succeeded. Two notable achievements include the city's implementation of green building policies and its recycling program. In 2000, Seattle adopted a sustainable building policy and became the first city in the nation to adopt LEED, the U.S. Green Building Council's green building rating system, as the municipal design standard and performance measurement tool. In 2011, the Economist Intelligence Unit ranked the city as fourth greenest city in the United States, and first in terms of building. Seattleites' commitment to the three R's (Reduce, Reuse, Recycle) was demonstrated in 2011, when single-family homes recycled 70% of their waste (the national average is 34%), helping divert 50% of municipal waste away from landfills into recycling facilities or compost.

Reducing the environmental impact of single-car commutes has been more of a challenge. Seattle has significant traffic woes, and has struggled for years to implement working transit solutions. Unlike its neighbor to the south, Portland, Oregon, which boasts an efficient and extensive light rail system, Seattle's principal form of mass transit is still its bus system, though a series of light rail projects are currently under way. Large-scale transportation initiatives tend to get stalled, and funding squandered, in expensive and protracted squabbles over transit projects, such as the Monorail expansion (R.I.P. 2005) and the deep-bore tunnel project scheduled to replace the crumbling Alaska Way Viaduct. Nevertheless, more people in Seattle bike to work than in any other U.S. city, including Mayor McGinn, who has taxed motorists to raise money to make the city safer and more convenient for bicyclists and pedestrians by creating bike lanes and reducing on-street parking.

All in all, if environmental issues are close to your heart, Seattle is a great place to live, with plenty of green resources (the Seattle Times features a regular "ecoconsumer" column) and the political will and community support to back up environmentally beneficial policies. When you run into each other dragging your recycling bins to curb, you'll find that most of your neighbors are equally committed to reducing their own carbon footprints.

GREENING YOUR HOME

If you're a prospective home buyer, consider reducing your consumption of energy and resources by purchasing the smallest, most energy-efficient property that you need. If you purchase an older home, you can have it retrofitted to be more energy efficient (see below), or you can look for a newer property built to rigorous environmental standards. GreenWorks Realty (2850 SW Yancy St, 206-283-8181, http://greenworksrealty.com) is the first real estate broker in the nation to specialize in green properties, and a growing number of eco-brokers (www.ecobroker.com) can show you similarly eco-friendly homes in Seattle and its surrounding communities. If you're planning to have a new home built, you'll find that the city gives the green light (so to speak) to eco-friendly construction projects by expediting the permit process for green buildings (search for "Green Permitting" at www.seattle.gov/dpd).

You can also choose to live in a neighborhood where a majority of services are situated within walking distance, or one that is close to bus lines or other forms of public transit, thus reducing your reliance on a car. A handy online resource called **Walk Score** (www.walkscore.com) calculates the walking distance from any address to local businesses and amenities and assigns it a number between 0 and 100 that reflects the walkability of that address. The site also shows you nearby amenities and the distance to those services, and calculates the length of your commute by car, bike, and on foot. Many realtors advertise the Walk Scores of the properties they list; a score of 90 to 100 means a walker's paradise, whereas a very low Walk Score, between 0 and 24 for instance, means you will be car-dependent.

GREEN REMODELING

If you intend to remodel an existing structure, consider choosing a contractor who is committed to using salvaged building materials, or source them yourself. A list of local contractors and suppliers can be found on the Green Pages at Northwest Eco-building Guild's website (206-575-2222, www.ecobuilding.org). The SoDo district is home to a number of secondhand building material suppliers, including Second Use (7953 2nd Ave S, 206-763-6929, www.seconduse. com) and EarthWise (3447 4th Ave S, 206-624-4510, http://earthwise-salvage. com). Visit RE Store, in Ballard, for a constantly evolving selections of used bathroom sinks, doors, and vintage lighting fixtures (1440 NW 52nd St, 206-297-9119, www.re-store.org). Or check out Bedrock, tucked under the end of the Magnolia Bridge, with its kaleidoscopic collection of tiles crafted from recycled glass (1401 W Garfield St, 206-283-7625, www.bedrockindustries.com). If you need new materials, the flagship store of Ecohaus (4121 1st Ave S, 206-315-1974, www.ecohaus.com) carries a huge selection of eco-friendly building supplies, including bamboo flooring, composting toilets, and "stone" countertops made from recycled paper. Make sure that the paint you buy contains little or no volatile organic compounds, or VOCs. These solvents become gases at room temperature and aren't healthy for you or for the environment. Sources for "green" paint include Best Paint Co. (206-783-9938, wwwbestpaintco.com) and Miller Paints (multiple locations, www.millerpaint.com), which carries its own low-VOC brand Acro Pure. Notable environmentally friendly brands include Devine Color (888-MY-DEVINE, www.devinecolor.com) and Yolo Colorhouse (www.yolocolorhouse.com). Most larger national paint manufacturers also carry their own lines of low-VOC paint.

Consider installing a green roof on your property. Green roofs are covered with plants and grass that absorb rainwater and reduce runoff. They also keep a building cooler in the summer, warmer in the winter, and help cool and clean the air. Green roofs cost more than traditional roofs, but they last two to three times longer than traditional roofing materials.

ENERGY EFFICIENCY

Energy conservation has become a priority for many communities in the Puget Sound area. Official websites maintained by each city government are usually a good place to begin searching for information and resources to help you save energy and lower your utility bills. Seattle residents have access to cash rebates for sprinkler systems and toilets and other incentives for energy-efficient appliances, lighting, and weatherizing, including low-cost loans for energy-efficient upgrades and deeply discounted home energy audits.

Here are a few of the programs and services listed at the City of Seattle site (www.seattle.gov):

- The **HomeWise** program (206-684-0244) www.seattle.gov/housing/HomeWise), sponsored by the Seattle Office of Housing, provides free weatherization services for low-income tenants or home owners as well as low-interest home improvement loans for those who qualify.
- **The WashWise Rebate Program**, initiated in 2007, offers incentives to Washington state residents who purchase an Energy Star–rated clothes washer (866-632-4636, www.washwiserebate.com). Visit **www.energystar.gov** to read about the Energy Star program and learn how you can earn federal tax credits when you upgrade to energy-efficient appliances.

- **Community Power Works** (CPW) (206-449-1170, www.communitypow erworks.org) is a federally funded building upgrade program available to homeowners and businesses in central and southeast Seattle that will ultimately eliminate 70,000 metric tons of greenhouse gas emissions and create thousands of green jobs. Qualified homeowners have access to inexpensive energy assessments, certified contractors, and rebates, incentives, and loans to help pay for upgrades.
- Seattle City Light's **Energy Conservation** (206-684-3800, www.seattle.gov/ light/Conserve) page lists rebate programs for homes and businesses and tools for saving energy. City Light also sponsors a program called Powerful Neighborhoods, which distributes free compact fluorescent lightbulbs (CFLs), low-flow showerheads, and faucet aerators to designated neighborhoods.

The city of Seattle has invested a wealth of time and money into encouraging its residents to conserve energy not just because it's good for the planet but because it makes sound economic sense. Simply switching to LED (light-emitting diode) streetlights is expected to save the city $2.4 million in operating costs by 2014.

RENEWABLE ENERGY

While the majority of electricity used in the United States still comes from burning fossil fuels, many utility suppliers in the Puget Sound region now have programs that enable customers to purchase a portion or all of their electricity from renewable sources. **Green power** is electricity generated from wind, solar, geothermal, landfill gases, waves and tides, gas from wastewater treatment, hydropower, and other alternative fuel sources. Seattle City Light's **Green Up** program (206-684-8822, www.seattle.gov/light/Green) allows residential and business customers to buy electricity derived from solar, wind, and biomass (from animal waste) power generators based in the Northwest. You can choose the extent to which you participate in the program, whether 25%, 50%, or 100%, and pay a slightly higher electricity bill. Puget Sound Energy, which provides natural gas to Seattle and its suburbs, has its own **Green Power** program (800-562-1482, www.pse.com), consistently ranked as one of the most successful in the nation. Tacoma Power's **Evergreen Options** (253-502-8377, www.mytpu.org) allows its customers to purchase green power, and the Snohomish County Public Utility District sponsors the **Plant Power** program (425-783-1000, www.snopud.com).

Some homeowners take it a step farther and build their own power sources. If you install solar panels on your roof or erect a wind turbine to generate your own electricity, you can earn a federal tax credit for up to 30% of the cost of renewable energy improvements to your home. The Natural Resources Defense Council publishes an online guide to clean energy (www.nrdc.org, search

Consumer's Guide to Buying Clean Energy) that's worth a visit. Another site with information about tax credits for renewable energy is DSIRE, the Database of State Incentives for Renewables & Efficiency (www.dsireusa.org/incentives).

WATER CONSERVATION

It's easy to take water for granted when you're surrounded by it. A large part of the beauty of the Seattle area is due to the omnipresence of water, whether it falls from the sky or shimmers in lakes and on the surfaces of rivers that empty into Puget Sound. According to the **Partnership for Water Conservation** (877-411-2120, www.bewatersmart.net), the region's burgeoning population has diminished clean water supplies and led to reductions in stream flows, endangering fish populations. Did you know that a leaking toilet can waste 200 gallons of water a day? For years, public information campaigns have been counseling us to conserve water, so hopefully you've got the basics down: Take short showers, don't brush your teeth with the faucet running, put a brick in the toilet tank or install low-flow toilets, use aerating faucets, and shower-heads and front-loading washing machines that use water more efficiently. And don't let all that "liquid sunshine" go to waste! Buy a rain barrel, install it under your downspout, and use the water you harvest in your garden (but never for drinking). The Seattle Conservation Corps sells rain barrels for $75 each, plus tax and shipping. They can deliver rain barrels for a fee, or you can pick one up at their office at Magnuson Park (206-684-0910). The **Saving Water Partner-ship** (206-684-7283, www.savingwater.org), sponsored by Seattle-area utility companies, lists ways to conserve water inside, outside, and at work. See "Land-scaping," below, for additional ways to conserve water.

LANDSCAPING

A lush green lawn is an ecological disaster area. It may be heaven for your bare feet, but it's hell on the environment, requiring destructive amounts or water, fertilizer, and pesticides to keep it that way. As anti-lawn sentiment grows, many Seattle homes sport brown lawns during the (usually dry) summer months. Practice natural lawn care (www.savingwater.org/docs/natlawncare. pdf) or consider replacing an existing lawn with another garden feature. If you are landscaping your property, choose drought-resistant native plants, which tend to be more pest and disease resistant than non-native varieties. Natives need less water and control soil erosion better than non-native plants. The **Washington Native Plant Society** (206-527-3210, www.wnps.org) provides information about and sources for native plants. You might be surprised to learn that the ubiquitous Himalayan blackberry was actually introduced to the region by settlers. Clear out invasive plants such as English ivy and holly, Japa-nese knotweed, blackberry vines, and even attractive ornamentals like bamboo and the butterfly bush. The "Northwest Yard and Garden" section on the King

County website (www.kingcounty.gov) has useful information about natural landscaping or you can call (or e-mail) their Natural Lawn and Garden Hotline at 206-633-0224.

You'll likely notice signs around the neighborhood declaring that a garden is a Pesticide-Free Zone. Do the planet—and everyone on it—a favor and reduce or eliminate your use of pesticides and weed killers. Opt for earth-friendly forms of pest control and organic fertilizers. Local sources for organic and non-toxic garden products include **Swansons Nursery** (9701 15th Ave NW, 206-782-2583, www.swansonsnursery.com), **Goods for the Planet** (425 Dexter Ave N, 206-652-2327, www.goodsfortheplanet.com), and **Molbak's** in Woodinville (425-483-2000, www.molbaks.com), or you can order supplies online. **Seattle Tilth** (4649 Sunnyside Ave N, 206-633-0451, http://seattletilth.org) is an excellent resource for information about organic gardening.

The earth's changing climate is expected to dump even more rainfall on the Puget Sound region in years to come. Unmanaged runoff from storm water can lead to erosion, mudslides, and increased pollutants flowing into the Sound. Seattle Public Utilities sponsors the **Rain Wise** program to help residents manage the flow of storm water. The program encourages residents to plant trees and rain gardens, reduce paved areas on their property, and build cisterns to slow the runoff, offering rebates for construction costs (https://rainwise.seattle.gov/city/seattle/overview). See resources in "Water Conservation" above for information about efficient irrigation.

ENVIRONMENTALLY FRIENDLY PRODUCTS AND SERVICES

Growing consumer demand has created a mushrooming market for eco-friendly goods and services. Businesses that are not actually "green" may claim to be (see "A Word on Greenwashing" below) in order to profit from this trend. Here are a few resources for finding businesses and suppliers with bonafide green credentials:

- The **Chinook Book** (http://sea.chinookbook.net) contains more than 400 coupons for groceries, dining, travel, entertainment, garden supplies, and more that can be redeemed at sustainable businesses around the Puget Sound/Seattle region. Many stores and restaurants carry the book, which is published annually. If you have a smart phone, the Chinook Book has a free app that you can download at the Apple store.
- Online directories for environmentally friendly suppliers are all over the Internet. The **Greenopia.com** website (www.greenopia.com) lets you search for green products and services in your area. The site also posts sustainability ratings for products and corporations as well as relevant news and articles about green living.
- **Natural Choice Directory** (www.naturalchoice.net) helps you find businesses committed to sustainability. Here you'll find everything from green

dentistry (replace your old fillings with biocompatible materials) and non-toxic pest control, to green (phthalate-free) sex toys and vegan pet food.

- For free or a fee you can download **green apps** onto your smart phone or PDA that, among other things, help you make informed choices as a consumer. The free GoodGuide app gives you detailed information about the health, social, and environmental impacts of a given product when you type in its name or photograph its barcode.

A WORD ON GREENWASHING

When offered a choice, consumers are turning increasingly to "green" products and services. Some businesses attempt to profit by masquerading as earth friendly when they are, in fact, anything but. Greenwashing is "when a company or organization spends more time and money claiming to be 'green' through advertising and marketing than actually implementing practices that minimize environmental impact," according to the **Greenwashing Index** sponsored by the University of Oregon. You can visit this site (www.greenwashingindex.com) and others, such as the one maintained by Consumer Reports (www.greener-choices.com), to determine if a given product or service is as eco-friendly as it claims.

GREEN CLEANING

A number of useful guides have been published, such as Clean & Green by Annie Berthold-Bond, that can help you find less toxic household products for cleaning your home. If you prefer to hire someone else to do your dirty work, many local cleaning services specialize in green cleaning. The website **www.ecovian.com** rates local green services and posts customer reviews. If you're in the market for a new washing machine, dryer, or dishwasher, be sure to purchase one with an energy-efficient model with a high Energy Star rating of 75 or above, if possible (www.energystar.gov).

FOOD

Seattle has embraced the locavore movement, a commitment to eating locally grown, seasonal foods that has transformed the city's restaurant scene in recent years. Load up on locally grown produce at one of the region's weekly farmers' markets (see list in "Shopping for the Home"). An increasing number of area residents purchase a share in a **CSA** (Community Supported Agriculture programs), such as **New Roots Organics** (206-261-2500, http://newrootsorganics.com) or **Helsing Junction Farm** (360-273-2033, www.helsingfarmcsa.com), which deliver locally grown organic produce to your doorstep. With veggies this delicious, you might consider adopting a vegetarian diet, one of the most powerful things you can do for the environment. Livestock production contributes tons of greenhouse gases to the atmosphere. If you can't resist the temptations of the flesh, you can buy your meat from a local rancher, such as the folks at **Cascade Range Beef Company** (206-355-2468), who raise grass-fed animals without using antibiotics or hormones. Of course, the freshest produce is the kind you grow yourself: More Seattleites are cultivating their own vegetable gardens, raising chickens for eggs and even keeping bees in their backyards. If you don't have the space, you can get on the (very long) waiting list for your local **P-Patch** or community garden (www.seattle.gov/neighborhoods/ppatch). **Urban Garden Share** pairs would-be gardeners with available gardening space (www.urbangardenshare.org).

When shopping for food at the grocery store, buy fruits and vegetables that are certified organic. Another label to watch for is the **Salmon Safe** certification, which promises that a farm or vineyard isn't polluting the local watershed. When buying seafood, choose varieties from sustainable fisheries. The Monterey Bay Aquarium's **Seafood Watch** guide lists best choices for seafood and which ones to avoid (www.montereybayaquarium.org). You can download a wallet card or an app for your phone so you'll have it while you're shopping.

And in a city that literally worships the coffee bean, you'll want to make sure that your daily cup of joe is environmentally friendly, too. Seattle-based **Zoka** (multiple locations, www.zokacoffee.com) gets high marks for greenness.

GREEN MONEY

Green banking means promoting environmentally friendly practices and reducing your carbon footprint through your banking activities. Some financial institutions have adopted greener methods of operation and lending practices, in large part because there's a market for it: an increasing number of customers want to entrust their money to financial institutions committed to doing business in an environmentally conscientious manner. As a rule, smaller community banks and credit unions and online banks have a better environmental track record. One local bank committed to supporting green initiatives is **One PacificCoast Bank** (2720 3rd Ave, Ste #1, 206-340-2700, www.onepacificcoastbank. com), which focuses on economic and environmental sustainability. A national Internet bank that gets high marks for green banking is **ING Direct** (https:// home.ingdirect.com). Certain banks or mortgage lenders will let you qualify for a larger home loan if you are purchasing a "green" property, or one with more energy efficient features. **GreenStreet Lending**, a service of Umpqua Bank, offers loans for energy-efficiency and renewable energy home and small-business improvements (866-790-2121; www.umpquabank.com). Many financial institutions encourage their customers to go paperless and arrange to conduct their banking and pay their bills entirely on line. If you're not quite ready to give up your checkbook, you can opt for eco-friendly checks made with recycled paper. **Green Bank Report** (http://greenbankreport.com) is an excellent Internet resource for information about green banking practices.

Opportunities for green investing are growing as well, as more people opt to invest their money in environmentally responsible companies. **Light Green Advisors** (1420 5th Ave, 206-547-8645, www.lightgreen.com), an asset management firm specializing in environmentally beneficial investing, and **GoodFunds Wealth Management** (6009 34th Ave NW, 206-782-1205, www.goodfunds.com), both based in Seattle, specialize in sustainable responsible investment (SRI) services.

GREENER TRANSPORTATION

On average, people drive more in the Seattle metropolitan area than they do in Los Angeles. Finding alternative forms of transportation is a critical issue in Seattle, where so many residents still rely on their cars to get to work or to run daily errands. Currently, transportation represents the largest and fastest growing source of greenhouse gases (GHG), as well as water and air pollution, in Washington State, and the Puget Sound region's burgeoning population will only exacerbate this problem in years to come. Urban planners believe one key to the region's transit woes lies in the concept of **transit-oriented communities** (TOC): compact and walkable mixed-use neighborhoods designed to accommodate housing as well as shops, businesses, and services, in close proximity to a transit hub or station. Recent developments in outlying suburban communities such as Burien, Redmond, and Bellevue have been planned according to this model.

Of course, the most environmentally friendly thing you can do is give up your car and rely on your own legs (whether to walk, bicycle, or climb aboard public transit) to take you where you need to go. In 2010 the city of Seattle launched its **Walk Bike Ride Challenge**, a program of incentives to encourage residents to reduce single-occupant car trips and walk, bike, or take public transit whenever possible. Some families choose to share a single car; some people become members of a **car sharing** service such as Zipcar (206-682-0107, www.zipcar.com), which affords you access to a vehicle when you need it minus the expense of owning, insuring, and maintaining one.

However, such measures may not be practical for you. Another way to limit the amount of time you spend behind the wheel is to live in a neighborhood that's close to your workplace, or you can choose housing in proximity to a mass transit hub, so you can ride public transportation to work. (See also the **Transportation** chapter, which lists all local sources of public transit, along with many municipal resources geared to help commuters stay out of their vehicles.) If you must drive, you can purchase a fuel-efficient vehicle, such as a **hybrid**, which are now made by most car manufacturers. In Washington, individuals who purchase or lease high-mileage hybrid vehicles or cars powered by clean alternative fuels are exempt from certain sales and use taxes (visit http://dor.wa.gov; 800-647-7706 for more information) through 2016. In addition, Washington is one of six states participating in the EV Project, a federally (public-private) funded program to promote the use of **electric vehicles**. ECOtality, Inc., the company in charge of the project, is busy installing 14,000 of its Blink charging stations nationwide, thanks to a cooperative effort between the City of Seattle, Washington State, and the Obama administration. In 2011, the city's first public charging stations for electric vehicles were installed at CenturyLink Field. Drivers who own a Nissan Leaf or a Chevy Volt can use an app on their smart phone or PDA to locate the nearest Blink recharging station. No matter what type of car you drive, regular maintenance will help it burn fuel more efficiently and pollute less. If you're in the market for an auto club, you might consider joining the **Better World Club** (866-238-1137; www.betterworldclub.com). Based in Portland, this alternative to AAA is the nation's only eco-friendly roadside assistance service for cars and bikes.

ALTERNATIVE FUELS

As part of its larger pro-environmental agenda, Seattle has purchased hybrids and converted to using alternative fuels in many city-owned vehicles such as trucks and fire engines. In 2010, the city's Green Fleet won first place in a nationwide competition. Originally, the city of Seattle used **biodiesel** to power many of its vehicles. Biodiesel is produced from a variety of renewable resources including waste vegetable oils, animal fats, cooking oil, and soybean oil. The most commonly used form is B20, which is a blend of 20% biodiesel and 80% petroleum fuel, and most diesel engines can handle this with little or no adaptations. In 2009, in response to emerging evidence that its production may actually be worse for the environment than gasoline, the city put a hold on its biodiesel purchases. The city has also invested in a program that uses **electricity** to power its Green Fleet, and plans to add 35 Nissan Leafs to its motor pool by 2012. Seattle Children's Hospital, which runs the largest vanpool program in the United States, recently added the nation's first electric vehicle vanpools to its fleet. Electrically charged Segways are used for tasks such as parking enforcement and meter reading. Seattle also maintains an aging fleet of 159 electric trolley buses, a legacy of the old Seattle Transit system, which run on fourteen routes, connected to a rather unsightly grid of overhead wires. Replacement of these vehicles, either with new trolley buses or by diesel-hybrids, will begin in 2014. Two useful sources for information about alternative fuels include **Puget Sound Clean Cities Coalition** (206-689-4055; www.wwcleancities.org) and the **Seattle Electric Vehicle Association** (www.seattleeva.org).

GREEN RESOURCES

The following organizations represent just a select few of the multitude of resources on sustainability and environmental protection available in Seattle and its surrounding communities:

- **Cascadia Green Building Council**, 206-223-2028, http://cascadiabc.org; this chapter of the U.S. Green Building Council promotes green building by forging alliances with other environmentally progressive organizations.
- **The Community Coalition for Environmental Justice**, 206-720-0285, www.ccej.com, works to ensure that low-income people and people of color have equal access to environmental quality and services.
- **Earthshare Washington**, 206-622-9840, www.esw.org, promotes environmental education, volunteerism, and charitable giving by partnering with businesses across the state.
- **Environment New Service**, www.ens-newswire.com, an independently owned and operated international wire service that presents late-breaking environmental news in a fair and balanced manner.
- **Futurewise**, 206-343-0681, www.futurewise.org, a statewide public interest group working to promote healthy communities and cities while protecting farmland, forests, and shorelines today and for future generations.
- **The Green Seattle Partnership**, http://greenseattle.org, a public-private partnership formed in 2004 between the City of Seattle and the Cascade Land Conservancy, to create a sustainable network of forest parkland throughout the city.
- **Greendrinks**, www.greendrinks.org, is an informal social networking group for environmentalists and people interested in environmental issues.
- **Founded in 1906, The Mountaineers**, 206-521-6000, www.mountaineers.org, is the largest membership group in the Puget Sound Region for people interested in preserving, enjoying, and exploring the outdoors and wilderness areas. The club sponsors a wide range of social, and education outdoor activities.
- **The Nature Consortium**, 206-923-0853, www.naturec.org, is a grassroots organization committed to connecting people, the arts, and nature.
- **The Northwest EcoBuilding Guild**, 206-575-222, www.ecobuilding.org, a community of homeowners, builders, suppliers, and designers that encourages green building practices by providing open-source building materials to the construction industry and the public.
- **The city of Seattle's Office of Sustainability and Environment**, 700 5th Ave, #2748, 206-615-0817, www.seattle.gov/environment, information about sustainable urban planning and waste and toxics reduction, and how to reduce your environmental impact.

- **The Seattle Chefs Collaborative**, www.seattlechefs.org, works with chefs and the great food community to celebrate local foods and foster a more sustainable food supply.
- **The Sierra Club,** maintains a Green Home Provider list of businesses with green credentials (www.sierraclubgreenhome.com). A service or retailer must pass an application review to be listed as a **SCGH GreenCheck Provider**. Be advised that the program ultimately depends upon consumer verifications and is not an official accreditation process.
- **TreeHugger.com**, www.treehugger.com, is a source of green news and product information dedicated to making sustainability mainstream.
- **The Washington Environmental Council**, 206-631-2600, www.wecprotects.org, is an excellent resource for environmental news and information about current legislation.

F YOU NEED TEMPORARY QUARTERS WHILE YOU ARE LOOKING FOR A place to live, Seattle offers a variety of options. Those planning on staying in temporary housing for more than a couple of weeks should consider a sublet or short-term lease. Apartment sublets are often advertised in classifieds, particularly during the spring and summer when college students head out of town. The apartment search firms listed in the **Finding a Place to Live** chapter can assist you with finding a short-term lease, or see below under the Short Term Leases and Residence Hotels and Summer Only sections. For additional lodging options, and to get a packet of information on accommodations in Seattle or surrounding communities, try Seattle's Convention and Visitors Bureau (701 Pike Street, 206-461-5800, 866-732-2695, www.visitseattle.org) or the Washington State Department of Tourism (800-544-1800, www.experiencewa.com).

HOTELS AND MOTELS

As a port city, business hub, and tourist destination, Seattle has a large number of hotels and motels offering various levels of service and facilities. In general, the least expensive motels are those along Aurora Avenue North (Highway 99) north of downtown. These lodgings come with the security risks inherent to the high crime area of Aurora. They generally are not suitable for children or for adults uncomfortable with fast-paced urban settings, and for that reason are not listed here.

The following list of hotels and motels is by no means complete. For a more comprehensive listing, check the Yellow Pages under "Hotels and Other Accommodations" or search online. For up-to-the-minute room availability in Bellevue, Kent, Lynnwood, Renton, and Seattle, call **Seattle Hotel Reservations** at 888-254-0637 or visit www.seattle-hotel-reservation.com. **Hotel Hotline** is another reservation service. Call 800-311-4307 or visit www.hotelhotline.com. **AAA** travel guides are a good source for hotel and motel recommendations. Free to members, their listings are useful because AAA weeds out those hotels that are not up to their standards. **Quikbook** is a national, discount room-reservation service that costs nothing to join. It offers reduced room rates for many hotels. For a list of cities and hotels, and information about them, call 800-789-9887 or visit www.quikbook.com. Other companies include **Hotels.com** (800-246-8357, www.hotels.com) and the online discount travel companies **Expedia** (877-787-7186, www.expedia.com), **Orbitz** (888-656-4546, www.orbitz.com), and **Travelocity** (888-872-8356, www.travelocity.com).

Hotel prices fluctuate, based on the season, special events, and vacancy rates. Call ahead for reservations, and be sure to ask about special discounts or business rates. Often, hotels will offer a special "Internet only" rate, so be sure to check websites before you book.

LUXURY LODGINGS

A room at one of the following hotels costs $250 or more per night.

SEATTLE

- **Alexis Hotel**, 1007 1st Ave, 206-624-4844, reservations: 866-356-8894, www.alexishotel.com
- **The Edgewater Hotel**, 2411 Alaskan Way, 206-728-7000, 800-624-0670, www.edgewaterhotel.com
- **Fairmont Olympic Hotel**, 411 University St, 206-621-1700, 888-363-5022, www.fairmont.com/seattle
- **Hotel Monaco**, 1101 4th Ave, 206-621-1770, 800-715-6513, www.monaco-seattle.com
- **Hotel Vintage Park**, 1100 5th Ave, 206-624-8000, 800-853-3914, www.hotelvintagepark.com
- **The Inn at the Market**, 86 Pine St, 206-443-3600, 800-446-4484, www.innatthemarket.com
- **Pan Pacific Hotel,** 2125 Terry Ave, 206-264-8111, www.panpacific.com
- **Red Lion Hotel on Fifth Avenue**, 1415 5th Ave, 206-971-8000 or 800-325-4000, www.seattleredlionfifthavenue.com
- **The Sorrento Hotel**, 900 Madison St, 206-622-6400, 800-426-1265, www.hotelsorrento.com
- **W Hotel Seattle**, 1112 4th Ave, 206-264-6000, 877-WHOTELS, www.whotels.com

MIDDLE-RANGE LODGINGS

These hotels charge between $150 and $250 per night.

BELLEVUE

- **Courtyard by Marriott**, 11010 NE 8th St, 425-454-5888, www.marriott.com/bvudt
- **Hyatt Regency Bellevue**, 900 Bellevue Way NE, 425-462-1234, 800-233-1234, www.bellevue.hyatt.com

ISSAQUAH

- **Holiday Inn of Issaquah**, 1801 12th NW, 425-392-6421, 888-HOLIDAY, www.holidayinn.com

KIRKLAND

- **Comfort Inn**, 12204 NE 124th St, 425-821-8300, www.comfortinn.com
- **Courtyard by Marriott**, 11215 NE 124th St, 425-602-3200, 800-321-2211, www.marriott.com

REDMOND

- **Redmond Inn**, 17601 Redmond Way, 425-883-4900, 800-634-8080, www.redmondinn.com

RENTON

- **Holiday Inn Renton**, 1 S Grady Way, 425-226-7700, 800-860-7715, www.holidayinn.com

SEATTLE

- **The Arctic Club Seattle**, 700 3rd Ave, 206-340-0340, 800-222-TREE, http://doubletree1.hilton.com
- **Best Western Pioneer Square Hotel**, 77 Yesler Way, 206-340-1234, 800-800-5514, www.pioneersquare.com
- **Crowne Plaza**, 1113 6th Ave, 206-464-1980, 877-227-6963, www.ichotelsgroup.com
- **Hotel FIVE**, 2200 Fifth Ave, 206-441-9785, 866-866-7977, www.hotelfiveseattle.com
- **Mayflower Park Hotel**, 405 Olive Way, 206-623-8700, 800-426-5100, www.mayflowerpark.com
- **Renaissance Madison Hotel**, 515 Madison St, 206-583-0300, 888-236-2427, www.renaissancehotels.com
- **Sheraton Seattle Hotel & Towers**, 1400 6th Ave, 206-621-9000, 800-325-3535, www.sheraton.com/seattle
- **Silver Cloud Inn Lake Union**, 1150 Fairview Ave N, 206-447-9500, 800-330-5812, https://lakeunion.scinns.com
- **Silver Cloud Inn University District**, 5036 25th Ave NE, 206-526-5200, 800-205-6940, www.scinns.com/university

- **The Westin Seattle**, 1900 5th Ave, 206-728-1000, 800-937-8461, www.starwoodhotels.com/westin

BUDGET STAYS

You can stay at one of these hotels for less than $150.

BELLEVUE

- **Coast Bellevue Hotel**, 625 116th Ave, 425-455-9444, 800-716-6199, www.coasthotels.com
- **Hotel Sierra Bellevue**, 3244 139th Ave SE, 425-747-2705, 800-474-3772, www.hotel-sierra.com

BOTHELL

- **Comfort Inn & Suites**, 1414 228th St SE, 425-402-0900, 877-424-6423, www.comfortinn.com

EVERETT

- **Holiday Inn Downtown Everett**, 3105 Pine St, 425-339-2000, 888-HOLIDAY, www.holidayinn.com
- **La Quinta Inn Everett**, 12619 4th Ave W, 425-347-9099, 800-753-3757, www.lq.com

FEDERAL WAY

- **Best Western Plus Evergreen Inn and Suites**, 32124 25th Ave S, 253-529-4000, 800-780-7234, www.bestwestern.com
- **Comfort Inn**, 31622 Pacific Hwy S, 253-529-0101, 877-424-6423, www.comfortinn.com

KENT

- **Comfort Inn**, 22311 84th S, 253-872-2211, www.comfortinn.com
- **Hawthorn Suites,** 6329 S 212nd St, 253-395-3800, 800-337-0160, www.hawthorn.com

KIRKLAND

- **Baymont Inn**, 12223 NE 116th, 425-822-2300, 800-337-0550, www.baymontinns.com

LYNNWOOD

- **Hampton Inn & Suites**, 19324 Alderwood Mall Pkwy, 425-771-1888, 877-771-8555, www.hamptonseattlenorth.com

SEATTLE

- **Best Western Loyal Inn**, 2301 8th Ave, 206-682-0200, 800-780-7234, www.bestwestern.com
- **Hotel Seattle**, 315 Seneca St, 206-623-5110, 800-426-2439, www.thehotelseattle.com
- **Inn at Queen Anne**, 505 1st Ave N, 206-282-7357, 800-952-5043, www.innatqueenanne.com
- **Travelodge Seattle Center**, 200 6th Ave N, 866-446-4151, www.travelodgeseattlecenter.com
- **Travelodge University**, 4725 25th Ave NE, 206-525-4612, 888-637-4859, www.travelodge.com
- **University Inn**, 4140 Roosevelt Way NE, 206-632-5055, 866-866-7977, www.universityinnseattle.com

TUKWILA

- **Best Western River's Edge**, 15901 West Valley Hwy, 425-226-1812, 800-780-7234, www.bestwestern.com

SHORT-TERM LEASES AND RESIDENCE HOTELS

The following hotels and leasing companies offer full suites for rent by the day, week or month. Rooms include a kitchen or kitchenette, living room, and bedroom. Often maid service and other amenities are available.

- **Aboda Corporate Housing**, 425-861-0500, 888-389-0500, www.aboda.com
- **Accommodations Plus**, 425-455-2773, 800-583-1613, www.aplusnw.com
- **Alternative Suites International**, 206-860-1616, 888-900-4050, www.asuites.com
- **Homewood Suites**, 206 Western Ave W, 206-281-9393, 800-CALL-HOME, http://homewoodsuites1.hilton.com
- **Oakwood Corporate Housing**, 877-969-5142, www.oakwood.com
- **Pacific Guest Suites**, 425-454-7888, 800-962-6620, www.pacificguestsuites.com
- **University Motel Suites**, 4731 12th Ave NE, 206-522-4724, 800-522-4720, www.university-hotel.com

BED & BREAKFASTS

If you're in the mood for quaint or cozy, consider a bed and breakfast. Most of Seattle's B&Bs are outside the downtown area, so this may also be a good way to check out prospective neighborhoods. You may contact the inn directly (listed below), or try one of the local or national bed and breakfast registries. Locally, call **Seattle Bed & Breakfast Association** (206-547-1020, 800-348-5630, www.lodginginseattle.com), **Bed & Breakfast Association of Suburban Seattle** (www.seattlebestbandb.com), or **Pacific Reservation Service** (206-439-7677, 800-684-2932, www.seattlebedandbreakfast.com). Other sites include **InnSite** (www.innsite.com) and **Bed and Breakfast Inns Online** (www.bbonline.com).

- **11th Avenue Inn**, 121 11th Ave E, 206-669-4373, 800-370-8414, www.11thavenueinn.com
- **Bacon Mansion**, 959 Broadway E, 206-329-1864, 800-240-1864, www.baconmansion.com
- **Chambered Nautilus Bed & Breakfast**, 5005 22nd Ave NE, 206-522-2536, 800-545-8459, www.chamberednautilus.com
- **Chelsea Station Inn**, 4915 Linden Ave N, 206-547-6077, 800-400-6077, www.chelseastationinn.com
- **Gaslight Inn**, 1727 15th Ave, 206-325-3654, www.gaslight-inn.com
- **Mildred's Bed & Breakfast**, 1202 15th Ave E, 206-325-6072, 800-327-9692, www.mildredsbnb.com
- **9 Cranes Inn**, 5717 Palatine Ave N, 206-855-5222, www.9cranesinn.com
- **Sleeping Bulldog Bed & Breakfast**, 816 19th Ave S, 206-325-0202, www.sleepingbulldog.com
- **Villa Heidelberg Bed & Breakfast**, 4845 45th Ave SW, 206-938-3658, 800-671-2942, www.villaheidelberg.com
- **Wildwood Bed & Breakfast**, 4518 SW Wildwood Place, 206-819-9075, 800-840-8410, www.wildwoodseattle.com

ALTERNATIVE LODGINGS

HOSTELS

Hostels offer basic accommodations at low prices, but there are a few restrictions. Generally, you should expect to sleep in a shared room and use a common bathroom and shower, although some have private rooms at a higher price. Some hostels require membership in an international hostelling association, some restrict the number of nights you can stay, or limit the time that you can be in the hostel during the day. The wisest course is to call in advance to make sure that you qualify (and that you'll be happy with the house rules).

- **City Hostel Seattle,** 2327 2nd Ave, 206-706-3255, 877-8HOSTEL, www.cityhostelseattle.com
- **Green Tortoise Hostel**, 105-1/2 Pike St, 206-340-1222, 888-424-6783, www.greentortoise.net
- **Hostelling International**, 520 S King St, 206-622-5443, www.hiusa.org

WASHINGTON ATHLETIC CLUB

The Inn at the Washington Athletic Club offers hotel rooms for members of reciprocal clubs across the country, and their guests. Rates vary depending on membership status and time of year. For more information, or a list of reciprocal clubs, call 206-622-7900 or visit www.wac.net.

SUMMER ONLY

Summer housing on Seattle-area campuses is restricted to students, visiting conference attendees, and special-interest groups. If you're looking for an apartment or rental house in which to spend the summer (which *is* the best time of year in Seattle), concentrate your efforts in university neighborhoods where students vacate from June to September. The University District, adjacent to the University of Washington, is a good place to start. Also consider the Fremont area near Seattle Pacific University. Short-term and seasonal housing opportunities are listed in the classifieds section of *The Seattle Times* (www.seattletimes.com) and in the *Seattle Weekly* (www.seattleweekly.com) under "Vacation/Seasonal Rentals." Many listings for short-term housing can also be found on craiglist (http://seattle.craigslist.org) under "Sublets/Temporary" and "Vacation Rentals."

A FTER YOU'VE FOUND A HOME AND HAVE SETTLED IN A BIT, YOU'LL probably want to explore outside Seattle. The communities of the Puget Sound area and western Washington are wonderful places to visit. Just a short drive away (five hours at most) you'll discover mountain peaks, lush valleys, azure lakes and streams, delightful fields of flowers, and picturesque farms. For general travel information and a tourism packet, call the Washington State Tourism Office at 800-544-1800 or visit www.experiencewa.com.

Most of the locations listed in this chapter offer a variety of activities, lodgings, and other attractions. For information on outdoor sports like hiking, fishing, and skiing, read the **Sports and Recreation** chapter of this book. See also **Outdoor Guides** in **A Seattle Reading List**.

WHIDBEY ISLAND, SAN JUAN ISLANDS

Whidbey Island, northwest of Seattle, is one of the two longest islands in the United States (Long Island and Whidbey Island trade the honor back and forth as their measurements change with erosion). Whidbey Island is most easily reached by ferry from Mukilteo, but a longer route through Mount Vernon and Anacortes can save you the ferry fare. Whidbey has several picturesque towns, such as **Coupeville** and **Oak Harbor**. While visiting, make sure you try some mussels in a local seafood restaurant, and take the time to drive to **Deception Pass**, at the north end of the island. The view from the bridge is stunning, though not recommended for those afraid of heights. For a free **Island County Discovery Guide** and other tourist information, call 888-747-7777, or visit www.islandweb.org.

The **San Juan Islands** are reached by ferry, either from Anacortes or Bellingham, and are worth the trip. If possible, give yourself a long weekend or several days; the wait for the ferry can take several hours, especially on a holiday or summer weekend. There are several islands in the San Juans worth visiting, each with breathtaking views. Stay in a quaint bed and breakfast or hotel, or check for vacation rentals on the Internet or in Seattle newspapers. Camping is also available in the breathtaking Moran State Park on Orcas Island. You'll find secluded beaches, cozy coffee shops, and charming towns. If possible, take your bike or kayak, and tour the islands that way. Ferry rides between islands, especially if you're walking or taking a bicycle, are inexpensive, but you'll want to make sure that the dock is close enough to town, or you might be in for a long haul. For more information, contact the **Orcas Island Chamber of Commerce** at 360-376-2273 or http://orcasislandchamber.com, **San Juan Island Chamber of Commerce** at 360-378-5240 or www.sanjuanisland.org, **Lopez Island Chamber of Commerce** at 360-468-4664 or www.lopezisland.com, or the **San Juan Islands Visitors Bureau** at www.visitsanjuans.com, where you can download a free visitors guide.

SKAGIT VALLEY

Skagit Valley, located only a couple hours north of Seattle, is famous for its tulips, producing more of the flowers than the Netherlands. During the spring and summer, thousands of visitors come to the valley to see the colorful tulip fields. The entire month of April is given over to the Skagit Valley Tulip Festival. In addition to viewing acres of waving tulips, be sure to visit nearby **La Conner** or **Mount Vernon**. La Conner is a captivating village, with intimate cafés, homemade ice cream and candy shops, and scrumptious bakeries. A few antique malls on the edges of town attract Seattle collectors as well. Mount Vernon offers several antique malls, delicious eateries, and a local brewpub with excellent food. The Skagit Valley is also a well-known haven for artists, with the **Museum of Northwest Art** located in La Conner: 360-466-4446, www.museumofnwart.org. For more information, call the **Skagit Valley Tulip Festival Office** at 360-428-5959, or visit www.tulipfestival.org.

VICTORIA, VANCOUVER, AND HARRISON HOT SPRINGS, B.C.

Located on the southern tip of Vancouver Island, **Victoria, B.C.,** is a direct ferry ride from the Seattle Waterfront on the *Victoria Clipper*. It's a small but appealing city, with a lively waterfront and beautiful gardens. The **Butchart Gardens** in particular are worth a visit. Bus tours leave for the gardens several times a day from the waterfront. Children will enjoy the wax museum with its replicas of famous and historical figures. A trip to Victoria isn't complete without afternoon tea at the Empress Hotel, which presides over the waterfront. For visitor information call **Tourism Victoria** at 250-953-2033 or visit www.tourismvictoria.com.

A three-hour drive north of Seattle on I-5, **Vancouver, B.C.**, is a cosmopolitan port city offering great dining and shopping, including an extensive underground mall and Robson Street, which is lined with fashionable clothing boutiques, trendy cosmetics stores, and unique beauty and bath shops. Visit **Granville Island** for a bustling farmers' market during the day or live music and dancing at night. Rent bicycles and pack a picnic lunch to ride through beautiful **Stanley Park**, which overlooks the shipping activity in the bay. Music concerts and live theater performances draw many Seattle residents to Vancouver, since many tours stop at only one of the two cities. For more information, call 604-682-2222 or visit www.tourismvancouver.com.

If you're in the mood to relax and get away from the big city pace, consider a trip to the sleepy resort town of **Harrison Hot Springs, B.C.** From any point in this small town, you'll have a spectacular view of Harrison Lake and surrounding mountains. During spring and summer, you can charter a fishing boat, take a cruise on the lake, play golf, go parasailing, play tennis, swim in the lake or the public hot springs, hike, water ski, windsurf, or go horseback riding. Harrison Hot Springs is just a little more than four hours away from Seattle. A stay at the Harrison Hot Springs Resort offers a soak in private hot springs pools and complimentary high tea. For additional information on the town and neighboring communities call the **Harrison Hot Springs Chamber of Commerce** at 604-796-5581 or visit www.harrison.ca.

EAST OF THE CASCADES

Located on Highway 2 on the east side of the Cascade Mountains, Washington's own Bavarian village, **Leavenworth,** attracts many visitors. During the summer, the town is a destination for novice rock climbers, who scale boulders along Icicle Creek. In the fall, Leavenworth presents the music-filled and beer-soaked Oktoberfest celebration. In winter, the village offers nearby skiing at Stevens Pass, as well as Christmas festivals and concerts. For more information, or to order a guide, contact the **Leavenworth Chamber of Commerce** at 509-548-5807 or visit www.leavenworth.org.

Also east of the Cascades, **Lake Chelan** is a favorite among sun-seekers and water enthusiasts. The area is a favorite family destination, with plenty of water-based activities and houseboat rentals. At the southern tip of the lake, the town of Lake Chelan offers crowded bars, casual restaurants, and sporting goods shops. Condominiums and motels line the lakeshore, and there is public camping at nearby parks. Call ahead for reservations, though, because the area is usually packed during the summer months. At the northern tip of the lake, the tiny town of **Stehekin** is reachable only by ferry or boat from Chelan and is favored by hikers and those wishing a quieter vacation. For additional tourist information call 800-4-CHELAN, 509-682-3503, or go to www.lakechelan.org.

OLYMPIC PENINSULA AND MOUNTAINS

A short ferry ride across Puget Sound, the **Olympic Peninsula** has something for everyone. **Poulsbo** is a small Scandinavian-style village located 30 minutes east of the Bainbridge ferry terminal. Stop in for a fabulous donut at Sluys Poulsbo Bakery, home of the original recipe for Poulsbo Bread.

Drive south on Highway 101 along **Hood Canal** for scenic little fishing towns like **Quilcene,** clamming and oyster beaches, and spectacular vistas from **Mt. Walker.** Heading north on Highway 101, you'll find **Port Townsend**, where *An Officer and a Gentleman* was filmed. It features historic buildings, antique stores, unusual boutiques, and kite shops, and you can also catch a ferry to Whidbey Island from downtown.

Port Angeles, at the northern tip of the peninsula, offers ferry service to Victoria, B.C. **Hurricane Ridge**, located only 15 minutes away from Port Angeles, is always worth a visit. The mountaintop views from the ridge are sensational, even if you only drive to the parking lot and visitors' center. **Sequim** is famous for its fields of lavender and as the sunniest town in Western Washington, receiving only 16 inches of rain a year.

Nestled in the Olympic National Park, **Sol Duc Hot Springs**, 866-476-5382, www.olympicnationalparks.com, has cabins and a campground for visitors. Soak in the beautiful outdoor pools, take a short hike to the Sol Duc waterfall, or arrange for a massage from on-site massage therapists. Another short drive takes you to secluded **Ruby Beach**, one of the nicest sandy beaches on the Washington Coast. For more information on the Olympic Peninsula, visit the **Olympic Peninsula Visitor Bureau** at www.olympicpeninsula.org.

If you are interested in hiking or mountain climbing, get a copy of one of the many hiking guides to the Olympics. (See the **Literary Life** section of the **Cultural Life** chapter for a list of area bookstores.) If you enjoy mountain climbing, two mountains on the Peninsula are especially challenging: The Brothers is the twin-peaked mountain that is easily visible from Seattle, and Mount Olympus, while it cannot be seen from the city, is the tallest mountain in the Olympic range. To climb to the summit of either of these peaks, contact a local mountain climbing club or guide service (see the **Sports and Recreation** chapter for listings). Happily, there are many more hikes in the Olympics that are manageable for the average person. For information on **Olympic National Park**, call 360-565-3130 or visit www.nps.gov/olym.

THE COAST

A popular summer destination along the coast is the tourist town of **Ocean Shores**. Hotels line the beach, and popular activities include horseback riding on the beach, driving on the beach, beachcombing, kite flying, and a Fourth of July fireworks show over the ocean. For a free visitors guide, call the **Ocean Shores Chamber of Commerce** at 360-289-2451 or visit www.oceanshores.org. In the mood for a picturesque beach resort town and spectacular ocean view? Try either the southwest Washington coast or northern Oregon coast. **Long Beach**, at the far southwest tip of Washington, is said to be the world's longest beach. Several annual events are held in Long Beach, such as an international kite-flying festival, regional stunt kite competition, sand sculpture contest, and Fourth of July fireworks celebration. Contact the **Long Beach Peninsula Visitor's Bureau** at 360-642-2400 or 800-451-2542, or visit www. funbeach.com.

Across the mouth of the Columbia, the Oregon coast offers a stretch of beautiful beaches and ocean surf. **Seaside** is the best known destination, with affordable beach cottages and hotels and access to an expanse of white sandy beach. Other nearby towns attract fewer visitors, a plus for those in search of a private stretch of beach or a romantic getaway. If that's your preference, rent a cottage in **Gearhart** or reserve a room overlooking the ocean in **Cannon Beach**. For more information on these and other Oregon destinations, call the **Oregon Tourism Commission** at 800-547-7842 or visit www.traveloregon.com. The drive to Long Beach from Seattle is about four hours; Seattle to Seaside takes four to five hours, even in Friday rush hour traffic. If possible, give yourself a long weekend, but expect more crowds if it's a holiday.

MOUNT RAINIER

Majestic **Mount Rainier** will be a familiar sight soon after you move here, and definitely worth a visit. During the winter, **Crystal Mountain Ski Resort** bustles with activity while the rest of the mountain is deserted. In early spring, however, the roads begin to re-open and visitors flock to the area to hike, mountain climb, and camp. Many start their hikes from the mountain's most visited site, **Paradise,** which hosts a visitor center and historic lodge. Mount Rainier is a challenging hiking or climbing destination even for experienced climbers. Some short hikes near the base of the mountain are suitable for the average recreational hiker; look in a good hiking book or trail guide for details. For anything other than a day hike on a well-marked trail be sure to research your route carefully and take an experienced outdoorsman or guide with you. If you're interested in climbing to the summit, contact a local mountain climbing club or guide service (several are listed in the **Sports and Recreation** chapter). Don't let the beauty of the Cascades and Olympics fool you; people get lost and some die every year climbing mountains in Washington. For more information, call **Mount Rainier National Park** at 360-569-2211 or visit the National Park Service's Mount Rainier website at www.nps.gov/mora.

S PEND A YEAR IN SEATTLE AND THE DELIGHTFUL MIX OF EVENTS THAT take place here will amaze you. Residents embrace the few months of sunshine and the long, wet winter months with a variety of music, food, and arts festivals, and sporting events. Below is a list of annual highlights you won't want to miss. Unless otherwise noted, al events are held in Seattle. To find smaller events, and happenings in communities outside of Seattle, check your local newspaper or visit www.nwsource.com.

JANUARY

- **Martin Luther King, Jr. Celebration**—206-296-1002, www.mlkseattle.org; this annual celebration features a rally, a march, workshops, music, and entertainment.
- **Seattle Boat Show**—CenturyLink Field Event Center, 206-634-0911, www. seattleboatshow.com; the Northwest Marine Trade Association sponsors this annual event for boat enthusiasts and prospective buyers.
- **Seattle Wedding Show**—Washington State Convention & Trade Center, 425-744-6509, www.weddingshow.com; prospective brides flock to this event showcasing everything from gowns to honeymoons.

FEBRUARY

- **Lunar New Year Celebration**—Chinatown/International District, 206-382-1197, www.cidbiast.org; this traditional Chinese festival includes a colorful parade.
- **Festival Sundiata**—Seattle Center, 206-329-8086, www.festivalsundiata. org; this annual celebration commemorates African and African-American culture, history, and art, with exhibits and live performances.

- **Mardi Gras**—Pioneer Square, 206-622-2563 (New Orleans Creole Restaurant); Seattle's very own Fat Tuesday celebration takes place in bars throughout the city's historic district.
- **Northwest Flower and Garden Show**—Washington State Convention Center, 253-756-2121, www.gardenshow.com; a gardener's paradise, featuring seminars, displays, workshops, and vendors.
- **Seattle Home Show**—CenturyLink Field Event Center, 425-467-0960, www.seattlehomeshow.com; homeowners find thousands of ideas for improving their homes inside and out.
- **Seattle RV & Outdoor Recreation Show**—CenturyLink Field Event Center, 425-277-8132, www.mhrvshows.com; discover the biggest, newest, and best in recreational vehicles and outdoor recreation.
- **Vietnamese Lunar New Year Celebration**—Seattle Center, 206-706-2658, www.tetinseattle.org; the Vietnamese community celebrates Tet, its most important festival of the year.

MARCH

- **Daffodils in Bloom Celebration**—La Conner, 888-642-9284, www.laconnerchamber.com; fields ablaze with yellow blossoms are found just a short drive from Seattle.
- **Irish Week Festival**—Seattle Center, 206-223-3608, www.irishclub.org; sponsored by the Irish Heritage Club, this family festival celebrates St. Patrick's Day by presenting Irish films, history, dancing, language workshops, and a festive parade through downtown Seattle.
- **Moisture Festival**—Hale's Brewery in Fremont and other venues, 206-297-1405, www.moisturefestival.com; in celebration of the region's damp spring, performers at this annual neovaudeville show include aerialists, jugglers, magicians, torch singers, classically trained clowns, and the indescribable Godfrey Daniels. Early shows are for the whole family; later shows feature burlesque performances.
- **Seattle Bicycle Expo**—Warren G. Magnuson Park, 206-522-3222, www.cascade.org/expo; cycling enthusiasts enjoy exhibits, demonstrations, and presentations on all aspects of the sport.
- **VegFest**—Seattle Center, 206-706-2635, www.vegofwa.org; the largest event of its kind in the Northwest, where you can sample vegetarian food, watch cooking demos, and learn about the many benefits of a meat-free diet.
- **Whirligig**—Seattle Center, 206-684-7200, www.seattlecenter.com; the Seattle Center presents a fun-filled family event, with carnival activities for children.
- **Women's Show**—CenturyLink Field Event Center, 425-605-4131, www.nwwomenshow.com; fashion, fitness, and food combine to make this event a local favorite.

APRIL

- **Daffodil Festival**—253-840-4194, www.daffodilfestival.net; the highlight of this festival is the large parade that winds through the cities of Tacoma, Puyallup, Sumner and Orting.
- **Earth Day Puget Sound**—dozens of groups hold a variety of events throughout the region in recognition of Earth Day, including exhibits, activities, and music along Seattle's waterfront. Check your local newspaper for information.
- **Friends of the Seattle Public Library Book Sale**—Magnuson Park, 206-386-4098, www.splfriends.org; twice a year an enormous warehouse is converted into the biggest book sale in the city. Proceeds from the sale of books, art, music, and movies benefit the Seattle Public Library. While you'll find a separate section for appropriately priced rare and antique books, most items are a dollar or less.
- **MS Walk**—206-284-4254, http://walkwas.nationalmssociety.org; the MS Walk supports national research and local programs for people living with Multiple Sclerosis in western and central Washington.
- **Seattle Cherry Blossom Festival**—Seattle Center, 206-723-2003, www.seattlecenter.org; this annual festival celebrates both contemporary and traditional aspects of Japanese culture with artists, stage performances, children's entertainment, and exhibits.
- **Skagit Valley Tulip Festival**—Mount Vernon, 360-428-5959, www.tulipfestival.org; during the month of April, the Skagit Valley hosts the annual Tulip Festival, featuring tours of brilliantly colored fields of silky tulips, set against a backdrop of Mount Baker and the Cascade Mountains. Enjoy local art exhibits and special events, dine in local restaurants, visit nearby antique malls in La Conner or Mount Vernon, or send bulbs in your favorite colors to loved ones.
- **Take Our Daughters and Sons to Work Day**—800-676-7780, www.daughtersandsonstowork.org; organizations all over Puget Sound participate in this educational and fun day held on the fourth Thursday of every April.
- **World Rhythm Festival**—Seattle Center, www.swps.org, 206-684-7200; sponsored by the Seattle World Percussion Society, this three-day festival of drumming and dance celebrates percussive music from African, North and South American, Middle Eastern, and Indian traditions.

MAY

- **Bike to Work Month**—206-522-3222, www.cbcef.org; sponsored by the Cascade Bicycle Club, challenges, events, and lots of bike commuting are featured all month, with many area employers participating.
- **Chinese Culture and Arts Festival**—Seattle Center, 206-684-7200, www.seattlecenter.com; annually in May or early June, the Seattle Center hosts

two days of Chinese opera, dance, visual arts, ancient crafts, and children's activities.

- **Northwest Folklife Festival**—Seattle Center, 206-684-7300, www.nwfolklife. org; held every Memorial Day weekend, the Folklife Festival celebrates the folk arts communities of the Northwest. This popular and free event offers a blend of world music and dance performance, arts and crafts exhibits, musical and artistic workshops, and films and demonstrations focusing on multicultural and folk heritage in the Northwest.
- **Opening Day**—206-325-1000, www.seattleyachtclub.org; on the first Saturday of May, the Seattle Yacht Club sponsors the Opening Day celebration, which marks the first official day of the summer boating season, a Seattle tradition since 1909. Hundreds of gaudily decorated pleasure boats parade through the Montlake Cut and then tie up to one another in Lake Washington to watch the Windermere Cup rowing race. Even if you don't own a boat, you can enjoy the spectacle from the Montlake Bridge or from the sloping sides of the cut.
- **Pike Place Market Festival**—Pike Place Market, 206-682-7453, www.pikeplacemarket.org; held each Memorial Day weekend to celebrate the arrival of summer, this event features music stages, Northwest food and craft vendors, and beer and coffee gardens.
- **Seattle Cheese Festival**—Pike Place Market, www.seattlecheesefestival. com; artisanal cheeses, such as the varieties produced at Beecher's in the Market, take center stage at this festival where the public and the food service industry gather to sample hundreds of local and international cheeses. Other festival offerings include cheese-making demos, informative seminars and panels, and a wine garden.
- **Seattle Green Festival**—CenturyLink Field Event Center, 800-58-GREEN, www.greenfestivals.org/seattle; at this event devoted to sustainable practices and social justice you can learn about green building, green business, fair trade, and renewable energy, and find out how to repurpose your old computer. In 2010, the festival diverted 88% of its waste from winding up in a landfill.
- **Seattle Maritime Festival**—Seattle Waterfront, 206-787-3163, www.seattlepropellerclub.org; this annual event, held mostly on Pier 66, features the largest tugboat race in the world.
- **Syttende Mai**—Ballard, 206-930-3690, www.17thofmay.org; this annual Scandinavian festival is held in the Ballard neighborhood to commemorate Norwegian Constitution Day.
- **University District Street Fair**—University District, 206-547-4417, www.udistrictchamber.org; several blocks of University Way are closed to traffic for the longest running street fair in the nation, which features arts and crafts kiosks, music and dance performances, and lots of great food.

JUNE

- **Edmonds Arts Festival**—Frances Anderson Cultural Center, Edmonds, 425-771-6412, www.edmondsartsfestival.com; this free festival 20 miles north of Seattle attracts more than 75,000 spectators over Father's Day weekend.
- **Fremont Fair**—Fremont, 206-694-6706, www.fremontfair.com; located in "The Center of the Universe," as Fremont is fondly called, this festival features nude bicyclists and unusually costumed participants celebrating the summer solstice with a rowdy Solstice Parade, art booths, food, and music.
- **Georgetown Carnival**—Georgetown, www.georgetowncarnival.com; start the summer off right in one of the city's quirkier neighborhoods, with live music, a freak show, bicycle jousting, a trailer park mall, and other curiosities.
- **Komen Race for the Cure**—CenturyLink Field Event Center, 206-633-0303, www.komenpugetsound.org; proceeds from this popular 5K run fund research efforts and local breast health and breast cancer outreach efforts.
- **Lake Union Wooden Boat Festival**—the Center for Wooden Boats, 206-382-2628, www.cwb.org; in June or early July, maritime experts and wooden boats gather at the south end of Lake Union.
- **Olympic Music Festival**—360-732-4800, http://olympicmusicfestival.org; every Saturday and Sunday from June until September, thousands flock to rural Quilcene to hear "concerts in the Barn." Music performed in this pastoral setting is broadcast on Seattle's local classical station KING 98.1 FM and on NPR.
- **Out to Lunch Concert Series**—206-623-0340, www.downtownseattleevents.com; held at venues in downtown Seattle from noon to 1:30, beginning in June through July, this intimate concert series produced by the Downtown Seattle Association attracts many popular musicians and is free to the public.
- **Pagdiriwang**—Seattle Center, 206-684-7200, www.seattlecenter.com; a celebration of Philippine culture, this festival includes music, dance, and dramatic performances.
- **Seattle Pride**—Seattle Center, 206-322-9561, www.seattlepride.org; the Seattle Pride march, parade, and celebration are boisterous events that take place on the last weekend in June. The downtown parade ends at the Seattle Center where the celebration continues. Parade participants range from politicians to "dykes on bikes."
- **Zoo Tunes**—Woodland Park Zoo, 206-548-2688, www.zoo.org/zootunes; kid-friendly outdoor concerts on the Woodland Park Lawn, featuring acts like Taj Mahal and the Go-Gos, are held beginning in June through August, with each ticket good for one adult's and one child's admission.

JULY

- **Ballard Seafood Fest**—Ballard, 206-784-9705, www.seafoodfest.org; you'll find Viking helmets, salmon burgers, and a lutefisk-eating contest at this annual weekend celebration of Ballard's Scandinavian heritage and maritime history.
- **Bellevue Arts Fair**—Bellevue, 425-519-0770, www.bellevuearts.org; artists from across the country exhibit their work at the most successful arts and crafts festival in the Pacific Northwest.
- **Bite of Seattle**—Seattle Center, 425-295-3262, www.comcastbiteofseattle. com; "The Bite" showcases local restaurants, microbreweries, wineries, and coffeehouses. Local merchants and artisans open small booths to display and sell their wares, and musicians, jugglers, and other performers provide outdoor entertainment.
- **Capitol Hill Block Party**—South Capitol Hill, http://capitolhillblockparty. com; this three-day street party showcases over 70 of the best young Northwest bands and deejays on three stages, along with food and craft booths.
- **Chinatown International District Summer Festival**—Hing Hay Park, 206-382-1197, www.cidbiast.org; The ID, also known as the International District, celebrates summer with cultural entertainment, internationalth foods, arts and crafts, and community booths.
- **Family 4th**—Gasworks Park, Lake Union, 206-281-7788, http://familyfourth. org; the annual fireworks spectacular that *Time* magazine called one of the nation's "Top Five Fireworks Displays" takes place above Lake Union near downtown. Music blasting from large speakers in Gasworks Park accompanies the brilliant display. People fill the park to capacity, and other viewpoints along the lake are usually full of onlookers as well.
- **King County Fair**—King County Fairgrounds, Enumclaw, www.thekingcountyfair.com; Washington's oldest county fair includes nationally known entertainers, a professional rodeo, and all the usual fair fixin's.
- **Seafair**—206-728-0123, www.seafair.com; the Seafair festival begins in mid-July but lasts well into August, and offers something for everyone. The Milk Carton Derby at Green Lake, which usually kicks off Seafair, is a race of homemade boats kept afloat (or not) by milk cartons. A true community celebration, Seafair consists of numerous neighborhood festivals, kids' parades, and sidewalk sales. Athletic events include a triathlon and the Torchlight Run. Other events include the Annual Torchlight Parade, a performance by the Blue Angels, and the arrival of the Seafair Fleet—Naval and Coast Guard ships that can be toured on the Seattle Waterfront. The grand finale of this event is the Seafair hydroplane race (and qualifying races), which takes place on Lake Washington. During the races, Seward Park is packed, and everyone with access to a boat takes to the water to watch the excitement.

- **Seattle International Beerfest**—Seattle Center, 206-684-7200, www.seattlebeerfest.com; billed as "the ultimate world beer experience," connoisseurs of the suds can sample over 150 beers from over 15 different countries. One ticket allows re-entry on all three days of the festival, which includes live music. No kids allowed, but dogs are welcome.
- **Seattle to Portland Bicycle Classic**—206-522-3222, www.seattletoportland.com; the Cascade Bicycle Club annual ride is one of the best cycling events in the country, and covers more than 200 miles between Seattle and Portland, with up to 10,000 participants from all over the country and world.
- **Vashon Island Strawberry Festival**—Vashon Island, 206-463-6217, www.vashonchamber.com; though no longer carpeted with strawberry farms, Vashon still hosts a nostalgic three-day party in honor of the big red berry, complete with strawberry funnel cakes, carnival rides, classic cars, and a Grand Parade.

AUGUST

- **BrasilFest**—Seattle Center, 206-684-7200, www.brasilfest.com; this sultry celebration of South American soul and Brazilian style features performances, children's activities, workshops, and food.
- **Cambodian Cultural Heritage Celebration**—Seattle Center, 206-684-7200, www.seattlecenter.com; through storytelling, traditional music, dance, and crafts, learn about the customs and traditions of Cambodia.
- **Commencement Bay Maritime Fest**—Tacoma, 253-318-2210, www.maritimefest.org; dragon-boat races, a salmon bake, art show, harbor tours, and a two-day boat-building contest highlight this celebration of Tacoma's working waterfront. Sometimes held in September.
- **Danskin Triathlon**—www.danskintriathlon.net; thousands of women compete each August in the largest and longest-running triathlon series in multi-sport history. The annual event consists of a half-mile swim, 12-mile bike, and 3.1-mile run in and along Lake Washington.
- **Evergreen State Fair**—Monroe, 360-805-6700, www.evergreenfair.org; concerts and exhibits plus carnival and rodeo events pack twelve days in late August and early September.
- **Hempfest**—Myrtle Edwards Park, 206-781-5734, www.hempfest.com; attendees rally in support of legalized marijuana at the north end of the Seattle Waterfront.
- **Night Out**—206-684-2489; Seattle joins the rest of the country in promoting crime/drug prevention awareness. Residents turn on their porch lights and gather outdoors at block parties to strengthen neighborhood spirit and safety.
- **South Lake Union Block Party**—South Lake Union Discovery Center, 206-342-5900, www.slublockparty.com; scarf down a burger, get your face

painted, build your own boat, and watch a movie on the lawn at this fun-for-all party.

- **TibetFest**—Seattle Center, 206-684-7200, www.seattlecenter.com; this festival showcases Tibetan and Himalayan cultural arts, folk music, and dance.
- **Umoja Fest**—Central District, 877-505-6306, www.umojafamilyfest.com; Named after the Swahili word for "unity," this annual African heritage festival and parade features three days of live R&B, soul, jazz, blues, poetry and spoken word, fashion, dance, and more.

SEPTEMBER

- **Blackberry Festival**—Bremerton, 360-377-3041, www.blackberryfestival. org; Bremerton's waterfront is transformed every year during this three-day festival that includes a fun run, arts and crafts, music, and tons of blackberries.
- **Bumbershoot**—Seattle Center, 206-281-7788, www.bumbershoot.org; named after a slang term for umbrella, Bumbershoot is a Labor Day weekend event that has been a Seattle tradition since 1971. The festival that *Rolling Stone* magazine called "The Mother of All Arts Festivals" showcases more than 2,500 artists from all over the world, and draws more than 100,000 visitors each year. In addition to arts and crafts booths and dance performances, you'll find fortunetellers, street musicians, delicacies from local restaurants, and non-stop music concerts in multiple venues. The ticket price covers admittance to all of the exhibits and performances, but you'll need to stand in line to get seats for the headlining acts.
- **Fiestas Patrias**—Seattle Center, 206-903-0486, www.seattlefiestaspatrias. org; this Latin American cultural festival features traditional food, music, and dance performances.
- **Festa Italiana**—Seattle Center, 206-282-0627, www.festaseattle.com; this celebration showcases Italian food, music, art, and dance, including a bocce tournament, film festival, and a grape stomp competition.
- **Friends of the Seattle Public Library Book Sale**—Magnuson Park, 206-386-4098, www.splfriends.org; this is the fall installment of the popular biannual book sale, with over 200,000 items on sale.
- **Fremont Oktoberfest**—Fremont, 206-633-0422, www.fremontoktoberfest. com; as well as the mandatory beer garden, enjoy a fun run, live music, a carnival, and the highly popular chainsaw pumpkin carving contest.
- **Northwest AIDS Walk**—Volunteer Park, 206-328-8979, www.seattleaidswalk.org; this large and popular event supports the Lifelong AIDS Alliance.
- **PAWS Walk**—Magnuson Park, 425-412-4027, www.pawswalk.net; this festival for dogs and the people who love them includes a fundraising walk for the PAWS animal shelter, off-leash areas, contests, and canine-inspired artwork. You can also adopt a dog or get your dog microchipped.

- **The Puyallup Fair**—Puyallup Fairgrounds, 253-841-5045, www.thefair.com; also known as the Western Washington Fair, this event has been held in Puyallup (pyew-AL-lup) since 1900. If you decide to "do the Puyallup," give yourself a whole day. You'll want to sample a famous onion burger, tour a cattle barn, ride the roller coaster, watch a concert, and savor fresh corn on the cob. Or perhaps you'll decide to try your hand at bungee jumping, marvel at the hypnotist's skill, visit the prize-winning vegetable exhibit, and have several hot buttery scones. Don't assume this is a little country affair or you'll miss out on one of the best events of the year, and the biggest in the state. Puyallup is near Tacoma, less than an hour's drive from Seattle. The fair lasts for 2–3 weeks in September.
- **Salmon Homecoming Celebration**—Magnuson Park, 206-999-0532, www. salmonhomecoming.org; The Salmon Homecoming Alliance hosts this celebration that aims to build bridges between tribal and non-tribal communities while supporting a healthy salmon population.

OCTOBER

- **Arab Festival**—Seattle Center, 206-684-7200; held every other year in odd-numbered years, the Arab Festival features folk dancing, a traditional bazaar, food, cultural and educational booths, and children's activities.
- **Earshot Jazz Festival**—Seattle, 206-547-6763, www.earshot.org; the city's best jazz festival features over 50 concerts and events over a 2-week period in venues all over the city. Internationally famous acts abound.
- **Issaquah Salmon Days Festival**—Issaquah, 425-392-0661, www.salmon-days.org; Issaquah celebrates the return of salmon to its lakes, streams, and downtown hatchery with a parade, salmon bake, art, and music.
- **Pumpkin Prowl**—Woodland Park Zoo, 206-548-2500, www.zoo.org; costumed trick-or-treaters can stroll along paths decorated with carved pumpkins and spooky decorations and watch live entertainment.
- **Seattle Home Show 2**—CenturyLink Field Event Center, 425-467-0960, www.seattlehomeshow.com; the popular spring event is duplicated in the fall, with tips on winterizing your home.
- **Space City Mixer Halloween Bash**—www.spacecitymixer.com; locations and themes vary for this annual Halloween bash thrown by the city's largest social club, Space City Mixer, but you can expect to see some mind-blowing costumes, with a $1,000 prize at stake.

NOVEMBER

- **Apple Cup**—206-543-2200, www.gohuskies. com; the state football rivalry of the season pits the University of Washington Huskies against the Washington State University Cougars. The venue alternates between Husky Stadium in Seattle and Martin Stadium in Pullman, east of the Cascades.

- **Green Lake Frostbite Regatta**—206-684-4074, www.seattle.gov/Parks/boats/Grnlake.htm; just as the weather gets a little too cold and the wind picks up the bite of winter, two annual rowing events are held in Seattle. The Frostbite Regatta is a series of fairly short races, easily watched from the side of the lake with a hot cup of coffee in hand.
- **Head of the Lake Regatta**—206-547-1583, www.headofthelake.org; the Head of the Lake Race, which is held on a course that includes parts of both Lake Union and Lake Washington, is a three-mile race that tests the endurance of both rowers and spectators.
- **Heather Tartan Ball**—206-522-2541, www.sshga.org; break out your kilt and toast the haggis at this semiformal dance featuring pipe bands, Scottish country dancing, and a silent auction.
- **Hmong New Year Celebration**—Seattle Center, 206-684-7200, www.seattlecenter.com; this Laotian Hmong festival celebrates the lunar new year with art exhibits and dance performances.
- **Seattle International Auto Show**—CenturyLink Field Event Center, www.seattleautoshow.com; State Farm Insurance presents new and classic cars, trucks, motorcycles, SUVs and minivans, plus rare "supercars" and concept vehicles.
- **Seattle Marathon**—206-729-3660, www.seattlemarathon.org; this annual athletic event features a rolling course with scenic views, and a reputation for cold and rainy weather. The event also offers a marathon walk, half-marathon run and walk, and kids' marathon.
- **Winterfest**—Seattle Center, 206-684-7200, www.seattlecenter.com; an annual holiday event, this festival features school choirs, a public ice rink, a model train display, and all sorts of performances and shows. The five-week festival is a family favorite.
- **Yulefest**—Nordic Heritage Museum, Ballard, 206-789-5707, www.nordicmuseum.com; Ballard celebrates the holidays and its Scandinavian heritage the weekend before Thanksgiving.

DECEMBER

- **Christmas Ship Festival**—206-622-8687, www.argosycruises.com; boaters in Seattle celebrate the holiday season with a festive parade of lighted boats that tour Puget Sound, Lake Washington, and Lake Union during the weeks before Christmas. Shoreside revelers gather around bonfires and are treated to Christmas carols sung by choirs on the boats as they stop at area parks and beaches.
- **Community Hanukkah Celebration**—Stroum Jewish Community Center, Mercer Island, 206-232-7115, www.sjcc.org; listen to music, and enjoy arts and crafts and a candle lighting ceremony at this community Festival of Lights.

- **New Year's Eve at the Space Needle**—Space Needle, 206-905-2100, www. spaceneedle.com; for many years, the Space Needle has been the site of the liveliest New Year's celebration in Seattle. From the formal dinner dance at the revolving restaurant level to the casual party at the base of the needle, it has become a destination for New Year's revelers. Even if you decide to spend a quiet New Year's Eve at home, consider driving (or walking) to one of the many parks overlooking the Space Needle just before midnight. The fireworks display, which is set off from the top and sides of the structure, is spectacular. If you can't see it in person, local news stations broadcast the extravaganza.
- **The Nutcracker**—Seattle Center Opera House, 206-441-2424, www.pnb.org; no Christmas in Seattle would be complete without the annual production of *The Nutcracker* by Pacific Northwest Ballet. With marvelous sets by Maurice Sendak, this unique production is popular with all age groups.
- **Zoolights**—Point Defiance Zoo and Aquarium, Tacoma, 253-591-5337, www. pdza.org; more than half a million lights shimmer in the shapes of animals, nursery rhymes, and local landmarks.

ARCHITECTURE

- **Classic Houses of Seattle: High St**yle to Vernacular, 1870-1950 by Caroline T. Swope; covering the architectural styles and history of Seattle homes, from mansions to cottages.
- **National Trust Guide Seattle: America's Guide for Architecture and Histor**y **Travelers** by Walt Crowley; in-depth guide to the famous and not so famous landmarks and buildings in Seattle, including maps and photographs.
- **Shaping Seattle Architecture: A Historical Guide to the Architects** edited by Jeffrey Karl Ochsner; traces the history of Seattle's architecture through biographies of the area's best-known architects. Many famous Seattle buildings and houses are profiled in this book.
- **Seattle Architecture: A Walking Guide to Downtown** by Maureen R. Elenga; divided into nine tours, this guidebook begins at Pioneer Square and ends at the Seattle Center.

ART

- **Chihuly** by Donald Kuspit; a look at the career of internationally renowned glass artist Dale Chihuly in a coffee table–sized book full of stunning photos.
- **A Field Guide to Seattle's Public Art** edited by Steven Huss, contains five self-guided tours of Seattle's best-known public artworks, as well as essays by artists, writers, and historians.
- **Seattle, Washington: A Photographic Portrait** by Roger L. Johnson; the photographs of Seattle and the Puget Sound region are a visual feast of landscapes, people, and architecture.

COMMUNITY

- **Gay Seattle: Stories of Exile and Belonging** by Gary Atkins; tells the stories of the gay community in Seattle and its trials and triumphs over the last century.
- **Neighbor Power: Building Community the Seattle Way** by Jim Diers; provides stories and practical methods for building stronger communities and citizen activists.
- **Seattle's International District** by Doug Chin; chronicles the experiences of the diverse waves of immigrants who settled in this culturally rich neighborhood.

FAMILY AND PETS

- **Best Hikes with Dogs in Western Washington** by Dan Nelson; a useful guide to the region's most dog-friendly trails, published by The Mountaineers.
- **Best Hikes with Kids: Western Washington & the Cascades** by Joan Burton; an essential hiking guide for parents, this book describes day hikes and overnighters suitable for the entire family.
- **Bringing Out Baby: Seattle and the Eastside: Places to Take Babies and Toddlers** by Rebecca Johnston; addresses where to go with the under-three set.
- **The Dog Lovers' Companion to the Pacific Northwest: The Inside Scoop on Where To Take Your Dog** by Val Mallinson; using a "4 paws" rating system and Pick of the Litter lists, find the best places to take your canine companion.
- **Out and About Seattle with Kids: The Ultimate Family Guide for Fun and Learning** by Ann Bergman; this handbook can help families who are new to Seattle become acquainted with the city and its child-friendly diversions and resources.

FICTION

- **The Art of Deception** by Ridley Pearson; the 2002 thriller featuring Seattle detective Lou Boldt. Earlier titles set in the Emerald City include **Middle of Nowhere**, **The First Victim**, and **The Pied Piper**.
- **Broken for Use** by Stephanie Kaloos; the protagonist of this haunted tale of family conflict, secrets, and redemption is a divorced woman rattling around in a Seattle mansion after the death of her son. Seattle-based Kaloos is also the author of **Sing Them Home**.
- **Ed King** by David Guterson; a reimagining of the Oedipus Rex story set in Seattle. This Bainbridge Island–based author also wrote the award-winning **Snow Falling on Cedars** and **Our Lady of the Forest**.
- **Firetrap: A Novel of Suspense** by Earl W. Emerson; one of several mysteries by this author that take place in or around Seattle and feature firefighter sleuths. His previous series of books starring private eye Thomas Black still have a loyal following.

- *Half Asleep in Frog Pajamas* by Tom Robbins; a woman is in crisis in this typical Robbins wild ride set in Seattle.
- *The Highest Tide* by Jim Lynch; a 13-year-old boy's life is changed in a surprising way one summer in this beautiful novel set in the south end of Puget Sound.
- *Hotel Angeline: A Novel in 36 Voices;* a group of Seattle writers gathered in October 2010 to write a novel in six days, each completing a chapter in two hours before a live audience. The result of this literary experiment is a remarkably cohesive story about 14-year-old Alexis who inherits the task of running a Seattle residential hotel after the death of her mother.
- *Joy for Beginners* by Erica Bauermeister; at a Seattle dinner party to celebrate a friend's recovery from breast cancer, six women are challenged to face their own fears, with profound consequences.
- *Justice Denied* by J. A. Jance; one in an 18-book series of mysteries featuring fictional Seattle detective J. P. Beaumont. Others include *Long Time Gone, Breach of Duty,* and *Name Withheld*.
- *The Living* by Annie Dillard; this often heartrending novel by the Pulitzer Prize–winning author of *Pilgrim at Tinker Creek* details the trials of several 19th-century European families who settled north of Seattle on Bellingham Bay.
- *Long for This World* by Michael Byers; in the late 1990s a Seattle doctor must cope with a startling and world-changing discovery.
- *No Man's Land* by G. M. Ford; the fifth of a series following the investigative exploits of Seattle writer Frank Corso. Ford also wrote the successful Leo Waterman mystery novels about a Seattle private investigator.
- *War Dances* by Sherman Alexie; winner of the PEN/Faulkner Award for Fiction, a compelling collection of short stories and poems by the author of *Ten Little Indians, The Lone Ranger and Tonto Fistfight in Heaven, and Reservation Blues.*

FOOD & DINING

- *The Food Lover's Guide to Seattle* by Katy Calcott; a guide book to the city's freshest greens, best baguettes, and surliest fishmongers.
- *Pike Place Market Cookbook: Recipes, Anecdotes, and Personalities from Seattle's Renowned Public Market* by Braiden Rex-Johnson; with a foreword by Tom Douglas, this little gem is part cookbook, part market history.
- *Savor Greater Seattle Cookbook: Seattle's Finest Restaurants, Their Recipes, and Their Histories* by Chuck and Blanche Johnson; a combination cookbook and travel book celebrating the area's best restaurants.
- *Tom Douglas' Seattle Kitchen* by Tom Douglas; Seattle's favorite chef and owner of several restaurants shares some of his inspired recipes.

- *Zagat Survey: Seattle/Portland Restaurants*; the annual edition of this indispensable survey will help you find the right restaurant for every occasion.

HISTORY

- *Before Seattle Rocked: A City and Its Music* by Kurt E. Armbruster; a history of Seattle's music scene from the 1890s to the 1960s.
- *Eccentric Seattle: Pillars and Pariahs Who Made the City Not Such a Boring Place After All* by J. Kingston Pierce; an amusing romp through the characters and events of Seattle's past.
- *Grunge Is Dead: The Oral History of Seattle Rock Music* by Greg Prato; contains more than 130 interviews along with background history about the Seattle music scene and the evolution of great rock acts such as Pearl Jam, Nirvana, Soundgarden, and Alice in Chains.
- *Native Seattle: Histories from the Crossing-Over Place* by Coll Thrush; a study of the changing roles of native peoples in the urban history of Seattle.
- *Nisei Daughter* by Monica Itoi-Stone; a Japanese-American woman's story of a Seattle childhood interrupted by the WWII relocation of Japanese-Americans to internment camps. This book is standard reading in many Seattle classrooms.
- *Seattle and the Demons of Ambition* by Fred Moody; a portrait of the city's transformation beginning with the techno-boom of the late 1980s to the WTO riots (aka "The Battle of Seattle") in 1999.
- *Skid Road* by Murray Morgan; the now-famous account of early Seattle, from which the phrase "skid row" was coined.
- *Sons of the Profits* by William Speidel; an irreverent history of the colorful characters who populated Seattle in its early days from 1851 to 1901.

OUTDOOR GUIDES

- **100 Hikes in the Inland Northwest** by Rich Landers; the "100 Hikes" series published by Mountaineers Books also includes *100 Hikes in Washington's Alpine Lakes* by Vicky Spring, *100 Hikes in Washington's Glacier Peak Region*, *100 Hikes in Washington's North Cascades National Park Region*, and *100 Hikes in Washington's South Cascades and Olympics* by Ira Spring.
- *Birds of Seattle and Puget Sound* by Chris C. Fisher; essential field guide for Seattle bird watchers.
- *Nature in the City: Seattle: Walks, Hikes, Wildlife, Natural Wonders* by Maria Dolan and Kathryn True; fact-filled guide to the sometimes surprising places to experience the great outdoors in an urban environment.
- *Outside Magazine's Urban Adventure: Seattle* by Maria Dolan; discover the best spots for kayaking, hiking, biking, rock climbing, winter sports and more.

- **Take a Walk: 110 Walks Within 30 Minutes of Seattle and the Greater Puget Sound** by Sue Muller Hacking; a guide to walks in a range of easily accessible natural settings throughout the Puget Sound area. This updated edition includes details about walk length and difficulty, disabled access, connecting trails, as well as information for birders.

SPORTS

- *The Great Book of Seattle Sports Lists* by Mike Gastineau, Art Thiel, and Steve Rudman; Gastineau, a local sports radio deejay, and two sportswriters bring Seattle's sports history to life with this book of lists.
- *Notes from a 12 Man: A Truly Biased History of the Seattle Seahawks* by Mark Tye Turner; a passionate and funny "fanoir," covering the football team's greatest victories and most shameful defeats.
- *Out of Left Field: How the Mariners Made Baseball Fly in Seattle* by Art Thiel; from underdog team to the pride of a city, read about the rise of the Mariners.
- *Seattle Slew* by Dan Mearns; a biography of the city's most famous thoroughbred, from his Triple Crown glory to the illness that nearly took his life.

For help on finding 800 numbers, and especially for tips on how to reach an actual human being at hundreds of companies, go to http://gethuman.com.

AGING

- **American Association of Retired Persons (AARP)**, 866-227-7457, 877-434-7598 (TTY), www.aarp.org
- **King County Aging and Disability Services**, 206-684-0660, www.aging kingcounty.org
- **Mayor's Office for Senior Citizens**, 206-684-0500, www.seattle.gov/humanservices
- **Senior Information and Assistance Program**, 206-448-3110, 206-448-5025 (TTY), www.metro.kingcounty.gov
- **Senior Services of Seattle/King County**, 206-448-5757, 206-448-5025 (TDD), www.seniorservices.org

ALCOHOL AND DRUG ABUSE

- **Adult Children of Alcoholics (ACA)**, 206-722-6117, 800-562-1240
- **The Al-Anon & Alateen Information Service**, 206-625-0000, www.seattle-al-anon.org
- **Alcohol/Drug 24-Hour Help Line**, 206-722-3700, 800-562-1240, www.adhl.org
- **Alcohol Drug Teen Help Line**, 206-722-4222, 877-345-8336, www.theteen line.org
- **Alcoholics Anonymous**, 206-587-2838; Bellevue, 425-454-9192; Edmonds, 425-672-0987, www.seattleaa.org
- **Cocaine Anonymous**, 425-244-1150, 800-723-1923, www.ca.org

- **Highline Recovery Services**, 206-242-2260, www.highlinemedicalservices. org
- **King County Alcoholism and Substance Abuse Services & Information**, 206-296-5213, www.kingcounty.gov
- **King County Chemical Dependency Involuntary Commitment**, 206-296-7612
- **Nicotine Anonymous**, 877-879-6422, www.nicotine-anonymous.org
- **Salvation Army Adult Rehabilitation Center**, 206-587-0503, www.seattle. satruck.org
- **Women's Recovery Center**, 206-547-1955, www.apositivealternative.com

ANIMALS

- **Animal Bites**, 911
- **City of Seattle Pet Licenses**, 206-386-4262, www.seattle.gov/animalshelter/ licences.htm
- **Humane Society for Seattle/King County**, 425-641-0080, www.seattlehu mane.org
- **King County Regional Animal Services**, 206-296-7387, www.kingcounty. gov/safety/regionalAnimalServices.aspx
- **Progressive Animal Welfare Society (PAWS)**, 425-787-2500, www.paws.org
- **Seattle Animal Control Hotline (Lost Pets)**, 206-386-7387, www.seattle. gov/animalshelter
- **Seattle Animal Shelter**, 206-386-7387, www.seattle.gov/animalshelter

THE ARTS

- **4Culture**, 206-296-7580, www.4culture.org
- **Humanities Washington**, 206-682-1770, www.humanities.org
- **Seattle Arts Commission**, 206-733-9591, www.seattle.gov/arts
- **Washington State Arts Commission**, 360-753-3860, www.arts.wa.gov

AUTOMOBILES

- **American Automobile Association (AAA) of Washington**, 206-448-5353; Bellevue, 425-455-3933; Everett, 425-353-7222; Lynnwood, 425-775-3571; Renton, 425-251-6040; www.aaawa.com
- **City of Seattle—Abandoned Automobiles/Public Areas**, 206-684-8763, www.seattle.gov
- **City of Seattle—Illegally Parked Vehicles**, 206-625-5011, www.seattle.gov
- **City of Seattle—Inoperative Automobiles/Private Property**, 206-684-7899, www.seattle.gov
- **Department of Ecology**, 425-649-7000, www.ecy.wa.gov

- **King County Vehicle/Vessel License Information**, 206-296-4000, 206-296-2709 (TTY), www.kingcounty.gov/tranportation/licensing.aspx
- **Municipal Court of Seattle (parking tickets/traffic violations)**, 206-684-5600, 206-684-5210 (TTY), www.ci.seattle.wa.us/courts
- **Seattle Police Department Auto Impound**, 206-684-5441, www.seattle.gov/police
- **Washington State Department of Licensing**, 360-902-3900, www.dol.wa.gov
- **U.S. Department of Transportation Auto Safety Hotline**, 888-327-4236, www.nhtsa.gov

BIRTH AND DEATH RECORDS

- **King County Vital Statistics**, 206-296-4768, www.kingcounty.gov
- **State of Washington Department of Health Center**, Birth/Death/Marriage/Divorce Certificates, 360-236-4300, www.doh.wa.gov

CHAMBERS OF COMMERCE

SEATTLE

- **Ballard Chamber of Commerce**, 206-784-9705, www.ballardchamber.com
- **Central Area Chamber of Commerce**, 206-325-2864, www.scacc2108.org
- **Fremont Chamber of Commerce**, 206-632-1500, http://fremont.com
- **Greater Queen Anne Chamber of Commerce**, 206-283-6876, www.qachamber.org
- **Greater Seattle Chamber of Commerce**, 206-389-7200, www.seattlechamber.com
- **Greater University Chamber of Commerce**, 206-547-4417, www.udistrictchamber.org
- **Greenwood-Phinney Chamber of Commerce**, 206-355-5362, www.greenwood-phinney.com
- **Lake City Chamber of Commerce**, 206-363-3287, www.lakecitychamber.org
- **Magnolia Chamber of Commerce**, 206-284-5836, www.magnoliachamber.org
- **Northgate Chamber of Commerce**, www.northgatechamber.com
- **Southwest King County Chamber of Commerce**, 206-575-1633, www.swkcc.org
- **Wallingford Chamber of Commerce**, 206-632-0645, www.wallingfordchamber.org
- **West Seattle Chamber of Commerce**, 206-932-5685, www.wschamber.com
- **White Center Chamber of Commerce**, 206-412-5376, www.whitecenter-chamber.org

EASTSIDE

- **Bellevue Chamber of Commerce**, 425-454-2464, www.bellevuechamber.org
- **Greater Issaquah Chamber of Commerce**, 425-392-7024, www.issaquahchamber.com
- **Greater Kirkland Chamber of Commerce**, 425-822-7066, www.kirklandchamber.org
- **Greater Redmond Chamber of Commerce**, 425-885-4014, www.redmondchamber.org
- **Greater Woodinville Chamber of Commerce**, 425-481-8300, www.woodinvillechamber.org
- **Mercer Island Chamber of Commerce**, 206-232-3404, www.mercerislandchamber.org

WEST

- **Bainbridge Island Chamber of Commerce**, 206-842-3700, www.bainbridgechamber.com
- **Bremerton Chamber of Commerce**, 360-479-3579, www.bremertonchamber.org
- **Vashon-Maury Island Chamber of Commerce**, 206-463-6217, www.vashonchamber.com

NORTH

- **Everett Area Chamber of Commerce**, 425-257-3222, www.everettchamber.com
- **Greater Edmonds Chamber of Commerce**, 425-670-1496, www.edmondswa.com
- **Greater Bothell Chamber of Commerce**, 425-485-4353, www.bothellchamber.biz
- **Shoreline Chamber of Commerce**, 206-361-2260, www.shorelinechamber.org

SOUTH

- **Auburn Area Chamber of Commerce**, 253-833-0700, www.auburnareawa.org
- **Greater Federal Way Chamber of Commerce**, 253-838-2605, www.federalwaychamber.com
- **Greater Renton Chamber of Commerce**, 425-226-4560, www.gorenton.com
- **Kent Chamber of Commerce**, 253-854-1770, www.kentchamber.com
- **Tacoma-Pierce County Chamber of Commerce**, 253-627-2175, www.tacomachamber.org

CITY GOVERNMENTS

SEATTLE

- **City Attorney**, 206-684-8200, 206-233-7206 (TTY), www.seattle.gov/law
- **City Auditor**, 206-233-3801, www.seattle.gov/audit
- **City Council**, 206-684-8888, 206-233-0025 (TTY), www.seattle.gov/council
- **City Information**, 206-684-2489, 206-615-0476 (TTY), www.cityofseattle.net
- **Crime Prevention**, 206-684-7555, www.seattle.gov/police
- **Customer Service Bureau (complaints and information)**, 206-684-2489, www.seattle.gov/customerservice
- **Office for Civil Rights**, 206-684-4500, 206-684-4503 (TTY), www.seattle.gov/civilrights
- **Mayor's Office**, 206-684-4000, www.seattle.gov/mayor
- **Neighborhoods**, 206-684-0464, www.seattle.gov/neighborhoods
- **Seattle Chamber of Commerce**, 206-389-7200, www.seattlechamber.com

EASTSIDE

- **Bellevue**, 425-452-6800, www.ci.bellevue.wa.us
- **Duvall**, 425-788-1185, www.duvallwa.com
- **Issaquah**, 425-837-3000, www.ci.issaquah.wa.us
- **Kirkland**, 425-587-3000, 425-587-3111 (TTY/TTD), www.kirklandwa.gov
- **Mercer Island**, 206-275-7793 (City Clerk), www.mercergov.org
- **Newcastle**, 425-649-4444, www.ci.newcastle.wa.us
- **Redmond**, 425-556-2900, www.ci.redmond.wa.us
- **Snoqualmie**, 425-888-1555, www.ci.snoqualmie.wa.us
- **Woodinville**, 425-489-2700, www.ci.woodinville.wa.us

WEST

- **Bainbridge Island**, 206-842-7633, www.ci.bainbridge-isl.wa.us
- **Bremerton**, 360-473-5290 (City Clerk), www.ci.bremerton.wa.us

NORTH

- **Bothell**, 425-486-3256, www.ci.bothell.wa.us
- **Edmonds**, 425-775-2525, www.ci.edmonds.wa.us
- **Everett**, 425-257-8700, www.everettwa.org
- **Kenmore**, 425-398-8900, www.cityofkenmore.com
- **Lake Forest Park**, 206-368-5440, www.cityoflfp.com
- **Lynnwood**, 425-670-5000, www.ci.lynnwood.wa.us
- **Mountlake Terrace**, 425-744-6205 (City Manager), www.ci.mountlake-terrace.wa.us
- **Shoreline**, 206-801-2700, 206-546-0457 (TTY), www.cityofshoreline.com

SOUTH

- **Burien**, 206-241-4647, 206-248-5538 (TTY), www.burienwa.gov
- **Des Moines**, 206-870-6541, www.desmoineswa.gov
- **Federal Way**, 253-835-7000, www.ci.federal-way.wa.us
- **Kent**, 253-856-5200, www.ci.kent.wa.us
- **Normandy Park**, 206-248-7603, www.ci.normandy-park.wa.us
- **Renton**, 425-430-6400, www.ci.renton.wa.us
- **Sea-Tac**, 206-973-4800, www.ci.seatac.wa.us
- **Tacoma**, 253-591-5000, 800-833-6388 (TTY), www.cityoftacoma.org
- **Tukwila**, 206-433-1800, www.ci.tukwila.wa.us

CONSUMER COMPLAINTS AND SERVICES

- **Better Business Bureau of Alaska, Oregon, and Western Washington**, 206-431-2222, http://alaskaoregonwesternwashington.bbb.org
- **Customer Service Bureau (complaints and information)**, 206-684-2489, www.seattle.gov/customerservice
- **U.S. Consumer Product Safety Commission**, 301-504-7923 (general information), 800-638-2772 (consumer hotline), 301-595-7054 (TTY), www.cpsc.gov
- **Federal Trade Commission**, 877-382-4357, www.ftc.gov
- **State of Washington Attorney General's Office**, 360-753-6200, www.atg.wa.gov
- **State of Washington Consumer Protection Complaints and Inquiries**, 206-464-6684, 800-551-4636, www.atg.wa.gov/SafeguardingConsumers.aspx
- **State of Washington, Office of Insurance Commissioner**, 360-725-7080, 800-562-6900, www.insurance.wa.gov

COUNTY GOVERNMENTS

KING

- **King County Executive**, 206-296-4040, 206-296-0200 (TTY), www.kingcounty.gov/exec
- **King County Department of Development and Environmental Services**, 206-296-6600, 206-296-7217 (TTY), www.kingcounty.gov/property/permits
- **King County Health Services**, 206-296-4600, www.kingcounty.gov/healthservices
- **Metropolitan King County Council**, 206-296-1000, 206-296-1024 (TTY/TDD), www.kingcounty.gov/council

PIERCE

- **Pierce County Council**, 253-798-7777, 253-798-4018 (TDD), www.co.pierce. wa.us
- **Pierce County Executive**, 253-798-7477, www.co.pierce.wa.us
- **Tacoma-Pierce County Health Department**, 253-798-6500, 800-992-2456, www.tpchd.org
- **Pierce County Planning and Land Services Department**, 253-798-3739, www.co.pierce.wa.us

SNOHOMISH

- **Snohomish County Executive**, 425-388-3460, www.1.co.snohomish.wa.us/ Executive
- **Snohomish County Council**, 425-388-3494, 425-388-3700 (TTY), www1. co.snohomish.wa.us/departments/council
- **Snohomish Health District**, 425-339-5200, www.snohd.org
- **Snohomish County Planning and Development Services**, 425-388-3311, www1.co.snohomish.wa.us/departments/pds

CRIME

- **Crime in Progress**, 911
- **City of Seattle Crime Prevention**, 206-684-7555, www.seattle.gov/police

CRISIS LINES

CHILD ABUSE AND NEGLECT

- **New Beginnings for Battered Women and their Children**, (TTY/Voice) 206-522-9472, www.newbegin.org
- **State of Washington Department of Social and Health Services—Child Abuse Reporting**, (24-hours) 866-ENDHARM (363-4276), 800-562-5624 (evenings, weekends), 800-624-6186 (TTY); Seattle, 206-691-2300, 800-379-3395; 206-760-2068; White Center, 206-716-2400, 888-766-3510; East King County, 425-590-3000, 800-962-0073; South King County, 253-372-5930, 800-422-7880; Office of Indian Child Welfare, 206-923-4904, 800-379-3757; www.dshs. wa.gov
- **State of Washington Domestic Violence Hotline**, 800-562-6025, www. courts.wa.gov

CRISIS HOTLINE

- **Crisis Clinic 24-hour Crisis Line**, 206-461-3222, 206-461-3219 (TDD)

DOMESTIC ABUSE

- **Domestic Abuse Women's Network**, 425-656-7867, www.dawnonline.org
- **King County Domestic Violence Automated Information Service**, 206-205-5555, www.kingcounty.gov/courts/Clerk/Domestic Violence
- **National Domestic Violence Hotline**, 800-799-SAFE (7233), 800-787-3224 (TTY), www.thehotlinend.org
- **New Beginnings for Battered Women and Their Children**, (TTY/Voice) 206-522-9472, www.newbegin.org
- **State of Washington Adult Protective Services**, 866-ENDHARM (363-4276) (24-hour hotline), 866-221-4909, 800-977-5456 (TTY), www.aasa.dshs.wa.gov
- **State of Washington Domestic Violence Hotline**, 800-562-6025, www.courts.wa.gov

RAPE AND SEXUAL ASSAULT

- **Harborview Center for Sexual Assault and Traumatic Stress**, 206-744-1600, 206-744-1616 (TDD); http://depts.washington.edu/hcsats
- **King County Sexual Assault Resource Center**, 888-99-VOICE (998-6423) (24 hours), 425-226-5062, www.kcsarc.org

DISABLED, SERVICES FOR THE

See the **Helpful Services** chapter.

DISCRIMINATION

- **City of Seattle Office for Civil Rights**, 206-684-4500, 206-684-4503 (TTY), www.seattle.gov/civilrights
- **City of Seattle Office for Civil Rights, Hate Crimes Hotline**, 206-684-4500, 206-684-4503 (TTY), www.seattle.gov/civilrights
- **Hate Crimes in Progress**, 911
- **State of Washington Human Rights Commission**, 800-233-3247, 800-300-7525 (TTY), www.hum.wa.gov

EMERGENCY

- **Fire, Police, Medical**, 911
- **City of Seattle Office of Seattle Emergency Management**, 206-233-5076, www.seattle.gov/emergency
- **Federal Emergency Management Agency**, 425-487-4600, 800-621-FEMA (3362), www.fema.gov
- **King County Office of Emergency Management**, 206-296-3830, www.king-county.gov/safety/prepare
- **Pierce County Department of Emergency Management**, 253-798-7470, www.co.pierce.wa.us

- **Snohomish County Department of Emergency Management**, 425-388-5060, www1.co.snohomish.wa.us

FEDERAL OFFICES/CENTERS

- **Centers for Disease Control and Prevention**, 800-CDC-INFO (232-4636), www.cdc.gov
- **Consumer Product Safety Commission**, 301-504-7923 (general info), 800-638-2772 (consumer hotline), 301-595-7054 (TTY), www.cpsc.gov
- **Federal Citizen Information Center**, 888-878-3256, www.pueblo.gsa.gov
- **Federal Emergency Management Agency**, 425-487-4600, 800-621-FEMA (3362), www.fema.gov
- **Federal Information Center**, 800-333-4636, www.info.gov
- **Small Business Administration**, 206-553-7310, 800-827-5722, www.sbaonline.sba.gov
- **Social Security Administration**, 800-772-1213, 800-325-0778 (TTY), www.ssa.gov
- **U.S. Attorney, Western District of Washington**, 206-553-7970, 800-797-6722, www.justice.gov/usao/waw
- **U.S. Census Bureau**, 206-381-6200, 800-233-3308, www.census.gov
- **U.S. Government Bookstore**, 866-512-1800, http://bookstore.gpo.gov

GARBAGE

- **King County Hazardous Waste Management Program**, 206-296-4692, www.lhwmp.org
- **Seattle Public Utilities Household Hazardous Waste**, 206-296-4692, www.seattle.gov
- **Seattle Public Utilities Recycling and Disposal Station Information Line**, 684-3000, www.seattle.gov
- **Seattle Public Utilities Solid Waste Services, Missed Collection Hotline**, 206-684-3000, 206-233-7241 (TTY), www. seattle.gov
- **Wastemobile,** 206-296-4692, 888-869-4233, www.lhwmp.org

GREEN INFORMATION AND RESOURCES

See the **Green Living** chapter.

HEALTH AND MEDICAL CARE

STATE OF WASHINGTON

- **Washington State Healthcare Authority**, 800-660-9840, www.hca.wa.gov

- **State of Washington Department of Social and Health Services**, 888-436-6392, 877-501-2233, www.dshs.wa.gov
- **WithinReach**, 206-284-2465, http://withinreachwa.org

SEATTLE

- **Children's Hospital & Medical Center Resource Line**, 206-987-2500 (press 3), 866-987-2500, www.seattlechildrens.org
- **Columbia Public Health Center**, 206-296-4650, www.kingcounty.gov/healthservices
- **Community Health Access Program (CHAP)**, 206-284-0331, 800-756-5437, www.kingcounty.gov
- **Downtown Public Health Center**, 206-296-4755, www.kingcounty.gov/healthservices
- **Harborview Medical Center Sexually Transmitted Disease Clinic**, 206-744-3590, http://uwmedicine.washington.edu
- **King County Communicable Disease 24-Hour Report Line**, 206-296-4949, www.kingcounty.gov/healthservices
- **King County Environmental Health Services**, 206-205-4394, www.kingcounty.gov/healthservices
- **King County Family Health Hotline**, 800-322-2588
- **King County Health Services**, (TTY/Voice) 206-296-4600, www.kingcounty.gov/healthservices
- **King County HIV/AIDS Program**, 206-296-4649, www.kingcounty.gov/healthservices
- **King County Immunization Program Information**, 206-296-4774, www.kingcounty.gov/healthservices
- **King County Medical Society**, 206-621-9396, www.kcmsociety.org
- **North Seattle Public Health Center**, 206-296-4765, www.kingcounty.gov/healthservices
- **Northwest Hospital MED-INFO Physician Referral Line**, 206-633-4636, 206-364-0500, www.nwhospital.org
- **Seattle Indian Health Board**, 206-324-9360, www.sihb.org

SURROUNDING COMMUNITIES

- **Auburn Public Health Center,** 206-296-8400, www.kingcounty.gov/healthservices
- **Birch Creek (Kent) Public Health Center,** 206-296-4930, www.kingcounty.gov/healthservices
- **Eastgate Public Health Center**, 206-296-4920, www.kingcounty.gov/healthservices
- **Federal Way Public Health Center**, 206-296-8410, www.kingcounty.gov/healthservices

- **Highline Medical Center Physician Referral**, 206-444-8419, www.highline-medicalcenter.org
- **Kent Public Health Center**, 206-296-4500, www.kingcounty.gov/healthservices
- **Northshore Public Health Center**, 206-296-9787, www.kingcounty.gov/healthservices
- **Renton Public Health Center**, 206-296-4700, www.kingcounty.gov/healthservices
- **White Center Public Health Center**, 206-296-4646, www.kingcounty.gov/healthservices

HOUSING

- **Central Area Motivation Program (CAMP)**, 206-812-4940, www.campseattle.org
- **City of Seattle Office of Housing**, 206-684-0721, www.seattle.gov/housing
- **King County Housing Authority**, 206-574-1100, 800-833-6388 (TDD), www.kcha.org
- **King County Home Repair Assistance**, Seattle 206-684-0244, Auburn 253-931-3090, Bellevue 425-452-6884, Kent 253-856-5065, Renton 425-530-6650 (check city government websites for cities not listed)
- **Seattle Housing Authority**, 206-615-3300, www.seattlehousing.org
- **Seattle Office for Civil Rights Housing Discrimination**, 206-684-4500, 206-684-4503 (TTY), www.seattle.gov/civilrights
- **Tenants Union**, 206-723-0500, www.tenantsunion.org
- **Urban League of Metropolitan Seattle**, 206-461-3792, www.urbanleague.org
- **Department of Housing and Urban Development**, 206-220-5101, www.hud.gov

LEGAL REFERRAL

- **City of Seattle Attorney**, 206-684-8200, 206-233-7206 (TTY), www.seattle.gov/law
- **King County Bar Association, Lawyers Referral Service**, 206-267-7100, www.kcba.org
- **King County Prosecuting Attorney's Protection Order Advocacy Program**, 206-296-9547, http://protectionorder.org
- **Legal Action Center**, 800-223-4044, www.lac.org
- **Legal Voice (women's rights)**, 206-621-7691, www.nwwlc.org
- **Unemployment Law Project**, 206-441-9178, http://unemploymentlawproject.org
- **Volunteer Legal Services**, 206-623-0281

LIBRARIES

See the **Neighborhoods** chapter for branch libraries.
- **Everett Public Library**, 425-257-8000, www.epls.org
- **King County Library System**, 425-369-3200, 800-462-9600, www.kcls.org
- **Kitsap Regional Library**, 360-405-9100, www.krl.org
- **Pierce County Library System**, 253-536-6500, www.piercecountylibrary.org
- **Seattle Public Library**, 206-386-4636, www.spl.org
- **Sno-Isle Libraries**, 360-651-7000, www.sno-isle.org
- **Tacoma Public Library**, 253-591-5666, www.tpl.lib.wa.us
- **University of Washington Libraries,** 206-543-0242, www.lib.washington.edu

MARRIAGE LICENSES

- **King County Marriage Licenses**, 206-296-4021, www.kingcounty.gov/courts/marriage
- **Kitsap County Marriage Licenses**, 360-337-4935, www.kitsapgov.com
- **Pierce County Marriage Licenses**, 253-798-7435, www.co.pierce.wa.us
- **Snohomish County Marriage Licenses**, 425-388-3483, www1.co.snohomish.wa.us

PARKS

See the **Neighborhoods** chapter for community center locations, or the **Sports and Recreation** or **Greenspace and Beaches** chapters for individual parks.

SEATTLE AND KING COUNTY

- **King County Parks and Recreation Department**, 206-296-8687, www.king-county.gov/recreation/parks
- **Seattle Parks and Recreation Department**, 206-684-4075, 206-233-1509 (TTY), www.seattle.gov/parks

EASTSIDE

- **Bellevue Parks and Community Services Department**, 425-452-6885, www.bellevuewa.gov/parks-community-services.htm
- **Issaquah Parks and Recreation Department**, 425-837-3300, www.ci.issaquah.wa.us
- **Kirkland Department of Parks & Community Services**, 425-587-3300, www.kirklandwa.gov/depart/parks
- **Mercer Island Parks and Recreation**, 206-275-7609, www.mercergov.org
- **Newcastle Parks Department**, 425-649-4444, www.ci.newcastle.wa.us
- **Redmond Parks and Recreation**, 425-556-2300, www.ci.redmond.wa.us

- **Snoqualmie Parks and Recreation**, 425-831-5784, www.ci.snoqualmie.wa.us
- **Woodinville Recreation and Parks**, 425-877-2287, www.ci.woodinville.wa.us

WEST

- **Bainbridge Island Park and Recreation District**, 206-842-2306, www.biparks.org

NORTH

- **Bothell Parks and Recreation**, 425-486-7430, www.ci.bothell.wa.us
- **Edmonds Parks, Recreation & Cultural Services**, 425-771-0230, www.ci.edmonds.wa.us
- **Everett Parks and Recreation**, 425-257-8300, www.ci.everett.wa.us
- **Kenmore Parks and Recreation**, 425-398-8900, www.kenmorewa.gov
- **Lake Forest Park Parks**, 206-368-5440, www.cityoflfp.com
- **Lynnwood Parks, Recreation and Cultural Arts Department**, 425-670-5732, www.ci.lynnwood.wa.us
- **Mountlake Terrace Parks Services**, 425-776-9173, www.cityofmlt.com
- **Shoreline Parks, Recreation, and Cultural Services**, 206-801-2601, www.cityofshoreline.com

SOUTH

- **Burien Parks, Recreation and Cultural Services**, 206-988-3700, www.burienwa.gov
- **Des Moines Parks and Recreation Department**, 206-870-6527, www.desmoineswa.gov
- **Kent Parks, Recreation and Community Services**, 253-856-5050, www.kentwa.gov
- **Renton Parks and Trails**, 425-430-6600, http://rentonwa.gov
- **Sea-Tac Parks and Recreation**, 206-973-4670, www.ci.seatac.wa.us
- **Tacoma Metro Parks**, 253-305-1000, www.metroparkstacoma.org
- **Tukwila Parks and Recreation Department**, 206-768-2822, www.ci.tukwila.wa.us

POLICE

STATE OF WASHINGTON

- **Emergency**, 911
- **Washington State Patrol Non-Emergency**, 425-649-4370, 425-649-4367 (TTY), www.wsp.wa.gov

SEATTLE AND KING COUNTY

- **Emergency,** 911
- **King County Sheriff's Office Non-Emergency**, 206-296-3311, www.king county.gov/safety/sheriff
- **Seattle Police Department Non-Emergency**, 206-625-5011, www.seattle. gov/police
- **Seattle Police Department East Precinct**, 206-684-4300, www.seattle.gov/ police
- **Seattle Police Department North Precinct**, 206-684-0850, www.seattle. gov/police
- **Seattle Police Department South Precinct**, 206-684-4300, www.seattle. gov/police
- **Seattle Police Department West Precinct**, 206-684-8917, www.seattle.gov/ police
- **Seattle Police Department Southwest Precinct**, 206-733-9800, www. seattle.gov/police

EASTSIDE

- **Bellevue Police Department,** 425-452-6917, 877-881-2731, www.bellevuewa.gov
- **Issaquah Police Department**, 425-837-3200, www.ci.issaquah.wa.us
- **Kirkland Police Department**, 425-577-5656 (Voice/TTY), www.kirklandwa. gov
- **Mercer Island Police Division**, 206-275-7610, www.mercergov.org
- **Newcastle Police Department**, 425-296-3311, www.ci.newcastle.wa.us
- **Redmond Police Department**, 425-556-2500, www.ci.redmond.wa.us
- **Snoqualmie Police Division**, 425-888-3333, www.ci.snoqualmie.wa.us

NORTH

- **Bothell Police Department**, 425-486-1254, www.ci.bothell.wa.us
- **Edmonds Police Department**, 425-771-0200, www.ci.edmonds.wa.us/ police_dept.stm
- **Everett Police Department**, 425-257-8400, www.everettwa.org
- **Lake Forest Park Police Department**, 206-364-8216, www.cityoflfp.com/ police
- **Lynnwood Police Department**, 425-670-5600, www.ci.lynnwood.wa.us
- **Mountlake Terrace Police Department**, 425-670-8260, www.cityofmlt.com
- **Shoreline Police Department**, 206-801-2710, www.cityofshoreline.com

SOUTH

- **Kent Police Department**, 253-856-5800, www.ci.kent.wa.us

- **Renton Police Department,** 425-430-7500, http://rentonwa.gov/government
- **Sea-Tac Police Services,** 206-973-4900, www.ci.seatac.wa.us
- **Tacoma Police Department,** 253-591-5900, www.cityoftacoma.org
- **Tukwila Police Department,** 206-433-1808, www.tukwilawa.gov

POST OFFICE

- **Addresses**—see the **Neighborhoods** chapter for branch stations.
- **U.S. Postal Service,** 800-275-8777, www.usps.com

ROAD CONDITION INFORMATION

- **Washington State Department of Transportation Highway Information Line,** 511, www.wsdot.wa.gov

RECYCLING

- **City of Seattle Recycling Information,** 206-684-3000
- **State of Washington Recycling Information,** 800-RECYCLE (732-9253)

SCHOOLS

SURROUNDING COMMUNITIES

- **Auburn School District,** 253-931-4900, www.auburn.wednet.edu
- **Bellevue School District,** 425-456-4000, www.bsd405.org
- **Bremerton School District,** 360-473-1000, www.bremertonschools.org
- **Edmonds School District,** 425-431-7000, www.edmonds.wednet.edu
- **Federal Way Public Schools,** 253-945-2000, www.fwsd.wednet.edu
- **Highline Public Schools,** 206-433-2331, www.hsd401.org
- **Issaquah School District,** 425-837-7000, www.issaquah.wednet.edu
- **Kent School District,** 253-373-7000, www.kent.k12.wa.us
- **Lake Washington School District,** 425-936-1200, www.lwsd.org
- **Mercer Island School District,** 206-236-3330, www.misd.k12.wa.us
- **Northshore School District,** 425-408-6000, www.nsd.org
- **Renton School District,** 425-204-2300, www.rentonschools.us
- **Shoreline School District,** 206-393-6111, 206-393-3386 (TTY), www.shorelineschools.org
- **Tukwila School District,** 206-901-8000, www.tukwila.wednet.edu
- **Vashon Island School District,** 206-463-2121, www.vashonsd.wednet.edu

SEATTLE PUBLIC

- **Administrative Center,** 206-252-0010, www.seattleschools.org

- **Automated Enrollment Services Line**, 206-252-0410
- **Bilingual Family Center**, 206-252-7750
- **Central Enrollment Service Center**, 206-720-3533
- **Customer Service Center**, 206-252-0010
- **Highly Capable Services**, 206-252-0130
- **North Enrollment Service Center**, 206-252-0765
- **School Board**, 206-252-0040
- **South Enrollment Service Center**, 206-252-7732
- **Superintendent's Office**, 206-252-0167
- **Special Education Services**, 206-252-0058
- **Transportation Services**, 206-252-0900
- **Wait List Automated Info Line**, 206-252-0212
- **West Seattle Enrollment Service Center**, 206-252-8660

SHIPPING SERVICES

- **DHL Worldwide Express**, 800-225-5345, www.dhl-usa.com
- **FedEx**, 800-463-3339, www.fedex.com/us
- **United Parcel Service (UPS)**, 800-742-5877,
- **U.S. Postal Service Express Mail**, 800-275-8777, www.usps.com

SOCIAL SECURITY

- **Social Security Administration**, 800-772-1213, 800-325-0778 (TTY), www.ssa.gov

SPORTS

- **Everett AquaSox (Northwest League Baseball)**, 425-258-3673, http://www.milb.com/index.jsp?sid=t403
- **Seattle Mariners (Major League Baseball)**, 206-346-4000, http://seattle.mariners.mlb.com
- **Seattle Seahawks (National Football League)**,888-635-4295, www.seahawks.com
- **Seattle Sounders (Major League Soccer)**, 877-MLS-GOAL (657-4625), www.soundersfc.com
- **Seattle Storm (Women's National Basketball Association)**, 206-217-WNBA, www.wnba.com/storm
- **Seattle Thunderbirds (Western Hockey League)**, 206-448-PUCK, www.seattle-thunderbirds.com
- **Tacoma Rainiers (Pacific Coast League Baseball)**, 253-752-7707, http://tacoma.rainiers.milb.com
- **University of Washington Huskies (all teams)**, 206-543-2200, www.gohuskies.com

STATE OF WASHINGTON

- **Attorney General's Office**, 360-753-6200, 800-833-6384 (TTY), www.atg.wa.gov
- **General Information**, 800-321-2808, www.wa.gov
- **Governor's Office**, 360-902-4111, 800-833-6388 (TTY), www.governor.wa.gov
- **Legislative Hotline**, 800-562-6000
- **Secretary of State, General Information and Elections**, 360-902-4151, 800-422-8683 (TTY), www.sos.wa.gov

STREET MAINTENANCE

- **City of Seattle Street Repairs**, 206-684-ROAD (7623) (pothole and street repair hotline), 206-684-5118 (traffic signals), www.seattle.gov
- **King County Transportation Department Road Services Division**, 206-296-8100, 800-527-6237, 206-296-0933 (TTY), www.kingcounty.gov
- **State of Washington Department of Transportation**,350-705-7000; Emergency Maintenance, 206-440-4490; Maintenance Administration, 360-705-7850, www.wsdot.wa.gov

TAXES

CITY

- **City of Seattle Finance and Administrative Services**, 206-684-2489; City Business Tax, 206-684-8484, www.seattle.gov/rca

COUNTY

- **King County Department of Assessments**, 206-296-7300, 206-296-7888 (TTY), www.kingcounty.gov/assessor
- **King County Personal Property Tax Line**, 206-296-4290, 206-296-7888 (TTY), www.kingcounty.gov/assessor
- **King County Property Tax Advisor**, 206-205-6330, 206-205-6338 (TTY), www.kingcounty.gov/assessor
- **King County Real Estate Tax Information**, 206-296-7300, 800-833-6388 (TTY), www.kingcounty.gov/assessor

FEDERAL

- **Internal Revenue Service**, Federal Tax Questions, 800-829-1040, 800-829-4059 (TTY); 24-hour Recorded Tax Help, 800-829-4477; www.irs.gov
- **Internal Revenue Service Local Taxpayer Advocate**, 206-220-6037, 800-829-4059 (TTY), outside Seattle, 877-777-4778

STATE (NO INCOME TAX)

- **Washington State Department of Revenue**, 425-727-5300, 360-705-6718 (TTY), 800-647-7706, http://dor.wa.gov

TAXIS

- **Farwest Taxi**, 206-622-1717, www.farwesttaxi.net
- **Orange Cab**, 206-522-8800, www.orangecab.net
- **Stita Taxi,** 206-246-9999, www.stitataxi.com
- **Yellow Cab**, 206-622-6500, www.yellowtaxi.net

TOURISM

- **Canada, British Columbia**, 800-435-5622, www.hellobc.com
- **National Park Service**, 202-208-6843; Pacific West Region, 510-817-1300, www.nps.gov
- **National Park Service Campground Reservations**, 800-365-2267, www.nps.gov
- **Seattle's Convention and Visitors Bureau**, 206-461-5800, 866-732-2695, www.visitseattle.org
- **State of Idaho**, 208-334-2470, 800-635-7820, www.visitidaho.org
- **State of Oregon**, 800-547-7842, www.traveloregon.com
- **Washington State Department of Tourism**, 800-544-1800, www.experiencewa.com

TRANSPORTATION

AIRPORTS

- **Seattle-Tacoma International Airport**, 206-787-5388, www.portseattle.org/seatac
- **King County International Airport (Boeing Field)**, 206-296-7380, www.kingcounty.gov/transportation/kcdot/airport
- **Paine Field Airport (Everett)**, 425-388-5125, www.painefield.com
- **Renton Municipal Airport**, 425-430-7471, www.ci.renton.wa.us

BUSES

- **Community Transit**, 425-353-RIDE or 800-562-1375, www.commtrans.org
- **Everett Transit**, 425-257-7777, www.everettwa.org
- **Greyhound Bus Lines**, 800-231-2222, www.greyhound.com
- **Metro Transit**, 206-553-3000, http://www.metro.kingcounty.gov
- **Pierce Transit**, 253-581-8000, 800-562-8109, www.ptbus.pierce.wa.us
- **RapidRide,** 206-553-3000, http://www.metro.kingcounty.gov/travel-options

- **Seattle Personal Transit**, 206-716-3840, www.solid-ground.org/programs/transportation
- **Senior Services Volunteer Transportation**, 206-448-5740, www.seniorservices.org
- **ST Express**, 888-889-6368, www.soundtransit.org

LIGHT RAIL

- **Sound Transit**, 888-889-6368, www.soundtransit.org

TRAINS

- **Amtrak National Route Information**, 800-USA-RAIL, www.amtrak.com
- **Amtrak Seattle King Street Station**, 206-382-4125
- **Sounder Commuter Trains**, 206-398-5000, 800-201-4900, (TTY Relay 711), www.soundtransit.org

FERRIES

- **Washington State Ferries**, 206-464-6400, 888-808-7977, www.wsdot.wa.gov/ferries

RIDE-SHARING PROGRAMS

- **City of Seattle Commuter Services**, 206-386-4648, www.seattle.gov/transportation
- **Metro Transit Ridematch and Vanpool**, 888-814-1300, 800-833-6388 (TTY), www.rideshareonline.com

UTILITY EMERGENCIES

- **Puget Sound Energy**, 888-225-5773, 800-962-9498 (TTY), www.pse.com
- **Seattle City Light**, 206-684-3000, 206-223-0025 (TTY), www.seattle.gov/light
- **Seattle City Light 24-Hour Power Outage Hotline**, 206-684-7400
- **Seattle Public Utilities**, 206-684-3000, 206-233-7241 (TTY), www.seattle.gov/util
- **Seattle Public Utilities Missed Collection Hotline**, 206-684-7600
- **Seattle Public Utilities Sewer or Surface Drainage Emergencies**, 206-386-1800
- **Seattle Public Utilities Streets and Slide Emergencies**, 206-684-7508
- **Snohomish County Public Utility District**, 425-783-1000, www.snopud.com
- **Tacoma Public Utilities**, 253-502-8602 (for outages and fallen wires), www.mytpu.org

VOTING

- **King County Voter Registration**, 206-296-8683, www.kingcounty.gov/elections/registration
- **Washington Secretary of State, Voting and Elections Information**, 360-902-4180, www.sos.wa.gov/elections
- **Washington State Voter Registration Information**, 800-448-4881

WASHINGTON STATE LOTTERY

- **Regional Offices**, Everett 425-356-2902, Federal Way 253-661-5050
- **Winning Numbers**, 800-545-7510, www.walottery.com

WEATHER

- **National Weather Service Forecast Office**, 206-526-6087, www.wrh.noaa.gov/sew
- **KING 5 TV Weather**, www.king5.com/weather
- **KIRO TV Weather**, www.kirotv.com/weather
- **KOMO TV Weather**, www.komotv.com/weather

ZIP CODES

- **U.S. Postal Service**, 800-275-8777, www.usps.com

INDEX

The Newcomer's Handbook for Seattle, first published in 1999, was written by Amy Bellamy. The second edition (2002) was revised by Monica Fischer, and Maria Christensen updated the third edition in 2007. The most recent revision, including all photographs, is the work of Monique Vescia, who describes herself as follows:

MONIQUE VESCIA continues in the alliterative tradition of Newcomer's Handbook revisers whose first names begin with "M." She is both a relative newcomer to Seattle and a person with deep familial roots in the city. She grew up in Palo Alto, and earned graduate degrees in English and American literature before relocating from Brooklyn to Seattle in 2002. She lives with her husband and son in a lovely old house on Queen Anne that once belonged to her grandparents, where she spent many blackberry summers and gray Christmases as a child. She is a freelance writer and editor, and she keeps bees in her backyard.

RELOCATION RESOURCES

Utilizing an innovative grid and "static" reusable adhesive sticker format, *Furniture Placement and Room Planning Guide...Moving Made Easy* provides a functional and practical solution to all your space planning and furniture placement needs.

Moving with kids?

Look into *The Moving Book: A Kids' Survival Guide*.

Divided into three sections (before, during, and after the move), it's a handbook, a journal, and a scrapbook all in one. Includes address book, colorful change-of-address cards, and a useful section for parents.

Children's Book of the Month Club "Featured Selection"; American Bookseller's "Pick of the List"; Winner of the Family Channel's "Seal of Quality" Award

And for your younger children, ease their transition with our brand-new title just for them, *Max's Moving Adventure: A Coloring Book for Kids on the Move.* A complete story book featuring activities as well as pictures that children can color; designed to help children cope with the stresses of small or large moves.

NewcomersWeb.com

Based on the award-winning *Newcomer's Handbooks*, NewcomersWeb.com offers the highest quality neighborhood and community information in a one-of-a-kind searchable online database. The following areas are covered: Atlanta, Austin, Boston, Chicago, Dallas–Fort Worth, Houston, Los Angeles, Minneapolis–St. Paul, New York City, Portland (Oregon), San Francisco, Seattle, Washington DC, and the USA.

NEWCOMER'S HANDBOOKS®

Regularly revised and updated, these popular guides are now available for Atlanta, Boston, Chicago, China, London, Los Angeles, Minneapolis–St. Paul, New York City, Portland, San Francisco Bay Area, Seattle, Texas and Washington DC.

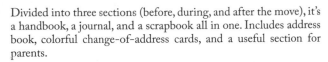

"Invaluable ...highly recommended" – Library Journal

If you're coming from another country, don't miss the *Newcomer's Handbook® for Moving to and Living in the USA* by Mike Livingston, termed "a fascinating book for newcomers and residents alike" by the *Chicago Tribune*.

6750 SW Franklin Street
Portland, Oregon 97223-2542
Phone 503.968.6777 • Fax 503.968.6779
FIRST BOOKS   **www.firstbooks.com**

READER RESPONSE

We would appreciate your comments regarding this fourth edition of the *Newcomer's Handbook® for Moving to and Living in Seattle: Including Bellevue, Redmond, Everett, and Tacoma.* If you've found any mistakes or omissions or if you would just like to express your opinion about the guide, please let us know. We will consider any suggestions for possible inclusion in our next edition, and if we use your comments, we'll send you a free copy of our next edition. Please e-mail us at readerresponse@firstbooks. com, or mail or fax this response form to:

Reader Response Department
First Books
6750 SW Franklin, Suite A
Portland, OR 97223-2542
Fax: 503.968.6779

Comments: _____

_____

_____

_____

_____

_____

_____

_____

_____

Name: _____

Address: _____

_____

Telephone: ( ) _____

Email: _____

6750 SW Franklin, Suite A
Portland, OR 97223-2542
USA
P: 503.968.6777
www.firstbooks.com